Mihai Nadin
The Civilization of Illiteracy

The Civilization
of
Illiteracy

MIHAI NADIN

Dresden University Press
1997

Dresden University Press
Dresden, Germany

Copyright 1997 © by
Dresden University Press

Die Deutsche Bibliothek – CIP-Einheitsaufnahme

Nadin, Mihai:
The Civilization of Illiteracy / Mihai Nadin. Dresden University Press. –
Dresden: Dresden Univ. Press, 1997
  ISBN 3-931-828-387

Printed in Germany

Girl of mine, thank you!

FOREWORD

I wish I could put in your hands the first page of the interconnected digital book suggested on the cover. This new page relates to those from which it issues forth. How the relation between them is shaped deserves more than a fleeting thought or a speculative remark. Let us imagine that this new digital book already exists. It will not only be a window to the author's mind, as are the books we know, but also to that of the readers.

The networked digital book has to be understood as a dynamic mapping of human interactions. It transcends the separation between writer and reader. Try to recall the bright images of cities we see at night from an airplane. They seem to come and go. On the ever-changing cognitive map of humankind, digital books are like such settlements, but of minds. Embodying centers of reciprocal interest, they serve as multimedia conduits for interactions facilitated by virtual reality interfaces. They are the journey, not the vehicle.

No other time than ours has had more of the future in it—and less of the past. The civilization we are entering is no promised land. It is a realm of challenge, with hurdles to overcome and frustrations to live with. Don't confuse it with the latest in techno-gewgaws and acronym babble. Or with the obsession for instant gratification by which we seem to live more and more.

Pioneers, inventors, entrepreneurs, even the politicians of the so-called Third Wave, forge ahead impatiently. Their optimism, as real or fake as it might be, is difficult to contain. The young take the lead, as they break free of an education that contributed the least to their innovative zest. Others hesitate. The literate heritage might not be perfect, but it protects from the often disquieting changes that we all—enthusiasts, pessimists, and critics—experience. In the palace of printed books, we were promised not only eternal truth and beauty, but also prosperity. Well, prosperity is here, even if not equally distributed, but truth and beauty are increasingly elusive.

Nations, having vested interests in the dominion of literacy, transformed it into a political slogan. Guardians of written laws, politicians, and the media—established as an effective power based on its own justification—defend literacy also. They are dedicated to its domination over alternative means of human expression and communication, even when they use such alternative means for their own benefit. We are experiencing the conflict between forces corresponding to a literate structure of human activity and the emerging post-literate structure. One of the results of the conflict is that the visual has already surpassed the written, though not always for the better.

Disenfranchised of permanence, many people become nostalgic for a past that exists only in their imaginations. They experience, painfully, a lost sense of continuity. Downsizing might cut the literate overhead of economic activity. It might increase efficiency. But it does not add to anyone's sense of security, even if those downsized understand why it takes place.

Those apprehensive of the change, or not prepared for it, are ready to take a turn onto Prozac Avenue. Synthetic maintenance of psychic balance is as justified as voyages in space or the mobotic performance of heart or brain surgery. Discoveries and inventions, sometimes contradicting our sense of history, and even of fairness, become not only the headline of the day, but also part of our daily routine. Publishing on the World Wide Web is an alternative to the mass media. Nevertheless, surfing the Internet or indulging in the current orgy of images can relatively soon become boring, if no meaningful goal animates the action.

The cutting-edge language and look of *Wired*—the magazine of the Netizens—and that of the fast growing number of Web publications, are a radical departure from the literate discourse of yester-year. It might be that their provocative "language" is more appropriate to the subject of a new civilization than the elaborate prose in which this book is written. Regardless, this is not another product of the cottage industry of predictions, as we know them from the reputable Naisbitt, Gilder, and Tofflers. A little knowledge is dangerous—today more than ever before! Not the highs of or the obsession with the stock market are of concern here, but rather an intellectual passion hopefully not unlike that embodied in the forces of our time.

Science and technology are themes of this intellectual expedition. But the subject is the ever-changing human being. To explain without explaining away the complexity of this juncture is more important to me than riding the coattails of today's sound-bite stars. Solid arguments, which suggest possibilities fundamentally different from what quite a few are willing to accept—or even entertain—make for a more deeply founded optimism.

This is a time of conflict, manifested in many instabilities. It is also a time of opportunities. Those not able or willing to recognize them might slow the dynamics, but will not stop the process of change. This applies to the USA and Canada, as it applies to the rest of the world—the advanced countries of Western Europe, Australia, and New Zealand; or the countries of Africa, Asia, Eastern Europe, and Latin America. A perspective fundamentally different from that of the Machine Age cannot emerge within the structures embodying their assumptions.

No nation, and no individual, has enough resources to afford a wait-and-see posture. The experience of the computer is telling: The next chip will be faster, cheaper, and will incorporate more processing possibilities. Those who postpone using the computer of today are missing not only a cycle of learning, but also everything that the current chip is making possible. We can never make up for lost time. This applies to the destruction of the Amazon Rain Forest as it applies, probably in a more critical way, to facilitating means of access to cognition, and to effective human interaction in the global world.

I hope you understand that behind the euphemism of this book's title lie the many languages and means of expression and communication that I should have used myself, and not only written about. If you get lost along the intellectual journey to which this book invites, it is my fault. If you agree with the argument only because it tired you, or because of my enthusiasm, it will be my loss. But if you can argue with me, and if your argument is free of prejudice, we can continue the journey together.

Try to reach me—as my thoughts try to reach you through this book. Unfortunately, I am not yet able to hand you that digital book that would directly connect us. Short of this, here is an address you can use:

nadin@code.uni-wuppertal.de

Let's keep on touch!

Mihai Nadin
Little Compton, USA
Wuppertal, Germany

TABLE OF CONTENTS

INTRODUCTION

LITERACY IN A CHANGING WORLD

THINKING ABOUT ALTERNATIVES

Preoccupation with language is, in fact, preoccupation with ourselves as individuals and as a species. While many concerns, such as terrorism, AIDS, poverty, racism, and massive migration of populations, haunt us as we hurry to achieve our portion of well-being, one at least seems easier to allay: illiteracy. This book proclaims the end of literacy, as it also accounts for the incredible forces at work in our restlessly shifting world. The end of literacy—a chasm between a not-so-distant yesterday and the exciting, though confusing, tomorrow—is probably more difficult to understand than to live with. Reluctance to acknowledge change only makes things worse. We notice that literate language use does not work as we assume or were told it should, and wonder what can be done to make things fit our expectations. Parents hope that better schools with better teachers will remedy the situation. Teachers expect more from the family and suggest that society should invest more in order to maintain literacy skills. Professors groan under the prospect of ill-prepared students entering college. Publishers redefine their strategies as new forms of expression and communication vie for public attention and dollars. Lawyers, journalists, the military, and politicians worry about the role and functions of language in society. Probably most concerned with their own roles in the social structure and with the legitimacy of their institutions, they would preserve those structures of human activity that justify literacy and thus their own positions of power and influence. The few who believe that literacy comprises not only skills, but also ideals and values, say that the destiny of our civilization is at stake, and that the decline in literacy has dreadful implications. Opportunity is not part of the discourse or argument.

The major accomplishment of analyzing illiteracy so far has been *the listing of symptoms:* the decrease in functional literacy; a general degradation of writing skills and reading comprehension; an alarming increase of *packaged* language (clichés used in speeches, *canned* messages); and a general tendency to substitute visual media (especially television and video) for written language. Parallel to scholarship on the subject, a massive but unfocused public opinion campaign has resulted in all kinds of literacy enterprises. Frequently using stereotypes that in themselves affect language quality, such enterprises plead for teaching adults who cannot read or write, for improving language study in all grades, and for raising public awareness of illiteracy and its various implications. Still, we do not really understand the necessary character of the decline of literacy. Historic and systematic aspects of functional illiteracy, as well as language degradation, are minimally addressed. They are phenomena that affect not only the United States. Countries with a long cultural tradition, and which make the preservation and literate use of language a public institution, experience them as well.

My interest in the subject of illiteracy was triggered by two factors: the personal experience of being uprooted from an East European culture that stubbornly defended and maintained rigid structures of literacy; and involvement in what are commonly described as new technologies. I ended up in the USA, a land of unstructured and flawed literacy, but also one of amazing dynamics. Here I joined those who experienced the consequences of the low quality of education, as well as the opening of new opportunities. The majority of these are disconnected from what is going on in schools and universities. This is how and why I started thinking, like many others, about alternatives.

My Mayflower (if I may use the analogy to the Pilgrims) brought me to individuals who do many things—shop, work, play or watch sports, travel, go to church, even love—with an acute sense of immediacy. Worshippers of the instant, my new compatriots served as a contrast to those who, on the European continent I came from, conscientiously strive for permanency—of family, work, values, tools, homes, appliances, cars, buildings. In contrast, the USA is a place where everything is *the present*, the coming moment. Not only television programs and advertisements made me aware of this fact. Books are as permanent as their survival on bestseller lists. The market, with its increasingly breathtaking fluctuations, might today celebrate a company that tomorrow disappears for good. Commencement ceremonies, family life, business commitments, religious practice, succeeding fashions, songs, presidents, denture creams, car models, movies, and practically everything else embody the same obsession. Language and literacy could not escape this obsession with change. Because of my work as a university professor, I was in the trenches where battles of literacy are fought. That is where I came to realize that a better curriculum, multicultural or not, or better paid teachers, or cheaper and better books could make a difference, but would not change the outcome.

The decline of literacy is an encompassing phenomenon impossible to reduce to the state of education, to a nation's economic rank, to the status of social, ethnic, religious, or racial groups, to a political system, or to cultural history. There was life before literacy and there will be life after it. In fact, it has already begun. Let us not forget that literacy is a relatively late acquisition in human culture. The time preceding writing is 99% of the entire story of the human being. My position in the discussion is one of questioning historic continuity as a premise for literacy. If we can understand what the end of literacy as we know it means in practical terms, we will avoid further lamentation and initiate a course of action from which all can benefit.

Moreover, if we can get an idea of what to expect beyond the safe haven now fading on the horizon, then we will be able to come up with improved, more effective models of education. At the same time, we will comprehend what individuals need in order to successfully ascertain their manifold nature. Improved human interaction, for which new technologies are plentifully available, should be the concrete result of this understanding of the end of the civilization of literacy.

The first irony of any publication on illiteracy is that it is inaccessible to those who are the very subject of the concern of literacy partisans. Indeed, the majority of the millions active on the Internet read at most a 3-sentence short paragraph. The attention span of students in high school and universities is not much shorter than that of their instructors: one typed page. Legislators, no less than bureaucrats, thrive on executive summaries. A 30-second TV spot is many times more influential than a 4-column in-depth article. But those who give life and dynamics to reality use means other than those whose *continued* predominance this book questions.

The second irony is that this book also presents arguments which are, in their logical sequence, dependent on the conventions of reading and writing. As a medium for constituting and interpreting history, writing definitely influences how we think and what we think about. I wondered how my arguments would hold up in an interactive, non-linear medium of communication, in which we can question each other, and which also makes authorship, if not irrelevant, the last thing someone would worry about. Since I have used language to think through this book, I know that it would make less sense in a different medium.

This leads me to state from the outset—almost as self-encouragement—that literacy, whose end I discuss, will not disappear. For some, *Literacy Studies* will become a new specialty, as Sanskrit or Ancient Greek has become for a handful of experts. For others, it will become a skill, as it is already for editors, proofreaders, and professional writers. For the majority, it will continue in *literacies* that facilitate the use and integration of new media and new forms of communication and interpretation. The utopian in me says that we will find ways to *reinvent* literacy, if not save it. It has played a major role in leading to the new civilization we are entering. The realist acknowledges that new times and challenges require new means to cope with their complexity. Reluctance to acknowledge change does not prevent it from coming about. It only prevents us from making the best of it.

Probably my active practice of literacy has been matched by all those means, computer-based or not, for coping with complexity, to whose design and realization I contributed. This book is not an exercise in prophesying a brave new world of people happy to know less but all that they have to know when they need to. Neither is it about individuals who are superficial but who adapt more easily to change, mediocre but extremely competitive. Its subject is language and everything pertaining to it: family and sexuality, politics, the market, what and how we eat, how we dress, the wars we fight, love, sports, and more. It is a book about ourselves who give life to words whenever we speak, write, or read. We give life to images, sounds, textures, to multimedia and virtual reality involving ourselves in new interactions. Transcending boundaries of literacy in practical experiences for which literacy is no longer appropriate means, ultimately, to grow into a new civilization.

PROGRESSING TOWARDS ILLITERACY?

Here is as good a place as any to explain my perspective. Language involves human beings in all their aspects: biology, sense of space and time, cognitive and manual skills, emotional resources, sensitivity, tendency to social interaction and political organization. But what best defines our relation to language is the pragmatics of our existence. Our continuous self-constitution through what we do, why we do, and how we do all we actually do—in short, human pragmatics—

involves language, but is not reducible to it. The pragmatic perspective I assume originated with Charles Sanders Peirce. When I began teaching in the USA, my American colleagues and students did not know who he was. The semiotic implications of this text relate to his work. Questioning how knowledge is shared, Peirce noticed that, without talking about the bearers of our knowledge—all the sign carriers we constitute—we would not be able to figure out how results of our inquiries are integrated in our deeds, actions, and theories.

Language and the formation and expression of ideas is unique to humans in that they define a part of the cognitive dimension of our pragmatic. We seem endowed with language, as we are with hearing, sight, touch, smell, and taste. But behind the appearance is a process through which human self-constitution led to the possibility and necessity of language, as it led to the humanization of our senses. Furthermore, it led to the means by which we constitute ourselves as literate as the pragmatics of our existence requires under ever-changing circumstances. The appearance is that literacy is a useful tool, when in fact it results in the pragmatic context. We can *use* a hammer or a computer, but we *are* our language. The experience of language extends to the experience of the logic it embodies, as well as to that of the institutions that language and literacy made possible. These, in turn, influence what we are and how we think, what we do and why we do. So does every tool, appliance, and machine we use, and so do all the people with whom we interact. Our interactions with people, with nature, or with artifacts we ourselves generated further affect the pragmatic self-constitution of our identity.

The literate experience of language enhanced our cognitive capabilities. Consequently, literacy became larger than life. Much is covered by the practice of literacy: tradition, culture, thoughts and feelings, human expression through literature, the constitution of political, scientific, and artistic programs, ethics, the practical experience of law. In this book, I use a broad definition of literacy that reflects the many facets it has acquired over time. Those readers who think I

8

stretch the term *literacy* too far should keep in mind all that literacy comprises in our culture. In contrast, illiteracy, no matter what its cause or what other attributes an individual labeled *illiterate* has, is seen as something harmful and shameful, to be avoided at any price. Without an understanding that encompasses our values and ways of thinking, we cannot perceive how a civilization can *progress* to illiteracy. Many people are willing to be part of *post-literate* society, but by no means are they willing to be labeled members of a civilization qualified as illiterate.

By *civilization of illiteracy* I mean one in which literate characteristics no longer constitute the underlying structure of effective practical experiences. Furthermore, I mean a civilization in which no one literacy dominates, as it did until around the turn of the century, and still does. This domination takes place through imposition of its rules, which prevent practical experiences of human self-constitution in domains where literacy has exhausted its potential or is impotent. In describing the post-literate, I know that any metaphor will do as long as it does not call undue attention to itself. What counts is not the provocativeness but that we lift our gaze, determined to see, not just to look for the comforting familiar.

This civilization of illiteracy is one of many literacies, each with its own characteristics and rules of functioning. Some of such partial literacies are based on configurational modes of expression, as in the written languages of Japan, China, or Korea; on visual forms of communication; or on synesthetic communication involving a combination of our senses. Some are numerical and rely on a different notation system than that of literacy. The civilization of illiteracy comprises experiences of thinking and working above and beyond language, as mathematicians from different countries communicating perfectly through mathematical formulae demonstrate. Or as we experience in activities where the visual, digitally processed, supports a human pragmatics of increased efficiency. Even in its primitive, but extremely dynamic, deployment, the Internet embodies the directions and possibilities of such a civilization. This brings us back to literacy's reason for being: pragmatics expressed in methods for increasing efficiency, of ensuring a desired outcome, be this in regard to a list of merchandise, a deed, instructions on how to make something or to carry out an act, a description of a place, poetry and drama, philosophy, the recording and dissemination of history and abstract ideas, mythology, stories and novels, laws, and customs. Some of these products of literacy are simply no longer necessary. That new methods and technologies of a digital nature effectively constitute an alternative to literacy cannot be overemphasized.

I started this book convinced that the price we pay for the human tendency to efficiency—that is, our striving for more and more at an ever cheaper price—is literacy and the values connected to it as represented by tradition, books, art, family, philosophy, ethics, among many others. We are confronted with the increased speed and shorter durations of human interactions. A growing number and a variety of mediating elements in human praxis challenge our understanding of what we do. Fragmentation and interconnectedness of the world, the new technology of synchronization, the dynamics of life forms or of artificial constructs elude the domain of literacy as they constitute a new pragmatic framework. This becomes apparent when we compare the fundamental characteristics of language to the characteristics of the many new sign systems complementing or replacing it. Language is sequential, centralized, linear, and corresponds to the stage of linear growth of humankind. Matched by the linear increase of the means of subsistence and production required for the survival and development of the species, this stage reached its implicit potential. The new stage corresponds to distributed, non-sequential forms of human activity, nonlinear dependencies. Reflecting the exponential growth of humankind (population, expectations, needs, and desires), this new stage is one of alternative resources, mainly cognitive in nature, compensating for what was perceived as limited natural means for supporting humankind. It is a system of a different scale, suggestively represented by our concerns with globality and higher levels of complexity. Therefore, humans can no longer develop within the limitations of an intrinsically centralized, linear, hierarchic, proportional model of contingencies that connect existence to production and consumption, and to the life-support system. Alternatives that affect the nature of life, work, and social interaction emerge through practical experiences of a fundamentally new condition.

Literacy and the means of human self-constitution based on it reached their full potential decades ago. The new means, which are not as universal (i.e., as encompassing) as language, open possibilities for exponential growth, resulting from their connectivity and improved involvement of cognitive resources. As long as the world was composed of small units (tribes, communities, cities, counties), language, despite differences in structure and use, occupied a central place. It had a unifying character and exercised a homogenizing function within each viable political unit. The world has entered the phase of global interdependencies. Many *local* languages and their literacies of relative, restricted significance emerge as instruments of optimization. What takes precedence today is interconnectivity at many levels, a function for which literacy is ill prepared. Citizens become *Netizens,* an identity that relates them to the entire world, not only to where they happen to live and work.

The encompassing system of culture broke into subsystems, not just into the "two cultures" of science and literacy that C. P. Snow discussed in 1959, hoping idealistically that a third culture could unite and harmonize them. Market mechanisms, representative of the competitive nature of human beings, are in the process of emancipating themselves from literacy. Where literate norms and regulations still in place prevent this emancipation—as is the case with government activity and bureaucracies, the military, and legal institutions—the price is expressed in lower efficiency and painful stagnation. Some European countries, more productive in impeding the work of the forces of renewal, pay dearly for their inability to understand the need for structural changes. United or not in a Europe of broader market opportunities, member countries will have to free themselves from the rigid constraints of a pragmatic framework that no longer supports their viability. Conflicts are not solved; solutions are a long time in coming.

One more remark before ending this introduction. It seems that those who run the scholarly publishing industry are unable to accept that someone can have an idea that does not originate from a quotation. In keeping with literacy's reliance on authority, I have acknowledged in the references the works that have some bearing on the ideas presented in this book. Few, very few indeed, are mentioned in the body of the text. The line of argument deserves priority over the stereotypes of referencing. This does not prevent me from acknowledging here, in addition to Leibniz and Peirce, the influence of thinkers and writers such as Roberto Maturana, Terry Winograd, George Lakoff, Lotfi Zadeh, Hans Magnus Enzensberger, George Steiner, Marshall McLuhan, Ivan Illich, Yuri M. Lotman, and even Baudrillard, the essayist of the post-industrial. If I misunderstood any of them, it is not because I do not respect their contributions. Seduced by my own interest and line of reasoning, I integrated what I thought could become solid bricks into a building of arguments which was to be mine. I am willing to take blame for its design and construction, remaining thankful to all those whose fingerprints are, probably, still evident on some of the bricks I used.

In the 14 years that have gone by since I started thinking and writing about the civilization of illiteracy, many of the directions I brought into discussion are making it into the public domain. But I should be the last to be surprised or unhappy that reality changed before I was able to finish this book, and before publishers could make up their minds about printing it. The Internet was not yet driving the stock market, neither had the writers of future shock had published their books churning prophecies, nor had companies made fortunes in multimedia when the ideas that go into this book were discussed with students, presented in public lectures, outlined to policy-makers (including administrators in higher education), and printed in scholarly journals. On starting this book, I wanted it to be not only a presentation of events and trends, but a program for practical action. This is why, after examination of what could be called the theoretical aspects, the focus shifts to the applied. The book ends with suggestions for practical measures to be considered as alternatives to the beaten path of the bandage method that only puts off radical treatment, even when its inevitability is acknowledged. Yes, I like to see my ideas tested and applied, even taken over and developed further (credit given or not!). I would rather put up with a negative outcome in discussions following publication of this book, than have it go unnoticed.

BOOK I.

CHAPTER 1: THE CHASM BETWEEN YESTERDAY AND TOMORROW

CONTRASTING CHARACTERS

The information produced in our time, in one day, exceeds that of the last 300 years. What this means can be more easily understood by giving some life to this dry evaluation originating from people in the business of quantifying data processing.

Zizi, the hairdresser, and her companions exemplify today's literate population. Portrayed by Hans Magnus Enzensberger, she is contrasted to Pascal, who at the age of sixteen had already published his work on conic sections, to Hugo Grotius, who graduated from college at fifteen, and to Melanchthon, who at the age of twelve was a student at the once famous Heidelberg University. Zizi knows how to get around. She is like a living address on the Internet at its current stage of development: more links than content, perennially under construction. She continuously starts on new avenues, never pursuing any to the end. Her well-being is supported by public money as she lives off all the social benefits society affords. Zizi's conversations are about her taxes, and characters she reads about in magazines, sees on television, or meets on vacation. As superficial as such conversations can be, they are full of catch phrases associated or not with the celebrations of the day. Her boyfriend, 34-year-old Bruno G., graduated with a degree in political economy, drives a taxi cab, and still wonders what he wants to do in life. He knows the name of every soccer team that has won the championship since 1936; he knows by heart the names of the players, which coach was fired when, and every game score.

Melanchthon studied reading, writing, Latin, Greek, and theology. He knew by heart many fragments from the classical writers and from the Bible. The world he lived in was small. To explain its workings, one did not need to master mathematics or physics, but philosophy. Since Melanchthon can no longer be subjected to multiple choice or to IQ tests, we will never know if he could make it into college today. The question posed about all the characters introduced is a simple one: Who is more ignorant, Melanchthon or Zizi?

Enzensberger's examples are from Germany, but the phenomena he brings to his readers' attention transcend national boundaries. He himself—writer, poet, publisher—is far from being an Internet buff, although he might be as informed about it as his characters are. As opposed to many other writers on literacy and education, Enzensberger confirms that the efficiency reached in the civilization of illiteracy (he does not call it that) makes it possible to extend adolescence well into what used to be the more productive time in the life of past generations. Everyone goes to college—in some countries college education is a right. This means that over half of the young people enter some form of higher education. After graduating, they find out that they still don't know what they want. Or, worse yet, that what they know, or are certified as knowing, is of no consequence to what they are expected to do. They will live, like Zizi, from social benefits and will get extremely angry at anyone questioning society's ability to provide them. For them, efficiency of human practical experiences translate into the right to not worry whether they will ever contribute to this efficiency. While still students, they demand, and probably rightly so, that everything be to the point. The problem is that neither they nor their teachers can define what that means. What students get are more choices among less significant subjects. That, at least, is how it looks. They probably never finish a book from cover to cover. Assignments are given to them in small portions, and usually with photocopied pages, which they are expected to read. A question-and-answer sheet is conveniently attached, with the hope that the students will read the pages to find the answers, and not copy them from more dedicated classmates.

That Zizi probably has a vocabulary as rich as that of a 16th-century scholar in the humanities can be assumed. That she likely uses fewer than 1,000 of these words only says that this is how much she needs in order to function efficiently. Melanchthon used almost all the words he knew. His work required mastery of literacy so that he could express every new idea prompted by the few new practical experiences of human self-constitution he was involved in or aware of. He spoke and wrote in three languages, two of which are used today only in the specialties they are part of. Two or three sentences from a tourist guidebook or from a tape is all Zizi needs for her next vacation in Greece or Italy. For her, travel is a practical experience as vital as any other. She knows the names of rock groups, and lip-syncs the songs that express her concerns: sex, drugs, loneliness. Her memory of any stage performance or movie surpasses that of Melanchthon, who probably knew by heart the entire liturgy of the Catholic Church. Like everyone else constituting their identities in the civilization of illiteracy, Zizi knows what it takes to minimize her tax burden and how to use coupons. The rhythm of her existence is defined more by commercial than natural cycles. And she keeps refreshing her base of practical information. Living in a time of change, this is her chance to beat *the system* and all the literate norms and constraints it imposes on her.

Melanchthon, despite his literacy, would have been lost between two consecutive tax laws of our time, and even more between consecutive changes in fashion or music trends, or between consecutive versions of computer software, not to say chips. He belonged to a system appropriate to a stable world of relatively unchanging expectations. What he studied would last him a lifetime. Zizi and Bruno, as well as their friend Helga—the *third* in Enzensberger's text—live in a world of unsettled, heterogeneous information, based on *ad hoc* methods delivered by magazines, or through the Internet, that one has only to scan or surf in order to find useful data.

At this juncture, readers familiar with the World Wide Web, whether passionate about it or strongly against it, understand why I describe Zizi as a living Internet address. To derive some meaning from this description, and especially to avoid the appearance of drawing a caricature of the Internet, we need to focus on the pragmatic context in which Zizi constitutes herself and in which the Internet is constituted as a global experience. The picture one gets from contrasting the famous Melanchthon to Zizi the hairdresser is not exactly fair, as it would be unfair to contrast the Library of Alexandria to the Internet. On the one hand, we have a tremendous collection representative of human knowledge (and the illusion of knowledge). On the other we have the embodiment of extremely effective methods for acquiring, testing, using, and discarding information required by human pragmatics. The world in which Melanchthon worked was limited to Central Europe and Rome. News circulated mainly by word-of-mouth. Melanchthon, like everyone who was raised with and worked amid books, was subjected to less information than we are today. He did not need an *Intel inside* computer or search engine to find what he wanted. He would not understand how anyone could replace the need for and pleasure of browsing by a machine called *Browser.* His was a world of associations, not matches, no matter how successful. Human minds, not machines, made up his cognitive world.

Literacy opened access to knowledge as long as this knowledge was compatible with the pragmatic structures it embodied and supported. The *ozone hole* of over-information broke the protective bubble of literacy. In the new pragmatic context, the human being, thirsty for data, seems at the mercy of the informational environment that shapes work, entertainment, life—in short, everything. Access to study was far from being equal, or even close to some standard of fairness, in Melanchthon's time of obsession with excellence. Information itself was very expensive. In order to become a hairdresser—were it possible and necessary 500 years ago—Zizi, as well as the millions who attend career training schools, would have had to pay much more for her training than she did in our age of unlimited equal access to mediocrity. Knowledge was acquired through channels as diverse as family, schools, churches, and disseminated in very few books, or orally, or through imitation.

Individuals in Melanchthon's time formed a set of expectations and pursued goals that changed minimally over their lifetime, since the pragmatic context remained the same. This ended with the dynamic practical experiences of self-constitution that led to the pragmatic context of our day. Ended also are the variety of forms of human cooperation and solidarity—as imperfect as they were—characteristic of a scale in which survival of the individual was essential for the survival and well-being of the community. They are replaced by a generalized sense of competition. Not infrequently, this takes the form of adversity, socially acceptable when performed by literate lawyers, for instance, yet undesirable when performed by illiterate terrorists.

More suggestive than precise, this description, in which Zizi and Melanchthon play the leading characters, exemplifies the chasm between yesterday and today. A further examination of what is going on in our world allows the observation that literate language no longer exclusively, or even dominantly, affects and regulates day-to-day activities. A great amount of language used in the daily routine of people living in economically advanced countries was simply wiped out or absorbed in machine transactions. Digital networks, connecting production lines, distribution channels, and points of sale spectacularly augment the volume and variety of such transactions. Practical experiences of shopping, transportation, banking, and stock market transactions require literacy less and less. Automation rationalized away the literate component of many activities. All over the world, regardless of the economic or technological level reached, communication-specific endeavors, such as advertisement, political campaigns, various forms of ceremonial (religious, military, athletic), make crystal clear that literate language use is subordinated to the function or purpose pursued.

The developments under scrutiny affect surviving pre-literate societies—the nomadic, animistic population of Sudan, the tribes of the Brazilian Amazon forests, remote populations of Africa, Asia, Australia—as they affect the literate and post-literate. Without going into the details of the process, we should be aware that commodities coming from such societies, including the commodity of labor, no less than their needs and expectations, are traded on the global market. In the African Sahara, TV is watched—sets connected to car batteries—as much as in the high mountains of Peru populated by illiterate Incas. As virtual points of sale, the lands with pre-literate societies are traded in the futures markets as possible tourist resorts, or as a source of cheap labor. Experiences of practical self-constitution as nomadic, animistic, and tribal are no longer confined to the small scale of the respective community. In the effective world of a global pragmatics of high efficiency, their hunger and misery shows up in ledgers as potential aid and cooperation programs. Don't read here only greed and cynicism, rather the expression of reciprocal dependencies. AIDS on the African sub-continent and the Ebola epidemics only capture the image of shared dangers. Across the Atlantic Ocean, the plants of the disappearing Amazon rain forest, studied for their healing potential, capture an image of opportunity. In such situations and locations, the pragmatics of literacy and illiteracy meet and interact.

CHOOSE A LETTER AND CLICK

Images substitute text; sounds add rhythm or nuance; visual representations other than written words become dominant; animation introduces dynamics where written words could only suggest it. In technologically advanced societies, interactive multimedia (or hypermedia) combine visual, aural, dynamic, and structural representations. Environments for personal exploration, organization, and manipulation of information proliferate in CD-ROM formats, interactive games, and tutorial networks. High fidelity sound, rich video resources, computer graphics, and a variety of devices for individualized human interaction provide the technological basis for what emerges as a ubiquitous computing environment.

The entire process can be provisionally summarized as follows: Human cooperation and interaction corresponding to the complexity of the undertakings of our age is defined by expectations of high efficiency. Relatively stable and well structured literate communication among the people involved is less efficient than rather fast and fragmentary contact through means other than those facilitated by, or based on, literacy. Stereotyped, highly repetitive or well defined unique tasks, and the literate language associated with them, have been transferred to machines. Unique tasks require strategies of specialization. The smaller the task assigned to each participant, the more effective the ways to carry it out at the expense of variety of forms and extent of direct human interaction, as well as at the expense of literacy-based interactions. Accordingly, human self-constitution today involves means of expression and communication no longer based on or reducible to literacy. Characteristics immanent in literacy affect cognitive processes, forms of human interaction, and the nature of productive effort to a lesser extent. Nevertheless, the reshaping of human pragmatics does not take place by general agreement or without conflict, as will be pointed out more than once.

While some fail to notice the decreased role of literacy and the deterioration of language in our life today, others surrender to illiteracy without even being aware of their surrender. We live in a world in which many people—especially those with more than undergraduate college education—complain about the low level of literacy while they simultaneously acquiesce to methods and necessities that make literacy less and less significant. Furthermore, when invoking literacy, people maintain a nostalgia for something that has already ceased to affect their lives. Their thinking, feeling, interpersonal relations, and expectations regarding family, religion, ethics, morals, art, dining, cultural and leisure activities already reflect the new illiterate condition. It is not a matter of personal choice, but a *necessary* development. The low level of literacy of those who receive an education from which society used to expect literate adults to graduate worries politicians, educators, and literacy professionals (writers, publishers, booksellers). They fear, probably for the wrong reasons, that people cannot live and prosper without knowing how to write or read at high levels of competence. What actually worries them is not that people write less well, or less correctly, or read less (some if at all), but that some succeed despite the odds. Self-styled champions of literacy, instead of focusing on change, spend money, energy, and intelligence, not in exploring how to optimally benefit from change, but on how to stop an inexorable process.

The state of affairs characteristic of the civilization of illiteracy did not come about overnight. Norbert Wiener's prophetic warning that we will become slaves of intelligent contraptions that take over intellectual faculties deserves more than a parenthetic reminder. Some commentators point to the disruption of the sixties, which put the educational system all over the world in turmoil. The events of the sixties, as much as the new machines Wiener discussed, are yet another symptom of, but not a reason for, the decline of literacy. The major hypothesis of this book is that illiteracy, in its relative terms mentioned so far, results from the changed nature of human practical experiences; that is, from the pragmatics corresponding to a new stage of human civilization. (I prefer to use *pragmatics* in the sense the Greeks used it: *pragma*, for *deeds*, from *prattein, to do*.) Regardless of our vocations—working in a large corporation or heading one's own business, farming, creating art, teaching language or mathematics, programming, or even participating in a university's board of trustees—we accept, even if with some reluctance, the rationalization of language. Our lives take place increasingly in the impersonal world of stereotype discourse of forms, applications, passwords, and word processed letters. The Internet, as World Wide Web, e-mail medium, data exchange, or chat forum effectively overrides constraints and limitations resulting from the participation of language in human pragmatics. Our world is becoming more and more a world of efficiency and interconnected activities that take place at a speed and at a variety of levels for which literacy is not appropriate.

Still, complex interdependencies are reflected in our relation to language in general, and in our use of it, in particular. It seems that language is a key—at least one among many—to the mind, the reason for which artificial intelligence is interested in language. It also seems to be a major social ingredient. Accordingly, no one should be surprised that once the status of language changes, there are also changes far beyond what we expect when we naively consider what a word is, or what is in a word or a rule of grammar, or what defines a text. A word on paper, one like the many on this page, is quite different from a word in the hypertext of a multimedia application or that of the Web. The letters serve a different function. Omit one from this page and you have a misspelling. Click on one and nothing happens. Click on a letter displayed on a Web page and you might be connected to other signs, images, sounds, and interactive multimedia presentations. These changes, among others, are the implicit themes of this book and define the context for understanding why illiteracy is not an accident, but a necessary development.

KEEPING UP WITH FASTER LIVING

Ours is a world of efficiency. Although more obvious on the computer screen, and on the command buttons and touch-sensitive levers of the machines we rely quite heavily upon, efficiency expectations met in business and financial life insinuate themselves into the intimacy of our private lives as well. As a result of efficiency expectations, we have changed almost everything we inherited in our homes—kitchen, study, or bathroom—and redefined our respective social or family roles. We do almost everything others used to do for us. We cook (if warming up prefabricated dishes in a microwave oven still qualifies as cooking), do the laundry (if selecting dirty sheets or clothes by color and fabric and stuffing them into the machine qualifies as washing), type or desktop publish, transport (ourselves, our children). Machines replaced servants, and we became their servants in turn. We have to learn their language of instructions and to cope with the consequences their use entails: increased energy demand, pollution, waste, and most important, dependence. Ours is a world of brief encounters in which "How are you?" is not a question reflecting concern or expecting a real answer, but a formula. Once it meant what it expressed and prefaced dialogue. Now it is the end of interaction, or at best the introduction to a dialogue totally independent of the question. Where everyone living within the model of literacy expected the homogeneous background of shared language, we now find a very fragmented reality of sub-languages, images, sounds, body gestures, and new conventions.

Despite the heavy investment society has made in literacy over hundreds of years, literacy is no longer adopted by all as a desired educational goal. Neither is it actively pursued for immediate practical or long-term reasons. People seem to acknowledge that they need not even that amount of literacy imposed upon them by obligatory education. For quite a few—speech writers, editors, perhaps novelists and educators—literacy is indeed a skill which they aptly use for making a living. They know and apply rules of correct language usage. Methods for augmenting the efficiency of the message they put in the mouths of politicians, soap-opera actors, businessmen, activists and many others in need of somebody to write (and sometimes even to think) for them are part of their trade. For others, these rules are a means of exploring the wealth of fiction, poetry, history, and philosophy. For a great majority, literacy is but another skill required in high school and college, but not necessarily an essential component of their current and, more important, future lives and work. This majority, estimated at ca. 75% of the population, believes that all one has to know is already stored for them and made available as an expected social service—mathematics in the cash register or pocket calculator, chemistry in the laundry detergent, physics in the toaster, language in the greeting cards available for all imaginable occasions, eventually incorporated, as spellers or writing routines, into the word processing programs they use or others use for them.

Four groups seem to have formed: those for whom literacy is a skill; those using it as a means for studying values based on literacy; those functioning in a world of pre-packaged literacy artifacts; and those active beyond the limitations of literacy, stretching cognitive boundaries, defining new means and methods of communication and interaction, constituting themselves in practical activities of higher and higher efficiency. These four groups are the result of changes in the condition of the human being in what was broadly (in fact, too broadly) termed *Post-Industrial Society*. Whether specifically identified as such or assuming labels of convenience, the conflict characteristic of this time of fundamental change has its locus in literacy; and more specifically in the direction of change towards the civilization of illiteracy.

At first glance, it is exceedingly difficult to say whether language, as an instrument of continuity and permanence, is failing because the rhythm of existence has accelerated increasingly since the Industrial Revolution, or the rhythm of existence has accelerated because human interaction is no longer at the mercy of language. We do not know whether this acceleration is due to, or nourished by, changes in language and the way people use it, or if changes in language reflect this acceleration. It is quite plausible that the use of images, moreover of interactive multimedia and network-based exchange of complex data are more appropriate to a faster paced society than texts requiring more time and concentration. But it is less clear whether we use images and synesthetic means of expression because we want to be faster, and thus more efficient, or we can be faster and improve efficiency if we use such means.

Shorter terms of human interaction and, for example, the change in the status of the family have something in common. The new political condition of the individual in modern society also has something in common with the characteristics of human interaction and the means of this interaction. But again, we do not really know whether the new socio-economic dynamics resulted from our intention to accelerate interactions, or the acceleration in human interaction is only the background (or a marginal effect) of a more encompassing change of our condition under circumstances making this change necessary. My hypothesis is that a dramatic change in the scale of humankind and in the nature of the relation between humans and their natural and cultural environments might explain the new socio-economic dynamics.

LOADED LITERACY

Languages, or any other form of expression and communication, are meaningful only to the extent that they become part of our existence. When people do not know how to spell words that refer to their existence, we suspect that something related to the learning of spelling (usually the learner) does not function as we assumed it should. (Obviously, literacy is more than spelling.) School, family, new habits—such as extensive television viewing, comics reading, obsessive playing of computer games, Internet surfing, to name some of the apparent culprits—come under scrutiny. Culture, prejudice, or fear of the unknown prevents us from asking whether spelling is still a necessity. Cowardly conformity stops us short from suspecting that something might be wrong with language or with those literacy expectations deeply anchored in all known political programs thrown into our face when our vote is elicited. When spelling and phonetics are as inconsistent as they are in English especially, this suspicion led to the examination and creation of alternative alphabets and to alternative artificial languages, which we shall examine. But spelling fails even in languages with more consistent relations between pronunciation and writing.

Because we inherited, along with our reverence for language, a passive attitude regarding what is logically permissible under the guise of literacy, we do not question implicit assumptions and expectations of literacy. For instance, the belief that command of language enhances cognitive skills, although we know that cognitive processes are not exactly reducible to language, is accepted without hesitation. It is ascertained that literate people from no matter what country can communicate better and learn foreign languages more easily. This is not always the case. In reality, languages are rather loaded systems of conventions in which national biases and other inclinations are extensively embodied and maintained, and even propagated, through speech, writing, and reading. This expectation leads to well intended, though disputable, statements such as: "You can never understand one language until you understand at least two" (signed by Searle).

There is also the implication that literate people have better access to the arts and sciences. The reason for this is that language, as a universal means of communication, is consequently the only means that ultimately explains scientific theories. Works of art, proponents of language argue, can be reduced to verbal description, or at least be better accessed through the language used to index them through labels, classifications, categories. Another assumption (and prejudice) is that the level of performance in and outside language is in direct relation to competence acquired in literacy. This prejudice, from among all others, will come under closer scrutiny because, though literacy is declining, language use deviating from that normed by literacy takes astonishing forms.

MAN PROPOSES, MAN DISPOSES

Knowledge of the connection between languages—taking the appearance of entities with lives of their own—and people constituting them—with the appearance of having unlimited control over their language—is essential for understanding the shift from a literacy-dominated civilization to one of multiple means of expression and communication. These means could be called *languages* if an appropriate definition of such *languages* (and the *literacies* associated with them) could be provided. In light of what has been already mentioned, the broader context of the changes in the status of literacy is the pragmatic framework of our existence. It is not only that the use of language has diminished or its quality decreased. Rather, it is the acknowledgment of a very complex reality, of a biologically and culturally modified human being facing apparent choices difficult, if not impossible, to harmonize. Life is faster paced, not because biological rhythms abruptly changed, but because a new pragmatic framework, of higher efficiency, came about.

Human interaction extends in our days beyond the immediate circle of acquaintances, or what used to be the family circle. This interaction is, however, more superficial and more mediated by other people and by various devices. The universe of existence seems to open as wide as the space we can explore—practically the whole planet, as well as the heavens. At the same time, the pressure of the narrower reality, of exceedingly specialized work, through whose product individual and social identification, as well as valuation take place, is stronger than ever before. On a different level, the individual realizes that the traditional mapping from one to few (family, friends, community) changes drastically. In a context of globality, the mapping extends to the infinity of those partaking in it.

Characteristic of the context of change in the status and function (communication, in particular) of literacy are *fragmentation* of everything we do or encounter and the need to coordinate. We become aware of the increased number and variety of stimuli and realize that previous explanations of their origin and possible impact are not satisfactory. *Decentralization* of many, if not all, aspects of existence, paralleled by strong *integrative forces* at work, is also characteristic of the dynamics of change. It is not communication alone, as some believe, that shapes society. More encompassing effective forces, relatively independent of words, images, sounds, textures, and odors continuously directed at society's members, from every direction and with every imaginable purpose, define social dynamics. They define goals and means of communication as well.

The gap between the performance of communication technology and the effectiveness of communication is symptomatic of the contradictory condition of contemporary humans. It often seems that messages have lives of their own and that the more communication there is, the less it reaches its address. Less than two percent of all the information thrown into mass media communication reaches its audience. At this level of efficiency, no car would ever move, no plane could take off, babies could not even roll over in their cribs! The dependency of communication on literacy proved to be communication's strength. It delivered a potential audience. But it proved to be its weakness, too. The assumption that among literate people, communication not only takes place, but, based on the implied shared background, is always successful, was found to be wrong time and again. Experiences such as wars, conflicts among nations, communities, professional groups (academia, a highly literate social group, is infamous in this respect), families and generations continuously remind us that this assumption is a fallacy. Still we misinterpret these experiences. Case in point: the anxiety of the business community over the lack of communication skills in the young people it employs. That the most literate segment of business is rationalized away in the massive re-engineering of companies goes unnoticed.

We want to believe that business is concerned with fundamental values when its representatives discuss the difficulties mid-level executives have in articulating goals and plans for achieving them in speech or writing. The new structural forms emerging in today's economy show that business-people, as much as politicians and many other people troubled by the current state of literacy today, speak out of both sides of their mouths. They would like to have it both ways: more efficiency, which does not require or stimulate a need for literacy since literacy is not adapted to the new socio-economic dynamics, and the benefits of literacy, without having to pay for them. The reality is that they are all concerned with economic cycles, productivity, efficiency, and profit in trying to figure out what a global economy requires from them. Re-engineering, which companies also called restructuring or downsizing, translates into efficiency expectations within an extremely competitive global economy. By all accounts, restructuring cut the literacy overhead of business. It replaced literate practical experiences of management and productive work with automated procedures for data processing and with computer-aided manufacturing. The process is far from over. It has just reached the usually placid working world of Japan, and it might motivate Europe's effort to regain competitiveness, despite all the social contracts in place that embody expectations of a past that will never return. In fact, all boils down to the recognition of a new status of language: that of becoming, to a greater extent than in its literate embodiment, a business tool, a means of production, a technology. The freeing of language from literacy, and the subsequent loss in quality, is only part of a broader process. The people opposing it should be aware that the civilization of illiteracy is also the expression of practical criticism in respect to a past pragmatic framework far from being as perfect as literacy advocates lead us to believe.

The pragmatics of literacy established a frame of reference in respect to ownership, trade, national identity, and political power. Distribution of ownership might not be new, but its motivations are no longer rooted in inheritance, rather in creativity and a selfish sense of business allegiance. One much circulated observation sums it up: If you think that the thousands of not yet fully vested Microsoft programmers will miss their chance to join the club of millionaires to which their colleagues belong, think again! It is not for the sake of the owner of a business, or of a legendary entrepreneur, and certainly not for the sake of idealism. It is for their own sake that more and more young and less young people use their chance in this hierarchy-free, or freer, environment in which they constitute their identity. What motivates them are arguments of competitiveness, not national identity, political philosophy, or family pride. All these and many other structural aspects resulting from the acquired freedom from structural characteristics of a pragmatic context defined by literacy do not automatically make society better or fairer. But a distribution of wealth and power, and a redefinition of the goals and methods through which democracy is practiced is taking place.

We know, too, that the coercion of writing was applied to what today we call minorities. Since writing is less natural than speaking and bears values specific to a culture, it has alienated individuality. Literacy implies the integration of minorities by appropriating their activity and culture, sometimes replacing their own with the dominant literacy in total disregard of their heritage. "If writing did not suffice to consolidate knowledge," observed Claude Lévi-Strauss, "it was perhaps indispensable in affirming domination. [...] the fight against illiteracy is thus identical with the reinforcement of the control of the citizen by authority." I shall not go so far as to state that the current attempt to celebrate multiplicity and to recognize contradiction brought about by irreducible differences among races, cultures, and practical experiences is not the result of literate necessities. But without a doubt, developments peculiar to the civilization of illiteracy, as this becomes the background for heterogeneous human experiences and conflicting value systems, brought multiplicity to the forefront. And, what is more important, illiteracy builds upon the potential of this multiplicity.

BEYOND THE COMMITMENT TO LITERACY

What seems to be the issue of putting the past in the right perspective (with the appearance of historic revisionism) is actually the expression of pragmatic needs in regard to the present and the future. The subject, in view of its many implications, deserves a closer examination outside, but not in disregard of, the political controversy it has already stirred up. Writing is a form of commitment that extends from the Phoenician agreements and Egyptian records, religious and legal texts on clay and in stone, to the medieval oath and later to contracts. Written language encodes, at many levels (alphabet, sentence structure, semantics, etc.), the nature of the relation among those addressed in writing. A tablet that the Egyptians used for identifying locally traded commodities addressed very few readers. A reduced scale of existence, work, and trade was reflected in very direct notation. For the given context, the tablets supported the expected efficiency. In the framework of the Roman Empire, labeling of construction materials—roof tiles, drainage pipes—distributed within and outside the Empire, involved more elaborate elements. These materials were stamped during manufacture and helped builders select what matched their needs. More people were addressed. Their backgrounds were more diverse: they functioned in different languages and in different cultural contexts. Their practical experience as builders was more complex than that of Egyptian dealers in grain or other commodities who operated locally. Stamping construction materials signaled a commitment to fulfill building needs and expectations. Over time, such commitments became more elaborate and separated themselves from the product. With literacy, they became formalized contracts covering various pragmatic contexts. They bear all the characteristics of literacy. They also become representative of the conflict between means of a literate nature and means appropriate to the levels of efficiency expected in the civilization of illiteracy.

A short look at contracts as we experience them today reveals that contracts are based on languages of their own, hard to decipher by even the average literate person. They quantify economic expectations, legal provisions, and tax consequences. Written in English, they are expected to address the entire world. In the European Community, each of the member countries expects a contract to be formulated in its own language. Consequently, delays and extra costs can make the transaction meaningless. Actually, the contract, not only the packaging and distribution labels, could be provided in the *universal* language of machine-readable bar codes. Ours is a pragmatic framework of illiteracy that results in the generation of *languages* corresponding to functions but pertinent to the fast-changing circumstances that make the activity possible in the first place. In a world of tremendous competition, fast exchange, and accelerated growth of new expectations, the contract itself and the mechanisms for executing it have to be efficient.

Relations to power, property, and national identity expressed in language and stabilized through the means of literacy were also embodied in myths, religions, poetry and literature. Indeed, from the epic poems of ancient civilizations to the ballads of the troubadours and the songs of the minstrels, and to poetry and literature, references were made to property and feelings, to the living and the dead. Records of life were kept and commitments were reiterated. Today many literates despair at the thought that these are displaced by the dead poetry or prose of the computer-generated variety. It is unquestionable that information storage and access redefined the scope of commitments and historic records, and ultimately redefined memory.

From whatever angle we look at language and literacy, we come back to the people who commit themselves in the practical experience of their self-constitution. While the relation of people to language is symptomatic of their general condition, to understand how and why this relation changes is to understand how and why human beings change. With the ideal of literacy, we inherited the illusion that to understand human beings is to understand human language. It is actually the other way around—if we understand language as a dynamic practical experience in its own right. There is a deeper level that we have to explore—that of the human activity through which we project our being into the reality of existence, and make it sensible and understandable to others. It is only in the act of expressing ourselves through work, contemplation, enjoyment, and wonder that we become what we are for ourselves and for others. Under pragmatic circumstances characteristic of the establishment of the species and its history up to our time, this required language and led to the need for literacy. As a matter of fact, literacy can be seen as a form of commitment, one among the successive commitments that individuals make and the human species enters. For over 2,500 years, these circumstances seemed to be eternal and dominated our existence. But as humankind outgrows the pragmatics based on the underlying structure of literacy, means different from language, that is, means different from those constituting the framework of literacy and of literacy-based commitments become necessary.

A MOVING TARGET

The context of the subject of change comprises also the terminology developed around it. The variation of the meanings assigned to the words *literacy* and *illiteracy* is symptomatic of the various angles from which they are examined. Literacy, as someone said (I found this credited to both John Ashcroft, once governor of Missouri, and to Henry A. Miller) has been a *moving target*. It has reflected changes in criteria for evaluating writing and writing skills as the pragmatic framework of human activity changed through time. Writing is probably more than 5,000 years old. And while the emergence of writing and reading are the premise for literacy, a notion of generalized literacy can be construed only in connection to the invention of movable type (during the 11th century in China, and the early 16th century in Western Europe), and even more so with the advent of the 19th century high-speed rotary press.

Within the mentioned time-frame, many changes in the understanding of what literacy connotes have come about. For those who see the world through the Book (*Torah, Bible, Koran, Upanishads, Wu Ching*), literacy means to be able to read and understand the Book, and thus the world. All practical rules presented in the Book constitute a framework accessed either through literacy or oral tradition. In the Middle Ages, to be literate meant to know Latin, which was perceived as the language of divine revelation. Parallel to the religious, or religion-oriented, perspective of literacy, many others were acknowledged: social—how writing and reading constitute a framework for social interaction; economic—how writing and reading and other skills of comprehending maps, tables, and symbols affect people's ability to participate in economic life; educational—how literacy is disseminated; legal—how laws and social rules are encoded in order to ensure uniform social behavior.

Scholars have looked at literacy from all these perspectives. In doing so, they have foisted upon the understanding of literacy interpretations so diverse and so contradictory that to follow them is to enter a maze from which there is no escape. One of Will Rogers' lines was paraphrased as: "We are all illiterate, only about different things." The formula deserves closer examination because it defines another characteristic of the context for understanding the relative illiteracy of our times. The degree of illiteracy is difficult to quantify, but the result is easy to notice. Everything carried into the self-constitution of the individual as warrior, lover, athlete, family member, educator or educated in literacy-based pragmatics is being replaced by illiterate means. Nobody expected that an individual who reads Tolstoy or Shakespeare will be a better cook, or devise better military plans, or even be a better lover. Nevertheless, the characteristics of literacy affected practically all pragmatic experiences, conferring upon them a unity and coherence we can only look back upon with nostalgia. Champions of sexual encounters, as much as innovators in new technologies and Olympic athletes are extremely efficient in their respective domains. Peak performance increases as the average falls in the range of mediocrity and sub-mediocrity. In this book I will examine many aspects of literacy pertinent to what is usually associated with it: the publications people write and read, communication at the individual and social levels, as well as many aspects of human activity that we do not necessarily consider in relation to literacy—military, sports, sex and family, eating—but which nevertheless were influenced by the pragmatic framework that made literacy possible and necessary.

With the evident demise of philosophy as the *science of sciences,* began fragmentation of knowledge. Doubt that a common instrument of access to and dissemination of knowledge exists is replaced by certitude that it does not. A so-called third culture, in the opinion of the author who brought it to public attention, "consists of rendering visible the deeper meanings of our lives" in ways different from those of literary intellectuals. This is not C.P. Snow's *third culture* of scientists capable of communicating with non-scientific intellectuals, but the illiterate scientific discourse that brings fascinating notions into the mainstream, via powerful metaphors and images (albeit in a trivialized manner). This is why the relation between science and literacy, as well as between philosophy and literacy, will be examined with the intention to characterize the philosophy and science of the civilization of illiteracy.

But are we really equipped with the means of exploration and evaluation of this wide-ranging change? Aren't we captive to language and literacy, and thus to the philosophic and scientific explanations based on them? We know that the system in place in our culture is the result of the logocratic view adopted. The testing of skills rated by score is to a great extent a measure of comprehension characteristic of the civilization of literacy. The new pragmatic framework requires skills related not only to language and literacy, but also to images, sounds, textures, motion, and virtual space and time. Knowing this, we have to address the relation between a relatively static medium and dynamic media. We should look into how literacy relates to the visual, in general, and, in particular, to the controversial reality of television, of interactive multimedia, of artificial images, of networking and virtual reality. These are all tasks of high order, requiring a broad perspective and an unbiased viewpoint.

Most important is the comprehension of the structural implications of literacy. An understanding of the framework that led to literacy, and of the consequences that the new pragmatic framework of existence has on all aspects of our lives will help us understand how literacy influenced them. I refer specifically to religion, family, state, and education. In a world giving up the notion of permanency, God disappears for quite a number of people. Still, there are many more churches, denominations, sects, and other religious factions (atheist and neo-pagan included) than at any other time. In the United States of America, people change life partners 2.8 times during their life span (if they ever constitute a family), and calculate the financial aspects of getting married and having children with the same precision that they use to calculate the expected return on an investment. The state has evolved into a corporation regulating the business of the nation, and is now judged on its economic achievements. Presidents of states act as super-peddlers of major industries on whose survival employment depends. These heads of state are not shy about giving up the ideals anchored in literate discourse (e.g., human rights). But they will raise a big fuss when it comes to copyright infringement, especially of software. The irony is that copyright is difficult to define in respect to digital *originals*. Through the literacy model, the state became a self-preserving bureaucratic machine rarely akin to the broad variety of options brought about by the pragmatic framework of the civilization of illiteracy.

Many more people than previous records mention become (or remain) illiterates after finishing the required years of schooling—a minimum of ten years—and even after graduating from college. Some people know how to read, even how to write, but opt for scanning TV channels, playing games, attending sports events, or surfing the Internet. *Aliteracy* is also part of the broader change in the status of literacy. Decisions to forego reading and writing are decisions in favor of different means of expression and communication. The new generation is more proficient in video games than in orthography. This generation will be involved in high-efficiency practical experiences structurally similar to the interactive toy and far removed from the expectation of correct writing. The Internet shapes the choices of the new generation in terms of what they want to know, how, when, and for what purpose more than newspapers, books, and magazines, and even more than radio or television does. And even more than schools and colleges do. Through its vast and expanding means and offerings, the Internet connects the individual to the globe, instead of only talking about globality. Networking, at many levels and in many ways, is related to the characteristics of our pragmatic framework. As rudimentary as it still is, networking excludes everything that is not fast-paced and to the point.

Can all these examples, part of the context of the discussion of literacy in our changing world, be interpreted as being in causal relation to the decline of literacy? That is, the less people are knowledgeable in reading and writing, or choose not to read or write, the less they believe in God or the more pagan they want to be? The more often they divorce, the less they marry or have children? The more they want or accept a bureaucratic machine to handle their problems, the more TV programs they watch and the more electronic games they play, the more they surf the infinite world of networks? No, not along this line of one-dimensional, linear, simplistic form of determinism. A multiplicity of factors, and a multiplicity of layers need to be considered. They are, however, rooted in the pragmatic framework of our continuous self-constitution. It is exhibited through the dynamics of shorter and faster interactions. It is embodied in the ever wider choices of ascertaining our identity. It takes the appearance of availabilities, fragmentation and global integration, of increased mediation. The dynamics described corresponds to the higher efficiency that a larger scale of human activity demands. To call attention to the multi-dimensionality of the process and to the many interdependencies, which we can finally uncover with the help of new technologies, is a first step. To evince their non-linearity, reflecting the meshing between what can be seen as deterministic and what is probably non-deterministic is another step in the argument of the book.

Without basing our discussion on human pragmatics, it would be impossible to explain why, despite all the effort and money societies invest in education, and all the time allocated for education—sometimes over a quarter of a lifetime—despite research of cognitive processes pertinent to literacy, people wind up less literate, but, surprisingly, not at all less efficient. Some would argue—the late Alan Bloom, a crusader for culture and literacy, indeed a brilliant writer of the epilogue of human culture and nostalgia for it, already did—that without literacy, we are less effective as human beings. The debate over such arguments requires that we acknowledge changes in the status of human beings and of human societies, and that we understand what makes such changes unavoidable.

THE WISE FOX

The world as it stands today, especially the industrialized world, is fundamentally different from the world of any yesteryear, the last decade and century, not to mention the past that seems more the time of story than of history. Alan Bloom's position, embraced by many intellectuals, is rooted in the belief that people cannot be effective unless they build on the foundation of historically confirmed values, in particular the great books. But we are at a point of divergences with no noticeably privileged direction, but with many, many options. This is not a time of crisis, although some want us to believe the contrary and are ready to offer their remedies: back to something (authority, books, some primitive stage of no-ego, or of the mushroom, i.e., psychedelic drugs, back to nature); or fast forward to the utopia of technocracy, the information age, the service society, even virtual reality or artificial life.

Humans are heuristic animals. Our society is one of creativity and diversity, operating on a scale of human interaction to which we exponentially add new domains: outer space, whose dimensions can be measured only in light years, and whose period of observation extends over lifetimes; the microcosmos, mirroring the scale in the opposite direction of infinitesimal differentiations; the new *continents* of man-made materials, new forms of energy, genetically designed plants and animals, new genetic codes, and virtual realities to experience new spaces, new times, and new forms of mediation. Networking, which at its current stage barely suggests things to come, can only be compared to the time electricity became widely available. Cognitive energy exchanged through networks and focused on cooperative endeavors is part of what lies ahead as we experience exponential growth on digital networks and fast learning curves of efficient handling of their potential.

The past corresponds to a pragmatic framework well adapted to the survival and development of humankind in the limited world of direct encounters or limited mediations. In terms pertinent to a civilization built around the notion of literacy, the current lower levels of literacy can be seen as symptomatic of a crisis, or even a breakdown. But what defines the new pragmatic context is the shift from a literacy-centered model to one of multiple, interconnected, and interconditioned, distributed literacies. It is well justified to repeat that some of the most enlightened minds overlook the pragmatics of bygone practice. Challenged, confused, even scared by the change, they call for a journey to the past: back to tradition, to discipline, to the ethics of our forefathers, to old-time religion and the education that grew out of it, to permanence, and hopefully to stability. Even those who wholeheartedly espouse evolutionary and revolutionary models seem to have a problem when it comes to literacy. All set to do away with authority, they have no qualms about celebrating the imperialism of the written word. Other minds confess to difficulties in coping with a present so promising and, at the same time, so confusing in its structural contradictions. What we experience, from the extreme of moral turpitude to a disquieting sense of mediocrity and meaninglessness, nourishes skeptical, if not fatalistic, visions. The warning is out (again): We will end up destroying humankind! Yet another part of the living present accepts the challenge without caring about the implications it entails. The people in this group give up their desire to understand what happens, as long as this makes life exciting and rewarding. Hollywood thrives on this. So do the industries of digital smoke-and-mirrors, always a step from fame, and not much farther from oblivion. Addresses on the Internet fade as quickly as they are set up. The most promising links of yesterday show up on the monitor as a "Sorry" message, as meaningful as their short-lived presence was. Arguing with success is a sure recipe for failure. Success deserves to be celebrated in its authentic forms that change the nature of human existence in our universe.

The future suggested in the labels *technocracy, information age,* and *service society* might capture some characteristics of today's world, but it is limited and limiting. This future fails to accommodate the development of human activity at the new scale in terms of population, resources, adaptation, and growth it has reached. Within this model, its proponents preserve as the underlying structure the current set of dependencies among the many parts involved in human activity, and a stubborn deterministic view of simplistic inclination. Unreflected celebration of technocracy as the sole agent of change must be treated with the same suspicion as its demonization. The current participation of technology in human activity is indeed impressive. So are the extent of information processing and information mining, and the new relation between productive activities and services. To make sense of disparate data and from them form new productive endeavors is a formidable task. Science, in turn, made available enormously challenging theories and extremely refined models of the world.

But after all is done and said, these are only particular aspects of a much more encompassing process. The result is a pragmatic framework of a new condition. Highly mediated work, distributed tasks, parallel modes, and generalized networking of rather loosely coordinated individual experiences define this condition. Within this framework, the connection between input (for instance, work) and output (what results) is of a different order of magnitude from that between the force applied on a lever and the outcome; or that between the energy necessary to accomplish useful tasks through engines or electric, or pneumatic devices, no matter how efficient, and the result. In addition, even the distinction between input and output becomes fuzzy. The wearable computer provides interoperability and interconnectedness—an increase in a person's heart rate can be a result of an increase in physical exertion or cause for communicating with a doctor's office or for alerting the police station (if an accident takes place). It might be that the next interaction will involve our genetic code.

The capacity for language and the ability to understand its various implications are only relatively interdependent, and thus only relatively open to scrutiny and understanding. This statement, as personal as it sounds, and as much as it expresses probably less resignation than uncertainty, is crucial to the integrity of this entire enterprise. Indeed, once within a language, one is bound to look at the world surrounding oneself from the perspective of that language as the medium for partial self-constitution and evaluation. Participating in its dynamics affects what I am able to see and describe. This affects also what I am no longer able to perceive, what escapes my perception, or even worse, filters it to the point that I see only my own thoughts. This dual identity—observer and integral part of the observed phenomena—raises ethical, axiological, and epistemological aspects almost impossible to reconcile. Since every language is a projection of ourselves—as participants in the human experience, yet as distinct instantiations of that experience—we do not see the world so much as ourselves in relation to it, ourselves in establishing our culture, and again ourselves in taming and appropriating the universe around us. The fox in Saint-Exupéry's *The Little Prince* says it much better: "One only understands the things one tames."

"BETWEEN US THE RIFT"

Huge industrial complexes where an immense number of workers participate in the production of goods, and densely populated urban centers gravitating around factories, make up the image characteristic of industrial society. This image is strikingly different from the new reality of interconnected, yet decentralized, individual activities going well beyond telecommuting. Various mediating elements contribute to increasingly efficient practical experiences of human self-constitution. The computer is one of the varied embodiments of these mediating elements, but by no means the only one. Through its functions, such as calculation, word, image, and information processing, and control of manufacturing, it introduces many layers between individuals and the object of their actions. The technology of interconnecting provides means for distributive task strategies. It also facilitates parallel modes of productive work. This is a world of progressive decentralization and interoperative possibilities. All kinds of machines can be an address in this interconnected world. Their operations can range from design tasks to computer-aided manufacturing. Distributed work and cognitive functions pertinent to it afford practical experiences qualitatively different from the mechanical sequencing of tasks as we know it from industrial modes of production.

Obviously, large portions of Africa, Asia, and Latin America, as well as part of the European and North American continents, do not necessarily fit this description in detail. Industrial activities still constitute the dominant practical experience in the world. Although nomadic and jungle tribes are part of this integrated world, the Industrial Revolution has not yet reached them all. In some cases, the stages leading to agriculture have not yet been attained. In view of the global nature of human life and activity today, I submit that despite the deep disparity in the economic and social evolution of various regions of the world, it is plausible to assume that centralized modes of production peculiar to industrial economies are not a necessary development. Efficiency expectations corresponding to the global scale of human activity can be reached only by development strategies different from those embodied in the pragmatic framework of industrial activity. It is therefore probable that countries, and even subcontinents, not affected by the Industrial Revolution will not go through it. Planners with an ecological bent even argue that developing countries should not take the path that led industrial nations to augment their population's living standard to the detriment of the environment or by depleting natural resources (*A German Manifest,* 1992).

Industrial production and the related social structures rely on literacy. Edmund Carpenter formulated this quite expressively: "Translated into gears and levers, the book became machine. Translated into people, it became army, chain of command, assembly line...." His description, made in broad strokes, is to the point. At the beginning of the Industrial Revolution, children and women became part of the labor market. For the very limited operation one had to perform, no literacy was necessary; and women and children were not literate. Still, the future development of the industrial society could not take place without the dissemination of literacy skills. For instance, industry made possible the invention, in 1830, of the steel pen indispensable to the compulsory elementary education that was later instituted. The production of steel needles seemed to extend domesticity, but actually created the basis for the *sweat* trades following what Louis Mumford called *carboniferous capitalism.* Gaslight and electricity expanded the time available for the dissemination of literacy skills. Housing improvements made possible the building of the individual library. George Steiner sees this as a turning point in the sense that a private context of the experience of the book was created.

As far as national structures were concerned, phenomena characteristic of the Industrial Revolution cannot be understood outside the wider context of the formation and consolidation of nations. Affirmation of national identity is a process intimately connected to the values and functions of literacy. The production process of the industrial age of mechanical machinery and electric power required not brute force, but qualified force. Administrative and management functions required more literacy than work on the assembly line. But literacy projected its characteristics onto the entire activity, thus making a literate workforce desirable. The market it generated projected the condition of the industry in the structure of its transactions. The requirements for qualified work expanded to requirements for qualified market activities and resulted in the beginnings of marketing and advertising. That market was based on the recognition of national boundaries, i.e., boundaries of efficiency, self-sufficiency, and future growth offering markets of a size and complexity adequate to industrial output. Nations replaced the coarse fragmentation of the world. They were no longer, as Jean-Marie Guéhenno notices, a disguise of tribal structures, but a political space within which democracy could be established.

Progression from competing individual life and temporary congregation in an environment of survival of the fittest to tribal, communal, local, confederate, and national life is paralleled by progression in the forms and methods of human integration. The global scale of human activity characteristic of our age is not an extension of the linear, deterministic relations between those constituting a valid human entity and the life-support system, called environment, that structurally define industrial society. Discontinuity in numbers (of people, resources, expectations, etc.), in the nature of the relations among people, in the forms of mediations that define human practical experiences is symptomatic of the depth and breadth of change. The end of nations, of democracy even, might be far off, but this end is definitory of the chasm before us. The United Nations, which does not yet comprise the entire world, is a collection of over 197 nations, and increasing. Some are only island communities, or newly proclaimed independent countries brought about by social and political movements. Of the over 240 distinct territories, countries, and protectorates, very few (if any) are truly autarchic entities. Despite never before experienced integration, our world is less the house of nations and discrete alliances among them, and more the civilization of a species in firm control (too firm, as some perceive) of other species.

Within the world, we know that there are people still coming out of an age of natural economy based on hunting, foraging, fishing, and rudimentary agriculture. While barter and the minimal language of survival is the only market process in such places, in reality, the world is already involved in global transactions. Markets are traded in their entirety, more often than not without the knowledge of those comprising these markets. This only goes to show again the precarious nature of national structures. National independence, passionately fought for, is less a charter for the future than the expression of the memory of the past (authentic or fake). Selling or buying extends to the entire economy, which while still at a stage difficult to entirely explain, is bound to change in a rhythm difficult to cope with by those supposed to control it, but inescapable in the context of worldwide market. That literacy and national identity share in this condition should not surprise anyone.

MALTHUS REVISITED

The Malthusian principle (1798) related growth of populations (geometric) to food supply increases (arithmetic): "Population, when unchecked, increases in a geometrical ratio. Subsistence increases only in an arithmetical ratio." The weakness of the principle is probably its failure to acknowledge that the equation of mankind has more than the two variables it considers: population and food supply. The experience of extensive use of natural resources, in particular through farming, is only one among an increasing number of experiences. Human beings constitute their own reality not only as one of biological needs, but also of cultural expectations, growing demands, and creativity. These eventually affect changes in what were believed to be primary needs and instincts. In many ways, a great deal of previously acknowledged sources of protein are exhausted. But in an ever more impressive proportion, the acceptable realm of sources of nutrition—proteins included—has been expanded so as to include the artificial. Hunting and gathering wild plants (not to mention scavenging, which seems to predate hunting) were appropriate when linear, sequential strategies of survival defined human behavior; so were herding and agriculture, a continuation of foraging under circumstances of changed subsistence strategies.

Language was formed, and then stabilized, in connection to this linear form of praxis. Linearity simply reflects the fact that one person is less effective than two, but also that one's needs are smaller than those of several. The experience of self-constitution in language preserves linearity. This preservation of linearity extends as long as the scale of the community and its needs and wants allowed for proportional interaction among its individuals and the environment of their existence. Industrial society is probably the climax of this optimization effort.

If the issue were only to feed mankind, the population census (over five billion people on record as of the moment these pages are being written, though less than four billion when I started) and the measure of resources would not yet indicate a new scale. But the issue is to accommodate geometrically growing populations and exponentially (i.e., non-linearly) diversifying expectations. Such expectations relate to a human being celebrating higher average ages, and an extended period of active life. We change anatomically, not necessarily for the better: we see and hear less well and have lower physical abilities. Our cognitive behavior and our patterns of social interaction change, too. These changes reflect, among other things, the transition from direct interaction and co-presence to indirect, mediated forms of the practical self-constitution of the human being.

The sequential nature of language, in particular its embodiment in literacy, no longer suits human praxis as its universal measure. The strategies of linearization introduced through the experience of literacy were acceptable when the resulting efficiency accommodated lower and less differentiated expectations. They are now replaced by more efficient, intrinsically non-linear strategies made possible by *literacies* structurally different from those rooted in the practice of so-called natural language. Accordingly, literacy loses its primacy. New literacies emerge. Instead of a stable center and limited choice, a distributed and variable configuration of centers and wide choice connect and disconnect areas of common or disjoint interest. There are still national ambitions, huge factories to be built, cities to be erected and others to be expanded, highways to be widened in order to accommodate more intercity traffic, and airports to be constructed so that more airplanes can be used for national and international travel. The inertia of past pragmatics has not yet been annihilated by the dynamics of a fundamental change of direction. Still, an integrated, yet decentralized, universe of work and living has been taking shape and will continue to do so. Interconnection made possible by digital technology, first of all, opens a wide range of possibilities for reshaping social life, political institutions, and our ability to design and produce goods. Our own ability to mediate, to integrate parts and services resulting from specialized activities is supported by machines that enhance our cognitive characteristics.

CAPTIVES TO LITERACY

Probably the most shocking discovery we sometimes make is that, in order to be able to undertake new experiences, we need to forget, to break the curse of literate memory, and to immerse ourselves in the structurally amnesiac systems of signs corresponding to and addressing our senses. Nathaniel Hawthorne's short story "Earth's Holocaust" was prophetic in this sense. In this parable, the people of a new world (obviously the United States of America) bring all the books they inherited from the old world to a great bonfire. Theirs is not an exercise in mindless book-burning. They conscientiously discard all the rules and ideas passed down through millennia that governed the world and the life they left behind. Old ideas, as well as new ones, would have to prove their validity in the new context before they would be accepted. Indeed, the awareness brought about by theories of the physical world, of the mind, of our own biogenetic condition made possible practical experiences of self-constitution that are not like anything experienced by humans before our time. The realization of relativity, of the speed of light, of micro- and macro-structures, of dynamic forces and non-linearity is already translated in new structures of interactions. Our systems of interconnection—through electric energy, telephone (wired and cellular), radio, television, communication, computer networks—function at speeds comparable to that of light. They integrate dynamic mechanisms inspired by genetics, physics, molecular biology, and our knowledge of the micro- and macro-structure.

Our life cycle seems to accept two different synchronizing mechanisms: one corresponding to our natural condition (days, nights, seasons), the other corresponding to the perceived scale and to our striving towards efficiency. The two are less and less dependent, and efficiency seems to dominate nature. Discovery of the world in its expanded comprehensive geographic dimensions required ships and planes. It also required the biological effort to adapt and the intellectual effort to understand various kinds of differences. In outer space, this adaptation proves to be even more difficult. In a world in a continuous flux of newer and newer distinctions, people constitute, instead of one permanent and encompassing literacy, several literacies, none of which bears the status of (quasi)eternal. Differentiation of human experience is so far reaching that it is impossible to reduce the variety to one literate language.

In the process of building rational, interpretive methods and establishing a body of knowledge that can be tested and practically applied, people often discard what did not fit in the theories they advanced, what did not obey the laws that these theories expressed. This was a necessary methodology that resulted in the progress we enjoy today. But it was also a deceptive method because what could not be explained was omitted. Where literacy was instilled, non-linguistic aspects—such as the irreducible world of magic, mystery, the esoteric (to name a few)—were done away with. Commenting upon *The Adventures of Huckleberry Finn*, Illich and Sanders pointed out that there is a whole world in Twain's novel that is inaccessible to the illiterate, but also a world of folklore and superstition that cannot be understood by those hostage to the beautiful kingdom of literacy. Folklore in many countries, and superstition, and mystery in all the varieties corresponding to human practical self-constitution are definitely areas from which we might gain better insight into life past, present, and future. They are part of the context and should not be left out, even though they may belong to the epoch before literacy.

All in all, since language was and still is the most comprehensive testimony to (and participant in) our experience as human beings, we may want to see whether its crisis says something about our own permanence and our own prejudices concerning the species. After all, why, and based on what arguments, do we see ourselves as the only permanence in the universe and the highest possible achievement of evolution? Literacy freed us in many respects. But it also made us prisoners of a number of prejudices, not the least a projection of self-awareness in direct contradiction to our own experience of never-ending change in the world.

CHAPTER 2: THE EPITOME OF THE CIVILIZATION OF ILLITERACY

In the opinion of foe and friend alike, America (the name under which the United States of America, appropriating the identifier of the two continents comprising the New World) epitomizes many of the defining characteristics of today's world: market oriented, technologically driven, living on borrowed means (financial and natural resources), competitive to the extreme of promoting adversarial relations, and submitting, in the name of democracy and tolerance, to mediocrity, demagoguery, and opportunism. Americans are seen as boastful, boorish, unrealistic, naive, primitive, hypocritical, and obsessed with money. Even to some of its most patriotic citizens, the USA appears to be driven by political opportunism, corruption, and bigotry. As still others perceive the USA, it is captive to militarism and prey to the seductive moral poison of its self-proclaimed supremacy. At times it looks like the more it fails in some of its policies, the more it wants to hear declarations of gratitude and hymns of glory, as in John Adams' lines: "The eastern nations sink, their glory ends/ And empires rise where sun descends." To the peoples just awaking from the nightmare of communism, the American political slogans have a familiar, though frightening, self-delusive ring.

On the other hand, Americans are credited with extraordinary accomplishments in technology, science, medicine, the arts, literature, sports, and entertainment. They are appreciated as friendly, open, and tolerant. Their willingness to engage in altruistic projects (programs for the poor and for children all over the world), indeed free from discrimination, makes for a good example to people of other nations. Patriotism does not prevent Americans from being critical of their own country. To the majority of the world, America represents a vivid model of liberal democracy in action within a federation of states united by a political system based on expectations of balance among local, state, and federal functions.

Jean Jacques Servan-Schreiber once made headlines writing about the American challenge (*Le Défi Américain*), more or less about the danger of seeing the world Americanized. Downtown Frankfurt (on the river Main) is called *Mainhattan* because its skyscrapers recall those of the island between the Hudson and East Rivers. The *Disneyland* near Paris, more of an import (the French government wanted it badly) than an export product, was called a "cultural Chernobyl." Tourists from all over the crumbled Soviet Empire are no longer taken to Lenin's Mausoleum but to Moscow's McDonald's. The Japanese, reluctant to import American-made cars and supercomputers, or to open their markets to agricultural goods (except marbled beef), will bend over backwards for baseball. Add to all this the symbolism of blue jeans, Madonna or Heavy Metal (as music or comic books), Coca-Cola, the television series *Dallas,* the incessant chomping on chewing gum and bubble-gum popping, Texan boots, and the world-wide sneaker craze, and you have an image of the visible threat of Americanization. But appearance is deceitful.

Taken out of their context, these and many other Americanized aspects of daily life are only exotic phenomena, easy to counteract, and indeed subject to counteraction. Italians protested the culture of fast food near the Piazza d'Espagna in Rome (where one fast food establishment rented space) by giving out free spaghetti carbonara and pizza. (They were unaware of the irony in this: the biggest exporter of pizza restaurants is no longer Italy, but the USA.) The rightist Russian movement protested McDonald's by touting national dishes, the good old high-calorie menu of times when physical effort was much greater than in our days (even in that part of the world). The Germans push native *Lederhosen* and *Dirndls* over blue jeans. The German unions protest attempts to address structural problems in their economy through diminishing social benefits with a slogan that echoes like a hollow threat: American conditions will be met by a French response, by which they mean that strikes will paralyze the country. The Japanese resisted the Disney temptation by building their own *lands* of technological marvels. When an athlete born in America, naturalized as Japanese, won the traditional Sumo wrestling championship, the Japanese judges decided that this would be his last chance, since the sport requires, they stated, a spirituality (translated by *demeanor*) that a foreign-born sportsman cannot have.

On closer examination, Americanization runs deeper than what any assortment of objects, attitudes, values, and imitated behavior tell us. It addresses the very core of human activity in today's global community. It is easy to understand why America appears to embody efficiency reached at the expense of many abandoned values: respect for authority, for environment, for resources, even human resources, and ultimately human values. The focus of the practical experience through which American identity is constituted is on limitless expectations regarding social existence, standard of living, political action, economic reward, even religious experience. Its encompassing obsession is freedom, or at least the appearance of freedom. Whatever the pragmatics affords becomes the new expectation and is projected as the next necessity. The right to affluence, as relative as affluence is in American society, is taken for granted, never shadowed by the thought that one's wealth and well-being might come at the expense of someone else's lack of opportunity. Competitive, actually adversarial, considerations prevail, such as those manifest in the morally dubious practices accepted by the legal and political systems. "To the victor go the spoils" is probably the most succinct description of what this means in real life.

The American way of life has been a hope and promise for people all over the world. The mixed feelings they have towards America does not necessarily reflect this. The entire world is probably driven by the desire for efficiency that makes such a standard of living possible more than by the pressure to copy the American style (of products, living, politics, behavior, etc.). This desire corresponds to a pragmatics shaped by the global scale of humankind, and by the contemporary dynamics of human self-constitution. Each country faces the battle between efficiency and culture (some going back thousands of years), in contrast to the USA, whose culture is always *in status nascendi*. The American anxiety over the current state of literacy is laden with a nostalgia for a tradition never truly established and a fear of a future never thought through. It is, consequently, of more than documentary interest to understand how America epitomizes a civilization that has made literacy obsolete.

FOR THE LOVE OF TRADE

As a country formed by unending waves of immigration, America can be seen, superficially though, as a civilization of many parallel literacies. Ethnic neighborhoods are still a fact of life. Here one finds stores where only the *native* language is spoken, with newspapers printed in Greek, Hungarian, German, Italian, Ukrainian, Farsi, Armenian, Hebrew, Romanian, Russian, Arabic, Japanese, Mandarin, Korean. Cable TV caters to these groups, and so do many importers of products reminiscent of some country where "food tastes real" and goods "last forever." All of these carried-over literacies are, in final analysis, means of self-constitution, bridges between cultures that will be burned by the third generation. In practicing the *literacy of origins,* human beings constitute themselves as split personalities between two pragmatic contexts. One embodies expectations characteristic of the context that relied upon literacy—homogeneity, hierarchy, centralism, tradition. The other, of the adopted country, is focused upon needs that effect the transition to the civilization of illiteracy—heterogeneity, horizontality, decentralism, tradition as choice, but not way of life.

Aspects of immigration (and in general of human migration) need to be addressed, not from the perspective of parallel literacies, but as variations within a unifying pragmatic framework. The de-cul-turization of people originating from many countries and belonging to many nations is probably a unique feature of America. It impacted all aspects of life, and continues to be a source of vitality, as well as tension. Immigrants arrive as literates (some more so than others) only to discover that their literacy is relatively useless. That things were not always like this is relatively well documented. Neil Postman reported that the 17th-century settlers were quite literate in terms characteristic of the time. Up to 95 percent of the men were able to read the Bible; among women the percentage reported is 62. They also read other publications, some imported from England, and at the beginning of the second half of the eighteenth century supported a printing industry soon to become very powerful.

In importing their literacies, the English, as well as the French and Dutch, imported all the characteristics that literacy implies and which went into the foundation of the American government. Over time, in the successive waves of immigration, unskilled and skilled workers, intellectuals, and peasants arrived. They all had to adapt to a different culture, dominated by the British model but moving farther away from it as the country started to develop its own characteristics. Each national or ethnic group, shaped through practical experiences that did not have a common denominator, had to adapt to others. The country grew quite fast, as did its industry, transportation system, farming, banking, and the many services made possible and necessary by the overall economic development. To some extent, literacy was an integral part of these accomplishments. The young country soon established its own body of literature, reflecting its own experience, while remaining true to the literacy of the former mother country. I say *to some extent* because, as the history of each of these accomplish-ments shows, the characteristics inherent in literacy were opposed, under the banner of States' rights, democracy, individuality, or progress.

With all this in mind, it is no wonder that Americans do not like to hear that they are a nation of illiterates, as people from much older cultures are sometimes inclined to call them (for right or wrong reasons). No wonder either that they are still committed to literacy; moreover, that they believe that it represents a panacea to the problems raised by fast technological cycles of change, by new modes of human interaction, and by circumstances of practical experiences to which they have to adapt. Educators and business-people are well aware, and worried, that literacy in the classical sense is declining. The sense of history they inherited makes them demand that effort and money be spent to turn the tide and bring America back to past *greatness,* or at least to some stability. Probably the nature of this greatness is misunderstood or misconstrued, since there is not much in the history of the accomplishments of the United States that could rank the country among the *cultural* giants of past and present civilizations.

Throughout its history, America always represented, to some degree, a break with the values of the old world. The Europeans who came to the Dutch, French, and English colonies had at least one thing in common: they wanted to escape from the pragmatics of hierarchy, centralized political and religious domination, and fixed rules of social and cultural life representing a system of order that kept them *in their place.* Freedom of religion—one of the most sought after—is freedom from a dominant, unified church and its vision of the unconditionally submissive individual. Cultivating one's own land, another hope that animated the settlers, is freedom from practical serfdom imposed by the landowning nobility on those lower on the hierarchy. John Smith's maxim that those who didn't work didn't eat was perhaps the first blow to the European values that ranked language and culture along with social status and privilege.

Most likely, the immigrants, highborn and low, did not come with the intention of overthrowing the sense and morals prevailing at the time. The phase of imitation of the old, characteristic of any development, extended from religious ceremonies to ways of working, enjoying, educating, dressing, and relating to outsiders (natives, slaves, religious sects). In this phase of imitation, a semi-aristocracy established itself in the South, emulating the English model. In protesting the taxes and punitive laws imposed by King George III, the upper-class colonials were demanding their rights as *Englishmen*, with all that this qualifier entailed. Jefferson's model for the free United States was that the agrarian state best embodied the classic ideals that animated him. Jefferson was himself the model of literacy-based practical experiences, a landed aristocrat who owned slaves, a man trained in the logic of Greece and Rome. His knowledge came from books. He was able to bring his various interests in architecture, politics, planning, and administration in focus through the pragmatic framework for which literacy was adequate. Although Jefferson, among others, rejected monarchy, which his fellow citizens would have set up, he did not hesitate to exercise the almost kingly powers that the executive branch of government entailed. His activity shows how monarchic centrality and hierarchy were translated in the new political forms of emerging democracies, within which elective office replaced inherited power. In the history of early America, we can see how literacy carries over the non-egalitarian model as it advanced equality in people's natural rights and before the law, the power of rules, and a sense of authority inspired by religion, practiced in political life, and connected to expectations of order.

Just as new trees sprout from the trunk of an old tree, so new paradigms take root within an old one. People immigrated to America to escape the old models. Challenged by the need to provide a framework for their own self-identification, they ended up establishing an alternative context for the unfolding of the Industrial Revolution. In the process, they changed in more ways than they could foresee. Politically, they established conditions conducive to emancipation from the many constraints of the system they left. Even their patterns of living, speaking, behaving, and thinking changed. In 1842, Charles Dickens observed of Americans that

> The love of trade is assigned as a reason for that comfortless custom...of married persons living in hotels, having no fireside of their own, and seldom meeting, from early morning until late at night, but at the hasty

public meals. The love of trade is a reason why the literature of America is to remain forever unprotected: "For we are a trading people, and don't care for poetry: though we do, by the way, profess to be very proud of our poets."

Dickens came from a culture that considered literacy one of the highest achievements of England, so much so that, according to Jane Austen, Shakespeare could be particularly appreciated by the English alone (cf. *Mansfield Park*). She gave cultivation of the mind the highest priority. Literature was expected to assist in defining values and pointing out the proper moral and intellectual direction. France was in a very similar position in regard to its culture and literature; so were the German lands and Holland. Even Russia, otherwise opposed to acknowledging the new pragmatic context of industrial production, was affected by the European Enlightenment.

De Toqueville, whose journey to America contributed to his fame, made his historic visit in the 1830's. By this time, America had time and opportunity to establish its peculiar character, so he was able to observe characteristics that would eventually define a new paradigm. The associated emerging values, based on a life relatively free of historic constraints, caught his attention:

> The Americans can devote to general education only the early years of life. [...] At fifteen they enter upon their calling, and thus their education generally ends at the age when ours begins. If it is continued beyond that point, it aims only towards a particular specialized and profitable purpose; one studies science as one takes up a business; and one takes up only those applications whose immediate practicality is recognized. [...] There is no class, then, in America, in which the taste for intellectual pleasures is transmitted with hereditary fortune and leisure and by which the labors of the intellect are held in honor. Accordingly, there is an equal want of the desire and power of application to these objects.

Opinions, even those of scholars of de Toqueville's reputation, are inherently limited in scope. Sent by the French government to examine prisons and penitentiaries in the New World, he wound up writing a study of how a highly literate European understood America's social and political institutions. Many of the characteristics of the civilization of illiteracy were emerging during the years of his visit. He highlighted the shortness of political cycles, the orality of public administration, the transience of commitments (the little there is of writing "is soon wafted away forever, like the leaves of the sibyl, by the smallest breeze"). Severance from the past, in particular, made this visitor predict that Americans would have to "recourse to the history of other nations in order to learn anything of the people who now inhabit them." What we read in de Toqueville is the expression of the surprise caused by discontinuity, by change, and by a dynamics that in other parts of the world was less obvious.

The New World certainly provided new themes, addressed and interpreted differently by Americans and Europeans. The more European cities of the Northeast—Boston, New York, Philadelphia—maintained cultural ties to the Old World, as evidenced by universities, scholars, poets, essayists, and artists. Nevertheless, Washington Irving complained that one could not make a living as a writer in the United States as one could in Europe. Indeed, many writers earned a living as journalists (which is a way of being a writer) or as civil servants. The real America—the one Dickens so lamented—was taking form west of the Hudson River and beyond the Appalachian Mountains. This was truly a world where the past did not count.

America finally did away with slavery (as a by-product of the Civil War). But at the same time, it started undoing some part of the underlying structure reflected in literacy. The depth and breadth of the process escaped the full understanding of those literate Founding Fathers who set the process in motion, and was only partially realized by others (de Toqueville included). It clearly affected the nature of human practical experiences of self-constitution as free citizens of a democracy whose chance to succeed lay in the efficiency, *not* in the expressive power, of ideas. America's industrial revolution took place against a background different from that of the rest of the world—a huge island indulging in relative autarchy for a short time. Forces corresponding to the pragmatics of the post-industrial age determined a course of opening itself and opening as much of the world as possible—regardless of how this was to be accomplished. The process still affects economic development, financial markets, cultural interdependencies, and education.

"THE BEST OF THE USEFUL AND THE BEST OF THE ORNAMENTAL"

Some will protest that over 150 years have gone by and the American character has been shaped by more than the love of trade. They will point to the literary heritage of Washington Irving, Mark Twain, Henry Wadsworth Longfellow, Ralph Waldo Emerson, Nathaniel Hawthorne, Henry James. Indeed, 20th-century American writers have been appreciated and imitated abroad. Faulkner and Hemingway are the best known examples. Today, American writers of lesser stature and talent are translated into the various European languages, for the same reasons that Disneyland was brought to France. Americans will point to theaters (which presented European plays) and opera houses, forgetting how late these acquisitions are, instituted when economic progress was on a sound track. Indeed, the response to these assertions is simple: the result of other influences is not a change of course, but a much faster movement in the direction America pursues.

A good example is given by education. The American colleges and universities founded in the 18th and early 19th centuries attempted to follow the traditional model of learning for its own sake; that is, moral and intellectual improvement through study of the age-old classics. This lasted until various interest groups, in particular businessmen, questioned the validity of an educational program that had little or no pragmatic value. These schools were in the East—Harvard, Brown, Yale, Columbia, William and Mary—and the curricula reflected that of the Old World. In general, only the elite of America attended them. The newer universities, the so-called Land Grant colleges, later called *state* universities (such as Ohio State University, Texas A & M), established west of the Allegheny River during the last quarter of the 19th century, did indeed pursue more pragmatic programs—agriculture and mechanics—to serve the needs of the respective state, not the nation.

In view of this demand for what is useful, it is easy to understand why American universities have become high (and sometimes not so high) level vocational schools, substituting for what high school rarely provided. Pragmatic requirements and anti-elitist political considerations collided with the literate model and a strange hybrid resulted. A look at how the course offerings changed over time brings clear evidence that logic, rhetoric, culture, appreciation of the word and of the rules of grammar and syntax—all the values associated with a dominant literacy—are relegated to specializations in philosophy, literature, or written communication, and to a vast, though confusing, repertory of elective classes, which reflect an obsession with *free choice* and a leveling notion of democracy. Literature, after being forced to give up its romantic claim to permanency, associates itself with transitory approaches that meet, with increasing opportunistic speed, whatever the current agenda might be: feminism, multiculturalism, anti-war rhetoric, economic upheaval. Human truth, as literary illusion or hope, is replaced by uncertainty. No wonder that in this context programs in linguistics and philology languish or disappear from the curriculum. Economics lost its philosophic backbone and became an exercise in statistics and mathematics.

When faced with a list of courses that a university requires, most students ask, "Why do I need...?" In this category fall literature, mathematics, philosophy, and almost everything else definable within literacy as formative subject matter or discipline. Blame for this attitude, if any can be uttered, should not be put on the young people processed by the university system. The students conform, as difficult as it might be for them to understand their conformity, to what is expected of them: to get a driver's license and a college diploma, and to pay taxes. The expectation of a diploma does not result from requirements of qualification but from the American obsession with equality. America, which revolted against hierarchy and inequality, has never tolerated even the appearance of individual superiority. This led to a democracy that opposed superiority, leveling what was not equal—rights or aptitudes, opportunities or abilities—at any price. College education as privilege, which America inherited from the Europe it left behind, was considered an injustice. Over time, commercial democracy turned college into another shopping mall. Today, diplomas, from BA to Ph.D., are expected just for having attended college, a mere prerequisite to a career, not necessarily the result of rigorous mental application leading to quality results. Young adults go to college because they heard that one can get a better (read higher paying) job with a college education.

The result of broadening the scope of university studies to include professions for which only training is required is that the value of a college diploma (but not the price paid for it) has decreased. Some say that soon one will need a college diploma just to be a street cleaner (*sanitation engineer*). Actually, a person will not need a diploma, but will just happen to have one. And the wage of a sanitation worker will be so high (inflation always keeps pace with demagogy) that a college graduate will feel more entitled to the job than a high school dropout. When Thomas Jefferson studied, he realized that none of his studies would help him run his plantation. Architecture and geometry were subordinate to a literacy-dominated standard. Nevertheless, education inspired him as a citizen, as it inspired all who joined him in signing the Declaration of Independence.

A context was established for further emancipation. The depth and breadth of the process escaped the full understanding of those who set the process in motion, and was at best partially realized by very few others, de Tocqueville included. It clearly affected the nature of human practical experiences of self-constitution as free citizens of a democracy whose chance to succeed lay in the *efficiency* of ideas, not in their expressive power. Inventiveness was unleashed;

labor-saving devices, machinery that did the work of tens and hundreds of men provided more and more immediate satisfaction than intellectual exercise did.

Americans do not, if they ever did, live in an age of the idea for its own sake or for the sake of the spirit. Maintaining mental faculties or uplifting the spirit are imported services. In the early history of the USA, the Transcendentalist movement, of *a priori* intuitions, was a strong intellectual presence, but its adherents only transplanted the seed from Europe. Those and others—the schools of thought associated with Peirce, Dewey, James, and Royce—rarely took root, producing a flower more appreciated if it actually was imported. This is not a country that appreciates the *pure* idea. America has always prided itself in its products and practicality, not thinking and vision. "A plaine souldier that can use a pick-axe and a spade is better than five knights," according to Captain John Smith. His evaluation summarizes the American preference for useful over ornamental.

Paradoxically though, business leaders argued for education and proclaimed their support for schools and colleges. At a closer look, their position appears somewhat duplicitous. American business needed its Cooper, Edison, and Bell, around whose inventions and discoveries industries were built. Once these were in place, it needed consumers with money to buy what industries produced. Business supported education as a right and took all the tax deductions it could in order to have this right serve the interests of industry and business. Consequently, in American society, ideas are validated only at the material level, in providing utility, convenience, comfort, and entertainment, as long as these maximize profit. "The sooner the better" is an expectation of efficiency, one that does not take into consideration the secondary effects of production or actions, as long as the first effect was profit. Not the educated citizen, but the person who succeeded in getting rich no matter how, was considered the "smart" fellow, as Dickens learned during his journey through America. Prompted by such a deeply rooted attitude, Sidney Lanier, of Georgia, deplored the "endless tale/ of gain by cunning and plus by sale." To value success regardless of the means applied is part of the American teleology (sometimes in complicity with American theology).

Bertrand Russell observed of Machiavelli that no one has been more maligned for simply stating the truth. The observation applies to those who have taken upon themselves the task of writing about the brave citizens of the free land. Dickens was warned against publishing his *American Notes*. European writers and artists, and visitors from Russia, China, and Japan have irritated their American friends through their sincere remarks. Not many Americans refer to Thorston Veblen, Theodore Dreiser, Henry James, or to Gore Vidal, but the evaluations these authors made of the American character have been criticized by the majority of their compatriots whose sentimental vision of America cannot cope with legitimate observations. Mark Twain felt that he'd rather be "damned to John Bunyan's heaven" than be obliged to read James's *The Bostonians*.

THE REAR-VIEW MIRROR SYNDROME

So why do Americans look back to a time when people "knew how to read and write," a time when "each town had five newspapers?" Big businesses, consolidated well before the invention of newer means of communication and mediation, have large investments in literacy: newspapers, publishing houses, and especially universities. But the promise of a better material life through literacy today rings tragically hollow in the ears of graduates who cannot find jobs in their fields of study. The advertisement most telling of this state of affairs is for a cooking school: "College gave me a degree in English. Peter Kump's Cooking School gave me a career."

Granted that literacy has never made anyone rich in the monetary sense, we can ask what the pragmatic framework set up in this part of the New World did accomplish that literacy could not. In the first place, escape from one dominant mode embodied in literate practical experiences facilitated the assertion of other modes of expression and communication. Peter Cooper, founder of the Cooper Union for the Advancement of Science and Art in New York City, made his fortune in railroads, glue, and gelatin desserts. He was truly illiterate: he could not read. Obviously he was not unintelligent. Many pioneers had a better command of their tools than of their pen. They *read* nature with more understanding than some university students read books. There are other cases of people who succeed, sometimes spectacularly, although they cannot read. The illiterate California businessman who taught high school social sciences and mathematics for eighteen years became known because television, for some reason, saw in him a good case for the literacy cause. People like him rely on a powerful memory or use an intelligence not based on literate conventions. Howard Gardner's theory of multiple *intelligences* (formerly known as *aptitudes*) seems to be ignored by educators who still insist that everyone learn to read and write—better said, conform to the conventions of literacy—as though these were the only ways to comprehend others and to function in life. There are few commentaries that contradict this attitude. William Burroughs thought that "Language is a virus from outer space." Probably it feels better to perceive language like this in view of the many abuses to which language is subjected, but also in view of the way people use it to deceive. A more direct criticism states:

> The current high profile of literacy is symptomatic of a speedy, ruthless transition from an industrial to an information-based economy. [...] Literacy, to be sure, is a powerful, unique technology. Yet literacy remains a human invention contained by social contract, and the maintenance of that contract in education betrays our ideas of humanity as surely as our use of literacy enforces them. (cf. Elsbeth Stuckey)

American experience shows that the imposition of a sole model of higher education, based on literacy, has economic, social, and cultural consequences. It is very costly. It levels instead of addressing and encouraging diversity. It introduces expectations of cultural homogeneity in a context that thrives on heterogeneity. The literate model of education with which the country flirted, and which still seems so attractive, negates one of America's sources of vitality—openness to alternatives, itself made possible by the stubborn refusal of centralism and hierarchy. Held in high esteem in the early part of American history, literacy came to students through schoolhouses in which Webster's *Speller* and McGuffey's *Reader* disbursed more patriotism (essential to a nation in search of an identity) and more awareness of what "life, liberty, and the pursuit of happiness" should mean than quality writing or the possibility to select good books for reading. Literacy with a practical purpose, and the variety of literacies corresponding to the variety of human practical experiences, is a discovery made in America. Understanding pragmatic requirements as opposed to pursuing literacy for the sake of literacy, at the price of rejecting its rewards, is where the road forks. But here America follows Yogi Berra's advice: "When you come to a fork in the road, take it."

In their search for new values, or when faced with competing answers to tough questions, people tend to look back to a time when everything seemed all right. And they tend to pick and choose the characteristics that led to this perceived state of affairs. Things were all right, some want to believe, when kids, plodding along country roads, winter or summer, went to school and learned to read. Therefore, most people assume that the environment propitious to literacy will bring back the golden age. No one wants to see that America was never reducible to this romantic picture. In the South, education never seemed to be a mission. Slaves and poor whites remained outside the idealized stream. Females were not encouraged to study. A Protestant viewpoint dominated subject matter (recall the Puritan alphabet primer).

Americans seem intent on ignoring accomplishments outside the domain of literacy and the dynamics of the non-literate United States. In admiration of real cultures, Americans do not want to hear or see that many of them, of proud and ancient ancestry, started questioning their own values and the education transmitting them.

The practical sense and pragmatism ascertained in the formation of America were adopted as causes worth fighting for. In Europe, students protested an education that did not prepare them for work. Thanks to universal education—European governments by and large offer publicly supported higher education, at no cost to the student, through college and graduate school—more young people received an education (in the classical sense of the word) and their ranks flooded the market. They discovered that they were not prepared for the practical experiences characteristic of the new pragmatics, especially the new forms of mediations that characterize work and that are making headway around the world. In Europe, there is a clear distinction between university studies and vocational studies. This has prevented universities from becoming the high-class vocational schools that they are in America, and has maintained the meaning of the diploma as a proof of intellectual endeavor. On the other hand, they remain ivory towers, not preparing students for the practical experiences of the new pragmatics. *Brotlose Kunst* (breadless art) is what the Germans now call such fields of study as literature, philosophy, musicology, religion, and any other purely intellectual endeavor.

Looking at a totally different culture, Americans tend to respond to Japan's economic success and criticism of our system by saying that our educational system must become more like that of America's leading competitor. They ignore the fact that Japan's high rate of productivity has less to do with the nation's high rate of literacy than does the indoctrination and character formation that Japanese schooling entails. Fundamental attitudes of conformity, team mentality, and a very strong sense of hierarchy, together with an almost sacred sense of tradition, are instilled through literate means. One does not have to be literate in any language in order to solder one circuit to another on an assembly line or to snap together modular components fabricated by advanced machines. What is necessary, indeed expected, is an ethic that calls for a sense of duty and pride in a job well done, a sense met by the social promise of permanency. All in all, the Japanese system allows for little variation from the consensus, and even less for the creation of new models. The only way Japan stepped out of the literate mode in the manufacturing world is in quality control. Ironically, this idea was developed by the American Edward Denning, but rejected by his compatriots, who literally stagnated in a hierarchic model originating from circumstances of literacy. This hierarchical model, now in obvious decline, gave to American businessmen the sense of power they could not achieve through education or culture.

The Japanese, living in a system that preserved its identity while actively pursuing plans for economic expansion, formed strategies of self-containment (severely tested in times of economic downturn), as well as methods of relating to the rest of the world. This condition is manifest in their talent for spotting the most profitable from other countries, making it theirs, and pursuing avenues of competition in which what is specifically Japanese (skills, endurance, collusion) and the appropriated foreign component are successfully joined. Almost the entire foundation of today's television, in its analog embodiment, is Japanese. But if for some reason the programming component would cease to exist, all the marvelous equipment that makes TV possible would abruptly become useless. In some ways, Japan has almost no interest in a change of paradigm in television, such as the revolutionary digital TV, because an enormous industry, present in almost every home where television is used, would have to reinvent itself. The expectation of permanency that permeates literate Japan thus extends from literacy to a medium of illiteracy. In the American context, of almost no stable commitments, digital television, along with many other innovations in computation and other fields, is a challenge, not a threat to an entire infrastructure. This example was not chosen randomly. It illustrates the dynamics of the change from a literacy-dominated civilization to one of many competing literacies. These emerge in the context of change from self-sufficient, relatively small-scale, homogeneous communities to the global world of today, so powerfully interconnected through television and through digital media of all kinds. As *illiterates,* Americans lead other nations in breakthroughs in medicine, genetics, networking, interactive multimedia, virtual reality, and inventiveness in general.

Obviously, it is easier to design a course of education assuming some permanency or maintaining it, regardless of pragmatic requirements. Diane Ravitch stated that it is hard to define what education will be needed for the future when we don't know what skills the jobs of the future will require. An optimal education, reflecting pragmatic needs of highly mediated practical experiences of distributed effort and networking, will have to facilitate the acquisition of new cognitive skills. Decentralized, non-sequential, non-deterministic experiences require cognitive skills different from those characteristic of literacy. Schools used to be able to prepare students to find their place in the workforce even before graduation. More schools than ever insist on churning out a strange version of the *literate* student who should go on to a college that is more (though still not enough) vocational school than university. The university, under the alibi of equal opportunity and more in consideration of its own agenda, has done more damage to education and literacy by forcing itself upon Americans as the only means to attain a better life. The result is crowded classes in which passive students are processed according to the industrial model of the assembly line, while the creative energy of faculty and students is redirected to a variety of ventures promising what a university cannot deliver. The very word *university* acknowledges one encompassing paradigm, prevalent in the Middle Ages, that the USA practically disposed of over a century ago. In an age of global reality and many paradigms, the university is in reality less universal and increasingly specialized.

In these times of change, America, founded on innovation and self-reliance, seems to forget its own philosophy of decentralization and non-hierarchy. By no surprise, the newer computer technology-based companies took the lead in decentralizing and networking the workplace, in re-engineering each and every business. Most businesspeople, especially in established companies, are reluctant to address matrix management methods or to use distributed forms of organization and decentralized structures. Consequently, after waves of corporate restructuring and resizing, presidents and chairmen (not unlike university presidents and school principals) are kings, and the laborer, when not replaced by a machine, is often a virtual serf. Surprisingly, the decentralized spirit of homesteading and the distribution of tasks and responsibilities, through which much of efficiency is reached, makes slow headway. But things are changing! If there is an engine at work pulling the world from its literacy-based pragmatics to the future of higher efficiency required by the new scale of human activity, it has the initials USA written on it. And it is—make no mistake about it—digital.

When not faithful to its own experience of pluralism and self-motivation, the USA faces the inherent limitations of literacy-based practical experience in a number of domains, the political included. America once had a number of political parties. Now it seems that it cannot effectively get beyond the literate dualistic model of two antagonistic parties, emulating the Tories and the Whigs of the empire to which it once belonged. European countries and several African and Asian states have multi-party systems that reflect sensitivity to differences and take advantage of the variety they allow for. Such systems enfranchise more of a country's citizenry than does the two-party system in the USA. Every four years, Americans demand greater choice in elections, but only one state, Alaska, considers it normal to have more than two parties, and, incidentally, a governor who is neither Republican nor Democrat.

The USA has a complex about literacy to the extent that every subject is now qualified as *literacy*—cultural literacy, computer literacy, visual literacy, etc.—whether literacy is involved or not. Literacy has become its own specialty. In addition, new *literacies*, effectively disconnected from the ideals and expectations of classical literacy, have emerged from practical experiences of human self-constitution in realms where writing and reading are no longer required. This would not be so bad if it were not blinding people to the truth about a major characteristic of humankind. Diversity of expression and multiplicity of communication modes define new areas of human accomplishment and open avenues for further unfolding of people's creative and economic potential. The new condition of language, in particular the failure of literacy, is at the same time a symptom of a new stage in human progress. It in no way reflects a failure of national policy or will. As a matter of fact, the new stage we are entering is a reflection of the human spirit unfolding, refusing to be held captive to a dominant mode that has outlived its usefulness. It may well be that the coming of age of America is part of this new stage. After all, many believe that the crisis of language is the crisis of the white man (cf. Gottfried Benn), or at least of Western civilization.

So, is the USA the epitome of the civilization of illiteracy? Yes, America is illiterate to the extent that it constituted itself as an alternative to the world based on the underlying structures of literacy. The new pragmatic framework that the USA embodies does not automatically free it from the seductive embrace of the civilization it negates, and the current *angst* over the state of literacy is a manifestation of this. As an embodiment of the civilization of illiteracy, America demonstrates how several literacies can work together by complementing each other. Such a pragmatics succeeds or fails on its own terms. Whenever the implicit founding principles of adaptation, openness, exploration and validation of new models, and pragmatically based institutions are pursued, the result is the expected efficiency. Sometimes, the price people seem to pay for it is very high— unemployment, dislocation, retrenchment, a loss of a sense of permanency that humans long for. The price includes the ability or willingness to consider all aspects involved in a situation—political, environmental, social, legal, religious. These aspects transcend the tangible and necessitate taking the broad view, which literate civilization allowed for, over the specialized, narrowly focused, short-sighted, parochial view. Other times, it looks as though there are no alternatives. But in the long run, no one would really want to go back to the way things were 200 years ago.

BOOK II.

CHAPTER I: FROM SIGNS TO LANGUAGE

Languages are very different. So are literacies. The differences go well beyond how words sound, how alphabets differ, how letters are put together, or how sentences are structured in the various languages used around the world. In some languages, fine distinctions of color, shape, gender, numbers, and aspects of nature are made while more general statements are difficult to articulate. Anthropologists noted that in some of the Eskimo languages many words could be identified for what we call (using one word) *snow* and for activities involving it; in Arabic, many names are given to *camel;* in Mexico, different names qualify ceramic pottery according to function, not form: *jarro* for drinking, *jarra* for pouring, *olla* for cooking beans, *cazuela* for cooking stews. The Japanese and Chinese distinguish among different kinds of rice: still in the paddy, long-grained, shucked, kernels. George Lakoff mentions the Dyirbal language of Australia where the category *balan* includes fire, dangerous things, women, birds, and animals such as platypus, bandicoot, and echidna.

In other languages, the effort to categorize reveals associations surprising to individuals whose own life experiences are not reflected in the language they observe. The questioning attitude in the *Talmud* (a book of interpretations of the Hebrew *Torah*) is based on 20 terms qualifying different kinds of questions. *Shuzan* is calculation based on the use of the abacus. *Hissan,* hiding the Japanese word *hitsu* that stands for the brush used for writing, is calculation based on the use of Arabic numerals. To be in command of a language such as Chinese (to be literate in Chinese) is different from being literate in English, and even more different from being *literate* in various tribal languages. These examples suggest that the practical experience through which language is constituted belongs to the broad pragmatic context.

There is no such thing as an *abstract* language. Among particular languages there are great differences in vocabulary, syntax, and grammar, as well as in the idiosyncratic aspects implicit in them, reflective of the experience of their constitution. Despite such differences—some very deep—language is the common denominator of the species *Homo Sapiens,* and an important constitutive element of the dynamics of the species. *We are our language.* Those who state that language follows life consider only one side of the coin. Life is also formed in practical experiences of language constitution. The influence goes both ways, but human existence is in the end dependent upon the pragmatic framework within which individuals project their own biological structure in the practical act through which they identify themselves

Changes in the dynamics of language can be traced in what makes language necessary (biologically, socially, culturally), what causes different kinds of language use, and what brought about change. Necessity and agents of change are not the same, although sometimes it is quite difficult to distinguish between them. Changed working habits and new life styles are, as much as the appropriate language characterizing them, symptomatically connected to the pragmatic framework of our continuous self-constitution. We still have ten fingers—a structural reality of the human body projected into the decimal system—but the dominant number system today is probably binary. This observation regards the simplistic notion that words are coined when new instances make them desirable, and disappear when no longer required. In fact, many times words and other means of expression constitute new instances of life or work, and thus do not follow life, but define possible life paths.

There are several sources from which knowledge about language constitution and its subsequent evolution can be derived: historic evidence, anthropological research, cognitive modeling, cultural evaluation, linguistics, and archaeology. Here is a quote from one of the better (though not uncontroversial) books on the subject: Language

> enabled man to achieve a form of social organization whose range and complexity was different in kind from that of animals: whereas the social organization of animals was mainly instinctive and genetically transmitted, that of man was largely learned and transmitted verbally through the cultural heritage, (cf. Jack Goody and Ian Watt, *The Consequence of Literacy*).

The general idea pertaining to the social implications of language is restrictive but acceptable. What is not at all explained here is how language comes into existence, and why instinctive and genetically transmitted organization (of animals) would not suffice, or even be tantamount to the verbally transmitted organization of human beings. As a matter of fact, language, as perceived in the text cited and elsewhere in literature, becomes merely a storing device, not a formative instrument, a working tool of sorts, even a tool for making other tools and for evaluating them.

Languages have to be understood in a much broader perspective. Like humans, languages have an evolution in time. What came before language can be identified. What remains after a certain language disappears (and we know of some that have disappeared) are elements as important as the language itself for our better understanding of what makes language necessary. The disappearance of a language also helps us realize how the life of a language takes place through the life of those who made it initially possible, afterwards necessary, and finally replaced it with means more appropriate to their practical life and to their ever-changing condition. Research into pre-linguistic time (I refer to anthropological, archaeological, and genetic research) has focused on items people used in primitive forms of work. It convincingly suggests that before a relatively stable and repetitive structure was in place, people used sounds, gestures, and body expressions (face, hands, legs) pretty much the way infants do. The human lineage, in its constitutive phases, left behind a wealth of testimony to patterns of action and, later, to behavioral codes that result in some sense of cohesion. Distant forebears developed patterns in obtaining food and adapting to changes affecting the availability of food and shelter.

Before words, tools probably embodied both potential action and communication. Many scholars believe that tools are not possible without, or before, words. They claim that cognitive processes leading to the manufacture of tools, and to the tool-making human being (*Homo Faber*), are based on language. In the opinion of these scholars, tools extend the arm, and thus embody a level of generality not accessible otherwise than through language. It might well be that nature-based "notation" (footprints, bite marks, and the stone chips that some researchers believe were the actual tools) preceded language. Such notation was more in extension of the biological reality of the human being, and corresponded to a cognitive state, as well as to a scale of existence, preparing for the emergence of language.

Research on emerging writing systems (the work of Scribner and Cole, for instance, and moreover the work of Harald Haarmann, who considers the origins of writing in the notations found at Vinca, in the Balkans, near present-day Belgrade) has allowed us to understand how patterns of sounds and gestures became graphic representations; and how, once writing was established, new human experiences, at a larger scale of work, became possible. Finally, the lesson drawn from dying languages (Rosch's studies of Dyirbal, reported by Lakoff) is a lesson in the foundation of such languages and their demise. What we learn from these is less about grammar and phonetics and more about a type of human experience. We also acquire information regarding the supporting biological structure of those involved in it, the role of the scale of humankind, and how this scale changes due to a multitude of conjectures.

The differentiation introduced above among pre-language notations, emerging languages, emerging systems of writing, and dying languages is simultaneously a differentiation of kinds and types of human expression, interaction, and interpretation of everything humans use to acknowledge their reality in the world they live in.

Drawing attention to oneself or to others does not require language. Sounds suffice; gestures can add to the intended signal. In every sound and in every gesture, humans project themselves in some way. Individuality is preserved through a sound's pitch, timbre, volume, and duration; a gesture can be slow or rapid, timid or aggressive, or a mixture of these characteristics. Once the same sound, or the same gesture, or the same sequence of sounds and gestures is used to point to the same thing, this stabilized expression becomes what can be defined, in retrospect, as a sign.

SEMEION REVISITED

Interest in various sign systems used by humans reaches well back to ancient times. But it was only after renewed interest in semiotics—the discipline dealing with signs (*semeion* is the Greek word for sign)—that researchers from various other disciplines started looking at signs and their use by humans. The reason for this is to be found in the fast growth of expression and communication based on means other than natural language. Interaction between humans and increasingly complex machines also prompted a great deal of this interest.

Language—oral and written—is probably the most complex system of signs that researchers are aware of. Although the word *language* comprises experiences in other sign systems, it is by no means their synthesis. Before the practical experience of language, humans constituted themselves in experiences of simpler means of expression and communication: sounds, rhythms, gestures, drawings, ritualized movement, and all kinds of marks. The process can be seen as one of progressive projection of the individual onto the environment of existence. The sign *I* of one's own individuality—as distinct from other *I's* with whom interaction took place through competition, cooperation, or hostility—is most likely the first one can conjure. It must be simultaneous with the sign of the *other,* since *I* can be defined only in relation to something *different*, i.e., to the other. In the world of the different, some entities were dangerous or threatening, others accommodating, others cooperating. These qualifiers could not be simply translated into identifiers. They were actually projections of the subject as it perceived and understood, or misunderstood, the environment.

To support my thesis about the pragmatic nature of language and literacy, a short account of the pre-verbal stage needs to be attempted here. Very many scholars have tried to discover the origin of language. It is a subject as fascinating as the origins of the universe and the origin of life itself. My interest is rather in the area of the nature of language, the origin being an implicit theme, and the circumstances of its origination. I have already referred to what are loosely called tools and to behavioral codes (sexual, or relating to shelter, food-gathering, etc.). There is historic evidence that can be considered for such an account, and there are quite a number of facts related to conditions of living (changes in climate, extinction of some animals and plants, etc.) that affect this stage. The remaining information is comprised of inferences based on how beings similar to what we believe human beings once were constituted their signs as an expression of their identity. These signs reflected the outside world, but moreover expressed awareness of the world made possible by the human's own biological condition.

The very first sentence of the once famous *Port-Royal Grammar* unequivocally considers speaking as an explanation of our thoughts by signs invented for this particular purpose. The same text makes thinking independent of words or any kind of signs. I take the position that the transition from nature to culture, i.e., from reactions caused by natural stimuli to reflections and awareness, is marked by both continuity and discontinuity. The continuous aspect refers to the biological structure projected into the universe of interactions with similar or dissimilar entities. The discontinuity results from biological changes in brain size, vertical posture, functions of the hands. The pre-verbal (or pre-discursive) is immediate by its very nature.

The discursive, which makes possible the manifest thought (one among many kinds) is mediated by the signs of language. Closeness to the natural environment is definitive of this stage. Although I am rather suspicious of claims made by contemporary advocates of the psychedelic, in particular McKenna, I can see how everything affecting the biological potential of the being (in this case psilocybin, influencing vision and group behavior) deserves at least consideration when we approach the subject of language.

Signs, through which pre-verbal human beings projected their reality in the context of their existence, expressed through their energy and plasticity what humans were. Signs captured what was perceived as alike in others, objects or beings, and likeness became the shared part of signs. This was a time of direct interaction and immediateness, a time of action and reaction. Everything delayed or unexpected constituted the realm of the unknown, of mystery. The scale of life was reduced. All events were of limited steps and limited duration. Interacting individuals constituted themselves as signs of presence, that is, of a shared space and time. Signs could thus refer to here and now as immediate instantiations of duration, proximity, interval, etc., but long before the notions of space and time were formed. Once distinctions were projected in the experience of signs, the absent or the coming could be suggested, and the dynamics of repetitive events could be expressed. It was only after this self-expression took place that a representational function became possible: a high-pitched cry not just for pain, but also for danger that might cause pain; an arm raised not only as an indication of firm presence, but also of requested attention; a color applied on the skin not only as an expression of pleasure in using a fruit or a plant, but also of anticipated similar pleasures—an *instruction* to be mimetically followed, to be imitated.

Being part of the expressed, the individuals projecting themselves in the expression also projected a certain experience related to the limited world they lived in. Signs standing for associations of events (clouds with rain, noise of hooves with animals, bubbles on a lake's surface with fish) were probably as much representations of those sequences as an expression of constituted experience shared with others living in the same environment. Sharing experience *beyond the here and now,* in other words, transition from direct and unreflected to indirect and reflected interaction, is the next cognitive step. It took place once shared signs were associated with shared common experiences and with rules of generating new signs that could report on new, similar, or dissimilar experiences. Each sign is a biological witness to the process in which it was constituted and of the scale of the experience. A whisper addresses one other person, maybe two, very close to each other. A shout corresponds to a different scale. Accordingly, each sign is its shorthand history and a bridge from the natural to the cultural.

Sequences, such as successions of sounds or verbal utterances, or configurations of signs, such as drawings, testify to a higher cognitive level. Relations between sequences or configurations of signs and the practical experience in which they are constituted are less intuitive. To derive from the understanding of such sign relations some practical rules of significance to those sharing a sign system was an experience in human interaction. Later in time, the immediate experiential component is present only indirectly in language. The constitution of the language is the result of the change of focus from signs to relations among them. Grammar, in its most primitive condition, was not about how signs are put together (*syntax*), nor of how signs represent something (*semantics*), but of the circumstances determining new signs to be constituted in a manner preserving their experiential quality—the *pragmatics.*

Consequently, language was constituted as an intermediary between stabilized experience (repetitive patterns of work and interaction) and future (patterns broken). Signs still preserved the concreteness of the event that triggered their constitution. In the use of language, the human being abandoned a great deal of individual projection. Language's degree of generality became far higher than that of its components (signs themselves), or of any other signs. But even at the level of language, the characteristic function of this sign system was the constitution of practical experiences, not the representation of means for sharing categories of experiences. In each sign, and more so in each language, the biological and the artificial collide. When the biological element dominates, sign experiences take place as reactions. When the cultural dominates, the sign or language experience becomes an interpretation, i.e., a continuation of the semiotic experience. Interpretation of any kind corresponds to the never-ending differentiation from the biological and is representative of the constitution of culture. Under the name culture as used above, we understand human nature and its objectification in products, organizations, ideas, attitudes, values, artifacts.

The practical experience of sign constitution—from the use of branches, rocks, and fur to the most primitive etchings (on stone, bone, and wood), from the use of sounds and gestures to articulated language—contributed to successive changes in ongoing activity (hunting, seeking shelter, collaborative efforts), as well as to changes in humans themselves. In the universe of rich detail in which humans affirmed their identity through fighting for resources and creatively finding alternatives, information did not change, but the awareness of the practical implications of details increased. Each observation made in the appropriation of knowledge through its use in work triggered possible patterns of interaction.

Once signs were constituted, sharing in the experience became possible. Genetic transmission of information was relatively slow. It dominated the initial phases during which the species introduced its own patterns within the patterns of the natural environment. Semiotic transmission of information, in particular through language, is much faster than genetic inheritance but cannot replace it. Human life is attested at roughly 2.5 million years ago, incipient language use roughly 200,000 years ago. Agriculture as a patterned experience emerged no more than 19,000 years ago, and writing less than 5,000 years ago (although some researchers estimate 10,000 years). The shorter and shorter cycles characteristic of self-constitution correspond to the involvement of means other than genetic in the process of change. What today we call mental skills are the result of a rather compressed process. Compare the time it took until motor skills involved in hunting, gathering, and foraging were perfected to the extent they were before they started to degenerate, relatively speaking, as we notice in our days.

THE FIRST RECORD IS A WHIP

Signs can be recorded—quite a few were recorded in and on various materials—and so can language, as we all know. But language did not start out as a written system. The African *Ishango Bone* predates a writing system by some thousands of years; the *quipus* of the Inca culture are a *sui generis* record of people, animals, and goods previous to writing. China and Japan, as well as India, have similar pre-writing forms of keeping records.

The polygenetic emergence of writing is, in itself, significant in several ways. For one, it introduced another mediating element disassociated from a particular speaker. Second, it constituted a level of generality higher than that of the verbal expression that was independent of time and space, or of other forms of record keeping. Third, everything projected into signs, and from signs into articulated language, participated in the formation of meaning as the result of the understanding of language through its use. Only at that moment did language gain a semantic and syntactic dimension (as we call them in today's terminology).

Formally, if the issue of literacy and the constitution of languages are connected, then this connection started with written languages. Nevertheless, events preceding written language give us the perspective of what made writing necessary, and why some cultures never developed a written language. Although referring to a different time-frame (thousands of years ago), this could help us comprehend why writing and reading need not dominate life and work today and in the future. Or at least it could help clarify the relation among human beings, their language, and their existence. After all, this is what we want to understand from the vantage point of today's world. We take the word for granted, wondering whether there was a stage of the wordless human being (about which we can only infer indirectly). But once the word was established, with the advent of the means for recording it, it affected not only the future, but also the perception of the past.

Conquering the past, the word gives legitimacy to explanations that presume it. Thus it implies some carrying device, i.e., a system of notation as a built-in memory and as a mechanism for associations, permutations, and substitutions. But if such a system is accepted, the origins of writing and reading are pushed back so far in time that the disjunction of *literate-illiterate* becomes a structural characteristic of the species at one of the periods of its self-definition. Obviously expanded far in time and seen in such a broad perspective, this notation (comprising images, the *Ishango Bone, quipus,* the Vinca figurines, etc.) contradicts the logocratic model of language. Mono- and poly-syllabic elements of speech, embodying audible sequences of sounds (and appropriate breathing patterns that insert pauses and maintain a mechanism for synchronization), together with natural mnemonic devices (such as pebbles, knots on branches, shapes of stones, etc.) are pre-word components of pre-languages. They all correspond to the stage of direct interaction. They pertain to such a small scale of human activity that time and space can be sequenced in extension of the patterns of nature (day-night, very close-less close, etc.).

This juncture in the self-definition of the species occurred when the transition, from selected natural marks to *marking,* and later to stable patterns of sounds, eventually leading to words, took place. This was an impressive change that introduced a linear relation in a realm that was one of randomness or even chaos. If catastrophes occurred (as many anthropologists indicate), i.e., changes of scale outside the linear to which human beings were not adapted, they resulted in the disappearance of entire populations, or in massive displacements. Rooted in experiences belonging to what we would call natural phenomena, this change resulted in rudimentary elements of a language. New patterns of interaction were also developed: naming (by association, as in clans bearing names of animals), ordering and counting (at the beginning by pairing the counted objects, one by one, with other objects), recording regularities (of weather, sky configurations, biological cycles) as these affected the outcome of practical activities.

SCALE AND THRESHOLD

Already mentioned in previous pages, the concept of *scale* is an important parameter in human development. At this point, it is useful to elaborate on the notion since I consider scale to be critical in explaining major transitions in human pragmatics. The progression from pre-word to notation, and in our days from literacy to illiteracy is paralleled by the progression of scale. Numbers as such—how many people in a given area, how many people interacting in a particular practical experience, the longevity of people under given circumstances, the mortality rate, family size—are almost meaningless. Only when *relations* among numbers and circumstances can be established is some meaningful inference possible. Scale is the expression of relations.

A crude scale of life and death is remote from underlying adaptive strategies as these are embodied in practical experiences of self-constitution. Knowledge regarding biological mechanisms, such as knowledge of health or disease, supports efforts to derive models for various circumstances of life, as humans project their biological reality into the reality of interactions with the outside world. We know, for instance, that when the scale of human activity progressed to include domesticated animals, some animal diseases affecting human life and work were transmitted to humans. Domestication of animals, a very early practical experience, brought humans closer to them for longer times, thus facilitating what is called a change of host for agents of such diseases. The common cold seems to have been acquired from horses, influenza from pigs, smallpox from cattle. We also know that over time, infectious diseases affect populations that are both relatively large and stationary. The examples usually given are yellow fever or malaria and measles (the latter probably also transported from swine, where the disease is caused by the larva of the tapeworm from which the word *measles* is derived). Sometimes the inference is made from information on groups that until recently were, or still are, involved in practical experiences similar to those of remote stages in human history, as are the tribes of the Amazon rain forest. Isolated hunter-gatherers and populations that still forage (the Kung San, Hadza, Pygmies) replay adaptive strategies that otherwise would be beyond our understanding. Statistical data derived from observations help improve models based only on our knowledge about biological mechanisms.

The notion of scale involves these considerations insofar as it tells us that life expectancy in different pragmatic frameworks varies drastically. The less than 30-year life expectancy (associated with high infant mortality, diseases, and dangers in the natural environment) explains the relatively stationary population of hunter-gatherers. Orders of magnitude of 20 years higher were achieved in what are called settled modes of life existing before the rise of cities (occurring at different times in Asia Minor, North Africa, the Far East, South America, and Europe). The praxis of agriculture resulted in diversified resources and is connected to the dynamics of a lower death rate, a higher birth rate, and changes in anatomy (e.g., increased height).

The hypotheses advanced by modern researchers of ancestral language families concerning the relation between their diffusion over large territories and the expanding agricultural populations is of special interest here. The so-called Neolithic Revolution brought about food production in some communities of people as opposed to reliance on searching, finding, catching or trapping (as with foragers and hunters). As conditions favored an increase in population, the nature of the relations among individuals and groups of individuals changed due to force of number. Groups broke away from the main tribe in order to acquire a living environment with less competition for resources. Alternatively, pragmatic requirements led to situations in which the number of people in a given area increased. With this increase, the nature of their relations became more complex.

What is of interest here is the direction of change and the interplay of the many variables involved in it. Definitely, one wants to know how scale and changes in practical experiences are related. Does a discovery or invention predate a change in scale, or is the new scale a result of it or of several related phenomena? Polygenetic explanations point to the many variables that affect developments as complex as those leading to discoveries of human practical experiences that result in increased populations and diversified pragmatic interactions. The major families of languages are associated, as archaeological and linguistic data prove, with places where the new pragmatic context of agriculture was established. One well documented example is that of two areas in China: the Yellow River Basin, where foxtail millet is documented, and the Yangtzi River Basin, where rice was domesticated. The Austronesian languages spread from these areas over thousands of miles beyond. We have here an interesting correlation, even if only summarily illustrated, between the nature of human experience, the scale that makes it possible, and the spread of language. Similar research bears evidence from the area called New Guinea, where cultivation of taro tubers is identified with speakers of the Papuan languages, covering large areas of territory as they searched for suitable land and encountered the opposition of foragers.

Natural abilities (such as yelling, throwing, running, plucking, breaking, bending) dominated a humankind constituted in groups and communities of reduced scale. Abilities other than natural, such as planting, cooking, herding, singing, and using tools, emerge consciously, in knowledge of the cause, when the change of scale in population and effort required efficiency levels relative to the community, impossible to achieve at the natural level. Such abilities developed very quickly. They led to the diversified means generated in practical experiences involving elements of planning (as rudimentary as it was at its beginning), reductionist strategies of survival and well-being (break a bigger problem into smaller parts, what will become the divide-and-conquer strategy), and coalition building. These involved acts of substitution, insertion, and omission, and continued with combinations of these at progressively higher levels. At a certain scale of human activity, the experience of work and the cognitive experience of storing information pertinent to work differentiated.

Do structural changes bring about a new scale, or does scale effect structural changes? The process is complex in the sense that the underlying structure of human activity is adapted to exigencies of survival fine tuned to the many factors influencing both individual and communal experiences. That scale and underlying structure are not independent results from the fact that *possibilities* as well as *needs* are reflected in scale. More individuals, with complementary skills, have a better chance to succeed in practical endeavors of increased complexity. Their needs increase, too, since these individuals bring into the experience not only their person, but also commitments outside the experience. The underlying structure embodies elements characteristic of the human endowment—itself bound to change as the individual is challenged by new circumstances of life—and elements characteristic of the nature of human relations, affecting and being affected by scale. Dynamic tensions between scale and the elements defining the underlying structure lead to changes in the pragmatic framework. Language development is just one example of such changes. Articulated speech emerged in the context of initial agricultural praxis as an extension of communication means used in hunting and food gathering. Notation and more advanced tools emerged at a later juncture. Crafts resulted from practical experiences made possible by such tools as work started to become specialized. Writing was made possible by the cognitive experiences of notation and reading (no matter how primitive the *reading* was). Writing emerged as practical human constitution extended to trade, to beyond the here-and-now and beyond co-presence. The underlying structure of literacy was well suited to the sequentiality characteristic of practical experiences, expression of dependencies, and deterministic processes.

As already stated, successive forms of communication came about when the scale of interaction among humans expanded from one to several to many. Literacy corresponded to a qualitatively different moment. If language can be associated with the human scale characteristic of the transition from hunting and foraging for food to producing it by means of agriculture, literacy can be associated with the next level of human interconditioning—production of means of production. One can use here the metaphor of critical mass or threshold, not to overwrite scale, but to define a value, a level of complexity, or a new *attractor* (as this is called in chaos theory). Critical mass defines a lower threshold—until this value, interaction was still optimally carried out by means such as referential signs, representations based on likeness, or by speech. At the lower threshold, individuals and the groups they belong to can still identify themselves coherently. But a certain instability is noticeable: the same signs do not express similar or equivalent experiences. In this respect, critical mass refers to number or amount (of people, resources they share, interactions they are involved in, etc.) and to quality (differences in the result of the effort of self-constitution). Former means are rendered inadequate by practical experiences of a different nature. New strategies for dealing with inadequacies result from the experience itself, as the optimization of the sign systems involved (signals, speech, notation, writing) result from the same. Notation became necessary when the information to be stored (inventories, myths, genealogies) became more than what oral transmission could efficiently handle. Critical mass explains why some cultures never developed literacy, as well as why a dominant literacy proves inadequate in our days.

SIGNS AND TOOLS

Practical experiences involving nature led to the realization of differences: colors that change with seasons, flora and fauna in their variety, variations in sky and weather. Human need is externalized through hunting (maybe scavenging), fishing, finding shelter, and seeking one's own kind, either under sexual drive or for some collaborative effort. Thus, multiplicity of nature is met by multiplicity of elementary operations. What resulted was a language of actions, with elements relevant to the task at hand. There was no real dialogue. In nature, screeches and hoots, in finite sequences, signal danger. Otherwise, nature does not understand human signs, images, or sounds. For attracting and catching prey, or for avoiding danger, sounds, colors, and shapes can be involved. What qualifies them as signs is the infinity of variations and combinations required by the practical context. Against the background of differences, human practical experiences resulted also in the realization of similarities in appearance and actions. Awareness of similarities was embodied in means of interaction. They became signs once the experience stabilized in the constitution of a group coherently integrating the sign in its activity.

Elementary forms of praxis maintained individuals near the object upon which they acted, or upon which needs and plans for their fulfillment were projected. *Extraction* of what was common to many tasks at hand translated into accumulation of experience. With experience, a certain distance between the individual, or group, and the task was introduced. The language of actions changed continuously. Evaluation started as a comparison. It evolved into inclinations, repetitive patterns, and selections until it translated into a rule to be followed. Interpretation of natural patterns connected to weather (what we call change of season, storm, drought, etc.), to observations concerning hunted animals, or digging for tubers, or to agriculture (as we define it in retrospect) resulted in the constitution of a repertory of observed characteristics and, over time, in a method of observation. Once observed, phenomena were *tested* for relevancy and thus became signs. They integrated the observer, who memorized and associated them with successful patterns of action. In a way, this meant that *reading*—i.e., observation of all kinds of patterns and associations to tasks at hand—was in anticipation of notation and writing, and probably one of the major reasons for their progressive appearance. This *reading* filtered the relevant, that characteristic—of an animal, plant, weather pattern—which affected the attainment of desired goals. Consequently, the language of actions gained in coherence, progressively involving more signs. Rituals are a form of sharing and collective memory, a *sui generis* calendar, characteristic of an implicit sense of time. They are a training device in both understanding the signs pertaining to work and the strategy of action to follow when circumstances changed. In rituals, the unity between what is natural and what is human is continuously reaffirmed.

Tools are extensions of the physical reality of the human being. They are relevant as means for reaching a goal. Signs, however, are means of self-reflection, and thus by their nature means of communication. Tools, which can be interpreted as signs, too, are also an expression of the self-reflective nature of humans, but in a different way. What defines them is the function, not the meaning they might conjure in a communicational context. By their nature, tools require integration. In retrospect, tools appear to us as instances of self-constitution at a scale different from the natural scale of the physical world in which individuals created them. The difference is reflected in their efficiency in the first place, but also in the implicit correlations they embody. Some are tools for individual use; others require cooperation with other persons.

Sign activity at such primitive stages of humankind marked the transcendence from accidental to systematic. The use of tools and the relative uniform structure of the tasks performed contributed to a sense of method. Tools testify to the close and homogenous character of the pragmatic framework of primitive humans. The syncretic nature of the signs of practical experiences were reflected in the syncretism of tools and signs. What we today call religion, art, science, philosophy, and ethics were represented, *in nuce,* in the sign in an undifferentiated, syncretic manner. Observations of repetitive patterns and awareness of possible deviations blended. Externalized in these complex signs, individuals strove towards making them understandable, unequivocal, and easy to preserve over time.

Think about such categories as *syncretism, understanding, repetitive patterns* in practical terms. A sign can be a beat. It should be easily perceived even under adverse conditions (noise from thunder, the howl of animals). Humans should be able to associate it with the same consequences (*Run!* should not be confused with *Halt!; Throw!* should not be confused with *Don't throw!* or some other unrelated action). This univocal association must be maintained over time. As practical experiences diversified, so did the generation of signs. Rhythm, color, shape, body expression and movement, as experienced in daily life, were integrated in rituals. Things were shown as they are—animal heads, antlers and claws, tree branches and trunks, huge rocks split apart. Their transformation was performed through the use of fire, water, and stones shaped to cut, or to help in shaping other stones.

It is quite difficult for us today to understand that for the primitive mind, likeness produced and explained likeness, that there was no connotation, that everything had immediate practical implications. What was shared, here and now, or between one short-lived generation and the next, was an experience so undifferentiated that sometimes even the distinction between action and object of action (such as hunting and prey, plowing and soil, collecting and the collected fruit, etc.) was difficult to make.

The process of becoming a human being is one of constituting its own nature. Externalizing characteristics (predominantly biological, but progressively also spiritual) to be shared within the emergent human culture is part of the process. We have come to understand that there is no such thing as the world on one side and a subject reflecting it on another. The appearance, which Descartes turned into the premise of the rational discourse adopted by Western civilization, makes us fall captive to representational explanations rather than to ontogenetic descriptions. Human beings identify themselves, and thus the species they belong to, by accounting for similarities and distinctions. These pertain to their existence, and sharing in the awareness of these similarities and distinctions is part of human interaction. As such, the world is constituted almost at the same time as it is discovered. This contradictory dynamics of identity and distinction makes it possible to see how language is something other than the "image of our thoughts," as Lamy once put it, obviously in the tradition of Descartes. Language is also something other than the act of using it. We make our language the way we continuously make ourselves. This making does not come about in a vacuum, but in the pragmatic framework of our interdependencies. The transition from directness and immediateness to indirectness and mediation, along with the notions of space and time appropriated in the process, is in many ways reflected in the process of language constitution. The emergence of signs, their functioning, the constitution of language, and the emergence of writing seem to point to both the self-definition and preservation of human nature, as these unfold in the practical act of the species' self-constitution.

CHAPTER 2: FROM ORALITY TO WRITING

Tracing the origin of language to early nuclei of agriculture, as many authors do (Peter Bellwood, Paul K. Benedict, Colin Renfrew, Robert Blust, among them), is tantamount to acknowledging the pragmatic foundation of the practical experience of language of human beings. Language is not a passive witness to human dynamics. Diversity of practical experience is *reflected* in language and *made possible* through the practical experience of language. The origins of language, as much as the origins of writing, lie in the realm of the natural. This is why considerations regarding the biological condition of the individual interacting with the outside world are extremely important. Practical experiences of self-constitution in language are constitutive of culture. The act of writing, together with that of tool-making, is constitutive of a species increasingly *defining* its own nature. Considerations regarding culture are accordingly no less important than those concerning the biological identity of the human being.

Let us point to some implications of the biological factor. We know that the number of sounds, for instance, that humans can produce when they push air through their mouths is very high. However, out of this practically infinite number of sounds, only slightly more than forty are identifiable in the Indo-European languages, as opposed to the number of sounds produced in the Chinese and Japanese languages. While it is impossible to show how the biological make-up of individuals and the structure of their experience are projected onto the system of language, it would be unwise not to account for this projection as it occurs at every moment of our existence. When humans speak, muscles, vocal chords, and other anatomical components are activated and used according to the characteristics of each. People's voices differ in many ways and so subtly that to identify people through voice alone is difficult. When we speak, our hearing is also involved. In writing, as well as in reading, this participation extends to sight. Other dynamic features such as eye movement, breathing, heartbeat, and perspiration come into play as well. What we are, do, say, write, or read are related. The experience behind language use and the biological characteristics of people living in a language differ to such an extent that almost never will similar events, even the simplest, be similarly accounted for in language (or in any other sign system, for that matter) by different persons.

The first history, or the personal inquiry into the probable course of past events, rests upon orality, integrates myths, and ends up with the attempt to refer events to places, as well as to time. Logographers try to reconstruct genealogies of persons involved in real events (wars, founding of clans, tribes, or dynasties, for example) or in the dominant fiction of a period (e.g., the epics attributed to Homer, or the book of *Genesis* in the Bible). In the transition from remembrance (*mnemai*) to documented accounts (*logoi*), human beings acquired what we call today consciousness of time or of history. They became aware of differences in relating to the same events.

The entire encoding of social experience, from very naive forms (concerning family, religion, illness) to very complex rules (of ceremony, power, military conduct) is the result of human practice diversified with the participation of language. The tension between orality and writing is, respectively, an expression of the tension between a more homogeneous way of life and the ever diversifying new forms that broke through boundaries accepted for a very long time. In the universe of the many Chinese languages, this is more evident than in Western languages. Chinese ideographic writing, which unifies the many dialects used in spoken Chinese, preserves concreteness, and as such preserves tradition as an established way of relating to the world. Within the broader Chinese culture, every effort was made to preserve characteristics of orality. The philosophy derived from such a language defends, through the fundamental principle of Tao in Confucianism, an established and shared mechanism of transmitting knowledge.

Unlike spoken language, writing is fairly recent. Some scholars (especially Haarmann) consider that writing did not appear until 4,000 to 3,000 BCE; others extend the time span to 6,000 BCE and beyond. To repeat: It is not my intention to reconstitute the history of writing or literacy. It makes little sense to rekindle disputes over chronology, especially when new findings, or better interpretations of old findings, are not at hand or are not yet sufficiently convincing. The so-called boundaries between oral and post-oral cultures, as well as between non-literate, literate, and what are called post-literate, or illiterate, cultures are difficult to determine. It is highly unlikely that we shall ever be able to discover whether images (cave drawings or petroglyphs) antecede or come after spoken language. Probably languages involving notation, drawings, etchings, and rituals—with their vast repertory of articulated gestures—were relatively simultaneous. Some historians of writing ascertain that without the word, there could be no image. Others reject the logocratic model and suggest that images preceded the written and probably even the spoken. Many speculate on the emergence of rituals, placing them before or after drawing, before or after writing. I suggest that primitive human expression is syncretic and polymorphous, a direct consequence of a pragmatic framework of self-constitution that ascertains multiplicity.

INDIVIDUAL AND COLLECTIVE MEMORY

Anthropologists have tried to categorize the experience transmitted in order to understand how orality and, later, writing (primitive notation, in fact) refer to the particular categories. Researchers point to the material surroundings—resources, in the most general way—to successful action, and to words as pertaining to the more general framework (time, space, goals, etc.). Speculation goes as far as to suggest that these human beings became increasingly dependent on arti-factual means of notation. As a consequence, they relied less on the functions of the brain's right hemisphere. In turn, this resulted in decreased acuteness of these functions. Some even go so far as to read here an incipient *Weltanschauung*, a perspective and horizon of the world. They are probably wrong because they apply an explana-tory model already influenced by language (product of a civilization of literacy) on a very unsettled human condition. In order to achieve some stability and permanence, as dictated by the instinctive survival of the species, this human condition was projected in various sequences of signs still unsettled in a language. The very objects of direct experience were the signs. This experience eventually settled and became more uniform through the means and constraints of orality.

Language is not a direct expression of experience, as the same anthropologists think. In fact, language is also less comprehensive than the signs leading to it. Before any conversation can take place, something else—experience within the species—is shared and con-stitutes the background for future sharing. Face to face encounter, scavenging, hunting, fishing, finding natural forms of shelter, etc., became themselves signs when they no longer were related only to survival, but embodied practical rules and the need to share. Sharing is the ultimate qualifier for a sign, especially for a language.

Tools, cave paintings, primitive forms of notation, and rituals addressed collective memory, no matter how limited this collective was. Words addressed individual memory and became means of indi-vidual differentiation. Individual needs and motivations need to be understood in their relation to those of groups. Signs and tools are elements that were integrated in differentiation. To understand the interplay between them, we could probably benefit from modern cognitive research of distributed and centralized authority. Tools are of a distributed nature. They are endlessly changed and tested in individual or cooperative efforts. Signs, as they result from human interaction, seem to emanate from anything but the individual. As such, they are associated with incipient centralized authority. These remarks define a conceptual viewpoint rather than describe a reality to which none of us has or can have access. But in the absence of such a conceptual premise, inferences, mine or anybody else's, are meaningless.

The distinctions introduced above point to the need to consider at least three stages before we can refer to language:

1. integration in the group of one's kind in direct forms of interaction: touching, passing objects from one to another, recognition through sounds, gestures, satisfying instinctual drives;
2. awareness of differences and similarities expressed in direct ways: comparison by juxtaposition, equalization by physical adjustment;
3. stabilization of expressions of sameness or difference, making them part of the practical act.

From the time *same* and *different* were perceived in their degree of generality, directness and immediateness was progressively lost. Layers of understanding, together with rules for generating coherent expressions, were accumulated, checked against an infinity of concrete situations, related to signs still used (objects, sounds, gestures, colors, etc.), and freed from the demand of unequivocal or univocal meaning. All these means of expression were socialized in the process of *production* (the making of artifacts, hunting, fishing, plowing, etc.) and *self-reproduction* until they became language. Once they became language—*talked about* things and actions—this language removed itself from the objects and the making or doing. This removal made it appear more and more as a given, an entity in itself, a reality to fear or enjoy, to use or compare one's actions to the actions of others. The time it took for this process to unfold was very long—hundreds of thousands of years (if we can imagine this in our age of the instant). The process is probably simultaneous to the formation of larger brains and upright posture. It included biological changes connected to the self-constitution of the species and its survival within a framework different from the natural. It nevertheless acknowledged the natural as the object of action and even change.

The functional need for distinctions explains morphological aspects; the pragmatic context suggests how the shift from the scale of one-to-one direct interaction to one-to-many by the intermediary of language takes place. Concreteness, i.e., closeness to the object, is also symptomatic of the limited shared universe. These languages are very localized because they result from localized experiences. They externalize a limited awareness, and make possible a very restricted development of both the experience and the language associated with it. As we shall see later on, a structurally similar situation can be identified in the world today, not on some island, as the reader might suspect, but on the *islands* of specialized work as we constitute them in our economies. Obsessed with (or driven by) efficiency, and oriented towards maximizing it, we use strategies of integration and coordination which were not possible in the ages of language constitution.

But let us get back to the place of the spoken (before the emergence of notation and the written) and its cultural function in the lives of human communities. The memory before the word was the memory of repeated actions, the memory of gestures, sounds, odors, and artifacts. Structuring was imposed from outside—natural cycle (of day and night, of seasons, of aging), and natural environment (riverside, mountainside, valley, wooded region, grassy plains). The outside world gave the cues. Participants acted according to them and to the cues of previous experience as this was directly passed from one person to another. Long before astrology, it was geomancy (association of topographical features to people or outcomes of activity) that inhabited people's *reading* of the environment and resulted in various glyphs (petroglyphs, geoglyphs). Initially remembering referred to a place, later on to a sequence of events. Only with language did time come into the picture. Remembrance was dictated minimally by instinct and was only slightly genetic in nature. With the word, whose appearance implied means for recognizing and eventually recording words, a fundamental shift occurred. The word entered human experience as a relational sign. It associated object and action. Together with tools, it constituted culture as the unity between who we are (identity), what our world is (object of work, contemplation, and questioning), and what we do (to survive, reproduce, change). At this moment, culture and awareness of it affected practical experiences of human self-constitution. Simultaneously, an important split occurred: genetic memory remained in charge of the human being's biological reality, while social memory took over cultural reality. Nevertheless, they were not independent of each other.

The nature of their interdependence is characteristic of each of the changes in the scale of humankind that interests us here. If we could describe what it takes for individuals to congregate, what they need to know or understand in order to hunt, to forage, to begin herding and agriculture, we would still not know how well they would have to perform. In retrospect, it seems that there was a predetermined path from the stage of primitive development to what we are today. Assuming the existence of such a path, we still do not know at what moment one type of activity no longer satisfied expectations of survival and other paths needed to be pursued. Once we involve the notion of scale in our cognitive modeling, we get some answers important for understanding not only orality and writing, but also the process leading to literacy and the post-literate.

CULTURAL MEMORY

Memory, in its incipient stages (comparable to childhood, at the beginning of human culture), as well as in its new functions today, deserves our entire attention. For the time being, we can confidently assume that before cultural memory was established, genetic memory, from genetic code to the inner clock and homeostatic mechanisms, dominated the inheritance mechanisms related to survival, reproduction, and social interaction. The emphasis brought by words is from inheritance to transmission of experience. Rituals changed; they integrated verbal language and gained a new status—syncretic projections of the community. Language opened the possibility to describe efficient courses of action. It also described generic programs for such diverse activities as navigating, hunting, fire-making, producing tools, etc. Expressions in language were of a level of generality that direct action and the ritual could not reach.

In images preceding words, thought and action followed a circular sequence: one was embedded in the other. A circular relation corresponded to the reduced scale of the incipient species: no growth, input and output in balance. Only when the circle was opened was a sense of progression ascertained. The circular framework can be easily defined as corresponding to the identity between the result of the effort and the effort. Obviously, chasing and catching prey required a major physical effort. The reward at this stage was nothing more nor less than satisfied hunger. Let us divide the result by the effort. The outcome of this division is a very intuitive representation of efficiency or usefulness. The circular stage maintained the two variables close to each other, and the ratio around the value of 1:1.

The framework of linear relations started with awareness of how efforts could be reduced and usefulness increased. The linear sequence of activities was deterministically connected—the stronger the person, the more powerful in throwing, thrusting and hauling; the longer the legs, the faster the run, etc. Language was a product of the change from the circular framework, embodied in foraging, but also a factor affecting the dynamics and the direction followed, i.e., agriculture. In language the circle was opened in the sense that sequences were made possible and generality, once achieved, generated further levels of generality. From direct interaction coordinated by instinct, biological rhythm, etc., to interaction coordinated by melodic sound, movement, fire signals, to communication based on words, the human species ascertained its existence among other species. It also ascertained a sense of purpose and progression.

The pragmatics of myths is one of progression. It extends well into our age, in forms that suit the scale of humankind—progression from tribal life to the *polis,* ancient cities—and its activities. In today's terminology, we can look at myths as algorithms of practical life. In the ritual, giving birth, selecting a mate, fruitful sexual relations—all related to reproduction and death—could be approached within the implicit circularity of action-reaction. In myths, the word of the language conveys a relatively depersonalized experience available to each and all. Since it was objectified in language, it took on the semblance of rules. In language, things are remembered; but also forgotten, or made forgotten, for reasons having to do with new circumstances of work and social life. Change in experience was reflected in the change of everything pertinent to the experience as it was preserved in language. Quite often, in the act of transmitting experience, details were changed, myths were transmuted. They became new programs for new goals and new circumstances of work.

Generally speaking, the emergence and cultural acquisition of language and the change of status of the human being from *Homo Faber* (tool-using human) to *Homo Sapiens* (thinking human) were parallel processes within the pragmatic framework of linear relations between actions and results. The pre-language stage of relatively homogeneous activities, of directness and immediateness, of relative equality between the effort and the result progressively came to an end. The need to describe, categorize, store, and retrieve the content of diversified, indirect, mediated experience was projected into the reality of language, within the experience of human self-constitution. The relevance of experience to the task at hand was replaced by the anticipated relevancy of structuring future tasks in order to minimize effort and maximize outcome.

FRAMES OF EXISTENCE

The oral phase of language made it difficult, if not impossible, to account for past events. Testimony in communities researched while still in the oral phase (see Lévi-Strauss, among others) shows that they could not maintain the semantic integrity of the discourse.

Words uttered in a never-ending now—the implicit notion of *present*—seem to automatically reinvent the past according to the exigencies of the immediate. The past, during the oral phase of language, was a form of present, and so was the future, since there are no instruments to project the word along the axis of time.

Orality is associated with fixed frames of existence and practical life. The culture of the written word resulted from the introduction of a variable frame of existence, within which a new pragmatic framework, corresponding to a growing scale of human activity, required a stable outline of language. This outline of language—over short time intervals it appears as a fixed frame of reference—can be associated with more mobile, more dynamic frames of existence and practical experiences, whose output follows the dynamic of the linear relations it embodies. Work and social interaction—in short, the pragmatic dimension of human existence—made the recording of language necessary and impressed linearity upon it.

A cuneiform notation, over 3,500 years old, testifies to a Sumerian who looked at the nightly skies and saw a lion, a bull, and a scorpion. More importantly, it demonstrates how a practical experience constitutes a cognitive filter: what people saw when they looked at something unknown and for which no name was constituted, and how disjoint worlds—the earthly environment and the sky—were put in relation at this phase of language constitution. This is even more important in view of the fact that as an isolated language, Sumerian survives only in writing, a product of that "budding flower" as A. and S. Sherrat described it, referring to the agricultural heartland of Southwest Asia where many language families originated.

Writing, which takes place in many respects at a higher cognitive level than the production and utterance of the word, or than in pictographic notation, is a multi-relational device. It makes possible relations between different words, between different sentences, between images and language. From its incipient phase, it also related disjoint worlds, but at a level other than that achieved in Sumerian cuneiform notation. Writing facilitates and further necessitates the next level of a language, which is the text, an entity in which its parts lose their individual meaning while the whole constitutes the message or is conjured into meaning. The experience already gained in visual records, such as drawing, rock engravings, and wood carvings, was taken over in the experience of the written word.

The pictorial was a highly complex notation with a vast number of components, some visible (the *written*), some invisible (the *phonetics*), and few rules of association. Within the pictorial, sequences are formed which narrate events or actions in their natural succession. What comes first in the sequence is also prior (in time) to everything else, or it has a more important place in a hierarchy. The male-female relation, or that between free individuals and slaves, between native and foreign was embedded here. Even the direction of writing (from left to right, right to left, top to bottom) encodes important information about the people constituting their identity in the practical experience of engraving letters on tablets or painting them on parchment. The very concrete nature of the pictograms prevents generalization. Expression was enormously rich, precision practically impossible to achieve.

The detailed history of writing makes up many chapters in the history of languages. It is also a useful introduction to the history of knowledge, aesthetics, and most likely cognitive science. This history also details processes characteristic of the beginning of literacy. Probably more than 30,000 years passed between the time of cave paintings and rock engravings and the first acknowledged attempt at writing. From the perspective of literacy, this time span comprised the liberation of the human being from the pictorially concrete and the establishment of the realm of conventions, of purposeful encoding. Abstract thinking is not possible without the cognitive support of abstract representations and the sharing of conventions (some implicit) they embody. The wedge-shaped letters of Sumerian cuneiform, the sacred engraved notations of Egyptian hieroglyphics, the Chinese ideograms, the Hebrew, Greek, and Roman alphabets—

all have in common the need to overcome concreteness. They offer a system of abstract notation for increasingly more complex languages.

Until writing, language was still close to its users and bore their mark. It was their voice, and their seeing, hearing, and touching. With writing, language was objectified, freed from the subject and the senses. The development towards written language, and from written language to initially limited and then generalized literacy, paralleled the evolution from satisfying immediate needs (the circular relation) to extending and increasing demand (the linear function) of a mediated nature. The difference between needs related to survival and needs that are no longer a matter of survival but of social status (power, ego, fear, pleasure, incipient forms of conviction, etc.) is represented through language, itself seen as part of the continuous self-constitution of the human being in a particular pragmatic framework.

THE ALIENATION OF IMMEDIACY

The term *alienation* requires a short explanation. Generally, it is used to describe the estrangement, through work, of human beings from the object of their effort. Awareness of having one's life turned into products, which then appear to those who made them as entities in themselves, open to anybody to appropriate them in the market, is an expression of alienation. There are quite a number of other descriptions, but basically, alienation is a process of having something that is part of us (our bodies, thoughts, work, feelings, beliefs, etc.) revealed as foreign. Rooting the explanation of this very significant process of alienation (and of the concept representing it in language) in the establishment and use of signs, makes possible the understanding of its pragmatic implications.

Awareness of signs is awareness of the difference between who we are and how we express our identity. In the case of signs representing some object (the drawing of the object or of the person, the name, social security number, passport, etc.), the difference between what is represented and the representation is as much an issue of appropriateness (why we call a table *table* or a certain woman *Mary*) as it is one of alienation. The conscious use of signs most probably results from the observation people make that their thoughts, feelings, or questions are almost always imperfectly expressed. Two things happen, probably at the same time:

1. No longer dealing directly with the object, or intended action, but with its representation, makes it more difficult to share with others experiences pertinent to the object.
2. The interpretation being no longer one of the direct object, or the intended action, but of its representation, it leads to new experiences, and thus associations—some confusing, and others quite stimulating.

The image was still close to the object; the confusion regarded actions. Writing is remote from objects, though actions can be better described since differentiation of time is much easier. We know by now that moving images, or sequences of photographs of the action, are even better for this purpose.

With the written word, even in the most primitive use of it, events become the object of record. Relations, as well as reciprocal commitments among community members, can also be put in the records. Norms can be established and imposed. A fundamental change, resulting from the increased productivity of the newly settled communities, is accounted for in writing. People no longer deal with work in order to live (in order to survive, actually), but with life dedicated to work. Writing, more than previously used signs (sounds, images, movements, colors), estranges human beings from the environment and from themselves. Some feelings (joy, sadness), some attitudes (anger, mistrust) become signs and, once expressed, can be written down (e.g., in letters, wills). In order to be shared, thoughts go through the same process, and so does everything else pertaining to life, activity, change, illness, love, and death.

It was stated many times that writing and the settlement of human beings are related. So are writing and the exchange of goods, as well as what will become known as labor division. While the use of verbal language makes possible the differentiation of human praxis, the use of written language requires the division between physical and non-physical work. Writing requires skills, such as those needed for using a stylus to engrave in wax or clay, quill on parchment, later the art of calligraphy. It implies knowledge of language and of its rules of grammar and spelling. There is a great difference between writing skills and the skills needed for processing animal skins, meat, various agricultural products, and raw materials. The social status of scribes proves only that this difference was duly acknowledged. It should be added here that the few who mastered writing were also the few who mastered reading. Nevertheless, some historic reference points to the contrary: in the 13th century, non-reading subjects were used as scribes because the accuracy of their *undisturbed* copying was better than that of those who read. This reference is echoed today in the use of non-English speaking operators to key-in texts, i.e., to transfer accumulated records into digital databases. And while the number of readers increased continuously, the number of *writers*, lending their hands as scribes to *real writers*, remained small for many centuries.

Literacy started as an elitist overhead expenditure in primitive economies, became an elitist occupation surrounded by prejudices and superstition, expanded after technological progress (however rudimentary) facilitated its dissemination, and was finally validated in the marketplace as a prerequisite for the higher efficiency of the industrial age. Primitive barter did not rely on and did not require the written word, although barter continued even after the place of written language became secure. In barter, people interact by exchanging whatever they produce in order to fulfill their immediate needs within a diversified production.

The alienation peculiar to barter and the alienation characteristic of a market relying on the mediating function of written language are far from being one and the same. In short, exchanging is fundamentally different from selling and buying. Products to be exchanged still bear the mark of those who sweat to produce them. Products to be sold become impersonal; their only identity is the need they might satisfy or sometimes generate. Myth, as a set of practical programs for a limited number of local human experiences, no longer satisfied exigencies of a community diversifying its experience and interacting with communities living in different environments. This contrast of market forms characteristic of orality and of incipient writing is related to the contrast between myth transmitted orally and mythology, associated with the experience of writing. Language in its written form appeared as a *sui generis* social memory, as potential history.

The obsession with genealogies (in China, India, Egypt, among the Hebrews, and in oral culture in general) was an obsession with human sequences stored in a memory with social dimensions. It was also an obsession with time, since each genealogical line is simultaneously a historic record—who did what, when and where; who followed; and how things changed. Most of these aspects are only implicit in genealogy. In oral culture, genealogies were turned into mnemonic devices, easily adjustable to new conditions of life, but still circular, and just as easily transformable from a record of the past into a command for the future. In its incipient phases as notation and record, genealogy still relied on images to a great extent (the family tree), but also on the spoken, maintaining a variability similar to that of the oral. Nevertheless, the possibility for more stabilized expression, for storing, for uniformity, and consistency was given in the very structure of writing. These were progressively reached in the first attempts to articulate ideas, concepts, and what would become the corpus of *theoria*—contemplation of things translated into language—on which the sciences and humanities of yesterday, and even some of today, are based. Theories are in some ways genealogies, with a *root* and *branches* representing hypotheses and various inferences. Written language extended the permanence of records (genealogies, ownership, theories, etc.) and facilitated access through relatively uniform codes.

In the city-states of ancient Greece, writing alerted people working within the pragmatic constraints of orality to the dangers involved in a new mechanism of expression and communication. Writing seemed to introduce its own inaccuracies, either because of a deliberate attitude towards certain experiences, or as a result of systematic avoidance of inconsistency, which ended up affecting the records of facts. As we know, facts are not intrinsically consistent in their succession. Therefore, we still use all kinds of strategies to align them, even if they are obliquely random. In the oral mode, as opposed to procedures later introduced through writing, consistency was maintained by a succession of adaptations in the sequence of conversations through which records were transmitted. Within oral communication, there is a direct form of criticism, i.e., the self-adjusting function of dialogue. Completeness and consistency are different in conversation (open-ended) than in written text, and even more different in formal languages.

Memory itself was also at issue. Reliance on the written might affect memory—which was the repository of a people's tradition and identity in the age of orality—because it provided an alternative medium for storage. The written has a different degree of expression and leaves a different impression than the oral. Writing, confined to those who read, could also affect constitution and sharing of knowledge. Writing was characterized as superficial, not reaching the soul (again, lacking expressiveness), interfering between the source of knowledge and the receiver of any lesson about knowledge. Spoken words are the words of the person speaking them. A written text seems to take on a life of its own and appears as external, alien. The written is given and does not account for differences among human beings; the spoken can be adapted or changed, its coherence dependent upon the circumstances of the dialogue. There are societies today (the Netsidik, the Nuer, the Bassari, to name a few) that still prefer the oral to the written. Within their pragmatic framework, the live expression of the human uttering the words in the presence of others conveys more information than the same words can in writing.

The memory of a literate society becomes more and more a repository of the various mediations in social life and loses its relation to direct experience. Things said (what the Greeks called *legomena*) are different from things done (*dromena*). The written word connects to other words, not to things done. And so does the sentence, when it acquires its status as a relatively complete unit of language. But the real change is brought about by the written, whether on papyrus, clay, scroll or tablet, or in stone or lead. Such a *page* connects to other written pages and to writing in general. Thus, things done disappear in the body of history, which becomes the collection of writings, eventually stored on bookshelves. The meaning of history is expressed in the variability of the connections ascertained from one text to another. When the *here and now* of *dromena* are expurgated, we remain only with the consciousness of sequences. This is a gain, but also a loss: the holistic meaning of experience vanishes.

How much of this kind of criticism, opposing the oral to the written, is relevant to the phenomena of our time cannot be evaluated in a simple statement. Language has changed so much that in order to understand texts originating at the time of this criticism, we have to translate and annotate them. Some are already reconstituted from writings of a later time (i.e., of a different pragmatic framework), or even from translations. There is no direct correspondence between the literacy of emergent writing and that of automated writing and reading. In some cases we have to define a contextual reference in the absence of which large parts of these recuperated texts make little sense, if any, to people constituted in literacy and in a pragmatic reality so different from that of thousands of years ago. Even written words are dependent on the context in which they are used. In other words, although it seems that written language is less alive than conversation, and less bound to change, it actually changes. We write today, using technologies for word processing, in ways different from any other practical experience of writing.

The criticism voiced in Plato's time cannot be entirely dismissed. Writing became the medium through which some human experiences were reified. It allowed for extreme subjectivity: In the absence of dialogue and of the influence of criticism through dialogue, the past was continuously reinvented according to goals and values of the writer's present. In orality-dominated social life, opinion (which Greeks called *doxa*) was the product of language activity, and it had to be immediate. In writing, truth is sought and preserved. What made Socrates sound so fierce (at least in Plato's dialogues) in his attacks against writing was his intuition of progressive removal from the source of thinking, hence the danger of unfaithful interpretation. Socrates, as well as Plato, feared indirectness and refered conclusively to memory and wisdom.

Situated between Socrates and Aristotle, Plato could observe and express the consequences of writing: "I cannot help feeling, Phaedrus, that writing is unfortunately like painting; for the creations of the painter have the attitude of life, and yet if you ask them a question they preserve a solemn silence." As one of the first philosophers of writing, Plato could not yet observe that writing is not simply the transcription of thoughts (of the words through which and in which humans think), that ideas are formed differently in writing than in speech, that writing represents a qualitatively new sign system in which meanings are formed and communicated through a mechanism once more mediated in respect to practical reality. The subject of confidence in language became the central theme of the Sophists' exercise, of Medieval philosophy, of Romanticism, and of the literature of the absurd (symptomatically popular in the years following World War 2).

Moving from the past to the present, we notice that memory is an issue of extreme importance today, too. Literacy challenges the reliability of memory across the board, even when memory is the repository of facts through which people establish themselves in the world of work. Professionals ranging from doctors, lawyers, and military commanders to teachers, nurses, and office personnel rely more on memory than do factory workers on an assembly line. The paradox is that the more educated a professional is, the less he or she needs to rely on literacy in the exercise of his or her profession, except in the initial learning process, which is made through books. With the advent of video and cassette tapes or disks, with digital storage and networks, literacy loses its supremacy as transmitter of knowledge.

What makes language necessary is also what explains its history and its characteristics. Language came to life in a process through which humans projected themselves into the reality of their existence, identified themselves in respect to natural and social environments, and followed a path of linear growth. Orality testifies to limited, circular experiences but corresponds to an unsettled human being in search of well being and security. It relied on memory for the most part and was assimilated in ritual. The written appeared in the context of several fundamental changes: diversified human praxis, settlement, and a market that outgrew barter, each related and influencing the other. Its main result was the division between mental and physical labor. It made speaking, writing, and reading—characteristics of literacy, as we know it from the perspective of literate societies—logically possible. In fact, it represented only the possibility of literacy, not its beginning. Once we understand how language works and what were some of the functions of language that corresponded to the new stage made possible by writing, we shall also understand how writing contributed to the future ideal of literacy.

CHAPTER 3: ORALITY AND WRITING TODAY: WHAT DO PEOPLE UNDERSTAND WHEN THEY UNDERSTAND LANGUAGE?

Sitting before your computer, you connect to the World Wide Web. What is of interest today? How about something in neurosurgery? Somewhere on this planet, a neurosurgeon is operating. You can see individual neurons triggering right on your monitor. Or you can view how the surgeon tests the patient's pattern recognition abilities, allowing the surgeon to *draw* a map of the brain's cognitive functioning, a map essential for the outcome of the operation. Every now and then the dialogue between surgeon and assistants is complemented by the display of data coming from different monitoring devices. Can you understand the language they are using? Could a written report of the operation substitute for the real-time event? For a student in neurosurgery, or for a researcher, the issue of understanding is very different from what it would be for a lay-person.

Tired of science? A concert is taking place at another Internet address. Musical groups from all over the world are sending their live music to this address. As a multi-threaded performance, this concert enables its listeners to select from among the many simultaneously performing groups. They sing about love, hope, understanding...all the themes that each listener is familiar with. Still, understanding every word the musicians use, do you understand what is taking place?

Moving away from the Internet, one could visit a factory, a stock exchange, a store. One could find oneself in subway in any city, witness a first-grade class in session, or pursue business in a government office. All these scenarios embody the various forms of self-constitution through practical activity. It seems that everyone involved is talking the same language, but who understands what? In seemingly simpler contexts, what do individuals understand today when they understand a written instruction or conversations, casual or official? The context is our day, which is different from that of any previous time, and, in particular, different from that of a literacy-dominated pragmatics. The answers to the questions posed above do not come easily. A foundation has to be provided for addressing such questions from a perspective broader than that afforded by the examples given.

A FEEDBACK CALLED CONFIRMATION

Understanding language is a process that extends far beyond knowledge of vocabulary and grammar. Where there is no sharing of experience beyond what a particular language sequence expresses, there is no understanding. This sounds like a difficult expectation. To be met, the non-expressed must be *present* in the listener, reader, or writer. Language must recreate the non-expressed, through the sequence heard, read, or written, and related to it, beyond the words recognized and the grammar used. Behind each word that people comprehend, there is either a common practical experience, or a shared pragmatic framework, or minimally some form of shared understanding, which constitute what is known as background knowledge. "The limits of my language mean the limits of my world," Wittgenstein promulgated. I would rephrase, in an attempt to connect knowledge and experience, "The limits of my experience are the limits of my world." Self-constitution in language is such an experience.

The first level of the indirect relation established between someone expressing something in language and someone else trying to understand it is concentrated in a semantic assumption: "I know that you know." But is it a sufficient condition to continue a conversation, let's say about a hunted animal, fire, or a tool, as long as the listener knows what the hunted animal or fire is? Many who study semantics think that it is, and accordingly devise strategies for establishing a shared semantic background. These strategies range from making sure that students in a class understand the same things when they use the same words, to publishing comprehensive dictionaries of what they perceive as the necessary shared knowledge in order to maintain cultural coherence at the appropriate scale of the group or community in question. In the final analysis, these strategies correspond to a semantically based model of cultural education driven by the Chomskyan distinction between competence and performance. They identify the problem in the incongruence of our individual dictionaries (vocabulary), not in the diversity of human practical experiences. The assumption is that once people understand what is in language, they apply it (pragmatics as "uses and effects of signs within the behavior in which they occur," according to J. Lyons). We know by now that after a certain stage of unifying influences corresponding to industrial society, this congruence becomes impossible when the scale of human experience changes. The examples given at the beginning of this chapter are evidence of this fact.

What I maintain throughout this book is that language is constituted in human experiences, not merely applied to them. Performance predates competence. Recognition, of an utterance, a written word, a sentence, is itself an experience through which individuals define each one of themselves. Within a limited scale of existence and experience, the homogeneity of the circumstance guaranteed the coherence of language use. As the number of people increases, and as they are involved in increasingly varied experiences, they no longer share a homogeneous pragmatic framework. Consequently, they can no longer assume the coherence of language. Progressively, ever diversifying practical experiences cause words, phrases, and sentences to mean more and different things at the same time. Instantiation of meaning is always in the experience through which individuals constitute their identity.

Examination of the various elements affecting the status of literacy in the contemporary world of fragmented practical experiences opens a new perspective on language. Within this perspective, we acknowledge how and when similar experiences make the unifying framework of literacy possible and necessary. We also acknowledge from which point literacy is complemented by *literacies* and what, if anything, bridges among such literacies. Direct experience and mediated experience are the two stages to be considered. In particular, we are interested in language at the level where direct experience is affected by the insertion of gestures, sounds, and *initial* words.

Indirectness implies awareness of a shared reference—the gesture, the sound, the word—that is simultaneously shared experience. At this level, there is no generality. Patterns of activity are patterns of self-constitution: in the act of hunting, the hunter projects physical abilities (running, seeing, ability to use the terrain, to grab stones, to target). In relation to other hunters, he projects abilities pertinent to coordination, planning, and reciprocal understanding. Within this pragmatic framework, a level of indirectness is constituted: confirmation, or what cybernetics identifies as feedback, in all biological processes. Along this line, the initial (unuttered and obviously unwritten) "I know that you know" becomes subsequently "I know that you know that I know." Coordination and hierarchy within the given task come into the picture. Indeed, if we consider the experience as the origin of meaning in language, the sequence of assumptions is even larger: "I know that you know that I know that you know." It corresponds to a cognitive level totally different from that of direct practical experiences.

In a way, this threefold sequence shows how syntax is enveloped in semantics, and both in the pragmatics that determines them. Applied to the hunting scene, it says, "I know that you know that I am over here, opposite you, we are both closing in on a hunted animal, and I know that you are aware that you might throw your spear in my direction; but the fact that we share in the knowledge of who is placed where will help us get the animal and not kill each other by accident." At a very small scale of human experiences, the sequence was realized without language. Patterns of activity captured its essence. At a larger scale, words replaced signs used for coordination. Writing established frames of reference and a medium for planning more complex activities. The language of drawings, for what eventually became artifacts, confirmed the sequence in the built-in knowledge. The Internet browser, a graphic interface to an infinity of simultaneous experiences of sharing information, frees participants from saying to each other, "Hello. I am here." It facilitates a virtual community of individuals who constitute the experience of real-time neurosurgery, or the virtual concert mentioned at the beginning of this section. In similar ways, new patterns of work in the civilization of illiteracy constitute our work-place, school, or government, based on the same pragmatic assumptions.

Between the primitive hunters and those who in our days identify their presence by all kinds of devices—a badge, a pager, a mobile phone, an access card, a password—there is a difference in the means and forms used to acknowledge the shared awareness that affects the outcome of the experience. Even the simple act of greeting someone we think we know implies the whole sequence of feedback (double confirmation, each participant's awareness, and shared awareness). This says, probably in too many words:

1. To understand language means to understand all the others with whom we share practical experiences of self-constitution.
2. All the others must realize this implicit expectation of communication.
3. Each new pragmatic context brings about new experiences and new forms of awareness.

This understanding can go something along the line of, "I know that you know that I know that you know" what the hunted animal is, what fire is, which tool can be used and how; or in today's context, what surgery is, what a brain is, what a virtual concert is, what a certain activity in a production cycle affects, what the function of a particular government office is. Otherwise, the conversation would stop, or another means of expression (such as recreating fire, or demonstrating a tool) would have to be used, as happened in the past and as frequently happens today: "I know that you know how to drive a car (or use a computer), but let me show you how."

Confirmation in language, gestures, and facial expression signals the understanding. Whenever this understanding fails, it fails on account of the missing confirmation. When this confirmation is no longer uniquely provided by means characteristic of literacy—let us recall modern warfare, technology controlling nuclear reactors, electronic transactions—the need for literacy is subject to doubt. Since the majority of instruction conveyed today is through images (drawings), or image and sound (videotapes), or some combination of media, it is not surprising that literacy is met with skepticism, if not by those who teach, at least by those who are taught. In the pragmatics of their existence they already live beyond the literate understanding. This applies not only to the Internet, but just as well to places of work, schools, government, and other instances of pragmatic activity.

PRIMITIVE ORALITY AND INCIPIENT WRITING

In addition to the general background of understanding, there are many levels, represented by the clues present in speech or writing, or in other forms of expression and communication. For example, a question is identified by some vocal expression accepted as interrogation. In writing, the question is denoted by a particular sign, depending on the particular language. But other clues, no less important, are more deeply seated. They refer to such things as intention, who is talking—man, woman, child, policeman, priest—the context of the talk, hierarchies—social, sexual, moral—and many other clues. Much extra-language background knowledge goes into human language and directs understanding from experience to language use. Dialogue is more than two persons throwing sentences at each other.

It is a pragmatic situation requiring as much language as understanding of the context of the conversation because each partner in the dialogue constitutes himself or herself for the other. Dialogue is the elementary cell of communication experience. Within dialogue, language is transcended by the many other sign systems through which human self-constitution takes place. Dialogues make it clear that understanding language becomes a supra- (or para-) linguistic endeavor. It requires the discovery of the clues, in and outside language, and of their relationship. But more importantly, it requires the reconstruction of experience as it is embodied in background knowledge.

By contrasting primitive orality to incipient writing, we can understand that the process of establishing conventions is motivated by the need to overrule concreteness and to access a new cognitive realm that a different pragmatic context necessitates. By understanding how experience affects their relation, we can consider orality and writing in successive moments of human pragmatics, i.e., within a concrete scale of humankind. Indeed, when writing emerged, elements of orality corresponding to a reduced scale of experience were reproduced in its structure because they were continued at the cognitive level. In our days, there is a far less pressing need to mimic orality in written signs. Some will argue that *4 Sale, 4-Runner, While-U-Wait,* and *Toys 'R' Us,* among other such expressions, are examples to the contrary. These attempts to compress language represent ways of establishing visual icons, of achieving a synthetic level better adapted to fast exchange of information. We see many more examples in interactive multimedia, or in the heavy traffic of Internet-based communication. There is no literacy involved here, and no literacy is expected in decoding the message. There is a strong new orality, with characteristics reminiscent of previous orality. But the dominant element is the visual as it becomes a new icon. The international depiction of a valentine-shaped heart to represent the word *love* is one example in this sense; the icons used in Europe on clothing care labels are others.

Time reference in texts today is made difficult by the nature of processes characteristic of our age: numerous simultaneous transactions, distributed activity, interconnection, rapid change of rules. These cannot be appropriately expressed in a written text. In the global world, *Now* means quite a different thing for individuals connected over many time zones. Sunrise experienced on the Web page of the city of Santa Monica can be immediately associated to poetic text through a link. But the implicit experience of time (and space) carried by language and made instrumental in literacy does not automatically refresh itself.

It took thousands of years before humans became acquainted with the conventions of writing. It is possible that some of these conventions were assimilated in the *hardware* (brain) supporting cognitive activity and progressively projected in new forms of self-constitution. The practice of writing and the awareness of the avenues it opened led to new conventions. Practical endeavors, originating in the conventions of space and time, implicit in the written (and the subsequent reading), resulted in changed conventions. For instance, the discovery that time and space could be fragmented, a major realization probably not possible in the culture of orality, resulted in new practical experiences and new theories of space and time.

Once writing became a practical experience and constituted a legitimate reality, at a level of generality characteristic of its difference from gestures, sounds, uttered words or sentences, associations became possible at several levels of the text. Some were so unexpected or unusual that understanding such associations turned into a real challenge for the reader. This challenge regarding understanding is obviously characteristic of new levels, such as the self-referential, omnipresent in the wired world of *home pages*. In some ways, language is becoming a medium for witnessing the relation between the conscious, unconscious, or subconscious, and language itself. The brain surgery mentioned some pages ago suppressed the patient's conscious recognition of objects or actions by inhibiting certain neurons.

The unnatural, nonlinguistic use of language is studied by psychologists, cognitive scientists, and artificial intelligence researchers in order to understand the relation between language and intelligence. This need to touch upon the biological aspects of the practical experiences of speaking, writing, or reading results from the premise pursued. Self-constitution of the human being takes place while the biological endowment is projected into the experience. Important work on what are called split-brain patients—persons who, in order to suppress epileptic attack, have had the connection between the two brain hemispheres severed—shows that even the neat distinction left-right (the left part of the brain is in charge of language) is problematic. Researchers learned that in each practical experience, our biological endowment is at work and at the same time subject to self-reflection. Projecting a word like *laugh* in the right field of vision results in the patients' laughing, although in principle they could not have processed the word. When asked, such patients explain their laughter through unrelated causes. If a text says "Scratch yourself," they actually scratch themselves, stating that it is because something itches. Virtual reality practical experiences take full advantage of these and other clinical observations. The absent in a virtual reality environment is very often as important as the present. On the back channels of virtual reality interactions, not only words but also data describing human reactions (turning one's head, closing the eyes, gesturing with the hand) can be transmitted. Once fed back, such data becomes part of the virtual world, adapted to the condition of the person experiencing it. This is why interest in cognitive characteristics of oral communication—of the primitive stages or of the present—remains important.

Background information is more readily available in oral communication. In orality, things people refer to are closer to the words they use. Human co-presence in conversation results in the possibility to *read* and *translate* the word under the guise of a willingness by others to show what a particular word stands for. In orality, the experience pertinent to the word is shared in its entirety. This is possible because the appropriate world of experience (corresponding to the circular scale of human praxis) is so limited that the language is in a one-to-one relation with what it describes. In some ways, the parent-child relation is representative of this stage in the *childhood* of humankind.

In the new orality of the civilization of illiteracy the same one-to-one relation is established through strategies of segmentation. The speaker and listener(s) share space and time—and hence past, present, and, to a certain degree, future. And even if the subject is not related to that particular space and moment, it already sets a reference mechanism in place by virtue of the fact that people in dialogue are people sharing a similar experience of self-constitution. *Far* is far from where they speak; *a long time ago* is a long time ago from the moment of the verbal exchange. The acquisition of *far, long (or short) time ago* is in itself the result of practical circumstances leading to a more evolved being. We now take these distinctions for granted, surprised when children ask for tighter qualifiers, or when computer programs fail because we input information with insufficient levels of distinction.

The realization of the frame of time and space occurred quite late in the development of the species, within the scale of linear relationships, and only as a result of repeated practical experiences, of sequences constituting patterns. Once the reference mechanism for both time and space was acknowledged and integrated in new experiences, it became so powerful that it allowed people to simplify their language and to assume much more than what was actually said. In today's world, space and time are constituted in experiences affected by the experience of relativity. Accordingly, the orality of the civilization of illiteracy is not a return to primitive orality, but to a referential structure that helps us better cope with dynamism. The space and time of virtual experiences are an example of effective freedom from language, but not from the experiences through which we acquired our understanding of time and space. Computers able to perform in the space of human assumptions are not yet on the horizon of current technological possibilities.

ASSUMPTIONS

Assumptions are a component of the functioning of sign systems. A mark left can make sense if it is noticed. The assumption of perception is the minimum at which expression is acknowledged. Assumptions of writing are different from those of orality. They entail the structural characteristics of the practical experiences in which the people writing constitute their identity. Literate assumptions, unlike any other assumptions in language, are extensions of linear, sequential experience in all its constitutive parts. They are evinced in vocabulary, but even more strongly in grammar. In many ways, the final test of any sign system is that of its built-in assumptions. Illiteracy is an experience outside the realm defined by the means and methods of literacy. The civilization of illiteracy challenges the need and justification of literate assumptions, especially in view of the way these affect human effectiveness.

The very fine qualifiers of time and space that we take for granted today were acknowledged only slowly, and initially at a rather coarse level of distinction. Despite the tremendous progress made, even today our experience with time and space requires some of the repertory of the primitive human. Movements of hands, head, other body parts (body language), changes in facial expression and skin color (e.g., blushing), breathing rhythm, and voice variations (e.g., intonation, pause, lilt)—all account for the *resurrection* in dialogue of an experience much richer than language alone can convey. Such para-linguistic elements are no less meaningful in new practical experiences, such as interaction with and inside virtual environments.

Para-linguistic elements consciously used in primitive communities, or unconsciously present, still escape our scrutiny. Their presence in communication among members of communities sharing a certain genetic endowment takes different forms. They are not reducible to language, although they are connected to its experience. Examples of this are the strong sense of rhythm among Blacks in

America and Africa, the sense of holistic perception among Chinese and Japanese. We can only conjecture, from words reconstituted in the main language strand (*proto-languages*), or in the mother tongue of humankind (*proto-world*), that words were used in conjunction with non-linguistic entities. Whether a mother-tongue or a *pre-Babel* language existed is a different issue. The hypothesis mimics the notion of a common ancestor of the species and obviously looks for the language of this possible ancestor. More important, however, is the observation that the practical experience of language constitution does not eliminate everything that is not linguistic in nature. Moreover, the para-linguistic, even when language becomes as dominant as it does under the reign of literacy, remains significant for the effectiveness of human activity. The civilization of illiteracy does not necessarily dig for para-linguistic remnants of previous practical endeavors. It rather constitutes a framework for their participation in a more effective pragmatics, in the process involving technological means capable of processing all kinds of cues.

In a given frame of time and space, para-linguistic signs acquire a strong conventional nature. The way the word for *I* evolved (quite differently than equivalents in different languages of the world: *ich, je, yo, eu, én, ani*, etc.), and the way words relating to *two* evolved (hands, legs, eyes, ears, parents), and so forth, gives useful leads. It seems, for instance, that the *pair* entered language as a modifier (i.e., a grammatical category), marked by non-linguistic signs (clasp, repetition, pointing). Some of the signs are still in use. The grammatical category and the distinction between one and two are related. The Aranda population (in Australia) combine the words for one and two in order to handle their arithmetic. Also, the distinction singular-plural begins with *two*. We take this for granted, but in some languages (e.g., Japanese), there is no distinction between singular and plural. In addition, it should be pointed out here that the same signs (e.g., use of a finger to point, hand signals) can be understood in different ways in different cultures. Bulgarians shake their head up and down to signal *no*, and side to side to signal *yes*.

Within a given culture, each sign eventually becomes a very strong background component because it embodies the shared experience through which it was constituted. In direct speech, we either know each other, or shall know each other to a certain extent, represented by the cumulative degrees of "I know that you know that I know that you know," defining a vague notion of knowledge within a multivalued logic. This makes speaking and listening an experience in reciprocal understanding, if indeed the conversation takes place in a non-linear, vague context impossible to emulate in writing. Dialogues in the *wired* world, as well as in transactional situations of extreme speed (stock market transactions, space research, military actions), belong to such experiences, impossible to pursue within the limitations of literacy.

Orality can be assertive (declarative), interrogative, and imperative (a great deal more so than writing). In the course of time, and due to very extended experience with language and its assumptions in oral form, humans acquired an intrinsic interactive quality. This resulted from a change in their condition: on the natural level there was the limited interactivity of action-reaction. In the human realm, the nucleus action-reaction led to subsequent sequences through which areas of common interest were defined. The progressive cognitive realization that speaking to someone involves their understanding of what we say, as well as the acknowledged responsibility to explain, whenever this understanding is incomplete or partial, is also a source of our interactive bent. Questions take over part of the role played by the more direct para-linguistic signs and add to the interactive quality of dialogue, so long as there is a common ground. This common ground is assumed by everyone who maintains the idea of literacy—how else to establish it?—as a necessity, but understood in many different ways: the common ground as embodied in vocabulary and grammar, in logic, spelling, phonetics, cultural heritage. Granted that a common language is a necessary condition for communication, such a common language is not simultaneously a sufficient condition, or at least not one of most efficient, for communication. Interactivity, as it evolved beyond the literate model, is based on the probability, and indeed necessity, to transcend the common language expectation and replace it with variable common codes, such as those we establish in the experience of multimedia or in networked interactions. Even the ability to interact with our own representation as an avatar in the Internet world becomes plausible beyond the constraining borders of literate identity.

TAKING LITERACY FOR GRANTED

In preceding paragraphs, we examined what is required, in addition to a common language, for a conversation to make sense. Scale is another factor. The scale that defines a dialogue is very different from the scale at which human self-constitution, language acquisition and use included, take place. Scale by itself is not enough to define either dialogue or the more encompassing language-oriented, or language-based, practical activity through which people ascertain their biological endowment and their human characteristics. There is sufficient proof that at the early stage of humankind, individuals could be involved only in homogeneous tasks. Within such a framework of quasi-homogeneous activity, dialogues were instances of cooperation and confirmation, or of conflict. Diversification made them progressively gain a heuristic dimension—choosing the useful from among many possibilities, sometimes against the logical odds of maintaining consistency or achieving completeness. A generalized language-supported practical activity involved not only heuristics ("If it seems useful, do it"), but also logic ("If it is right/If it makes sense"), through the intermediary of which truth and falsehood take occupancy of language experiences. Thus an integrative influence is exercised. This influence increases when orality is progressively superseded by the limited literacy of writing and reading.

The quasi-generalized literacy of industrial society reflected the need for unified and centralized frameworks of practical experience, within a scale optimally served by the linearity of language. In our days, people constitute themselves and their language through experiences more diverse than ever. These experiences are shorter and relatively partial. They are only an instant in the more encompassing process they make possible. The result is social fragmentation, even within the assumed boundaries of a common language, which nations are supposed to be, and paradoxically survive their own predicted end. In reality, this common language ceases to exist, or at least to function as it used to. What exists are provisional commitments making up a framework for activities impossible to carry out as a practical experience defined by literacy. Within each of these fast-changing commitments, partial languages, of limited duration and scope, come into existence. Sub-literacies accompany their lives. Experience as such opens avenues to more orality, under post-literate conditions—in particular, conditions of increased efficiency made possible by technology that negates the pragmatics of literacy. The most favorable case for the functioning of language—direct verbal communication—becomes a test case for what it really means to speak the same language, and not what we assume a common language accomplishes when written or read by everyone.

Instances of direct verbal communication today (in the family and community, when visiting foreign countries, at work, shopping, at church, at a football stadium, answering opinion polls or marketing inquiries, in social life) are also instances of taking for granted that others speak our own language. Many researchers have attempted to evaluate the effectiveness of communication in these contexts. Their observations are nevertheless not independent of the assumed premise of literacy as a necessity and as a shared pragmatic framework. Some recent research on the cognitive dimension of understanding language does not realize how deep the understanding goes. One example given is the terse instruction on a bottle of shampoo: "Lather. Rinse. Repeat." It is not a matter of an individual's ability to read the instructions in order to know how to proceed. One does not need to be literate, moreover, one does not even need to *create lan-*

guage in order to use shampoo, if one is familiar with the purpose and use of shampoo (i.e., with the act). Indeed, for most individuals, the word *shampoo* on a bottle suffices for them to use it correctly with no written instructions at all. Icons or hieroglyphics can convey the instructions just as well, even better, than literacy can. These, by the way, are coming more into use in our global economy. It is even doubtful that most individuals read the instructions because they are familiar not just with the conventions that go into using shampoo, but, deeper still, the conventions behind the words of the instructions. Should an adult, even a literate adult, who was totally unfamiliar with the concept of washing his or her hair be presented with a bottle of shampoo, the entire experience of washing the hair with shampoo would have to be demonstrated and inculcated until it became part of that adult's self-constitutive repertory. Such analyses of language only scrape the surface of how humans constitute themselves in language.

Literacy forces certain assumptions upon us: Literate parents educate literate children. A sense of community requires that its members share in the functionality of literacy. Literate people communicate better beyond the borders of their respective languages. Literacy maintains religious faith. People can participate in social life only if they are literate. Considering such assumptions, we should realize that the abstract concept of literacy, resulting from the assumption that a common language automatically means a common experience, only maintains false hope. Children of literate parents are not necessarily literate. Chances are that they are already integrated in the illiterate structures of work and life to the same degree children of illiterate parents are. This is not a matter of individual choice, or of parental authority.

On the digital highway, on which a growing number of people define their coordinates, with the prevalent sign @ taking over any other identification, communities emerge independent of location. Participation in such communities is different in nature from literate congregations maintained by a set of reciprocal dependencies that involved spelling as much as it involved accepting authority or working according to industrial production cycles.

In all of today's communication, not only is the literate component no longer dominant, it is undergoing the steepest percentile fall in comparison to any other form of communication. In this framework, states and bureaucracies are putting up a good fight for their own survival. But the methods and means of literacy on which their entire activity—regulation, control, self-preservation—is based have many times over proven inefficient. These statements do not remove the need to deal with how people understand writing, to which literacy is more closely connected than it is to speech. To discover what makes the task of understanding language more difficult as language frees itself from the constraints of literacy within the new pragmatic framework is yet another goal we pursue.

TO UNDERSTAND UNDERSTANDING

Incipient writing was pictorial. This was an advantage in that it regarded the world directly, immediately perceived and shared, and a disadvantage in that it did not support more than a potential generality of expression. It maintained notation very close to things, not to speech. Image-dominated language came along with a simplified frame of space and time reference. Things were presented as close or far apart, as successive events or as distant, interrupted events. Anyone with a minimal visual culture can *read* Chinese or Japanese ideograms, i.e., *see* mountain, sky, or bird in the *writing*. But this is not reading the language; it is *reading* the natural world from which the notation was *extracted*, reconstituting the reference based on the iconic convention.

Alphabetic writing annihilates this frame of experience based on resemblance. Unless time is specifically given, or coordinates in space intentionally expressed, time and space tend to be assimilated in the text, and more deeply in the grammar. It is a different communication, mediated by abstract entities whose relation to experience is, in turn, the result of numerous substitutions, the record of which is not at the disposal of the reader. Between *tell* in English and the root *tal* (or *dal*) in proto-language (with the literal meaning of *tongue*), there is a whole experiential sequence available only implicitly in the language. In the nostratic phylum (root of many languages, the Indo-European among them), *luba* stands for *thirst*; the English *love* and the German *Liebe* seem to derive from it, although when we think of love we do not associate it with the physical experience of thirst.

Clues in written language are clues to language first of all, and only afterwards clues to human experience. Accordingly, reading a text requires an elaborate cognitive reconstruction of the experience expressed, and probably a never-ending questioning of the appropriateness of its understanding. When a text is read, there is nobody to be questioned, nobody to actively understand the understanding, to challenge it. The *author* exists in the text, as a projection, to the extent that the author exists in the manufactured objects we buy in order to use (glasses to drink water, chairs to sit on), or in whose production we participate in some way. After all, each text is a reality on paper, or on other means of storage and display. Clues can be derived from names of writers and from historic knowledge. What cannot be derived is the reciprocal exchange which goes on during conversation, the cooperative effort under circumstances of co-presence.

Regardless of the degree of complexity, the interactive component of orality cannot be maintained in writing. This points to an intrinsic limitation relevant to our attempt to find out why literacy does not satisfy expectations characteristic of practical experiences requiring interactivity. The metaphoric use of interactivity, as it is practiced to express an animistic attitude according to which, for instance, the text is alive, and we interact with it in reading, interpreting, and understanding it, addresses a different issue. Difficulties in language understanding can be overcome, but not in the mechanical effort of improving language skills by learning 50 more words or studying a chapter in grammar. Rather, one has to build background knowledge through extending the experience (practical, emotional, theoretical, etc.) on which the knowledge to be shared relies.

But once we proceed in this direction, we step out from the unifying framework of literacy, within which the diversity of experiences is reduced to the experience of writing, reading, and speaking. When this reduction is no longer possible—as we experience more and more under the new conditions of existence—understanding language becomes more and more difficult. At the same time, the result of understanding becomes less and less significant for our self-constitution in human experiences. If no other example comes to mind, the reader should reflect upon the many volumes that accompany the software you've bought in recent years. Their language is kept simple, but they are still difficult to comprehend. Once comprehended, the pay-off is slim. This is why the illiterate strategy of integrating on-line the instructions one needs to work with software is replacing literate documentation. These instructions can be reduced to graphic representations or simple animations. The framework is specialization, for instance, in providing instructions in a form adequate to the task. Within specialized experience, even writing and reading are subject to specialization. Literacy turns into yet another distinct form of human praxis instead of remaining its common denominator.

Writing, in this context, makes it clear that language is not enough for understanding a text. Under our own scrutiny, writing becomes a form of praxis in itself, contributing to the general fragmentation of society, not to its unification. This happens insofar as specialized writing becomes part of the general trend towards specialization and generates specialized reading. Some explanation is necessary.

Even when writers strive to adapt their language to a specific readership, the result is only partially successful, precisely because the experiences constituted in writing are disjoint. Indeed, the practical experience to be shared, and the subsequent practical experience of writing are different, pertinent to domains not reducible to each other. Sometimes the writer falls captive to the language (that very specialized subset of language adapted to a specific field of knowledge) and mimics natural discourse by observing grammar and rhetoric devices. Other times, the writer translates, or explains, as in popular magazines on physics, genetics, arts, psychology. Within this type of interpretive discourse either details are left out, or more details are added, with the intention of broadening the common base. Expressive devices, from simple comparisons (which should bridge different backgrounds) to metaphors, expose readers to a new level of experiences. Even if readers know what comparisons are and how metaphors work, they still cannot compensate for the unshared part of experience, with whose help a text makes sense. A legal brief, a military text, an investment analysis, the evaluation of a computer program are examples in this sense. The language they are written in looks like English. But they refer to experiences that a lawyer, or military officer, or broker, or computer programmer is likely to be familiar with.

Writers, speakers, readers, and listeners are aware of the adjustments required to comprehend these and many other types of documents. While a direct conversation, for which time spent with others is required, can be a frame for adjustment, a printed page is definitely less so. The reader can, at best, transmit a reaction in writing, or write to request supplementary explanation, that is, to maintain the spirit of conversation. The experience of writing and reading is becoming less a general experience or cultural identifier, and more a specialized activity. Writing can be *read* by machines. In order to serve the blind, such machines read instructions, newspaper articles, and captions accompanying video images. The synthetic voice, as much as a synthetic eye or nose, a syntactic touch-sensitive device, or taste translator, operates in a realm devoid of the life that went into the text (image, odor, texture, taste) and which was supposed to be contributed by the reader (viewer, smeller, toucher, taster).

Literacy, projected as a universal and permanent medium for expression, communication, and signification, nourished a certain romanticism or democracy of art, politics, and science. It embodied an axiomatic system: since everybody should speak, write, and read, everybody *can* and *should* speak, write, and read; everybody *can* and *should* appreciate poetry, participate in political life, understand science. This was indeed relatively true when poetry, politics, and science were, to a certain degree, direct forms of human praxis with levels of efficiency appropriate to the scale of human activity constituted in linear, homogeneous practical experiences. Now that the scale changed, dynamics accelerated, mediation increased, and non-linearity is accepted, we face a new situation. Paradoxically, the poet, the speech-writer, and the science-writer not only fail to address everybody, but they, as part and result of the mechanism of labor division, also contribute to the generation of partially literate human beings. In other words, they contribute to the fragmentation of society, although they are all devoted (some passionately) to the cause of its unity. In reaction to claims that literacy carried through time, a general deconstructionist attitude challenges the permanency of philosophical tractate, of scientific systems, of mathematics, political discourse and, probably more than anything else, of literature. The method applied is coherent: make evident the mechanisms used to create the illusion of permanence and truth. Texts thus appear as means to an end that does not directly count. What results is an account of the technology of expression, embraced by all who grew skeptical of the universality of science, politics and literature. When each sign (independent of the subject) becomes its own reference, and the experience it embodies is, strictly speaking, that of its making, the deconstructionist project reaches the climax. Nike's™ advertisement is not about sneakers, even less about the celebrities who wear them. It is a rather hermetic self-referential experience. Its understanding, however, is based on the fast-changing experience of revealing one's illiterate identity.

WORDS ABOUT IMAGES

The written, as we know, almost constantly appeared together with other referential systems, especially images. In this respect, a question regarding what we understand when we understand language is whether images can be used as an aid to understanding texts. Doubtless, pictures (at least some of them) are, by their cognitive attributes, better bearers of interpretation clues than are some words or writing devices. Images, more so than texts, can stand in for the absent writer. To the extent that they follow conventions of reality, pictures can help the individual reconstitute, at least partially, the frame of time and space, or one of the two. However, this represents only one side of the issue. The other side reveals that images are not always the best conveyors of information, and that what we gain by using them comes at a cost in understanding, clarity, or context dependence.

First of all, what is gained through the abstraction of the words is almost entirely lost through the concreteness of the image. The very dense medium of writing stands in sharp contrast to the diluted medium of images. Their respective complexity is not the same. To download text on the network is quite different from displaying images. If this were the only reason, we would be alert to the differences between images and texts. When the complexity of the image reaches high levels, decoding the image becomes as tedious as decoding texts, and the result less precise. All this explains why people try to use a combination of images and words. It also helps in understanding strategies for their combination. As a strategy of relating text and image, redundancy helps in focusing interpretation. The strategy of complementing helps in broadening the interpretation. Other strategies, ranging from contrasting texts and images to paraphrasing texts through images, or substituting texts for images, or images for text, result in forceful ways of influencing interpretation by introducing explanatory contexts. A very large portion of today's culture—from the comic strip to picture novels and advertisements, to soap operas on the Internet—is embodied in works using such and similar strategies.

What interests us here is whether images can replace the experience required to understand a text. If the answer is affirmative, such images would be almost like the partner in conversation. As products of human experience, images, just like language, embody that particular experience. This automatically makes the problem of understanding images more involved than just seeing them. But we knew this from written language. Seeing words or sentences or texts on paper (in script or in print) is only preliminary to understanding. The naturalness of images (especially those resembling the physical universe of our existence) makes access to them sometimes easier than access to written language. But this access is never automatic, and should never be taken for granted. In addition, while the written word does not invite to imitation, images play a more active role, triggering reactions different from those triggered by words. The code of language and visual codes are not reducible to each other; neither is their pragmatic function the same.

Research reports are quasi-unanimous in emphasizing that the usefulness of pictures in increasing text comprehension seems not to depend on the mere presence of the image, but on the specific characteristics of the reader. These make clear the role played by what was defined as background knowledge, without which texts, images, and other forms of expression stabilized as languages make little sense, if any, to their readers, viewers, or listeners. In order to arrive at such conclusions, researchers went through real-time measurements of the so-called processing of texts, in comparison to picture-text processing. The paradigm employed uses eye movement recordings and comprehension measures to study picture-text interactions. Pictures helped what the researchers defined as poor readers. For skilled readers, pictures were neutral when the information was important. The presence of pictures interfered with reading when the information in the text was less important. Researchers also established that the type of text—expository or narrative—is not a factor and that pictures can help in recall of text details. This has been known for at least 300 years, if not longer. Actors in Shakespeare's time were prompted to recall their lines through visual cues embodied in the architecture of the theater. After all was measured and analyzed, the only dependable conclusion was that the effects of images on comprehension of written language are not easy to explain. Again, this should not come as a surprise as long as we use literacy-based quantifiers to understand the limits of literacy. Whether images are accidental or forced upon the reader, whether the text is quasi-linear or very sophisticated (i.e., results from practical experiences of high complexity), the relation does not seem to follow any pattern. Such experiments, along with many others based on a literacy premise, proved unsuitable for discovering the sources and nature of reading difficulties.

Eye movement and comprehension measures used to study picture-text interactions only confirmed that today there are fewer commonalties, even among young students (not to mention among adults already absorbed in life and work) than at the time of the emergence of writing and reading. The diversification of forms of human experience, seen against the background of a relatively stable language adopted as a standard of culture, hints at the need to look at this relation as one of the possible explanations for the data, even for the questions that prompted the experiments in the first place. These questions have bearing on the general issue of literacy. Why reading, comprehension, and recall of written language have become more uncertain in recent years, despite efforts made by schools, parents, employers, and governments to improve instruction, remains unanswered. Regardless of how much we are willing to help the understanding of a text through the use of images, the necessity of the text, as an expression of a literate practical experience, is not enhanced. Conclusions like these are not easy to draw because we are still conditioned by literacy. Experiences outside the frame of literacy come much more naturally together because their necessity is beyond the conditioning of our rational discourse. This is how I can explain why on the Internet, the tenor of social and political dialogue is infinitely more free of prejudice than the information provided through books, newspapers, or TV. These observations should not be misconstrued as yet another form of technological determinism. The emphasis here, as elsewhere in the book, is on new pragmatic circumstances themselves, not on the means involved.

The research reported above, as any research we hear about in our days, was carried out on a sample. A sample, as representative as it can be, is after all a scaled-down model of society. The issue critical to literacy being the scale of human practical existence, scaled-down models are simply not suited for our attempt to understand language changes when the complexity of our pragmatic self-constitution increases. We need to consider language, images, sounds, textures, odors, taste, motion, not to mention sub-verbal levels, where survival strategies are encoded, and beliefs and emotions are internalized, as they pertain to the pragmatic context of our existence. Literacy is not adequate for satisfactorily encoding the complexity and dynamics of practical experiences corresponding to the new scale that humankind has reached. The corresponding expectations of efficiency are also beyond the potential of literacy-based productivity. Ill-suited to address the mediated nature of human experience at this scale, literacy has to be integrated with other *literacies*. Its privileged status in our civilization can no longer be maintained.

Korzybski was probably right in stating that language is a "map for charting what is happening both inside and outside of our skins." At the new stage that civilization has reached, it turns out that none of the maps previously drawn is accurate. If we really want details essential to the current and future development of our species, we have to recognize the change in metrics, i.e., in the scale of the charted entity, as well as in dynamics. The world is changing because we change, and as a result we introduce new dimensions in this world.

Even when we notice similarities to some past moment—let us take orality as an example—they are only apparent and meaningless if not put in proper context. Technology made talking to each other at long distances (tele-communication) quite easy, because we found ways to overcome the constraints resulting from the limited speed of sound. The most people could do when living on two close hills was to visit, or to yell, or to signal with fire or lights. Now we can talk to somebody flying on an airplane, to people driving or walking, or climbing Mount Everest. Cellular telephony places us on the map of the world as precisely as the global positioning system (GPS) deployed on satellites. The telephone, in its generalized reality as a medium for orality, defies co-presence and can be accessed virtually from anywhere. Telephony as a practical experience in modern communication revived orality under circumstances of highly integrated, parallel, and distributed forms of human activity on a global scale. On the digital networks that increasingly represent the medium of self-constitution, we are goal and destination at the same time. In one click we are wherever we want to be, and to a great extent what we want to be or are able to do. With another click, we are only the instantiation of someone else's interest, acts, knowledge, or questioning. The use of images belongs to the same broad framework. So does television, omnipresent and, at times, seemingly omnipotent. We became connected to the world, but disconnected from ourselves. As bandwidth available for interacting through a variety of backchannels expands from copper wire to new fiberglass data highways, a structure is put in place that effectively resets our coordinates in the world of global activity. Defying the laws of physics, we can be in more than one place at the same time. And we can be more than one person at the same time. Understanding language under such circumstances becomes a totally new experience of self-constitution.

Still, understanding language is understanding those who express themselves through language, regardless of the medium or the carrier. Literacy brought to culture the means for effectively understanding language in a civilization whose scale was well adapted to the linear nature of writing and reading, and to the logic of truth embodied in language. However, literacy lacks heuristic dimensions, is slow, and of limited interactivity. It rationalizes even the irrational, taking into bureaucratic custody all there is to our life. Common experience, in a limited framework characteristic of the beginning of language notation, is bound to facilitate interpretation and support conflicting choices. Divergent experiences, many driven by the search for the useful, the efficient, the mediating, experiences having less in common among themselves, make language less adapted to our self-constitution, and thus less easy to understand. In such a context, literacy can be perceived only as a phenomenon that makes all things it encomapsses uniform; therefore literacy is resisted. Far from being only a matter of skill, literacy is an issue of shared knowledge formed in work and social life. Changes in the pragmatic framework brought about the realization that literacy today might be better suited to bridging various fragmented bodies of knowledge or experiences, than to actually embodying them. Literacy might still affect the manner in which we use specialized languages as tools adapted to the various ways we see the world, the manner in which we try to change it and report on what happens as a result. But even under these charitable assumptions, it does not follow that literacy will, or should, continue to remain the panacea for all human expression, communication, and signification.

CHAPTER 4: THE FUNCTIONING OF LANGUAGE

To function is a verb derived from experiences involving machines. We expect from machines uniform performance within a defined domain. In adopting the metaphor of *functioning* to refer to language, we should be aware that it entails understandings originating from human interaction involving sign systems, in particular those eventually embodied in literacy. The argument we want to pursue is straightforward: identify language functions as they are defined through various pragmatic contexts; compare processes through which these functions are accomplished; and describe pragmatic circumstances in which a certain functioning mechanism no longer supports practical experiences at the efficiency level required by the scale of the pragmatic framework.

EXPRESSION, COMMUNICATION, SIGNIFICATION

Traditionally, language functions either are associated with the workings of the brain or defined in the realm of human interaction. In the first case, comprehension, speech production, the ability to read, spell, write, and similar are investigated. Through non-invasive methods, neuropsychologists attempt to establish how memory and language functions relate to the brain. In the second case, the focus is on social and communicative functions, with an increasing interest in underlying aspects (often computationally modeled). My approach is different in that it bases language functions in the practical experience, i.e., pragmatics, of the species. Language functions are, in the final analysis, embodied in sign processes.

Preceding language, signs functioned based on their ontogenetic condition. As marks left behind—footprints, blood from an open wound, teethmarks—signs facilitated associations only to the extent that individuals directly experienced their coming into being. Cognitive awareness of such marks led to associations of patterns, such as action and reaction, cause and effect. Biting that leaves behind teethmarks is an example. Pointers to objects—broken branches along a path, obsidian flakes where stones had been processed, ashes where a fire had burned—and, even more so, symptoms—strength or weakness—are less immediate, but still free of intentionality. Imitation brought the unintentional phase of sign experience to an end. In imitative signs, which are supposed to resemble whatever they stand for, the mark is not left, but produced with the express desire to share.

The function best describing signs that are marks of the originator is *expression*. *Communication* is the function of bringing individuals together through shared experiences. *Signification* corresponds to an experience that has signs as its object and relies on the symbolic level. It is the function of endowing signs with the memory of their constitution in practical experiences. Signification expresses the self-reflective dimension of signs. Expression and communication, moreover signification, vary dramatically from one pragmatic framework to another.

Expressions, as simili of individual characteristics and personal experience, can be seen as *translations* of these characteristics and of the experience through which they come into being. A very large footprint is a mark associated with a large foot, human or animal. It is important insofar as it defines, within a limited scale of experience, a possible outcome essential to the survival of those involved. Expressions in speech are marked by co-presence. The functioning of language within orality rested upon a shared experience of time and space, expressed through *here* and *now*. In writing, expression hides itself in the physical characteristics of the skill. This is how we come, for example, to graphology—an exercise in associating patterns of the marks somebody wrote on paper to psychological characteristics. Literacy is not concerned with this kind of expression, although literacy is conducive to it and eventually serves as a medium for graphology. Rather, literacy stipulates norms and expectations of correct writing. People adopting them know well that within the pragmatics based on literacy, the efficiency of practical experiences of self-constitution is enhanced by uniform performance. As we search in our days for the fingerprints of terrorists, we experience the function of expression in almost the reverse of previous pragmatic contexts. Their marks—identifiers of parts used to trigger explosions, or of manufacturers of explosives—are accidental. Terrorists would prefer to leave none.

The analysis can be repeated for communication and signification. What they have in common is the progressive scale: expression for kin, expression for larger groups, collective expression, forceful expression as the scale of activity increases and individuals are gradually being negated in their characteristics. Communication makes the process even more evident. To bring together members of a family is different from achieving the togetherness of a tribe, community, city, province, nation, continent, or globe. But as available resources do not necessarily keep up with increased populations, and even less with the growth in need and expectations, it is critical to integrate cognitive resources in experiences of self-constitution. Communication, as a function performed through sign systems, reached through the means of literacy higher levels than during any previous pragmatic phase. Another increase in scale will bring even higher expectations of efficiency and, implicitly, the need for means to meet such expectations. Only as practical experiences become more complex and integrate additional cognitive resources do changes—such as from pre-verbal to verbal sign systems, from orality to writing, and from writing to literacy, or from literacy to post-literacy—take place. In other words, once the functioning of language no longer adequately supports human pragmatics in terms of achieving the efficiency that corresponds to the actual scale of that pragmatics, new forms of expression, communication, and signification become necessary.

These remarks concern our subject, i.e., the transitional nature of any sign system, and in particular that of orality or that of literacy, in two ways:

1. They make us aware of fundamental functions (expression, communication, signification) and their dependence on pragmatic contexts.
2. They point to conditions under which new means and methods pertinent to effective functioning complement or override those of transcended pragmatic contexts.

As we have seen, prior to language experiences, people constituted their identity in a phase of circular and self-referential reflection. This was followed by a pragmatics leading to sequential, linear practice of language and language notation. With writing, and especially with literacy, sequentiality, linearity, hierarchy, and centralism became characteristics of the entire practical experience. Writing was stamped by these characteristics at its inception, as were other practical activities. With its unfolding in literacy, it actively shaped further practical experiences. The potential of experiences sharing in these characteristics was reached in productive activities, in social life, in politics, in the arts, in commerce, in education and in leisure.

The advent of higher-level languages and of means for visualization, expanding into animation, modeling, and simulation in our day, entails new changes. Their meaning, however, will forever escape us if we are not prepared to see what makes them necessary. Ultimately, this means to return to human beings and their dynamic unfolding within a broader genetic script. To make sense of any explanatory models advanced, here or elsewhere, we need to understand the relation between *cultural structure*—in which sign systems, literacy, and post-literate means are identified—and *social structure*, which comprises the interaction of the individuals constituting society. The premise of this enterprise is as follows: Since not even the originators of the behaviorist model believed that we are the source of our behavior (Skinner went on record with this in an interview shortly before his death), we can look at the individuals constituting a human community as the *locus of human interactions*. Language is only one agent of integration among many. The shift from the natural to the cultural—with its climax in literacy—was actually from immediacy, circularity, discreteness, and the physical realm to indirectness, sequentiality, linearity, and metaphysics. What we experience in our time is a change of course, to the civilization of illiteracy, characterized by many mediating layers, configuration, non-linearity, distribution of tasks, and meta-language. In the process, the functioning of language is as much subject to change as the human beings constituted in succeeding practical experiences of a fundamentally new nature.

THE IDEA MACHINE

Functioning of language cannot be expressed in rotations per second (of a motor) or units of processed raw materials (of a processing machine). It cannot even be expressed in our new measurement of bits and bytes and all kinds of flops. Expressions, opportunities for exchange of information, and evaluations are the output of language (to keep to the machine model and terminology). But more important is another output, definitive of the cognitive aspect of human self-constitution: thoughts and ideas.

We encounter language as we continuously externalize our biological and cultural identities in the act of living as human beings. Attempts within primitive practical experiences to capture language in some notation eventually freed language from the individual experience through sharing with the entire group practicing such notation. Even in the absence of the originator of whatever the notation conveyed, as long as the experience was shared, the notation remained viable. Constituted in human praxis, notation became a reality with an apparent life of its own. It affected interactions as well as a course of action, to the degree that notation could describe it. Notation predates writing, addressing small-scale groups involved in relatively homogenous practical experiences. As the scale grew and endeavors required different forms of interaction, the written evolved from various co-existing notations based on constitutive experiences with their own characteristics. Together with the experience of writing, an entire body of linear conventions was established.

Circumstances that made possible the constitution of ideas and their understanding deserve attention because they relate to a form of activity that singles out the human being from the entire realm of known creatures. Ideas, no matter how complex, pertain to states of affairs in the world: physical, biological, or spatial reality embodied in an individual's self-constitution. They also pertain to the states of mind of those expressing them. Ideas are symptomatic of human self-constitution, and thus of the languages people have developed in their praxis. What we want to find out is whether there is an intrinsic relation between literacy and the formation and understanding of ideas. We want to know if ideas can be constituted and/or understood in forms of expression other than verbal language, such as in drawings, or in the more current multimedia.

Humans not only express themselves to (enter into contact with) one another through their sign systems, but also *listen* to themselves, and look at themselves. They are at once originators (*emitters,* as the information theory model considers them) and receivers. In speech, signs succeed themselves in a series of self-controlled sequences. Synthesis, as the generation of new expression by assembling what is known in new ways appropriate to new practical experiences, is continuously controlled by self-analysis.

Pre-verbal and sub-verbal unarticulated languages (at the signal level of smell, touch, taste, or language of kinesic or proxemic type) participate in defining sensations directly, as well as through rudimentary specification of context. The relationship of articulated language and unarticulated sub-verbal languages is demonstrated at the level of predominantly natural activities as well as at the level of predominantly socio-cultural activities. One example: Under the pragmatic conditions leading to language, olfaction played a role comparable to sight and hearing, effectively controlling taste. This changed as experience mediated through language replaced direct experience. Within the pragmatics of higher efficiency associated with literacy, the sense of smell, for example, ended up being done away with. The decrease of the weight of biological communication, in this case of chemo-physical nature, is paralleled by the increase of importance of the *immaterial,* not substance-bound, communication. Granted, there are no ideas, in the true definition of the word, that can be expressed in smell. But practical experiences involving the olfactory and the gustatory, as well as other senses, affect areas of human practical experiences beyond literacy. Identification of kin, awareness of reproduction cycles, and alarm can all be simulated in language, which slowly assumed or substituted some of the functions of *natural* languages.

WRITING AND THE EXPRESSION OF IDEAS

When the sign of speech became a sign of language (alphabets, words, sentences), the process described above deepened. The concrete (written, stabilized) sign participated in capturing generality via the abstraction of lines, shapes, intersections, in wax, in clay, on parchment, or on another medium. The succession of individual signs (letters, words) was metamorphosed into the sign of the general. For centuries, writing was only a *container* for speech, not operational language. This observation does not contradict the still controversial Saphir-Whorf hypothesis that language influences thinking. Rather, the observation makes clearer the fact that active influence did not originate from language itself, but is a result of succeeding practical experiences. Had a recorder of spoken language, let us imagine, been invented before writing, a need or use for literacy would have taken very different forms.

Humans did not dispose of a system of signs as a person disposes of a machine or of elements to be assembled. They were their own *scripts,* always re-constituting in notation an experience they had or might have had. In other words, the functioning of languages is essentially a record of the functioning of human beings. The Hebrew alphabet started as shorthand notation reduced to consonants by scribes who retained only the root of the word before recording its *marks* on parchment. Due to the small scale and shared pragmatics of readers, this shorthand sufficed. In Mayan hieroglyphics, and in Mesopotamian ideographs, as well as in other known forms of notation, the intention was the same: to give *clues* so that another person could *give life* to the language, could resuscitate it. Increased scale and consequently less homogenous practical experiences forced the Hebrew scribes to add diacritical marks indicating vowels. The written language of the Sumerians and Mesopotamians also changed as the pragmatic framework changed.

That writing is an experience of self-constitution, reflected in the structure of ideas, might not sound convincing enough unless the biological component is at least brought up. Derrick de Kerkhove noticed that all languages written from right to left use only consonants. The cognitive reading mechanism involved in deciphering them differs from that of languages using vowels, too, and written from left to right. Once the Greeks took over the initially consonantal alphabet of the Phoenicians and Hebrews, they added vowels and changed the direction of writing—at the beginning using the *Bustrophedon* (*how the oxen plow*), i.e., both directions. Afterwards, the direction corresponding to a cognitive structure associated with sequentiality was adopted. Consequently, the functioning of the Greek language changed as well. Ideas resulting in the context of pre-Socratic and Socratic dialogue have a more pronounced deductive, speculative nuance than those expressed in the analytic discourse of written Greek philosophy.

One can further this thought by noticing the so-called bias against the left-hand that is deeply rooted in many languages and the beliefs they express. It seems that the right (hand and direction) is favored in ways ranging from calling things *right*, or calling servants of justice *Herr Richter* (*Master Right*, the German form of address for a judge), or favoring things done with the right hand, on the right side, etc. The very idea of what is right, what is just, human rights, originates from this preference. The left hand is associated, in a pragmatic and cognitive mode dominated by the right, with weakness, incompetence, even sin. (In the *New Testament*, sinners are told to go to the left side of God after judgment.) While the implicit symbolism is worth more than this passing remark, it is worthwhile noticing that in our days, the domination of the right in writing and in literacy expectations is coming to an end. The efficiency of a right-biased praxis is not high enough to satisfy expectations peculiar to globality. The process is part of the broader experience through which literacy itself is replaced by the many partial literacies defining the civilization of illiteracy.

Since ideas come into being in the experience of language, their dissemination and validation, critical to the efficiency of human effort at any given scale, depends on the portability of the medium in which they are expressed. Through writing, the portability of language was no longer reducible to the mobility of those speaking it. Ideas expressed in writing could be tested outside the context in which they originated. This associated the function of dissemination through language to the function of validation in the pragmatic context. A tablet, a papyrus scroll, a codex, a book, or a digital simile have in common their condition as a record resulting from practical experiences; but it is not what they have in common that explains their efficiency. Portability is telling of pragmatic requirements so different that nothing before the digital record could be as pervasive and globally present. Except for a password, we need nothing with us in order to access knowledge distributed today through networks. We are freeing ourselves from space and time coordinates. Literacy cannot function within such broad parameters. The domain of alternatives constitutes the civilization of illiteracy.

FUTURE AND PAST

Do we need to be literate in order to deal with the future? Reciprocally: Is history, as many believe, the offspring of writing? Moreover, is it a prerequisite for understanding the present? These are questions that resonate loudly in today's political discourse and in the beliefs of very many people. Let us start with the future, as the question raises the issue of what it takes to deal with it.

Pre-sensing (premonition) is the natural form of diffuse perception of time. This perception can be immediate or less immediate. It is extended not from now to what was (stored in one's memory or not), but to what might be (a sign of danger in the natural environment, for instance). The indexical signs participating in these representations are footprints, feathers, bloodstains. Speech makes premonition and feeling explicit, but not wholly so. It transforms accumulated signs (past) into the language of the possible (future). In fact, in the practical experience of re-constituting the past we realize that each past was once a future.

Still, as we want to establish some understanding of the unfolding of the present into the future, we come to realize that while possibilities expand, the future becomes less and less determined in its details. Try to tell this to the champions of technology who predicted the paperless office and who now predict the networked world. Alternatively, tell this to those who still constitute their identity in literacy-dependent practical experiences: politicians, bureaucrats and educators. Neither of the two categories mentioned seems to understand the relation between language and the future expressed in it, or in any sign system, as plans, prophecies, or anticipations.

An idea is always representative of the practical experience and of the cognitive effort to transcend immediate affection. Monoarticulated speech (signaling), as well as ideographic writing, result from experiences involving the pragmatic-affective level of existence. One cries or shouts, one captures resemblance in an image when choices are made and feelings evoked. There are no ideas here, as there is very little that reaches beyond the immediate. Ideas extend from experiences involving the pragmatic-rational level. Speech can serve as the medium for making plans explicit. Drawings, diagrams, models, and simulations can be described through what we say. Indeed, before *writing* the future, human beings expressed it as speech, undoubtedly in conjunction with other signs: body movement, objects known to relate to danger and thus to fear, or successful actions associated with satisfaction. When finally set in clay tablets or papyrus, the language regarding the future acquired a different status—it no longer vanished, as the sounds or gestures used before. Writing accompanies action, and even lasts past the experience. This permanency gave the written word an aura that sounds, gestures, even artifacts, could not achieve. Even repetition, a major structural characteristic of rituals, could not project the same expectation of permanency as writing. Probably this is what prompted Gordon Childe to remark that "The immortalization of a word in writing must have seemed a supernatural process; it was surely magical that a man long vanished from the land of the living could still speak from a clay tablet or a papyrus roll."

Within the context of religion, the aura shifts from the mythomagical—transmitted clues for successful action—to the mystical—the source of the successful clues is a higher authority. Even social organization, which became necessary when the scale of humankind changed, was not very effective in the absence of documents with a prescriptive function. Recognized in ancient Chinese society, this practical need was expressed in its first documents, as it was in Hindu civilization, in the Hebrew and the Greek, and by the civilizations to follow, many taking an obvious cue from the Roman Empire.

Language use for prescriptive purposes does not necessitate or even imply literacy. This holds true as much for the past as for the present. There was a time, corresponding to increased mobility of people, when only those foreign to a land were supposed to learn how to write and read. The requirement was pragmatic: in order to get used to the customs by which the native population lived, they had to gain access to their expression in language. Nevertheless, once promises are made—a promise relates structurally to the future—the record becomes more and more written, although quite often *sealed* by the oral, as we know from oath formulae and from oath gestures that survived even in our days. In all these, linear relations of cause-and-effect were preserved and projected as the measure, i.e. rationality, for the future.

In contemporary society, the language characteristic of the past is used as a decorum. Global scale and social complexity are no longer efficiently served by linear relations. Subsequently, means for formulating ideas regarding the future make literacy not only one of the many *languages* of the time to come, but probably an obstacle in the attempt to more efficiently articulate ideas for the future. Keep in mind that almost all people dedicated to the study of the future work on computational models. The outcome of their effort is shorter and shorter on text, which is replaced with dynamic models, always global in nature. Linearity is effectively supplanted by non-linear descriptions of the many interlocking factors at work. Moreover, self-configuration, parallelism, and distributive strategies are brought to expression in simulations of the future.

As far as history is concerned, it is, whether we like it or not, the offspring of writing. Ivan Illich and Barry Sanders state bluntly: "The historian's house is on the island of writing.... Where no words are left behind, the historian finds no foundations for his reconstructions." Indeed, history results from concern with records that are *universally* accessible, hence within the universe of those sharing in literacy. We never know whether a grammar is a summary of the history of a language, or its program for the future. Grammars appear in various contexts because people recognize the need to verify the *voices* within a language. Histories appear also, motivated by the same stimulus, not so much to do justice to some army, general, king or party, but to maintain coherent records, make them speak in one and only one voice, and probably link the records to recreate the continuum from which they emerge.

While the future and the self-constitution of the human being in new pragmatic contexts are directly related, the past is connected to human practical experiences in indirect ways. The unifying element of the various perspectives of the future is in the new experience. In the absence of such a unifying perspective, writing history becomes an end in itself, notwithstanding the power exercised by examples. From the beginning of the Middle Ages, the written record and the analytic power of language sufficed for constituting history and shaping historic experience. But once the methods of historic research diversified, probably as much as the pragmatics of human existence did, new perspectives were introduced. Some of these have practical implications: What were the plants used in primitive societies? How was water supply handled? How were the dead disposed of? Other perspectives had ideological, political, or cultural ramifications. In each of these pragmatically determined instances, history started escaping the prison of literacy.

Linguistic archaeology, anthropological and especially paleoanthropological history, computational history, are only some of the post-literate forms of practical experiences constituting a new domain of history. This domain is characterized by the use of non-traditional tools, such as genetics, electronic microscopy, computational simulation, artificial life modeling, and inferences supported by artificial intelligence. Memetics, or the life of ideas and awareness of them, pertains no less to the past than to the present and future. It sprang from genetics and bears the mark of an implicit Darwinian mechanism. Its focus on ideas made it the catch phrase of a generation feeling dangerously severed from its relation to history, and no less endangered by a future falling too fast upon this generation. Technological extensions of memetics (the so-called memetic engineering) testify to expectations of efficiency which history of the literate age never seemed to care about or even to acknowledge.

Based on the awareness thus gained, we would have to agree that the relative dissolution of literacy and the associated ideals of universality, permanency, hierarchy, and determinism, as well as the emergence of *literacies*, with the resulting attitudes of parochialness, transitoriness, decentralization, and indeterminacy are paralleled by the dissolution of history and the emergence of specialized histories. Hypertext replaces sequential text, and thus a universe of connections is established. The new links among carefully defined fields in the historic record point to a reality that escapes the story (in history), but are relevant to the present. The specialized historian reports not so much about the past, but about particular aspects of human self-constitution from the past that are significant in the new frame of current experience. It sometimes seems that we reinvent the past in patches, only to accommodate the present pragmatics and to enforce awareness of the present. The immanent sequentiality and linearity of the pragmatic framework within which languages emerged and which made, at a later juncture, literacy and history necessary, is replaced by non-sequentiality and non-linear relations better adapted to the scale of humankind's existence today. They are also better adapted to the complexity of the practical process of humankind's continuous self-constitution. In addition, primitive, deterministic inferences are debunked, and a better image of complexity, as it pertains to the living subject, becomes available.

As an entry in a database (huge by all means), the past sheds its romantic aura, only to align itself with the present and the future. The illiterate attitude, reflected, for instance, in the ignorance of the story of the past, results not from lack of writing and reading skills. It is not caused by bad history teachers or books, as some claim. Decisive is the fact that our pragmatic framework, i.e. our new practical experiences of self-constitution, is disconnected from the experiences of the past.

KNOWING AND UNDERSTANDING

Probably one of the most important aspects of current pragmatics is the connection between *knowing* and *understanding*. We are involved in many activities without really understanding how they take place. Our e-mail reaches us as it reaches those to whom we send messages, even though most people have no idea how. The postal system is easier to understand. We know what happens: letters are delivered to the post office, sorted, and sent to their destinations by bus, train, plane, or boat. Determining the paths of an e-mail message is trivial for a machine, but almost impossible for a human being. As the complexity of an endeavor increases, chances that individuals constituting themselves in the activity know how everything works and understand the various mechanisms involved decrease. Still, the efficiency of the experience is not diminished. Moreover, it seems that knowledge and understanding do not necessarily affect efficiency.

This statement is valid for an increasing number of practical experiences in the pragmatics of the civilization of illiteracy—not for all of them. We can conceive of complex diagnostic machines; but there is something in the practical experience of medicine, for example, that makes one physician better than another. We can automate a great deal of other activities—accounting, tax preparation, design, architecture—but there is something implicit in the activity that will qualify a certain individual's performance as above and beyond our most advanced science and technology. There are managers who know close to nothing about what their company produces but who understand market mechanisms to such an extent that they end up winners regardless of whether they head a bank, a cracker-producing factory, or a giant computer company. These managers constitute themselves within the experience of language—the language of the market more than the language of the product. Therefore, it is useful to examine the evolution of knowledge and understanding within succeeding pragmatic frameworks, and the role language plays as a mediating element in each of these frameworks.

The sign of language represents the contradictory unity of the phonetic and semantic units. Within a limited scale of experience, literacy meant to know what is behind the written word, to be able to resuscitate it, and to even give the word new life. As the scale increases, literacy means to take for granted what is behind the written word. This implies that dictionaries, including *personal* dictionaries, as they are formed in constituting our language, are congruent. Learning language is not reducible to the memorization of expressions. The only way to learn is to *live* the language. With knowledge acquired and expressed in language comes understanding.

Humans are not born free of experience. Important parts of it are passed along in the biological endowment. Others are transmitted through ever new human interactions, including those of reciprocal understanding. Neither are humans born free of the evolutionary cycle of the species. The relative decline of the olfactory in humans was mentioned some pages ago. With the relative loss of sensory experience, knowledge corresponding to the respective sensorial perception diminishes. Linguistic performance is the result of living and practicing language, of existence as language. Relating oneself to the world in language experience is a condition for knowing and understanding it. The *language* of the natural surrounding world is not verbal, but it is *articulated* at the level of the elementary sensations (Merleau-Ponty's *participative perception*) that the world occasions, when human beings are engaged in the practical attempt to constitute themselves, for instance, by trying to change or to master their world. They perceive this world, after the experience, as stabilized meanings: clouds offer the hope of rain; thunder can produce fire; running deer are probably pursued by predators; eggs in a nest testify to birds. The complexity of the effort to master the world surrounding us increases over time. Tasks originating in the context leading to literacy are of a different degree of complexity than those faced in industrial society and than those we assume today.

Between the senses and speech—hence between nonverbal and verbal languages—numerous influences play a role. Words obviously have a cognitive condition different from perceptions and are processed differently. Speech adds intellectual information to the sensorial information, mainly in the form of associations, capable of reflecting the present and the absent. Interestingly enough, we do not know everything that we understand; and we do not understand everything that we know. For instance, we might know that in non-Euclidean geometries, parallels meet. Or that water, a liquid, is made up of oxygen and hydrogen, two gases. Or that the use of drugs can lead to addiction. Nevertheless, we do not necessarily understand how and why and when.

Within the civilization of literacy the expectation is that once we know how to write something, we automatically know and understand it. And if by some chance the knowledge is incomplete, inconsistent, or not maintained, if it loses its integrity through some corruption, it can be resuscitated through reading or can be made consistent by comparing it to knowledge accumulated by others, and eventually redeemed. As writing has failed us repeatedly within practical experiences that transcend its characteristics and necessity, we have learned that the relative stability of the written is a blessing in disguise. Compared to the variability of the speech, it is more stable. But this stability turns out to be a shortcoming, exactly because knowledge and understanding are context dependent. Within relatively stable contexts this shortcoming is noticed only at rare intervals. But with the expectation of higher efficiency, cycles of human activity get shorter. Increased intensity, the variability of structures of interaction, the distributed nature of practical involvement, all require variable frames of reference for knowledge and understanding. As a result of these pragmatic characteristics, we witnessed progressive use of language in equivocal and ambiguous ways. Acceptable, and even adequate, in the practical experience of poetry, drama and fiction, of disputable relevance in political and diplomatic usage, ambiguity affects the literate formulation of ideas and plans pertinent to moral values, political programs, or scientific and technological purposes.

The same pragmatic characteristics mentioned above make necessary the integration of means other than language and its literate functioning in the acquisition and dissemination of knowledge. This addresses concerns raised in the opening lines of this section. Fast-changing knowledge can be acquired through means adapted to its dynamics. As these means, such as interactive multimedia, virtual reality programs, and genetic computation, change, the experience of accessing knowledge becomes, in addition, one of understanding the transitory means involved in storing and presenting it. Many practical experiences are based on knowledge that no other means, literacy-based means included, could effectively make available. From advanced brain surgery at neuronal levels to the deployment of vast networks, which support not only e-mail but also many other meaningful human interactions—from space exploration to memetic engineering—focused understanding and a whole new gamut of highly efficient practical experiences, involving knowledge never before available, make up the pragmatic framework of the civilization of illiteracy.

UNIVOCAL, EQUIVOCAL, AMBIGUOUS

At least 700 artificial languages are on record. Behind each of these there is a practical experience in respect to which natural language functions in a less than desirable manner. There is a language on record that addresses left-hand/right-hand biases. There is one, authored by S. H. Elgin, in which gender biases are reversed (*Láadan*). And there is *Inda,* a language constructed like a work of art. There are exotic languages written for certain fictional worlds: J.R.R. Tolkien's *Elvish*, or the language of the Klingons of *Star Trek* fame, or Anthony Burgess's *Nadsat*, the language of the yobbs in *A Clockwork Orange.* And there are scientifically oriented attempts to structure a language: James Cooke Brown invented *Loglan* to be a logic language. Sotos Ochado (almost 100 years before Brown) invented a language based on the classifications of science. Some artificial languages of the past correspond to obvious pragmatic functions. *Ars Magna*, designed by Ramon Llul (celebrated in history books dedicated to precursors of the digital age), was to be a language of missionaries. *Lingua Ignota*, attributed to the legendary Abbess Hildegard, is a language of practical monastic experiences extended well beyond the performance of the liturgy.

When we acknowledge these languages we implicitly acknowledge attempts to improve the performance of language functions. In some cases, the effort is driven by the goal of transcending barriers among languages; in others, of getting a better description of the world, with the implicit hope that this would facilitate mastery of it. Awareness of the fact that language is not a neutral means of expression, communication, and signification, but comes loaded with all the characteristics of our practical endeavors, prejudices included, motivated attempts to generate languages reflecting an improved view of the world. Regardless of the intention, and especially of the success they had, such languages allow us a closer look at their cognitive condition, and hence at their contribution to increases in the efficiency of human practical activities.

Increased expressive power, as in the artificial languages invented by Tolkien and Burgess, or in the language of the Klingons, is an objective relatively easy to comprehend. Propagated by means of literacy and within the literate experience, such languages are accepted primarily as artistic conventions. Precision is the last quality they aim for; expressive richness is their goal. These are languages of sublime ambiguity. Those seeking precision will find it in *Loglan*, or better yet in the languages of computer programming. Disseminated by means contradicting and transcending the assumptions of literacy, and within a pragmatics requiring means of higher efficiency, programming languages, from *Cobol* and *Fortran* to *C*, *C++*, *Lisp*, or *Java*, are accepted for their functionality. They are not for poetry writing, as the family of expressive artificial languages are not for driving a computer or its peripherals. These are languages of never-failing univocality. With such languages, we can control the function, and even the logic of the language. These languages are conceived in a modular fashion and can be designed to optimally serve the task at hand. Among the functions pursued are provability, optimization, and precision. Among the logics that can be used are classical propositional logic, intuitionistic propositional logic, modal logic, temporal logic, and others.

Reflecting human obsession with a universal language, some artificial constructs advance hypotheses regarding the nature of universality. Dedicated, like many before him, to the idea of a universal language, François Sondre (1827) invented a language based on the assumption that music comes the closest to transcending boundaries among various groups of people. Imagine a theory expressed as a melody, communication accomplished by music, or the music of the law and law enforcement. There is in such a language enough room for expression and precision, but almost no connection to the pragmatic dimension of human self-constitution. If time is, as we know, encoded in music, the experience of space is only indirectly present. Accordingly, its functioning might address the universality of harmony and rhythm, but not aspects of pragmatics which are of a different nature.

A category of so-called *controlled languages* is also establishing itself. A controlled language is a subset (constrained in its vocabulary, grammar, and style) of a natural language adapted to a certain activity. Artificial languages are products inspired and motivated by the functioning of our so-called *natural* language. Their authors wanted to fix something, or at least improve performance of the *language machine* in some respect. In order to understand the meaning of their effort, we should look into how language relates the people constituted in the language to the world in which they live. Let's start with the evolution of the word and its relation to the expression of thoughts and ideas, that is, from the univocal (one-to-one relation to what is expressed) to the ambiguous (one-to-many relation).

Systems of univocal signs participate in the production of ideas only to a small degree. As an outgrowth of signals, initial signs are univocal. Feathers are definitely not from fish or mammals; blood stains are from wounds; four-legged animals leave different marks than biped humans. Polysemy (more than one meaning assignable to the sign) is a gradual acquisition and reflects the principle of retroaction of meaning on the carrier: words, drawings, sounds, etc. A drawing of an animal points to what is depicted, or to things associated with the animal: the softness of fur, savage behavior, meat, etc.

Philosophy and literature (and the arts, in general) became possible only at a certain level of language development brought about by the practical experience of society confronted with new tasks related to its survival and further evolution. The philosopher, for example, resorts to *common* speech (verbal language) but uses it in an *uncommon* way: metasemically, metaphorically, metaphysically. Ancient philosophy, important here for its testimony regarding language and literacy, is still so metaphoric that it can be read as literature, and actually was enjoyed as such. Modern philosophy (post-Heidegger) shows how *relations* (which it points out and dwells upon) have absorbed the *related*. As a formalized argumentation, freed of restrictions characteristic of literacy, but also so much less expressive than the philosophy of the written word and the endless interpretations it makes possible, philosophy generates its own motivations and justifications. Its practical consequences, within a pragmatics based on different forms of semiotic functioning than those of literacy, diminish constantly.

The distance between the verbal and the significance of the idea is itself a parameter of the evolution from nature to culture. Words such as *space, time, matter, motion,* become possible only after experience in writing. But once written, there is nothing left of the direct, probably intuitive, human experience of space and time, of experience with matter in its various concrete forms, or of the experience of motion (of the human body or other bodies, some flying, some swimming, running, falling). Visual representations—other forms of *writing*—are closer to what they report about: the Cartesian coordinates for space, the clock for a cyclical perception of time, etc. They express particular instances of relations in space or time, or particular aspects of matter or motion.

The word is arbitrary in relation to the idea it embodies. The idea itself, getting its life in instances of activity, is knowledge practically revealed in the order of nature or thought. In expressing the idea, rational rigor and expressiveness collide. Synthesizing ideas is an instance of the self-constitution of the human being. Ideas express the implicit will of the human being to externalize them (what Marcuse called "the imperative quality" of thought). Once written, words not only defy the ephemerality of the sounds of speech, but also enter the realm of potentially conflicting interpretations. These interpretations result from the conversion of the way we use words in different pragmatic contexts.

To be literate means to be in control of language, but it also means acceptance and awareness of being hostage to the experiences of the past in which its rules were shaped. When spelling, for instance, is disassociated from the origin of the word, a totally arbitrary new realm of language is established, one in which transitory conventions replace permanency (or the illusion of permanency), and the appearance of super-temporality of ideas is questioned. Each idea is the result of choices in a certain paradigm of existence. Its concrete determination, i.e., realization as meaning, comes through its insertion in a pragmatic context. When the context changes, the idea might be confirmed, contradicted (it becomes equivocal), or open to many interpretations (it becomes ambiguous). To give an example, the idea of *democracy* went through all these stages from its early embodiment in Greek society to its liberal application, and even self-negation, in the civilization of illiteracy. It means one thing—the power of people—but in different contexts, depending on how *people* was defined and how power was exercised. It means so many things in its new contexts that some people really wonder if it actually means anything at all anymore.

Literacy made communication of ideas possible within a scale of humankind well served by linear relations and in search of proportional growth. But when ideas come to expression in a faster rhythm, and turn in shorter cycles from the univocal to the ambiguous stage, the medium of literacy no longer does justice either to their practical function or to the dynamics of an individual's continuous self-constitution. Moreover, it seems that ideas themselves, as forms of human projection, are less necessary under the new projection of pragmatic circumstances we examine. What once seemed almost as the human's highest contribution impacts today's society less and less. We live in a world dominated by methods and products, within which previous ideas have, so it seems, cultural significance, at most. Knowledge is reduced to information; understanding is only operational. Artificial languages, which keep multiplying, are more and more geared towards methods and products. In the interconnected world of digitally disseminated information, we do not need Esperanto, but rather languages that unify the increasing variety of machines and programs we use in our new experiences on the World Wide Web. Efficiency in this world refers to transactions which do not necessarily involve human beings. Independent agents, active in business transactions of what emerges as the *Netconomy,* act towards maximizing outcome. Such agents are endowed with rules of reproduction, movement, fair trade, and can even be culturally identified. Even so, the Netconomy is more a promise than a reality. The functioning of such agents allows us to see how the metaphor of language functioning reverts to its literal meaning in the civilization of illiteracy.

MAKING THOUGHTS VISIBLE

At a minimum, the object for which the written sign—the word, sentence, or text—stands is the sign of speech. But writing came a relatively long way before reaching this condition. In prelinguistic forms, graphic representation had its object in reality—the *re-presentation* of the absent. What is present need not be represented. The direction impressed on visual representation is from past to present. What must be retained is the originating tendency of distancing in respect to the present and the direct, what I called the alienation of immediacy. Initial representations, part of a rather primitive repertory, have only an expressive function. They retain information about the absent that is not seen (or heard, felt, smelled) for future relationships between human beings and their environment. The image belongs to nature. That which is communicated is the way of seeing or perceiving it, not what is actually seen. The execution of the written sign is not its realization as information, as is the case with pictographic representations, some leading to the making of things (tools, artifacts). What matters is not how something is written, but *what* it means. A relatively small number of signs—the alphabet, punctuation and diacritical marks—participate in the infinite competence of writing.

No matter how we conceive of human thought, its stabilization comes about with that of writing. The present captured in writing loses its impact of immediate action. No written word has ever reached the surface without being *uttered* and *heard,* that is, without being *sensed.* The possibility of meaning (intended, assigned) stems from the establishment of language within human praxis. It is not accidental (cf. Leroi-Gourhan) that spatial establishment (in village-type settlements) and the establishment of language in writing (also spatial in nature) are synchronous. But here a third component, the language of drawings, no matter how primitive, helping in the making of things related to shelter and to work, needs to be acknowledged, too.

This is the broader context leading to the great moment of Greek philosophy in the temporal context of *alphabetization,* and the cultural context of all kinds of forms of craftsmanship, architecture probably in the lead. Socrates, as the philosopher of thinking and discovering truth through dialogue, defended oral culture. Or at least that is what Plato wanted us to believe when he mentioned Socrates' opposition to writing. The great artisans of Socrates' time shared this attitude. For building temples, conceiving tools, creating all kinds of useful objects, writing is not a prerequisite. Heuristics and maieutics, as methods of questioning human choices, those of craftsmen included, and generating new options, are essentially oral. They presuppose the philosopher's, or the architect's, physical presence. Not too much has changed since, if we consider how the disciplines of design and engineering are taught and exercised. But a lot is changing, as design and engineering practical activities rely more and more on digital processing. Computational practical experiences, as well as genetic engineering or memetics, are no longer in continuation of those founded on literacy.

ALPHABET CULTURES AND A LESSON FROM APHASIA

The history of culture has recorded numerous attacks against writing, culminating, probably, in Marshall McLuhan's philosophy (1964): alphabetic cultures have uniformized, fragmented, and sequentialized the world, generating an excessive rationalism, nationalism, and individualism. Here we have, in a succinct list, the indictment made of *Gutenberg's Galaxy*. Commenting on E. M. Forster's *A Passage to India*, McLuhan remarked: "Rational, of course, has for the West long meant uniform and continuous and sequential. In other words, we have confused reason with literacy, and rationalism with a single technology." That McLuhan failed to acknowledge the complementary language of design and engineering, with its own rationality, is a shortcoming, but does not change the validity of the argument. The consequences of these attacks—as much as they can be judged from the historical perspective we have since gained—have nevertheless not been the abatement of writing or of its influence. In the same vein, the need to proceed to an oral-visual culture has been idealistically suggested (Barthes' well known plea of 1970 can be cited).

There is no doubt that all the plans devised by architects, artisans, and designers of artifacts belong to a praxis uniting oral (instructions to those transposing the plan into a product) and visual cultures. Many such plans, embodying ideas and concepts probably as daring as those we read in manuscripts and later in books, vanished. Some of the artifacts they created did withstand the test of time. Even if the domination of the written word somehow resulted in a relatively low awareness of the role drawings played over time, experiences were shaped by them and knowledge transmitted through them. Drawings are holistic units of a complexity difficult to compare to that of a text.

The meaning conferred by the intermediary of writing is brought about through a process of generalization, or re-individualization: What is it for the individual reading and understanding it? It inversely travels the route that led from speech to writing, from the concrete to the abstract, from the analytic to the synthetic function of language. At any given time, it looks as though we have, on the one hand, the finite reality of signs (alphabet, words, idiomatic expressions) and, on the other, the practically infinite reality embodied in the language sequences or ideas expressed. In view of this, the question arises regarding the source of ideas and the relation between signs (words, in particular) and their assigned meanings, or the content that can be communicated using the language. Meaning is conjured in Western culture through *additive* mechanisms, similar to those of mixing pigments. In Eastern culture, meaning is based on *subtractive* mechanisms, similar to those of mixing light.

Alphabetic writing, although more simple and stabilized, is really more difficult than ideographic writing. The experience from which it results is one of abstraction. Henceforth, it subjects the readers of the alphabetic text to the task of filling the enormous gap separating the graphic sign from its referent with their own experience. The assumption of the literate practical experience is that literacy can substitute for the reference through history or culture. Readers of ideographic texts have the advantage of the concreteness of the representation. Even if Chinese characters stand for specific Chinese words, as John DeFrancis convincingly showed, the experience of that writing system remains different from that of Western alphabets. Since every language integrates its own history as the summary of the practical activity in which it was constituted, reading in a language of a foreign experience means that one must step-by-step invent this writing.

Research undertaken in the last 15 years shows that at a certain stage, aphasia brings on a regression from alphabet to image reading as design, as pictographic, iconic reading. Letters lose their linguistic identity. The aphasic reader sees only lines, intersections, and shapes. Ideas expressed in writing crumble like buildings shaken by an earthquake. What is still perceived is the similarity to concrete things. The decline from the abstract to the concrete can be seen as a socio-cultural accident taking place against the background of a natural (biological) accident.

In our days we encounter symptoms similar to those described above, testifying to a sort of collective aphasia in reverse. Indeed, writing is *deconstructed* and becomes graffiti notation, shorthand statements freed of language, and defying literacy. For a while, graffiti was criminalized. Later on it was framed as art, and the market absorbed the new product among the many others it negotiates. What we probably refused to see is how deep the *literacy* of graffiti goes, where its roots are, how wide the extensions, and how much aphasia in its *writing* and *reading*. After all, it was not only in the New York subway that trains were literally turned into *moving papers* or *moving books, issued* as often as authority was circumvented. Much of the public hated graffiti because it obliterated legitimate communication and a sense of neatness and order that literacy continuously reinforced. But many also enjoyed it. Rap music is the musical equivalent of graffiti. Gang rituals and fights are a continuation of these. Messages exchanged on the data highways—from e-mail to Web communication—often display the same characteristics of aphasia. Concreteness is obsessively pursued. :) (*the smiley*) renders expressions of pleasure useless, while

(: (*the grince*) warns of being *flamed.* On the digital networks of today's furious exchange of information, collective aphasia is symptomatic of many changes in the cognitive condition of the people involved in its practical experiences. Neither opportunistic excitement nor dogmatic rejection of this far-reaching experience can replace the need to understand what makes it necessary and how to best benefit from it. More private languages and more codes than ever circulate as kilo- and megabytes among individuals escaping any form of regulation.

On the increasingly rewarding practical experiences of networking, literacy is challenged by transitory, partial literacies. Literacy is exposed in its infatuation and emptiness, although not discarded from among the means of expression and communication defining the human being. It is often ridiculed for not being appropriate to the new circumstances of the practical and spiritual experience of a humankind that has outgrown all its clothes, toys, books, stories, tools, and even conflicts.

A legitimate follow-up question is whether the literate experience of the word contributes to its progressive lack of determination, or the change of context affects the interpretation, i.e., the semantic shift from determinate to vague. Probably both factors play a role in the process. On the one hand, literacy progressively exhausts its potential. On the other, new contexts make it simultaneously less suited as the dominant medium for expression, communication, and signification of ideas. For instance, the establishment of a vague meaning of *democracy* in political discourse leads to the need for *strong* contexts, such as armed conflicts, for ascertaining it. In the last 10 years we have experienced many such conflicts, but we were not prepared to see them in conjunction with the forces at work in facilitating higher levels of efficiency according to the new scale that humankind has reached.

There is also the attempt to use language as context free as possible—the generalities of all demagogy (liberal, conservative, left or right, religious or emancipated) can serve as examples. But so can all the crystal ball readings, palm readings, horoscopes, and tarot cards, revived in recent years against the background of illiteracy. None of these is new, but the relative flourishing of the market of vagueness and ambiguity, reflective of a deviant functioning of language, is. Together with illiteracy, they are other symptoms of the change in pragmatics discussed in this book.

These and other examples require a few more words of explanation regarding changes in the functions of language. It is known that the oldest preserved cave drawings are marks (indexical signs) of an oral context rather than representations of hunting scenes (even though they are often interpreted as such). They testify more to those who drew them than to what the drawing is about. The decadent literacy of mystified messages does the same. It speaks about their writers more than about their subject, be this history, sociology, or anthropology. And the increased oral and visual communication, supported by technology, defines the post-literate condition of the human cognitive dimension. The transition from speech to writing corresponds to the shift from the pragmatic-affective level of human praxis to the pragmatic-rational level of linear relations among people and their environment. It takes place in the context of the evolution from the syncretic to the analytic. The transition from literacy to literacies corresponds to the pragmatics of non-linear relations, and results from the evolution from analytic to synthetic. These affirmations, at least as far as the civilization of literacy is concerned, apply to the universe of European cultures and their later extensions. The cultures of the Far East are characterized by language's tendency to *present,* not to *explain.* The analytical structure of logical thought (which will be discussed in another chapter) is actually formed in the sentence structure of speech, which is fundamentally different in the two cultures mentioned. The imperative energy of the act of expressing confers on the Chinese language, for example, a continuous state of birth (speech in the act). The preeminence of the act in Oriental culture is reflected by the central position the verb occupies. Concentration around the verb guides thought towards the relationship between *condition* and *conditioned.*

The experience of logic characteristic of European cultures (under the distinctive mark of classical Greek philosophy) shows that the main instrument of thinking is the noun. It is freer than the verb (tied to the forms it specifies), more stable, capable of reflecting identity, invariance, and the universal. The logic founded on this premise is oriented toward the search for unity between species and genus. European writing and Oriental ideographic writing have each participated in this process of defining logic, rhetoric, heuristics, and dialectics. From a historic perspective, they are complementary. Recalling the history of knowledge and history *per se,* we can say that the European Occident achieved the meaning of knowledge and world control, while the Orient achieved self-knowledge and self-control. It would seem utopian (and with vast historical, social, ideological, and political implications) to imagine a world harmoniously uniting these meanings. However, this would imply, as the reader can easily surmise, changes in the status of literacy in both cultures. This is exactly the direction of the changes we witness, as languages function towards convergence in the two cultures mentioned.

Literacy is not only a medium of exchange between cultures; it also sets boundaries among them. This holds true for both Western and Far Eastern (and any other) civilization. Japan, for instance, despite the spectacular effort of assimilation and development of new technologies, maintains inside its national boundaries a framework quite well suited to its traditional literacy. Outside, it assimilates other literacies. In different ways, this holds true for China. It is willing to build its internal network (Intranet) without connecting it to the all-encompassing net (Internet) through which we experience some aspects of globality.

The organization of hierarchy, which made the object of many studies telling the West why Japan succeeds better in economic terms, is centered around the unity *semmai-kohai*, i.e., senior-junior. Within the pragmatic framework of a literacy different from that of the Western world, a logic and ethics pertinent to the distinction mentioned evolved. The moral basis of the precedence of the senior over the junior is pragmatic in nature. The Chinese formula (*cho-jo-no-jo*) results from a practical experience encoded not only in language but also in the system of ranking. In fact, what is acknowledged is both experience and performance, expressed by the Japanese in the categories of *kyu*, referring to proficiency, and *dau*, referring to cumulative results. The system applies to economic life, calligraphy, wrestling (*sumo*), and flower arrangement (*ikebana*), as well as to social rank. In the dynamics of current changes, such systems are also affected.

From the viewpoint of language functions, we notice that national language can serve for insulation, while adopted language—English, in particular—can serve as a bridge to the rest of the world. Nevertheless, Japanese society, like all contemporary societies, is more and more confronted with the world in its globality, and with the need to constitute appropriate means for expression, communication and signification pertinent to the global world. While Japan is an example of many literate prejudices at work, rigidly hierarchic, discriminating against women and foreigners, dogmatic, it also exemplifies the understanding of changing circumstances for human practical experiences of self-constitution as Japanese, and as members of the integrated world community as well. Consequently, new *literacies* emerge within its homogeneous cultural environment, as they emerge in countries such as China, Korea, and Indonesia, and in the Arab nations. As a result, we experience changes in the nature of the relations between the cultures of the Far East, Middle East, the Indian subcontinent and the West. The process expands, probably more slowly than one might expect, to the African and South American continents.

Global economy requires new types of relations among nations and cultures, and these relations need to correspond to the dynamics of the new pragmatic framework that has emerged against the background of the new scale of human activity. The identity urge expressed in the multiculturalism trend of our days will find in the past its most unreliable arguments. The point is proven by the naive misrepresentation of past events, facts, and figures through the activists of the movement. Multiculturalism corresponds to the dynamics of the civilization of illiteracy: from the uniqueness and universality of one dominating mode to plurality, not limited to race, lifestyle, or cultures. Whoever sees multiculturalism as an issue of race, or feminism as one of gender (against the background of history), will not be able to design a course of action to best serve those whose *different* condition is now acknowledged. A different condition results in different abilities, and thus different ways of projecting one's identity in the practical experience of self-constitution. The past is irrelevant; emphasis is always on the future.

CHAPTER 5: LANGUAGE AND LOGIC

Around the time computers entered public life, a relatively unknown writer of science fiction described the world of *non A (A)*. It is our planet Earth in the year 2560, and what *non A* denotes is the non-Aristotelian logic embodied in a super-computer game machine that rules the planet. Gilbert Gosseyn (pronounced *Go Sane*, with an obvious pun intended) finds out that he is more than just one person.

Anyone even marginally educated in the history of logic will spontaneously associate the experience described here with Levy-Bruhl's controversial *law of participation*. According to this law, "In the collective representations of primitive mentality, objects, beings, phenomena can be, in a way we cannot understand, themselves and something different at the same time." The relatively undifferentiated, syncretic human experience at the time of the inception of notation and writing testifies to awareness of very unusual connections. Research of artifacts originating with primitive tribes makes clear the relative dominance of *visual thinking* and *functioning* of human beings along the line of what we would today call multi-valued logics.

The world of *non A*, although placed by its author in some fictional future, seems to describe a logic prevalent in a remote time. Even today, as anthropologists report, there are tribes in the Amazon jungles and in remote Eskimo territories whose members claim to be not only the beings they are, but also something else, such as a bird, plant, or even a past event. This is not a way of speaking, but a different way of ascertaining identity. Inferences in this pragmatic context go beyond those possible in the logical world of truth and falsehood that Aristotle described. Multi-valued logic is probably a good name for describing the production of such inferences, but not necessarily the explanation we seek for why it is that self-constitution involves such mechanisms, and how they work. Moreover, even if we could get both questions answered, we would still wonder—because our own self-constitution involves a different logic—what the relation is between the language experience and the logical framework of those living in the *non A* world of ancient times. Practical experiences with images, dominant in such tribes, explains why there is a logical continuum, instead of a clear-cut association with truth and falsehood, or with present and absent. Multi-valued logics of different types, corresponding to different pragmatic contexts, were actually tamed when language was experienced in its written form and thinking was stabilized in written expressions. Awareness of connections distinctly integrated in human experience and quantified in a body of intelligible knowledge progressively clears the logical horizon. As many-valued logics were subdued, entities were constituted only as what the experience made them to be, and no longer simultaneously many different things.

The change from orality to the practical experience of written language affected many aspects of human interaction. Writing introduced a frame of reference, ways to compare and evaluate, and thus a sense of value associated with limited choices. Orality was controlled by those exercising it. The written, stabilized in marks on a surface, gave rise to a new type of questioning, based on its implicit analyticity. Over time written language led to associations. Some were in relation to its visual aspect. Other associations were made to writing patterns, a kind of repetition. Integrative by its nature, writing stimulates the quest for comparing experiences of self-constitution by comparing what was recorded. The expectation of accurate recording is implicit in the experience of writing. The rather skeletal incipient written language makes visible connections which within orality faded away.

A very raw definition of logic can be *the discipline of connections*— "if something, then something else"—that can be expressed in many ways, including formal expressions. Connections established in orality are spontaneous. With writing, the experience is stabilized and a promise for method is established. This method leads to inferences from connections. What I am trying to suggest is that although there is logic in orality, it is a *natural* logic, reflecting natural connections, as opposed to connections established in writing. Writing provides the X-ray of the elusive body of experience in whose depths awareness of connections and their practical implications was starting to take shape.

Time and space awareness are gained relatively slowly. In parallel, connections to experiences in time and space are expressed in an incipient awareness of how they affect the outcome of any practical experience. No less than signs, logic is rooted also in the pragmatics of human self-constitution, and probably comes into existence together with them. Co-presence, of what is different or what is alike, incompatibilities, exclusions, and similar time or space situations bcome disassociated from actions, objects, and persons and form a well-defined layer of experience. Mechanisms of inference, from objects, actions, persons, situations, etc., evolve from simpler configurations or sequences of connections. Writing is more effective than rituals or oral expression in capturing inferences, although not necessarily in providing a mechanism for sharing. What is gained in breadth is lost in depth.

As human practical experiences get more effective they also become more complex. The cognitive effort substitutes more and more for the physical. Stabilized in inferences based on increasingly more encompassing cycles of activity—agriculture is definitely more extensive than hunting or food gathering—experience is transmitted more and more in its skeletal form, deprived of the richness of the individual characteristics of those identified through it. Less information and more sequences of successful action—this is how from the richness of connections logic of actions takes shape. The accent is on time and space, or better yet on what we call, in retrospect, references. As writing supplants time-based means of expression and communication (rituals, first of all), temporal logic begins to lose in importance.

Once the pragmatic horizon of human life changes, literacy, in conjunction with the logic it houses, constitutes its invisible grid, its implicit metrics. The understanding of anything that is not related to our literate self-constitution remains outside this understanding. Literate language is a reductionist machine, which we use to look at the world from the perspective of our own experience. Aware of experiences different from ours, at least of their possibility, we would like to understand them, knowing perfectly well that once captured in our experience of language, their own condition is negated. Oral education maintained the parent-child continuum, and memory, i.e., experience, was directly transmitted. Literacy introduced means for handling discontinuity and, above all, differences. It stored, in some form of record, everything pertaining to the experience. But as record, it constituted a new experience, with its own inherent values.

As a reductionist device, writing reduces language to a body of accepted ways of speaking, recording, and reading governed by two kinds of rules: pertinent to connections (logic), and pertinent to grammar. The process was obviously more elaborate and less focused. In retrospect, we can understand how writing affected the experience of human self-constitution through language. It is therefore understandable why those who, following the young Wittgenstein, take the logic of language for granted, seeing only the need to bring to light what is concealed in the signs of language, are wrong. Language does not have an intrinsic logic; each practical experience extracts *logic* from the experience and contaminates all means of human expression by the inference from what is possible to what is necessary.

LOGICS BEHIND THE LOGIC

The function of coordination resulting from the use of language evolved over time. What did not change is the structure of the coordinating mechanism. Logic as we know it, i.e., a discipline legitimized by literate use of language, is concerned with structural aspects of various languages. The attempt to explain how and why conditions leading to literacy were created, after the writing entered the realm of human experience, can only benefit from an understanding of the coordinating mechanism of writing and literacy, which includes logic but is not reducible to it. This mechanism consisted of rules for correct language use (grammar), awareness of connections specific to the pragmatic framework (logic), means of persuasion (rhetoric), selection of choices (heuristics), and argumentation (dialectics). Together, they give us an image of how complex the process of self-constitution is. Separately, they give us insight into the fragmented experiences of language use, rationality, conviction, selection, actions, and beliefs. There is a logic behind the (relative) normal course of events, and also behind any crisis, if we want to extend the concept of logic so as to include the rational description or explanation of whatever might have led to the crisis. And there are logics behind the logic, as Descartes, the authors of the *Port Royale Logic* (actually *The Art of Thinking*), Locke, and many others saw it. The logic of religion, the logic of art, of morality, of science, of logic itself, the logic of literacy, are examples of the variety people consider and establish as their object of interest, subjecting such logic to the test of completeness (does it apply to everything?), consistency (is it contradictory?), and sometimes transitivity.

Independent of the subject (religion, art, ethics, a precise science, literacy, etc.), human beings establish the particular logic as a network of reciprocal relations and functional dependencies according to which truth (religious, artistic, ethical, etc.), relevant to the practical experience in more than one way, can and should be pursued. This logic, an extension of the incipient awareness of connections, became a formal system, which some researchers in philosophy and psychology still believe is somehow attached to the brain (or to the mind), ensuring its correct functioning. Indeed, successful action was seen as a result of logic, *hard-wired* as part of the biological endowment. Other researchers perceived logic as a product of our experience, in particular thinking, as this applies to our self-constitution in the natural world and the world we ourselves created. As a corpus of rules and criteria, logic applies to language, but there is a logic of human actions, a logic of art, a logic of morals, etc., described by rules for preserving consistency, maintaining integrity, facilitating causal inference and other relevant cognitive operations, such as articulating a hypothesis or drawing conclusions.

An old question sneaks in: Is there a universal logic, something that in its purity transcends differences in language, in biological characteristics, in differences, *period?* The answer depends on whom one asks. From the perspective assumed so far, the answer is definitely no. Differences are emphasized, even celebrated here, precisely because they extend to the different logics that pertain to various practical experiences. Formulated as such, the answer is elusive because, after all, logic is expressed through language, and once expressed, it constitutes a body of knowledge which in turn participates in practical human experiences. No stronger proof of this can be given than the Boolean logic embedded in computer hardware and programming languages. A more appropriate answer can be given once we notice that major language systems embody different logical mechanisms that pertain to language's coordinating function.

The main logical systems require our attention because they are related to what makes literacy necessary and, under new pragmatic conditions, less necessary, if not superfluous. Since the civilization of illiteracy is viewed also from the perspective of the changes resulting in a new scale of human praxis, it becomes necessary to see whether in the global world *forces of uniformity* or *forces of heterogeneity and diversity,* embodied in various literacies and the logic attached to them, or associated with their use, are at work. As almost all scholars agree, Aristotle is the father of the logic that applies to the Western language system. Writing helped to encode his logic of proper inference from premises expressed in sentences. Literacy gave this logic a house, and a sense of validity and permanency that scholars accept almost as religion. For Eastern systems, contributions of equal value and relevance can be found in the major writings of ancient China and Japan, as well as in Hindu documents. Instead of a superficial overview of the subject, I prefer to quote Fung-Yu-lan's precise observation regarding the particular focus of Chinese philosophy (which is also representative of the Far East): "Philosophy must not be simply the object of cognition, it must also be the object of an experience." The resulting expression of this endeavor differs from the Indian, in search of a certain state of mind, not formulations of truth, and from Western philosophical statements. It takes the form of concise, often enigmatic, and usually paradoxical statements or aphorisms. A very good presentation of this experience is given in a famous text by Chuang-tzu: "The words serve to fix the ideas, but once the idea is grasped, there is no need to think about words. I wish I could find somebody who has ceased to think of words and have him with me to talk to."

The logic of the Indo-European languages is based on the recognition of the object-action distinction, expressed in language through the noun and the verb. For over 2,000 years, this logic has dominated and maintained the structure of society, of the *polis*, to use Aristotle's term. Indeed, he defined the human as *zoon politikon*—community (*polis*), animal (*zoon*)—and his logic is an attempt to discover what was the cognitive structure that ensured proper inference from premises expressed in sentences. Probably as much as some who today hope for a similar achievement through formal languages, he wanted logic to be as independent as possible of the language used, as well as independent of the particular language spoken by people belonging to different communities.

Parallel to the language housing Aristotle's logic was a different system in which the verb (referring to action) was assimilated in the object, as in the Chinese and Japanese languages. Every action became a noun (hunting, running, talking), and a non-predicative language mode was achieved. Aristotle's construction goes like this: If a is b (The sky is covered), and if b is c (the cover are clouds), then a is *c* (cloudy sky). Non-predicative constructions do not come to a conclusion but continue from one condition to another, as in approximately: Being covered, covers being clouds, clouding being associated with rain, rain...and so on. That is, they are open-ended connections *in status nascendi*. We notice that Aristotelian logic derives the truth of the inference from the truth of the premise, based on a formal relation independent of both. In non-predicative logic, language only points to possible chains of relations, implicitly acknowledging that others are simultaneously possible without deriving knowledge, or without subjecting conclusions to a formal test of their truth or falsehood. To the abstract and formal representation of knowledge inference, it opposes a model of concrete and natural representation in which distinctions regarding quality are more important than quantity distinctions.

Based on observations already accumulated, first of all that ideographic writing keeps the means of expression very close to the object represented in language, we can understand why languages expressed in ideographic writing are not adapted to the kind of thinking Aristotle and his followers developed and which culminated in the Western notion of science, as well as in the Western system of values. The successive rediscovery of Far Eastern modes of representation and of the philosophy growing out of this very different way of thinking, as well as of the interest in subtleties rather uncommon to our culture, resulted in the many attempts we witness to transcend the boundaries between these fundamentally different language structures. The purpose is to endow our language, and thus our thinking and emotional life, with dimensions structurally impossible within the Western framework of existence.

The logic of dependency—the Japanese *amé*—is one of embedded relations and many conjectures resulting in a logic of actions, a different way of thinking, and a different system of values. These are partially reflected in the periodic misunderstandings between the Western world and Japan. Of course, it can be simplified as to mean that if a company and an employee accept it, and they do so since *amé* is structurally embedded in the life of people, both parties will be faithful to each other no matter what. *Amé* can also be simplified to mean a mutual relationship within families (all prejudices included), or among friends. But as we get closer to the practical experience of *amé* (Takeo Doi's writing on the "anatomy of dependence" helps us a great deal in this attempt), we realize that it constitutes a framework, marking not only distinct decisions (logically justified), but an entire context of thinking, feeling, acting, evaluating. It is reflected in the attitude towards language and in the education system, inculcating dependency as a logic that takes priority over the individual. Evidently, the only way to integrate the logic of *amé* into our logic—if indeed we think that this is right, moreover that it is possible—is through practical experience. Although *amé* seems to point to some limits inherent in our language, it actually reveals limits in our self-constitution, as part of establishing a network of generalized mutual relationships as part of our experience.

It should be added that practically a mirrored phenomenon occurs in the Far East, where what can be perceived as the limitations of the language system and the logic it supports (or embodies), triggered an ever-growing interest in Western culture and many attempts to copy or to quickly assimilate it in vocabulary and behavior. From the Indian universe comes not only the mysticism of the Vedic texts, but also the stubborn preoccupation with the human condition (both the aspect of conditioning and of what Mircea Eliade called *de-conditioning*). This resulted in the attraction it exercises on many people looking for an alternative to what they perceive as an over-conditioned existence, usually translated as pressure of performance and competitive attitudes. Some opted out of literacy, and generally out of their culture, in search of liberation (*mukti*), a practical experience of lower preoccupation with the useful and higher spiritual goals, and of obstinate refusal of logic. (Some really never fully appropriated or internalized the philosophy, but adopted a lifestyle emulating commercialized models, the exotic syntax of escapism.)

In short, and trying not to preclude future discussion of these phenomena, the historic development of language and logic within the many cultures we know of—more than the Western and Far Eastern mentioned—bears witness to the very complex relation between who and what people are: their language and the logic that the language makes possible and later embodies. The hunter in the West, and the hunter in the Far East, in Africa, India, Papua, the fishermen, the forager, etc. relate in different ways to their environment and to their peers in the community. The way their relatively similar experiences are embodied in language and other means of expression plays an important role in forms of sharing, religion, art, in the establishment of a value system, and later on education and identity preservation. There are common points, however, and the most relevant refer to relations established in the work process, as these affect efficiency. These commonalties prove relevant to understanding the role language, in conjunction with logic, exercises on various stages of social and economic development.

A PLURALITY OF INTELLECTUAL STRUCTURES

Since scale (of humankind, of groups performing coherent activities, of activities themselves) plays such an important role in the dynamics of human self-constitution through practical activities involving language, it is only fair to question whether logic is affected by scale. Again, the answer will depend upon who is asked. Logic as we study it has nothing to do with scale. An inference remains preserved no matter how many people make it, or study it, for that matter. But this reflects the universalistic viewpoint. Once we question the constitution of logic itself, and trace it to practical experiences resulting in the awareness of connections, it becomes less obvious that logic is independent of scale. Actually, some experiences are not even possible without having reached a critical mass, and the relation between *simple* and *complex* is not one of progression. But it is certainly a multi-valued relation, granted with elements of progression.

The practical experience of a tribe (in Africa, North America, or South America) is defined at the scale of relations inside the tribe, and between the tribe and the relatively limited environment of existence. The logic (or pre-logic, to adapt the jargon of some anthropologists) specific to this scale corresponds to the dominance of instincts and intuitions, and is expressed within the visually dominant means of expression and communication characteristic of what is called the primitive mentality. From all we know, memory plays a major role in shaping patterns of activity. The power of discrimination (through vision, hearing, smell, etc.) is extraordinary; adaptability is much higher than that of humans in modern societies. These tribe members live in a phase of disjoint groups, unaware even of biological commonalties among such groups, focused on themselves in pursuing survival strategies not much different from those of other living creatures who share the same environment. Once these groups start relating to each other, the practical experiences of self-constitution diversify. Cooperation and exchange increase, and language, in many varieties, becomes part of the self-constitution of various human types.

Languages originate in areas associated with the early nuclei of agriculture. These are places where the population could increase, since in some ways the pragmatics was effective enough to provide for a greater number of people. Probably primitive agriculture is the first activity in which a scale threshold was reached and a new quality, constituted in the practical experience of language, emerged. It is also an activity with a precise logic embodied in the awareness of a multitude of levels where connections are critical for the outcome of the activity, i.e., for the well being of those practicing it. The sacredness of place, to which the Latin root of the word culture (*cultus*) refers, is embodied in the practical activity with everything pertinent to human experience. Logic captures the connection between the place and the activity. In a variety of embodiments—from ways to sequence an action to the use of available resources, how to pursue a plan, craft tools, etc.—logic is integrated in culture and, in turn, participates in shaping it. It is a two-way dependency which increases over time and results in today's logical machines that define a culture radically different from the culture of the mechanical contraption. There are differences in the type of intelligence, which need to be acknowledged. And there are differences resulting from the variety of natural contexts of practical life, which we need to consider. Commonalties of the survival experience and further development should also be placed in the equation of human self-constitution.

Within the pragmatics of the post-industrial, the logic extracted from practical experiences of self-constitution in the world and the logic constituted in experiences defining the world of the human are increasingly different. We no longer *read* the logic of language and infer from it to the experience, but project our own logic (itself a practical result of self-constitution) upon the experience in the world. The *algebra of thought,* a *cross section* of rational thinking that Boole submitted with his calculus of logics, is a good example, but by no means the only one. Languages are created in order to support a variety of logical systems, e.g., autoepistemic, temporal and tense propositional, modal, intuitionist.

One would almost expect the emergence of a universal logic and a universal language (attempts were and are made to facilitate such a universalism). Leibniz had visions of an ideal language, a *characteristica universalis* and a *calculus ratiocinator.* So did many others, from the 17th century on, not realizing that in the process of diversification of human experiences, their dream became progressively less attainable. In parallel, we gave up the logical inheritance of the past: logic embedded in a variety of autarchic primitive practical experiences that various groups (in Africa, Asia, Europe, etc.) had up to our time is rapidly becoming a cultural reference. The scale that such experiences embody and the logic appropriate to that scale are simply absorbed in the larger scale of the global economy. We are simply no longer in the position to effectively unveil the logic of magical experiences, not even of those rational or rationalizable aspects that refer to the plants, animals, and various minerals used by the peoples preceding us for avoiding disease or treating illness.

In our days, the cultures swinging from the sacred to the profane, from the primitive to the over-developed, come closer together. This happens not because everyone wants this to happen, not even because all benefit (in fact, many give up an identity—their own way of life—for a condition of non-identity that characterizes a certain style of living). The process is driven by the need to achieve levels of efficiency appropriate to the scale humankind reached. The various groups of people are integrated as humans in the first place (not as tribes, nations, or religions), and consequently a pragmatic framework of increasing integration is progressively put in place.

The Euro-centrist (or Western) notion that all types of intelligence develop towards the Western type (and thus the Western practice of language culminating in literacy) has been discredited many times. The plurality of intellectual structures has been acknowledged, unfortunately either demagogically or in lip-service to the past, but never as an opening to the future. Literacy eradicated, for valid practical reasons—those of the Industrial Revolution—heterogeneity, and thus variety from among the experiences through which people constitute themselves in the universe of their experience. When those reasons are exhausted, because new circumstances of existence and work require a new logic, literacy becomes a hindrance, without necessarily affecting the role of the logic inhabiting it.

The scale of human life and activity, and the associated projection of expectations beyond human survival and preservation, lead less to the need for universal literacy than to the need for several *literacies* and for a rich variety of logical horizons. Since the coordinating mechanism consists of logic, rhetoric, heuristics, and dialectics, the new scale prompts the emergence of new rhetorical devices, among other things. It suffices to think about persuasion at the level of the global village, or about persuasion at the level of the individual, as the individual can be filtered in this global village through mechanisms of networking and multimedia interactivity. Logical mechanisms of mass communication are replaced by logical considerations of increased individual communication. Think about new heuristic procedures at work on the World Wide Web, as well as in market research and in Netconomy transactions. Consider a new dialectic, definitely that of the infertile opposition between what is proclaimed as very good and excellent, as we try to convince ourselves that mediocrity is eradicated by consensus. Fascinating work in multi-valued logic, fuzzy logic, temporal logic, and many areas of logical focus pertinent to computation, artificial intelligence, memetics, and networking allow progress well beyond what the science fiction of the world of *non A* presented us with.

THE LOGICS OF ACTIONS

Between the relatively monolithic and uniform ideal of a literate society convinced of the virtues of logic, and the pluralistic and heterogeneous reality of partial literacies that transfer logic to machines, one can easily distinguish a change in direction. Persons with a rather adequate literate culture, educated in the spirit of rationality guarded by classic or formal logic, are at a loss when facing the sub-literacies of specialized practical endeavors, or the *illogical* inferences made within new fields of human self-constitution. Let us put their attitude in some perspective. At various stages in human evolution—for instance, transition from scavenging to hunting, or from hunting and foraging to herding and agriculture—people experienced the effects of the erosion of some behavioral codes and projected their new condition in new practical patterns. One type of cohesion represented in the declining behavioral code was replaced by another; one logic, deferring the code, was followed by others. When interaction among groups of different types of cohesion occurred, logic was severely challenged. Sometimes, as a result, one logic dominated; other times, compromise was established. Primitive stages are remarkably adaptive to the environment.

Our stage, remote in many ways from the wellspring (*Ursprung*), consists of an appropriated environment within which the effort is to provide a pragmatic framework for high efficiency. Logic, rhetoric, heuristics, and dialectics interact inside this framework. In other words, human evolution goes from sensorial anchoring in the natural world to an artificial (human crafted) world superimposed on the concrete reality—and eventually extended into artificial life, one from among the most recently established fields of scientific inquiry. Within this world, humans no longer restrict the projection of their natural and intellectual condition through one (or very few) comprehensive sign systems. Quite to the contrary, the effort is towards segmentation, with the aim of reaching not global cohesion, but local cohesiveness, corresponding to local optima. The complexity and the nature of the changes within this system result in the need for a strategy of segmentation, and a logic, or several, supporting it. In the interaction between a language and the humans constituted in it, as the embodiment of their biological characteristics and of their experience, logical conflicts are not excluded. After all, the logic of actions, influenced by heuristics as well, and the logic inherent to literacy are not identical.

Actions bring to mind agents of action and thus the logic integrated in tools and artifacts. The assumption that the same logic housed in language is involved in the expression leading to the making of tools and other objects related to people's activity went unchallenged for a long time. Even today, designers and engineers are educated according to an ideal of literacy that is expected to reflect in their work the rationality exemplified in the literate use of language. Complementing most of the development of humankind's language, drawings have expressed ideas about how to make things and how to perform some operations that are part of our continuous experience of self-constitution in practical activity. Each drawing embodies the logic of the future artifact, no matter how useful or even how ephemeral. There is a large record of literate work from which logical aspects of thinking can be derived. There is a rather small record of drawing, and not too many surviving artifacts. They were conceived for precise practical experiences and usually did not outlast the experience, or the person who embodied it. Roads, houses, tools, and other objects indeed survived, but it is not until better tools for drawing itself and better paper became available that a *library* of engineering was established.

As a hybrid between art and science, engineering accepts the logic of scientific discovery only in order to balance it against the logic of aesthetic expectations. In the pragmatic framework of the civilization of illiteracy, engineering definitely has a dominant position in respect to the self-constitution of the human being in language-based practical experiences. This is due to the impact it has on the efficiency of human practical experiences and on their almost endless diversification.

There is a phase of conflict, a phase of accommodation, and a phase of complementarity when some means (such as language and the means for visualization used by designers and engineers) replace others, if they do not render them useless. In our time of experiences involving many more people than ever, of distributive transactions, of heterogeneity, and of interactions that go beyond the linearity of the sequence, the structural characteristics of literacy interfere with the new dynamics of human development as this is supported by very powerful technologies embodying a variety of logical possibilities. At this time, the implicit logic of literacy and the new logics (in the plural) collide in the pragmatic framework.

Within the logic of the literate discourse, followed *volens nolens* in this book, it should be clear that the attempt to salvage literacy is the attempt to maintain linear relations, determinism, hierarchy (of values), centralization—which fostered literacy—in a framework requiring non-linearity, decentralization, distributed modes of practical experiences, and unstable value (among others). The two frameworks are logically incompatible. This does not mean that literacy has to be discarded altogether, or·that it will disappear, as cuneiform notation and pictographic writing did, or that it will be replaced by drawing or by computer-based language processing. The linear will definitely satisfy a vast number of practical activities; so will deterministic explanations and centralism (political, religious, technological, etc.), and even an elitist sense of value. But instead of being a universal standard, or even a goal (to linearize everything that is not linear, to ascertain sequences of cause and effect, to find a center and practice centrality), it will become part of a complex system of relations, free of hierarchy—or at least with fast changing hierarchies—valueless, adaptive, extremely distributed.

Of no less significance is the type of logic (and for that matter, rhetoric, heuristics, and dialectics) housed in language, i.e., projected from the universe of human self-constitution in the system of inferences, knowledge, and awareness of the being characteristic of literate frameworks of practical experiences. Language successfully captured a dualistic logic indebted to the values of truth and falsehood, and supported experiences embodied in the abstract character of logical rationality. It was complemented by logical symbolism and logical calculus, very successful in formalizing dualism, and in eliminating logical models not fitting the dualistic structure.

Literacy instilled bivalent logic as another of its invisible layers—something is written or not, the written is right or wrong—allowing only quite late, and actually in the realm of logical formalism, the appearance of multi-valued schemes. The non-linearity, vagueness, and fuzziness characteristic of the post-industrial pragmatic framework opened avenues of high human efficiency, better adapted to the scale of humankind that required efficiency and eventually made efficiency its major goal. Literacy is ill endowed for supporting multi-valued logic, although it was always tempted to step in its vast territories. Even some of the disciplines built around and in extension of literacy (such as history, philosophy, sociology) are not able to integrate a logic different from the one seated in the practical experience of reading and writing. This explains, for instance, computationalism as a new horizon for science, within which multi-valued logic can be simulated even if the computer's underlying structure is that of Boolean logic. The literate argument of science and multimedia's non-linear heuristic path to science are fundamentally different. Each requires a different logic and results in a different interaction between those who constitute their identity in the practical experience of scientific experiments and those who constitute their identity in co-participation.

It took longer in the world of predicative logic and in the science based on analytic power to accept fuzzy logic and to integrate it in new artifacts, than it took in the world of non-predicative logic and in the science based on the power of synthesis. Within the universe of non-predicative language, fuzzy logic made it into the design of control mechanisms for high-speed trains, as well as into new efficient toasters. It was accepted in Japan while it was still debated among experts in the Western world, until 1993, when a washing machine integrating fuzzy logic was introduced in the market. This fact can go on record as more than a mere example in a discussion regarding the implications of the global economy for the various language systems and the logical coordinating mechanisms specific to each.

Progress in understanding and emulating human thinking shows a progression from a literacy-based model to a model rooted in the new pragmatic framework. Rule-based, pattern-matching systems generalize predicate calculus; neural networking is devoted to mimicking the way minds work, in a synthetic neuron-plex array; fuzzy logic addresses the limitations of Boolean calculus and the nondeterminism of neural networks, and concentrates on modeling imprecision, ambiguity, and undecidability as these are embodied in new human practical experiences.

Within the civilization of literacy, recollection and the logic attached to it are predominantly made through *quoting*. In the literate framework, to know something means to be able to write about it, thus reconfirming the logic of writing. Lives are subject to memories, and diaries are our interpreted life, written with some reader in mind: the beloved, one's children, a posterity willing to acknowledge or understand. The literate means of sharing in successive practical experiences contain the expected logic and affect both the experience and its communication. Everything seems to originate in the same context: to know means to re-live the experience. The literate gnoseology, with its implicit logic, is based on continuously remaking, reconstituting the experience as a language experience. This is why every form of writing based on the structure embodied in literacy—literary or philosophic, religious, scientific, journalistic, or political—is actually rewriting.

The civilization of illiteracy is one of *sampling*, a concept originating in genetics. To understand what this means, it is useful to contrast *quotation* and *sampling*. Literate appropriation in the form of quotation takes place in the structure of literacy. Sequences are designed to accept someone else's words. A quote introduces the hierarchy desired or acknowledged by invoking authority or questioning it. Authorship is exercised by producing a context for interpretation and maintaining literate rules for their expression. Interpretations are determined by the implicit expectation of reproducing the deterministic structure of literacy, i.e., its inner logic. The quote embodies centralism by establishing centers of interest and understanding around the quoted.

Illiterate appropriation corresponds to a dissolution of hierarchy, to an experience of dissolving it and doing away with sequence, authorship, and the rules of logical inference. It questions the notion of elementary meaningful units, extending choices beyond well formed sentences, beyond words, beyond morphemes or phonemes (which always mean a lot to linguists, but almost nothing to the people constituting themselves in literate language experiences), and beyond formal logic. These techniques of sampling lead to actual undoing. Rhythms of words can be appropriated, as writers did long before the technology of musical sampling became available. So can the structure of a sentence be appropriated, the *feel* of a text, or of many other forms of expression that are not literacy-based (the visual arts, for instance). Anything pertaining to a written sentence—and for that matter to music, painting, odor, texture, movement (of a person, of images, leaves on a tree, stars, rivers, etc.)—can be selected, decomposed into units as small as one desires, and appropriated as an echo of the experience it embodies. Genetic configurations, as they apply to plants and other living entities, can be sampled as well. Genetic splicing maintains the relations to the broader genetic texture of plants or animals. Spliced, a word, a sentence, or a text still maintains relations to the experience in which it was constituted.

These relations are enormously relativized, subjected to a logic of vagueness. When they relate to what we write, they are empowered by emotional components that the literate experience expelled from literate expression. There is room for variation, for spontaneity, for the accidental, where before the rigor and logic of good writing stood guard against anything that might disturb. When they relate to a biological structure, they concern specific characteristics, such as composition or perisability. Within the culture of sampling, the expectation of a shared body of *literacy* and its attached logic are quite out of touch with the dynamics of discarding the past as having no other significance than as an extended alphabet from which one can choose, at random or with some system, *letters* fitting the act. The *letters* are part of a *sui generis* alphabet, changing as practical experiences change, interacting with many logical rules for using them or for understanding how they work. In this new perspective, interpretation is always another instance of constituting the *language*, not only using it. Biological sampling, along with the associated splicing, also regards the living as a *text*. Its purpose is to affect some components in order to achieve desired qualities related to taste, look, nutritional value, etc. This is the core of genetic engineering, a practical experience in which the logic of life, expressed in DNA sequences and configurations, takes precedence over the logic of language and literacy, even if the *text* metaphor, so prominent in genetics, plays such a major role. It is worth recalling that the word *text* derives from the Latin word for *to weave*, which was later applied to coherent collections of written sentences.

Sampling does not necessarily transform everything into the gray mass of information. In their practical experiences, people sample emotions and feelings as they sample foods in supermarkets, sample entertainment programs (television sampling included), sample clothing, and even partners (for special occasions or as potential spouses, partners in business, or whatever else). As opposed to quoting, sampling—periodic, random, or sequential—results in the severing from what literacy celebrated as tradition and continuity. And it challenges authorship. With increased sampling as a practical experience of diversification, the human being acquires a very specific freedom not possible within boundaries of the literate experience. Tradition is complemented by forms of innovation impossible within a pragmatic framework of progression and dualistic (true-false) experience. This becomes even more clear when we understand that sampling is followed by synthesis, which might be neither true nor false, but *appropriate* (to some degree). In the case of music, a device called a *sequencer* is used for this purpose. The composite is synthetic. A new experience, significant in itself at formal levels corresponding to the constitution of *ad hoc* languages and their consumption in the act, becomes possible. The *mixmaster* is a machine for recycling arbitrarily defined constitutive units such as notes, rhythms, or melodic patterns freed from their pragmatic identity. What is significant is that the same applies to the biological *text*, including the biology of the human being. In some ways, genetic mutation acquires the status of a new means for synthesizing new plants and animals, and even new materials.

The artistic technique of collage is based on a logic of choices beyond those of realistic representations. Logical rules of perspective are negated by rules of juxtaposition. Collage, as a technique, anticipates the generalized stage of sampling and compositing. It changes our notion of intellectual property, trademark, and copyright, all expressions of a logic firmly attached to the literate experience. The famous case of Dr. Martin Luther King's *plagiarism* reflected aspects of primitive culture carried over to the civilization of illiteracy: there is no authorship; once something becomes public, it is free to be shared. In the same vein, there is no Malcolm X left in the poetry resulting from sampling his speeches, or anyone else's for that matter.

Post-modern literature and painting result from sampling exercises governed by an ear or eye keen to our day's vernacular of machines and alienation. The same applies to plants, fruits, and microbes insofar as sampling does not preserve previous identities, but constitutes new ones, which we integrate in new experiences of our own self-constitution. From the perspective of logic, the procedure is of interest to the extent that it establishes domains of logical appropriateness. Logical identity is redefined from a dynamic perspective. From a pragmatic viewpoint, certain experiences might be maximized by applying a certain logic to them. Moreover, within some experiences, complementary logics—each logic assigned to a precise aspect of the system—can be used together in strategies of layered management of the process, or in parallel processes, checked against each other at defined instances. Strategies for maximizing market transactions, for instance, integrate various decision-making layers, each characterized by a different logical assumption. We experience a process of replacing the rigid logical framework of literate condition with many logical frameworks, adapted to diversity.

In conclusion, one more aspect should be approached. Is it enough to say that language expresses the biological and the social identity of the human being? To deal with language, and more specifically with the embodiment of language in literacy, means to deal with everything that makes the human being the bio-socio-politico-cultural entity that defines our species. The logical appears to be an underlying element: bio-*logical,* socio-*logical,* etc. The hierarchy will probably bother some, since it seems that language assumes a higher place among the many factors participating in the process of human self-constitution. Indeed, in order for the human being to qualify as *zoon politikon,* as *Homo Sapiens,* or *Homo Ludens* (playful man) or *Homo Faber,* he or she must first qualify for the interactions which each designation describes: on the biological level, with other human beings, within structures of common interest, in the realm of a human being's own nature. This is why humans define themselves through practical experiences involving signs.

At the various levels at which such signs are generated, interpreted, comprehended, and used to conceive new signs, human identity is ascertained. This is what prompted Felix Hausdorf to define the human being as *zoon semeiotikon*—semiotic animal, sign-using animal. Moreover, Charles Sanders Peirce considered semiotics as being the logic of vagueness. Signs—whether pictures, sounds, odors, textures, words (or combinations), belonging to a language, diagram, mathematical or chemical formalism, new language (as in art, political power, or programming), genetic code, etc.—relate to human beings, not in their abstraction but in the concreteness of their participation in our lives and work.

MEMETIC OPTIMISM

John Locke knew that all knowledge is derived from experience. But he was not sure that the same applies to logic or mathematics. If we define experience as self-constitutive practical activity, whose output is the ever-changing identity of the individual or individuals carrying out the experience, logic derives from it, as do all knowledge and language. This places logic not outside thought, but in experience, and raises the question of logical replication. Dawkins defined the replicator as a biological molecule that "has the extraordinary property of being able to make copies of itself." Such an entity is supposed to have fecundity, fidelity, longevity. Language is a replicator; or better yet, it is a replicative medium. The question is whether duplication can take place only by virtue of its own structural characteristics, or whether one has to consider logic, for instance, as the rule of replication. Moreover, maybe logic itself is replicative in nature.

This discussion belongs to the broader subject of memetics. Its implicit assumption is that memes, the spiritual equivalent of genes, are subject to mechanisms of evolution. As opposed to natural evolution, memetic evolution is through more efficient orders of magnitude, and faster by far.

In experiences of cultural transfer (sharing of experience as a practical experience itself) or of inheritance—genetic or memetic, or a combination of both—something like a *gene of meaning* was suspected to exist. Were it to exist, that would not mean, within our pragmatic system, that signification is carried over through memetic replication, but that practical experiences of human self-constitution involve the act of conjuring meaning under the guise of various logics pertinent to sign processes. Replication is, then, not of information, but of fundamental processes, conjuring of meaning being one of them. Evolution of language, as well as of logic, belongs to cultural evolution. Meme mutation and spread of a reduced scale, such as the scale of finite artificial languages and limited logical rules, can be described in equations similar to those of genetics. But once the scale changes, it is doubtful that we could encode the resulting complexity in such formalizations.

Be this as it may, expression, communication, and signification, the fundamental functions of any sign system, regardless of its logic, are endowed with replicative qualities. Logic prevents corruption, or at least provides means for identifying it. The easiest way to understand this statement is to relate it to the many replications involved in the manipulation of data in a computer. The *Error* message announcing corruption of data corresponds to a replication process that went astray. Like all analogies, this one is not infallible: a certain logic, against whose rules the replication is tested, might simply prove to be inadequate to processes of replication that are different in nature. Indeed, if the logic implicit in the experience of literacy were to authenticate semiotic processes characteristic of the civilization of illiteracy, the *Error* message of corruption would overrun the monitor. All that occurs in the experience of networking and all that defines virtuality pertain to a logical framework that is by no means a memetic replication of the Aristotelian or some other logical system intrinsic to the experience of literacy. Memes residing in the brain's neuronal structure, as a pattern of pits on a CD-ROM, or in an HTML (hypertext markup language) Web format can be replicated. Interactions among minds correspond to a different dynamic realm, the realm of their reciprocal identification.

BOOK III.

BOOK III.

CHAPTER 1: LANGUAGE AS MEDIATING MECHANISM

Mention the word *mediation* today, or post it on the Internet. Swarms of lawyers will come after you. From the many meanings *mediation* has acquired over time, *dispute resolution* is the practical activity that has appropriated the word. Nevertheless, in its etymology, mediation attests to experiences that pre-date lawyers as they pre-date the earliest attempt to introduce laws.

Mediation, along with heuristics, is definitory of the human species. From all we know, nature is a realm of action and reaction. The realm of human activity implies a third element, an *in-between*, be this a tool, a word, a plan. This applies to primitive experiences of self-constitution, as well as to current embedded mediating activities: mediation of mediation *ad infinitum*. In each mediation there is the potential for further mediation. That is, the inserted third can be divided in turn. A lever used to move a very heavy object can be supplemented by another one, or two or more, all applied to the task at hand. Each tool can progressively evolve into a series of tools. Each individual called upon to mediate can call upon others to perform a chain of related or unrelated mediations.

The same holds true for signs and language. Mediation is the practical experience of reducing to manageable size a task that is beyond the abilities of an individual or individuals identified through the task. Mediation is a mapping from a higher scale of complexity to a scale that the persons involved in a task can handle. This chapter will examine various phases of mediated human experiences. We shall examine at which pragmatic junctures language and, subsequently, literacy provide mediating functions. More important, we will define the conditions that require mediations for which literacy is no longer adequate.

Since tools, in their mediating function, will be frequently brought into the argument, a distinction needs to be made from the outset: Signs, language, artificial languages, and programs (for computers and other devices) are all mediating entities. What distinguishes these from tools is their caoability for self-replication. They are, as much as humans constituting their identity in semiotic processes, subject to evolutionary cycles structurally similar to those of nature. Their evolution is, as we know, much faster than genetic evolution. The genetic make-up of the human species has changed relatively little, while the mediating elements that substantially contributed to the increase in human efficiency underwent many transformations. Some of these are no longer evolutionary, but revolutionary, and mark discontinuities. Genetic continuity is a background for pragmatic discontinuity. The moments of discontinuity correspond to threshold values in the scale of human activity. They regard mediating devices and strategies as dynamic components of the pragmatic framework.

THE POWER OF INSERTION

Self-constitution in mediating and mediated practical experiences is different from self-constitution in direct forms of praxis. In direct praxis, the *wholeness* of the being is externalized. But it is the *partial* being—partial in respect to the human's biological and intellectual reality—that is projected in mediated practical experiences. The narrow, limited, and immediate scope of direct human activity explains why no mediation, or only accidental mediation (unintended mediation), characterizes the pragmatic framework. In the long run, mediation results in the severed relation between individuals and their social and natural environments. As we shall see, this fact has implications for literacy. A long chain of mediations separates the working individual from the object to be worked upon, be this object raw material, processed goods, thoughts, or other experiences.

It is not easy to immediately realize the pervasiveness of mediation and its effects on human activity and self-constitution. People introduce all the intermediaries they need in order to maintain efficiency. Because we notice only the immediate layer with which we come into contact—the tool we use or the object we act upon—we have difficulty in recognizing the pervasiveness of mediation. The multitude of intermediaries involved in fabricating one finished product is far beyond our direct involvement.

Division, in the context of labor, means to break a task into smaller parts that are easier to rationalize, understand, and execute. Division engenders the specialization of each mediating element. To specialize means to be involved in practical experiences through which skills and knowledge pertinent to activity segmented through labor division are acquired. Whether division of physical work or of intellectual activity, at the end of the process there is a large number of components which have to be assembled. Even more important, the quantity of pieces, the order in which various pieces come together, and the intermediary sequences of checks and balances (if something does not work, it is better to find out before the entire product is assembled) are essential. All these constitute the *integration* aspect, which requires the element of coordination through tools and methods.

The segmentation of work in order to reach higher efficiency is not arbitrary. The goal is to arrive at coherent units of simpler work, which in some ways are like the letters of an alphabet. In this model, production resembles writing different words by combining available letters. Segmentation of work takes place concomitant with the effort to conceive of tools appropriate to each segment in order to ensure the desired efficiency. In effect, to specialize means to be aware of and to master tools that correspond to a step in the sequence leading to the desired result—the final word, in keeping with our example. Conversely, what sometimes looks like excessive specialization in our day—e.g., in medicine, physics, mathematics, electronics, computer science, transportation—is the result of the propensity of each mediating element to engender a need for further mediations, which reflect expectations for efficiency. Simultaneously with the differentiation of work, language changed, becoming itself more differentiated.

The efficiency reached in specialization is higher than that of direct action and of low levels of labor division. With each new specialization of a mediating element, humans constitute a body of practical knowledge, in the form of experience, that can be used again and again. This body of knowledge reflects the complexity of the task and the scale in which it is exercised. For instance, stones (the Latin *calcula)* were used to represent quantities (just as the early English used *stone* as a measure of weight). Over the centuries, this practice led to the body of knowledge known as *calculus* and to coherent applications in various human endeavors. The physical presence of stones gave way to easier methods of calculation: the abacus, as well as to marks recorded on bone, shell, leather, and paper, to a number system, and to symbols for numbers. The vector of change starts at the materiality and heads towards the abstract—that is, from objects to signs.

Computers were invented as a tool for calculation, as well as for other activities. They are the result of the labor of philosophers, logicians, mathematicians, and finally technologists, who changed calculation from a physical to a cognitive practical experience. Boolean logic, binary numbers, and electronic gates are mediating elements that enhance the effectiveness of calculation by high orders of magnitude. As things stand today, computer technology has led to myriad specialties: design and production of chips; information processing at various levels; manufacture of components and their integration as machines; networking; visualization techniques; the creation of machine languages for rendering the illiterate input, and on and on. This development exemplifies the active character of each mediation, especially the open-endedness of the mediation process.

As an insertion, mediation proves powerful also in terms of the cognitive awareness it stimulates. Through mediating elements, such as signs, language, tools, and even ideas, the individual gets a different perspective on the practical experience. The distance introduced through mediation, between actions and results, is one of space—the lever, not the hand, touches the stone to be moved—and duration—the time it takes to execute an action. With each inserted third, i.e., with each mediation, seeds are planted for what will eventually result in a totally new category of practical experiences: the conception of plans. The power of insertion is actually that of acquiring a sense and a direction for the future.

MYTH AS MEDIATING PRE-TEXT

Among the mediating elements mentioned so far, language performs its role in a particular way. Tools (such as pulleys, levers, gears, etc.) extend the arms or the legs, that is, the human body; language extends the coordinating capability of humans. Words, no matter how well articulated, will not turn the stone or lift the trunk of the fallen tree. They can be used to describe the problem, to enlist help, to discuss how the task can be accomplished, to render intelligible the sequence of accomplishing it. Once writing was developed, coordination was extended to apply from those physically present to people who could read, or to whom a text could be read if one did not have reading skills.

Language is in extension and succession of the pragmatic phase of immediate and direct appropriation of objects. As Leonard Bloomfield—probably a bit hasty in his generalization—observed, "...the division of labor (...) is due to language." Although different in nature from physical tools, language is instrumental: It is applied on something and embodies characteristics of human beings constituted in a practical experience that made language possible and necessary.

The mediating nature of early words and early articulated thoughts derived from their practical condition: medium for self-constitution (the voice externalizes the anatomy pertinent to producing and hearing sounds), and medium of exchange of experience (pertinent to nature or to others in the group). Early words are a record of the self-awareness of the human, denoting body parts and elementary actions. They also reflect the relational nature of the practical experience of those constituting viable groups. Researchers infer this from words, identified in proto-languages, that point to an *other*, or to coalitions, or to danger. What distinguished words from animal sounds was their coherence in extending the practical experience of appropriating a uniform survival strategy.

Cave paintings, always regarded as a sequence of animal representations, constitute what can be called a coherent image of a small universe of human life. They are an inventory of a sort—of fauna as opposed to humans, and as a reference to animals different from humans—and a statement regarding the importance of each kind of animal to human beings. By relating animals and drawings of *man* and *woman,* they also show that there is a third element to be considered: incipient implied symbolism. This is not to say that we have language, even less a visual language, articulated in the Paleolithic. But at Lascaux, Niaux, Altamira, and at the caves in northern China, in images preserved in the caves along the Lena River in Russia, there are some patterns, such as the co-presence of bison and horses, and the hinted association with male and female, for example, which show that the visual can go beyond the immediate and suggest a frame of work with mytho-magical elements.

Indeed, myths are singular mediating entities. They convey experience and preserve it in oral societies. Magic is also a mediating element, metaphysical in nature. Magic, in the pre-literacy context, inserts, between humans and everything they cannot understand, control, or tame, something (actions, words, objects) that stands for

Civilization of Illiteracy: Book III

the practical implications of this failure. An amulet, for example, stands for the lack of understanding of what it takes to be protected from evil forces. Spells and gestures intended to scare away demons belong to the same phenomenon. Though not without purpose, magic is action with no *immediate* practical purpose, triggered by events language could not account for. Myth is a *pre-text* for action with a practical, experiential purpose. Each myth contains rules for successful activity.

The context in which language, as a complex sign system, was structured was also the context of social mediation: division of social functions and integration in a cohesive social structure. In syncretic forms of social life, with low efficiency, and limited self-consciousness, there is little need for or possibility of mediation. Once human nature was constituted in the reality of practical, mytho-magical relations, both labor division and mediation became part of the new human experience. Tools for plowing, processing skins, and sharing experience (in visual or verbal form) kept the human subject close to the object of work or human relation. It is probably more in respect to the unknown and unpredictable that mediation, via priests and shamans in various rituals, was used in forms of magical practice. Cave paintings, no less than cuneiform, and later phonetic writing, constituted intermediaries inserted in the world in which human beings asserted their presence or questioned the presence of others.

The centralized state, which is a late form of social organization, the church, and schools are all expressions of the same need to introduce in a world of differences elements with uniformizing and integrating power. What we today call *politics* simply belongs to the self-constitution of the individual as member of the *politeia,* the community. By extension, politics means to effectively participate in the life of the community. The nature of this participation changed enormously over time. It started as participation in magic and ritual, and it evolved in participation in symbolic forms, such as *mancipatio,* conventions embodied in *normative* acts. In the framework of participation, we can mention goal determination and forms of organization and representation, as well as the payment of taxes to support the mediators of this activity. At the beginning, participation was an issue of survival; and survival, of natural condition, remained the unwritten rule of social life for a very long time. While in oral language there is no mediating element to preserve the *good* and the *right*, in written language, law mediates and *justice*, as much as *God* (actually a plurality of gods and goddesses) or *wisdom*, are inserted in community affairs.

DIFFERENTIATION AND COORDINATION

Mediation also implies breaking the immediate connection, to escape the domination of the present—shared time and space—and to discover relations characteristic of adjacency, i.e., neighboring in time and space. Adjacency can be in respect to the past, as expressed through the practice of keeping burial records. It can also be in respect to the future. The magic dimension of the ritual focused on desired things—weather, game, children—exemplifies this aspect. The notion of adjacency can pertain also to neighboring territories, inhabited by others involved in similar or slightly different practical forms of experience. Regardless of the type of adjacency, what is significant is the element that separates the immediate from the mediated. The expanding horizon of life required means to assimilate adjacency in the experience of continuous human self-constitution. Language was among such means and became even more effective when a medium for storing and disseminating—writing—was established. In orality-dominated social life, *opinion* was the product of language activity, and it had to be immediate. In writing, *truth* was sought and preserved. Accordingly, logic centered around the true-false distinction.

Literate societies are societies which accept the value of speaking, writing, and reading, and which operate under the assumption that literacy can accomplish a unifying function. Mediation and the associated strategy of integration relied on language for differentiation of tasks and for coordination of resulting activities and products. Language projects both a sense of *belonging* to and *living* in a context of life. It embodies characteristics of the individuals sharing perceptions of space and time integrated in their practical experiences and expressed in vocabulary, grammar, and idioms, and in the logic that language houses.

Language is simultaneously a medium of uniformity and a means of differentiation. Within continuously constituted language, individual expression and various non-standard uses of language (literary and poetic, probably the most notorious of these) are a fact of life. In the practical constitution of language for religious or judicial purposes, or in order to give historic accounts of scientific phenomena, expression is not uniform. Neither is interpretation. As we know from early attempts at history, there is little difference between languages used to describe relations of ownership (of animals, land, shelter) and texts on astronomy or navigation, for instance. The lunar calendar and the practical experience of navigation determined the coherence of writings on the subject. There is very little difference in the work of people who accounted for numbers of animals and numbers of stars. Once differentiation of work took place, language allowed for expressions of differences. Behind this change of language is the change of the people involved in various aspects of social life, i.e., their projection into a world appropriated through practical experiences based on the human ability to differentiate—between useful and harmful, pleasant and unpleasant, similar and dissimilar.

In order to distinguish the level at which a language is practiced, people become aware of language's practical consequences, of its pragmatic context. Plato's dialogues can be read as poetry, as philosophy, or as testimony to the state of language-based practical experiences in use at the time and place in which he was active. What is not clear is how a person operating in and constituting himself in the language identifies the level of an oral or written text, and how the person interprets it according to the context in which it was written. The question is of more than marginal importance to our understanding of how Plato related to language or how people today relate to language: either by overstating its importance or by ignoring it to the extent of consciously discarding language, or certain aspects of it.

Here is where the issue of mediation becomes critical. The inserted third—person, text, image, theory—should *understand* both the language of the reader and the language of the text. More generally, the third should at any instance understand the language of the entities it mediates between. States, as political entities, are constituted on this assumption; so are legal systems, religion, and education. Each such mediating entity introduces elements into the social structure that will finally be expressed in language and assimilated as accepted value. They will become the norm. The process is sometimes extremely tight. Retroaction from mediating function to language and back to action entails progressive fine-tuning, never-ending in fact, since human beings are in continuous biological and social change.

Mediations lead to segmentation. The coordination of mediations is necessary in order to recover the integrality (wholeness) of the human being in the output of the practical experience. Mediations, although coordinated by language or other mediating means, and subject to integration in the outcome of activity, introduce elements of tension, which in turn require new mediation and thus progressive specialization. When the sequence of mediations expands, the complexity of integration can easily exceed the degree of complexity of the initial task. The efficiency reached is higher than that of direct action or of low levels of labor division. With each new mediation, the human being constitutes a body of practical knowledge that can be used again and again. The necessary integrative dimension of mediations makes the strategy of using mediating entities, along with the appropriate coordination mechanism, socially relevant and economically rewarding. One can speak of mediation between rational and emotional aspects of human life, between thought and language, language and images, thought and means of expression, communication and signification. Regardless of its particular aspect, mediation is an experience of cognitive leverage.

INTEGRATION AND COORDINATION REVISITED

From the entire subject of mediation, two questions seem more relevant to our understanding of literacy and of its dynamics:
1. Why, at a certain moment in human evolution, does literacy become the main mediating instrument?
2. Under which circumstances is language's mediating function assumed by other sign systems?

Let us answer the questions in the order they are posed.

Language is not the only mediating instrument people use. In the short account given so far, other mediating entities, such as images, movements, odors, gestures, objects (stones, twigs, bones, artifacts) were mentioned. Also mentioned was the fact that these are quite close to what they actually refer to (as indexical signs), or to what they depict based on a relation of similarity (as iconic signs). However, even at this level of reduced generality and limited coherence and consistency, human beings can express themselves beyond the immediate and direct.

The cave paintings of the Paleolithic age should be mentioned again in this respect. The *immediate* is the cave itself. It is shelter, and its physical characteristics are perceived in direct relation to its function. The surprise comes in noticing how these characteristics become part of the practical experience of sharing what is not present by involving a mediating element. The drawings are *completions, continuations, extensions* of the ridges of the stone walls of the cave. This is not a way of speaking. A better quality photograph, not to mention the actual drawings in the caves, reveals how the lines of the relief are extended into the drawing and made part of them. The first layer of exchange of information among people is comparison, focused on similarities, then on differences. We infer from here that, before drawing—a practical experience involving a major cognitive step—the human beings seeking shelter in the cave noticed how a certain natural configuration—cloud, plant, rock formation, the trail left by erosion—looked like the head or tail of an animal, or like the human head, for example.

The completion of this look-alike form—when such a completion was physically possible—was an instance of practical self-definition and of shared experience. When the act of completion was physically performed, probably by accident at the beginning, the immediate natural (the cave) was appropriated for a new function, something other than merely shelter. The shape of the wings of galleries in the Altamira or Niaux caves suggests analogies to the male-female distinction, a sexual identifier but also a first step towards distinctions based on perceived differences. The selection of a certain cave from among others was the result of an effort, no matter how primitive, to *express.* Together, this selected physical structure and the added elements became a *statement* regarding a very limited universe of existence and its shared distinctions. Further on, the animals depicted, the sequence, the addition of mytho-magical signs (identification of more general notions such as hand, wound, or different animals) make the painted cave an expression of an inserted thought about the *world,* that is, about the limited environment constituting the world. In the case of Egyptian pictographic writing, we know that images were used as mediating devices in such sophisticated instances as the burial of pharaohs and in their life after death. In the universe of ideographic languages (such as Chinese and Japanese), the mediating function of images constituting the written is different. Combinations of ideograms constitute new ideograms. Accordingly, self-constitution in language takes over experiences of combining different things in order to obtain something different from each of the combined ingredients. In some ways, the added efficiency facilitated by mediations was augmented by formal qualities that would eventually establish the realm of aesthetic practical experiences. This should come as no surprise, since we know from many practical experiences or the remote past that formal qualities often translate into higher functionality.

Language use, which opened access to generality and abstraction, allowed humans to insert elements supporting an optimized exchange of information in the structure of social relations, and to participate in the conventions of social life. There is not only the trace of the immediate experience in a word, there is also the shared convention of mediated interactions. Language, in its development over time, is thus a very difficult-to-decode dynamic history of common praxis. We understand this from the way the use of the ax, millstone, or animal sacrifice expanded, along with the appropriate vocabulary and linguistic expression, from the universe of the Semites to the Indo-Europeans. Reconstructed vocabulary from the region of the Hittite kingdom testifies to the landscape (there are many words for mountains), to trees (the Hittites distinguished various species), to animals (leopard, lion, monkey), and to tools (wheel-based means of transportation).

Language is not only a reflection of the past, but also a program for future work. The nuclei of agriculture where language emerged (in China, Africa, southeastern Europe) were also centers of dissemination of practical experience. Writing, even when it only records the past, does it for the future. Progress in writing resulted in better histories, but moreover in new avenues for future praxis. In the ideal of literacy, the individual states a program of unifying scope in a social reality of diverse means and diverse goals. Literacy as such is an insertion between a rather complex social structure, nature, and among the members of society. Within a culture, it is a generic code which facilitates dialogue among the members of the literate community and among communities of different languages. Its scope is multidimensional. Its condition is one of mediation.

A major mediating element in the rationale of industrial society, literacy fulfilled the function of a coordinating mechanism for mediations made otherwise than through language, along the assembly line, for instance. Obviously conceived on the linear, sequential model of time and language, the assembly line optimally embodied requirements characteristic of complex integration. Once the reductionist practice of dividing work into smaller, specialized activities became necessary, the results of these activities had to be integrated in the final product. At the level of technology of industrial society, literacy-based human practical experiences of self-constitution defined the scope and character of labor division, specialization, integration, and coordination.

LIFE AFTER LITERACY

The answer to the second question posed a few pages back is not an exercise in prophecy. (I'll leave that to the priests of futurology.) This is why the question concerns *circumstances* under which the dominant mediating function of language can be assumed by other sign systems. The discussion involves a *moving target* because today the notion of literacy is a changing representation of expectations and requirements. We know that there is a *before* to literacy; and this *before* pertains to mediations closer to the natural human condition. Of course, we can, and should, ask whether there is an *after,* and what its characteristics might be. Complexities of human activity and the need to ensure higher efficiency explain, at least partially, complexities of interhuman relations and the need to ensure some form of human integration.

What this first assessment somehow misses is the fact that, from a certain moment on, mediation becomes an activity in itself. Means become an end in themselves. When individuals constituted themselves in structurally very similar experiences, mediation took place through the insertion of rather homogeneous objects, such as arrows, bows, levers, and tools for cutting and piercing. Interaction was a matter of co-presence. Language resulted in the context of diversification of practical human experiences. Self-constitution in language captured the permanence and the perspective of the whole into which variously mediated components usually come together. Later on, literacy freed humans from the requirement of co-presence. Language's mediating capabilities relied on space and time conventions built into language experience over a very long time and interiorized by literate societies.

Characteristics of writing specific to different notational systems resulted from characteristics of practical experiences. Literacy only indirectly reflects the encoding of experience in a medium of expression and communication. Moreover, the shift from a literacy-dominated civilization to one of partial literacies involves the encoding of the experience in media that are no longer appropriate for literate expression. We *write* to tape or to digital storage. We publish on networks. We convert texts into machine-readable formats. We edit in non-linear fashion. We operate on configurations or on mixed data types (that constitute multimedia). Experiences encoded in such media reflect their own characteristics in what is expressed and how it is expressed.

Although there are vast qualitative differences in linguistic performance within a literate society, a common denominator—the language reified in the *technology of literacy*—is established. The expectation is a minimum of competence, supposed to meet integration requirements at the workplace, the understanding of religion, politics, literature, and the ability to communicate and comprehend communication. But as literacy became a socially desirable characteristic, language became a tool—at least in some professions and trades—and the command of language became a marketable skill. For example, during periods of greater political activity in classical Greece and Rome, the practical experience of rhetoric was a discipline in itself. Orators, skilled in persuasion, for which language is necessary, made a career out of language use. The written texts of the Middle Ages were also intended to foster the rhetorical skills of the clergy in presenting arguments. In our time, speechwriters and ghostwriters have become the language professionals, and so have priests, prophets, and evangelists (of all *religions*).

But what is only an example of how language can become an end in itself has become a very significant development in human praxis. Not only in professions such as expository writing (for journalists, essayists, politicians, and scientists), poetry, fiction, dramaturgy, communications, but also in the practice of law (normative, enforcement, judicial), politics, economics, sociology, and psychology has language become a principal tool. Nevertheless, the language used in such endeavors is not the standard, national, or regional language, but a specialized subset, marginally understood by the literate population at large. While the grammar governing such sub-languages is, with some exceptions, the grammar of the language from which they are derived, the vocabulary is more appropriate to the subject matter. Moreover, while sharing language conventions and the general frame of language, these sub-languages project an experience so particular that it cannot be properly understood and interpreted without some *translation and commentary*. And each commentary (on a law, a new scientific theory, a work of art or poetry) is yet another insertion of a *third*, which refers to the initial object sometimes so indirectly that the relation might be difficult to track and the meaning is lost.

A similar process can be identified in our present relation to the physical environment. Many things mediate between us and the natural environment: our homes, clothes, the food processing industry. Even *natural* artifacts, such as gardens, lakes, or water channels, are a buffer against nature, an insertion between us and nature. Constituted in our language are experiences of survival and adaptation: the vocabulary of hunting, fishing, agriculture, animal husbandry, coping with changes in weather and climate, and coping with natural catastrophes such as floods and earthquakes. The mediating function of language is different here than on the production line.

Mediated practice leads to distributed knowledge along successive or parallel mediations that are not at all literacy-based or literacy-dependent. Within the global scale of human experience, it makes sense to use a global perspective (of resources, factors affecting agriculture, navigation, etc.) in order to maximize locally distributed efforts. For example: people involved in various activities must rely on persons specialized to infer from observation (of plants, trees, animals, water levels in rivers and lakes, wind direction, changes in the earth's surface, biological, chemical, atmospheric factors) and generate predictions regarding natural events (drought, plant or animal disease, floods, weather patterns, earthquakes). What we acknowledge here is the new scale of the practical experience of meteorology, as well as methods of collecting and distributing information through vast networks of radio, television, and weather services. Both the means for acquiring the information and for disseminating it are visual. Local networks subscribe to the service and receive computer-generated maps on which clouds, rain, or snow are graphically depicted. The equations of weather forecasting are obviously different from local observations of wind direction, precipitation, dew point, etc. The chaotic component captured and the necessity to visually display information as it changes over time are not reducible to equations or direct observation. It is hard to imagine having weather predicted through very mediated meteorological practice, and even harder to imagine forecasting earthquakes or volcanic activity from remote stations, such as satellites. Still, weather patterns display dynamic characteristics that made the metaphor of the butterfly causing a hurricane the most descriptive explanation of how small changes—caused by the flapping of the butterfly's wings—can result in impressive consequences—the hurricane. The language of the forecast only *translates* into *common* language the data (the majority in visual form) that represents our new understanding of natural phenomena.

There is yet another aspect, which is related to the status of knowledge and our ways of acquiring, transmitting, and testing it. Our knowledge of phenomena such as nuclear fusion, thermonuclear reaction, stellar explosions, genes and genetic codes, and complex dynamic systems is no longer predominantly based on inductions from observed facts to theories explaining such facts. It seems that we project theories, founded on abstract thinking, onto physical reality and turn these theories into means of adapting the world to our goals or needs, which are much more complex than survival. Memetics is but the more recent example in this respect. It projects the abstract models of natural evolution into culture, focusing on replicative processes for the production of phenomena such as ideas, behavioral rules, ways of thinking, beliefs, and norms. Mediation probably qualifies for a memetic approach, too. Theories require a medium of expression, and this is represented by new languages, such as mathematical and logical formalisms, chemical notation, computer graphics, or discourse in some pseudo-language. The formalism of memetics reminds many of us of formal languages, as well as of the shorthand used in genetics. The goal is to describe whatever we want to describe through computational functions or through computable expressions.

Since experiential space and time are *housed* in our language, we can account for only a three-dimensional space and a homogeneous time that has only one direction—from past to future. Nevertheless, we can conceive of multidimensional spaces and of non-homogeneous time. To describe the same in language, especially through literate expression, is not only inadequate, but also raises obstacles. With the advent of digital technology, a language of two letters—zero and one—and the *grammar* of Boolean logic, we have stepped into a new age of language, no longer the exclusive domain of the human being. Such a language introduces new levels of mediation, which allow for the use of machines by means of *sentences,* i.e., sequences of encoded commands triggered by a *text* written in a language other than natural language. Physical contact is substituted by language, inserted in processes of complexity impossible to control directly or even to relate to in forms characteristic of previous scientific and technological praxis.

Indeed, there are instances when the speed of a process and the requirement of sequencing make direct human control not only impossible, but also undesirable. This mediation is then continued by sequences automatically generated by machines, i.e., mediation generating new mediation. Although the structure of all these new languages (which describe phenomena, support programming, or control processes) is inspired by the structure of natural language, they project experiences which are not possible in the universe of standard language. New forms of interaction, higher speeds, and higher precision become available when such powerful cognitive tools are designed as custom-made instruments for advancing our understanding of phenomena that evade analytic or even small-scale synthetic frameworks.

The discussion of mediation brought up other sign systems that assume the mediating function characteristic of literacy. Not only artificial languages—instruments of knowledge and action, new pragmatic dimensions, in fact—but also natural languages are increasingly used in a mediating capacity. I would submit to the reader the observation that the visual, primarily, and other sensory information are recuperated and used in ways that change human experience. Where words no longer suffice, visualized images of the unseen constitute a mediating language, allowing us to understand phenomena otherwise inaccessible—the micro- or remote universe, for instance. Touch, smell, and sound can be articulated and introduced as *statements* in a series of events for which written and spoken language are no longer adequate. Virtual reality is synthesized as a valid simulation of *real* reality. Virtual realities can be experienced if we simply put on body-sensitive gloves, headgear (goggles and earphones), special footwear, or a whole suit. Powerful computer graphics, with a refresh rate high enough to maintain the illusion of space and motion, make a virtual space available. Within this space, one's own image can become a partner of dialogue or confrontation. Journeys *outside* one's body and *inside* one's imagination are experienced not only in advanced laboratories, but also in the new entertainment centers that appeal to children as well as adults. Such projections of oneself into something else represent one of the most intriguing forms of interaction in the networked world. The experience of self-constitution as an avatar on the Internet is no longer one of a unique self, but of multiples.

Language guards the entrance to the experience, but once the human subject is inside, it has only limited power or significance. Mediations other than through language dominate here, invoking all our senses and deep levels of our existence, for which literacy produced only psychoanalytic rhetoric. In other words, we notice that while language constituted a projection of the human being in the conventions of abstract systems of expression, representation, and communication, it also exercised an impoverishing function in that it excluded the wealth of senses—possibly including common sense—and the signs addressing them. Language made of us one monolithic entity. In the meantime, we have come to realize that the transitions between our many inner states can be a source of new experiences.

The answer to the question regarding alternatives to literacy is that part of the mediating function of language has extended to specialized languages, and to sign systems other than verbal language, when those systems are better adapted to the complexities of heretofore unencountered challenges. Virtual reality is not a linear reality but an integrating, interacting reality of non-linear relations between what we do and what results. Among these newly acquired, different mediating entities, relations and interdependencies are continuously established and changed at an ever faster pace. It appears that once human activity moves from the predominantly object level to the *meta* condition (one of self-awareness and self-interpretation), we have several languages and several contingent literacies instead of a dominant language and dominant literacy. When writing is replaced by multimedia along the communication channels of the networked world, we seem to enjoy rediscovering ourselves as much richer entities than we knew or were told about through literate mediation.

The entire transition is the result of pragmatic needs resulting from the fundamental change in continuous human self-constitution and the scale in which it is exercised. Mediations break activities into segments that are more intensive and shorter than the cycle from which they were extracted. Therefore, mediation results in the perception of the reality of faster rhythms and of time contraction. Massive distribution of tasks, finer levels of parallelism, and more sophisticated integrating and coordinating mechanisms, result in new pragmatic possibilities, for which literacy is not suitable, and even counter-productive. This entire transition comprises another vector of change: from individual to communal survival, from direct work to highly mediated praxes, from local to global to universal, from the visible to the invisible of macro and micro-universe, from the real to the virtual. Mediation, in its newest digital forms of enmeshed nature and evolving culture, causes boundaries to disappear between the elements involved in practical experiences of our self-constitution.

CHAPTER 2: LITERACY, LANGUAGE AND MARKET

Markets are mediating *machines*. In our time, the notion of a machine is very different from that of the industrial Machine Age associated with the pragmatics of the civilization of literacy. Today, the term *machine* is evocative of software rather than hardware. *Machine* comprises input and output, process, control mechanisms, and the expectation of predictable functioning. Here is where our difficulties start. At best, markets appear as erratic to us. *Market prediction* seems to be an oxymoron. Every time experts come up with a formula, the market acts in a totally new manner.

An amazing number of transactions, ranging from bargaining at a garage sale to multi-prong deals in derivatives, continuously subject the outcome of practical experiences of human self-constitution to the test of market efficiency. There is nothing that can escape this test: ideas, products, individuals, art, sports, entertainment. Like a tadpole, the market seems to consume itself in transactions. At times, they appear so esoteric to us that we cannot even fathom what the input of this machine is and what the output. But we all expect the charming prince to emerge from the ugly frog!

What can be said, without giving away the end of the story too early, is that the functioning of this growing mechanism of human self-evaluation could never take place at its current dynamics and size in the pragmatic framework of literacy. All over the world, market processes associated with previous pragmatic frameworks—barter is one of them—are relived in bazaars and shopping malls. But if anyone wants to see practical experiences of the civilization of illiteracy unfolding in their quasi-pure manner, one has only to look at the stock market and commodities exchanges and auctions conducted over the Internet. Moreover, one must try to envision those invisible, distributed, networked transactions in which it is impossible to define who initiated a transaction, continued another one, or brought a deal to an end, and based on what criteria. They, too, seem to have a life of their own.

Mediating machine also evokes the notion of machine as program. Although some stockbrokers have second thoughts about how their role is diminished through the mediation of entities that cannot speak or write, programmed trading on the various stock exchanges is a matter of course. Computational economists and market researchers, who design programs based on biological analogies, genetics, and dynamic system models, can testify to the truth of this statement.

PRELIMINARIES

In viewing the market in its relation to the civilization of literacy, and that of illiteracy, we must first establish a conceptual frame of reference for discussing the specific role of language as a mediating element characteristic of the market. In particular, we should examine the functions filled by literacy in allowing people to diversify markets and make them more effective. When the limits of literacy's mediating capabilities are reached, its efficiency becomes subject to doubt. This does not happen outside the market, as some scholars, educators, and politicians would have us believe, or want to happen. It is within the market that this stage is acknowledged, rendering intellectual travail itself a product negotiated in the market, as literacy itself already is.

To establish the desired conceptual frame of reference, I take the perspective of market as a sign process through which people constitute themselves. Consequently, transactions can be seen as extensions of human biology: products of our work embody the structural characteristics of our natural endowment and address needs and expectations pertinent to these characteristics. These products are extensions of our personality and our culture, as constituted in expectations and values characteristic of the human species becoming self-aware and defining goals for the future. With language, and more so with literacy, markets become interpretive affairs, *projective instantiations of what we are*, in the process of becoming what we must be as the human scale reaches yet another threshold. Human self-constitution through markets reflects attained levels of productive and creative power, as well as goals pertinent initially to survival, later to levels of well-being, and now to the complexity of the global scale of current and future human activity.

From barter to the trading of commodities futures and stock options, from money to the cashless society, markets constitute frameworks for higher transaction efficiency, often equated with profit. The broad arguments, such as the market as semiosis, often stumble upon specific aspects: Semiosis or not, practical experience or not, how come a rumor sends a company's stock into turmoil while an audited report goes unnoticed? The hidden structure of the processes discussed throughout this book might have more to do with explanations and predictive models than the many clarifications empowered by academic aura.

PRODUCTS 'R' US

The reality of the human being as sign-using animal (*zoon semiotikon*) corresponds to the fact that we project our individual reality into the reality of our existence through semiotic means. In the market, the three entities of sign processes meet: that which represents (*representamen*), that which is represented (*object*), and the process of interpretation (*interpretant*). These terms can be defined in the market context. The *representamen* is the repertory of signs that are identified in the market. These can be utility (usefulness of a certain product), rarity, quantity, type of material used to process the merchandise, imagination applied to the conception and creation of a product, and the technology used and the energy consumed in the manufacturing process, for example. People can be attracted by the most unexpected characteristics of merchandise, and can be enticed to develop *addictions* to color, form, brand name, odor. Sometimes the representamen is price, which is supposed to reflect the elements listed above, as well as other pricing criteria: a trend, a product's *sexiness;* a buyer's gullibility, ego, or lack of economic sense. The price represents the product, although not always appropriately. The *object* is the product itself, be it a manufactured item, an idea, an action, a process, a business, or an index. Except for the market based on exchange of object for object, every known market object is represented by some of its characteristics. That these representations might be far removed from the object only goes to show how many mediating entities participate in the market.

Nothing is a sign unless interpreted as a sign. Someone has to be able to conjure, or endow, meaning and constitute something (an idea, object, or action) as part of one's self-constitution. This is the *interpretant*—understood as process, because interpretations can go on *ad infinitum*. For example: bread is food; an academic title acknowledges that a course of study was successfully completed; computers can be used as better typewriters or for data mining. As a sign, bread can stand for everything that it embodies: our daily bread; a certain culture of nourishment; the knowledge involved in cultivating and processing grain, in making dough, building the ovens, observing the baking process. Symbolic interpretation, relating to myth or religion, is also part of the interpretation of bread as a sign. Interpretation of an academic title follows a similar path: educational background (university attended, title conferred), context (there are streets on which mostly lawyers and doctors live), function (how the title affects one's activity), and future expectations (a prospective

Nobel Prize winner). Likewise with computers: *Intel inside,* or *Netscape* browser, networked or stand-alone, a *Big Blue* product, or one put together in the back alleys of some far Eastern country.

According to the premise that nothing is a sign unless considered as such, interpretation is equivalent to the constitution of human beings as the sign, *represented through their product.* A product is *read* as being useful; a product can be liked or disliked; a product can generate needs and expectations. Self-constituting individuals validate themselves (succeed or fail) through their activity as represented by the product of this activity, be it tangible or intangible, a concrete object, a process (mediations are included here), an idea. These *readings* are also part of the process of interpretation. A conglomerate of the *readings* mentioned above is the mug shot of the abstract consumer, behind whom are all the others who constitute their individuality through the transactions that make up the market. A used car or computer salesman, a small retailer, and a university professor identify themselves in different ways *in* and *through* the market. Each is represented by some characteristic feature of his or her work. Each is interpreted in the market as reliable, competent, or creative in view of the pragmatics of the transaction: Some people need a good used car, some a cheap, used computer, others a leather wallet, others an education or counsel. The forms of interpretation in the market are diverse and range from simple observation of the market to direct involvement in market mechanisms through products, exchange of goods, or legislation.

As a place where the three elements—what is marketed (object), language or signs of marketing (representamen), and interpretation (leading to a transaction or not)—come together, the market can be direct or mediated, real or symbolic, closed or open, free or regulated. A produce market, a supermarket, a factory outlet, and a shopping mall are examples of real market space. The market takes on mediated, conventional, and symbolic aspects in the case where, for example, the product is not displayed in its three-dimensional reality but substituted by an image, a description, or a promise. Mail-order houses, and the stock and futures markets belong here, even though they are derived from direct, real markets. Once upon a time, Wall Street was surrounded by various exchanges filled with the odors, tastes, and textures of the products brought in by ships. It is now a battery of machines and traders who read signs on order slips or computer screens but know nothing of the product that is traded.

In our day, the stock market has become a data processing center. Pressures caused by the demand for optimal market efficiency were behind this transformation. Nevertheless, the time involved in the new market semiosis is as real and necessary as the time of transactions in the market based on barter or on direct negotiations; that is, only the amount of time needed to ensure the cooperation of the three elements mentioned above, as human beings constitute themselves in the pragmatic context of the market. The pragmatic context affects market cycles and the speed at which market transactions take place. This is why a deal in a bazaar takes quite a bit of time, and digital transactions triggered by programmed trading are complete before anyone realizes their consequences. Market regulations always affect the dynamics of mediations.

THE LANGUAGE OF THE MARKET

Language signs and other signs are mediating devices between the object represented in the market and the interpretant—the human beings constituting themselves in the process of interpretation, including satisfaction of their needs and desires. No matter what type of market we refer to, it is *a place and time of mediations*. What defines each of the known markets (barter, farmers' markets and fairs, highly regulated markets, so-called free markets, underground markets) is the *type of mediation* more than the merchandise or the production process. Of significance is the dynamic structure involved. It is obvious that if anything anticipated our current experience of the market, it was the ritual.

Objects (things, money, ideas, process), the *language* used to express the object, and the *interpretation,* leading or not to a transaction, constitute the structural invariable in every type of socio-economic environment. In the so-called free market (more an abstraction than a reality) and in rigidly planned economies, the relation among the three elements is the variable, not the elements themselves. Interpretation in a given context can be influenced in the way associations are made between the merchandise and its representations.

The history of language is rich in testimony to commerce, from the very simple to the very complex forms of the latter. Language captures ownership characteristics, variations in exchange rates, the ever-expanding horizon of life facilitated through market transactions. It is within this framework that written records appear, thus justifying the idea that, together with practical experiences of human self-constitution, market processes characteristic of a limited scale of exchange of values are parents to notation, to writing and to literacy.

Expectations of efficiency are instantiated, within a given scale of human activity, in market quantities and qualities. Nobody really calculates whether rice production covers the needs of humankind at any given instance, or if enough entertainment is produced for the billions living on Earth today. The immense complexity of the market machine is reflected in its dynamics, which at a certain level of its evolution could no longer be handled by, or made subject to the rules and expectations of literacy. Market processes follow a pattern of self-organization under the guise of many parameters, some of which we can control, others that escape our direct influence upon them. Languages of extreme specialization are part of market dynamics in the sense that they offer practical contexts for new types of transactions. *Netconomy* started as a buzzword, joining *net, network,* and *economy.* In less than one year, the term was used to describe a distributed commercial environment where extremely efficient transactions make up an increasing part of the global economy. But the consequences of the Netconomy are also local: distribution channels can be eliminated, with the effect of accelerating commercial cycles and lowering prices. Computers, cars, software, and legal services are more frequently acquired through the virtual shops of the Netconomy.

To see how the practical experience of the market freed itself from language and literacy, let us now examine the market process as semiosis in its various aspects. As already stated, in trading products, people trade themselves. Various qualities of the product (color, smell, texture, style, design, etc.), as well as qualities of its presentation (advertising, packaging, vicinity to other products, etc.), and associated characteristics (prestige, ideology) are among the implicit components of this trade. Sometimes the object *per se*—a new dress, a tool, wine, a home—is less important than the image it projects. Secondary functions, such as aesthetics, pleasure, conformity, override the function of fulfilling needs. In market semiosis, desire proves to be just as important, if not more so, than need. In a large part of the world, self-constitution is no longer just a question of survival, but also one of pleasure. The higher the semiotic level of the market in a context of decadent plenty—the number of sign systems involved, their extent and variety—the more obvious the deviations from the rule of merely satisfying needs.

Human activity that aims at maintaining life is very different from the human activity that results in surplus and availability for market transaction. In the first case, a subsistence level is preserved; in the second, new levels of self-constitution are made possible. Surplus and exchange, initially made possible through the practical experience of agriculture, constituted a scale of human activity that required human constitution in signs, sign systems, and finally language. Surplus can be used in many ways, for which sign and later language differentiation became progressively necessary. Rituals, adornment, war, religion, means of accumulation, and means of persuasion are examples of differentiations. All these uses pertained to settled patterns of human interaction and led to products that were more than mere physical entities to be consumed. To repeat, they were projections of individual self-constitution.

Behind each product is a cycle of conception, manufacture, and trade, and an attached understanding of utility and permanence. With the advent of writing and reading, from its rudimentary forms to the forms celebrated in literacy, and its participation in the constitution of the market, the avenue was opened towards using what was produced in surplus to cover the need to maintain life, so that more surplus could be generated. The market of merchandise, services, slaves, and ideas was completed by the market of salaried workers, earning money for their life's salt, as Roman soldiers did. These belong to the category of human beings constituting themselves in the pragmatic framework of an activity in which production (work) and the means of production separated. The language through which workers constituted themselves underwent a similar differentiation. As work became more alienated from the product, a language of the product also came into being.

THE LANGUAGE OF PRODUCTS

Exchanging goods pertinent to survival corresponds to a scale of human praxis that guarantees coherence and homogeneity. People who have excess grain but need eggs, people who offer meat because they need fruit or tools, do not require instructions for using what they obtain in exchange for what they offer. *Small worlds,* loosely connected, constitute the universe of their existence. The rather slow rhythm of production cycles equals that of natural cycles. A relatively uniform lifestyle results from complementary practical experiences only slightly differentiated in structure. Together, these characteristics constitute a framework of direct sharing of experience. This market, as limited as it is, forms part of the social mechanism for sharing experience.

Today's markets, defined by a complexity of mediations, are no longer environments of common or shareable experience. Rather, they are frameworks of validation of one type of human experience against another. This statement requires some explanation. Products embody not only material, design, and skills, but also a language of optimal functioning. Thus they project a variety of ways through which people constitute themselves through the language of these products. Accordingly, the market becomes a place of transaction for the many *languages* our products *speak*. The complexity of everything we produce in the pragmatic framework of the civilization of illiteracy is the result of expectations made possible by levels of human efficiency that literacy can only marginally support.

This comes at a cost, in addition to the dissolution of literacy: the loss of a sense of quality, because each product carries with itself not only its own language, but also its own evaluation criteria. The product is one of many from which to choose, each embodying its own justification. Its value is relative, and sometimes no value at all dictates the urge to buy, or the decision to look for something else. Rules of grammar, which gave us a sense of order and quality of literate language use, do not apply to products. Previous expectations of morality were anchored in language and conveyed through means of literacy. The morality of partial literacies embodied in competing products no longer appears to participants in the market as emanating from high principles of religion or ethics, but rather as a convenient justification for political influence. Through regulation, politics inserts itself as a self-serving factor in market transactions.

TRANSACTION AND LITERACY

A visit to a small neighborhood store used to be primarily a way of satisfying a particular need, but also an instance of communication. Such small markets were spaces where members of the community exchanged news and gossip, usually with an accuracy that would put today's journalism to shame. The supermarket is a place where the demands of space utilization, fast movement of products, and low overhead make conversation counterproductive. Mail-order markets and electronic shopping practically do away with dialogue. They operate beyond the need for literacy and human interaction. Transactions are brought to a minimum: selection, confirmation, and providing a credit card number, or having it read automatically and validated via a networked service.

Literacy-based transactions involved all the characteristics of written language and all the implications of reading pertinent to the transaction. Literacy contributed to the diversification of needs and to a better expression of desires, thus helping markets to diversify and reach a level of efficiency not possible otherwise. With required education and laws prohibiting child labor, the productive part of people's lives was somehow reduced, but their ability to be more effective within modes adapted to literacy was enhanced. Thus market cycles were optimized by the effects of higher productivity and diversified demands. From earliest times (going back to the Phoenician traders), writing and the subsequent literacy contributed to strategies of exchange, of taxation—which represents the most direct form of political intervention in the market—and regulations regarding many aspects of the constitution of human beings in and through the market. Written contracts expressed expectations in anticipation of literacy-supported planning.

There are many levels between the extraction and processing of raw material and the final sale and consumption of a product. At each level, a different language is constituted, very concrete in some instances, very abstract in others. These languages are meant to speed up processing and transaction cycles, reduce risk, maximize profits, and ensure the effectiveness of the transaction on a global level. Literacy cannot uniformly accommodate these various expectations. The distributive nature of market transactions cannot be held captive to the centralism of literacy without affecting the efficiency of market mediation. The ruin left after 70 years of central planning in the Soviet Union and its satellite countries—highly literate societies—is proof of this point. The expected speed of market processes and the parallelism of negotiations require languages of optimal functionality and minimal ambiguity. Sometimes transactions have to rely on visual arguments, well beyond what teleconferencing can offer. Products and procedures are modified during negotiations, and on-the-fly, through interactive links between all parties involved in the effort of designing, manufacturing, and marketing them. As fashion shows become prohibitively expensive, the fashion market is exploring interactive presentations that put the talent of the designer and the desire of the public one click away from each other.

The expectation of freedom results in the need to ignore national or political (and cultural and religious) allegiances, which, after all, means freedom from the literate mode of a national language, as well as from all the representations and definitions of freedom housed in literate discourse. Indeed, since sign systems, and language in particular, are not neutral means of expression, one individual has to specialize in the signs of other cultures. There are consulting firms that advise businesses on the cultural practices of various countries. They deal in what Robert Reich called *symbol manipulation,* semiotic activity *par excellence.* These firms explain to clients doing business in Japan, for instance, that the Japanese have a penchant for exchanging gifts. Business cards, more symbolic than functional, are of great importance. These consultants will also advise on customs that fall outside values instilled through literacy, such as in which countries bribery is the most *efficient* way to do business.

WHOSE MARKET? WHOSE FREEDOM?

A market captive to moral or political concepts expressed in literate discourse soon reaches the limits of its efficiency. We face these limits in a different way when ideals are proclaimed or negotiations submitted to rules reflecting values attached to expectations—of a certain standard of living, fringe benefits—frozen in contracts and laws. Many European countries are undergoing the crisis of their literate heritage because outdated working relations have been codified in labor laws. Contracts between unions claiming to represent various types of workers are not subject to criteria for efficiency at work in the market.

On the other hand, the freedom and rights written into the U.S. Constitution are totally forgotten in the global marketplace by people who take them for granted. An American—even a member of a minority group—who buys a pair of brand-name sneakers is totally ignorant of the fact that the women, and sometimes the children, making those sneakers in faraway countries earn less than subsistence wages. It is not the market that is immoral or opportunistic in such cases, but the people who constitute their expectations for the most at the lowest cost. Would literacy be a stronger force than the demand for efficiency in bringing about the justice discussed in tomes of literature? To read morality in the market context of competition, where only efficiency and profit are written, is a rather futile exercise, even though it might alleviate pangs of conscience. Markets, the expression of the people who constitute them, are realistic, even cynical; they call things by their names and have no mercy on those who try to reinvent an idealized past in the transaction of futures.

For reasons of efficiency only, markets are frameworks for the self-constitution of human beings as free, enjoying liberties and rights that add to their productive capabilities. It will probably irk many people to read here that markets, instances of terrible tension and amorality, are the cradle of human freedom, tolerance (political, social, religious, intellectual), and creativity. To a great extent, it was a fight over market processes that led to the American Revolution. Now that Soviet-style communism has fallen, the flow of both goods and ideas is slowly and painfully taking place, in ways similar to that in the West, in the former Soviet Bloc. Democratic ideals and the upward distribution of wealth are on a collision course. But the compass is at least set on more freedom and less regulation. Only mainland China remains in the grip of centralized market control. The struggle between open markets and the free flow of ideas going on there today can have only one outcome. It may take time, but China, too, will one day be as free as its neighbors in Taiwan. Market inter-action is what defines human beings, facilitating the establishment of a framework of existence that includes others.

Some people would prefer a confirmation of culture as the more encompassing framework, containing markets but not reducible to them. Culture itself is an object in the market, subjected to transac-tions involving literacy, but not exclusively. Here new languages are used to expedite the exchange of goods and values. When literacy reaches the limits of its implicit capabilities, new transaction lan-guages emerge, and new forms of freedom, tolerance, and creativity are sanctioned through the market mechanism. There is a price attached here, too. New constraints, new types of intolerance, and new obstacles come about. An example is the preservation of wildlife at the expense of jobs. Efficiency and wide choice entail a replace-ment of what are known as traditional values (perceived as eternal, but usually not older than 200-300 years) with what many would have a hard time calling value: mediocrity, the transitory, the expedi-ent, and the propensity for waste.

The market circumvents literacy when literacy affects its efficien-cy and follows its own course by means appropriate to new market conditions. In the quest for understanding how markets operate, the further cultivation of explanations originating from previous prag-matic circumstances is pointless. The time-consuming detour might result in nostalgia, but not in better mastery of the complexities implicit in the practical experience of human self-constitution in the market.

NEW MARKETS, NEW LANGUAGES

With the descriptive model of markets as sign processes, allusion was made to the open character of any transaction. With the discussion regarding the many phases through which markets are constituted, allusion was made to the distributed nature of market processes. In order to further explain the changed condition of human self-constitution in the market of a radically new scale and dynamics, we need to add some details to both characteristics mentioned.

Like any other sign process, language processes are human processes. The person speaking or writing a text continues to constitute his identity in one or the other, while simultaneously anticipating the constitutive act of listening to or interpreting the potential or intended *readership*. Visual, auditory, tactile, olfactory, verbal, or written expression, as well as combinations of these, which composes the language of performance, dance, architecture, etc., are in the same condition. A viewer or viewers can associate an image with a text, music, odors, textures, or with combinations of these. Furthermore, the association can continue and can be conveyed to others who will extend it *ad infinitum,* sometimes so far that the *initial* sign (which is the *initial* person interpreting that sign in anticipation of the interpretation given by others), i.e., the image, text, or music that triggered the process, is forgotten.

Expanding this concept to the products of human activity, we can certainly look at various artifacts from the perspective of *what they express*—a need specifically fulfilled by a machine, a product, a type of food or clothing, an industry; *what they communicate*—the need shared by few or many, the way this need is addressed, what it says about those constituted in the product and those who will confirm their identity by using it, what it says about opportunity and risk taking; and *what they signify*—in terms of the level of knowledge and competence achieved.

This is not to say that the milk we buy from a farmer or in the supermarket, the shoes, cars, homes, vacation packages, and shares in a company or options in a stock are all signs or language. Rather, they can be interpreted as signs standing for an object (the state of manufacturing, quality of design, competence, or a combination of these) to be interpreted in view of the framework for the pragmatics of human self-constitution that the pragmatics makes possible. There are many instances when a word simply dies on the lips of the speaker because nobody listens or nobody cares to continue interpreting it. There are as many instances when a product dies because it is irrelevant to the pragmatic framework of our lives. There are other instances when signs lose the quality of interpretability.

A company that goes public is identified through many qualifiers. Its potential growth is one of them—this is why Internet-oriented companies were so highly valued in their initial public offerings. Potential can be conveyed through literate descriptions, data regarding patents, market analysis, or an intuitive element that there is more to this new market sign than only its name and initial offering price. At a small scale of human experience, the neighbors wanted to own some of the action; at a larger scale, literacy conveyed the information and acted as a co-guarantor. At today's scale, many similar businesses are already in place, others are emerging; supply and demand meet in the marketplace where one's risk can be someone else's gain. Literacy is no longer capable of providing the background for the dynamics of change and renewal. If literacy could still control market transactions, Netscape—synonymous with the Internet browser—would have never made it; nor the companies that develop software facilitating telephone calls via the Internet.

In the markets of relative homogeneity, language proved to be an appropriate means of coordination. For as long as the various contexts making up today's global market were not as radically different as they are becoming, literacy represented a good compromise. But when market transactions themselves shift from exchanging goods against goods, or the exchange of goods for some *universal* substitute (gold, silver, precious stones with qualities of permanency), or even for a more conventional unit (money), for more abstract entities, such as the *Ecu* (the *basket* of currencies of the European Community), the Eurodollar, or the e-money transacted over networks, literacy is replaced by the *literacies* of the segmented practical instances of each transaction. Shares of an Italian or Spanish company, futures on the American commodities market, bonds for Third World investment funds—they all come with their own rules of transaction, and with their own languages.

The specialization that increases market efficiency results in a growing number of literacies. These literacies bring to the market the productive potential of companies and their management value. They encode levels of expected productivity in farming (and a certain wager on weather conditions), entrepreneurial risks assumed within the context of progressive globalization of the economy. In turn, they can be encoded in programs designed to negotiate with other programs. In addition, the mechanisms assuring the distributed nature of the market in the global economy insert other *literacies*, in this case, the literacy of machines endowed with search and heuristic capabilities independent of literacy.

Market simulations trigger intelligent trade programs and a variety of intelligent agents, capable of modifying their behavior, and achieve higher and higher transaction performance. In short, we have many mediations against the background of a powerful integrative process: the pragmatic framework of a highly segmented economy, working in shorter production cycles, for a global world. In this process, almost nothing remains sequential, and nothing is centralized. Put in different words, almost all market activity takes place in parallel processes. Configurations, i.e., changing centers of interest, come into existence on the ever fluid map of negotiations. Being a self-organizing nucleus, each deal has its own dynamics. Relations among configurational nuclei are also dynamic. Everything is distributed. The relations between the elements involved are non-linear and change continuously. Solidarity is replaced by competition, often fiercely adversarial. Thus the market consumes itself, and the sequels of literacy, requiring provisional and distributed literacies.

Each time individuals project their identity in a product, the multi-dimensional human experience embodied in the product is made available for exchange with others. In the market, it is reduced to the dimension appropriate to the given context of the transaction. Human behavior in the market is symptomatic of the self-awareness of the species, of its critical and self-critical capabilities, of its sense of the future. The progressive increase of the abstract nature of market transactions, the ominous liberation from literacy, and adoption of technologies of efficient exchange define a sense of future which can be quite scary for people raised in a different pragmatic context.

We are beyond the disjunctive models of socialist ideologies of bourgeois property, class differences, reproduction of labor power, and similar categories that emerged in the pragmatic framework that made literacy (and human constitution through literacy) possible and necessary. Property, as much as markets, is distributed (sometimes in ways that do not conform with our sense of fairness). People define their place in the continuum of a society that in many ways does away with the exceptional and introduces a model based on averaging and resulting in mediocrity. The human being's self-constitutive power is not only reproduced in new instances of practical activity, but also augmented in the pragmatics of surplus creating higher surplus. Along with the sense of permanency, humans lose a sense of the exceptional as this applies to their products and the way they constitute themselves through their work.

F TRANSIENT

When a product is offered with a lifetime warranty and the manufacturer goes bankrupt within months from the date of the sales transaction, questions pertaining to ethics, misrepresentation, and advertisement are usually asked. Such incidents, to which no one is immune, cannot be discarded since the experience of market transactions is an experience in human values, no matter how relative these are. Honesty, respect for truth, respect for the given word, written or not, belong to the civilization of literacy and are expressed in its books. The civilization of illiteracy renders these and all other books senseless. But it would be wrong to suggest that markets of the civilization of illiteracy corrupt everything and that, instead of confirming values, they actually empty values of significance. Markets do something else: They integrate expectations into their own mechanisms. In short, they have to live up to expectations not because these were written down, but because markets would otherwise not succeed. How this takes place is a longer story, starting with the example given: What happens to a lifetime warranty when the manufacturer goes bankrupt?

The pragmatic framework of human self-constitution in language through the use of the powerful means of literacy is one of stability and progressive growth. The means of production facilitated in this framework are endowed with qualities, physical, first of all, that guarantee permanency. The industrial model is an extension of the model of creation deeply rooted in literacy-dominated human activity. Machines were powerful and dominating. They, as well as the products they turned out, lasted much longer than the generation of people who use them.

After participating in the complex circumstances that made the Industrial Revolution possible, literacy was stimulated and supported by it. Incandescent lighting, more powerful than the gas or oil lamp, expanded the time available for reading, among other activities. Books were printed faster and more cheaply because paper was produced faster and more cheaply, and the printing press was driven by stronger engines. More time was available for study because industrial society discovered that a qualified workforce was more productive once machines become more complicated. All this happened against the background of an obsession with permanency reflected also in the structure of the markets. As opposed to agricultural products, subject to weather and time, industrial products can be accepted on consignment.

Literacy was a mediating tool here since transactions became less and less homogeneous, and the institution of credit more powerful due to the disparity between production and consumption cycles. The scale of the industrial market corresponded to the scale of industrial economy. Industrial markets are optimally served by the sequential nature of literacy and the linearity inherent in its structure. Production cycles are long, and one cycle follows the other, like seasons, like letters in a word. Remember when new model automobiles came out in October, and only in October? A large manufacturer embodied permanence and so did its product. In this framework, a lifetime warranty reflects a product's promised performance and the language describing this performance.

This is no longer the case in the civilization of illiteracy. From the design of the product, to the materials used and principles applied, almost nothing is meant to last beyond a cycle of optimal efficiency. It is not a moral decision, neither is it a devious plan. Different expectations are embodied in our products. Their life cycle reflects the dynamics of change corresponding to the new scale of human self-constitution, and the obsession with efficiency. Products become transient because the cycles of relative uniformity of our self-constitution are shorter.

We know that life expectancy has increased, and it may well be that people past the peak of their productive capability will soon represent the majority of the population. Nonetheless, the increased level of productivity facilitated by mediating strategies is independent of this change. Longer life means presence in more cycles of change (which translates into other changes, such as in education and training, family life). What was once a relatively homogeneous life becomes a succession of shorter periods, some only loosely connected. In comparison to centuries of slow, incremental development, relatively abrupt change testifies to a new human condition.

Where once literacy was necessary to coordinate the variety of contributions from many people—who projected as much permanency in their products, even if the individuals were more literate in drawing than in writing—new forms of coordination and integration are now in place. The corresponding pragmatics is characterized by intension and distribution, and the products capture the projected sense of change that dominates all human experiences. Thus conditions were created for markets of the transient, in which lifetime functioning of ingenious artifacts is promised, because the lifetime meant is as short as the cycle of the entire line. The fact that the manufacturer goes bankrupt is not even surprising since the structural characteristics of the obsession with efficiency results in manufacturing entities that last as long (or as short) as the need for their product, or as long as the functional characteristics of the product satisfy market expectations. This is how expectations are integrated in market mechanisms. Since mediation is now exercised through many *literacies* integrated in the product, it is clear why, together with the exhausted lifetime warranty, we throw away not only manufactured items, but also the literacy (and literacies) embodied in them. Each transaction in the transient corresponds to a pragmatics that transforms the Faustian promise into an advertising slogan.

MARKET, ADVERTISEMENT, LITERACY

First, the indictment: "If I were asked to name the deadliest subversive force within capitalism—the single greatest source of its waning morality—I should without hesitation name advertising." These words belong to a commentator of the ill-reputed supply side economics, Robert L. Heilbroner, but could have been signed by many sharing in this definition. Now comes the apologia: "The historians and archaeologists will one day discover that ads of our times are the richest and most faithful daily reflections that any society ever made of its entire range of activities." McLuhan's words, as familiar as they are, bear the imprint of his original thinking. The issue is not to take sides. Whether admired or despised, ignored or enjoyed, advertisement occupies an inordinately important place in our life today. For anyone who went through the history of advertisement, it becomes obvious that the scale of this activity, which is indeed part of the market, has changed radically.

It used to be true that only 50 to 60 percent of the investment in advertisement resulted in higher sales or brand recognition. Today, the 50 to 60 percent has shrunk to less than 2 percent. But of the 2 percent that impacts the market, 2 percent (or less) results in covering the entire expense of advertisement. Such levels of efficiency—and waste, one should add, in full awareness that the notion is relative—are possible only in the civilization of illiteracy. The figures (subject to controversy and multiple interpretation) point to efficiency as much as to the various aspects of the market. Our concern with advertisement is not only with how literate (or illiterate) advertisement is, but also with how appropriate literacy means can be to address psychological, ethical, and rational (or irrational) aspects of market transactions.

A look at advertisements through the centuries is significant to the role of literacy in society and in the world of merchandising. Word-of-mouth *advertising* and hanging signs outside a business reflect the literacy levels of an age of small-scale market transactions. The advertisements of the end of the 19th and beginning of the 20th century exemplify the levels of literacy and the efficiency expected from it for merchandising in the context and scale of that time. The ads contain more text than image and address reason more than the senses. In the age of the magazine and newspaper, advertisers relied on the power of verbal persuasion. Honesty or value was not the issue here, only its appearance. The word committed to paper, black on white, had to be simple and true.

In Europe, advertisement took a different style at this time, but still reflected value. Manufacturers engaged many well known artists of the time to design their ads. Henri Toulouse-Lautrec, El Lissitzky, and Herbert Bayer are among the best known. To the highly literate but more artistically inclined Europeans of the time, such ads for upscale products and events were more appealing. Probably taking their cue from Europe, American designers experimented with image advertising after World War II, and graphic design took off in the USA. With the advent of more powerful visualization media, and based on data from psychology to support its effectiveness, the image began to dominate advertising. As ambiguously as an image can be interpreted, its efficiency in advertising was confirmed in rising sales figures.

In the rare cases when literacy is used today, it is usually for its visual impact. In an attempt to relate to the qualities of the black-on-white advertisement of earlier times, Mobil started a series of ads in the mid-1980's. To those not semiotically aware, the ad was simply text appealing to the reader's reason. Literacy rediviva! To people attuned to semiotics, the ad was a powerful visual device. The simple tombstone style evoked relations between literacy and values such as simplicity, honesty, the permanence of the idea, the dominance of reason. The visual convention was actually stronger than the literacy element, used as an alibi in these ads. Indeed, the people who hand out the Clio awards for advertising were so taken in as to award Mobil a first prize for these ads.

Markets are far from being simple causal phenomena. A market's easy switch from a well structured, rational interpretation and ethical conduit, to irrationality and misrepresentation is revealed in the new forms markets take, as well as in their new techniques for transactions and the associated advertisement. The term *irrationality* describes a contradiction of common sense rules (or economic theories setting them forth) of exchange of goods. During the 1980's, this occurred in the oil market, the art market, the market for adoptable children, and in new stock market offerings.

The literate discourse of theories or of an advertisement can only acknowledge the irrationality and suggest explanations. There are schools of market analysis based on game theory, psychodrama, cyclical modeling, the phases of the moon, etc., etc., each producing newsletters, giving advice, trying to render understandable economic and financial phenomena difficult to predict. Language-like explanations and advice are part of advertising, part of market language, forming its own literacy and keeping many captive to it. But even the most literate participant cannot stop the process since the literacy involved in what some perceive as an aberration is different from the literacy embodied in the product traded or in its advertisement. Irrational elements are present in the market, as in life, at all times, but not to the extent to which the language of the market reflects hysteria (as on Black Monday in 1987 on the New York Stock Exchange) or simply ceases its pragmatic function.

We all deplore the continuous shrinking of the intimate sphere of our lives, but admit, in the act of constituting ourselves in the space and time of market transactions, the integrating power that the market exercises, ignoring how close the relation between the two aspects is. Literacy was once a protective medium and entailed rules of discretion and decency. Illiteracy makes us fear; it allows us to become more efficient, but at the same time we become subject to intrusion by all the means that capture our identity. People making purchases on-line will not hesitate to write down their personal data and credit card numbers, trusting in a sense of privacy that is part of the code of literate behavior. Of all people, the computer-literate should realize the power of the Net for searching, retrieving, and sorting such information for all types of uses imaginable.

In the civilization of illiteracy, advertisement is no longer an integrative device that addresses a non-differentiated market but a device that addresses powerful distinctions that can capture smaller groups, even the individual. "Tell me what you want to buy or sell and I'll tell you who you are," is a concise way of declaring how market semiosis X-rays its participants. The enormous marketing efforts associated with a new brand of cereal, software, a political campaign, a role in a movie, or a sports event result in advertisement's becoming a language in itself, with its own *vocabulary* and *grammar.* These are subject to rapid change because the pragmatics of the activities they represent change so fast. "Tell me what you buy and I'll tell you who you are"—mug shots of all of us are taken continuously, by extremely inventive digital devices, while the market fine-tunes us. Buying products ended long ago. *Products now buy us.*

Advertising in the civilization of illiteracy is no longer communication or illustration. It is an information processing activity, bizarre at times, extremely innovative in the ability to cross reference information and fine-tune the message to the individual. Automatic analysis of data is complemented by refinement methods that adjust the weight of words in order to fit the addressee. In the reality of the market and its attendant advertising, languages pertaining to art, education, ideology, sexuality, are integrated at a high level of sophistication in the infinite series of mediations that constitute the pragmatic framework of human existence. Nothing is more valuable than the knowledge of who we are. One can risk stating that brokers of information about each of us will probably fare best in this market of many competing partial literacies.

When markets rely more and more on mediations, and market cycles become faster and faster, when the global nature of transactions requires mechanisms of differentiation and integration far beyond the scope of language, literacy ceases to play a dominating role. The literate message assumed that the human being is the optimal source of information and the ideal receiver. The illiterate message can send itself automatically, as image or as speech, as video or as Internet spamming, whatever best hits its human target, to people's addresses. Whether we like it or not, face-to-face negotiations have already become fax-to-fax and are bound to be converted into program-to-program dealings. The implications are so far-reaching that emotional reactions, such as enthusiasm or disgust, are not really the best answer to this prospect.

Market pragmatics in our civilization is defined by the need to continuously expand surplus to meet a dominant *desire and expectation driven* exchange of goods and services. These desires and expectations correspond to the global scale of human interaction for which a dominant literacy is poorly suited. Hundreds of literacies, representing hundreds of forms of human self-constitution around the world, are integrated in the supersign known as the *market*.

The market—in its narrow sense as transaction, and as a sign process joining structure and dynamics—focuses all that pertains to the relation between the individual and the social environment: language, customs, mores, knowledge, technology, images, sounds, odors, etc. Through the market, economies are ascertained or subjected to painful restructuring. Recent years brought with them turmoil and economic opportunity as an expression of new pragmatic characteristics. Competition, specialization, cooperation, were all intensified. An exciting but just as often disconcerting growth path of economic activity generated markets of high performance. Just-in-time, point-of-sale, and electronic interchanges came into being because the human pragmatic made them necessary.

This is why it is difficult to accept views, regardless of their public acclaim, that explain the dynamics of economic life through technological change. The increased speeds of economic cycles are not parallel but related to the new practical experiences of human self-constitution. Cognitive resources became the main commodity for economic experiences. And the market fully confirms this through mechanisms for accelerated transactions and through sign processes of a complexity that technology has really never reached. New algorithms inspired by dynamic systems, intelligent agent models, and better ways to handle the issues of opportunity and prediction are the expression of cognitive resources brought to fruition in a context requiring freedom from hierarchy, centralism, sequentiality, and determinism. As exciting as the model of the economy as ecosystem is (I refer to Rothschild's *bionomics*), it remains an essentially deterministic view.

No semiosis triggers forces of economic change. But sign processes, in the form of elaborate transactions, reflect the change in the pragmatic condition of the human being. All those new companies, from fast food chains to microchip makers and robot providers that convert human knowledge into the new goods and services, are the expression of the necessity of this pragmatic change. Diversity and abundance might be related to competition and cooperation, but what drives economic life, market included, is the objective need to achieve levels of efficiency corresponding to the global scale human activity has reached. Central planning, like any other centralized structure, including that of businesses, does not come to an end because of technological progress, but in view of the fact that it prevents efficient practical experiences.

Markets of the civilization of illiteracy, like the economy for which they stand, are more and more mediated. They go through faster cycles, their swings wilder, their interdependency deeper than ever. The literate experience of the market assumed that the individual was the optimal source of information and the ideal receiver. Decision-making was an exclusively human experience. The illiterate message of complex data processing and evaluation can send itself automatically and reach whatever has to be reached in a given context: producers of raw materials, energy providers, manufacturers, a point-of-sale unit. As shoppers start scanning their purchases by themselves, information regarding their buying patterns makes it quickly into programs in charge of delivery, production, and marketing. Face-to-face negotiations, many times replaced by fax-to-fax or e-mail-to-e-mail transactions, are converted into more program-to-program dealings. Instead of mass markets, we experience point-cast markets. Their pragmatics is defined by the need to continuously meet *desire* and *expectation* instead of need. Their dynamics, expressed in nuclei of self-organization, is in the last instance not at all different from that of the human beings self-constituted in their reality.

CHAPTER 3: LANGUAGE AND WORK

Work is a means of self-preservation beyond the primitive experience of survival. Actually, one can apply the word *work* only from the moment awareness of human self-constitution in practical experiences emerged from these experiences. Awareness of work and the beginnings of language are probably very close to one another.

By work we understand patterns of human activity, not the particulars of one or another form of work. This defines a functional perspective first of all, and allows us to deal with replication of these patterns. Interaction, mutation, growth, spreading, and ending are part of the pattern. For anyone even marginally informed, it is quite clear that work patterns of agriculture are quite different from those of the pre-industrial, industrial, or post-industrial age. Our aim is to examine work patterns of the civilization of literacy in contrast to those of the civilization of illiteracy.

That agriculture was determined, in its specific aspects, by different topography and climatic biological context is quite clear. Nevertheless, the people constituting their identity in experiences of cultivating the land accomplished it in coherent ways, regardless of their geographic location. Their language experience testifies to an identifiable set of concerns, questions, and knowledge which is, despite the fragmented picture of the world, more homogenous than we could expect. If, by contrast, one considers a chip foundry of today's high technology, it becomes clear how chip producers in Silicon Valley and those in Chinese provinces, in Russia, or in a developing country of Eastern Europe, Asia, or Africa share the same language and the same concerns.

The example of agriculture presents a bottom-up structure of pre-literate nature, based mainly on reaction. Reaction slowly but surely led to more deliberate choices. Experience converged in repetitive patterns. The more efficient experiences were confirmed, the others discarded. A body of knowledge was accumulated and transmitted to everyone partaking in survival activities. In the case of the chip foundry, the structure is top-down: Goals and reasons are built in, and so is the critical knowledge of a post-literate nature required for achieving high efficiency. Skills are continuously perfected through reinforcement schemes. Activity is programmed. An explicit notion of the factory's goals—high quality, high efficiency, high adaptability to new requirements—is built into the entire factory system.

In both models, corresponding to real-life situations, language is constituted as part of the experience. Indeed, coordination of effort, communication, record keeping, and transmission of knowledge are continuously requested. As a replicative process, work implies the presence of language as an agent of transfer. Language pertinent to the experience of agriculture is quite different from the language pertinent to the modern production of chips. One is more natural than the other, i.e., its connection to the human being's natural stage is stronger than that of the activity in the foundry. In the chip age of the civilization of illiteracy, languages of extreme precision become the means for an efficient practical experience. Their functions are different from those of natural language, which by all means still constitutes a medium for human interaction.

All these remarks are meant to provide a relatively comfortable entry to the aspects of the changing relation between language and work. The terminology is based on today's fashionable lingo of genetics, and of memetics, its counterpart. Still, I would suggest more than caution, because memetics focuses on the quantitative analysis of cultural dynamics, while semiotics, which represents the underlying conception, is concerned primarily with qualitative aspects.

As we have already seen, evolutionary biology became a source of metaphors for the new sciences of economics, as well as for the acquisition and dissemination of knowledge, or the replication of ideas. Many people are at work in the new scientific space of memetic considerations. The majority are focused on effective procedures, probably computational in nature, for generating mechanisms that will result in improved human interactions. As exciting as all this is, qualitative considerations might prove no less beneficial, if indeed we could translate them in effective practical experiences. If the purposeful character of all living organisms can be seen as an inevitable consequence of evolution, the dynamics of human activity, reflected in successive pragmatic frameworks, goes beyond the mechanism of natural selection. This is exactly where the sign perspective of human interaction, including that in work, differentiates itself from the quantitative viewpoint. As long as selection itself is a practical experience—choose from among possibilities—it becomes difficult to use selection in order to explain how it takes place.

In the tradition of analogies to machines—of yesterday or of today—we could look at work as a machine capable of self-reproduction (von Neumann's concept). In the new tradition of memetics, work would be described as a replicative complex unit, probably a *meta-meme*. But both analogies are focused ultimately on information exchange, which is only a limited part of what sign processes (or semioses, as they are called) are. This is not to say that work is reducible to sign processes or to language. What is of interest is the connection between work and signs, or language. Moreover, how pragmatic frameworks and characteristics of language experiences are interconditioned is a subject that involves a memetic perspective, but is not reducible to it.

Comparisons of the efficiency of *direct* human practical experiences to that of mediated forms—with the aid of tools, signs, or languages—suggest one preliminary observation: The efficiency of the action mediated through sign systems is higher than that of direct action. The source of this increase in efficiency is the cognitive effort to adapt the proper means (how work is done) to the end (what is accomplished) pursued. In retrospect, we understand that this task is of a tall order—it involves observation, comparison, and the ability to conceive of alternatives. As we learn from attempts involving the best of science and the best of technology, the emulation of such cognitive processes, especially as they evolve over time, is not yet within our reach.

Language, together with all other sign systems, is an integral part of the process of constitution and affirmation of human nature. The role it plays in the process is dynamic. It corresponds to the different pragmatic contexts in which human beings project their structural reality into the reality of their universe of life. The biophysical system within which this projection took and takes place underwent and still undergoes major changes. They are reflected in the biophysical reality of the human being itself. To be part of a changing world and to observe this change places the human being simultaneously *inside* and *outside* the world: inside as part of it, as a genetic sequence; outside as its *conscience,* expressed in all the forms through which awareness, including that of work, is externalized.

Whether a very restricted (limited by the pragmatic horizon of primitive human beings), or a potentially universal system of expression, representation, and communication, language cannot be conceived independent of human nature. Neither can it be conceived independent of other means of expression, representation, and communication. The necessity of language is reflected in the degree to which evolutionary determination and self-determination of the individual or of society, correlate. Language is constituted in human practical experiences. At the same time, it is constitutive, together with many other elements of human praxis: biological endowment, heuristics and logic, dialectic, training. This applies to the most primitive elements of language we can conceive of, as well as to today's productive languages. Embodied in literacy, language accounts for the ever-deepening specialization and fragmentation of human praxis. The replacement of the literate use of language by the *illiteracy* of the many languages dismissing it in work, market transactions, and even social life is the process to which we are at the same time witnesses and agents of change.

Sign systems of all kinds, but primarily language, housed and stored many of the projects that changed the condition of praxis. The major changes are: from direct to mediated, from sequential to parallel, from centralized to decentralized, from clustered (in productive units such as factories) to distributed, from dualistic (right or wrong) to multi-valued (along the continuum of acceptable engineering solutions), from deterministic to non-deterministic and chaotic, from closed (once a product is produced, the problem-solving cycle is completed) to open (human practical experiences are viewed as problem generating), from linear to non-linear. Each of these changes, in turn, made the structural limits of language more and more evident. Practical experiences in the design of languages, in particular the new languages of visualization, are pushing these limits in order to accommodate new expectations, such as increased expressiveness, higher processing speed, inter-operability—an image can trigger further operations.

Globality of human practical experience succeeds against the background of the emergence of many languages that are very specific, though global in scope in that they can be applied all over the world. The chip factory already mentioned—or, for that matter, an integrated pizza or hamburger production facility—can be delivered turn-key in any corner of the world. The languages of mathematics, of engineering, or of genetics might independently be characterized by the same sequentiality, dualism, centralism, determinism that made natural language itself incapable of handling complexities resulting from the new scale of human activity. Once integrated in practical experiences of a different nature, such as those of automation, they all allow for a new dynamics. Obviously, they are less expressive than language—we have yet to read a DNA sequence poem, or listen to the music of a mathematical formula—but infinitely more precise.

WE ARE WHAT WE DO

In the contemporary world, communication is progressively reified and takes place more and more through the intermediary of the product. Its source is human work. Characteristics of the languages involved in the work are also projected into them. A new underlying structure replaces that which made literacy possible and necessary. In the physical or spiritual reality of the product, specialized languages are re-translated into the *universal* language of satisfying needs, or creating new needs, which are afterwards processed through the mediating mechanisms of the market. Reification (from the Latin *res:* transformation of everything—life, language, feeling, work—into *things*) is the result of the alienating logic of the market and its semiosis.

Markets abstract individual contributions to a product. In the first place, language itself is reified and consumed. Markets reify this contribution, turning life, energy, doubts, time, or whatever else—in particular language—into the commodity embodied in the product. The very high degree of integration leads to conditions in which high efficiency—the most possible at the lowest price—becomes a criterion for survival. The consequence is that human individuality is absorbed in the product. People literally put their lives, and everything pertaining to them—natural history, education, family, feelings, culture, desires—in the outcome of their practical experiences. This absorption of the human being into the product takes place at different levels. In the second place, the individual constituted in work is also reified and consumed: the product *contains* a portion of the limited duration of the lives of those who processed it.

Each form of mediated work depends upon its mediating entities. As one form of work is replaced by another, more efficient, the language that mediated is replaced by other means. Languages of coordination corresponding to hunting, or those of incipient agriculture, made way for subsequent practical experience of self-constitution in language. This applies to any and all forms of work, whether resulting in agricultural, industrial, artistic, or ideological products. The metaphors of genetics and evolutionary models can be applied. We can describe the evolution of work in memetic terminology, but we would still not capture the active role of sign processes. Moreover, human reproduction, between its sexual and its cultural forms, would become meaningless if separated from the pragmatic framework through which human self-constitution takes place.

To illustrate how language is consumed, let us shortly examine what happens in the work we call education. In our day, the need for continual training increases dramatically. The paradigm of a once-for-life education is over, as much as literacy is over. Shorter production cycles require changes of tools and the pertinent training. A career for life, possible while the linear progress of technology required only maintenance of skills and slight changes of knowledge, is an ideal of the past. Efficiency requirements translate into training strategies that are less costly and less permanent than those afforded through literacy. These strategies produce educated operators as training itself becomes a product, offered by training companies whose list of clients includes fast food chains, nuclear energy producers, frozen storage facilities, the U.S. Congress, and computer operations. The market is the place where products are transacted and where the language of advertising, design, and public relations is consumed. Training, too, focused more and more on non-literate means of communication, is consumed.

Man built machines which imitated the human arm and its functions, and thus changed the nature of work. The skills needed to master such machines were quite different from the skills of craftsmen, no longer transmitted from generation to generation, and less permanent. The Industrial Revolution made possible levels of efficiency high enough to allow for the maintenance of both machines and workers. It also made possible the improvement of machines and required better qualified operators, who were educated to extract the maximum from the means of production entrusted to them.

At present, due to the integrative mechanisms that humans have developed in the processes of labor division, natural language has lost, and keeps losing, importance in the population's practical experience. The lower quality of writing, reading, and verbal expression, as they apply to self-constitution through work and social life, is symptomatic of a new underlying structure for the pragmatic framework. Literacy-based means of expression and communication are substituted, not just complemented, by other forms of expression and communication. Or they are reduced to a stereotyped repertory that is easy to mechanize, to automate, and finally, to do away with. Overseeing an automated assembly line, serving a sophisticated machine, participating in a very segmented activity without having a real overview of it, and many similar functions ultimately means to be part of a situation in which the subject's competence is progressively reduced to fit the task. Before being rationalized away, it is stereotyped. The language involved, in addition to that of engineering, is continuously compressed, trimmed according to the reduced amount of communication possible or necessary, and according to situations that change continuously and very fast.

Today, a manual for the maintenance and repair of a highly sophisticated machine or weapon contains fewer words than images. The words still used can be recorded and associated with the image. Or the whole manual can become a videotape, laser disk, or CD-

ROM, even network-distributed applications, to be called upon when necessary. The machine can contain its computerized manual, displaying *pages* (on the screen) appropriate to the maintenance task performed, generating synthesized speech for short utterances, and for canned dialogues. Here are some oddly related facts: The Treasury designs dollar bills that will *tell* the user their denomination; cars are already equipped with machines to *tell* us that we forgot to lock the door or fasten our seat belt; greeting cards contain voice messages (and in the future they will probably contain animated images). We can see in such gadgets a victory of the most superficial tastes people might have. But once the gratuitous moment is over, and first reactions fade away, we face a pragmatic situation which, whether synthesized messages are used or not, reflects an underlying structure better adapted to the complexities of the new scale of humankind.

The holographic dollar bill that declines its name might even become useless when transactions become entirely electronic. The *voice* of our cars might end up in a museum once the generalized network for guiding our automobiles is in place, and all we have to do is to punch in a destination and some route expectations ("I want to take the scenic route"). Moreover, the supertech car itself might join its precursors in the museum once work becomes so distributed that the energy orgy, so evident on the rush-hour clogged highways, is replaced by more rational strategies of work and life. Telecommuting is a timid beginning and a pale image of what such strategies might be. The speaking greeting card might be replaced by a program that *remembers* whose birthday it is and, after searching the *mugshot* of the addressee (likes rap, wears artificial flowers, is divorced, lives in Bexley, Ohio), custom designs an *original* message delivered with the individualized electronic newspaper when the coffee is ready. A modest company manufacturing screensavers, using today's still primitive applications in the networked world, could already do this.

Anticipation aside, we notice that work involves means of production that are more and more sophisticated. Nevertheless, the market of human work is at a relatively low level of literacy because human being do not need to be literate for most types of work. One reason for this is that the new machines incorporate the knowledge needed to fulfill their tasks. The machines have become more efficient than humans. The university system that is supposed to turn out literate graduates for the world of work obeys the same expectations of high efficiency as any other human practical experience. Universities become more and more training facilities for specific vocations, instead of carrying on their original goal of giving individuals a universal education in the domain of ideas.

The statement concerning the literacy level does not reflect the longing of humanists but the actual situation in the manpower market. What we encounter is the structurally determined fact that natural language is no longer, at least in its literate form, the main means of recording collective experience, nor the universal means of education. For instance, in all its aspects—work, market, education, social life—the practical experience of human self-constitution relies less on literacy and more on images. Since the role of images is frequently mentioned (formulated differently, perhaps), the reader might suspect this is only a way of speaking. The actual situation is quite different. Pictographic messages are used whenever a certain norm or rule has to be observed. This is not a question of transcending various national languages (as in airports or Olympic stadiums, or with traffic signals, or in transactions pertinent to international trade), but a way of living and functioning. The visual dominates communication today.

Words and sentences, affected by long-time use in various social, geographical, and historical contexts, became too ambiguous and require too much educational overhead for successful communication. Communication based on literacy requires an investment higher than the one needed for producing, perceiving, and observing images. Through images a positivist attitude is embodied, and a sense of relativity is introduced. Avoiding sequential reading, time and money consuming instruction, and the rigidity of the rules of literacy, the use of images reflects the drive for efficiency as this results from the new scale of human survival and future well-being. The change from literacy-oriented to visually-oriented culture is not the result of media development, as romantic media ecologists would like us to believe. Actually, the opposite is true. It is the result of fundamental ways of working and exchanging goods, within the new pragmatic framework that determined the need for these media in the first place, and afterwards made possible their production, dissemination, and their continuous diversification.

The change under discussion here is very complex. Direct demands of mediated praxis and the new, highly mediative means of mass communication (television, computers, telecommunication, networks), acting as instruments of integrating the individual in the mechanism of a global economy, are brought to expression in this mutation. Transition from language to languages, and from direct to indirect, multimediated communication is not reducible to abandoning logocentrism (a structural characteristic of cultures based on literacy) and the logic attached to it. We participate in the process of establishing many centers of importance that replace the word, and compete with language as we know it. These can be found in subculture, but also within the entrenched culture. One example is the proliferation of electronic cafés, where clients sipping their coffee on the West Coast can carry on a dialogue with a friend in Barcelona; or contact a Japanese journalist flying in one of the Soviet space missions; or receive images from an art exhibit opening in Bogota; or play chess with one of the *miracle sisters* from Budapest. These experiences take place in what is known generically as cyberspace.

THE DISPOSABLE HUMAN BEING

While it is true that just as many different curves can be drawn through a finite number of points, consistent observations can be subsumed under various explanations. Observations regarding the role and status of literacy might result in explanations that put radically different glosses on their results, but they cannot escape confirming the sense of change defined here. This change ultimately concerns the identity humans acquire in illiterate experiences of self-constitution.

Progressively abandoning reading and writing and replacing them with other forms of communication and reception, humans participate in another structural change: from centralization to decentralization; from a centripetal model of existence and activity, with the traditional system of values as an attraction point (religious, aesthetic, moral, political values, among others) to a centrifugal model; and from a monolithic to a pluralistic model. Paradoxically, the loss of the center also means that human beings lose their central role and referential value. This results in a dramatic situation: When human creativity compensates for the limited nature of resources (minerals, energy, food supply, water, etc.), either by producing substitutes or by stimulating efficient forms of their use, the human itself becomes a disposable commodity, more so the more limited its practical self-constitution is.

Within the pragmatics characteristic of the underlying literacy, machines were changed less often; but even when changed, the human operator did not have to be replaced. A basic set of skills sufficed for lifelong activity. Engineering was concerned with artifacts as long lasting as life. The pragmatic framework of illiteracy, as one of rapid change and progressively shorter cycles, made the human more easily replaceable. At the new scale of human activity, the very large and growing commodity of human beings decreases in value: in its market value, and in its spiritual and real value. The sanctity of life gives way to the intricate technology of life maintenance, to the mechanics of existence and the body-building shops. In the stock market of spare parts, a kidney or a heart, mechanical or natural, is listed almost the same way as pork bellies and cement, van Gogh's paintings, CD players, and nuclear headscrews. They are quoted and transacted as commodities. And they support highly specialized work, compensated at the level of professional football or basketball.

Projected into and among products of short-lived destiny, the human beings working to make them project a morality of the disposable that affects their own condition and, finally, the dissolution of their values. As a result of high levels of work efficiency, there are enough resources to feed and house humankind, but not enough to support practical experiences that redeem the integrity of the individual and the dignity of human existence. Within a literate discourse, with an embedded ideology of permanency, the morality of the disposable makes for good headlines; but since it does not affect the structural conditions conducive to this morality, it soon gets lost in the many other literate commentaries, including those decrying the decline of literacy.

The broader picture to which these reflections belong includes, of course, the themes of disposable language. If basic skills, as defined by Harvard professor and Secretary of Labor Robert Reich, Massachusetts Institute of Technology economics professor Lester Thurow, and many educators and policy-makers, become less and less meaningful in the fast-changing world of work, it is easy to understand why little weight can be attached to one or another individual. Under the guise of basic skills, young and less than young workers receive an education in reading and writing that has nothing to do with the emergent practical experiences of ever shorter cycles. Companies in search of cheap labor have discovered the USA, or at least some parts of it, and achieve here efficiencies that at home, under labor laws originating from a literate pragmatics, are not attainable. Mercedes-Benz, BMW, Porsche, and many Japanese companies train their labor force in South Carolina, Mississippi, Arkansas, and other states. The usefulness of the people these companies train is almost equal to that of the machine, unless the workers are replaced by automation.

The technological cycle and the human cycle are so closely interwoven that one can predicate the hybrid nature of technology today:

machines with a live component. As a matter of fact, it is interesting to notice how progressively machines no longer serve us, but how we serve them. Entirely equipped to produce high quality desktop publishing, to process data for financial transactions, to visualize scientific phenomena, such machines require that we feed the data and run the program so that a meaningful output results. In the case in which the machine might not know the difference between good and bad typography, for example, the human operator supplies the required knowledge, based on intangible factors such as style or taste.

SCALE OF WORK, SCALE OF LANGUAGE

Within each framework, be that of agriculture, pre-industrial, industrial, or post-industrial practical experiences, continuity of means and methods and of semiotic processes can be easily established. What should most draw our attention are discontinuities. We are going through such a discontinuity, and the opposition between the civilization of literacy and the civilization of illiteracy is suggestive of this. Evidently, within the new practical experiences through which our own identity is constituted, this is reflected in fast dynamics of economic change. Some industries disappear overnight. Many innovative ideas become work almost as quickly, but this work has a different condition. Discontinuity goes beyond analogy and statistical inferences. It marks the qualitative change which we see embodied in the new relations between work and language.

One of the major hypotheses of this book is that discontinuities, also described in dynamic systems theory as phase shifts, occur as scale changes. Threshold values mark the emergence of new sign processes. As we have seen, practical experiences through which humans continuously ascertain their reality are affected by the scale at which they take place. Immediate tasks, such as those characteristic of direct forms of work, do not require a division into smaller tasks, a decomposition into smaller actions. The more complex the task, the more obvious the need to divide it. But it is not until the scale characteristic of our age is reached that decomposition becomes as critical as it now is. In industrial society, and in every civilization prior to it, the relation between the whole (task, goal, plan) and the parts (subtasks, partial goals, successive plans) is within the range of the human's ability to handle it. Labor division is a powerful mechanism for a *divide and conquer* strategy applied to tasks of growing complexity. The generation of choices, and the ability to compensate for the limited nature of resources as these affect the equation of population growth, integrate this rule of decomposition.

Literacy, itself a practical experience of not negligible complexity, helps as long as the depth of the division into smaller parts, and the breadth of the integrative travail do not go beyond litercy's own complexity. When this happens, it is obvious that even if means belonging to literacy were effective in managing very deep hierarchies in order to allow for re-integration of the *parts* in the desired *whole*, the management of such means would itself go beyond the complexity we are able to cope with. Indeed, although very powerful in many respects, when faced with many pragmatic levels independent of language, literacy (through which language attains its optimal operational power) appears flat. Actually, not only literacy appears flat, but even the much glorified human intelligence.

Distinctions that result from deeper segmentation of work, brought about by the requirements of a scale of population and demand of an order of magnitude exponentially higher than any experience an individual can have, can no longer be grasped by single minds. Since the condition of the mind depends on interaction with other minds within practical experiences of self-constitution, it results that means of interaction different from those appropriate to sequentiality, linearity, and dualism are necessary. This new stage is not a continuation of a previous stage. It is even less a result of an incremental progression. The wheel, once upon a time a rounded stone, along with a host of wheel-based means of practical experiences, opened a perspective of progression. So did the lever, and probably alphabetic writing, and the number system. This is why the old and new could be linked through comparisons, metaphors, and analogies in a given scale of humankind. But this is also why, when the scale changes, we have to deal with *discontinuity* and avoid misleading *translations* in the language of the past.

A car was still, in some ways, the result of incremental progression from the horse-drawn carriage. An airplane, and later a rocket, are less along a line of gradual change, but still conceptually close to our own practical experience with flying birds, or with the physics of action and reaction. Nevertheless, a nuclear reactor is well beyond such experiences. The conceptual hierarchy it embodies takes it out of the realm of any previous pragmatic experience. The effort here is to *tame* the process, to keep it within a scale that allows for our use of a new resource of energy. The relation between the sizes actively involved—nuclear level of matter compared to the enormous machinery and construction—is not only beyond the power of distinction of individual minds, but also of any operators, unless assisted by devices themselves of a high degree of complexity. The Chernobyl meltdown suggests only the magnitudes involved, and how peripheral to them are the literacy-based experiences of energy management.

The enormous satellite and radio-telephonic network, which physically embodies the once fashionable concept of *ether,* is another example of the scale of work under the circumstances of the new scale of human activity; and so are the telephone networks—copper, coaxial, or fiberglass. The conceptual hierarchies handled by such networks of increasingly generalized communication of voice, data, and images make any comparison to Edison's telephone, to letters, or to videotapes useless. The amount of information, the speed of transmission, and the synchronicity mechanisms required and achieved in the network—all participate in establishing a framework for remote interaction that practically resets the time for all involved and does away with physical distances. Literacy, by its intrinsic characteristics, could not achieve such levels.

Finally, the computer, associated or not with networks, makes this limit to our ability to grasp complexities even more pressing. We have no problems with the fact that a passenger airplane is 200 times faster than a pedestrian, and carries, at its current capacity, 300-450 passengers plus cargo. The computer chip itself is a conceptual accomplishment beyond anything we can conceive of. The depth encountered in the functioning of the digital computer—from the whole it represents to its smallest components endowed with functions integrated in its operation—is of a scale to which we have no intuitive or direct access. Computers are not a better abacus. Some computer users have even noticed that they are not even a better cash register. They define an age of semiotic focus, in that symbol manipulation follows language processing. (The word *symbol* points to work become semiotic praxis, but this is not what I am after here.)

In addition to the complexity it embodies, the computer makes another distinction necessary. It replaces the world of the continuum by a world of discrete states. Probably this distinction would be seen only as qualitative, if the shift from the universe of continuous functions and monotonic behavior—whatever applies to extreme cases applies to everything in between—were not concretized in a different condition of human self-constitutive practical experience.

In the universe of literacy-based analog expectations, accumulation results in progress: know more (language, science, arts), have more (resources), acquire more (real estate). Even striving—from a general attitude to particular forms (do better, achieve higher levels)—is inherent in the underlying structure of the analog. The digital is not linear in nature. Within the digital, one small deviation (one digit in the phrase) changes the result of processing so drastically that retracing the error and fixing it becomes itself a new experience, and many times a new source of knowledge.

In a written sentence, a misspelling or a typographical error is almost automatically corrected. Through literacy, we dispose of a model that tells us what is right. In the digital, the *language* of the program and the data on which programs operate are difficult to distinguish (if at all). Such machines can manipulate more symbols, and of a broader variety, than the human mind can. Free of the burden of previous practical experiences, such machines can refer to potential experiences in a frame of reference where literacy is entirely blind. The behavior of an object in a multi-dimensional space (four, five, six, or more dimensions), actions along a timeline that can be regressive, or in several distinct and unrelated time frames, modeling choices beyond the capability of the human mind—all these, and many more, with practical significance for the survival and development of humankind are acceptable problems for a digital computer.

It is true, as many would hasten to object, that the computer does not formulate the problem. But this is not the point. Neither does literacy formulate problems. It only embodies formulations and answers pertinent to work within a scale of manageable divisions. The less expressive language of zeros and ones (yes-no, open-closed, white-black) is more precise, and definitely more appropriate, for levels of complexity as high as those resulting from this new stage in the evolution. The generality of the computer (a general-purpose machine), the abstraction of the program of symbol manipulation, and the very concrete nature of the data upon which it is applied represent a powerful combination of reified knowledge, effective procedures for solving problems, and high resolution capabilities. Those who see the computer as only the principal technological metaphor of our time (according to J. D. Bolter) miss the significance of the new metrics of human activity and its degree of necessity as it results from awareness of the limits of our minds (after the limits of the body were experienced in industrial society).

Edsger Dijkstra, affirming the need for an orthogonal method of coping with radical novelty, concludes that this "amounts to creating and learning a new foreign language that *cannot* be translated into one's mother tongue." The direction he takes is right; the conclusion is still not as radical as the new scale of human activity and the limits of our self-constitution require. Coming to grips with the radical change that he and many, many others ascertain, amounts to understanding the end of literacy and the *illiteracy* of the numerous languages required by our practical experience of self-constitution. This conspectus of the transformation we experience may foster its own forms of fresh confusion. For instance, in what was called a civilized society, language acted as the currency of cultural transactions. If higher level needs and expectations continue to drive the market and technology, will they eventually become subservient to the illiterate means they have generated? Or, if language in one of its illiterate embodiments cannot keep pace with the exponential growth of information, will it undergo a restructuring in order to become a parallel process? Or will we generate more inclusive symbols, or some form of preprocessing, before information is delivered to human beings? All these questions relate to work, as the experience from which human identities result together with the products bearing their mark.

The active condition of any sign system is quite similar to the condition of tools. The hand that throws a stone is a hand influenced by the stone. Levers, hammers, pliers, no less than telescopes, pens, vending machines, and computers support practical experiences, but also affect the individuals constituting themselves through their use. A gesture, a written mark, a whisper, body movements, words written or read, express us or communicate for us, at the same time affecting those constituted in them. How language affects work means, therefore, how language affects the human being within a pragmatic framework. To deal with some aspects of this extremely difficult problem we can start with the original syncretic condition of the human being.

INNATE HEURISTICS

Conceptual tools that can be used to refer to the human being in its syncretic condition exist only to the degree to which we identify them in language. In every system we know of, variety and precision are complementary. Indeed, whether human beings hunt or present personal experiences to others, *they attempt to optimize their efforts*. Too many details affect efficiency; insufficient detail affects the outcome. There seems to be a structural relation of the nature of *one to many*, between our *what* and our *how*. This relation is scrutinized in the pragmatic context where efficiency considerations finally make us choose from among many possibilities. The optimum chosen indicates what, from the possibilities humans are aware of, is most suitable for reaching the goal pursued. Moreover, such an optimum is characteristic of the pragmatics of the particular context. For example, hunting could be performed alone or in groups, by throwing stones or hurling spears, by shooting arrows, or by setting traps.

The syncretic primitive being was (and still is, in existing primitive cultures) involved in a practical experience in its *wholeness*: through that being's biological endowment, relation to the environment, acquired skills and understanding, emotions (such as fear, joy, sorrow). The specialized individual constitutes himself in experiences progressively more and more partial. Nevertheless, the two have a *natural* condition in common. What distinguishes them is a strategy for survival and preservation that progressively departs from immediate needs and direct action to *humanized* needs and mediated action. This means a departure from a very limited set of options ("When hungry, search for food," for example), to multiplying the options, and thus establishing for the human being an innate heuristic condition. This means that *Homo Sapiens* looks for options. Humans are creative and efficient.

My line of reasoning argues that, while verbal language may be innate (as Chomsky's theory advances), the heuristic dimension characteristic of human self-constitution certainly is. In hunting, for instance, the choice of means (defining the *how*) reflects the goal (to get meat) and also the awareness of what is possible, as well as the effort to expand the realm of the possible. The major effort is *not* to keep things the way they are, but to multiply the realm of possibilities to ensure more than mere survival. This is known as progress.

The same heuristic strategy can be applied to the development of literacy. Before the Western alphabet was established, a number of less optimal writing systems (cuneiform, hieroglyphics, etc.) were employed. The very concrete nature of such languages is reflected in the limited expressive power they had. Current Chinese and Japanese writing are examples of this phenomenon today. In comparison to the 24-28 letters of Western alphabets, command of a minimum of 3,000 ideographic signs represents the entry level in Chinese and Japanese; command of 50,000 ideographic signs would correspond to the Western ideal of literacy. Behind the letters and characters of the various language alphabets, there is a history of optimization in which work influenced expression, expression constituted new frames for work, and together, generative and explanatory models of the world were established. The *what* and the *how* of language were initially on an order of complexity similar to that characteristic of actions. Over time, actions became simpler while languages acquired the complexity of the heuristic experience.

The *what* and the *how* of mediation tools of a higher order of abstraction than language, achieved even higher complexities. Such complexities were reflected in the difference in the order of magnitude between human work and outcome, especially the choices generated. Parallel to the loss of the syncretic nature of the human being at the level of the individual, we notice the composite syncretism of the community. Individual, relatively stable, wholeness was replaced by a faster and faster changing community-related wholeness. Language experiences were part of this shift. Self-constituted in the practical use of language, the human being realized its social dimension, itself an example of the acquired multiplication of choice.

Indeed, within the very small scale of incipient humanity corresponding to the stage of self-ascertainment (when signs were used and elements of language appeared), population and food supply were locked in the natural equation best reflected in the structural circularity of existence and survival. It is at this juncture that the heuristic condition applies: the more animals prey on a certain group, this group will either find survival strategies (adaptive or other kinds), or indeed cease to be available as food for others. But once the human being was ascertained, evidence shows that instead of focusing on one or few ways to get at its food sources, it actually diversified the practical experience of self-constitution and survival, proceeding from one, or few, to many resources. *Homo Habilis* was past the scavenging stage and well into foraging, hunting, and fishing during the pre-agricultural pragmatic frame. What for other species became only a limited food supply, and resulted in mechanisms of drastic growth control (through famine, cannibalism, and means of destroying life), in the human species resulted in a broadening of resources. In this process, the human being became a working being, and work an identifier of the species.

Language acquisition and the transition from the natural experience of self-constitution in survival to the practical experience of work are co-genetic. With each new scale that became possible, sequences of work marked a further departure from the universe of action-reaction. The observation to be made, without repeating information given in other chapters, is that from signs to incipient language, and from incipient language to stabilized means of expression, the scale of humankind changed and an underlying structure of practical experiences based on sequentiality, linearity, determinism (of one kind or another), and centralism established a new pragmatic framework. Individual syncretism was replaced by the syncretism of communities in which individuals are identified through their work.

Writing was a relatively late acquisition and occurred as part of the broader process of labor division. This process was itself correlated to the diversification of resources and types of practical experiences preserving syncretism at the community level. Not everyone wrote, not everybody read. The pragmatic framework suggested necessitated elements of order, ways of assigning and keeping track of assignments, a certain centralism, and, last but not least, organizational forms, which religion and governing bodies took care of. Under these circumstances, work was everything that allowed for the constitution, survival, change, and advancement of the human species. It was expressed in language to the degree such expression was necessary. In other words, language is another *asset* or *means* of diversifying choices and resources.

Over time, limited mediation through language and literacy became necessary in order to optimize the effort of matching needs with availabilities. This mediation was itself a form of work: questions asked, questions answered, commitments made, equivalencies determined. All these defined an activity related to using available resources, or finding new ones. When productivity increased, and language could not keep up with the complexities of higher production, variety, and the need for planning, a new semiosis, characteristic of this different pragmatic level, became necessary. Money, for example, introduced the next level of mediation, more abstract, that translated immediate, vital needs into a comparative scale of means to fulfill them. The context of exchange generated money, which eventually became itself a resource, a high level commodity. It also entailed a language of its own, as does each mediation. With the advent of means of exchange as universal as language, the *what* and *how* of human activity grew even more distant. Direct trade became indirect. People making up the market no longer randomly matched needs and availability. Their market praxis resulted in an organizing device, and used language to further diversify the resources people needed for their lives. This language was still rudimentary, direct, oral, captive to immediacy, and often *consumed* together with the resource or choice exhausted (when no alternative was generated). This happens even in our day.

In its later constitution in practical activity, language was used for records and transactions, for plans and new experiences. The logic of this language was an extension and instantiation of the logic of human activity. It complemented the heuristic, innate propensity for seeking new choices. Influenced by human interaction in the market, and subjected to the expectation of progressively higher efficiency, human activity became increasingly mediated. A proliferation of *tools* allowed for increased productivity in those remote times of the inception of language. Eventually tools, and other artifacts, became themselves an object of the market, in addition to supporting self-constitutive practical experiences of the humans interacting with them. As a mediating element between the processor and what is processed, the tool was a means of work and a goal: better tools require instructed users. If they use tools properly, they increase the efficiency of activity and make the results more marketable. Tools supported the effort of diversification of practical experiences, as well as the effort of expanding the subsistence base. The means for creating tools and other artifacts fostered other languages, such as the language of drawing, on which early engineering also relied. Here, an important point should be made. No tool is merely used. In using it, the user adapts to the tool, becoming to some extent, the used, the tool of the tool. The same is true of language, writing, and literacy. They were developed by humans seeking to optimize their activity. But humans have adapted themselves to the constraints of their own inventions.

At the inception of writing, the tension between an *imposed written precision* (as relative as this might appear from our perspective today)—keeping language close to the object, allowing into the language only objects that pictograms could represent—and a *rather diverse*, however very unfocused, oral language resulted in conflicts between the proponents of writing and the guardians of orality (as documented in ancient Greek philosophy). The written needed to be freed from the object as much as the human being from a particular source of protein, or a particular food source. It had to support a more general expression (referring to what would become families, types, classes of objects, etc.), and thus to support practical efforts to diversify the ways of survival and continuous growth in number. The oral had to be tamed and united with the written. Taming could, and did, take place only through and in work, and in socially related interaction. The practical effort to embody knowledge resulting from many practical experiences of survival into all kinds of artifacts (for measuring, orientation, navigation, etc.) testifies to this. Phonetic writing, the development of the effort to optimize writing, better imitated oral language. Personal characteristics, making the oral expressive, and social characteristics, endowing the written with the hints that bring it close to speech, are supported in the phonetic system. The theocratic system of pictographs and what others call the democratic language of phonetic writing deserve their names only if we understand that languages are both *constitutive* and *representative* of human experience. Undifferentiated labor is theocratic. Its rules are imposed by the object of the practical experience. Divided labor, while affecting the integrity of those becoming only an instance of the work process, is participatory, in the sense that its results are related to the performance of each participant in the process. Practical experience of language and experience of divided labor are intrinsically related and correspond to the pragmatic framework of this particular human scale. Labor division and the association of very abstract phonetic entities to very concrete language instantiations of human experience are interdependent.

THE REALM OF ALTERNATIVES

In defining the context of change leading from an all-encompassing literacy to the civilization of illiteracy, I referred to the Malthusian principle (Population, when unchecked, increases geometrically, while food sources increase arithmetically). What Malthus failed to acknowledge is the heuristic nature of the human species, i.e., the progressive realization of the creative potential of the only known species that, in addition to maintaining its natural condition, generates its own a-natural condition. In the process of their self-constitution, humans generate also the means for their survival and future growth beyond the circularity of mere survival strategies. The 19th century economist Henri George gave the following example of this characteristic: "Both the jayhawk and the man eat chicken, but the more jayhawks, the fewer chickens, while the more men, the more chickens." (Just think about the Purdue chicken industry!) The formula is flawed. Humans also intervene in the jayhawk-chicken relation; the number of animals and birds in a certain area is affected by more elements than what eats what; and the population increase is meaningless unless associated with patterns of human practical experiences. Species frequently become extinct due to human, not animal, intervention. Despite all this, Henri George's characterization captured an important aspect of the human species, as it defined itself in the human scale that made literacy possible and necessary.

George's time corresponded to some interesting though misleading messages that followed the pattern of Malthus' law. People were running out of timber, coal, and oil for lamps, just as we expect to run out of many other resources (minerals, energy and food sources, water, etc.). Originators of messages regarding the exhaustion of such resources, regardless of the time they utter them, ignore the fact that during previous shortages, humans focused on alternatives, and made them part of new practical experiences. This was the case leading to the use of coal, when the timber supply decreased in Britain in the 16th century, and this will be the case with the shortages mentioned above: for lighting, kerosene was extracted from the first oil wells (1859); more coal reserves were discovered; better machines were built that used less energy and made coal extraction more efficient; industry adapted other minerals; and the strict dependence on natural cycles and farming was progressively modified through food processing and storage techniques.

The pragmatic framework of current human praxis is based on the structural characteristics of this higher scale of humankind. It affects the nature of human work and the nature of social, political, and national organization within emerging national states. A retrospective of the dynamics of growth and resource availability shows that with language, writing and reading, and finally with literacy, and even more through engineering outside language experience, a

276

coherent framework of pragmatic human action was put in place, and used to compensate for the progressive imbalance between population growth and resources.

Our time is in more than one way the expression of a semiosis with deep roots in the pragmatic context in which writing emerged. Engineering dominates today. In trying to define the semiosis of engineering, i.e. how the relation between work we associate with engineering and language evolved, we evidence both continuity—in the form of successive replications—and discontinuity—in the new condition of the current engineering work. Our reference can be made to both the dissemination of the writing system based on the Phoenician alphabet, and the language of drawing that makes engineering possible.

Phoenician traders supplied materials to the Minoans. The Minoan burial culture involved the burial of precious objects that embodied the experience of crafts. These objects were made out of silver, gold, tin, and lead. In time, increased quantities of such metals were permanently removed from the market. Phoenicians, who supplied these materials, had to search farther and farther for them, using better tools to find and preprocess the minerals. The involvement of writing and drawing in the process of compensation between perceived needs and available resources, and the fact that searches for new resources led to the dissemination of writing and craftsmanship should be understood within the dynamics of local economies.

Up to which point such a compensatory action, implying literacy and engineering skills, is effective, and when it reached its climax, possibly during the Industrial Revolution, is a question that can be put only in retrospect. Is there a moment when the balance was tilted towards the means of expression of and the communication specific to engineering? If yes, we do not know this moment; we cannot identify it on historic charts. But once the potential of literacy to support human practical experiences of self-constitution in a new pragmatic framework was exhausted, new means became necessary. To understand the dynamics of the changes that made the new pragmatic framework of the civilization of illiteracy necessary is the object of the entire book. While engineering contributed to them, they are not the result of this important practical experience, but rather a cause of how it was and is affected by them. The stream of diversified experiences that eventually gushed forth through new languages, the language of design and engineering included, resulted in the awareness of mediation, which itself became a goal.

MEDIATION OF MEDIATION

With the risk of breaking the continuity of the argument, I would like to continue by suggesting the implications of this argument for the reality to which this book refers: the present. First, a general thesis derived from the analysis so far: The market of direct exchange, as well as the market of mediated forms, reflect the general structure of human activity—direct work vs. mediated forms of work—and are expressed in their specific languages. From a certain moment in human evolution, tools, as an extension of the human body and mind, are used, some directly, some indirectly. Today we notice how, through the intermediary of commands transmitted electronically, pneumatically, hydraulically, thermally, or in some other way, the mediation of mediation is introduced. Pressing a button, flipping a switch, punching a keyboard, triggering a relay—seen as steps preparing for entirely programmed activities—means to extend the sequence of mediations. Between the hand or another body part and the processed material, processing tools and sequences of signs controlling this process are introduced. Accordingly, language, as related to work, religion, education, poetry, exchange in the market, etc., is restructured. New levels of language and new, limited, functionally designed languages are generated and used for mediating. The language of drawings (more generally the language of design) is one of them. Relations among these different levels and among the newly designed languages are established.

But how is this related to the innate heuristic condition of the human being and to the working hypothesis advanced regarding the change in the scale of humanity? Or is it only another way of saying that technology, resulting from engineering interpretations of science, defines the path to higher levels of efficiency, and to the relative illiteracy of our time? The increase in population and the dynamics of diversification (more choices, more resources) at this new scale assume a different dimension. It is irrelevant that resources of one type or another are exhausted in one economy. As a matter of fact, Japan, Germany, England, and even the USA (rich in the majority of resources in demand) have exhausted whatever oil, copper, tin, diamonds, or tungsten was available. Due to many factors, farmland in the western world is decreasing, while the quantities and different types of food consumed per capita have increased substantially. Faced with the challenge posed by the national, linear, sequential, dual, deterministic nature of the pragmatic framework that generated the need for literacy, humans discover means to transcend these limitations—globality, non-linearity, configuration, multi-valued logic, non-determination—and embody them in artifacts appropriate to this condition.

The new scale necessitated creative work for multiplying available resources, for looking at needs and availabilities from a new perspective. Those who see globality in the Japanese sushi restaurant in Provence or in the Midwest, in the *McDonalds* in Moscow or Beijing, in multinational corporations, in foreign investments mushrooming all over, miss the real significance of the term. Globality applies to the understanding that we share in resources and creative means of multiplying them independent of boundaries (of language, culture, nations, alliances, etc.), as well as in high efficiency processing equipment. This understanding is not only sublime, it has its ugly side. The world would even go to war (and has, again and again) to secure access to critical resources or to keep markets open. But it is not the ugly side that defines the effective pragmatics. Nor does it define the circumstances of our continuous self-definition in this world of a new dynamics of survival needs and expectations above and beyond such needs.

Where literacy no longer adequately supports creative work based on higher levels of efficiency, it is replaced by languages designed and adapted to mediation, or to work destined to compensate for an exhausted resource, or by machines incorporating our literacy and the literacies of higher efficiency. Hunting and fishing remain as mere sport, and foraging declined to the level at which people in a country like the USA no longer know that in the woods there are mushrooms, berries, and nuts that can be used as food. Even agriculture, probably the longest standing form of practical experience, escapes sequentiality and linearity, and adds industrial dimensions that make agriculture a year-round, highly specialized, efficient activity. We share resources and even more in the globality of the life support system (the ecology); in the globality of communication, transportation, and technology; and, last but not least, in the globality of the market. The conclusion is that, once again, it is not any recent discovery or trend that is the engine of change, from local to national to global, but the new circumstances of human experience, whose long-lasting effect is the altered individual.

Freed from the human operator and replaced by technology that ensures levels of efficiency and security for which the living being is not well adapted to provide, many types of work are simultaneously freed from the constraints of language, of literacy in particular. There is no need to teach machines spelling, or grammar, or rules of constructing sentences. There is even less of a need to maintain between the human being and the machine a mediating literacy that is awkward, inefficient, stamped by ambiguity, and burdened by various uses (religious, political, ideological, etc.). The new languages, whether interfaces between machines or between humans and machines, are of limited scope and duration. In the dynamics of work, these new languages are appropriately adapted to each other.

Our entire activity becomes faster, more precise, more segmented, more distributed, more complex. This activity is subordinated to a multi-valued logic of efficiency, not to dualistic inferences or truth or falsehood.

Some might read into the argument made so far a vote against the many kinds of activists of this day and age: the ecologists who warn of damage inflicted on the environment; Malthusians tireless in warning of upcoming famine; the zero-population-growth movement, etc. Some might read here a vote for technocracy, for the advocates of limitless growth, the optimists of despair, or the miracle planners (free marketers, messianic ideologists, etc.). None is the case. Rather, I submit for examination a model for understanding and action that takes into account the complexity of the problem instead of explaining complexities away and working, as literacy taught us to, on simplified models. Mapping out the terrain of the descriptive level of the relation between language and work under current pragmatic circumstances will assist in the attempt to plot, in some meaningful detail, the position so far described.

CHAPTER 4: LITERACY AND EDUCATION

Education and literacy are intimately related. One seems impossible without the other. Nevertheless, there was education before the written word. And there is education that does not rely on literacy, or at least not exclusively. With this in mind, let us focus, in these preliminary words, on what brought literacy into education, and on the consequences of their reciprocal relation.

The state of education, like the state of many other institutions embodying characteristics of literacy-based practical experiences, is far from what is expected. Literacy carried the ideal of permanency into the practical experience of education. In a physical world perceived as limited in scale and fragmented, captive to sequentiality, characterized by periodic changes and intercommunal commitments aimed at maintaining permanency, literacy embodied both a goal and the means for achieving it. It defined a representative, limited set of choices. Within this structure, education is the practical experience of stabilizing optimal modes of interaction centered around values expressed in language. Education based on literacy is adapted to the dynamics of change within the reduced scale of humankind that eventually led to the formation of nations—entities of relative self-sufficiency. Within national boundaries, population growth, resources, and choices could be kept in balance.

Purposely simplified, this view allows us to understand that education evolved from its early stages—direct transmission of experience from one person to another, from one generation to another—to religion-based educational structures. Filtered by a set of religious premises, education later opened a window beyond the immediate and the proximity of life, and evolved, not painlessly, into schools and universities concerned with knowledge and scholarship. This, too, was a long process, with many intermediate steps, which eventually resulted in the generalized system of education we now have in place, and which reflects the separation of church and state. Liberal education and all the values attached to it are the foundational matrix of the current system of general education.

If you give someone a hammer, every problem looks like a nail. If you give someone an alphabet, every problem becomes one of literacy and education—this would probably be a good paraphrase, applicable to the discussions on education in our day. It should not follow, however, that with the World Wide Web, education is only a matter of on-line postings of classes and the accidental matching of educational needs to network availabilities. In our world of change and discontinuity, the end of literacy, along with the end of education based on literacy, is not a symptom, but a necessary development, beyond on-line studies. This conclusion, which may appear to be a criticism of the digital dissemination of knowledge, might seem hasty at this point in the text. The arguments to follow will justify the conclusion.

„KNOW THE BEST"

Resulting from our self-constitution in a world obsessed with efficiency and satisfaction, the insatiable effort to exhaust the new—only to replace it with the newer—puts education in a perspective different from that opened by literacy. Education driven by literacy seems to be condemned to a *sui generis* catch-up condition, or "damned if you do, damned if you don't." In the last 30 years, education has prepared students for a future different from the one education used to shape in a reactive mode. Under the enormous pressure of expectations (social, political, economic, moral) it simply cannot fulfill, unless it changes as the structure of the pragmatic framework changed, the *institution* of education has lost its credibility. Classes, laboratories, manuals, any of the educational methods advanced, not to mention the living inventory of teachers, account for contents and ways of thinking only marginally (if at all) linked to the change from a dominant literacy to numerous literacies. IBM, fighting to redefine itself, stated bluntly in one of its educational campaigns, "Since 1900, every institution has kept up with change, except one: Education."

More money than ever, more ideals and sweat have been invested in the process of educating the young, but little has changed either the general perception of education or the perception of those educated. The most recent laboratory of the high school or university is already outdated when the last piece of equipment is ordered. The competence of even the best teachers becomes questionable just as their students start their first journey in practical life. The harder our schools and colleges try to keep pace with change, the more obvious it becomes that this is a wrong direction to pursue, or that something in the nature of our educational system makes the goal unreachable—or both of these alternatives. Some people believe that the failure is due to the bureaucracy of education. Much can be said in support of this opinion. The National Institute for Literacy is an example of how a problem can become a public institution. Other people believe that the failure is due to the inability of educators to develop a good theory of education, based on how people learn and what the best way to teach is. Misunderstanding the implications of education and setting false priorities are also frequently invoked. Misunderstanding too often resulted in expensive government projects of no practical consequence.

Other explanations are also given for the failure of education—liberalism, excessive democracy in education, rejection of tradition, teaching and learning geared to tests, the breakdown of the family. (Listing them here should not be misconstrued as an endorsement.) It seems that every critic of today's education has his or her own explanation of what each thinks is wrong. Some of these explanations go well back, almost to the time when writing was established: education affects originality, dampens spontaneity, and infringes upon creativity. Education negates naturalness during the most critical period of development, when the minds of young people, the object of education, are most impressionable.

Other arguments are more contemporary: If the right texts (whatever *right* means) were to be taught, using the best methods to put them in a light that makes them attractive, education would not lose out to entertainment. Some groups advocate the digest approach for texts, sometimes presented in the form of comic strips or Internet-like messages of seven sentences per paragraph, each sentence containing no more than seven words. These explanations assume the permanence of literacy. They concentrate on strategies, from infantile to outlandish, to maintain literacy's role, never questioning it, never even questioning whether the conditions that made it necessary might have changed to the degree that a new structure is already in place. Educators like to think that their program is defined through Matthew Arnold's prescription, "Know the best that is known and thought in the world," an axiom of tradition-driven self-understanding. This attitude is irrelevant in a context in which *best* is an identifier of wares, not of dynamic knowledge. Some educators would follow Jacques Barzun's recommendation: "serious reading, serious teaching of reading, and inculcation of a love for reading are the proper goal of education."

IDEAL VS. REAL

Schools at all levels of education purport to give students a *traditional* education and promise to deliver the solid education of yesteryear. Contrast this claim to reality: Under the pressure of the market in which they operate, schools maintain that they prepare students for the new pragmatic context. Some schools integrate practical disciplines and include training components. Courses in computer use come immediately to mind. Some schools go so far as to sign contracts guaranteeing the appropriateness of the education they provide. In the tradition of the service industry, they promise to take back pupils unable to meet the standardized criteria. Every spring, a reality check is made. In 1996, a poll of 500 graduating seniors revealed that only 7% succeeded in answering at least 15 of 20 questions asked. Five of these were on math, the rest on history and literature—all traditional subject matter.

Experts called to comment on the results of this poll—E.D. Hirsch, author of *Cultural Literacy* and active in having his educational ideas implemented; Diane Ravitch, former Assistant Secretary of Education; and Stephen Balch, president of the National Association of Scholars, constitute themselves in the pragmatic framework of literacy-based education. They declare, and appropriately so, that educational standards are declining, that education is failing to produce the type of citizen a democracy needs. As reputable as they undoubtedly are, these scholars, and many of those in charge of education, do not seem to realize what changes have been taking place in the real world. They live in the richest and probably most dynamic country in the world, with one of the lowest unemployment rates, and the highest rate of new business creation, but fail to associate education with this dynamism. If education is failing, then something positive must be replacing it.

In modern jargon, one can say that until education is re-engineered (or should I say *rethought?*), it has no chance of catching up with reality. In its current condition of compromise, education will only continue to muddle along, upsetting both its constituencies: those captive to an education based on the literacy model, and those who recognize new structural requirements.

The reality is that the universality implicit in the literacy model of education, reflected in the corpus of democratic principles guaranteeing equality and access, is probably no longer defensible in its original form. Education should rather elaborate on notions that better reflect differences among people, their background, ethnicity, and their individual capabilities. Instead of trying to standardize, education should stimulate differences in order to derive the most benefit from them. Education should stimulate complementary avenues to excellence, instead of equal access to mediocrity. Some people may be *uneducatable*. They might have characteristics impossible to reduce to the common denominator that literacy-based education implies. These students might require *alternative* education paths in order to optimally become what their abilities allow them to be, and what practical experience will validate as relevant and desired, no matter how different.

Equal representation, as applied to members of minority students or faculty, ethnic groups, sexes or sexual preferences, and the handicapped, introduces a false sense of democracy in education. It takes away the very edge of their specific chances from the people it pretends to help and encourage. Instead of acknowledging distinctions, expectations of equal representation suggest that the more melting in the pot, the better for society, regardless of whether the result is uniform mediocrity or distributed excellence. Actually the opposite is true: equal opportunity should be used in order to preserve distinctive qualities and bring them to fruition.

As a unified requirement, literacy imparts a sense of conformity and standardization appropriate to the pragmatic framework that made standardized education necessary. Numerous alternative means of expression and communication, for which education has only a deaf ear, facilitate the multiplication of choices. In a world confronted with needs well beyond those of survival, this is a source of higher efficiency. The necessary effort to individualize education cannot, however, take place unless the inalienable right to study and work for one's own path to self-improvement is not respected to the same extent as liberty and equality are.

The globality of human praxis is not a scenario invented by some entrepreneur. It is the reflection of the scale at which population growth, shared resources, and choices heading to new levels of efficiency become critical. In our world many people never become literate; many more still live at the borderline between human and animal life, threatened by starvation and epidemics. These facts do not contradict the dynamics that made alternatives to literacy necessary. It is appropriate, therefore, to question the type of knowledge that education imparts, and how it impacts upon those who are educated.

RELEVANCE

Schools and universities are criticized for not giving students relevant knowledge. The notion of *relevance* is critical here. Scholars claim that knowledge of facts pertaining to tradition, such as those tested in the graduating class of 1996, are relevant. Relevant also are elements of logical thinking, enough science in order to understand the wealth of technologies we use, foreign languages, and other subject matter that will help students face the world of practical experience. Although the subjects listed are qualified as significant, they are never used in polls of graduating students.

Critics of the traditional curriculum dispute the relevance of a tradition that seems to exclude more than it includes. They also challenge implicit hierarchical judgments of the people who impose courses of study. Multiculturalism, criticism of tradition, and freedom from the pressure of competition are among the recommendations they make. Acknowledging the new context of social life and praxis, these critics fail, however, to put it in the broader context of successive structural conditions, and thus lack criteria of significance outside their own field of expertise.

With the notion of relevance, a perspective of the past and a direction for the future are suggested. That literacy-based education, at its inception, was xenophobic or racist, and obviously political, nobody has to tell us. Individuals from outside the *polis*, speaking a different mother tongue, were educated for a political reason: to make them useful to the community as soon as possible. Conditions for education changed dramatically over time, but the political dimension remains as strong as ever. This is why it can only help to dispense with certain literate attitudes expressing national, ethnic, racial, or similar ambitions. It is irrelevant whether Pythagoras was Greek and whether his geometry was original with him. It is irrelevant whether one or another person from one or another part of the world can be credited with a literary contribution, a work of art, or a religious or philosophic thought. What counts is how such accomplishments became relevant to the people of the world as they involved themselves in increasingly complex practical experiences. Moreover, our own sense of value does not rest on a sports-driven model—the first, the most, the best—but on the challenge posed by how each of us will constitute his own identity in unprecedented circumstances of work, leisure, and feeling. Relevance applies to the perspective of the future and to the recognition that experiences of the past are less and less pertinent in the new context.

What should be taught? Language? Math? Chemistry? Philosophy? The list can go on. It is indeed very hard to do justice by simply nodding yes to language, yes to math, yes to chemistry, but not *yes* wholesale, without putting the question in the pragmatic context. This means that education should not be approached with the aura of religion, or dogmatism, assumed up to now: The teacher knew what eternal truth was; students heard the lectures and finally received communion.

All basic disciplines have changed through time. The rhythm of their change keeps increasing. The current understanding of language, math, chemistry, and philosophy does not necessarily build on a progression. Science, for example, is not accumulation. Neither is language, contrary to all appearance. Rules learned by rote and accepted as invariable are not needed, but procedures for accessing knowledge relevant to our dynamic existence are. To memorize all that education—no matter how good or bad—unloads on students is sheer impossibility. But to know where to find what a given practical instance requires, and how one can use it, is quite a different matter.

Should square dancing, Heavy Metal music, bridge, Chinese cuisine be taught? The list, to be found in the curriculum of many schools and colleges, goes on and on. The test of the relevance of such disciplines (or subjects) in a curriculum should be based on the same pragmatic criteria that our lives and livelihoods depend on. New subjects of study appear on course lists due to structural changes that make literacy useless in the new pragmatic context. They cannot, however, substitute for an education that builds the power of thinking and feeling for practical experiences of increased complexity and dynamism.

Education needs to be shaped to the dynamics of self-constitution in practical experiences characteristic of this new age of humankind. This does not mean that education should become another TV program, or an endless Internet voyage, without aim and without method. We must comprehend that if we demand literacy and efficiency at the same time, ignoring that they are in many ways incompatible, we can only contribute to greater confusion. Higher education was opened to people who merely need training to obtain a skill. These students receive precious-looking diplomas that exactly resemble the ones given to students who have pursued a rigorous course of education. Once upon a time, literacy meant the ability to write and read Latin. Therefore, diplomas are embellished with Latin *dicta*, almost never understood by the graduates, and many times not even by the professors who hand them out. In the spirit of nostalgia, useless rituals are maintained, which are totally disconnected from today's pragmatic framework.

The progressively increased mediation that affects efficiency levels also contributes to the multiplication of the number of *languages* involved in describing, designing, coordinating, and synchronizing human work. We are facing new requirements—those of parallelism, non-linearity, multi-valued logic, vagueness, and selection among options. Programming, never subject to wrong or right, but to optimal choice, and always subject to further improvement, is becoming a requirement for many practical experiences, from the arts to advanced science. Requirements of globality, distribution, economies of scale, of elements pertinent to engineering, communication, marketing, management, and of service-providing experiences need to be met within specific educational programs. The fulfillment of these requirements can never be relegated to literacy.

We have seen that the broader necessity of language, from which the necessity of literacy is derived, is not defensible outside the process of human self-constitution. Language plays an important role, together with other sign systems, subordinated to language or not. In retrospect, we gain an understanding of the entire process: natural instincts are transmitted genetically and only slightly improve, if degeneration does not occur, in the interaction among individuals sharing a habitat. The conscious use of signs takes newborns from the domain of nature and eventually places them in the realm of culture. In this realm, life ceases to be a matter of biology only, and takes on non-natural, social and cultural dimensions. To live as an animal is to live for oneself and for very few others (mainly offspring). To live as a human being is to live through the existence of others, and in relation to others. Established before us and bound to continue after us, culture absorbs *newcomers* who not only begin their existence through their parents, but who also get to know culture and to adapt to it, or revolt against it.

Education starts with the experience of the absent, the non-immediate, the successive. In other words, it implies experiences resulting from comparisons, imitation of actions, and formation of individual patterns corresponding to human biological characteristics. Only much later comes the use of language, of adjectives, adverbs, and the generation of conventions and metaphors, some part of the body of literacy, others part of other languages, such as the visual. With the constitution of the family, education begins, and so does another phase in labor division. The initial phase probably marked the transition from a very small scale of nomadic tribal life to the scale within which language settled in notation and eventually in writing. The generality of sequences, words, phonetics, nouns, and actions was reached in the practical experience of writing. The language of drawings, resulting from different experiences and supporting the making of objects, complemented the development of writing. When the scale of humankind corresponding to incipient literacy was reached, literacy became the instrument for imparting experiences coherent with the experience of language and its use. This account is inserted here as a summary for those who, although claiming historic awareness, show no real instinct for history. This summary says that education is the result of many changes in the condition of humankind and makes clear that these alterations continue. They also entail a responsibility to improve the experience of education and re-establish its connection to the broader framework of human activity, instead of limiting education to the requirements of cultural continuity.

It has been said, again and again, that what we are we had to learn to become. Actually, we are who and what we are through what we do in the context of our individual and social existence. To speak, write, and read means to understand what we say, what we write, and what we read. It is not only the mechanical reproduction of words or sound patterns, which machines can also be programmed to perform. The expectation of speaking, reading, and writing is manifested in all human interactions. To learn how to speak, write, and read means both to *gain skills* and to *become aware* of the pragmatic context of interhuman relations that involve speaking, writing, and reading. It also means awareness of the possibility to change this context.

To educate today means to integrate others, and in the process oneself, in an activity-oriented process directed towards sharing the knowledge necessary to gain further knowledge. Its content cannot be knowledge in general, since the varieties of practical experiences cannot be emulated in school and college. Within the pragmatic framework that made literacy possible, it sufficed to know how an engine functioned in order to work with different machines driven by engines. Literacy reflected homogeneity and served those constituted as literate in controlling the parameters within which deviations were allowed. The post-industrial experience, based on an underlying digital structure, is so heterogeneous that it is impossible to cope with the many different instances of practical requirements. The skills to orient us towards where to find what we need become more important than the information shared. Ownership of knowledge takes a back seat; what counts is *access*, paralleled by a good understanding of the new nature of human praxis focused on cognition. Education should, accordingly, prepare people to handle information, or to direct it to information processing devices. It has to help students develop a propensity for understanding and explaining the variety in which cognition, the raw material of digital engines, results from our experiences.

The unity between the various paths we conceive in projecting our own biological reality into the reality of the world housing us and the result of our activity is characteristic of our mental and emotional condition. It defines our thinking and feeling. At some moment in time, after the division between physical and intellectual work took place, this thinking became relatively free of the result. The abstraction of thinking, once attained, corresponds to our ability to be in the process, to be aware of. it, to judge it. This is the level of theories. The dynamics of the present affects the status of theories, both the way we shape them and how we communicate them. At least in regard to the communication of theory, but also to some of its generation, it is worthwhile to examine, in the context of our concern with education in this age, the evolution of the university.

TEMPLES OF KNOWLEDGE

Education became the institution, the *machine* of literacy, once the social role of a generalized instrument of communication and coordination was established. This happened simultaneously with the reification of many other forms of human praxis: religion, the judiciary, the military. The first Western universities embodied the elitist ideal of literacy in every possible way: exclusivity, philosophy of education, architecture, goals, curriculum, body of professors, body of students, relation to the outside world, religious status. These universities did not care for the crafts, and did not acknowledge apprenticeship. The university, more than schools (in their various forms), extended its influence beyond its walls to assume a leading role in the spiritual lives of the population, while still maintaining an aura about itself. This was not just because of the religious foundation of universities. The university housed important intellectual documents containing theories of science and humanities, and encompassing educational concepts. These documents emphasized the role of a universal education (not only as a reflex of the Church's *catholic* drive) in which fundamental components constructed a *temple of knowledge* from which theories were dispensed throughout the Western world. Through its concept and affirmed values, the university was intended as a model for society and as an important participant in its dynamics. Tradition, languages (opening direct access to the world of classic philosophy and literature), and the arts were understood in their unity. Engineering and anything practical played no part in this.

Compared to the current situation, those first universities were ahead of their time almost to the effect of losing contact with reality. They existed in a world of advanced ideas, of idealized social and moral values, of scientific innovation celebrated in their metaphysical abstraction. There is no need to transcribe the history of education here. We are mainly interested in the dynamics of education up to the turn of the century, and would like to situate it in the discussion caused by the apparent, or actual, failure of education to accomplish its goals today. When universities were founded, access to education was very limited. This makes comparison to the current situation in universities almost irrelevant. It explains, however, why some people question the presence of students who would not have been accepted in a college a century ago, even 50 years ago. Yes, the university is the bearer of prejudices as well as values.

The relevance of historic background is provided by the understanding of the formative power of language, of its capacity for storing ideas and ideals associated with permanency, and for disseminating the doctrine of permanency and authority, making it part of the social texture. Religion insinuated itself into the sciences and humanities, and assumed the powerful role of assigning meaning to various discoveries and theories. Education in such universities was for eternity, according to a model that placed humanity in the center of the universe and declared it exemplary because it originated from the Supreme power. The university established continuity through its entire program, and did so on the foundation of literacy. As an organization, it adopted a structure more favorable to integration and less to differentiation. It constituted a counter-power, a critical instrument, and a framework for intellectual practice. Although many associate the formula "Knowledge is power" with the ideology of the political left, it actually originated in the medieval university, and within conservative power relations for which literacy constituted the underlying structure.

Looking at the development of the medieval university, one can say that it was the embodiment of the reification of language, of the Greek *logos* and of the Roman *ratio*. The entire history of reifying the past was summarized in the university and projected as a model for the future. Alternative ways of thinking and communicating were excluded, or made to fit the language mold and submit, without exception, to the dominating rationality. Based on these premises, the university evolved into an institution of methodical doubt. It became an intellectual machine for generating and experimenting with successive alternative explanations of the universe, as a whole, and of its parts, considered similar in some way to the whole they constituted.

The circumstances leading to the separation of intellectual and educational tasks were generated by an interplay of factors. The printing press is one of them. The metaphors of the university also played an important role. But the defining element was practical expectations. As people eventually learned, they could not build machines only by knowing Latin or Greek, or by reciting litanies, but by knowing mathematics and mechanics. Some of this knowledge came from Greek and Latin texts preserved by Moslem scholars from the desolation following the fall of the Roman empire. People also had to know how to express their goals, and communicate a plan to those who would transform it into roads, bridges, buildings, and much more. Humans could not rely on Aristotle's explanation of the world in order to find new forms of energy. More physics, chemistry, biology, and geology became necessary. Access to such domains was still primarily through literacy, although each of these areas of interest started developing its own *language*. Machines were conceived and built as metaphors of the human being. They embodied an animistic view, while actually answering needs and expectations corresponding to a scale of human existence beyond that of animistic practical experiences.

Industrial experience, a *school* of a new pragmatic framework, would impart awareness of creativity and productivity, as well as a new sense of confidence. Work became less and less homogeneous, as did social life. Once the potential of literacy reached its limits of explaining everything and constituting the only medium for new theories, universities started lagging behind the development of human practice. What separates Galileo Galilei's physics from the Newtonian is less drastic than what separates both from Einstein's relativity theory, and all three of these from the rapidly unfolding physics of the cosmos. In the latter, a different scale and scope must be accounted for, and a totally new way of formulating problems must be developed. Humans project upon the world cognitive explanatory models for which past instruments of knowledge are not adequate. The same applies to theories in biology, chemistry, and more and more to sociology, economics, and the decision sciences. It is worth noting that scale, and complexity therein, thus constitutes a rather encompassing criterion, one that finally affects the theory and practice of education.

COHERENCE AND CONNECTION

Education has stubbornly defended its turf. While it fell well behind the expectations of those in need of support for finding their place in the current pragmatic context, a new paradigm of scientific and humanistic investigation was acknowledged—computation. Together with experimental and theoretical science, computation stimulated levels at which the twin concerns for intellectual coherence and for the ability to establish connections outside the field of study could be satisfied. Computation made it into the educational system without becoming one of education's underlying structures. The late-incoming Technology Literacy Challenge that will provide two billion dollars by the year 2001 acknowledges this situation, though it fails to address it properly. In other countries, the situation is not much better. Bureaucracies based on rules of functioning pertinent to past pragmatics are not capable of even understanding the magnitude of change, in which their reason for being disappears.

In some colleges and private high schools, students can already access the computer network from terminals in their dormitories. Still, in the majority, computing time is limited, and assigned for specific class work, mainly word processing. Too many educational outlets have only administrative computers for keeping track of budget execution and enrollment. In most European countries the situation is even worse. And as far as the poor countries of the world are concerned, one can only hope that the disparity will not deepen. If this were the case with electricity, we would hear an uproar. Computing should become as pervasive as electricity.

This view is not necessarily unanimously accepted. Arguments about whether education needs to be computerized or whether computers should be integrated across the board go on and on among educators and administrators with a say in the matter. It should be noticed that failure to provide the appropriate context for teaching, learning, and research affects the condition of universities all over the world. These universities cease to contribute new knowledge.

They become instead the darkroom for pictures taken elsewhere, by people other than their professors, researchers, and graduate students. Such institutions fathom a relatively good understanding of the past, but a disputable notion of the present and the future, mainly because they are hostages to literacy-based structures of thought and activity, even when they use computers.

To function within a language means to share in the experiences which are built into it. Natural language has a built-in experience of space and time; programming languages contain experiences of logical inference or of object-oriented functioning of the world. These experiences represent its pre-understanding frame of reference. Knowledge built into our so-called natural languages was for a long time common to all human beings. It resulted in communities sharing, through language, the practical experiences through which the community members constituted themselves in space and time. The continuity of language and its permanence reflected continuity of experience and permanence of understanding. Within such a pragmatic framework, education and the sharing of experience were minimally differentiated from each other. Progressively, language experience was added to practical experience and used to differentiate such an experience in new forms of praxis: theoretic work, engineering, art, social activism, political programs. Diversity, incipient segmentation, higher speeds, and incremental mediations affected the condition of self-constitutive human experiences. Consequently, literacy progressively ceased to represent the optimal medium for sharing, although it maintains many other functions. Indeed, plans for a new building, for a bridge, for engines, for many artifacts cannot be expressed in literate discourse, no matter how high the level, or how well literate competency is served by education or impacts upon it.

Accelerated dynamics and a generalized practice of mediations, by means not based on literacy, become part of human praxis in the civilization of illiteracy and define a new underlying structure. Language preserves a limited function. It is paralleled by many other sign systems, some extremely well adapted to rationalization and automation, and becomes itself subject to integration in machines adept at sign processing (in particular information processing). The process can be exemplified by a limited analogy: In order to explore in depth the experience embodied in Homer's texts, one needs a knowledge of ancient Greek. In order to study the legal texts of the Roman Empire, one needs Latin, and probably more. But in order to understand algebra—the word comes from the Arabic *al-jabr/jebr*, meaning *union of broken parts*—one really does not need to be fluent in Arabic.

Literacy embodies a far less significant part of the current human practical experience of self-constitution than it did in the past. Still, literacy-based education asserts its own condition on everything: learning what is already known is a prerequisite to discovering the unknown. In examining the amount and kind of knowledge one needs to understand past experience and to make possible further forms of human praxis, we can be surprised. The first surprise is that we undergo a major shift, from forms of work and thinking fundamentally based on past experience to realms of human constitution that do not repeat the past. Rather, such new experiences negate it altogether, making it relatively irrelevant. Freed from the past, people notice that sometimes the known, expressed in texts, obliterates a better understanding of the present by introducing a pre-understanding of the future that prevents new and effective human practical experiences. The second surprise comes from the realization that means other than those based on literacy better support the current stage of our continuous self-constitution, and that these new means have a different underlying structure.

Searle, among many others, remarked that, "Like it or not, the natural sciences are perhaps our greatest single intellectual achievement as human beings, and any education that neglects this fact is to that extent defective." What is not clearly stated is the fact that sciences emerged as such achievements once the ancillary relation to language and literacy was overcome. *Mathematization* of science and engineering, the focus on computational knowledge, the need to address design aspects of human activity (within sociology, business, law, medicine, etc.), all belong to alternative modes of explanation that make literate speculation less and less effective. They also opened new horizons for hypotheses in astronomy, genetics, anthropology. Cognitive skills are required in the new pragmatic context together with meta-cognitive skills: how to control one's own learning, for example, in a world of change, variety, distributed effort, mediated work, interconnection, and heterogeneity.

We do not yet know how to express and quantify the need for education, how to select the means and criteria for evaluating performance. If the objective is only to generate attitudes of respect for tradition and to impart good manners and some form of judgment, then the result is the emulation of what we think the past celebrated in a person. In the USA, the bill for education, paid by parents, students, and private and public sources, is well over 370 billion dollars a year. In the national budget alone, 18 different categories of grants—programs for building basic and advanced skills in 50,000 schools, programs for Safe and Drug-free schools, programs for acquiring advanced technology, scholarships, and support for loans—quantify the Federal part of the sum. State and local agencies have their own budgets allowing for $5,000 to $12,000 per student. If a class of 25 students is supported by $250,000 of funding, something in the equation of financing education does not add up. The return on investment is miserable by all accounts. Knowing that close to one million students drop out each year—and the number is growing—at various stages of their education, and that to reclaim them would cost additional money, we add another detail to the picture of a failure that is no longer admissible. In other countries, the cost per person is different. In a number of countries (France, Germany, Italy, some countries in Eastern Europe), students attend school years beyond what is considered normal in the USA. Germany discusses, forever it seems, the need to cut schooling. Are 12 or 13 years of schooling sufficient? How long should the state support a student in the university? With the reunification of the country, new needs had to be addressed: qualified teachers, adequate facilities, financing. Japan, while maintaining a 12-grade system, requires more days of schooling (230 per year compared to 212 in Germany and 180 in the USA). France, which regulates even pre-school, maintains 15 years of education. Still, 40% of French students commit errors in using their language. When, almost 360 years ago, Richelieu introduced (unthinkable for the American mentality) the *Académie Française* as the guardian of the language, little did he know that a time would come when language, French or any other, would no longer dominate people's life and work, and would not, despite money invested and time spent to teach, make all who study literate.

The new pragmatic context requires an education that results in abilities to distinguish patterns in a world of extreme dynamism, to question, to cope with complexity as it affects one's practical existence, and with a continuum of values. Students know from their own experience that there is no intrinsic determination to the eternity and universality of language—and this is probably the first shock one faces when noticing how large illiterate populations function and prosper in modern society. The economy absorbed the majority of the dropout population. The almost 50% of the American population considered functionally illiterate partakes, in its majority, in the high standard of living of the country. In other countries, while the numbers are different, the general tenor is the same. Well versed in the literacy of consumption, these people perform exactly the function expected: keep the economic engine turning.

PLENTY OF QUESTIONS

Industrial society, as a precursor to our pragmatic framework, needed literacy in order to get the most out of machines, and to preserve the physical and intellectual capability of the human operator. It invested in education because the return was high enough to justify it. A qualified worker, a qualified physician, chemist, lawyer, and businessman represented a necessity for the harmonious functioning of industrial society. One needed to know how to operate one machine. Chances were that the machine would outlast the operator. One needed to study a relatively stable body of knowledge (laws, medical prescriptions, chemical formulas). Chances were that one and the same book would serve father, son, even grandson. And what could not be disseminated through literacy was taught by example, through the apprenticeship system, from which engineering profited a lot. What education generated were literate people, and members of a society prepared for relations without which machines made little or no sense at all. The more complex such relations, the longer the time needed for education, and the higher the qualifications required from those working as educators.

Education ensured the transmission of knowledge, filling *empty containers* sent by parents, from settled families, as incoming students to schools and colleges. Industrial society simultaneously generated the products and the increased need for them. Some would argue that all this is not so simple. Industrialists did not need educated workers. That is why they transferred a lot of work to children and women. Reformists (probably influenced by religious humanism) insisted on taking children out of the factories. Children were taught to read in order to uplift their souls (as the claim went). Finally, laws were enacted that forbade child labor. As this happened, industry got what it needed: a relatively educated class of workers and higher levels of productivity from employment that used the education provided. Under the right pragmatic conditions, an educated worker proved to be a good investment.

Alan Bloom detailed many of the motives that animated industrial philanthropists in supporting education. I beg to differ and return to the argument that industrial society, in order to use the potential of machine production, had to generate the need for what it produced. Indeed, the first products are the workers themselves, projecting into machine-based praxis their physical attributes, but foremostly skills such as comprehension, interaction, coordination. All these attributes belong to the structural condition of literacy.

Industrial products resulting from qualitatively new forms of human self-constitution were of accidental or no interest to illiterates. What would an illiterate do with products, such as new typewriters, books, more sophisticated household appliances? How would an illiterate interact with them in order to get the most out of each artifact? And how could coordination with others using such new products take place? We know that things were not exactly divided along such clear-cut borders. Illiterate parents had literate children who provided the necessary knowledge. The trickle-down effect was probably part of the broader strategy. But all in all, the philanthropists' support of education was an investment in the optimal functioning of a society whose scale necessitated levels high enough for efficient work. Education was connected to philanthropy, and it still is, as a form of wealth distribution. But it is not love for the neighbor that makes philanthropists' support of education necessary, rather the sheer advantage resulting from money given, estate or machines donated, chairs endowed. Cynical or not, this view results from the perception one experiences when noticing how generosity, well supported by public money, ends up as a self-serving gesture: donations that resulted in buildings, scholarships, endowments, and gifts named after the benefactor. The obsession with permanence—some live it as an obsession with eternity, others as a therapeutic ego massage—is but one of the overhead costs associated with literacy.

Lines from the Prologue to the *Canterbury Tales* come to mind: "Now isn't it a marvel of God's grace/that an illiterate fellow can outpace/the wisdom of a heap of learned men?" How a manciple (probably equivalent to a Residence Life Administrator and Cafeteria Head combined) would perform today is worth another tale. Education, as a product of the civilization of literacy, has problems understanding that literacy corresponds to a development in which written language was the medium for the spoken. Nevertheless, it did learn that today we can store the spoken in non-written form, sometimes more efficiently, and without the heavy investment required to maintain literacy. As an industry, with the special status of a not-for-profit organization, education in the USA competes in the market for its share, and for high returns. Endowments qualify many universities as large businesses that are buffered from the reality of economics.

With or without the aid of philanthropy, learning has to free itself from its subordination to literacy and restrictive literate structures, as it previously freed itself from its subordination to the church, in whose bosom it was nurtured. Obviously, if this new awareness manifests itself only in mailing out videotapes instead of printed college catalogues, then we may ask whether it is educators, or only marketers, who understand the current dynamics. The same should be asked when some professors put their courses on tape, in the belief that canned knowledge is easier for the student to absorb. On-line classes break with the mold, but they are not yet the answer, at least as long as they do not belong to a broader vision reflected in different priorities and appropriate content.

There is nothing intrinsically bad about involving media in education, but the problem is not the medium for storage and delivery. Media labs that are covered by dust because they convey the same useless information as the classes they were supposed to enhance only prove that a fundamental change is necessary. Fundamental, for instance, is the skewed notion that knowledge is transferred from professors—who know more—to students—who know less. Actually, we face a reality never before experienced: students know more than their teachers, in some disciplines. In addition, knowledge still appropriate to a subject a short time ago—call it history, politics, or economics, and think about classes in Soviet and East European studies—has been rendered useless. Physics, mathematics, and chemistry underwent spectacular renewal. This created situations in which what the textbooks taught was immediately contradicted by reality.

Should education compete with the news media? Should it become an Internet address for unlimited and unstructured browsing? Should education give up any sense of foundation? Or should universities periodically refresh their genetic make-up in order to maintain contact with the most recent theories, the most recent research techniques, the most recent discoveries? These are more than enough questions for a pen still writing one word at a time, or for a mouth answering questions as they pile up. Without posing these questions—to which some answers will be attempted at the conclusion of this book—no solution can be expected. The willingness of educators and *everyone* affected by education to formulate them, and many more, would bear witness to a concern that cannot be addressed by some miraculous, all-encompassing formula. The good news is that in many parts of the world this is happening. Finally!

THE EQUATION OF A COMPROMISE

As the scale of humankind changed, and the efficiency of human practical experience corresponding to the scale ascertained itself as the new rationality, the practical experience of self-constitution had to adjust to new circumstances of existence and activity. There is no magic borderline. But there is a definite discontinuity between what constituted the relatively stable underlying structure of literacy and what constitutes the fast-changing underlying structure of the pragmatic framework. Because in our own self-constitution literacy is only one among many media for achieving the efficiency that the new scale requires, we come to realize, even if public discourse does not exactly reflect it, that we cannot afford literacy the way we have until now. And even if we could, we should not. People recognize, even if only reluctantly, that the *literacy machine*, for some reason still called *education*, endows the new generation with a skill of limited significance. The resulting perspective is continuously contradicted by the ever new and ever renewing human experiences through which we become who we are. Education based on the paradigm of literacy is, as we have seen, a luxury which a society, rich or poor, cannot afford. Conditions of human life and praxis require, instead of a skill and perspective for the whole of life, a series. Skill and perspective need to be understood together. Their application will probably be limited in time, and not necessarily directly connected to those succeeding them.

Nobody seriously disputes the relevance of studying language, but very few see language and language-based disciplines as the prerequisite for the less than life-long series of different jobs students of today will have. Although colleges maintain a core curriculum that preserves the role of language and the humanities, the shift towards the languages of mathematics—a discipline that has diversified spectacularly—and of visual representation is so obvious that one can only wonder why the voices of mathematicians are not heard over those of the Modern Language Association. Mathematics prepares for fields from technical to managerial, from scientific to philosophic, and from design to legal. The realization that calculus is first of all a language, and that the goal of education is fluency in it, corresponds to an awareness that musicians had for the longest time with respect to musical scores, but the champions of literacy always refused to accept. The same holds true for the disciplines of visualization: drawing, computer graphics, design. In today's education, the visual needs to be studied at least as much as language-dependent subjects.

Against the background of deeper changes, education is focusing on its on redefinition. The major change is from a container model of education—the child being the empty container who needs to be filled with language, history, math, and not much more—to a heuristic education. Our pragmatics is one of process, as the pragmatics of education finally should be. Education needs to be conducive to interaction and to the formation of criteria for choices from among many options. But change does not come easily. Still using the impertinence of literacy, some educators call the container model "teaching students to think." They do not realize that students think whether we teach them to or not! Students of all ages are aware of change, and familiar with modes of interaction, among themselves and with technology, closer to their condition than to that of their teachers. The majority of the new businesses on the Internet are instigated by students and supported by their inventiveness and dedication. They have became agents of change in spite of all the shortcomings of education. And students have become educators themselves, offering environments for conveying their own experience.

TO BE A CHILD

No one can declare better ways of teaching without considering the real child. In a world of choice and free movement, children are more likely to come from families that will consist of a single parent. Many children will come from environments where discrimination, poverty, prejudice, and violence have an overpowering influence. Such an environment is significant for a society dedicated to democratic ideals. We have to face the fact that childrearing and education are being transferred from family to institutions meant to *produce* the educated person. With the best of motives, society has created *factories* for *processing* children. These socio-educational entities are accepted quite obligingly by the majority of the people freed from a responsibility affecting their own lives. "Everything will be fine, as long as the education of the new generation basically repeats the education of the parents," sums up the expectations regarding these institutions.

Although we know that, generally speaking, cycles (of production, design, and evaluation) are getting shorter, we maintain children in education well past the time they even fit in classroom chairs. One needs to see those adults forced to be students, full of energy, frustrated that their patience, not their creative potential, is put to the test. Dropping out of high school or college is not indicative of a student's immaturity. Society's tendency to decide what is best for the next generation has determined that only one type of education will ensure productive adults. Society refuses to consider humans in the variety of their potential. From the *Projection of Education Statistics to the Year 2006*, we learn that the total private and public elementary and secondary school enrollment in the USA will increase from 49.8 million in 1994 to 54.6 million. Of the 49.8 million in 1994, only 2.5 million graduated high school, and by the year 2006 the number will not exceed 3 million. Students themselves seem to be more aware of the excessively long cycle of education than do the experts who define its methods, contents, and goals. This creates a basis for conflict that no one should underestimate.

Growing up in an environment of change and challenge is probably rewarding in the long run. But things are not very simple. The pressure to perform, peer pressure, and one's youthful instincts to explore and ascertain can transform a student's life in an instant. The distance between paradise (support and choice without worry) and hell (the specter of disease, addiction, abandonment, disappointment, lack of direction) is also shorter than prior generations experienced it. Hundreds of TV channels, the Internet, thousands of music titles (on CD, video, and radio stations), the lure of sports, drugs, sex, and the hundreds of fashion labels—choosing can be overwhelming. Literacy used to organize everything neatly. If you were in love, *Romeo and Juliet* was proper reading material. If you wished to explore Greece, you started with Homer's epics and worked your way up to the most recent novel by a contemporary Greek writer.

The problem is that drugs, AIDS, millions of attractions, the need to find one's way in a world less settled and less patient, do not fit in the neat scheme of literacy. The language of genetics and the language of personality constitution are better articulated through means other than books. Heroes, teachers, parents, priests, and activists are no longer icons, even if they are portrayed to be better than they were in reality. Bart Simpson, the underachiever, "mediocre and proud of it," is a model for everyone who is told that what really counts is to feel good, period.

Still, some young people go to school or college full of enthusiasm, hoping to get an education that will guarantee self-fulfillment. All that is studied, over a long period of time and at great financial sacrifice, comes not even close to what they will face. Tehy might learn how to spell and how to add. But they soon discover that in real life skills other than spelling and arithmetic are expected. What bigger disappointment is there than discovering that years of pursing a promise bring no result? If, after all this, we still want both literacy and competence for experiences which literacy does not support, and often inhibits, we would have to invest beyond what society is willing and able to spend. And even if society were to do so, as it seems that it feels it must, the investment would be in imposing useless skills and a primitive perspective on the new generation, until the time comes when it can escape society's pressure. Education in our day remains a compromise between the interests of the institution of education (with tens of thousands of teachers who would become unemployed) and a new pragmatic framework that few in academia understand.

One of the elements of this equation is the practical need to extend education to all, and if possible on a continuous basis. But unless this education reflects the variety of literacies that the pragmatic framework requires, admitting everyone to everything results in the lowest general level of education. The variety of practical experiences of self-constitution requires that we find ways to coordinate access to education by properly and responsibly identifying *types of creativity*, and investing responsibility in their development. Continuous education needs to be integrated in the work structure. It has to become part of the reciprocal commitments through which the new pragmatic framework is acknowledged.

To all those dedicated to the human aspects of politics, business, law, and medicine, who deplore that the technicians of policy-making can no longer find their way to our souls, all this will sound terrifying. Nevertheless, as much as we would like to be considered as individuals, each with our own dignity, personality, opinions, emotions, and pains, we ourselves undermine our expectations in our striving for more and more, at a price lower than what it costs society to distinguish us. Scale dictates anonymity, and probably mediocrity.

Ignorance of literacy's role in centuries of productive human life dictates that it is time to unload the literacy-reflected experiences for which there is no reference in the new pragmatic context.

WHO ARE WE KIDDING?

Scared that in giving up literacy training we commit treason to our own condition, we maintain literacy and try to adapt it to new circumstances of working, thinking, feeling, and exploring. In view of the inefficiency built into our system of education, we try to compromise by adding the dimension characteristic of the current status of human experience of multiple partial literacies. The result is the transformation of education into a packaging industry of human beings: you choose the line along which you want to be processed; we make sure that you get the literacy alibi, and that we train you to be able to cope with so-called entry-level jobs. Obviously, this evolves in a more subtle way. The kind of college or university one attends, or the tuition one pays, determines the amount of subtlety. Students accept the function of education insofar as it mediates between their goals and the rather scary reality of the marketplace. This mediation differs according to the level of education, and is influenced by political and social decision making.

As an industry for processing the new generation, education acts according to parameters resulting from its opportunistic search for a place between academia and reality. Education acknowledges the narrow domains of expertise which labor division brought about, and reproduces the structure of current human experience in its own structure. Through vast financial support, from states, private sources, and tradition-based organizations, education is artificially removed from the reality of expected efficiency. It is rarely a universe of commitments. Accordingly, the gap between the literate language of the university and the languages of current human practice widens. The tenure system only adds another structural burden.

When the highest goal of a professor is to be freed of teaching, something is awfully wrong with our legitimate decision to guarantee educators the freedom necessary for exercising their profession.

Behind the testing model that drives much of current education is the expectation of effective ranking of students. This model takes a literate approach insofar as it establishes a dichotomy (aptitude vs. achievement) that makes students react to questions, but does not really engage them or encourage creative contributions. The result is illustrative of the relation between what we do and how we evaluate what we do. An expectation was set, and the process of education was skewed to generate good test results. This effectively eliminates teaching and learning for the sake of a subject. Students are afraid they will not measure up and demand to be taught *by the book*. Teachers who know better than the book are intimidated, by students and administration, from trying better approaches. Good students are frustrated in their attempts to define their own passion and to pursue it to their definition of success. Entrepreneurs at the age of 14, they do not need the feedback of stupid tests, carried out more for the sake of bureaucracy than for their well-being. Standardized tests dominated by multiple-choice answers facilitate low cost evaluations, but also affect patterns of teaching and learning. Exactly what the new pragmatics embodies—the ability to adapt and to be proactive—is counteracted through the experience of testing, and the teaching geared to multiple-choice instruments.

The uncoupling of education from the experiential frame of the human being is reflected in education's language and organization, and in the limiting assumptions about its function and methods. Education has become a self-serving organization with a bureaucratic "network of directives," as Winograd and Flores call them, and motivational elements not very different from the state, the military, and the legal system. Like the organizations mentioned, it also develops networks of interaction with sources of funding and sources of power, some driven by the same self-preserving energies as education itself. Instead of reflecting shorter cycles of activity in its own structure, it tends to maintain control over the destiny of students for longer periods of time. Even in fields of early acknowledged creativity—e.g., computer programming, networking, genetics, and nanotechnology—education continues to apply a policy that takes away the edge of youth, inventiveness, and risk.

The lowest quality of education is at the undergraduate level in universities, where either graduate assistants or even machines substitute for professors too busy funding their research, or actually no longer attuned to teaching. This situation exists exactly because we are not yet able to develop strategies of education adapted to new circumstances of human work and to the efficiency requirements which we ourselves made necessary. The "network of recurrent conversations," to use Winograd's terminology again, or the "language game" that Wittgenstein attributed to each profession, hides behind the front of literacy and thus burdens education. Once accreditation introduces the language game of politics, education distances itself even more from its fundamental mission. Accreditation agencies translate concerns about the quality of education into requirements, such as the evaluation of colleges and universities based on scores on exit tests taken by students. These are supposed to reflect academic achievement. In other cases, such scores are used for assessing financial support. The paradox is that what negatively affects the quality of education becomes the measure of reward. Test results are often used in politicians' arguments about improved education, as well as a marketing tool. In fact, to prepare students for performance makes performance a goal in itself. Thus it should come as no surprise that the most popular book on college campuses—today's education factories—is a guide to cheating.

Many times comparisons are made between students in the USA and in Japan or in Western European countries. In many ways these comparisons are against the pervasive dynamics of integration that we experience. Still, there are things to consider—for instance, that Japanese students spend almost the same amount of time watching TV as American students do, and that they are not involved in household tasks. Noticeable differences are in reading. The Japanese spend double the number of hours that American students do in reading. Japanese students spend more time on schoolwork (the same 2-to-1 ratio), but much less on entertainment. Should Japan be considered a model? If we see that Japanese students rank among the best in science subjects, the answer seems to be positive. But if we project the same against the entire development of students, their exceptional creative achievements, the answer becomes a little more guarded. With all its limitations, the USA is still more attuned to pragmatic requirements. This is probably due more to the country's inherent dynamics than to its educational institutions. Largely unregulated, capable of adaptive moves, subject to innovation, the USA is potentially a better network for educational possibilities.

What caused the criticism in these pages of evaluation is the indecisiveness that the USA shows—the program for school reform for the year 2000 is an example of this attitude—and the difficulty it has in realizing the price of the compromise it keeps supporting. Once Japanese businesses started buying American campuses, the price of the compromise became clear. Universities in the USA were saved from bankruptcy. Japanese schools, whose structured programs and lack of understanding of the new pragmatics made for headlines, were able to evade their own rigid system of education, reputed for being late in acknowledging the dynamics of change. Abruptly, the *Americanization* of world education—study driven by multiple-choice tests with a dualistic structure—was short-changed by a *Japanization* movement. But in the closer look suggested above, it is evident that the Japanese are extricating themselves from drastic literacy requirements that end up hampering necessary accommodations in the traditional Japanese system of values. Although caution is called for, especially in approaching a subject foreign to our direct experience and understanding, the trend expressed is telling in its many consequences.

A legitimate question to be expected from any sensible reader refers to alternatives. Let us first notice that, due to the new pragmatic framework, we are more and more in the situation to disseminate every and any type of information to any imaginable destination. The interconnectivity of business and of markets creates the global economy. In contrast, our school and college systems, as separate from real life, and conceived physically outside our universe of existence, are probably as anachronistic as the castles and palaces we associate with the power and function of nobility; or as anachronistic as the high stacks of steel mills we associate with industry, and the cities we associate with social life. Some alumni might be nostalgic for the Gothic structures of their university days. The physical reference to a time "when education meant something" is clear—as is the memory of the campus, yet another good reason to look at the homecoming party in anticipation of the football game, or in celebration of a good time (win or lose).

To make explicit the shift from a symbolism of education, coordinated with the function of intellectual accomplishment, to a stage when debunking this symbolism, still alive in and outside Ivy League universities, is an urgent political and practical goal is only the beginning. There is no justification for maintaining outmoded structures and attitudes, and investing in walls and campuses and feudal university domains. As one of the successful entrepreneurs of this time put it, "anything that has to do with brick and mortar and its DISPLAY is—to use some poetic license—dead." The focus has to be on the dynamics of individual self-constitution, and on the pragmatic horizons of everyone's future.

Fixing and maintaining schools in the USA, as well as in almost any country in the world, would cost more than building them from scratch. The advantage of giving up structures inappropriate to the new requirements of education is that, finally, at least we would create environments for interaction, taking full advantage of the progress made in technologies of communication and interactive learning. There is no need to idealize the Internet and the World Wide Web at their current stage. But if the future will continue to be defined more by commerce expectations than by educational needs, no one should be surprised that their educational potential will come to fruition late.

Humans do not develop at the same pace, and in the same direction. Each of us is so different that the main function of education should be not to minimize differences through literacy and literacy-based strategies that support a false sense of democracy, but to identify and maximize differences. This will provide the foundation for an education that allows each student to develop according to possibilities evinced through the relations, language-based or not, that people enter into. The content of education, understood as process, should be the experience, and the associated means of creating and understanding it. Instead of a dominant language, with built-in experiences more and more alien to the vast majority of students, the ability to cope with many sign systems, with many languages, to articulate them, adapt them to the circumstance, and share them as much as the circumstance requires, should become the goal. Some would counter, "This was attempted with courses labeled *modern math* and resulted in no one's understanding it, or even simple math." There is some truth in this. The mathematically gifted had no problem in learning the new math. Students who were under the influence of literate reasoning had problems. What we need to do is to keep the mind open, allow for as much accumulation as necessary, and for discarding, if new experiences demand an open mind and freedom from previous assumptions. Some students will settle (in math or in other subjects) for predominantly visual signs, others for sounds, some for words, for rhythm, for any of the forms through which human intelligence comes to expression. Interactive multimedia are only some of the many media available. Other possibilities are yet to emerge. The Internet is in the same situation. A framework for individual selection, for tapping into learning resources and using them to the degree desired and acknowledged as necessary by praxis, would be the way to go. Not only literacy, in the accepted sense, but mathematical literacy, biological, chemical, or engineering *literacy*, and visual thinking and expression should be given equal consideration. Cross-pollination among disciplines traditionally kept in isolation will definitely enhance creativity by doing away with the obsessive channeling practiced nowadays.

Education needs to shift from the atomistic view that isolates subjects from the whole of reality to a holistic perspective. This will acknowledge types of mediation as effective means of increasing the efficiency of work, the requirements of integration, and the distributed nature of practical experiences in the world today. *Collaborative effort* needs to be brought to the forefront of the educational experience. We can define communities of interest, focused on some body of experience (which can be incorporated in an artifact, a book, a work of art, or someone's expertise). Education should provide means for sharing experiences. A variety of different interests can be brought into focus through sharing and collaborative learning. There are many dimensions to such an approach: the knowledge sought, the experience of the variety of perspectives and uses, the awareness of interaction, the skills for intercommunication, and more. Implicit is the high expectation of sharing, while at the same time maintaining motivations for individual achievement and individual reward. This becomes critical at a time when it becomes more and more evident that resources are finite, while expectations still grow exponentially. The change from a standardized model, focused on the quick fix that leads to results (no matter how high a cost), to the collaborative model of individuality and distinction re-establishes an ethical framework, which is urgently needed. Competition is not excluded, but instead of conflict—which in the given system results in students who cut pages from books so that their colleagues will fail—we ought to create an environment of reciprocally advantageous cooperation. How far are we from such an objective?

In the words of Jacques Barzun, a devoted educator committed to literacy, education failed to "develop native intelligence." In an interesting *negative* of what people think education accomplishes, he points to the appearance of success: "We professed to make ideal citizens, super-tolerant neighbors, agents of world peace, and happy family folk, at once sexually adept and flawless drivers of cars." All this is nothing to be ashamed of, but as educational goals, they are quite off the target. Citizenship in the society of the new pragmatic context is different from citizenship in previous societies. Tolerance requires a new way to manifest it, such as the integration of what is different and complementary. Peace, yes, even peace, means a different state of affairs at a time when many local conflicts affect the world. As far as family, sex, and the culture of the car are concerned, nothing can point more to the failure of education. Indeed, education failed to understand all the factors involved in contemporary family life. It failed to understand sexual relations. Faced with the painful reality of the degradation of sexual relations, education resorted to the desperate measure of dispensing condoms, an extension of what was gloriously celebrated as *sex education*. The flawless drivers never heard the criticism voiced by citizens concerned with energy waste. We made students rely on cheap gasoline and affordable cars to bring them to school and college, instead of understanding that education needs to be decentralized, distributed, and—why not—adapted to the communication and interaction possibilities of our times. The Green Teens who are active against energy waste might be well ahead of their educational system, but still forced to go through it. Moreover, education should be seen in the broader context of the other changes coming with the end of the civilization of literacy: the status of family, religion, law, and government.

While education is related to the civic status of the individual, the new conditions for the activity of our minds are also very important. Ideally, education addresses all the facets of the human being. New conditions of generalized interconnection almost turn the paradigm of continuing education into continuous education that corresponds to changes in human experience unfolding under even more complex circumstances. It might well happen that for some experiences, we shall have to recuperate values characteristic of literacy. But better to rediscover them than to maintain literacy as an ideal when the perspectives for new forms of ascertaining ourselves as human beings require more, much more, than literacy.

BOOK IV.

CHAPTER 1: LANGUAGE AND THE VISUAL

Photography, film, and television have changed the world more than Gutenberg's printing press. Much of the blame for the decline in literacy is attributed to them, especially to movies and television. More recently, computer games and the Internet have been added to the list of culprits. Studies have been conducted all over the world with the aim of discovering how film and television have changed established reading habits, writing ability, and the use and interpretation of language. Patterns of publishing and distribution of information, including electronic publication and the World Wide Web (still in its infancy), have also been analyzed on a comparative basis. Inferences have been drawn concerning the influence of various types of images on what is printed and why, as well as on how writing (fiction, science, trade books, manuals, poetry, drama, even correspondence) has changed.

In some countries, almost every home has a television set; in others even more than one. In 1995, the number of computers sold surpassed that of television sets. In many countries, most children watch television and films before they learn to read. In a few countries, children play computer games before ever opening a book. After they start to read, the amount of time spent in front of a TV set is far greater than the time dedicated to books. Adults, already the fourth and fifth generations of television viewers, are even more inclined to images. Some images are of their choice—TV programs at home, movies in the theater, videotapes they buy, rent, or borrow from the library, CD-ROMs. Other images are imposed on the adult generations by demands connected to their professions, their health, their hobbies, and by advertisement. After image-recording and playing equipment became widely available, the focus on TV and video expanded. In addition to the ability to bring home films of one's choice, to buy and rent videotapes, laser discs, and CD-ROMs on a variety of subjects, we are able to produce a video archive for family, school, community, or professional purposes. We can even avail ourselves of cable TV to generate programs of local interest. The generalized system of networking (cable, satellites, airwaves), through which images can be *pumped* from practically any location into schools, homes, offices, and libraries, affects even further the relation of children and adults among themselves and the relation of both groups to language and to literacy in contemporary life. Anyone with access to the printing presses of the digital world can *print* a CD-ROM. Access to the Internet is no more expensive than a magazine subscription. But the Internet is much more exciting because we are not only at the receiving end.

The subject, as almost all have perceived and analyzed it, is not the impact of visual technology and computers on reading patterns, or the influence of new media on how people write. At the core of the development described so far is the fundamental shift from one dominant sign system, called *language,* and its reified form, called *literacy,* to several sign systems, among which the visual plays a dominant role. We would certainly fail to understand what is happening, what the long-lasting consequences of the changes we face are, and what the best course of action is, if we were to look only at the influence of technology. Understanding the degree of necessity of the technology in the first place is where the focus should be. The obsession with symptoms, characteristic of industrial pragmatics, is not limited to mechanics' shops and doctors' offices.

New practical experiences within the scale of humankind that result in the need for alternatives to language confirm that the focus cannot be on television and computer screens, nor on advertisement, electronic photography, and laser discs. The issue is not CD-ROM, digital video, Internet and the World Wide Web, but the need to cope with complexity. And the goal is to achieve higher levels of efficien-

Civilization of Illiteracy: Book IV

cy corresponding to the needs and expectations of the global scale that humankind has reached.

So far, very few of those who study the matter have resisted the temptation to fasten blame on television watching or on the intimidating intrusion of electronic and digital contraptions for the decline of literacy. It is easier to count the hours children spend watching TV—an average of 16,000 hours in comparison to 13,000 hours for study before graduation from high school—than to see *why* such patterns occur. And it is as easy to conclude that by the time these children can be served alcohol in a restaurant or buy it in stores, they will have seen well over a million commercials. Yet no one ever acknowledges new structures of work and communication, even less the unprecedented wealth of forms of human interaction, regardless of how shallow they are. That particular ways of working and living have for all practical purposes disappeared, is easily understood. Understanding *why* requires the will to take a fresh look at necessary developments.

Some of today's visual sign systems originate in the civilization of literacy: advertisement, theatrical and para-theatrical performance, and television drama. They carry with them efficiency expectations typical of the Machine Age. Other visual sign systems transcend the limits of literacy: concrete poetry, *happening,* animation, performance games that lead to interactive video, hypermedia or interactive multimedia, virtual reality, and global networks. Within such experiences, a different dynamics and a focus on distinctions, instead of on homogeneity, are embedded. Most of these experiences originate in the practical requirement to extend the human being's experiential horizon, and the need to keep pace with the dynamics of global economy.

HOW MANY WORDS IN A LOOK?

In a newspaper industry journal (*Printers' Ink,* 1921), Fred R. Barnard launched what would become over time a powerful slogan: "One look is worth a thousand words." To make his remark sound more convincing, he later reformulated it as "One picture is worth a thousand words," and called it a proverb from China. Few slogans were repeated and paraphrased more than this one. Barnard wanted to draw people's attention to the power of images. It took some years until the new underlying structure of our continuous practical self-constitution confirmed an observation made slightly ahead of its time. It should be added that, through the millennia, craftsmen and the forerunners of engineering used images to design artifacts and tools, and to plan and build cities, monuments, and bridges. They realized through their own experience how powerful images could be, although they did not compare them to words.

Images are more concrete than words. The concreteness of the visual makes images inappropriate for describing other images. However, it does not prevent human beings from associating images with the most abstract concepts they develop in the course of their practical or theoretical experience. Words start by being relatively close to what they denote, and end up so far removed from the objects or actions they name that, unless they are generated together with an object or action (like the word *calculator*, from *calculae,* stones for counting), they seem arbitrary. Reminiscences of the motivation of words (especially onomatopoeic qualities, i.e., phonetic resemblance to what the word refers to, such as *crack* or *whoosh*) do not really affect the abstract rules of generating statements, or even our understanding of such language signs.

Images are more constrained, more directly determined by the pragmatic experience in whose framework they are generated. *Red* as a word (with its equivalencies in other languages: *rot* in German, *rouge* in French, *rojo* in Spanish, 赤 (aka) in Japanese, *adom* in Hebrew, and красный in Russian) is arbitrary in comparison to the color it designates. Even the designation is quite approximate. In given experiential situations, many nuances can be distinguished, although there are no names for them. The red in an image is a physical quality that can be measured and standardized, hence made easier to process in photography, printing, and synthesis of pigments. In the same experiential framework, it can be associated with many objects or processes: flowers, blood, a stoplight, sunset, a flag. It can be compared to them, it can trigger new associations, or become a convention. Once language translates a visual sign, it also loads it with conventions characteristic of language—red as in revolution, cardinal red, redneck, etc.—moving it from the realm of its physical determination (wavelength, or frequency of oscillation) to the reality of cultural conventions. These are preserved and integrated in the symbolism of a community.

Purely pictorial signs, as in Chinese and Japanese writing, relate to the structure of language, and are culturally significant. No matter to which extent such pictorial signs are refined—and indeed, characters in Chinese and Kanji are extremely sophisticated—they maintain a relation to what they refer to. They extend the experience of writing, especially in calligraphic exercise, in the experience conveyed. We can impose on images—and I do not refer only to Chinese ideograms—the logic embodied in language. But once we do, we alter the condition of the image and transform it into an illustration.

Language, in its embodiment in literacy, is an analytic tool and supports analytic practice quite well. Images have a dominantly synthetic character and make for good composite tools. Synthesizing activities, especially designing, an object, a message, or a course of action, imply the participation of images, in particular powerful diagramming and drawing. Language describes; images constitute. Language requires a context for understanding, in which classes of distribution are defined. Images suggest such a context. Given the individual character of any image, the equivalent of a distributional class for a language simply does not exist.

To look at an image, for whatever practical or theoretical purpose, means to relate to the *method* of the image, not to its components. The method of an image is an experience, not a grammar applied to a repertory, or the instantiation of rules of grammar. The power of language consists of its abstract nature. Images are strong through their concreteness. The abstraction of language results from sharing vocabulary and grammar; the abstraction of images, from sharing visual experience, or creating a context for new experiences.

For as long as visual experience was confined to one's limited universe of existence, as in the case of the migrating tribes, the visual could not serve as a medium for anything beyond this changing universe of existence. Language resulted from the need to surpass the limitations of space and time, to generate choices. The only viable alternative adopted was the abstract image of the phonetic convention, which was easier to *carry* from one world to another, as, for instance, the Phoenicians did. Each alphabet is a condensed visual testimony to experiences in the meanwhile uncoupled from language and its concrete practical motivations.

Writing visualizes language; reading brings the written language back to its oral life, but in a tamed version. Whether the Sumerian, Aramaic, Hebrew, Greek, Arabic, Latin, or Slavic alphabet, the letters are not neutral signs for abstract phonetic language. They summarize visual experiences and encode rules of recognition; they are related to anthropologic experience and to cognitive processes of abstracting. The mysticism of numbers and their meta-physical meanings, of letters and combinations of letters and numbers, of shapes, symmetry, etc. are all present. With alphabets and numbers the abstract nature of visual representation took over the phonetic quality of language. The concreteness of pictorial representation, along with the encoded elements (what is the experience behind a letter? a number? a certain way of writing?), simply vanished for the average literate (or illiterate) person. This is part of the broader process of acculturation—that is, breaking through experiences of language. Experts in alphabets show us the levels at which the image of each letter constituted expressive levels significant in themselves. Nevertheless, their *alphabetic literacy* is as relevant to writing as much as a good description of the various kinds of wheels is relevant to the making and the use of automobiles.

The current use of images results from the new exigencies of human praxis and developments in visualization technology. In previous chapters, some of these conditions were mentioned:

1. the global scale of our activity and existence;
2. the diversity made possible by the practical experiences corresponding to this globality;
3. the dynamics of ever faster, increasingly mediated, human interaction;
4. the need to optimize human interaction in order to achieve high levels of efficiency;
5. the need to overcome the arcane stereotypes of language;
6. the non-linear, non-sequential, open nature of human experiences brought to the fore through the new scale of humankind.

The list is open-ended. The more our command of images improves, the more arguments in favor of their use. None of these arguments should be construed as a blank and non-critical endorsement of images. We know that we cannot pursue theoretic work exclusively with images, or that the meta-level (language about language) cannot be reached with images. Images are factual, situational, and unstable. They also convey a false sense of democracy. Moreover, they materialize the shift from a positivist conception of facts, dominating a literacy-based determinism, to a relativist conception of chaotic functioning, embodied, for instance, by the market or by the new means and methods of human interaction. However, until we learn all there is to know about the potential of images in areas other than art, architecture, and design, chances are that we shall not understand their participation in thinking and in other traditionally non-image-based forms of human praxis.

Images are very powerful agents for activities involving human emotions and instincts. They shy away from *literal* truth, insofar as the logic of images is different from the logic inhabiting human experiences of self-constitution in language. Imagery has a *protean* character. Images not only represent; they actually shape, form, and constitute subjects. Cognitive processes of association are better supported visually than in language. Through images, people are effectively encultured, i.e., given the identity which they cannot experience at the abstract level of acculturation through language. The world of *avatars,* dynamic graphic representations of a person in the virtual universe of networks, is one of concreteness. The individuals literally remake themselves as visual entities that can enter a dialogue with others.

Within a given culture, images relate to each other. In the multitude of cultures within which people identify themselves, images translate from one experience to another. Against the background of globality, the experience of images is one of simultaneous distinctions and integration. Distinctions carry the identifiers of the encultured human beings constituted in new practical experiences. Integration is probably best exemplified by the metaphor of the *global village* of teleconnections and tele-viewing, of Internet and World Wide Web interactions.

The characteristics of images given here so far need to be related to the perspective of changes brought about by imaging technologies. Otherwise, we could hardly come to understand how images constitute languages that make literacy useless, or better yet, that result in the need for complementary partial literacies.

THE MECHANICAL EYE AND THE ELECTRONIC EYE

The photo camera and the associated technology of photo processing are products of the civilization of literacy in anticipation of the civilization of illiteracy. The metaphor of the eye, manifest in the optics of the lens and the mechanics of the camera, could not entirely support new human perceptions of reality without the participation of literacy. Camera use implied the shared background of literacy and literacy-based space representations. The entire discussion of the possibilities and limitations of photography—a discussion begun shortly after the first photographic images were produced, and still going on in our day—is an exercise in analytical practice.

Some looked at photography as writing with light; others as mechanical drawing. They doubted whether there was room for creativity in its use, but never questioned its documentary quality: shorthand for descriptions difficult, but still possible, in writing. The wider the framework of practical experiences involving the camera, the more interesting the testimony of photography proved. This applies to photography in journalism and science, as well as in personal and family life. With photography, images started to substitute for words, and literacy progressively gave way to imagery in a variety of new human experiences related to space, movement, and aspects of life otherwise not visible.

Testimony of the *invisible*, made available to many people through the photographic camera, was much stronger, richer, and more authentic than the words one could write about the same. Early photographs of the Paris sewer system—the latter a subject of many stories, but literally out of sight—exemplify this function. Before the camera, only drawing could capture the visible without changing it into words or obscure diagrams. Drawing was an interpreted representation, not only in the sense of selection—what to draw—but also in defining a perspective and endowing the image with some emotional quality. The camera had a long way to go before the same interpretive quality was achieved, and even then, in view of the mediating technology, it was quite difficult to define what was added to what was photographed, and why.

Today's cameras—from the disposables to the fully automated—encapsulate everything we have to know to operate them. There is no need to be aware of the eye metaphor—which is undergoing change with the advent of electronic photography—and even less of what diaphragm, exposure time, and distance are. The experience leading to photography and the practical experience of automated photography are uncoupled. To take a picture is no longer a matter of expertise, but a reflex gesture accompanying travel, family, or community events, and discrete moments of relative significance. Thus photographic images took over linguistic descriptions and became our diaries. As confusing as this might sound, a camera turns into an extension of our eyes (actually, only one), easier to use than language, and probably more accurate. In some way, a camera is a *compressed language* all set for the generation of *visual sentences.* If scientific use of photography were not available, a great deal of effort would be necessary to verbally describe what images from outer space, from the powerful electronic microscope, or from under the earth and under water, reveal to us. In Leonardo da Vinci's time, the only alternative was drawing, and a very rich imagination!

The camera has a built-in space concept, probably more explicit than language has. This concept is asserted and embodied in the geometry of the lens and is reflected in some of the characteristics of photographic images. They are, mainly, two-dimensional reductions of our three-dimensional universe of experience, also influenced by light, film emulsion, type of processing, technology and materials used for printing, but primarily by physical properties of the lens used. Once our spatial concept improved and progress in lens processing was made, we were able to change the lens, to make it more adaptive (wide angle, zoom) to functions related to visual experiences. We were also able to introduce an element of time control that helped to capture dynamic events.

Another important change was brought about by Polaroid's concept of almost instant delivery of prints. It is with this concept—compressing two stages of photographic representation into one and, in initial developments, giving up the possibility of making copies—that we reached a new phase in the relation between literacy and photography. As we know, the traditional camera came with the implicit machine-focused conversation: What can *I* do with it? The Polaroid concept changed this to a different query: What can *it* do for me? This change of emphasis corresponds to a different experience with the medium and is accompanied by the liberation of photography from some of the constraints of the system of literacy. "What can *I* do?" concerns photographic knowledge and the selection made by photographers, persons who constitute their identity in a new practical experience. "What can *it* do?" refers to knowledge embodied in the hardware. The advertisement succinctly describes the change: "Hold the picture in your hand while you still hold the memory in your heart." As opposed to a written record, an instant image is meant for a short time, almost as a fast substitute for writing.

A more significant change occurs when photography goes electronic, and in particular, digital. Both elements already discussed— the significance of the smallest changes in the input on the result, and the quality aspect of digital vs. analog—are reflected in digital photography. I insist on this because of the new condition of the image it entails and our relation to the realm of the visual. Language found its medium in writing, and printing made writing the object of literacy. Images could not be used with the same ease as writing, and could not be transmitted the way the voice is. When we found ways to have voice travel at speeds faster than that of sound, by electromagnetic waves used in telephone or radio transmission, we consolidated the function of language, but at the same time freed language of some of the limitations of literacy. Digital photography accomplishes the same for images.

A written report from any place in the world might take longer to produce, though not to transmit, than the image representing the event reported. Connected to a network, an electronic camera sends images from the event to the page prepared for printing. The understanding of the image, whose printing involved a *digital* component (the raster) long before the computer was invented, requires a much lower social investment than literacy. The complexity is transferred from capturing the image to transmitting and viewing it. Films are used to generate an electronic simile of our photographic shots. At the friendly automated image shop, we get colorful prints and the shiny CD-ROM from which each image can be recalled on a video screen or further processed on our computers.

From the image as testimony, as literacy destined it to be, to the image as pretext for new experiences—medium of visual relativity and questionable morality—everything, and more, is possible. Images can mediate in fast developing situations—transactions, exchange of information, conflicts—better than words can. They are free of the extra burden words bear and allow for global and detailed local interpretation. Electronic processing of digital photography supports comparison, as well as manipulation, of images in view of unprecedented human experiences requiring such functions. The metaphor of the *one-eye*, which the photographic camera embodies, led to a flat world. Cyclopes see everything flat. Unfortunately, but by no accident, this metaphor was taken over in computer graphics. Images on the computer screen are held together by the conventions of monocular vision. Digital photography can be networked and endowed with dynamic qualities. But what makes digital photography more and more a breakthrough, in respect to its incipient literate phase, is that we can build 3D cameras, that is, technical beasts with two eyes (and if need be, with more). This leads to practical experiences in a pragmatic framework no longer limited to sequences or to reductionist strategies of representation.

WHO IS AFRAID OF A LOCOMOTIVE?

The image of a locomotive moving in the direction of the spectators made them scream and run away when moving pictures were first shown to the public. Movement enhanced the realism of the image, captured on film to the extent of blurring the borderline between reality and the newly established convention of cinematographic expression. In the movies of the silent era, the literacy-based realism of the image—actually an illustration of the script—successfully compensated for the impossibility of providing the sound of dialogue. The experience of literacy and that of *writing movement* onto film were tightly coupled. Short scenes, designed with close attention to visual details, could be understood without the presence of the word, because of the shared background of language. The convention of cinematography is based on sharing the extended *white page* on which the projection of moving images takes place. Humor was the preferred structure, since the mechanical reproduction of movement had, due to rudimentary technology and lack of sound, a comic quality in itself. Later, music was inserted, then dialogue. Everyone was looking forward to the day when image and sound would be synchronized, when color movies would become possible.

It adds to the arguments thus far advanced that cinematographic human experience, an experience dominantly visual, revealed the role of language as a synchronizing device, while the mechanics of cameras and projectors took care of the optical illusion. Cinematography also suggested that this role could be exercised by other means of expression and communication as well. Language is related to body movement, and often participates in the rhythmic patterns of this movement. Before language, other rhythmic devices better adapted to the unsettled self-constitutive practical experience of the *Homo Hominis* were used to synchronize the effort of several beings involved in the endeavor of survival. Although there is no relation between the experience of cinematography and that of primitive beings on the move after migrating herds of animals, it is worth pointing out the underlying structure of synchronicity. The means involved in achieving this synchronicity are characteristic of the various stages in human evolution. At a very small scale of existence, such as autarchic existence, the means were very simple, and very few. At the scale that makes the *writing of movement* possible, these means had become complex, but were dominated by literacy. With cinematography, a new strategy of synchronization was arrived at. In many ways, the story of how films became what they are today is also the story of a conflict between literacy and image-based strategies of synchronization.

The intermediary phases are well known: the film accompanied by music ("Don't kill the pianist"), recorded sound, sound integrated in the movie, stereophonic sound. Their significance is also known: emulate the rhythm of filmed movement, provide a dramatic background, integrate the realism of dialogue and other *real* sounds in the realism of action, expand the means of expression in order to synthesize new realities. Some of the conventions of the emerging film are cultural accomplishments, probably comparable to the convention of ideographic writing. They belong, nevertheless, to a pragmatic context based on the characteristics of literacy. They ensue also from an activity that will result in higher and higher levels of human productivity and efficiency. Each film is a *mold* for the many copies to be shown to millions of spectators. The personal touch of handwriting is obfuscated by the *neutral* camera—a mechanical device, after all. That the same story can be told in many different ways does not change the fact that, once told, it addresses enormous numbers of potential viewers, no longer required to master literacy in order to understand the film's content. The experience of filmmaking is industrially defined. It also bears witness to the many components of human interaction, opening a window on experiences irreducible to words; and it points to the possibility of going beyond literacy, and even beyond the first layers of the visible—that is, to appropriate the imaginary in the self-constitution of the human being.

Some of the changes sketched above occurred when cinematography, after its phase of *theater on film*, started to compress language, and to search for its own expressive potential. Compression of language means the use of images to diminish the quantity of words necessary to constitute a viable filmic expression, as well as the effort to *summarize* literature. Indeed, in view of the limitations of the medium, especially during its imitative phase, it could not support scripts based on literary works that exceeded film's own complexity. Cinematography had also to deal with the limited span of its viewers' attention, their lack of any previous exposure to moving images, and the conditions for viewing a film. When, later on, filmmakers compressed entire books into 90 to 120 minutes, we entered a phase of human experience characterized by substituting written with non- or para-linguistic means.

The generations since the beginning of cinematography learned the new filmic convention while still involved in practical experiences characteristic of literacy. Conventions of film, as a medium with its own characteristics, started to be experienced relatively recently, in the broader context of a human praxis in the process of freeing itself from the constraints of literacy. Films are an appropriate medium for integration of the visual, the aural, and motion. People can record on film some of their most intricate experiences, and afterwards submit the record to fast, slow, entire, or partial evaluation. The experience of filming is an experience with space and time in their interrelationship. But as opposed to the space and time projected in language, and uniformly shared by a literate community, space and time on film can be varied, and made extremely personal. Within the convention of film, we can uncouple ourselves from the physical limitations of our universe of existence, from social or cultural commitments, and generate a new frame for action. The love affair between Hollywood and emerging technologies for creating the impossible in the virtual space of digital synthesis testifies to this. But we cannot, after all, transcend the limitations of the underlying structure on which cinematography is based. Generated near the height of the civilization of literacy, cinematography represents the borderline between practical experiences corresponding to the scale for which literacy was optimal, and the new scale for which both literacy and film are only partially adequate. It is even doubtful that the film medium will survive as an alternative to the new media because it is, for all practical purposes, inefficient.

Cinematography influenced our experience with language, while simultaneously pointing to the limits of this experience. A film is not a visually illustrated text, or a *transcription* of a play. Rather, it is a mapping from a universe of sentences and meanings assigned to a text, to a more complex universe, one of consecutive images forming (or not) a new coherent entity. In the process, language performs sometimes as language (dialogue among characters), other times as a *pre-text* for the visual cinematographic *text*.

Before film, we moved only in the universe of our natural, physical existence, on the theatrical stage, or in the universe of our imagination, in our dreams. The synchronizing function of language made this movement (such as working, going from one place to another, from one person to another) socially relevant. Our movement in language descriptions (do this, go there, meet so-and-so) is an abstraction. Our movement recorded on film is the re-concretized abstraction. This explains the role of filmed images for teaching people how to carry out certain operations, for educating, or for indoctrinating them, or for acquainting them with things and actions never experienced directly. It also explains why, once efficiency criteria become important, film no longer addresses the individual, or small groups; rather, it addresses audiences at the only scale at which it can still be economically justified. The industry called Hollywood (and its various copies around the world) is based on an equation of efficiency that keys in the globality of the world, of illiteracy, and of the distribution network already in place. On an investment in a film of over $100 million, five continents of viewers are needed, and this is still no guarantee of breaking even. It is not at all clear whether *Dreamworks,* the offspring of the affair between Hollywood and the computer industry, will eventually create its own distribution channels on the global digital network.

The temptation to ask whether the *language* of moving images made literacy superfluous, or whether illiteracy created the need for film, and the risk of falling prey to a simplifying cause-and-effect explanation should not prevent us from acknowledging that there are many relations among the factors involved. Nevertheless, the key element is the underlying structure. Books embody the characteristics of language and trigger experiences within the confines of these characteristics. When faced with practical requirements and challenges resulting from a new scale of existence, the human being constitutes alternatives better adapted to a dynamics of change for which books and the experience they entail are only partially appropriate.

Books in which even literate people sometimes got lost, or for which we do not have time or patience, are interpreted for us, condensed in the movie. The fact is that more than a generation has now had access to established works of fiction and drama, as well as scientific, historic, or geographic accounts only through films. A price was paid—there is no equivalent between the book and film—and is being paid, but this is not the issue here. What is the issue is the advent of cinematography in the framework in which literacy ceased to support experiences other than those based on its structure.

Films are mediating expressions better adapted than language to a more segmented reality of social existence. They are also adapted to the dynamics of change and to the global nature of human existence. They prepared us for electronic media, but not before generating those strange *books* (or are they?) that transcribe films for a market so obsessed with success that it will buy the rudimentary transcription together with the paraphernalia derived from the stage design and from the costumes used by the characters. We can find substitutes for coal or oil or tin, but seemingly not for success and stars. As a result, everything they touch or are associated with enters the circuit of our own practical existence. An American journalist ended his commentary occasioned by Greta Garbo's death: "Today they no longer make legends, but celebrities."

BEING HERE AND THERE AT THE SAME TIME

Four generations old (or maybe five), but already the medium of choice—this statement does not define television, but probably captures its social significance. It can be said from the outset that while cinematography is at the borderline between the civilization of literacy and that of illiteracy, television definitely embodies the conflict between the two. In fact, television irreversibly tipped the balance in favor of the visual. The invention of television took place in the context of the change in scale of humankind. Primarily, television occasions the transition from the universe of mechanics and chemistry, implicit in film making and viewing, to that of electricity, in particular electronics, and, more recently, digital technology.

Television, as a product of this change in the structure and nature of human theoretic and practical experience, results from the perceived pragmatic need to capture and transmit dynamic images. Electricity was already the medium for capturing and transmitting sound at the speed of electrons along telephone networks. And since images and actions are influenced by the light we view them in, it followed that light is what we actually wanted to record and transmit. This is television. Cumbersome and still owing a lot to mechanics, television started as a news medium, allowing for almost instantaneous connection between the source of information and the audience. It was initially mostly illustrative. Today, it is constitutive, in the sense that it not only records news, *it makes news.* It constitutes a generalized mass-medium supporting entertainment and ritual (political, religious, military).

Literacy corresponds to the experiences of human self-definition in the world of *classical* physics and chemistry. It is based on the same underlying structure, and projects characteristics of this experience. Electricity and electronics correspond to very fast processes (practically instantaneous), high leverage of human action, diversity, more varied mediating elements, and feedback. The film camera has the main characteristics of literacy. It can be compared to the printing press. But the comparison is only partially adequate since it *writes movements* to film, and lets us *read* them together on the shared *white page* called the screen. Between recording the movement and viewing it, time is used for processing and duplication.

Television is structurally different, capturing movement and everything else belonging to what we call reality, in order to make it immediately available to the viewer. Electronic mediation is much more elaborate, has many more layers than cinematography, and as a result is much more efficient. Film mapped from the selected world of movement, in a studio, on the street, or in a laboratory, to a limited viewership: public in a movie theater. It requested that people share the screen on which its images were projected. Television maps from many cameras to the entire world, and all can simultaneously partake in its images. Television is distributed and introduces simultaneity in that several events from several locations can be broadcast on the TV screen. By comparison, cinematography is centralized. Filming is limited to the location where it is being carried on. Cinematography is intrinsically sequential in that it follows the narrative structure and constitutes a closed entity. Once edited for showing, the film cannot be interrupted to insert anything new.

There are still many who see the two as closely related, and others who see the use of television only as a carrier (of film, for instance). They ignore the defining fact that film and television, despite some commonalties, belong to practical experiences impossible to reconcile. In fact, while film passed the climax of its attraction, television became the most pervasive medium. Due to the use of television in education, corporate communication, sports, artistic and other performances, such as space exploration and war, television impacts upon social interaction without being an interactive medium. A televised event can address audiences close to the world's entire population. When recording images for television became possible, television supported continued human experiences of decentralization, which previous communication technologies could not provide. The video camera and the video cassette recorder, especially in its digital version, make each of us *own* not only the receivers of the language of images and sounds, but also *emitters*, the *sources*, the private Hollywood studios. That is, they make us live the *language of TV*, and substitute it for literacy. Interactive TV will undoubtedly contribute even more in this direction.

It is already the case that instead of writing a letter, some people make a video and send it to family and authorities, and to TV stations interested in viewer feedback and news stories. The massive deployment of troops in the *Desert Storm* operation made clear how the shift from literate to illiterate communication integrates video communication. Together with the telephone, television and video dominated communication patterns of the people involved. Subsequent troop deployments confirmed the pattern of illiterate communication.

Among the many networks through which the foundation of our existence is continuously altered, cable TV plays a distinct role. Many consider it more important than libraries, probably for the wrong reasons. Whether living in thickly populated urban clusters or in remote locations, people are physically connected through multi-channeled communication networks, and even through interactive media. Cable TV is often seen only as another entry to our home for downloading classical programs as well as pornography and superstition. The full utilization of the electronic avenue as a multi-lane, bi-directional highway through which we can be receivers of what we want to accept, and senders of visual messages to whomever is interested and willing to interact with these messages, is still more a goal than a reality. With computer-supported visual communication integrating digital television, we will dispose of the entire infrastructure for a visually dominated civilization. In the age of Internet, wired or wireless networks become part of the *artificial nervous system* of advanced societies. Whether in its modem-based variant, or through other advanced schemes for transporting digital information and supporting interaction, the cable system already contributes to the transformation of the nature of many human practical experiences. These can be experiences of entertainment, but also of learning, teaching, even work.

There is a negative side to all this development, and a need to face consequences that over time can accumulate beyond what we already know and understand. Children growing up with TV miss the experience of movement. Jaron Lanier discussed the "famous childhood zombiehood," an expression of staring into nothing, a limited ability to see beyond a television image, the desire for instant gratification, and a lack of basic common sense appreciation for doing work in order to achieve satisfaction. Games developed around video technology train children to behave like laboratory rats that learn a maze by rote. They grow up accepting the politics of telegenic competition, a poor substitute for competence and commitment. Their vote is focused on brands, regardless of whether they regard political choices or cereals. Addressed *en masse,* such viewers gel in the mass image of polls that rapidly succeed one another. That technology makes possible alternatives to literacy embodied in the visual is unquestionable. To what extent these alternatives carry with them previous determinations and constraints, or they correspond to a new stage in human civilization, is the crux of the matter. The degree of necessity and thus the efficiency of any new form of visual expression, communication, or interaction can be ascertained only in how individuals constitute themselves through practical activities coherently integrating the visual. There is no higher form of empowerment than in the fulfillment of our individual possibilities. Telegenic or not, a president or a TV star has little, if any, impact on our fulfillment in the interconnected world of our time.

Television implies a great deal of language, but such language frees the audience from the requirement of literacy. You do not need to know how to write or read to watch TV; you need to be in command of a limited part of spoken language in order to understand a TV show, even to actively participate in it—from going on a game show to using cable networks, videotex, or interactive programs, exploring the Internet, or setting up a presence on the network.

Growing up with TV results in stereotypes of language and attitudes representing a background of shared expressions, gestures, and values. To see in these only the negative, the low end, is easier than to acknowledge that previous backgrounds, constituted on the underlying structure of literacy, have become untenable under the new pragmatic circumstances. Due to its characteristics, television belongs to the framework of rapid change typical of the dynamics of needs and expectations within the new scale of humankind. There are many varied implications to this: it makes each of us more passive, more and more subject to manipulations (economic, political, religious), robbing (or freeing) us from the satisfaction of a more personal relation (to others, art, literature, etc.). Nobody should underestimate any of these and many other factors discussed by media ecologists and sociologists. But to stubbornly, and quite myopically, consider TV only from the perspective and expectations of literacy is presumptuous. We have to understand the structural changes that made TV and video possible. Moreover, we have to consider the changes they, in turn, brought about. Otherwise we will miss the opportunities opened by the practical experience of understanding the new choices presented to us, and even the new possibilities opened. There is so much more after TV, even on 500 channels and after video-on-demand!

Language is not an absolute democratic medium; literacy, with intrinsic elitist characteristics, even less. Although it was used to ascertain principles of democracy, literacy ended up, again and again, betraying them. Because they are closer to things and actions, and because they require a relatively smaller background of shared knowledge, images are more accessible, although less challenging. But where words and text can obscure the meaning of a message, images can be immediately related to what they refer to. There are more built-in checks in the visual than in the verbal, although the deceptive power of an image can be exploited probably much more than the power of the word. Such, and many other considerations are useful, since the transfer of social and political functions from literacy (books and newspapers, political manifestos, ceremonies and rituals based on writing and reading) to the visual, especially television, requires that we understand the consequences of this transfer. But it is not television that keeps voters away from exercising the right to elect their representatives in the civilization of illiteracy, and not the visual that makes us elect actors, lawyers, peanut farmers, or successful oilmen to the highest (and least useful) posts in the government. Conditions that require the multitude of languages that we use, the layers of mediation, the tendency to decentralization, to name a few, resulted in the increased influence of the visual, as well as in some of the choices mentioned so far.

High definition television (HDTV) helps us distinguish some characteristics of the entire development under discussion—for instance, how the function of integration is carried out. Integration through the intermediary of literacy required shared knowledge, and in particular, knowledge of writing and reading. Integration through the intermediary of modern image-producing technology, especially television and computer-aided visual communication, means access to and sharing of information. Television has made countries which are so different in their identity, history, and culture (as we know the countries of the world to be) seem sometimes so similar that one has to ask how this uniformity came about. Some will point to the influence of the market process—advertisements look much the same all over the world. Others may note the influence of technology—an electronic eye open on the world that renders uniform everything within its range. The new dynamics of human interaction, required by our striving for higher efficiency appropriate to the scale of humankind, probably explains the process better. The similarity is determined by the mechanism we use to achieve this higher efficiency, i.e., progressively deeper labor division, increased mediation, and the need for alternative mechanisms for human integration, that is reflected in TV images. This similarity makes up the substratum of TV images, as well as the substratum of fashion trends, new rituals, and new values, as transitory as all these prove to be.

Literacy and television are not reciprocally exclusive. If this were not the case, the solution to the lower levels of literacy would be at hand. Nevertheless, all those who hoped to increase the quality of literacy by using television had to accept that this was a goal for which the means are not appropriate. Language stabilizes, induces uniformity, depersonalizes; television keeps up with change, allows and invites diversity, makes possible personalized interaction among those connected through a TV chain of cameras and receivers. Literacy is a medium of tedious elaboration and inertia. TV is spontaneous and instantaneous. Moreover, it also supports forms of scientific activity for which language is not at all suited. We cannot send language to *look* at what our eyes do not see directly, or *see* only through some instruments. We cannot anticipate, in language, processes which, once made possible on a television screen, make future human experience conceivable. I know that in these last lines I started crossing the border between television and digital image processing, but this is no accident. Indeed, human experience with television, in its various forms and applications, although not at all closed, made necessary the next step towards a *language of images* which can take advantage of computer technology and of networking.

With the advent of HDTV, television achieves a quality that makes it appropriate for integration in many practical experiences. Design (of clothes, furniture, new products) can result from a collaborative effort of people working at different sites, and in the manufacture of their design during a live session. Modifications are almost instantaneously integrated in the sample. The product can be actually tested, and decisions leading to production made. Communication at such levels of effectiveness is actually integrated in the creative and productive effort. The language is that of the product, a visual reality in progress. The results are design and production cycles much shorter than literacy-based communication can support.

HDTV is television brought to a level of efficiency that only digital formats make possible. The reception of digital television opens the possibility to proceed from each and every image considered appropriate to storing, manipulating, and integrating it in a new context. Digital television reinstates activity, and is subject to creative programming and interactivity. The individual can make up a new universe through the effort of understanding and creative planning. It is quite possible that alternative forms of communication, much richer than those in use today, will emerge from practical experiences of human self-constitution in this new realm. That in ten years all our TV sets, if the TV set remains a distinct receiver, will be digital says much less than the endless creative ideas emerging around the reality of digital television.

VISUALIZATION

Whenever people using language try to convince their partner in dialogue, or even themselves, that they understood a description, a concept, a proof, and answer by using the colloquial "I see," they actually express the practical experience of *seeing through language*. They are overcoming the limitations of the abstract system of phonetic language and returning to the concreteness of seeing the image. Way of speaking equals way of doing—this sums up one of the many premises of this book. We extract information about things and actions from their images. When no image is possible—what does a thought look like, or what is the image of right, of wrong, of ideal?—language supports us in our theoretic experiences, or in the attempt to make the abstract concrete. Language is rather effective in helping us identify kinds of thoughts, in implementing social rules that encode prescriptions for distinguishing between right and wrong, for embodying the just in the institution of justice, and ideals in values. But the experience of language can also be an experience of images.

Once we reach the moment when we can embody the abstract in a concrete theory, in action, in new objects, in institutions, and in choices, and once we are able to form an image of these, share the image, make it part of the visual world we live in, and use it further for many practical or intellectual purposes, we expand the literate experience in new experiences. So it seems that we tend to visualize everything. I would go so far as to say that we not only visualize everything, but also listen to sounds of everything, experience their smell, touch, and taste, and recreate the abstract in the concreteness of our perceptions. The domination of language and the ideal of literacy, which instills this domination as a rule, was and still is seen as the domination of rationality, as though to be literate equals being rational, *volens nolens*. In fact, the rationality associated with language, and expressed with its help, is only a small part of the potential human rationality. The measure (*ratio*) we project in our objectification can as well be a measure related to our perceptive system. It is quite plausible to suspect that some of the negative effects of our literate rationality could have been avoided had we been able to simultaneously project our other dimensions in whatever we did.

The shift from a literacy-dominated civilization to the relative domination of the visual takes place under the influence of new tools, further mediations, and integration mechanisms required by self-constitutive practical experiences at the new human scale. The tools we need should allow us to continue exploring horizons at which literacy ceases to be effective, or even significant. The mediations required correspond to complexities for which new languages are structurally more adequate. The necessary integration is only partially achievable through literate means since many people active in the humanities and the sciences gave up the obsession of final explanations and accepted the model of infinite processes.

Images, among other sign systems, are structurally better suited for a pragmatic framework marked by continuous multiplication of choices, high efficiency, and distributed human experience. But in order to use images, the human being had to put in place a conceptual context that could support extended visual praxis. When the digital computer was invented, none of those who made it a reality knew that it would contribute to more than the mechanization of number crunching. The visionary dimension of the digital computer is not in the technology, but in the concept of a *universal language*, a *characteristica universalis*, or *lingua Adamica*, as Leibniz conceived it.

This is not the place to rewrite the history of the computer or the history of the languages that computers process. But the subject of visualization—presented here from the perspective of the shift from literacy to the visual—requires at least some explanation of the relation between the visual and the human use of computers. The binary

346

number system, which Leibniz called *Arithmetica Binaria* (according to a manuscript fragment dated March 15, 1679), was not meant to be the definitive alphabet, with only two letters, but the basis for a universal language, in which the limitations of natural language are overcome. Leibniz tried hard to make this language utilizable in all domains of human activity, in encoding laws, scientific results, music. I think that the most intriguing aspect, which has been ignored for centuries, was his attempt to visualize events of abstract nature with the help of the two symbols of his alphabet. In a letter to Herzog Rudolph August von Braunschweig (January 2, 1697), Leibniz described his project for a medal depicting the Creation (*Imago Creationis*). In this letter, he actually introduced digital calculus. Around 1714, he wrote two letters to Nicolas de Remond concerning Chinese philosophy. It is useful to mention these here because of the binary number representation of some of the most intriguing concepts of the *Ih-King*. Through these letters, we are in the realm of the visual, and in front of pages in which, probably for the first time, *translations* from ideographic to the sequential, and finally to the digital, were performed. It took almost 300 years before hackers, trying to see if they could use the digital for music notation, discovered that images can be described in a binary system.

This long historic parenthesis is justified by two thoughts. First, it was not the technology that made us aware of images, or even opened access to their digital processing, but intellectual praxis, motivated by its own need for efficiency. Second, visualization is not a matter of illustrating words, concepts, or intuitions. It is the attempt to create tools for generating images related to information and its use. A text on a computer screen is, in fact, an image, a visualization of the language generated not by a human hand in control of a quill, a piece of lead or graphite, a pencil or a pen. The computer does not know language. It *translates* our alphabet into its own alphabet, and then, after processing, it *translates* it back into ours. Displayed in those stored images which, if in lead, would constitute the contents of the lower and upper cases of the drawers in each typography shop, this literacy is subject to automation.

When we write, we visualize, making our language visible on paper. When we draw, we make our plans for new artifacts visible. The mediation introduced by the computer use does not affect the condition of language as long as the computer is only the *pen, keyboard,* or *typewriter.* But once we encode language rules (such as spelling, case agreement, and so on), once we store our vocabulary and our grammar, and mimic human use of language, what is written is only partially the result of the literacy of the writer. The visualization of text is the starting point towards automatic creation of other texts. It also leads to establishing relations between language and non-language sign systems. Today, we dispose of means for electronically associating images and texts, for cross-referencing images and texts, and for rapidly diagramming texts. We can, and indeed do, print electronic journals, which are refereed on the network. Nothing prevents such journals from inserting images, animation and sounds, or for facilitating on-line reactions to the hypotheses and scientific data presented. That such publications need a shorter time to reach their public goes without saying. The Internet thus became the new medium of publication, and the computer its printing press—a printing press of a totally new condition. Individuals constituting their identity on the Internet have access to resources which until recently were available only to those who owned presses, or gained access to them by virtue of their privileged position in society.

The visual component of computer processing, i.e., the graphics, relies on the same language of zeros and ones through which the entire computer processing takes place. As a result of this common *alphabet* and *grammar* (Boolean logic and its new extensions), we can consider language (image *translations,* or number-image relations such as diagrams, charts, and the like), and also more abstract relations. Creating the means to overcome the limitations of literacy has dominated scientific work. The new means for information processing allow us to replace the routine of phenomenological observation with processing of diverse languages designed especially to help us create new theories of very complex and dynamic phenomena.

The shift to the visual follows the need to change the accent from quantitative evaluations and language inferences based on them, to qualitative evaluations, and images expressing such evaluations at some significant moments of the process in which we are involved. Let us mention some of these processes. In medicine, or in the research for syntheses of new substances, and in space research, words have proven to be not only misleading, but also inefficient in many respects. New visualization techniques, such as those based on molecular resonance, freed the praxis of medicine from the limitations of word descriptions. Patients explain what they feel; physicians try to match such descriptions to typologies of disease based on data resulting from the most recent data. When this process is networked, the most qualified physician can be consulted. When experimental data and theoretic models are joined, the result is visualized and the information exchanged via high-speed broadband digital networks.

Based on similar visualization techniques, we acquire better access to sources of data regarding the past, as well as to information vital for carrying through projects oriented towards the future. Computed tomography, for instance, visualized the internal structure of Egyptian mummies. Three-dimensional images of the whole body were created without violating the casings and wrappings that cover the remnants. The internal body structure was visualized by using a simulation system similar to those utilized in non-intrusive surgery.

The design and production of new materials, space research, and nano-engineering have already benefited from replacing the analytical perspective ingrained in literacy-based methods with visual means for synthesis. It is possible to visualize molecular structures and simulate interactions of molecules in order to see how medicine affects the cells treated, the dynamics of mixing, chemical and biochemical reactions. It is also possible to simulate forces involved in the so-called docking of molecules in virtual space. No literacy-based description can substitute for flight simulators, or for visualization of data from radio astronomy, for large areas of genetics and physics.

Not the last among examples to be given is the still controversial field of artificial intelligence, seduced with emulating behaviors usually associated with human intelligence in action. But it should not surprise anybody that while the dynamics of the civilization of illiteracy requires freedom from literacy, people will continue to preserve values and concepts they are used to, or which are appropriate to specific knowledge areas. Paradoxically, artificial intelligence is, in part, doing exactly this.

When people grow up with images the same way prior generations were subjected to literacy, the relation to images changes. The technology for visualization, although sometimes still based on language models, makes interactivity possible in ways language could not. But it is not only the technology of visualization applied within science and engineering that marks the new development. Visualization, in its various forms and functions, supports the almost instantaneous interaction between us and our various machines, and among people sharing the same natural environment, or separated in space and time. It constitutes an alternative medium for thinking and creativity, as it did all along the history of crafts, design, and engineering. It is also a medium for understanding our environment, and the multitude of changes caused by practical experience involving the life support system. Through visualization, people can experience dimensions of space beyond their direct perception, they can consider the behavior of objects in such spaces, and can also expand the realm of artistic creativity.

The print media, as an overlapping practical experience uniting literacy and the power of sight, are more visual today than at any previous time. We are no longer subjected—sometimes with good reason, other times for dubious motives—to the sequentiality of literacy-dominated modes of communication. An entire shared *visual language* is projected upon us in the form of comic strips, advertisements, weather maps, economic reports, and other pictorial representations. Some of these representations are still printed on paper. Others are displayed through the more dynamic forms at public information kiosks, or through interactive means of information dissemination, such as computer-supported networks and non-linear search environments, which Ted Nelson anticipated back in 1965. The World Wide Web embodies many of his ideas, as well as ideas of a number of other visionaries.

Parallel to these developments, we are becoming more and more aware of the possibilities of using images in human activities where they played a reduced role within literacy—civic action, political debate, legal argumentation. Lawyers already integrate visual testimony in their cases. Juries can see for themselves the crime being committed, as well as the results of sophisticated forensic tests. Human destinies are defended with arguments that are no longer at the mercy of someone's memory or another's talent for rhetoric or drama. The citizen is frequently addressed by increasingly visual messages that explain how tax dollars are spent and why he or she should vote for one or another candidate. In becoming the *Netizen,* he or she will participate in social interactions fundamentally new in nature. On the Net, politicians claiming credit for some accomplishment can be immediately challenged by the real image. Political promises can be modeled and displayed while the campaign speech is given. A decision to go to war can be subjected to an instant referendum while the simulation of the war itself, or of alternatives, is played on our monitors. But again, to idealize these possibilities would be foolish. The potential for abusive use of images is as great as that for their meaningful application.

Many factors are at work slowing down the process of educating *visually literate* individuals. We continue to rediscover the wheel of reading and writing without advancing comprehensive programs for visual education. Illustrative visual alternatives, advanced more as an alibi for the maintenance of literacy-dominated communication, are by the nature of their function inappropriate in the context of higher efficiency requirements. Utilized as alternatives, these materials can be, and often are, irrelevant, ugly, insignificant, and expensive. More often than not, they are used not to enhance communication, but to direct it, to manipulate the addressee. It will take more than the recognition of the role of the visual to understand that *visual literacy,* or probably several such literacies, comprising the variety of visual languages we need, less confining, less permanent, and less patterned, are necessary in order to improve practical experiences of self-constitution through images. We are yet to address the ethical aspects of such experiences, especially in view of the fact that the visual entails constraints different from those encoded in the letter of our laws and moral principles.

In discussing the transition to the visual, I hope to have made clear that the process is not one of substituting one form of literacy for another. The process has a totally different dynamics. It implies transition from a dominating form of literacy to a multitude of highly adaptive sign systems. These all require new competencies that reflect this adaptability. It also requires that we all understand integrative processes in order to make the best of individual efforts in a framework of extremely divided and specialized experiences of self-constitution. If seeing is believing, then believing everything we see in our day is a challenge for which we are, for all practical purposes, ill prepared.

CHAPTER 2: UNBOUNDED SEXUALITY

> "Freedom of speech
> Is as good as sex."
> Madonna

The Netizens were up in arms: The Communications Decency Act must be repealed. Blue ribbons appeared on many Websites as an expression of solidarity. This Act was prompted by the American government's attempt to prevent children from accessing the many pornographic outlets of the Internet. This first major public confrontation between a past controlled by literate mechanisms and a future of illiterate unrestricted freedom seemed to be less about sex and more about democracy. But that the two are related, and defined within the current pragmatics of human self-constitution, has escaped both parties to the dispute.

SEEKING GOOD SEX

In *Economic-Philosophical Manuscripts,* Karl Marx (a product of the civilization of literacy) addressed alienation: "We thus arrive at the result that man feels that he acts freely only in his animal functions—eating, drinking, procreation, or at most using shelter, jewelry, etc.—while in his human functions, he feels only animal. What is animal becomes human and what is human becomes animal." How an analysis of industrial capitalism, with its underlying pragmatic structure reflected in literacy, can anticipate phenomena pertinent to the post-industrial, and reflected in illiteracy, is not easy to explain.

Although he referred to economic self-constitution, his description is significant in more than one way. Sexuality is of concern in the civilization of illiteracy insofar as the human being in its multi-dimensionality is of concern. This might sound too broad to afford any meaningful inference from the condition of literacy to the condition of human sexuality, but it is an existential premise. Through sexuality humans project their natural condition and the many influences, language included, leading to its humanization. An understanding of the multiple factors at work in conditioning human experiences as intimate as sexual relations, depends upon the understanding of the pragmatic framework in which they unfold. Child pornography on the Internet is by no means the offspring of our love affair with technology. Neither is pornography being invoked for the first time as a justification for censorship. Nevertheless, the commotion regarding the Communications Decency Act constitutes a new experience that is intimately related to the condition of human existence in today's world.

"SWF seeks unemployed SWM grad student for hideaway weekends, intimate dinners, and cuddling. Must know how to read, and be able to converse without extensive use of 'you know' or 'wicked.'" This announcement (dated October 6, 1983) is one among many that use qualifying initials, but with one twist: "Must know how to read."—moreover, to be articulate. What over ten years ago was formulated innocently (hideaway, intimate dinner, cuddling) would today be expressed quite bluntly: "Looking for good sex." What does reading, and possibly writing, have to do with our emotional life, with our need and desire to love and be loved; that is, what does reading have to do with sex?

Long before *Homo Sapiens* ascertained itself, reproduction, and all it comprises in its natural and form, ensured survival. Do literacy, language, or sign systems affect this basic equation of life? Mating seasons and habits shed some light on the natural aspect. Colors, odors, mating calls, specific movements (*dances*, fights, body language) send sexual signals. Molecular biology places the distinction between hominids and chimpanzees at four million years ago. After all this time of freeing themselves from nature, even to the extent of self-constitution in the practical experience of artificial insemination, human beings still integrate color, odor, mating calls, and particular movements into the erotic. But they also integrate the experience of their self-constitution in language. Since the time hominids distinguished themselves, the sexuality of the species started differentiating itself from that of animals. For example, humans are permanently attractive, even after insemination, while animals attract each other only at moments favorable for reproduction. Along the timeline from the primitive being to our civilization, sex changed from being an experience in reproduction to being *predominantly* a form of pleasure in itself.

Instead of the immediacy of the sexual urge, projected through patterns subject to natural cycles, humans experience ever more mediated forms of sexual attraction and gratification, which are not necessarily associated with reproduction. An initial change occurred when humanized sexual drive turned into love, and became associated with its many emotions. The practical experience of language played an important part in extending sexual encounters from the exclusive realm of nature to the realm of culture. Here they acquired a life of their own through practical experiences characteristic of the syncretic phase of human practical experiences, mostly rituals. During the process of differentiating these experiences— constitution of myths, moral and ethical self-awareness, theater, dance, poetry—sexual encounters were subjected to various interpretations.

The birth of languages and the establishment of sex codes, as primitive as they were, are related to the moment of agriculture, a juncture at which a certain autonomy of the species was reached. Rooted in the biological distinction between male and female, labor division increased the efficiency of human effort. Divisions were also established, some under the model of male domination, others under the model of female domination, pertinent to survival activities, and later on to incipient social life. Eventually, labor division *consecrated* the *profession* of prostitution, and thus the practice of satisfying natural urges in a context in which nature was culturized. The prototypical male-dominated structure of the sexual relation between man and woman marked the history of this relation more than female domination did. It introduced patterns of interaction and hierarchies today interpreted wholesale as harmful to the entire development of women.

What is probably less obvious is the relation among the many aspects of the pragmatic context in which such hierarchies were acknowledged. Moreover, we do not know enough about how these hierarchies were transformed into the underlying consciousness of the populations whose identities resulted from experiences corresponding to the pragmatic context. The implicit thesis of this book is that everything that made language and writing possible, and progressively necessary, led to a coherent framework of human practical experiences that are characterized by sequentiality, linearity, hierarchy, and centralism, and which literacy appropriated and transmits. Consequently, when the structural framework no longer effectively supports human self-constitution, the framework is modified. Other aspects of human existence, among them sexuality, reflect the modification.

Reading and writing have much to do with our emotional life. They remove it from the *immediacy* of drive, hope, pain, and disappointment and give it its own space: human striving, desire, pleasure.

They are associated with an infinity of qualifiers, names, and phrases. With language, feelings are given a means for externalizing, and they are stabilized. Expectations diversify from there. Structural characteristics of the context that makes language necessary simultaneously mark the very object of the self-constitutive experience of loving and being loved. There are many literary and visual testimonies to how the erotic was constituted as a realm of its own: From *Gilgamesh*, the *Song of Solomon*, *Kama Sutra*, Ovid's *Art of Love*, through *Canterbury Tales* and the *Decameron*, to the erotic literature of 18th- and 19th-century Europe, down to the many current romance novels and handbooks on lovemaking. No matter which of them is examined, one inference becomes clear: the pragmatic context of the continuous human self-constitution effects changes in the way people are attracted to each other. Love and integration of sexual experiences, in the manifold of acts through which hominids move from the self-perpetuation drive to new levels of expectation and new intensities of their relations, is also pragmatically conditioned.

Writing, as a practical experience of human self-constitution, is conducive to relations between male and female that are different from random or selective mating. It is bound to continue along a time sequence severed from the natural cycle of mating, reshaped into the marriage contract and the family alliance. Literacy, as a particular practical experience of language, regulates the sexual, as it regulates, in a variety of forms, all other aspects of human interaction. In the literate erotic experience, expectations pertinent to the pragmatics of a society in search of alternative means of survival evolve into norms. The inherited experience of female-male relations, affected through the experience of rituals, myths, and religion, is condensed in literacy. Encoding hierarchy, some languages place women in a secondary position. There is almost no language in which this does not happen. "Many men and women" is in Arabic ("rijaalan kafiiran wa-nisaa'aa") literally "men many women." In Japan, women speak a *Japanese* reserved to their sex alone. In the English wedding ceremony, the woman had to repeat that she would "love, honor, and *obey*" the husband. To this day, Orthodox Jewish men give thanks to God that He did "not make me a woman."

With the demise of literacy, the sexual experience is divorced from procreation. Statistics of survival in the past world of limited available resources, of natural catastrophes, of disease, etc., cease to play any role in the illiterate sex encounters. Sexuality becomes a diversified human experience, subject to divisions, mediations, and definitely to the influence of the general dynamics of the world today. As markets become part of the global economy, so does sexuality, in the sense that it allows for experiences which, in limited communities and within prescribed forms of ceremony (religious, especially), were simply not possible. From the earliest testimony regarding sexual awareness up to the present, everything one can imagine in respect to sex has been tried. So often placed under the veil of secrecy and mystery, sex is no less frequently and vividly, to say the least, depicted. Yet a rhetorical question deserves to be raised: Does anyone know everything about sex?

THE LAND OF SEXUAL UBIQUITY

Borges, in his own way, would have probably mapped the sexual realm: Freud aside, to know everything about sex would require that one be everyone who ever lived, lives, and eventually will live. Such a Borgesian map is indeed detailed but leads no further than ourselves. Connect all sex-related matter that is on the Internet today—from on-line striptease and copulation to legitimate sex education and the passionate defense of love—and you will still not have more than a partial image of sexuality. When one considers all the books, videotapes, songs, radio and television talk-shows, private discussions and public sermons, the subject of sex would still not be exhausted. If sex were an individual matter—which it is, to a large extent—how could we meaningfully approach the subject without the risk of making it a personal confession, or worse, a pretentious discourse about something any author would unavoidably know only through the many and powerful filters of his or her culture? But maybe sex is less private than we, based on prejudice, ignorance, or discretion, assume.

Ritualized sex was a public event, sometimes culminating in orgies. It took a lot of *taming,* or acculturation, for sex to become an intimate affair. Myths acknowledged sexual habits and propagated rules coherent within the pragmatic framework of their expression. Like myths, many religions described acceptable and unacceptable behavior, inspired by the need to maintain the integrity of the community and to serve its goals of survival through lineage and propriety rights, especially when males began to dominate in society. Art, science, and business appropriated sex as a subject of inquiry, or as a lucrative activity. Sex is a driving force for individuals and communities, an inescapable component of any experience, no matter how remote from sex.

Sexual ubiquity and the parallel world of self-awareness, embodied in forms of expression, communication, and signification different from the actual sexual act, are connected in very subtle ways. Once sexual experiences are appropriated by culture, they become themselves a sign system, a symbolic domain, a language. Each sexual encounter, or each unfulfilled intention, is but a *phrase* in this language *written* in the *alphabet* of gestures, odors, colors, smells, body movement, and rhythm.

We are the sexual sign: *first,* in its indexical condition—a definite mark left, a genetic fingerprint testifying to our deepest secrets encoded in our genetic endowment; *second,* in iconicity, that is, in all the imitations of others as they constitute their identity in the experience of sexuality. As many scholars have hastened to point out, we are also the sign in its symbolism. Indeed, phallic and vulvar symbols populate every sphere of human expression (and obsession). Nevertheless, our own self-constitution in the sexual act confirms a double identity of the human species: *nature,* involved in the struggle for survival, where the sheer power of numbers and strategies for coping with everything destructive make for continuous selection (Darwin's law of natural selection); and *culture*, in which humans pursue a path of progressive self-definition, many times in conflict with the natural condition, or what Freud and his followers defined as the psychological dimension. The two are related, and under specific circumstances one dominates the other. In my opinion, Peirce's encompassing notion that the sign is the person who interprets it *integrates* the two levels.

In the pragmatic framework, experiences of self-constitution result from the projection of natural characteristics in the activity performed, as well as from the awareness of the goals pursued, means incorporated, and meanings shared. Does the pragmatic perspective negate explanations originating from other, relatively limited, perspectives? Probably not. An example is furnished by the theories explaining sexuality from the viewpoint of the conflict between sex (*libido*) and self-preservation (*ego*) instincts, later substituted by the conflict between life instincts (*Eros*) and the death instinct (*Thanatos*, self-destruction). Such theories introduce a language layer into a subject which, although acknowledged, was simply not discussed, except in religious terms (mainly as prohibitions), or in poetry. As with any other dualistic representation, such theories also end in speculation, opposing the experience to the scheme adopted. The scheme functions in extreme cases, which psychoanalysis dealt with, but explains sexual *normalcy*—if such a thing can be defined, or even exists—to a lesser extent, and inconsistently. The labels remain unchanged—*Eros, Logos, Thanatos*—while the world undergoes drastic alterations. Some of these alterations affect the very nature of the sexual experience as human beings unfold under new pragmatic circumstances, some of extreme alienation.

THE LITERATE INVENTION OF THE WOMAN

The case I am trying to make is for the acknowledgment of the conflict between a new state of affairs in the world and our perspectives,

Civilization of Illiteracy: Book IV

limited or not by the literate model of sexuality. The current situation recalls the world before literacy, before the expectation of homogeneity, and before the attempt to derive order and complexity through linear progression. The atom of that sexual world was the genderless human being, a generic existence not yet defined by sexual differentiation. The male-female distinction came as a surprise— the realization of seeing the same and its *negative*, as in the case of a stone and the hole that remains after it is unearthed. Some read the genderless world as androcentric, because the generic human being it affirmed had a rather masculine bent. The significance of whatever such a genderless model embodied needs to be established in the pragmatic realm: how does *difference* result from *same*, if this same is an archetypal body with characteristics celebrated copiously over time? Painting, medical illustration, and diagrams, from the Middle Ages to the 17th century, focus on this genderless person, who seems today almost like a caricature.

The pragmatics of the time period just mentioned were conducive to a different image of genders. The sense of excitement associated with human advances in knowing nature certainly spilled over into every other form of human experience, sex included. A new scale of *mankind* required that the efficiency of human activity increase. This was a time of many innovations and groundbreaking scientific theories. It was also a time of diversified, though still limited, sexual experiences, made possible by a framework of creativity different from the framework of the Middle Ages. Discoveries in many domains shook the framework of thinking according to Platonic archetypes, appropriated by the Catholic Church and used as explanatory models for all things living or dead. Pragmatics required that the one-sex model be transcended because limits of efficiency (in thinking, medical practice, biological awareness, labor division) were reached within the model. The world of practical experiences of this time unfolded in the Industrial Revolution. With literacy established, some sexual attitudes, consonant with the pragmatic circumstance, were enforced. Others were deemed unacceptable, and qualified as such in the literate language of church, state, and education. From the ubiquity of natural sexuality to what would become sexual self-awareness and sexual culture, no matter how limited, the journey continued in leaps and bounds.

To acknowledge the woman as a biological entity, with characteristics impossible to reduce to male characteristics, was not due to political pressure—as Thomas Lacquer, a remarkable writer on the subject, seemed to believe—but to pragmatic needs. It simply made sense to know how the body functions, to acknowledge morphology, to improve the quality of life, however vaguely acknowledged as such, by addressing the richness of the human being. Interestingly enough, the order in nature and matter found by science contradicted the new experience of variety, sexuality included, made possible by the scientific revolution. A gulf opened between reality and appearance, motivating a healthy empirical program, well extended in the realm of sexual encounters.

Back in the *medium aevum*, Maximus of Torino thought that "the source of all evil is the woman," probably embodied in the prototypical Eve. The social importance of women in the context of the empirical program, leading to the need for generalized literacy and better knowledge of the human body, discredited this prejudice of the Middle Ages, and of any age since. Sexuality made the transition to the two-sex world with a vengeance. Reproduction still dominated, since incipient industry needed more qualified workers in its own *reproduction cycles,* and productivity triggered the need to maintain consumption. But the *unnatural* dimension widened as well. The context was population growth, limited means of birth control, and levels of production and consumption characteristic of the pragmatics of high efficiency.

Those who think that the relation between industry, sexuality, and reproduction is far-fetched should recall the birth policies of countries obsessed with industrial growth. In what was communist Romania, workers were needed to do what there were no machines to do: to produce for the benefit of the owners of the means of production.

To a similar end, the Soviets handed out medals to mothers of many children. The government structure, bearing the characteristics of literacy, clashed with the harsh pragmatic framework existing in the former communist countries. The result of the clash was that women avoided birth at all cost.

AHEAD TO THE PAST

Longer life and the ability to enjoy the fruits of industry altered attitudes towards sex, especially reproduction. Sexuality and marriage were postponed to the third decade of life as people acquired more training in their quest for a better life. Children were no longer a matter of continuity and survival. After decades of denying the strength of nature's drive towards self-perpetuation of a species, today we again recognize that sexual life starts very early. But this realization should not have come as a surprise. Juliet's mother was worried that Juliet was not married at the age of 13. Beyond the realization of early sexuality, we notice that adolescents have multiple sex partners, that the *average* American is bound to have 37 sex partners in his or her lifetime, that prohibitions against sodomy are ignored, and that half the population is involved in group sex. Statistics tell us that 25% of the adult population uses pornography for arousal and another 30% uses contraptions bought in sex shops; 33-1/3% of married couples have extra-marital affairs; the average marriage lasts 5 years; the open practice of homosexuality increases 15% annually. Incest, bestiality, and sexual practices usually defined as perverse are reaching unheard of proportions. It's not that changes in sexual experience take place, but that practices known from the earliest of times assert themselves, usually by appealing to the literate notion of freedom. As with many aspects of the change human society undergoes, we do not know what the impact of these sex practices will be. Probably that is the most one can say in a context that celebrates permissiveness as one of the highest accomplishments of modern society. Such changes challenge our values and attitudes, and make many wonder about the miserable state of morality. We already know about the cause and physical effects of AIDS. We do not even know how to wonder what other diseases might come upon humanity if the human relation with animals moves in the direction of bestiality. "Is this the price we pay for democracy?" is asked by people accused of having a conservative leaning. Enthusiasts celebrate an age of unprecedented tolerance, indulgence, and freedom from responsibility. But no matter to which end of the spectrum one leans, it should be clear that these considerations are part of the pragmatics of sexuality in the civilization of illiteracy. Shorter cycles are characteristic not only of production, but also of sexual encounters. Higher speed (however one wants to perceive it), non-linearity, freedom of choice from many options, and the transcendence of determinism and clear-cut dualistic distinctions apply to sexuality as they apply to everything else we do.

Although it is a unique experience, impossible to transmit or compare, and very difficult to separate from the individual, sex is widely discussed. Media, politicians, and social scientists have transformed it into a public issue; hypocrites turn it into an object of derision; professionals in sexual disorders make a good living from them. Sex is the subject of economic prognosis, legal dispute, moral evaluation, astrology, art, sports, and so on. One should see what is made public on the World Wide Web. Highly successful networked pages of pornographic magazines are visited daily by millions of people, as are pages of scientific and medical advice. Questions referring to sexuality in its many forms of expression increase day by day. Questions about sex have also extended to areas where the sexual seems (or seemed) excluded—science, technology, politics, the military. For example, the contraceptive pill, which has changed the world more than its inventors ever dreamed of, and more than society could have predicted, has also changed part of the condition of the sexual. The abortion pill (with a name—RU486—that reminds us of computer chips) only accentuates the change, as do many scientific and technological discoveries conceived with the purpose of sexually stimulating the individual or augmenting sexual pleasure.

Emancipation—social, political, economic, as well as emancipation of women, children, minorities, nations—has also had an impact on sexual relations. As such, emancipation results from different pragmatic needs and possibilities, and reflects the weaker grip of literate norms and expectations. Emancipation has reduced some of sexuality's inherent, and necessary, tension. It freed the sexual experience from most of the constraints it was subjected to in a civilization striving for order and control. Still, individual erotic experiences have often culminated not in the expected revelations, stimulated by the use of drugs or not, but in deception, even desperation. This is explained by the fact that, more than any activity that becomes a goal in itself, sexuality without the background of emotional contentment constitutes individuals as insular, alienated from each other, feeling used but not fulfilled. Lines of a similar sway were written by opponents of sexual emancipation, and as a suggestion of a price humans pay for excess. These lines were articulated also by firm believers in tolerance, free spirits who hardly entertain the thought of punishment (divine or otherwise).

Concerns over human sexuality result from the role of scale and the erotic dimension. Within a smaller scale, one does not feel lost or ignored. Small-scale experiences are constraining, but they also return a sense of care and belonging. The broader the scale, the less restrictive the influence of others, but also the more diminished the recognition of individuality. In the modern megalopolis, the only limits to one's sexual wishes are the limits of the individual. Nonetheless, at such a scale, individuality is continuously negated, absorbed in the anonymity of mediocre encounters and commercialism. The realization that scale relates not only to *how* and *how much* we produce, and to changes in human interaction, but also to deeper levels of our existence is occasioned by the sexual experience of self-constitution in a framework of permissiveness that nullifies value. The human scale and the altered underlying structure of our practical experiences affect drives, in particular the sexual drive, as well as reproduction, in a world subjected to a population explosion of exponential proportions.

The entire evolution under consideration, with all its positive and negative consequences, has a degree of necessity which we will not understand better by simply hiding behind moral slogans or acknowledging extreme sexual patterns. No person and no government could have prevented erotic emancipation, which is part of a much broader change affecting the human condition in its entirety. The civilization of illiteracy is representative of this change insofar as it defines a content for human experiences of self-constitution, including those related to sexuality, which mark a discontinuity in sexual patterns. Sex dreams turn into sex scripts on virtual reality programs within which one can make love to a virtual animal, plant, to oneself, projected into the virtual space and time of less than clear distinctions between what we were told is right and wrong. Telephone sex probably provides just as much arousal, but against fees that the majority of callers can hardly afford. Less than surprising, lesbians and gays make their presence known on the Internet more than in literate publications. Discussions evolve, uncensored, on matters that can be very intimate, described in titillating terms, sometimes disquietingly vulgar, obscene, or base, by literate standards. But there are also exchanges on health, AIDS prevention, and reciprocal support. Gay and lesbian sexuality is freely expressed, liberated from the code language used in the personal columns of literary publications.

FREUD, MODERN HOMOSEXUALITY, AIDS

The godfather of modern homosexuality is Freud (independent of his own sexual orientation), insofar as sexual expression remains a symbolic act. Homosexuality, evading natural selection and eliciting acceptance as an expression of a deeply rooted human complex, is part of the ubiquitous sexual experience of the species. The fact that homosexuality, documented in some of the earliest writings as a taboo, along with incest and bestiality, predated Freud does not contradict this assertion. Homosexual Eros has a different finality than heterosexual Eros. The extent of homosexuality under the structural circumstances of the civilization of illiteracy is not only the result of increased tolerance and permissiveness. Neither is it merely the result of freedom resulting from an expanded notion of liberal democracy. It is biologically relevant, and as a biological expression, it is projected into practical experiences constitutive of individuals, men or women, acknowledged as different because their practical experience of self-constitution identifies them as different. Their experience, though necessarily integrated in today's global world, has many consequences for them and for others.

While research has yet to confirm the hypothesis of structural peculiarities in the brain and genes of homosexuals, the specifics of the self-constitution process through practical experiences in a world subject to natural selection cannot be overlooked. Genetics tells us that the borderline between genders is less clear-cut than we assumed. Be this as it may, homosexuality takes place under a different set of biological and social expectations than do heterosexuality and other forms of sexuality. It is an act in itself, with its own goal, with no implicit commitment to offspring, and thus different in its intrinsic set of responsibilities and their connection to the social contract. But for this matter, so is heterosexuality under the protection of the pill, the condom, or any other birth control device or method, abortion included.

A different sense of future, moreover an expectation of instant gratification, is established in the sexual experience of homosexuality. Exactly this characteristic acknowledges the underlying structure of the pragmatics of high efficiency that makes homosexual experiences possible, and even economically acceptable. Acknowledged also is the scale of humankind. Survival is much less affected by fruitless sexuality than within a limited scale of existence and activity. The freedom gained through birth control methods and the freedom to practice non-reproductive sexual relations, such as homosexual love, are in some ways similar. It is impossible not to notice that the development under discussion displays a shift from a domain of vulnerability in regard to the *species*—any imbalance in procreation, under conditions of severe selection, affects the chances of survival—to the domain of the *individual*.

The extreme case of AIDS (acquired immune deficiency syndrome), which is transmitted sexually (among other ways), reintroduced moral concerns at a time when morality was almost dropped from erotic language and expelled from the human erotic experience. The frenzy of sexual freedom and the confusion resulting from the spread of AIDS present contradictory images of a much broader development that affects human erotic behavior, and probably much more than that. Nobody, no doomsayer on record, whether coming from a literate perspective or already integrated in the pragmatics of the civilization of illiteracy, predicted the new vulnerability which AIDS makes so painfully evident, inside and outside the homosexual segment of the population. The integrated global nature of human life brought Africa, with its large AIDS-infected population, close to countries that reached a different (not to use the word *higher*) level of civilization. AIDS impacted on the sense of invulnerability, assumed by individuals in industrialized countries as almost a right. This invulnerability is now drastically tested, despite the enormous effort to address AIDS. The disease suddenly put globality in a new light. Statistics connect the sense of danger experienced in Hollywood by HIV-infected movie stars, fashion designers, and dancers to the desperation of the disenfranchised in the First World—drug addicts, the urban poor, and prostitutes—and to the disenfranchised and working poor of the Third World.

Far from being a new phenomenon, the homosexual and lesbian preference, or lifestyle as it is euphemistically called, reaches a status of controversial acceptance in the civilization of illiteracy. The paradox is that while the choice of homosexuality over heterosexuality is facilitated by the pragmatic context of the civilization of illiteracy, the activism of homosexuality solicits recognition within the structures characteristic of literacy. It is very ironic that gay activism, stimulated by the many consequences of the AIDS epidemic, attempts to reverse time, fighting for equal access to exactly those means in which the values and prejudices that condemn homosexuality are embedded. It looks like homosexuals want to rewrite the book or books in which they are damned, instead of freeing themselves from them. Homosexuals want their voice to be heard in church and politics. They want their cause present in ethical writings, and their rights encoded in new laws and rules. They want to enlighten others by making their experience known as art, literature, and social discourse. The genetic condition of the homosexual choice needs to be considered together with the variety of contexts pertaining to the diversity of the civilization of illiteracy that make its unfolding possible.

There is a need to be aware that, between the function of procreation and divergent sexual behavior, a whole gamut of human cultural experience continues to unfold and challenges settled standards. This experience goes beyond language and the literate structure of a linear, sequential, hierarchic, centralized, deterministic pragmatics of limited choice. Human language, as a projection of human beings living within a context appropriate to their self-preservation and development, participated in the taming of our sexual drive. Illiteracy leads to its endless diversification, affecting sexuality in all its manifestations, such as patterns of mobility and settlement, family and community life, social rules, and the encoding of values in moral, economic, and educational systems.

Orality and sexuality were characterized by immediateness, and a reduced sense of space and time. Sex equaled instinct. With writing, and thus the possibility of what later would become literacy, a new set of underlying elements was acknowledged. Sexuality was subjected to the experience of accepted rules—the *do's and don'ts* appropriate to expectations of efficiency, and their resulting values, corresponding to the scale of humankind and the natural condition.

Reproduction still dominated sexuality, while rules of optimal human interaction, encoded in religion or social expectations, started to permeate erotic behavior. To a great extent, language in its literate form expresses the awareness of the various erotic dimensions as they were socially acknowledged at any given time. Literacy enrolled sexuality in the quest for higher productivity and sustained consumption characteristic of the pragmatics associated with the Industrial Revolution. Once conditions making literacy necessary are overruled by new conditions, sexuality undergoes corresponding changes. Basically, sexuality seems to return to immediateness, as it integrates many mediating elements. Sexuality unfolds in an unrestricted set of varieties, escaping some of its natural determination. In keeping with the shorter and shorter cycles of human activity, sexuality turns into an experience of transitory encounters. Since it is a form of human expression, it ascertains its condition as yet another sign system, or language, among the many participating in the practical experiences of our new pragmatic context. It now bridges dramatically between life and death, in a world where the currency of both life and death is, for all practical purposes, devaluated.

SEX AND CREATIVITY

Experts from fields as different as brain research, cognitive science, and physiology agree that a distinct similarity between the practical experience of self-constitution in sexual acts and in creative efforts of art, scientific discovery, and political performance can be established. It seems that they all involve a progression, reach a peak, experienced as enormous pleasure and relief, and are followed by a certain feeling of emptiness. Like any creative experience, the erotic experience is one of expression. To express means to constitute oneself authentically, and to project hope that the experience can impact others. From this stems the possible language, or semiotics, of the erotic: how it is expressed, what the erotic *vocabulary* (of sounds, words, gestures, etc.) and *grammar* are. The semiosis of the erotic includes the participation of the language of sexual relationships, without being limited to it.

Having reached this understanding, we can apply it to the observation that *Homo Eroticus* is a subject who continuously negates naturalness (from what and how we eat to how we dress, etc.) while simultaneously regretting the loss. Not surprisingly, sexuality is continued in the practice of producing, reading, viewing, and criticizing erotic literature, printed images, video, film documentaries, CD-ROM, or virtual reality. Real-time interactive erotic multimedia captures even more attention. In parallel, humans try to be authentic, unique, and free in their intimate sphere. They scan through image-dominated books, some more than vulgar, subscribe to magazines, face their own sexuality on videotapes, register for sex initiation seminars, or take advantage of group sex encounters. Millions land on pornographic Websites or create their own sex messages in the interconnected world. They do all this in an attempt to free themselves from natural necessity and from the conformist frame of literate Eros, including the many complexes explaining painful real or imaginary failures.

Living in an environment in which science and technology effectively support human experiences of overcoming the constraints of space, time, and material existence, humans *freed* sexuality from the influence of natural cycles. These, as we know, can even be altered as pragmatic conditions might require for sportswomen and ballerinas. New *totems* and *taboos* populate this environment in which *Eros,* as a reminder of distant phases of anthropological evolution, continues to be present. Like any other creative act, the sexual act involves imagination, and the urge to explore the unknown. It is irrepeatable, yet another instance of discovering one's identity in the uniqueness of the experience.

Although continuously programmed through endlessly refined means, humans maintain a nostalgia for the authentic, but accept, more often unconsciously than not, a mediocre syntax of the sexual impressed upon them from the world of celebrity and success. This syntax is a product of erotic experts, writers, and imagemakers. It is a contentless semantics—the meaning of erotic encounters fades in the meaning of the circumstance—and an absurd pragmatics—sexuality as yet another form of competition, deliriously celebrated by mass media.

While artificial insemination was a scientific breakthrough, it is also symptomatic of the process analyzed here, in particular of the changes in the underlying structure leading to the civilization of illiteracy. Artificial insemination is part of this background; so is the entire genetic research that resulted in our ability to design not only new plants and animals with expected characteristics, but also human beings. Specialization reached a point where the market can satisfy a new type of consumption, in this case represented by artificial insemination, under acceptable economic conditions. Whether a pill, or *aesthetic* insemination, will ever make those who desire to be artists become creative is still to be seen. (The same holds true for science, politics, and any other creative career.) But we have already seen the dissemination of tools (mainly computer-based) that give many the illusion of becoming abruptly talented, as some women discover that they are abruptly fecund because they found the right pill, or the right gynecologist, to make the impossible happen.

As part of contemporary society's generalized illiteracy, erotic illiteracy is eloquently illustrated by the pervasiveness of sex in art. The transition from pornography to artistic pornography corresponds to the search of those human obsessions that legitimize art's appropriation of territories considered taboo. As some see it, once freed from the constraints implicit in the pragmatic framework relying on literacy, art and sexuality intensified their reciprocal influence. Aesthetic concerns changed from elaboration and method to improvisation and process. The expectation of education or therapeutics gave way to triggering excitement, more obliquely sexual excitement. Striptease has moved from the back alleys of bigoted enjoyment into movie theaters, museums, prime time television, the Internet. And so has the language of arousal, the voice of pleasure, the groan of post-coital exhaustion, or disappointment from teleporn services to the pay-per-session Websites, where credit card numbers are submitted without fear of their being used beyond payment for the service. In certain countries still under a literate regimen, the problem of pornography has been solved by administrative prohibitions; in others, a solution arises from blind market logic.

The market acknowledges the various aspects of sexuality in the civilization of illiteracy through products and services geared towards all those involved. Many market semioses work in this direction—from the pornographic sites on the Internet to the *red light* districts where risk can be generously rewarded. Sometimes the market's attention leads to unexpected changes in what is marketed, and how previous acceptable codes of sexual behavior are revised and new codes publicly sanctioned. The many forms of advertisement catering to homosexuals, *sexploitation,* gendered sexuality, group experiences, while never using one qualifier or another, are quite explicit in identifying their public and the patterns of behavior characteristic for this public. Means used for this purpose correspond to those of the civilization of illiteracy. There is, probably, no other medium of more precise narrow casting of sexual wares, from legitimate to scandalously base, than that of the networked world.

In the framework of literacy, the erotic (as all other creative contributions) was idealized in many respects. Language projected the erotic experience as one that transcended sexuality, leading to stable and selective male-female relationships within the boundaries of the family characteristic of industrial society. In time, various value representations, symptomatic of a peculiar understanding of the differences between man and woman, and stored in the language of customs and rituals, took over the substance of the erotic and made *form* predominant. Literacy and the ceremonies celebrating the erotic—especially marriage and wedding anniversaries—are connected far beyond what most would accept on first reflection. The fact that the civilization of illiteracy took over these ceremonies, and created a *service* sector able to provide a substitute for an instance that used to signify commitment only proves how ubiquitous the expectation of high efficiency is. The vows that made marriage a social event, sanctioning the implicit sexual component of the contract, and sometimes celebrating more prejudice than tolerance, are expectations expressed in literate language and submitted for public validation. Whether newlyweds knew what they signed—or did not know how to sign—does not change the fact that the *institution* was acknowledged in the integrating reality of language.

EQUAL ACCESS TO EROTIC MEDIOCRITY

Once the homogeneous image of society breaks, and sexuality more than previously turns into another market commodity (prostitution, in its hetero- and homosexual forms), once morals and direct commitments are substituted by rules of efficiency and population control, the language of the erotic is emptied. It is useless to accuse people of lower moral standards without understanding that, under new conditions of human experience, these standards simply embody ways of achieving the efficiency that this civilization of illiteracy strives for. To *own* your partner, as the marriage certificate is interpreted by some, and to buy pleasure or perversion as one buys food or clothing, are two different contexts for the self-constitution of the individual. It is much cheaper—and I cringe to state this so bluntly—to buy sexual pleasure, regardless how limited and vulgar it can be, than to commit oneself to a life of reciprocal responsibility, and unavoidable moments of inequity. The economic equation is so obvious that facing it, one ends up discouraged. But this equation is part of the broader equation of high expectations defining the illiterate practical experience of self-constitution in a world of a very large scale. In this equation, access to pornographic sites on the Internet can indeed appear to some as an issue of freedom of speech or freedom of choice.

Even those living outside the platinum and diamond belt of wealth and prosperity partake in the illiterate expression of sexuality as this created global markets of prostitution, pornography, and vulgarity, or widely opened the doors to sexual experimentation. From food, music, and photography, to video, films, and clothing, almost everything seems to address sexuality, moreover, to stimulate it. Crime and sex drive the market (the art market included) more than anything else. All age groups are addressed on their own biological and cultural terms; all backgrounds, including ethnic and religious, are involved in the fabric of sex messages. One million children are forced yearly into the sex market, the majority of them from poor countries. People who do not know how to read or write, and who probably never will, live under the seduction of the Calvin Klein label and will imitate the lascivious moves of the models through which they learn about them. Enormous numbers of people who might not have appropriate shelter, or enough food, buy Madonna videos and indulge in the fantasy that sexual freedom embodies in their particular illiterate expression.

Today, humans no longer share a literate notion of the sexual, but display a multitude of attitudes and involve themselves in a variety of experiences, which include the expectation of a common denominator, such as the family used to be. Humans tamed their own nature and discovered, at the peak of what seemed to become a collective sense of invulnerability, that there are still points of individual vulnerability. Some are reviving hopes of chastity and *clean* marriages, of generalized heterosexuality—in short, of a return to the safe shores of an idealized erotic experience of the past. Sexuality, however, always had its bright and dark sides. Suffice it to recall the explicit images in the ruins of Pompeii, or those in Indian and Japanese art. Sometimes, not even our most aggressive sex magazines, porno shops, Hollywood crap, and Internet sites equal their boldness. But people have managed to hide the dark side, or at least what could be construed as such, and to propagate, through literacy, the sublime erotic poem, the clean erotic novel, the romance, the love songs and dances, and everything else testifying to the sublime in love. What is new in the context of the civilization of illiteracy is that one side no longer excludes the other. To be is to be different, even if the biological equation of only two sexes seems so limiting.

Becoming more indirect and transitory, human relations affect sexuality and the ability to cope with what is defined as deviant erotic behavior in respect to tradition. AIDS will not turn back events that made the current pragmatic context necessary. Rather, it will add to the demystifying of love and sex, and thus effectively bridge between genetic research and the self-perpetuation drive of the species, rationalized in formulas meeting higher levels of efficiency, resources, and human reproduction. Such formulas, more sophisticated than the progressions Malthus used, are already tested by various organizations concerned with strategies for avoiding human self-destruction by overpopulation. A condom is cheaper than giving birth; all the pills women swallow over a lifetime are far less costly than taking care of one child. It should not surprise that Japan, committed to all the values of literacy and the sexuality attached to them, is reluctant to adopt the pill. The country has a very low birth rate, so low that its leaders are justified in fearing that soon Japan will not have enough people to fuel the economy through production and consumption. Still, Japan sees a relation between the pill and the state of morality as part of the cultural homogeneous fabric on which it relies. Nobody really doubts that the globality of human experience, to which Japan contributed through its productive genius probably more than any country, will catch up with it. Sexually, the literate Japanese are no less daring than the illiterate Americans.

To continuously tend towards having more at the cheapest price—in many ways an expression of rape of other people's work and resources—means to exhaust not only the object, but also the subject. Rape, one of the most heinous crimes people commit, generalized in political and economic rape, projects sexuality and its powerful action even outside the biological realm of human life. To want all (especially all at once) means to want nothing in particular. At the end of the total sexual experience lies nothing but disappointment for some; for others, the next experience. Profoundly subjective, deeply individual, unique and irrepeatable, human sexuality has meaning only to the extent that it remains an integrating factor, relating individual destiny to that of the species. The similarity between the creative and sexual acts might explain why changes similar to those occurring in erotic experience can be identified in the artistic, scientific, or political practice of the civilization of illiteracy. Unless we understand the many implications of such changes, we would only leap into a vortex of wild conjecture. Family is the part of the experience of human self-constitution in which such implications are most likely to have a profound effect.

CHAPTER 3: FAMILY: DISCOVERING THE PRIMITIVE FUTURE

A paradox has developed: Homosexuals want to establish families and to have them acknowledged by society. Adults who have children choose to avoid the family contract. Well over 30% of the children born in the USA are born out of wedlock. In the pragmatic equation of human self-constitution, these facts bear deeper signification.

Commenting before a television camera after a celebrity divorce trial, an onlooker remarked that there is more communication in preparing a pre-nuptial agreement than during a marriage. As exaggerated and imprecise (communication between whom—the couple or their representatives?) as this remark probably is, it nevertheless captures some traits of family life in our age. Indeed, families are constituted on the basis of economic agreements, mediated by lawyers and financial consultants. The risk of family breakdown is carefully integrated in the calculations establishing the viability of the marriage. Children are part of the calculation—minus the long-lasting emotional effects—as are the odds for illness, disability, and liabilities, such as living parents and siblings who might need assistance, or obligations due to previous marriages. The curves registering amount of time the recently married spend together reveals that once the agreement is signed, dialogue shrinks to less than eight hours a week, which is well below the time spent watching television—almost seven hours a day—or devoted to physical exercise. If surfing the Net is part of the newlyweds' life, there is even less dialogue.

Typically, both partners in the marriage work, and this affects other aspects of family life besides dialogue. When children arrive, the time parents spend with them decreases progressively from the days following birth through the critical years of high school. It is reported that on the average, youngsters in the USA get their parents' attention for less than four hours a week. In some European countries, this time can reach eight to ten hours. On the Asian sub-continent, many children lose contact with their parents before the age of six. Statistics show that over a quarter of the American student population planning to enroll in college never discuss their high school programs, or necessary preparation courses, with their fathers. Close to half this amount never discuss their plans with their mothers (single or not). The same holds true for students in Italy, France, and Belgium.

Divorce percentages, abortion rates, number of partners over one's lifetime, and hours spent with the family in meaningful exchange of ideas or in common tasks express a condition of the family that reflects the dynamics of today's human practical experiences. Over 16 million children under the age of eighteen years live with one parent (mainly the mother). Economics (income level, joblessness, opportunity) plays a critical role in the life of the young and of their progenitors.

All the changes leading to the civilization of illiteracy affect the experience of family life, and result in radical changes of the family model itself. Faster rhythms of experiences leading to casual relationships and to forming a family are on record. Shorter cycles during which the experience is exhausted result in increasingly unstable relations and families. Permanence is no longer the expectation in marriage. Throughout society, clear-cut distinctions between morally right and wrong are being replaced by situation ethics. Increased mediation, through counselors, lawyers, doctors, and financial planners, explains the new efficiency of the family as short-lived interaction and cooperation. The factors mentioned characterize the new pragmatic framework of human existence in which a new kind of interpersonal commitment is made and a new type of family is established, not unlike the short-lived corporations that are exhausted as soon as their product's potential has been reached.

In this pragmatic framework, family-like interactions harking back to the civilization of literacy, with its hierarchy and central authority and the promise of stability and security, are considered the only alternative to the new situation of the family. The people who consciously seek this alternative discover that the family is bound by relatively loose connections and that reciprocally advantageous distributed tasks replace family unity. Mediated and segmented experiences and vague commitments, which evolve into a frame of vague morality, dominate family life today. Marriages of expediency, undertaken to solve some difficulty—such as resident status in some countries, health insurance, care for one's old age, better chances at a career—illustrate the tendency.

Once the conditions for the perpetuation and dissemination of values associated with literacy are no longer granted, at the current globally integrated scale of humankind, family life changes fundamentally. Even the notion of family is questioned. Family unity, reflected in the coherent pragmatic framework afforded by literacy, is replaced by individual autonomy and competition. An array of options greater than the one feasible at the scale characteristic of agricultural or industrial economy, presents itself to adults and children in their practical experiences of self-constitution. Nobody escapes the temptation of trying and testing in the multiple of choices that are characteristic of the civilization of illiteracy.

There are many facets to what is called *family*. The concept displays ample variety in its perceived or construed meaning. Sexual instincts manifested as attraction, associated with the awareness of the consequence of reproduction, might lead the list in defining what it took to establish a family. At the same level of importance is the need to establish a viable unity of economic, cultural, and psychological significance, a framework, sanctioned by religious and political entities, for carrying out obligations significant to the community. These, and a number of additional elements, such as morality based on the pragmatics of health, inter-generational exchange of information and aid, social functions ensuring survival and continuity through cooperation and understanding with other families, are tightly connected. The nature of this interconnectedness is probably a much better identifier of what, under given socio-historical circumstances, is considered and experienced as family.

TOGETHERNESS

Dictionaries point to the broader meaning of an extended notion of family—all living in a household—with the root of the word extending to all the servants, as well as to blood relations and descendants of the same progenitor. What is probably missing from such a definition is the understanding of interconnectedness, more specifically, awareness of the role played by agents of connection, among which language, in general, and literacy, in particular, become relevant.

Much has been written concerning the change from animal-like sexual drive to the formation of family; much, too, about the many specific forms of practical experiences through which families were established and maintained. The history of the human family captures the nature of the relations between man and woman, parents and offspring, near and distant kin, and between generations. Natural aspects of production and reproduction, and cultural, social, political, and ethnic elements are also expressed through the family. Its reality extends even to the area of interdependencies between the language of individuals constituting families as viable survival units, and the language of the community within which family is acknowledged. Whether female- or male-dominated, as the pragmatic context afforded, the family ascertains a sense of permanency against the background of need and flux. It is another constitutive practical experience involving the projection of individual biological characteristics in the context of life and work, an experience that progressively extended beyond biology into its own domain of expectations and values, and finally into its own effectiveness.

In search of a family nucleus, we arrive at female, male, offspring. The biological structure is maintained by some bond, probably a combination of factors pertaining to survival (the economy of family), emotions, sexual attraction (which includes psychological aspects), and ways of interacting with the extended family and with other families (social aspects). But beyond this, little else can be stated without causing controversy. Within each family, there is a maternal and a paternal line. In some family types, mother and father together feed the children, introduce them to survival tactics, and train their family instincts. In other cases, only one parent assumes these functions. The implicit linearity of family relations unfolds through new family associations.

Anthropological research reports in detail how families are established. The pragmatic aspect is decisive. In Melanesia, the goal is to acquire brothers-in-law who will join the woman's family in hunting, farming, and other activities. Margaret Mead described the rule of not marrying those one fights. Expressed in language, this rule has a normative quality. Nevertheless, in some tribes in Kenya, enemies marry to ensure that they become friends. The language expressing this strategy is more suggestive than imperative. Research also documents variations from the nuclear model. The Nayar, a population in India, consecrates a family in which children belong to the maternal line; fathers visit. The woman can have as many lovers as she desires. The semiosis of naming children reflects this condition. Rules established over time in some countries are indicative of peculiar pragmatic requirements: polygamy in societies where marriage is the only form of protection and fulfillment for women; polyandry in societies with a high man to woman ratio; uxorilocation (the new couple resides in the wife's home territory), and virilocation (the new couple resides in the husband's home territory).

The scale at which family self-constitution takes place affects its effectiveness. When this scale reaches a certain threshold or critical size, structural changes take place. The family, in its various embodiments, and within each specific pragmatic framework, reflected these major changes in the human scale of mankind at many levels. From the first images documenting families over 25,000 years ago, in the Paleolithic Age, to the paintings at Sefar (Tassili des Ajjer, 4th century BCE), and to many other subsequent forms of testimony, we have indicators of change in family size, the nature of family hierarchy, inheritance mechanisms, restrictions and prohibitions (incest foremost), and above all, change in the family condition when the pragmatic context changes. The testimony extends to *cemeteries:* It matters who is buried with whom or close to whom; to the *evolution of words:* What Beneviste called *glottochronology;* to *contracts.* Marriage contracts, such as the cuneiform tablet of Kish, dated 1820 BCE, or contracts documenting the sale of land, in which the family tree of the sellers is reproduced as testimony that the entire family accepts the transaction, shed light on the evolution of family. When Aristotle stated "Each city is made up of families," he acknowledged that a stage of stabilized family relations had been reached, well adapted to the stabilizing pragmatic framework facilitated by the new practical experience of writing.

By Aristotle's time, *togetherness* was designated through a name. The expectation at this scale of human relations was: without a name there is no social existence. Characteristics of sign processes pertinent to self-constitution as members of various family types become characteristic of the family. That is, the structure of family-based semiotic processes and the structure of the family are similar. Rudimentary signs, incipient language, oral communication, notation, and writing are stages in the semiosis of means of expression and communication. The sign processes of family develop in tandem.

At the time literacy became possible and necessary, it embodied an idiom of effective relations, both synchronically—at a given instance of those relations—and diachronically—over time, such as from one generation to another, each attached to the same use of language in writing, reading, and speaking. It is precisely the need to achieve efficiency, in every human endeavor, that assigns to the family the function of co-guarantor of tradition. Even before the possibility of literacy, language carried the *do's* and *don'ts* transmitting rules, based on the practical experience, that ensured survival through cooperation and new ways to satisfy direct needs and respond to expectations— rules that affected the efficiency of each practical experience.

The family appropriated these requirements, shaping them into a coherent framework for efficient togetherness. Directness, sequentiality, linearity, centralism, cooperation, and determinism marked the family experience as it marked other experiences of human self-constitution. Family members relied directly on each other. As one male assumed the role of provider, and the female, or females, of caretaker, a certain structure of dependence was put in place, resulting in hierarchy and sub-hierarchies. Family activity involved repetitive and sequential phases related to survival: reproductive cycles of animals; the progression of seasons and its relation to agriculture (rainy and dry, cold and hot, long days and short days). The pragmatics of survival seemed determined; there was little choice in method and timing. The family took shape in a world of cause-and-effect, which also determined religious practices.

The source of each rule for successful family life was direct practical experience; the test of validity was the effectiveness appropriate to the specific scale of humanity. The *do's* changed over time, as experience confirmed their efficiency. They became a body of accepted knowledge from which moral ideals are extracted, laws derived, and political action inspired within the context of literacy. In the industrial equation, output (products, end results, increase or profit) should equal or exceed input (raw materials, energy, human effort). The *don'ts,* adopted by religion, law, and rudimentary medical praxis, were engraved in language even more deeply. They were encoded together with punishments that reflected the urgency behind preserving the integrity of the family-based pragmatic framework, in the experience of the agricultural and, later on, the industrial model. The association between act and result was continuously scrutinized in a world of action and reaction. In a world of experience mediated through literacy, rules were followed for their own sake; or rather, for the sake of the permanence that literacy embodied.

That at some time sexual relations outside marriage could be the cause of so many prohibitions and dire punishment, mainly for women, does not bear as much significance on the state of morals as upon the pragmatic implications of the act of infidelity and wantonness. These implications refer to lineage, continuity, and inheritance, psychological effects on other family members, health, and status of offspring born out of wedlock. Rules regarding family integrity were encoded in the language of custom, ritual, and myth. Later on they were encoded in the language of religion, philosophy, ethics, law, science, ideology, and political discourse. Eventually, they were recorded in the rules of the market. Filtered over time through a variety of experiences resulting in success or failure, they are acknowledged in culture, and adopted in the language of education, and probably most directly in the language of market transactions. To give birth meant to continue the sequence and enhance the chances of survival; to rear children to adulthood meant to afford new levels of efficiency. More people could be more effective in ensuring survival in a pragmatic framework of direct action and immediacy. Beyond a certain scale, it became effectively impossible to coordinate the complex of families that went into the entire family. City life, even in early cities, was not propitious to extended families. During this period, the strategy of labor division took over undifferentiated, direct execution of tasks.

Over time, as the scale of human experience changed, community expectations were reflected in what used to be the domain of the individual or that of families. The term *over time* needs some clarification. The first phases to which we refer are of very slow change. From the initial indications of family-like relations up to the establishment of language families, the time span is greater than 15,000 years. From nuclei practicing agriculture to the first notation and writing, the time is in the range of 4,000 to 5,000 years. From then on, the cycles became more compressed: less than 2,000 years to the time religions were established, another 1,000 years to settlement in cities. Each moment marks either progressive changes in the pragmatic framework or radical change, when the scale of human life and work required different means to meet efficiency expectations. Language acquisition, settlement of populations, development of writing, the emergence of philosophy, science and technology, the Industrial Revolution, and the civilization of illiteracy are the six changes in the scale of humankind, each with its corresponding pragmatic framework. Many agents of influence contribute to the change from one pragmatic framework to another: climactic conditions, natural selection, the environment, religions, communal rules, distribution of resources, and the experience of the market. Regardless of the difference in languages, language use is probably the common experience through which natural changes are acknowledged and social differentiation effected.

Exactly what made literacy necessary—the need to achieve levels of efficiency corresponding to the human scale that led to industrial society—made the corresponding type of family necessary. Families reproduced the needed working force and transmitted the literacy required to attain the efficiency of qualified work. Such work was accomplished in a setting fundamentally different from that of immediate, direct, practical experiences with nature (farming, animal husbandry), or small-scale craftsmanship. Literacy was fostered by the family as a means of coordination and as a universal language of human transactions. This is how family fulfills the function of co-guarantor of education. Conversely, among the forms through which the future contract of literacy was acknowledged, family is one. The pragmatic need for permanency reflected in the expectation of the stable family has many consequences inside and outside family life. These can be witnessed in the spirit and letter of contractual obligations people enter under the coordinating power of the literate commitment. Education, law, politics, religion, and art are impregnated with this spirit. As the ultimate family—the homogeneous family of families—the nation asserts its permanency as a reflection of the permanency of its constituent *atoms*. When deterioration occurs in the conditions that make literacy possible and necessary, many of the permanencies associated with literacy, including the interpersonal relations adapted to it, or the homogeneity of nations, fail. As we entertain the prospect that nations, as definable political entities, might disappear, we automatically wonder whether the family, as a definable social entity, will survive—and if yes, in what form.

FAMILY FAILS?

The downfall of nations and empires has been attributed to the breakdown of the family. The weakening of family has been cited as a cause of the decline and fall of the Roman Empire. Anti-abortionists and other traditionalists in the United States blame the breakdown in traditional family values for many of the social ills of our day. Now that the royal children in Great Britain are divorced, people wonder how long the monarchy will last.

One of the symptoms of the civilization of illiteracy is the perceived breakdown of family. Simultaneously, other institutions, such as schools, the church, the military, embodying permanency and stability, are undergoing drastic reassessment. In a broad sense, a transition from one way of life to another has been taking place. But things are a little more confusing since what used to be is not always actually replaced by something else, but rescaled, turned into a possibility among many, in a dynamics of ever-expanding diversity and wider choices. Many have argued that the breakdown of the traditional family was inevitable. They bring up cultural, ideological, and socioeconomic arguments—from the liberation of women and children to the exhausted model of the patriarchal structure. All these arguments are probably partially right. After previous economies of scarcity and limited means of production, human experience at the global scale has brought about a wealth of choices and means of affluence that question the very premise of the family contract.

In a context of rapid change from the practical experience of authority to the pragmatics of endless choice, subsumed under the heading of freedom, the permanency of the family structure comes under the methodical doubt of our new patterns of praxis. The tension between choice and authority was experienced in family life in the specific context of human relations based on hierarchy and centralism. New questions have a bearing on sexuality, parent-child relations, interactions among families, and the whole social fabric. Likewise, the transition of what was projected as self-control—with elements of self-denial, for the sake of family, a form of internalized authority—to the discovery of new frontiers, and the alternative pursuit of self-indulgence, follows the same path. These new frontiers and alternatives make values appear relative and undermine the spirit of sharing implicit in the traditional experience of family. Sharing is replaced by strategies of coordination and wealth preservation, all involving many mediating elements, such as political power, the legal system, taxation, charity.

It is argued, probably with good reason, that the high rate of divorce—the socially sanctioned breakdown of a family, but probably only *relatively* indicative of the breakdown—is not meaningful unless put in a broader context: how many people still marry, how many remarry, how much longer people live. The high rate of divorce at the end of World War II is symptomatic of events above and beyond the structural characteristics of family constitution, reconstitution, or breakdown. The rate of divorce in the years following the war, especially in the last 10-15 years, is nevertheless connected to the underlying structure of a pragmatic framework within which permanency, whether that of language, family, values, nations, laws, art, or anything else, becomes a liability because it affects the dynamics of change. One out of two marriages—and the proportion is changing quite fast—ends in divorce. This is, nevertheless, only one aspect of broader modifications making such a rate more of a qualifier than an accident in human pairing.

The dynamics of reproduction—births per marriage, average number of children per family, children living with one parent, infant mortality—is significant from the perspective of one of the most important functions of family. In the pragmatic context of today's integrated world, the need to have many children in order to maintain continuity and viability is different, even in Bangladesh, Afghanistan, or Africa, than at any previous time. The species has practically freed itself from the direct pressure of natural selection. What is at work, even in areas of extreme poverty, is a perverted mechanism of interdependencies echoing what herders in East Africa expressed as: "He who has children does not sleep in the bush." The family has ceased to be the sole source of welfare. Its functions are taken over by the community, the state, even international organizations. The fact that in some parts of the world this structural change is not acknowledged, and very high birth rates are on record, shows that the result of ignoring the pragmatic exigencies of this new age adds to the burden, not to the solution.

Another phenomenon difficult to assess is the single woman who decides to give birth. If individual or social material resources are available, moral and educational needs or expectations still remain to be addressed. Individualism fostered to the extreme partially explains the trend, but cannot satisfactorily indicate the many aspects of this new phenomenon characteristic of the civilization of illiteracy. If one reads the statistics, single parenthood appears like a sure winner in the lottery of poverty and frustration. The problems of children who will be growing up with a mother single by choice will be the source of much sociological and psychoanalytical research in the future. But existence is more than numbers in ledgers, or psychological predicaments. Self-fulfillment, the instinct to nurture and to ensure continuity are all at work in such cases.

THE HOMOSEXUAL FAMILY

No group has done more in the way of forcing us to rethink the definition and role of family as homosexuals have. Within the civilization of illiteracy, homosexuals assert their identity in the public eye. Gay and lesbian groups fight for the ratification of the homosexual family, which could not even be conceived of within the pragmatics associated with literacy. Their fight corresponds to a practical experience that is not motivated by the self-perpetuation drive of the species, but by other forces. These are economic, social, and political—the right to enjoy the same benefits as members of heterosexual families. Interestingly enough, social principles adopted in the age when pragmatics required that society support childbirth, family nurturing, and education are extended today, under totally different circumstances, in ignorance of the necessities that were reflected in these principles. A tax deduction was an expression of social co-participation, since society needed more people, better educated youth, a stable framework of family life. The economy and the military could not succeed without the fresh flesh of new generations.

Gays and lesbians challenge the traditional notion of family in a context that no longer requires hierarchy and that redefines roles that have become stereotypes and undemocratic. They propose a model on a continuum in which each partner can be provider and assume household duties to any degree. There are no clear-cut roles, no clear-cut hierarchy, and no long-term commitments. Children are not the consequence of sexual relations but of desire and choice. This choice has two aspects of special significance for the pragmatics of our age. One concerns the human desire to form an alliance in the form of family, which seems almost instinctual. It may be difficult to recognize a natural inclination in a context (homosexuality) that negates propagation of the species. It is this threat to survival that caused so many taboos to be placed on homosexuality in the first place. These taboos took on other dimensions when encoded in a literacy that ignored the pragmatics.

The second aspect has to do with the extent to which homosexuals' desire for a family constitutes its own validity in the pragmatic framework of our time. To what extent does the desire to have a family reveal characteristics of human self-constitution in the current context? In a world in which there is a high rate of births out of wedlock, a world in which the traditional family is no guarantee of relationships free of abuse and exploitation, a world with great numbers of children in orphanages or in foster care, any desire to place children in a loving family context is worthy of attention.

What constitutes a family in an age whose pragmatics is not defined by the values perpetuated in and through literacy? The new definition might go along these lines: main provider (the father role); second provider (the mother role), who is also manager of the household. The two roles are not polarized; each provider participates in household work and in salaried work outside the home, as circumstances require. A child is a dependent under the age of 18 years (or 22 years if in college), for whom the providers are legally responsible. A grandparent is qualified through age and willingness to assume the role. Aunt/uncle is someone with fraternal ties to the providers. The definitions can go on. In considering these literate definitions, we can see that they apply to the situation of the current traditional family as well, in which father and mother both work, in which a child may live with and be cared for by a parent's second or third spouse, in which distance from or lack of blood relations calls for *ad hoc* relatives. The most vital implications concern our culture as it has been passed down over the centuries through literate expression, laden with values that literacy perpetuates and endows with an aura, in defiance of the new pragmatics and the new scale in which humans operate.

The homosexual family and its occasional focus on adopting children reflects the fact that we live in a world of many options, and consequently of very relative values. Their desire for a family, under circumstances that are far from being conducive to family life, is as valid as that of an unmarried woman who wants to give birth and rear a child (the one-parent household). It is as valid as the desire of infertile couples who use every means the market offers to have a child, through costly medical intervention or by hiring surrogates. In the civilization of illiteracy, each person forms his or her own definition of family, just as people form their own definitions of everything else. The only test of validity is, ultimately, effectiveness. In the long run, the biological future of the species will also be affected, one way or another, as part of the effectiveness equation.

TO WANT A CHILD

The new pragmatics ultimately affects the motives behind forming a family in the civilization of illiteracy. Marriage, if at all considered, has become a short-term contract. Its brevity contradicts marriage's reason for being: continuity and security through offspring and adaptation to life cycles. The attitudes with which partners enter the family contract result in a dynamic of personal relations outside of that sanctioned by society. Vows are exchanged more as a matter of performance than of bonding. Natural instincts are systematically overridden through mediating mechanisms for providing nourishment, acquiring health care, and settling conflicts. Child rearing is the result of pragmatic considerations: What does a couple, or single parent, give up in having a child? Can a mother continue working outside the home?

In order to correctly qualify answers to these questions, we would need to acknowledge that many characteristics of the individuals constituting a family, or seeking alternatives to it, are reflected in the family experience, or in experiences that are parallel to it. Economic status, race, religion, culture, and acculturation play an important role. Literacy assumed homogeneity and projected expectations of uniformity. The new pragmatic framework evidences the potential of heterogeneous experiences. Data indicating that the average numbers of divorces, single-parent households, number of partners, etc. vary drastically among groups of different biological, cultural, and economic backgrounds shows how necessary it is to realistically account for differences among human beings.

Let us take a look at some statistical data. But before doing that, let us also commit ourselves to an unbiased interpretation, free of any racial prejudice. Almost 60% of Black children in the USA are living in a one-parent household. Of these children, 94% live with their mothers. It was documented that 70% of the juveniles in long-term correctional facilities grew up without a father. To make any inference from such data without proper consideration of the many factors at work would only perpetuate literacy-based prejudices, and would not lead to a better understanding of the new circumstances of human self-constitution. Our need to understand the dynamics of family and what can be done to effect a course of events that is beneficial to all involved cannot be served unless we understand the many characteristics of the practical experience of self-constitution of the Black family, or of any non-standard Western family.

Under the expectations of literacy, a prototypical family life was to be expected from all. As the expectation of homogeneity is overridden by all the forces at work in the civilization of illiteracy, we should not be surprised by, and even less inclined to fasten blame on people who constitute themselves in ways closer to their authenticity. Multiplication of choice is—let me state again—part of the civilization of illiteracy. Modern, *enlightened* laws introduced in some African countries prohibit polygamous families. With this prohibition in place, a new phenomenon has occurred: Husbands end up having extra-marital affairs and support neither their lovers nor their children, which they did under polygamy. Paradoxically, activists in the Women's Liberation movement are seriously considering the return to polygamy, as an alternative to the increasing number of *deadbeat dads* and the misery of abandoned wives and children. There is no necessary relation between the two examples, rather the realization that within the civilization of illiteracy, tradition comes very powerfully to expression.

CHILDREN IN THE *ILLITERATE* FAMILY

Nobody can characterize families of the past (monogamous or polygamous) as unfailingly unified and showing exemplary concern for offspring. Children, as much as wives and husbands, were abused and neglected. Concern over education was at times questionable. The projected ideal of authority and infallibility resulted in the perpetuation of patterns of experiences from which we are still fighting to free ourselves. Notwithstanding these and other failures, we still have to acknowledge that a shift, from individual and family responsibility to a diffuse sense of social responsibility, characterizes the process affecting the status of children. The family in the civilization of illiteracy embodies expectations pertinent to progressively mediated practical experiences: from childbirth—an almost industrial experience—to education; from entering the family agreement, mediated by so many experts—lawyers, priests, tax consultants, psychologists—to maintaining a sense of commonalty among family members; from embodying direct interaction and a sense of immediacy to becoming instances of segmentation, change, and interaction, and instances of competition and outright conflict. The institution of the family must also counteract sequentiality and linearity with a sense of relativity that allows for more choices, which the new human scale makes possible. This new pragmatic framework also allows for higher expectations.

Like any other institution, the institution of marriage (and the bureaucracy it has generated) has its own inertia and drive to survive, even when the conditions of its necessity, at least in the forms ascertained in the past, are no longer in place. In short, the breakdown of the family, even if equated with the failure of the individuals constituting it—children included—is related to the new structural foundation of a pragmatic framework for which it is not suited as a universal model, or to which it is only partially acceptable. This does not exclude the continuation of family. Rather, it means that alternative forms of cooperation and interaction substituting the family will continue to emerge. Just as literacy maintains a presence among many other literacies, the family is present among many forms of reciprocal interdependence, some expanding beyond the man-woman nucleus. To understand the dynamics of this change, a closer look at how the new pragmatic framework of the civilization of illiteracy affects experiences pertinent to family is necessary here.

The history of the family, independent of its various embodiments (matriarchal, patriarchal, polygamous, monogamous, restricted or extended, heterosexual or homosexual), is in many respects the history of the appropriation of the individual by society. The offspring of primitive humans belonged to nobody. If they survived to puberty, they continued life on their own, or as members of the group in which they were born, as nameless as their parents. Children and parents were amoral and competed for the same resources. The offspring of the humans constituting their own identity, and their own universe *parallel* to that of nature, belonged more and more to what emerged as the family, and by extension to the community (tribe, village, parish). The child was marked, named, nurtured, and educated, as limited as this education might have been. It was given language and, through the experience of work, a sense of belonging. In all known practical experiences—work, language, religion, market, politics—the succession of generations was specifically acknowledged. Rules, some pertaining to the preservation of biological integrity, others to property and social life, were established in order to accommodate relations between generations.

Over centuries, family *ownership* of children decreased while that of society increased. This is reflected in the various ways church, school, social institutions, and especially the market claim each new generation. In this process, mediation becomes part of family life: the priest, the teacher, the counselor, the language of advertisement, direct marketing, and much, much more is insinuated between children and their parents. The process intensifies as expectancies of better life for less effort become predominant. Responsibilities, procreation included, are distributed from the parents to the practical experiences of genetics. Test-tube production of babies is an alternative to natural procreation. As a matter of fact, both procreation and adoption are dominated by strong selective methods and design procedures. Genetic traits are identified and matched in the genetic banks of adoptable children. Surrogate mothers are selected and contracted based on expectations of behavior and heredity. Sperm banks offer selections from high IQ or high physical performance *bulls*. Other mediators specify ideal *cows*, surrogate mothers whose offspring are treated like any other commodity—"satisfaction guaranteed." If the product is somehow unsatisfactory, the dissatisfied parents get rid of it.

Obviously, the language and literacy expected for the success of the biochemical reaction in the test tube is different from that involved in the constitution of the family. It is also different from the literacy involved in the change from instinctual sexual encounters to love, procreation, and child rearing. In each of the procedures mentioned, new languages—of genetics, for example—introduce levels of mediation that finally affect the efficiency of procreation. As nightmarish as some of these avenues might seem, they are in line with the entire development towards the new pragmatics: segmentation—the task is divided into sub-tasks—networking—to identify the desired components and strategies for synthesis—and task distribution. Children are not yet made on the Internet, but if the distinction between matter and information suggested by some geneticists is carried through, it would not be impossible to conceive of procreation on networks.

A NEW INDIVIDUALITY

The process of mediation expands well further. Family life becomes the subject of practical experiences involving family planning, health, psychology, socialized expectations of education, the right to die. The *private* family owned their offspring and educated it to the level of its own education, or to the level it deemed advantageous, consistent with the progress of literacy. To the extent that this family was involved in other experiences, such as religion, sport, art, or the military, children grew up partaking in them. Once one aspect of the relation between environment, home, family, and work changes—for example, living in the city reshapes the nature of the dependence on the environment, the house is one of several possible, family members work at different jobs—the family is made more and more part of a bigger family: society. In turn, this belonging dissolves into solitary individualism. Nothing any longer buffers the child from the competitive pressure that keeps the economic engine running. Industrial society required centers of population while it still relied on relatively nuclear families that embodied its own hierarchy. The human scale reflected in industrial society required the socialization of family in order to generate an adequate workforce, as well as the corresponding consumption. With networking, children as much as adults are on their own, in a world of interactions that breaks loose from any conceivable constraints. There is no need to fantasize here, rather to acknowledge a new structural situation of consequences beyond our wildest imagination.

Literacy unified through its prescriptions and expectations. It facilitated the balance between the preserved naturalness and the socialized aspect of family. It projected a sense of permanency and shielded the family from the universe of machines threatening to take over limited functions of the body: the mechanical arm, the treadmill. As a human medium for practical experiences involving writing and reading, literacy seemed to represent a means of resistance against the inanimate. It helped preserve human integrity and coherence in a world progressively losing its humanity due to all the factors that the need for increased efficiency put in place (machines, foremost). It eventually became obvious that procreation had to be kept within limits, that there is a social cost to each child and to each mother giving birth. Moreover, family structural relations needed to be reconsidered for the expected levels of efficiency to be maintained and increased, as expectations took over desires. The new pragmatic framework is established as this borderline between the possible and the necessary. The civilization of illiteracy is its expression.

At the family level, the civilization of illiteracy corresponds to increased segmentation, affecting the very core of family life, and mediation. The family can no longer be viewed as a whole by the many mediating entities constituting the market. The market is with us from birth to death. It deals in every aspect of life, and extends the pressure of competition in each moment of our existence. The market segments medical care. It is most likely that each family member sees a different doctor, depending on age, sex, and condition. It segments education, religion, and culture. It is not uncommon that family members constitute their identity in different religious experiences, and some of them in none, as it is not uncommon that their educational needs run the gamut from a modicum of instruction to never-ending study. They live together, or find togetherness on the network matrix—one running a business on some remote continent, the other pursuing solitary goals, and some adapting to foreign cultures (less than to foreign languages).

The market has broken society into segments and the family into parts on which it concentrates its message of consumption. There is not one market entity that views the family as a whole. Children are targeted on the basis of their economic, cultural, and racial back-ground for everything from food to clothing to toys and recreation. And so are their respective natural or adoptive parents, grandparents, and relatives. We can all decry this as manipulation, but in fact it corresponds to the objective need to increase commercial efficiency through narrow marketing. Accordingly, a new moral condition emerges, focused on the individual, not on the family. Part of the broader pragmatic framework, this process stimulates the relative illiteracy of the partners constituting the family. This illiteracy is reflected in varied patterns of sexual behavior, in new birth control strategies, in a different reciprocal relation between men and women, or between individuals of the same sex, and in as-yet undefinable codes of family behavior. The condition of the child in the civilization of illiteracy corresponds to the same dynamics. Children are less and less cared for at home, often entrusted to specialized caretakers, and finally started on their way through the vast machine called the education system.

DISCONTINUITY

It makes no sense to decry the hypocrisy of double (or multiple) standards and the loss of a morality associated with the misery of people obliged to remain together by forces they consider legitimate (religion foremost). In the dynamics of the civilization of illiteracy, forces kept under the control of rules and norms established in the practical experience of literacy are unleashed. It would be difficult to speak about progress where one sees the demise of family, the erosion of private life, the increased number of one-parent households, of early and very early maternity, of incest, rape and increased child abuse, of obsession with contraceptives or ignorance of their use, and the threat of drugs and sexually transmitted diseases. Still, before hurrying value judgments, one would be better advised to consider the entire picture and to assess what makes all these occurrences possible, indeed, what makes them necessary.

It might well be true that what we perceive as the sources of morality and happiness—the family, children, love, religion, work, and the satisfaction associated with all of these—are exhausted. It might well be that fresh sources must be sought, or invented, or at least not eliminated because they do not fit the mold of previous choices. Even the thought that morality and happiness are altogether unnecessary deserves to be considered. They are loaded with the expectation of permanency and universality rendered impossible in the new pragmatic framework of permissiveness, local values, instant gratification, change, and interconnectedness.

The nuclear family of the civilization of literacy has been absorbed in the illiterate dynamics of societal functioning. It is coming out of the experience restructured. On the other hand, socially acceptable patterns of development are encouraged through the public education system, where the chief objective is the socialization of children, not the dissemination of knowledge. Ethnic characteristics are progressively, although timidly, acknowledged. The seemingly losing battle against drugs leads many parents and social researchers to wonder whether legalization would be more efficient than spending immense amounts of money and energy to fight the underground market. In this world of mediation, science and technology make genetic engineering possible in the form of influencing the profile of the offspring, ways to avoid what does not fit the fashionable, ways to induce early in development (almost at the embryonic stage) preferences and cognitive characteristics.

Together with everything pertaining to the human being self-constituted in the framework of the civilization of illiteracy, the family goes public in the stock market of the many enterprises involved in the self-perpetuation and the well being of the species. Its value is no longer a matter of those constituting it, of its goals and means, but of the return on the investment society makes in it. As a competitive unit within the pragmatic framework associated with literacy, the family freed itself from the constraints implicit in literacy that affect its efficiency. It became a contract, one among the growing number, in whose expression literacy gives way to the alternative litigation language of the law, in respect to which, with the exception of lawyers, everyone else is illiterate. Favorable taxation supports children—euphemistically called *deductions* when they are really *additions*—but not beyond what is socially expected of them, at least in the USA: to become agents of consumption and increased efficiency as soon as possible. In this sense, the tensions between generations are simply refocused—society is willing to make available social help in the form of transitory family substitutes. The problem is not addressed, only its symptoms. The languages of counseling and psychiatry at work here are another instance of specialized literacy. They substitute for family communication while projecting limited and limiting psychological explanations upon all those involved.

In an age that expects efficiency to lead to satisfaction, if not happiness, the family relies on specialists when problems arise: psychiatrists, counselors, specialized schools. Sometimes the specialists are imposed when society perceives a need to intervene, especially in cases of suspected child abuse. It is reflective of the pragmatics of our time that the elderly receive attention in the market of mediations and specializations on a less obvious level. They are considered only to the extent that they are viable consumers. Once upon a time, and still in isolated cases, such as the Amish and Mennonites in the USA, age was to be honored for its own sake, a value kept alive through literacy. While many elderly enjoy the benefits of better healthcare and economic sufficiency, they effectively divorce themselves from the family in enjoying what the market offers them. Their participation in the family is a matter of choice more than necessity. The success of the Internet among the elderly, in need of communication and support groups, is a very telling phenomenon. Networks of reciprocal support, as nuclei of self-organization, emerge independent of any form of social intervention. Their viability is based on this dynamics.

The struggle between the value of life in the civilization of literacy and that of illiteracy can be seen in hospitals and nursing homes where the aged are treated on machine-based analogies, abandoned or entrusted to specialists in the care of the dying. While aging and death cannot be eliminated, the market provides ways to avoid them as long as we can afford to.

It used to be that the new generation continued the family work—farming, carpentry, pottery, law, business, banking, publishing. This happened in a context of continuity and relative permanence: the work or business remained relatively unchanged. Literacy was appropriate for the transfer of know-how, as it was for the maintenance of family-based values and successive assumption of responsibilities regarding the family, moreover the community. These pragmatic elements no longer exist the way they did.

Today, even within the same generation, the nature of business evolves, and so does the nature of the values around which family is established. In addition, ownership changes as well; businesses are more and more integrated in the market; they become public entities; their shares are traded with no regard to the object those shares represent. The consequence is what we perceive as lack of family continuity and bonding. The new nature of the family contract is such that its basis of affection is eroded. Sequentiality of work is replaced by cycles of parallel activity during which generations compete as adversaries. This is why the family contract is shifted more and more to the market, depersonalized, indexed like one among many commodities. This contract is no longer literacy-bound, but rooted in circumstances of distributed activities of intense competition and networking. Once demythified, family relations are reassessed; continuity is severed. The market acknowledges the segmentation of family—no longer an economic entity in its own right—and in turn accentuates it. The *baby business*, the *infant market, teenagers,* and so on to the *senior* market are well focused on their respective segments as these embody not just age groups, but foremostly expectations and desires that can be met at the level of each individual.

No matter how intense the desire to maintain a neutral discourse and to report facts without attaching teleological conclusions to them, it turns out that the language of family, probably more than the language of science, machines, or even art, religion, sports, and nourishment, involves our very existence. Where should somebody place himself in order to maintain some degree of objectivity? Probably at the level of the structural analysis. Here, everything affecting the status of family and the condition of morality appears as a network of changing interrelations among people involved in the practical experiences of defining what a human being is. It seems, at times, that we relive experiences of the primitive past: the child knew only his or her mother; women started giving birth at an early age (almost right after menarche); children were on their own as soon as they could minimally take care of themselves. But we also build an ideal image of the family based on recollections of the less distant past: permanent marriages ("until death"), respect for parents, mother cooking meals for which the whole family sits down, father bringing wood for the family hearth, children learning by participating, assuming responsibilities as their maturity permitted. This idealized image is also the bearer of prejudices: women's subservient role, the authoritarian model passed from one generation to another, frustration, unfulfilled talents.

So the paradox we experience is that of a primitive future: more animality (or, if you want a milder term, *naturalness*) in comparison to a civilized (or at least idealized) past. There is no cause for worry, especially in view of the realization that despite our success in labeling the world (for scientific and non-scientific purposes), the majority of human behavior is determined (as already pointed out) independent of labels. Taking into account that the notion of permanency is related to relatively stable frames of reference makes it easier to explain why the high mobility of our age results in changes, both physical and psychological, that undermine previous expectations.

Losing the discipline of the natural cycle that affected human work for centuries, human beings freed themselves from a condition of subservience, while at the same time generating new constraints reflected in the nature of their reciprocal relations. What does it mean to become used to something—environment, family, acquaintances—when this something is changing fast, and with it, we ourselves?

The Industrial Revolution brought about the experience of labor-saving machinery, but also of many new dependencies. In Henri Steele Commanger's words, "Every time-saving machine required another to fill the time that had been saved." One might not agree with this description. But it would be hard to contradict its spirit by taking only a cursory look at all the contraptions of illiteracy filling the inventory of the modern household: radio, photo camera, TV set, video recorder, video cassette player, Walkman™, CD player, electronic and digital games, laser disc player, CD-ROM, telephone, computer, modem. The one-directional communication supported by some of these machines affected patterns of interaction and resulted in audiences, but not necessarily in families, at least not in the sense acknowledged in practical experiences of family life. With the two-directional communication, supported by digital networks, human interaction takes on a new dimension. Choices increase. So do risks.

Once the substance of one's experience is substituted by mediations, even the rationale for communication changes, never mind the form. Families separated by virtue of assignments (war, business) at remote locations, or in pursuit of various interests (sport, entertainment, tourism), exchange videotapes instead of writing to each other, or focus on telephone conversations meant to signal a point of reference, but not a shared universe of existence and concerns. They discover e-mail and rationalize messages to a minimum. Or they become a Web page, available to whoever will surf by. All these changes—probably more can be acknowledged—took place concomitant with changes in our expectations and accepted values. With the increased gamut of choice, attachment to value decreases. When all emotions come from soap operas, and all identity from the latest fashion trend, it becomes difficult to defend notions such as sensitivity and personality. When love is as short as the random encounter, and faith as convincing as reading a person's palm or tarot cards, it is impossible to ascertain a notion of reciprocal responsibility or the moral expectation of faithfulness. On the other hand, when the need to achieve levels of efficiency dictated by a scale of humankind never experienced before and by expectations and desires in continuous expansion is as critical as we make it, something is given up—or, to put it the other way around, somebody has to pay for it. With the sense of globality—of resources, actions, plans—comes the pressure of integration of everybody into the global market, and the expectations of consumption attached to it. Many-to-many communication is not just a matter of bandwidth on digital networks, but of self-definition, also.

The family used to reflect the perceived infinity of the universe of existence., despite the family's finite and determined internal structure. With the awareness of limited resources, in particular those of the natural support system, comes the realization that alternative practical experiences of life and cooperation become necessary in order to generate new pragmatic frameworks for increased efficiency and enhanced dynamism. The indefinite expansion of what people want and the progressive incorporation of higher numbers of human beings into the market through which affluence, as much as misery, can be achieved, results in the devaluation of life, love, of values such as self-sacrifice, faithfulness, fairness. The moral literate philosophers of the 19th century—Ralph Waldo Emerson, Thomas Carlyle, William James—thought that the answer lay in our recognition that the world is not only for enjoyment. One can imagine a TV debate (interrupted by commercials, of course) between them and the romantic proponents of the ideology of progress—John Maynard Keynes, Adam Smith, David Hume. It's safe to wager that the audience would zap over their literate debate, while they would enjoy the illiterate 30-second spots. None of the philosophers would establish a Web site, as none would be terribly excited about the discussion forums on the Internet—not a place for intellectual debate. Who would read their elegant prose? To say more at this point would almost preempt the argument: The family in the civilization of illiteracy ascertains new forms of human interaction. It departs from the expectation of conformity for a model that acknowledges many ways to live together and, even more important, how we transcend our own nature in this process. We might, after all, be much more than we know, or trust that we could become.

CHAPTER 4: A GOD FOR EACH OF US

On the Memetic Algorithms Web page on the Internet, H. Keith Henson illustrates the lifelike quality of memes by recounting an episode from his time as a student (University of Arizona, 1960). Having to fill out a form on which religious affiliation was to be disclosed, he chose the denomination *Druid*, after having initially tried MYOB (the acronym for Mind Your Own Business). As he stated, "It was far too good a prank to keep it to myself." Replication mechanisms, in addition to a healthy dose of social criticism, soon had the university record almost 20% of the student body as Reform Druids, Orthodox Druids, Southern Druids, Members of the Church of the nth Druid, Zen Druids, Latter-Day Druids, and probably a number of other variations. Once the question regarding religious affiliation was removed from the entry form, the chain of replication and variation was interrupted.

There are many aspects of the relation between religion and language embedded in the anecdote. In some of the themes to be discussed in the coming pages, the humorous aspects will resonate probably less than questions on how religious experiences extend from early forms of human awareness to the current day.

Using, or even inventing, advanced technology, asking the most probing questions, experiencing injustice and pain, being subjected to antireligious indoctrination, or even repression, does not result in the abandonment of religion. Ignorance, primitive living conditions, extreme tolerance and liberalism, the possibility to freely choose one's religious affiliation from the many competing for each soul might lead to skepticism, if not to outright rejection of Divinity. In other words, conditions that seem to support religious beliefs do not automatically lead to practical experiences of human self-constitution as religious. Neither do adverse conditions generate atheists, or at least not the same kinds. There is no simple answer to the question of why some people are religious, some indifferent, and others actively against religion. Enlightenment did not result in generalized atheism; the pressure of the church did not generate more believers. Scientific and technological progress of the magnitude we experience did not erase the verb *to believe* from among the many that denote what people do, or no longer do, in our day. To believe, and this applies to religion as it applies to all other forms of belief, is part of the practical experience of human self-constitution. It involves our projection in a world acknowledging distinctions that are pragmatically significant and synchronized with the dynamics of life and work.

The world of nature is not one of belief but of situations. We humans perceive the world, i.e., project ourselves as entities, forming images of the surroundings in our mind, through many filters. One of them is our continuously constituted beliefs, in particular, our religious faith. Webster's dictionary (probably as good a source as any reference book) defines religion as "belief in a divine superhuman power or powers to be obeyed and worshipped as the creator(s) and ruler(s) of the universe." Religion today is far less a coherent and consistent practical experience than it was in previous pragmatic frameworks.

The manifold relation between literacy and religion can be meaningfully understood by explaining the pragmatic context of the constitution of religion. Its further development into different theologies, and its embodiment in various churches and other institutions connected to religion, also help in this understanding. The centralized and hierarchic structure of religion, the basic notions around which theology evolves, and the dynamics of change in religion and theology that reflect adaptive strategies or goals of changing the world to make it fit a theology, have a strong bearing on the values that formed and transformed literacy. Truly, language and religion, especially language after the experience of writing, developed practically in tandem. The transition from ritual to myth to incipient religion is simultaneously a transition from primitive expression, still tightly connected to body movement, image, and sound, to a more self-organized system of expression becoming communication. During the process, presented here in compressed form, writing appears as a result of interactions between the experiences of language and religion.

That writing is a premise for pragmatic requirements that will eventually lead to literacy has already been generously explained. It has also been pointed out that with writing emerges the perspective of literacy into whose reality many more practical experiences will eventually crystallize. Literacy and religion are intertwined in ways different from those characteristic of other human practical experiences. In the historic overview to be provided, these peculiarities will be pointed out. Expression, as a practical experience of human self-constitution, interrupts the slow cycle of genetic replication, and inaugurates the much shorter cycles of memetic transmission— along the horizontal axis of those living together, and along the vertical axis in the quickly succeeding sequence of generations. The role of scale of human experience, the relation between religious, ethical, aesthetic, political, and other aspects, the relation between individual and community, and between right and wrong will also be addressed in their context. In addition, logical, historic, and systemic arguments will be employed to clarify what religions have in common.

In anticipation of a short history, it should be clarified that living in a religion of one God (such as Judaism, Christianity, Islam), or of many (as the Hindu world entertains), or of a mixture of pantheism and mysticism (as in the Chinese or Japanese worlds), even living in animism, does not imply identification with its history, nor even with its national or ethnic confines or premises. Islamic enthusiasm and Christian retreat in our day is not a matter of the validity of one religion over the other, but rather a matter of their pragmatic significance. United in accepting Allah as their God, or a broadly defined way of living according to the Koran, Muslims are far less united than the less religious, and less homogeneous, Christians. But in giving up the clear-cut distinctions between right and wrong, and especially involving relativity in the search for options leading to higher efficiency, we constitute ourselves in a framework of vagueness and relativity—different from the transcendental value of Hinduism, or from the clear-cut values of contemporary Islam—which can no longer rely on the certainty embodied in literacy-based praxis, and which leads us to subject human existence to doubt.

In realizing the broad consequences of a pragmatics based on the desire to achieve levels of efficiency appropriate to a given scale of human experience, we can understand why some conflicts involving forces identifying themselves with religions from the past against forces of the present appear as religious conflicts. The most vivid examples can be found in Bosnia-Herzegovina and in the southern republics of the defunct Soviet Union. Through a religious past to which they have lost any meaningful connection, Orthodox Serbs, Catholic Croats, and Muslim Bosnians try to reconnect to the world of experiences to which they traditionally belong. In the Central Asian conflicts, allegiances are confused—Sunni from Tadjikistan align themselves with the Shiites of Iran, while the Uzbeks pursue the hope of a new pan-Turkish empire.

In a different vein, the sanctity of life celebrated in Taoism, as well as in Judaism and Christianity, ends at the doors of the shiny palace of cheap, replaceable values of planned obsolescence, eventually of the human being itself. In hope of redemption, many give their lives, probably not understanding that they close the cycle of potential practical experiences just as drug addicts, suicidals, and murderers do, obviously in different contexts and with different motivations. This might sound too strong, but it is no more extreme than the extremes of existence and faith, or lack thereof.

Friends and foes of religion will agree that, for better or worse, it has played an important role in the history of humankind. The complement to this agreement is less clear: We cannot define what replaced, or could replace, religion. The new world order brought about by the downfall of communism in the Soviet Union and East Europe raises even more questions regarding religion: Are the extremist—not to say fanatical—forms of religion that replace official atheism religion or disguised forms of ethnic or cultural identification? To which extent do they reflect pragmatic reintegration in the global economy or *safe* isolationism? Practical experiences of religious nature were all affected by a change in their details: different ways of preserving religious doctrine, a different attitude towards authority, a change from self-denial to indulgence, but not in the fundamental acceptance of Divinity.

Characteristics of religions are still in flux. For instance, religious events embedded in various cultures take on a merely ceremonial role in today's world, aligning themselves with the newest in music, imagery, interactive multimedia, and networks. Believers as well as casual spectators have access to religious ceremonies through Websites. Probably even more telling is the appropriation of social, political, and moral causes, as religion ascertains itself in our time as open, tolerant, and progressive, or conversely as the guardian of permanent values, justifying its active role outside its traditional territory. This ascertainment is dictated by the pragmatic framework of the dynamic reality in which religion operates, and not by the memetic replication of its name. This is, of course, the reason for not limiting our discussion to variation and replication, no matter how exciting this might appear.

BUT WHO MADE GOD?

The variety of religions corresponds to the variety of pragmatic circumstances of human identification. Regardless of such differences, each time children, or adults, are taught that God made the world, the oceans, the sun, stars, and moon, and all living creatures, they ask:

But who made God? Trying to answer such a question might sound offensive to some, impossible to others, or a waste of time. Still, it is a good entry point to the broader issue of religion's roots in the pragmatic framework. The commonalties among the majority of religions, to which comparative studies (especially those of Mircea Eliade) point, are significant at the structural level. We have, on the one hand, all the limitations of the individual human—one among many, mortal, subject to illness and defeat, object of passion and seduction, deceitful, limited in understanding of the various forces affecting one's projection as part of nature, and as part of the human species. On the other hand, there is the uniqueness of the immortal, untouchable, impervious, omniscient, entity (or entities) able to understand and unleash forces far more powerful than those of nature or of men, an entity (or entities) upon which depends the destiny of all that exists. Through belief, all the limitations of the human being are erased. It is quite instructive, as well as impressive, how every limitation of the human being, objective and subjective, is counteracted and given a life of its own in the language housing the progression from man to gods or to God, on one side, and to the practice of religion, on the other.

The various gods constituted in the world's religious texts also recount what people do in their respective environment, natural or tamed to some degree. They tell about what can go wrong in their life and work, and what community rules are most appropriate to the pragmatic context. The value of rain in the Middle East, the fine-tuning of work to seasonal changes in the Far East, the significance of hope and submission in the Indian subcontinent, the increased role of animal domestication, the extension of farmland, the role of navigation in other parts of the world are precisely encoded in the various religions and in their books. These books are bodies of explanations, expectations, and norms pertinent to practical experiences, written in very expressive language, ambiguous enough to accommodate a variety of similar situations, but precise in their identification of who is part of the shared religious experience, and who is outside, as foreign and undesirable, or foreign and subject to enticement.

THE PLURALITY OF RELIGIOUS EXPERIENCES

What makes religion necessary is a subject on which it would be foolish to expect any degree of consensus. What makes it possible, at least in the forms experienced and documented from ancient times to the modern, is language, and soon after language, writing—although Japanese Shintoism, like Judaism, began before writing—and reading, or more to the point, the Book. For the Judeo-Christian religions, as well as for Islam, the Book is the sufficient condition for their development and persistence. When the Book grew into books, it actually became the center of religious praxis. This is reflected in the nature of religious rituals, an extension of mytho-magical experiences previous to writing. They were all meant to disseminate the Book, and make its rules and prescriptions part of the life of the members of the respective community.

The timeline of the practical experience of religious human self-constitution suggests significant commonalties among the various religions. The way the notion of God was constituted is only one of these commonalties. What separates religion from pre-religious expression (such as animism) is the medium in which each is articulated. The subject is relatively constant. Acknowledgment of forces beyond individual understanding and desire to overcome confusion or fear in facing difficult and inexplicable aspects of life and death go hand in hand. A perceived need to pursue avenues of survival which promise to be successful because of the implied expectation that forces residing in the unknown would be, if not directly supportive, at least not actively opposed, is also discernible.

But when rationalizing the coming of age of religion, one automatically faces the broader issue of the source of religion. Is it given to humans by some perceived superior force? Does it result from our involvement with the environment of our existence and from the limits of our experience? When praxis began to differentiate, mytho-magical experiences proved unadaptable to the resulting pragmatic framework.

Farming and animal husbandry replaced scavenging, hunting, and foraging. Communities started to compete for resources (manpower included). Efficiency of human work increased, resulting in more forms of exchange and leading to accumulation of property. Relations among people within communities became complex to the extent that arguments, attributed to forces outside direct practical experiences, were necessary to instill and maintain order. The process was multi-faceted, and still involved myths, the magical, and rituals. All three—still retraceable in some parts of the world—were carried over to religion, progressively forming a coherent system of *explanations* and *prescriptions* meant to optimize human activity. The sequence is known: Practical experiences conveyed by example from one individual to another, or orally from one to several.

Where the unknown forces were ritually conjured in new forms of human practical self-constitution, these practical experiences were progressively unified and encoded in forms apt to further support the new scale achieved in the insular communities around the world. Abraham, accepted almost equally by Jews, Christians, and Muslims, lived at around 2,000 BCE and proclaimed the existence of one supreme God; Moses in the 13th century BCE; the six sacred texts of the Hindus were compiled between the 17th and 5th centuries BCE; Taoism—the Chinese religion and philosophy of *the path*—came to expression around 604 BCE, and Confucius's teachings on virtue, human perfectibility, obedience to Providence, and the role of the sage ruler shortly afterwards; Buddhism followed within decades, affirming the Four Noble truths, which teach how to exist in a world of suffering and find the path to inner peace leading to Nirvana. This listing is meant to highlight the context in which the practical experience of religious self-constitution was expressed in response to circumstances of life and work that necessitated a coherent framework for human interaction.

The *Torah,* containing the five books of Moses dedicated to the basic laws of Judaism, was written around 1,000 BCE. It was followed by the other books (Prophets and Writings) and form the *Old Testament.* The Greeks, referring to all seven books (the Septuagint), called the entire work *ta biblia* (books). This collection of books is dedicated to the theme of creation, failure, judgment, exodus, exile, and restoration, and introduced prescriptions for conduct, diet, justice, and religious rites. The themes were presented against the broad background in which laws pertinent to work, property, morals, learning, relations between the sexes, individuals, tribes, and other practical knowledge (e.g., symptoms of diseases, avoidance of contamination) were introduced in normative form, though in poetic language.

The pragmatic framework explains the *physics* of the prescriptions: What to do or not do in order to become useful in the given context, or at least not to be harmful. It also explains the *metaphysics:* why prescriptions should be followed, short of stating that failure to do so affects the functioning of the entire community. What was kept in writing from the broader oral elaborations that constituted the covenant (testament) for practical experience was the result of pragmatic considerations. Writing was done in consonantal Hebrew, a writing system then still at its beginning, on parchment scrolls, and thus subject to the limitations of the medium: How much text could be written on such scrolls in a size that facilitated reading and portability.

Between these books and what much later (translations notwithstanding) came from the printing presses following Gutenberg's invention, there is a difference not only in size, but also in sequence and in substance. Over time, texts were subject to repeated transcriptions, translations, annotation, revision, and commentary. The book that appeared to be given once and for all kept changing, and became subject to interpretations and scrutiny ever so often. Still, there is a fundamental element of the continuity of its expressed doctrine: life and work, in order to be successful, must follow the prescribed patterns. Hence the implicit expectation: read the book, immerse yourself in its spirit, renew the experience through religious services meant to extol the word.

But since alternate explanatory systems were progressively developed—science not the last—parallel to relative fixed pragmatic frames sanctioned in early religion, a certain separation of religion from practical experience took place. Religion consecutively constituted its own domain of human praxis, with its own division of labor, and its own frame of reference. Christianity, Islam, the Protestant Reformation, and various sectarian movements in China, Japan, the Indian subcontinent (neo-Confucianism, Zen, the Sikh religious movement) are such developments.

We have heard about such expatiations and hear as well about conflicts triggered around them, but fail to put these conflicts in the perspective that explains them. Within a given context, a new growth triggers reactions. Members of the Baha'i religion (a faith that began in the 19th century) are subjected to the repression of Muslims because its program is one of unity of religions, not subordination of some to others. The expectation of universal education, or active promotion of equality between sexes, corresponds to a pragmatics different from that from which Islam emerged, and for that matter, many other religions. The Religious Society of Friends, i.e., the Quaker movement, was a reaction to the corruption of the church as an institution. It spells out a program in line with the requirements of the time: reaching consensus in meetings, doing away with sermons, pursuing a program of education and non-violence. It was also subjected to repression, as each schism was, by the powers that were in place.

These and many other developments mark the long, as yet unfinished, process of transition from religion to theology and church, and even to business, as well as the process of permutation of religion into culture, in particular from religion to secular culture and market. The Book became not only many different books, but also varied experiences embodied in organized religion. Alternative perspectives were submitted as different ways to practice religion within a pragmatic context acknowledged by religion.

AND THE WORD BECAME RELIGION

In the circular structure of survival in nature, there was no room for metaphysical self-constitution, i.e., no practical need to wonder about what was beyond the immediate and proximate, never mind life and death. When the practical experience of self-constitution made rudiments of language (the language of gestures, objects, sounds) possible, a sense of time—as sequences of durations—developed, and thus a new dimension, in addition to the immediate, opened. This opening grew as awareness of oneself in relation to others increased in a context of diversified practical experiences. Acknowledging others, not just as prey, or as object of sexual drive, but as associates (in hunting, foraging, mating, securing shelter), and even the very act of association, resulted in awareness of the power of coordination. Thus the awareness, as diffuse as it still was, of time got reinforced. Be-Hu Tung ventured a description of the process:

> In the beginning there was no moral or social order. People knew only their mothers, not their fathers. Hungry, they searched for their food. Once full, they threw the rest away. They ate their food with skin and hair on it, drank blood and covered themselves in fur and reeds.

He described a world in its animal phase, still dependent on the cycles of nature, perceiving and celebrating repetition.

Myth and ritual responded to natural rhythms and incorporated these in the life cycle. Once human self-constitution extended beyond nature, creating its own realm, observance of natural rhythms took new forms. This new forms were more able to support levels of efficiency appropriate to the new condition achieved in the experience of farming. It was no longer the case that survival equaled finding and appropriating means of subsistence in nature. Rather, natural cycles were introduced as a matrix of work, modulating the entire existence. Once the experience of religion was identified as such, religious praxis adopted the same matrix. In almost all known religions, natural cycles, as they pertain to reproduction, work, celebrations, education, are detailed. Cooperation and coordination progressively increased. A mechanism of synchronization beyond the one that only accommodated natural cycles became necessary. In retrospect, we understand how rules of interaction established in the nature-dominated pragmatic framework turned into the commandments of what would be asserted through written religion.

We also understand how animistic pre-religious practice—embodied in the use of masks and charms, in worship of the untouched natural object (tree, rock, spring, animal), and the employment of objects meant to keep harm away (tooth, bone, plant) took new forms in what can be defined as the semiotic strategy of attaching the religious word (more broadly, the Book) to the life of each member of the religious community. The need to establish the community, and to identify it through action, was so pressing that ceremonies were put in place to bring people together for at least a few times during the year. In Egyptian hieroglyphics, one can distinguish an affection for *coordination of effort*, expressed in the depiction of rowers on boats, builders of pyramids, warriors. The written word of the Hebrews was inspired by the experience of hieroglyphics, taking the notion of coordination to a more abstract level. This level provided a framework for synchronizing activity that brought ritual closer to religion. This added a new dimension to ceremonies based on natural cycles, gradually severing the link to the practical experience of interaction with nature.

Notation evolving into the written word was still the domain of the very few. Accordingly, religious reminders were strongly visual, as well as aural, a state of affairs that continued in the religions that sprouted from Judaism and established themselves after the fall of the Roman Empire. The populations adhering to these religions were largely illiterate, but derived important characteristics from religions based on the written word—the Word that was equated with God. Nailed to the doorways or inscribed over portals, converted into many types of charms, the words of a religious creed became elements of the synchronizing mechanism that religion embodied in the pragmatic framework of its constitution. Prayer punctuated the daily routine, as it continues to do in our day. The seasons and the cycles of nature, embodied in the mytho-magical, were reinterpreted in religious celebrations, which referenced the natural cycle, and appropriated pre-religious rituals. Cycles of activity aimed at maintaining and increasing the outcome of work for survival were thus confirmed. A community's well-being was expressed by its ability to satisfy the needs of its members and achieve a pattern of growth. Still heavily dependent upon natural elements (rain, floods, wind, insects, etc.), as well as subjected to attacks from neighbors, communities developed strategies for better use of resources (human included), storage, and defense mechanisms. These strategies were carefully encoded in the respective religious covenants.

The religions that have survived and developed seem to gravitate around a core of very practical writings and associated visual reminders of the power they invoke in connection to the pragmatic identity of the community. The book was the standard; those who constituted the *organization* of religion—the priesthood—could usually read the book. Scribes, even some of the priests, could write and add to the book. The majority listened and memorized, resorting to better memory than we exercise today, memory that their practical experience required. They subscribed to religious patterns, or carried out rituals on a personal or communal level.

It is helpful to keep in mind that religious involvement was facilitated by the fact that religion is not only pragmatically founded, but also pragmatically ascertained and tested. Rules for farming, hunting, preparing food; rules for hygiene and family relations; rules for conducting war and dealing with prisoners and slaves were expressed against the background of an accepted supreme reference, before evolving into future ethical rules and legal systems. Those rules which were not confirmed, progressively lost authority, were "erased" from the people's memory, and ceased to affect the rhythm of their lives. The written word survived the oral, as well as the living who uttered it or wrote it down. This word, abstracted from voice, gesture, and movement, and abstracted from the individual, was progressively assigned a more privileged place in the hierarchy. The writings seemed to have a life of their own, independent of the scribes, who were believed to be only copiers of everlasting messages entrusted to them.

Written words express the longing for a unified framework of existence, thought and action. Within such a framework, observance of a limited number of rules and procedures could guarantee a level of efficiency appropriate to the scale at which human activity took place. This is a world of human practical experiences transcending natural danger and fear. It is a universe of existence in which a species is committed to its further self-definition in defiance of nature while still dependent upon it. Religion as a human experience appears in this world as a powerful tool for the optimization of the effort involved, because it effectively constitutes a synchronizing mechanism. In the practical experience of religious writing and the associated experience of reading or listening to a text, the word becomes an instrument of abstraction. Accordingly, it is assigned a privileged position in the hierarchy of the many sign systems in use. Memetic replication appropriately describes the evolution of religious ideas, but not necessarily how these ideas are shaped by the pragmatic framework.

Tablets, scrolls, and books are blueprints for effective self-constitution within a community of people sharing an understanding of rules for efficient experiences. The outcome is guaranteed by the implicit contract of those self-constituted as believers in the supernatural from which the rules supposedly emanate. In search of authority, this world settled for unifying motivations. The rules of animal, and sometimes even human, sacrifice, and those of religious offerings were based on the pragmatics of maintaining optimal productivity (of herds, trees, soil), of entering agreements, maintaining property, redistributing wealth, and endowing offspring. The immediate meaning of some of the commitments made became obscured over time as scale changed and the association to nature weakened. The rules were subsequently associated with metaphysical requirements, or simply appropriated by culture in the form of tradition. To ensure that each individual partook in the well-being of the community, punishments were established for those violating a religious rule. Immediate punishment and, later, eternal punishment, although not in all religions, went hand in hand as deterrents.

The involvement of language, in particular of writing and reading, is significant. As already stated, the individual who could decipher the signs of religious texts was set apart. Thus reading took on a mystical dimension. The division between the very few who wrote and read and the vast majority involved in the religious experience diminished over a very long time. More than other practical experiences, religion introduced the unifying power of the written word in a world of diversity and arbitrariness. Under the influence of Greek philosophy, the *Word* was endowed with godlike qualities, implicitly becoming a god. Seen from a given religious perspective, the rest of the world fails because it does not accept the word, i.e., the religion. The irreligious part of the world could be improved by imposing the implicit pragmatics that the religion carried; it could submit to the new order and cease to be a threat. At this time, religion entered the realm of the abstract, divorced from the experience with nature characteristic of religions originating in the oral phase of human self-constitution. It is at this time that religion became dogma.

All over the globe, in the worlds of Hinduism, Taoism, Confucianism, Judaism, Christianity, and later Islam, the conflict between communities embracing a certain creed and others, in pre-religious phases or dedicated to a different religion, is one of opposing pragmatics in the context of increased differentiation. In other words, a different religious belief is a threat to the successful practical self-constitution of one group. To get rid of the threat is a pragmatic requirement, for which many wars were fought. Some are still going on. With each religion that failed, a pragmatic requirement failed, and was replaced by others more appropriate to the context of human self-constitution. That these conflicts appeared under the aegis of conflicting deities, represented by leaders regarded as representatives of divinity, only goes to show how close the relation is between the underlying structure of human activity and its various embodiments.

In a world of unavoidable and even necessary diversity, religion maintained islands of unity. When interaction increased among the various groups, for reasons essentially connected to levels of efficiency required for current and future practical experiences, patterns of common activity resulted in patterns of behavior, increased commonalty of language, accepted (or rejected) values, and territorial and social organization. The commonalty of language, as well as the commonalty of what would become, during the Middle Ages, national identity (language and religion being two of the identifiers), increased steadily.

From among the major changes that religion underwent, the most significant are probably its *reification* in the institution of the church and the constitution of vast bodies of discourse regarding its intrinsic logic, known as theology. Once asserted as an institution, religion became the locus of specific human interaction that resulted in patterns based on the language (Latin, for some in the Western Christian world, and Arabic in the Islamic East) in which religion was expressed. Religious practical experience progressively distanced itself from the complexities of work and socio-political organization, and constituted a form of praxis independent of others, although never entirely disconnected from them. The organization of religion concerns the pattern of religious services at certain locations: temple, church, mosque. It concerns the institution, one among many: the military, the nobility, guilds, banks, sometimes competing with them. It also concerns education, within its own structure or in coordination, sometimes in conflict, with other interests at work.

A multitude of structural environments, adapted to the practical aspects of religious experience appear, while religion progressively extricated itself, or was eliminated, from the pragmatics of survival and existence. The institution it became dedicated itself to pursuing its own repetitive assignments. At the same time, it established and promoted its implicit set of motivations and criteria for evaluation. In many instances, the church constituted viable social entities in which work, and agriculture in particular, was performed according to prescriptions combining it with the practice of faith. Rules of feudal warfare were established, the day of rest was observed, education of clergy and nobility were provided. From the Middle Ages to the never abandoned missionary activity in Africa, Asia, and North and South America, the church impacted community life through actions that sometimes flew in the face of common sense. The effort was to impose new pragmatics, and new social and political realities, or at least to resist those in place.

Whether in agreement or in opposition, the pattern of religious experience was one of repeated self-constitution of its own entity in new contexts, and of pursuing experiences of faith, even if the activity as such was not religious. In this process, the church gained the awareness of the role of scale, and maintained, though sometimes artificially, entities, such as monasteries, where scale was controllable. Autarchy proved decreasingly possible as the church tried to extend its involvement. The growing pragmatic context had to be acknowledged: increased exchange of goods, reciprocal dependencies in regard to resources, the continuous expansion of the world— a consequence of the major discoveries resulting from long-distance travel. In recent years the challenge has come from communication—in particular the new visual media—requiring strategies of national, cultural, social, and even political integration.

From the scrolls of the *Torah* and from the sacred texts of the *Rig Veda* and Taoism, to the books of Christianity, to the *Koran*, to the illuminated manuscripts copied in monasteries, and to the Bible and treatises printed on the presses of Fust and Schöffer (Gutenberg's usurpers) in Mainz, Cologne, Basel, Paris, Zurich, Seville, and Naples—over 4,000 years can be seen as part of the broader history of the beginning of literacy. This history is a witness to the process, one of many variations, but also one of dedication to the permanency of faith and the word through which it is reified.

Replications of all kinds mark the memetic sequence, and so religion appears in retrospect as propagation of a special kind of information, generated in the human mind as it started labeling what we know, as well as what is beyond our direct understanding. What did not change, although it was rendered relative, is the acknowledgment and acceptance of a supreme authority, known as God, or described through other names such as Allah and Myo-Ho-Ren-Ge, and the nature of the practical experience of self-constitution as believer. If Abraham, Moses, Jesus, Mohammed, Confucius, and the Japanese and Indian religious leaders were alive today, they would probably realize that if religion had any chance, it could no longer be founded on the written text of the Book or books, but in the practical experiences of the civilization of illiteracy. By no accident, the first category on one of the Web sites dedicated to religion is entitled *Finding God in Cyberspace.*

THE EDUCATED FAITHFUL—A CONTRADICTION IN TERMS?

The pragmatic requirement of optimally transmitting experience essential to a group's permanency was recognized as one of the main functions of language. It should come as no surprise that education was carried out, if not exclusively then at least to a high degree, in religion. Neither should it surprise that religion appropriated literacy as one of its programs once the scale of human activity that made literacy necessary was reached. In the context of nation-states that adopted religion as one of their identifiers, the entire history of the relation between society and religion can be seen in a different light. As we know from history, the quest for power frequently brought state and religion into conflict, although one needed and relied on the other. In the unifying pragmatic framework of industrial society, their alliance was sealed in literacy programs. These were simultaneously programs for higher efficiency and for the maintenance of values rooted in religious belief, as long as these did not adversely affect the outcome of work or of market transactions.

Parallel to the initially dominant religious view of life, change, origins, and future, alternative views were expressed as the result of self-observation and observation of the outside world. Philosophy, influenced by religion and by religious explanations of the world, of men, of society and its change, is one example. Sciences would diverge from philosophy, multiplying alternate models and explanatory contexts. These were usually carefully construed so as not to collide with the religious viewpoint, unless they bluntly rejected it, regardless of the consequences of such an attitude. There were also heresies based on an individual's notions, or holdovers from past religions. During the Renaissance, for instance, such holdovers derived from studies of the Bible, which led to the Reformation. Ideas not rejected as heresy were usually within the scope of the church. These ideas were expressed by men and women who founded orders. They were put into practice by religious activists or made into new theologies. There is no religion that does not go through its internal revisions and through the pain of dividing schisms. On today's list of religious denominations, one can find everything, from paganism to cyberfaith. The rational explanation for this multiplication into infinity is not different from the explanation of any human experience. Multiplication of choices, as innate human characteristic, applies to religious experiences as it does to any other form of pragmatic human self-constitution. The practical experience of science, diverging more and more from philosophy and from religious dogma, also followed many paths of diversification. So did the unfolding of art, ethics, technology, and politics. The unifying framework offered by the written word, as interpreted by the monolithic church, was progressively subjected to distinctions that the experience of literacy made possible. When people were finally able to read the Bible for themselves—a book that the Catholic church did not allow them to read even after the Reformation—protest started, but it started after the Renaissance, when political entities were strong enough to defy the papacy with some degree of success.

The illiterate warriors of centuries ago and the sometimes illiterate, at least unlettered, worshipper and military insurgent of today belong to very different pragmatic frameworks. The former did not have to be able to read or write in order to fight for a cause superficially (if at all) related to the Book. One had only to show allegiance to the institution guarding souls from hell. In the scale characteristic of these events, individual performance was of extreme importance to the community, as we know from the stories of King Frederick, Joan of Arc, Jan Hus—or, to change the reference, from the story of Guru Nanak (the first guru of the Sikhs, a religion prompted by the Muslims' persecution of Hindus at about the time Columbus was on his last expedition to the New World), Martin Luther, George Fox (founder of the Quaker movement), and many others. The educated faithful of the past probably obtained access to the established values of culture and to the main paradigms of science as these confirmed the doctrine defended by the church. An educated faithful in contemporary society is torn between accepting a body of knowledge ascertaining permanency, while experiencing change at a pace for which no religion can prepare its followers. Indeed, from the unity of education and faith—one meant to reinforce the other—the direction of change is towards their contradiction and disparity. The secular web is not only that of the Internet infidels, but also of a broad segment of the population that has no need for either.

CHALLENGING PERMANENCY AND UNIVERSALITY

For many, the survival of religion is itself a miracle. For many more, it is indicative of human aspects not sufficiently accounted for in science, art, or social and political life. Its role in a new pragmatic framework of fast change, mediated activity, alienation, decentralization, and specialization, is obviously different from that it played in the time of religious constitution and in a reduced scale of humankind. Religion did not start out to deceive, but to explain. Its practices, while seeming violent, empty, extreme, demagogic, cunning, or even ridiculous at times, fulfilled a purpose deemed pragmatic at its inception. The old and familiar are reassuring, if only by resort to endurance. The promise of redemption and paradise gain in attraction the more people face change and uncertainty. While the original purpose of religion was modified over time, the practice is kept up precisely because novelty and progress, especially in their radical form, are difficult to cope with. Once old values are questioned in the light of succeeding pragmatic circumstances, under new patterns of self-constitution, the result is complacency and deception, if there is no alternative. Religion and literacy ultimately find themselves in the same predicament.

Religious diversification reflects each new scale at which human practical experience takes place. Changes in the pragmatic framework in which people constitute themselves as religious result in tension between the variability of the elements involved in work or new aspects of social life and the claims of the eternal. This tension triggers numerous rethinkings and consequent rewritings of the books, as well as the generation of numerous new books of new forms of faith. Christianity and Islam are revisions; within them other revisions (schisms) took place, such as the Roman and Orthodox churches, the Sunni and Shiite. Other sects and religions, schisms, and reformations and protestations (movements claiming to reconstitute the original status, whatever that means), are to a great extent rewritings based on acknowledging new contexts—that is, new pragmatic requirements. Once upon a time, the Book was supposed to address everyone in the small community in which it came to expression. Over time, many books addressed their own constituencies—adherents to certain teachers, to particular saints, or to some subset of the religious doctrine—within a larger community. The success of these sub-groups grew in proportion to the diversification of human praxis and to the function of education exercised on a broader and broader scale.

From the religion of small-scale human activity to the churches of universal ambitions, many modifications in the letter and the spirit of the respective books occurred. They ultimately reflect alterations of values that religious institutions had to adapt to and justify. The tribes that accepted the Book as a unifying framework—embodiment of tradition which became law—as well as the followers of the prescriptions in the Hindu scriptures of *Veda* and *Upanishad,* the followers of the Enlightened One (Buddha), the practitioners of Taoism and Confucianism, also acknowledged a sense of community. It is the same sense of community held, at a different scale and with different goals, by the nation-state.

The spread of religions, parallel to military conquest, resulted in the spread of the respective religious books, and of the letters that the books were written in. This is not necessarily the same as the spread of literacy. Religion established its own *state,* the Holy Roman Empire (which is now down to the size of Vatican City) that transcended national boundaries and languages, and was considered *universal.* In the language of Islam, *umma* is the world community of Muslims, while *wattan* is the Motherland. The Muslim armies, defeated at Poitiers by the Catholic Charles Martel, were also disseminating the religion, language, and culture of the world community they envisioned. The Crusades, in turn, and the religious wars that plagued Europe did not spread literacy as much as they attempted to defend or establish the dominance of a way of living meant to ensure an order that promised eternal life.

In the scale of today's human practical experience, efficiency in general is almost independent of individual performance. It is independent of the degree of faith, ethical behavior, family status, and other characteristics of what religion calls good, and which ethics appropriates as a desired set of social expectations. Within a small scale of existence and work, things belong together: the practical and the spiritual, politics and morals, the good and the useful. Religion is their syncretic expression. The need for specialization and mediation changed the nature of pragmatic relations. Various realms of human practical experience are severed from each other. As this takes place, the religiously grounded system of values based on unity and integration—after all, this is what monotheism, in its various embodiments, represents—is submitted to the test of new circumstances of human self-constitution.

Among the many explanations of the events of the late sixties, at least the phenomenon of the attraction exercised by the various *churches of meditation* and their gurus is reflective of the crisis of monotheism, and of the culture that grew around it. An increasing number of esoteric, exotic, scientific, or pseudoscientific sects today bear witness to the same. The difference is that these sects are no longer isolated, that almost the entire religious dimension of people is connected to some sect, be it even one that used to be a dominant church.

Religion-based values or attitudes are carried over into the new segmented practical experiences of work, family, and society, and thus into the realm of politics, law, and market relations. Originating from sexual drive, love is one of the experiences from which family, friendship, art, and philosophy derived over time. Once written in the Book as a different form of love, once ascertained as a practical experience, it bridges between its natural biological basis and its cultural reality as a characteristic of a framework of human interaction in which individuals project their biological and cultural identity. Written about in religious books, love starts a journey from naturalness to artifact. Expressed as intelligence, temperament, appearance, or physical ability (our natural endowment), love is subjected, in conjunction with the experience of writing the Book, to a set of expectations expressed as though they originated from outside the experience.

In this process, there is no passive participant. The written word is permeated by the structural characteristics of the act of preferring somebody to somebody else, one course of action from among many, and, more generally, something over something else, according to religious values. The implicit expectation of permanency (of faith, love, or ownership) results from the pragmatic reasons acknowledged by the Book(s). A consensus essential for the survival and well being of the community is reached by acknowledging forces from outside, and accepting their permanent and quasi-universal nature. In a universe of immediacy and proximity, change other than that experienced in natural cycles is not anticipated.

Divinity makes sense only if constituted in practical experiences from which a notion of eternity and universality result. The written words exalting unity, uniqueness, eternity, and the promise of a better future are the result of the practical experience, since in the realm of nature only the immediate and the proximate are acknowledged. Forever marked by this experience of time and space beyond the immediate, the written language of religion, together with the written language of observations connected to the awareness of natural cycles (the moon, the seasons, plagues), remains a repository of the notion of permanency, universality, and uniqueness, and an instrument for hierarchical differentiation.

Whenever constituted in activities related to or independent of religion, language, as a product of and medium for human identification, projects these structural characteristics upon whatever the object of practical experience is. Once written, the word seems to carry into eternity its own condition. With the advent of literacy, as this is made possible and necessary by a different scale of human praxis, literacy itself would appear as endowed with the quality of eternity and universality, triggering its own sense of exaltation and mission, lasting well into our day. For millions of citizens from countries south of Russia, who once gave up their roots to show allegiance to the Soviet Empire, to return to Arabic writing after being forced to adopt the Cyrillic means rediscovering and reconnecting to their eternity. That some of them, caught in the geo-political confrontation of their neighbors, adopt the Roman alphabet of their Turkish Muslim brothers, does not change the expectation.

RELIGION AND EFFICIENCY

In the literate forms of language experiences, not only religion, but also science and the humanities, literature, and politics are established and subjected to the practical test of efficiency. Each projects a notion of permanency and universality, which is influenced by the practical experience of religion, sometimes in contradiction to the archetypal experience resulting in the notion (or notions) of God (or gods). Now that the pragmatic framework of the very ample scale of human practice makes permanency and universality untenable, the tendency to escape from the confines of religion becomes evident. There is a strong sense of relativism in science, an appropriate self-doubt in humanistic discourse, and an appropriate understanding of the multiplicity and open-endedness in almost every aspect of our social and political life.

This was not achieved through and in literacy, but in disregard of it, through the many partial literacies reflecting our practical self-constitution. The reality of the global nature of human experience, of interconnectedness, of its distributed nature, and of the many integrative forces at work, renders the centralism implied in the Book(s) obsolete for many people. At the same time, let it also be noted that this reality makes the Book even more necessary than ever for many, and at different levels of their practical life. The many religious literacies of these days—promoting permanent modes of life, exotic and less exotic codes of behavior, ways of eating and dressing, hopes for a happy future or some form of afterlife—maintain dualistic schemes of good and bad, right and wrong, sacred and secular in a world of extremely subtle and painfully vague distinctions. The question whether love and reason can undergird community awareness, social action, political activism, and education if, as seems to be the case, their connection to faith continues to decline, belongs to the same dualistic perspective. This perspective is common to both partisans and enemies of religion. It used to be the backbone of the ideology of religious suppression—either under communism, or wherever a dominant religion takes upon itself the eradication of any other religion. And it is becoming the argument of the many emancipatory movements promoting the *religions* of atheism and agnosticism as a substitute for religion. The subject is ultimately one of faith, concerning very intimate aspects of individual self-assessment, but not necessarily the institution of creed. Still captive to dualism, brought about and nourished by experiences constitutive of literacy, we have problems coping with a world where the enemy is us and where religion is different from what it was at the time of its inception, or the time we were first were exposed to it.

In view of these developments, we wonder how the rules and values established in the original religious framework are to survive. If the literacy through which these rules come to us is seen only as a vessel, a means of expressing values and criteria for evaluation, then any other means could perform the same function. The Crystal Cathedral of television fame, no less than the Web sites of many churches, proves the point.

Since we are our language, and we constitute ourselves as spiritual and physical entities in the experience of language, writing cannot be seen as a passive medium, nor reading as a mechanical rendition. Accordingly, the medium through which religion is expressed affects the religion, changes its condition. Applied to contemporary religious experience, this argument is confirmed again and again. From the entire practical experience of religion, what survives is the liturgy, transformed into a performance of limited cathartic impact.

Merchandising completes this new condition of faith. For millennia, a community considered its priests vital to its survival. In the civilization of illiteracy, the situation is reversed. Ministers, and to some extent priests, depend on a community for their survival. Ministers are in the business of selling themselves as much as they are in the business of selling their church or even God. Some evangelists remain independent in the sense that they package their own programs for presentation to large crowds in tents, in auditoriums, or on television. These religious enterprises create a vast business empire around a persona. As long as the enterprise can deliver what the preacher promises—through his performance and the merchandise he sells to the faithful—then the tele-congregants—no less fascinated by celebrity than the rest of society—will *buy* him.

A newer phenomenon is less personality dependent and more message-oriented, but the goal is the same: ministers need to make a living. Relying on information polled from hundreds of middle-class non-churchgoers, some enterprising ministers came up with a product bound to please: nothing boring or aggressive; cost-efficiency; comfortable seating; no organ. According to a study by the Harvard Business School, the resulting church was the embodiment of the phrase "knowing your customers and meeting their needs." Church attendance grew by relying on customer recommendation. Soon, the ministers franchised their operation in localities with a target market: 25-to-40-year-old *seekers* ("a growing market"), with middle to upper middle class salaries.

Other seekers look in different directions. Almost anyone with a message can establish a religion, and sometimes entire sects are based on just a few words from the Bible (the Seventh-Day Adventists, for example, or the snake handlers of the Appalachians, or the Pentecostals). Participatory forms of worship are another trend. They may derive inspiration from the book, but they aim to involve avenues of perception not bound to literacy: song, dance, meditation, the inhaling of aroma, touching minerals. Some religions hark back to nature, animism, and what can be called neo-paganism, as in the Wikka religion. No matter how far back some of these religions claim to go, they are religions of the civilization of illiteracy. They do not repeat the original pragmatic framework but respond to today's framework of self-constitution and the individual needs or desires of the people who constitute themselves as religious through these new manifestations.

While observations made in language can be subjected to confirmation, religious assumptions are expressed through the *inner* reality of language, and are only subject to language correctness. It is impressive how language houses concepts for which there is no referent in practical experience, but which are constituted exactly because some aspects of practical experience cannot be otherwise explained. In the history of how ideas, generalities, and abstractions are formed, the experience of religion is of particular interest. Values and beliefs that cannot be submitted to the physical senses, but can be comprehended through language—written, read, sung, danced, and celebrated—are transmitted through religion.

Many assume that the new status of religion in our day is due not only to market pressure and obsession with consumption, but also to the advancement of science: Supposed to debunk the rationality of faith and offer its own rationality as the basis of new ways of understanding the origin of life, the role of human beings, the source of good and evil, and the nature of transcendence, science introduces a positivist conception of facts, irreconcilable with that of the relativity of religious *images*. Research in artificial intelligence discovered that "97% of human activity (is) concept-free, driven by control mechanisms we share not only with our simian forebears, but with insects." If this is indeed true, the role of rationality, religious or scientific, in our practical experiences of self-constitution has to be revisited. The various manifestations of religion subtly address this need because they recognize dimensions of human experience that cannot be reduced to scientific explanations and logic, or cannot be explained without explaining them away in the process. One interesting tendency in the civilization of illiteracy is less to assimilate the new science and technology—as was the case only 20-30 years ago—and more to subject it to what religion considers right.

Fundamentalism of any kind corresponds to the dynamics of this illiterate society, in the sense that it promotes a very limited and limiting subset of the language of religion, in a world segmented into more religious denominations than ever before. If over 350,000 registered churches serve the religious needs of the population.in the USA, and almost as many meeting places are available to small groups of believers, nobody will seriously argue that people are less religious, rather that they are religious in a different way, often integrating the latest in science and technology. Among the most active Internet forums, religion maintains a presence supported by the best that technology can offer. With each new scientific theory unveiling the deeper structure of matter, more subtle forms of interconnectedness among phenomena, new sources of creativity, and new limits of the universe, the need for religion changes. To cope with complexity means either to have a good command of it—which seems less and less possible—or to accept a benevolent underwriting. The challenge of complexity generates its own need for creed. Social, economic, and political realities are not always encouraging. Integration based on pragmatic motives increases, as does individual anxiety. No matter how much we learn about death, we are still not free of its frightening randomness. Realistically speaking, the belief in an afterlife and the dedication to cryonics are less far apart than they seem at first glance.

RELIGIOSITY IN THE CIVILIZATION OF ILLITERACY

Some will argue, probably with good reason, that religion in the civilization of illiteracy is but another form of consumerism, or at least of manipulation. No matter what the religious occasion, and if it is still indeed of religious motivation, the market celebrates its highest results in anticipation of holidays (the former *holy days*). The 40,000 car dealerships, many designed as car cathedrals, and almost 35,000 shopping malls get more visitors during the holiday season than do churches. In addition, even ceremonies whose significance is fundamentally different today than during previous periods, generate more business than religious awareness. The language of ceremonies is entrusted to consultants in marriage, confirmation, baptism, bar mitzvah, and death. Texts related to circumstances of practical experiences different from those of our day are written and read, or, to be more precise, performed without either understanding what kind of pragmatics made them necessary or realizing the discrepancy between past and present pragmatics. This is why they ring so hollow in our day.

When permanence is exalted, faithfulness promised, acceptance of biblical or other precepts (of the Koran, of Far Eastern pantheistic religions) ascertained, literacy and religion are only mimicked. *Talaba,* the 100 rubles (or whatever the currency of choice) per month paid by Shiite missionaries from Iran, brings many Tadjiks, Uzbeks, and Turkmenians to the new religious schools of Islam. Chances are that a higher bidder from another religion would spoil the game. Under the new pragmatic circumstances of human self-constitution, change, variety, self-determination, individualism, negation of authority, divine or secular, and skepticism are decisive for reaching the levels of efficiency demanded by a dynamic scale of existence.

Today's world is not one of generalized atheism. It is, rather, one of many partial religious literacies, sharing in some basic symbolism, although not necessarily in a unifying framework for its consistent interpretation. Many do not believe, for reasons of science or convenience, in the religious explanation of the origin of the universe and life. Or they do not care for the message of love and goodness embedded in almost every current manifestation of faith. They see in every religious book the handwriting of some groups who, in order to impose their values, invented the image of a supreme force in order to achieve, if not authority, at least credibility.

We live in an environment of compromise and tolerance, infinite distinctions, fast sequences of failure and success, challenged authority and generalized democracy. In today's huge and ineffective social mechanism, in the integrated and networked world, individual failure does not affect the performance of the system. Illiteracy, while dangerous under circumstances characteristic for the pragmatic of the recent past, only marginally affects the levels of efficiency reached. Religiosity, of consequence in the same pragmatic framework, plays no role whatsoever in the illiterate practical experiences of human self-constitution. Calling such assessments *heresies,* as some might be inclined to do, does not really answer the question of whether religious law can still serve, alone or together with other laws, as the binding tie of community—as it does not address the broader issues of whether literacy can serve as the binding tie of community. Because of their pragmatic nature, characteristics of religion and structural characteristics of language are fundamentally similar. If we want to understand the condition of religion today, we have to specifically address the pragmatic circumstances of self-constitution within the civilization of illiteracy.

In the events of tele-evangelism there is no place for literacy. But the video church, and computer-aided religion, the bible on CD-ROM, or CD-I, the vacation village for believers, and religious tourism are mainly forms of entertainment. Their validity is divorced from the concept of the exalted individual, critical in the context of a small-scale community. Consequently, the religious dimension of transcendence is annihilated. Ours is the time of the eternal instant, not of some vague eternity promised as reward after the present. Partially banalized through abuse of the word, concepts such as dignity, decency, and human values have become the clichés of the video church, with as many gospels as there are preachers. Religiosity today differs from the religiosity of previous pragmatic frameworks insofar as it corresponds to the accentuated insularity of the individual.

As long as the viewer is only a digit away on his or her remote control from a pornography channel, from the latest quote on the stock market, of from a commercial message—for denture adhesive, gastric relief, and home pregnancy tests—it is difficult, if not impossible, to distinguish between sanctity and triviality, righteousness and venality. The global community of tele-viewing is splitting into smaller and smaller groups. And TV, as a pulpit of missionary activity, reveals itself as only syntactically different from the missionary work of advertisement. *Mass* religion proves to be as impersonal as the market. In effect, it severs the relations between religion and the mysterious, still unexplained aspects of human existence. A virtual reality package can be as good as the performance of having the blind see, and the cripple leave the wheelchair to enter the 100-meter dash. The virtual cathedral, the stadium, and the mass audience addressed in front of the camera are themselves of a scale inadequate to both the teaching disseminated and the nature of religious experience, no matter how far the effort to change the vocabulary goes.

The language of the books is rooted in experiences to which the tele-viewer no longer has a direct relation. They cannot be substituted in a medium adapted to change and variety. The categories that religious discourse centers on—faith, goodness, transcendence, authority, sin, punishment—were established in a pragmatic framework totally different from that of the present. Today, existence offers variety, immediate satisfaction, and protection from the whims of nature. The sense of danger has changed. The equity accumulated by the church in these categories may be enough to entitle claims of ownership, given people's inertia, but not to maintain them as effective means of affecting current practical experiences. It might well be true that three out of five Americans now believe there is a hell, and that people in other countries share the same assumption, but this has no bearing on their self-constitution in the world of quickly changing scenarios for fulfillment outside faith. Networking and distributed work are better synchronized with the pragmatics of high efficiency of our day. Software for interactive multimedia keeps track of a person's religious patterns, and provides prayer and interpretation integrated in the same package.

In its attempt to adapt to a new framework of human activity, religion adopted social causes (renouncing its metaphysics), scientific terminology (renouncing agnosticism), or the means of entertainment (renouncing its asceticism). With each step outside the boundaries of religion, the transcendental dimension is sacrificed. This dimension is embedded in the medium of literacy through which religious practical experience became a fixture in society. When the word does not satisfy, believers resort to other means of expression, some older than religion. It is not unusual to have a religious celebration during the day in some Catholic churches in Brazil, and at night, on the same altar, a chicken sacrificed to Yemenyá. The literate celebration, of European import, and the illiterate sacrifice to which a different group of believers connects, are impossible to reconcile. In this framework, freedom of choice, as vulgar or trivial as those choices might be, takes precedence over authority. In Brazil, "Graças a Deus!" is paired with the practice of African cults (Candomblé, Umbanda, Macumba), just as "Allah-hu-akbar" is with shamanistic or Buddhist celebrations in Azerbaidjan and Kazakhstan. These are particular expressions of religion in the civilization of illiteracy, as much as TV evangelism is. For as much as religion was submitted to the word, performance always seems to get the upper hand.

To blindly ascertain permanence against the background of change would only further undermine religious practice. This is why the new religions focus on the immediate and produce the reward as fast as it is expected. The continuous proliferation of new religious denominations, soon to be as many as there are people who constitute the networks of human interaction in today's pragmatic context, reflects also the ability of the church to adapt. But this was not religion's reason for being in the first place, and will not represent more than what actually happens when we all wear the same shoes, or shirts, or hats but read a different label on each, when we all eat the same food that is only packaged differently, when we all vote for the same politics (or lack of same) while maintaining party affiliations. When each has his or her own god, God ceases to exist.

With the end of the civilization of literacy, partial religious literacies emerge, developing their own languages, their own organizations, their own justification. The heterogeneity of the world, its intrinsic relativity, and its dynamics of change mark religious practical experiences in ways not dissimilar to those of scientific, artistic, political, educational, moral, and many other experiences. Consumption of the language of religion in ceremonies and holidays that promote the expectation of more and cheaper, on which the quest for unlimited satisfaction of needs and desires is based, does not qualify anyone as religious or literate. Neither does secularism for that matter, no less illiterate, and no less subjected to the same expectation of high efficiency which undermines the core of any religion.

SECULAR RELIGION

In our day of increased secularism, the extent to which religion permeates people's lives, whether faithful, indifferent (neutral), or actively antireligious, is probably difficult to assess. The separation of church and state is powerfully anchored in constitutions and declarations of independence, while new presidents, kings, emperors, state officials, and members of the judiciary still swear on the books of their religious faith, invoke their respective gods as the ultimate judge (or help), and openly, or covertly, participate in the rituals inherited from theological practical experiences. The dominant symbolism of our day has a religious aura. It seems that both the faithful and the secularists of all nuances entered a mutual agreement in sanctioning what came to be known as *civil religion*. People pledge allegiance to the flag, get emotionally carried away when the national anthem is played, and partake in the celebration of holidays, never questioning their justification. These elements of civil religion come to us in perverted forms, divorced from the pragmatic context within which they were constituted. To swear on the Bible was specifically prohibited ("You are not to swear at all, not by heaven, for it is God's throne, nor by earth, for it is his footstool..." Matthew 5:33-36). Swearing-in ceremonies used to take place in the open in order to make them manifest to the gods. In some countries a window is still opened when an oath of office is recited. Holidays, meant as occasions of religious recollection, or to instill a sense of solidarity, remain only what each person makes of them. Even more, in countries making a point of avoiding the domination of one religion over another, the holidays of the dominant religion become the holidays of the entire nation, enjoyed foremostly as market celebrations.

To notice the contradictory nature of the presence of religion in contexts of secular practical experiences, some directly contrary to religious beliefs, means to notice how some of the motivations of religion expatiate in a context contradicting the legitimacy of the theological experience in our day and age. This became clear even within the particular circumstances of revolutions whose stated goal was to eradicate religion through state oppression or by education. The French Revolution discovered, soon after the king and other members of the power elite were decapitated, that the authority of its ideals, embodied in the call for liberty, equality, fraternity, was not enough, despite being housed in the same body of literacy as religion was, to substitute for the higher authority of Divinity.

The Soviet Revolution hoped that theater or cinematography would substitute for religion, or at least for church. Some of its ideologues experimented with a secular god-building strategy, inventing a *sui generis* higher force to which people could relate, and on which hope could be placed. They tried, very much in the spirit of the utopian Marx, to deify the collective force of the working class in order to inspire a religious sense of community. Enormous energy was invested in designing new rituals. Many of the atheist artists of the Russian avant-garde served the cause they thought opened the gates of artistic freedom and universal love. Their own escape from the realm of literacy into the realm of imagery—intended to replace the confining texts of religion and ideology—should have warned them about the impossibility of the task at hand. Disappointed by their own naiveté, but incapable of acknowledging failure, some of them wound up embracing the new civic religion of gods and holidays, as shallow as the *theology* around which they were built.

What we identify in all these elements is the continuation of structural characteristics pertinent to religion and to the medium of its expression, i.e., literacy in a fundamentally different context. The encompassing principles of tolerance, equality, and freedom contradict the spirit on which religion and literacy were based. They weaken our convictions of what is right and efficient in view of the desired end, and of endurance as a group. The decline of morals in a context in which moral behavior does not affect efficiency is not due to the decline in religiosity, but to the general perception, justified or not, that morality and religion do not count; or that they play no role in making people happy. The sanctity of life gone, there is little sanctity left in forms of celebrating it: birthdays, communions, marriage, funerals. Between birth and death, the audience at our rites of passage diminishes painfully. We know that death is very personal, but communities, for pragmatic reasons, used to confront death and its consequences, many related to inheritance, not relegate it to specialists in the various aspects of dying. Death is reduced to a biological event leading only to biochemical decomposition: No fun, no direct practical significance for others, except in the inheritance process, a market event for funeral parlors and pushy clergy.

Appropriation of life events in the civilization of illiteracy equals the structuring of small languages of post-literate celebrations, taken over by baptism, communion, and marriage consultants, all alienated from the religious meaning they had, moreover from the initial pragmatic motivation. Literacy stood as the rulebook for all these direct, integrated, sequentialized, deterministic occurrences. The illiterate celebrates the randomness and the relative and makes everything a festival of randomness—crime, deadly disease, a riot, a bargain, a love affair.

Religion and church tried to instill permanency. Baptism was the initiation rite that opened the cycle. Confirmation entailed acceptance in the community. Marriage, once and forever, introduced a sense of unity and continuity. The last rites freed one from life for an afterlife in which the deceased still watched over the living faithful.

Today, each of these moments is associated with a civil ritual: birth is recorded in the town or city hall. The child must have a social security number by the age of two. At age five, children must enter school. Children no longer join the community as responsible members at the age of 12 or 14 years, but they are given rights that they sometimes cannot handle. Marriage and the establishment of family come much later than in earlier pragmatic contexts. Extracted from the religious context, family life is a strange mixture of biological convenience and contractual obligations. Death, always the focus of religion, is defined in terms of its effects on efficiency. The fine distinction between clinical death and total death only shows how priests, the final witnesses to the end of a life, are replaced by the technologists who keep the heart beating under the alibi of "sanctity of life." Life ends as it begins, as an entry in the record books, for tax purposes.

Japanese parents-to-be might still consult an *ekisha* (a sort of fortune teller) in order to choose the proper name for a newborn infant, already thinking about the marriage (names should fit in order to ensure harmony); others will have difficulty in understanding the similarity between choosing a name and the observance of agricultural cycles, as both were religiously encoded in minute rules centuries ago. These people will even cringe at the discourse in a monastery where the priest might indulge in the discussion of the unity between inner order (of the individual) and outer order. The fact that *mandala*, traded all over the world, once represented that order escapes their personal experience.

Religions distinguished between nature and cosmos. Whether explicitly stated or not, nature was seen as earthbound, the source of our existence, the provider. Cosmos, beyond our reach, should not be interfered with. The experience of extraterrestrial research expanded the notion of nature. In today's integrated world, resources and environmental concerns also contribute to the expanded notion of nature pertinent to our activity and life. Our worries about pollution of earth, oceans, and skies are not religious in nature. Neither is the distinction between what is feasible and what is desirable. The Ten Commandments tell us what we should not do, while the devil called desire whispers into our ears that nothing is forbidden unless we really do not care for it. The relation between the wholeness of the being and its parts is subject to maintenance, just as the automobile is. Once gods were described as jealous and intolerant. Now they are presented as accommodating a world of diversified experiences and heterogeneous forms of worship, including Satanism. Our pragmatic context is one of generalized pluralism, embodied in the many choices we pursue in the practical experience of self-constitution. When the pragmatics of self-constitution can be based on rationality, the churches of the civilization of illiteracy are houses of secular religion.

CHAPTER 5: A MOUTHFUL OF MICROWAVE DIET

Have you ever ordered a pizza over the Internet? It is an experience in *illiterate* cooking. The image on the screen allows clients to prepare the most individualized pizza one can think of: they decide what the shape, size, and thickness of the crust will be; which spices and how much; what kind of cheese; and which toppings. They can arrange these the way they want, layer them, and control how much tomato sauce, if any, should be used. Done? Ask your children, or your guests, whether they want to correct your design. The on-line chef is open to suggestions. All set? The pizza will be delivered in 20 minutes—or it's free. The entire transaction is illiterate: selection is made by clicking an image. With each choice, prices are automatically calculated and listed. Addition is as error-free as it can get. Taxes are calculated and automatically transferred to the IRS. A voice announces over the Internet, "Food is ready! Thank you for your order. And please visit us again."

No, this is not fantasy. Pizza shops and hamburger joints figure visibly on the Internet (still in its infancy). Their structure and functioning, as well as the expectations connected to them, are what defines them as belonging to the civilization of illiteracy. But the picture of what people eat and how their food is prepared is more complicated than what this example conveys. This chapter will describe how we arrived at this point, and what the consequences of the fundamental shift from the civilization of literacy in our relation to food are.

How does one connect food to literacy? In the first place, how we eat is as important as what we eat and how we prepare it. There is a culture of dining, and an entire way of viewing food—from obtaining raw ingredients to preparation and to eating—that reflects values instilled in the civilization of literacy. Food and eating in the civilization of illiteracy are epitomized not only by the pizza outlet on the Internet, by McDonald's, Burger King, and the frozen dinner waiting to be thrown into the microwave oven, but also by the vast industry of efficient production of primary and secondary foodstuffs, the anonymous, segmented processing of nutrition. It is not an individual's literacy that characterizes the meal, but the pragmatic framework in which people emerge and how they project their characteristics, including dietary and taste expectations, in the process.

The hunger-driven primitive human and the spoiled patron of a good Italian restaurant have in common only the biological substratum of their need, expressed in the very dissimilar acts of hunting and, respectively, selecting items from a menu. Primitive beings are identified by projecting, in the universe of their existence, natural qualities pertinent to the experience of feeding themselves: sight, hearing, smell, speed, force. Restaurant patrons project natural abilities filtered through a culture of eating: taste, dietary awareness, ability to select and combine. These two extremes document a commonalty of human self-constitution. Nevertheless, what is of interest in the attempt to understand food and eating in the civilization of illiteracy are actually *differences*. The nuclei of ancient incipient agriculture, which were also the places of origin for many language families, are distinct pragmatic frameworks relevant also to the experience of cooking. Within agriculture, *absolute* dependencies on nature are changed to *relative* dependencies, since more food is produced than is needed for survival. The food of this period is cause for some of the rituals associated with the elements involved in producing it. The layers between animal hunger and the new hunger, filter new experiences of satisfaction or illness, of pleasure or pain, of self-control or abuse. Symbolism (concerning fertility, agriculture, power) confirms patterns of successful or failed practical experiences against the background of increased awareness of the biological characteristics of the species. Notation and writing contribute to the change of balance between the natural and the cultural. But the difference between the primitive eater and the person who awaits his dinner at a table derives from the distinctive conditions of their existence.

In the pragmatic framework that constitutes the foundation for literacy, expectations regarding food were already in place: slow rhythm, awareness of the environment, environment and natural cycles, labor division according to sex and age (the female was usually the homemaker and cook). Food preparation was characterized by its intrinsic sequentiality, by linear dependencies among its variables. Cooking was inspired and supported by the sequence of seasons, local stock, and relative immediacy of needs, affected by weather conditions, intensity of effort, and celebration pertinent to seasons or special events. In short, the relation to food was governed by the same principles that notation and writing were.

In the civilization of illiteracy, personal attitudes towards preparing food and eating, whether at home or in a restaurant, are affected by a different pragmatic framework. Probably more is known about food in the civilization of illiteracy than at any other time in the history of agriculture and cuisine. But this knowledge does not come from the direct experience of the food, i.e., how it is grown and processed. Human beings in the civilization of illiteracy know better *why* they eat than *what* they eat. It is not what is in the food that concerns many people, but what the food is supposed to do for them: maintain and service the body through the proper balance of vitamins, minerals, and protein; help people cope with residue; and, eventually, conjure meaning as a symbol in a universe of competing symbolisms. Fashion extends to food, too!

People feed themselves today according to expectations different from those of primitive human beings—hunters, farmers, craftsmen, and workers involved in pre-industrial experience. Needs are different, and food resources are different. Many layers of humanity stand between an individual projecting animal hunger in a world of competing animals and an individual expressing desire for French cuisine, in its authentic variations, in its snobbish form, or in its *fast food* versions, fresh or frozen, regular or dietetic. Pizza, spaghetti, falafel, sushi, tortillas, cold cuts, and egg rolls figure no less on the list of choices. Many filters, in the form of various taboos and restrictions, as well as personal tastes, are at work. Meaning is incidentally elicited as one chooses the recipe of a celebrity cook, or decides on a certain restaurant.

The hungry primitive human, the human beings working the land in the agricultural phase, the farmers, craftsmen, soldiers, and scholars of the pre-industrial age expected only that food would still their hunger. More is expected from the eating experience today, and some of these expectations have nothing to do with hunger. People take it for granted that they can buy any type of food from anywhere in the world, at any time of the year. Globality is thus acknowledged, just as the sequence of seasons is ignored. In between these two extremes is the literate eating experience, with its own expectations.

The experience of eating reflected a way of life, a way of self-constitution as civilized, progressive, literate. Here are the words of Charles Dickens, recorded during his visit to the United States in 1842. He gave a vivid summary of American eating habits west of the big eastern cities (Boston, New York) as he observed them on steamboats and in inns where stagecoaches stopped for the night in Pennsylvania, Ohio, and Missouri.

> I never in my life did see such listless, heavy dulness [sic] as brooded over these meals: the very recollection of it weighs me down, and makes me, for the moment, wretched. Reading and writing on my knee, in our little cabin, I really dreaded the coming of the hour that summoned us to table; and was as glad to escape from it again as if it had been a penance or a punishment. Healthy cheerfulness and good spirits forming part of the banquet, I could soak my crusts in the fountain with Le Sage's strolling players, and revel in their glad enjoyment: but sitting

down with so many fellow-animals to ward off thirst and hunger as a business; to empty each creature his Yahoo's trough as quickly as he can, and then to slink sullenly away; to have these social sacraments stripped of everything but the mere greedy satisfaction of the natural cravings; goes so against the grain with me, that I seriously believe the recollection of these funeral feasts will be a waking nightmare to me all my life.

Dickens was the epitome of the literate experience, and he was addressing a literate audience that had literate expectations in the experience of dining: what time meals were held, who sat where and next to whom, the order in which certain foods were served, how long a meal should last, what topics could be discussed. Literate characteristics persist in the literate frameworks of political and formal dinners: hierarchy (who sits where), the order in which food is presented, the types of dishes and eating utensils.

FISHING IN A VIDEOLAKE

Many questions come to mind with respect to how, and what, and when, people eat and drink. Human beings still project their reality in the environment through biological characteristics—the ability to see, smell, taste, move, jump, etc.—but some in *unnatural* ways. Not only do we help vision with glasses and hearing with aid devices, but even taste and smell are helped through the appropriate chemistry, in order to buffer some odor and enhance others. From odorless garlic to tofu smelling of pork chops, everything is within the possibility of biochemistry. At the extreme, nutrition is altogether removed from the context of nature. This is the case not just with people who are fed artificially, through tubes, pills, or special concoctions.

What does this have to do with literacy? How is it influenced, if at all, by the increased illiteracy of the new condition of human activity? The answers are far from being trivial. An editorialist from Germany, a country of solid, if not necessarily refined, eating instincts, went to great lengths to explain the alienation of nourishment in our age. The final scene he described is comic and sad at the same time. Some artificially obtained nutritive substance, molded in the shape of fish, is fried and served to a video-literate who eats the food while watching a videotape about fishing. The *ersatz* experience of tele-viewing is probably disconnected from the experience of river, trees, sunshine, and fish biting the hook, not to mention the taste of fresh fish. Dwindling stocks of fish is one reason why we can no longer afford the nourishment that results from direct involvement with nature. Not everyone can or wants to be a hunter, a fisherman, or a farmer. The romanticism of literacy, and of the utopian ideologies it helps express, would lead some to believe that this is possible, even desirable. But maybe not, since the new scale of humankind does not go unnoticed, even by those still clinging to the continuity and per-manency embodied in literacy.

Values, rules, and expectations such as health considerations, effi-ciency, and taste are embodied in programs and procedures for which machines are built, new substances designed, and waste reprocessed. It might make some people shiver, but about 50% of a person's aver-age caloric intake is the result of artificial synthesis and genetic engi-neering. Louis de Funés (in a 1976 French film directed by Claude Zidi) almost wound up as part of the food processed at *Tricatel*, a new factory that produces tasteless food based on the rules and looks of French cuisine, which the factory effectively undermines. The come-dian, performing as a food inspector, has to decide what the *real* thing is and what is the fake. Competing with this burlesque, a national program, *Awakening of Taste,* under the aegis of the Minister of Cul-ture, was set up to encourage French students in primary schools to rediscover the true national cuisine. That such a program parallels the effort of the Académie Française to maintain the purity and integrity of the language is a convenient argument concerning the interdependence of the ideal of literacy and that of *haute cuisine.*

The movie satirizes the human being's relation to food and tech-nology. Eating something reminiscent of a fish, whether farmed or synthetically produced, while having video nostalgia for fishing is not an exception. In the mental gardens we plant each spring, when magazines and television shows present images of the beautiful tomatoes we might enjoy in a few months, there is a virtual space for every practical experience we gave up in order to satisfy our desire for more at the lowest price. The tomato in the civilization of illiteracy, hydroponic or garden grown, ripens faster, is perfect in form, and tastes almost like we think it should.

Irony and science fiction aside, we are indeed engineering proteins, carbohydrates, fats, vitamins, and minerals. They are designed to optimally maintain the human being and enhance his or her performance. This can be seen as a new phase in the process of transferring knowledge pertinent to nourishment from the encompassing and dominating medium of literacy to the many partial literacies—chemical, biological, genetic—of the civilization of illiteracy. Having in mind the image of where we currently stand and the direction in which we are heading, we can trace human self-constitution with the practical experience of food.

LANGUAGE AND NOURISHMENT

The relation between what people eat, how they prepare their food, how they serve and how they eat it, is accounted for in language, especially in its literate use, in many ways. Experiences of our continuous constitution through work, personal life, habits, defense, and aggression are expressed through language and other manifestations of our nature and culture. The same holds true for such peculiarities as the way people eat, entertain, dress, make love, and play. Language, as one among many expressive means, is a medium for representation, but also for diversifying experiences. It supports the research of new realms of existence, and participates in the maintenance of the integrity of human interdependencies as they develop in work, leisure, and meditation.

When the question "Why are there fewer alcoholics in China, Korea, Japan, and India?" was asked, answers were sought in culture. Reformulated as "Why can't Asians tolerate alcohol?" the question shifted the focus from what we do or do not do—the filters of exclusion or preference—to biology. Environmental, cultural, social, psychological, and cognitive characteristics can be acknowledged once the biological substratum is brought to light. Many people of Asian origin display an intolerance to alcohol that is due to a metabolism peculiar to their race. The intolerance to alcohol is associated with the lack of a catalytic enzyme, which under normal circumstances does not affect the functioning of the body. Only when alcohol is consumed do unpleasant symptoms appear: the face becomes flushed, skin temperature rises, the pulse quickens. Europeans, black Africans, and North American Indians are not affected in the same way. But they are subject to other genetically determined food sensitivities. For example, lactose intolerance is highest in Blacks.

The example given above tells us that the projection of biological characteristics into the universe of people's existence results in the image of *differences* among various groups of people and among individuals. People noticed these peculiarities before science existed in order to explain them. Relating the effect to a cause—a certain food or drink—people incorporate this relation into their body of experiences. Established connections become rules that are intended to ensure optimal individual and group functioning. Rules pertaining to food and ways of eating were eventually encoded and transmitted through literate means.

In short, patterns of work and life are affected. They point to various levels at which human practical experiences and the experience of nourishment are interconditioned. A first level regards nourishment and our biological endowment. A second level is nourishment and the environment—what we can afford from the world surrounding us. A third level is nourishment and self-consciousness—what best suits our life and work. Over time the interdependency changes.

And at moments when the scale of mankind reaches a threshold, it is drastically redefined—as in our times, for instance.

On a larger scale, food- and drinking-related instances prompt vast servicing activities and the establishment of networks of distributed tasks. Today, diet engineers, caterers, geneticists, nutritionists, are set up to provide whatever fits the occasion, the guest list, dietary prescriptions, and astrological or medical recommendations. A formal dinner can become a well mediated activity, with many prefabricated components, including table manners—if the commissioning party so desires. Associated or not to the menu, a preparatory seminar in what to wear, how to use utensils (if more than plastic spoons and knives are used), what kind of conversation with the entrée, and which jokes before, or after, or instead of the wine, educates for the event. In fact, the buffet, a configuration from which each can assemble his or her menu, not unlike the on-line order form for the Internet pizza, is more and more preferred. It is less confining than the literacy-based sequence of the three-course meals—structured as introduction, thesis, and conclusion, known under the labels appetizer, main entrée, dessert.

SEQUENCE AND CONFIGURATION REVISITED

With writing and reading, the experience of feeding oneself and one's family expanded to partaking in the experience of food preservation and sharing. French Assyriologist Jean Bottero read recipes, in cuneiform writing on clay tablets from around 1700 BCE, for food cooked at important occasions for people in power. That this was "cuisine of striking richness, refinement, sophistication, and artistry" should not necessarily impress us here. But the description of the ingredients, some no longer known or in use, of the sequence, and the context (celebration) deserve attention: "Head, legs and tail should be singed. Take the meat. Bring water to boil. Add fat. Onions, *samidu,* leeks, garlic, some blood, some fresh cheese, the whole beaten together. Add an equal amount of plain *suhutium*." This is a stew of kid, a meal for an exceptional occasion.

The pragmatic framework that made this cooking possible also made writing possible and necessary. Over time, this connection became even closer. Between the experiences of language and that of eating and drinking, a continuum of interactions can be noticed. Language distinctions pertinent to the practical experience of cultivating plants, taking care of animals, processing milk, and seasoning food expanded from satisfying needs to creating desires associated with taste. New knowledge is stimulated by experiences different from nourishment, such as new forms of work (cooking included), use of new resources, new tools, and new skills. And so is the expression of logic in the act of preparing, serving, and eating the food. On reading a book of recipes from the Tiberian era of the Roman Empire—*De Re Culinaria* (The Art of Cooking, attributed to Gaelius Apicius) and *De Re Rustica* (by Cato)—one can discern how things have changed over 1600 years. Apicius expressed many distinctions in foods and in ways of cooking and eating. He also expressed a certain concern for health. "Digging one's grave with one's teeth," as the expression came to life in connection with gluttony (crisp tongues of larks, dormice marinated in honey, tasty thighs of ostrich are listed), was replaced by elaborate recipes to relieve an upset stomach or to facilitate digestion. The books do not say what everyone ate, and there are reasons to believe that there was quite a difference between the menu of slaves and that of their owners. Advances in identifying plants and in processing food go in tandem with advances in medicine. Writings from other parts of the world, especially China, testify to similar developments.

It was already remarked, by no other than Roland Barthes, that the two basic language systems—one based on ideographic writing, the second on the phonetic convention—put their characteristic stamp on the menus of the Far Eastern and Western civilizations. A Japanese menu is an expression of a configuration. One can start with any of the dishes offered simultaneously. Combinations are allowed. Eating is part of the Japanese culture, a practical experience of self-constitution with strong visual components, refined combinations of odors, and participation of almost all senses. It also reflects the awareness of the world in which the Japanese constitute themselves. Japanese food is focused on what life on an island affords, plus/minus influences from other cultures, resulting from the mobility of peoples. The more concrete writing system of the Far East and the more down-to-earth nourishment, i.e., the closeness to what each source of nutrition is (raw fish, seaweed, rice, minimal processing, strict dietary patterns based on combinations of nutritional *ideograms*), are an expression of the unity of the pragmatic framework within which they result.

A Western menu is a sequence, a one-directional linear event with a precise culmination. Eating proceeds from the *introduction* to the *conclusion*, "from soup to nuts." A meal has a progression and projects expectations associated with this progression. Within the *language of our food*, there are *well formed sentences* and *ill-formed sentences*, as well as a general tendency experience gastronomic pleasure. A literate society is a society aware of the rules for generating and enjoying meals according to such rules. The rules are based on experiences transmitted from one generation to the next, not necessarily in written form, but reflecting the intrinsic sequentiality of language and its abstract writing system. Goethe fired his cook (Lina Louise Axthelm) because she could not realize the distinction between healthy meals and the more sophisticated art of preparing them according to rules of literacy and aesthetic distinction.

ON COOKS, POTS, AND SPOONS

Cooking food—a practical experience that followed catching prey—represents an important moment in human self-definition. As a form of praxis, it parallels the experience of self-constitution through language. It extends, as language does, far beyond satisfying immediate needs, allowing for the establishment of expectations above and beyond survival. Cooking implies generality, but also integrates elements of individuality. Some foods taste better, are more easily digested, support specific practical experiences. For example, some foods enhance prowess. When eaten before a hunt, they can trigger lust for chasing the animal. Some foods stimulate sexual drive, others induce states of hallucination. Cooking was, in many ways, a journey from the known into the unknown. Together with the sensorial experience, intellectual elements were involved in the process. They are observations, of similarities and dissimilarities of certain procedures, of substances used, of the influence of weather, season, tools, etc.; simple inferences, discoveries—the effect of fire, salt, spices. The experience of preparing food, together with many other practical experiences on which it depends or which are connected to it, opens avenues of abstraction. Cooking improves the quality of individual life, and thus empowers members of a community to better adapt to pragmatic expectations.

The constitution of the notion of food quality, as an abstraction of taste, and crafting of tools appropriate to the activity, is of special interest. An example: Pottery, in the natural context where it was possible, became the medium for preserving and cooking. In other contexts, carved stone, carved wood, woven branches, or metal was used, for storing or for cooking, according to the material. Progressively, tools for preparing and tools for eating were crafted, and new eating habits were acknowledged. When the multiple interdependency food-container-cooking-preservation was internalized in the activity of preparing food, a framework for new experiences was established. Some of these experiences, such as how to handle fire, transcend nourishment. The significance of this process can be succinctly expressed: cooked food, which we need to associate to the tools used, is food taken out of the context of nature and introduced in the context of culture. The experience of cooking involves other experiences and then expands into other domains unrelated to nourishment. This experience requires instruments for cooking, but even

456   *Civilization of Illiteracy: Book IV*

more an understanding of the process involved, of the effects of combinations and additions, and a strategy for delivery to those for whom cooking was undertaken.

Satisfying hunger in the fight for survival is an individual experience. Preparation of food requires time. In the experience of achieving time awareness, cooking played a role not to be ignored. If time can be used for different purposes by different people, associated in view of shared goals, then some can tend to the need of prepared food for others, while in turn partaking in their effort of hunting, fishing, agriculture, and craftsmanship. It was a simple strategy of labor assignments, affected by tribal life, family, rituals, myth, and religion: knowledge gained in preparing food disseminated without the need for specialized activity. But once pragmatic circumstances of life required it, some people assumed the function and thus, once a critical mass of efficiency was reached, what we today call *the cook* was identified. From the not-too-many written recipes that come down to us through the centuries, as well as from religious writings containing precise, pragmatically motivated restrictions, we learn enough about the stabilizing role of writing upon food preparation. We also gain understanding of the new functions played by food preparation: celebration of events, sacrifice to gods, expression of power.

People learn to cook and to eat at the same time. In this process, they come to share values beyond the immediacy of plants, fruits, and a piece of meat. Mediations pertinent to the art of cooking and eating are also part of the language process and become language. Culinary restrictions, such as those set down in some religions, are but an example of this process. They encode practical rules related to survival and well-being, but also to some conventions beyond the physical reality of the food. Language makes such rules the rules of the community; writing preserves them as requirements and thus exercises an important normative role.

Each pragmatic context determined what was acceptable as food and the conditions of food preparation, henceforth the condition of cooks and their particular role in social life. Many cooks, serving at courts of royalty, in monasteries, in the military, became the object of folk tales, fiction, of philosophers' comments. No cook seems to have been highly educated, but all their *clients* tried to impress through the food served and the wines, or other drinks, accompanying them. In such circumstances, the symbolic function of food indeed takes over the primary function of satisfying hunger. Thus the cook, like the singer and the dancer and the poet, contributes his part to what becomes the art of living. It is probably worth pointing out that memory devices similar to those used by poets and musicians are used by cooks, and that improvisation in preparing a meal plays an important part.

Writing entered the kitchen; and some of the last to resist literacy, when it became a pragmatic requirement, were those who cooked for others. Orality is more stubborn, for many reasons, when it involves the secrecy of food preparation. There are good reasons for this, some obvious even in our day of cracking the most guarded secrets. Indeed, labor division does not stop at the gates of factories. The segmentation of life and labor, increased mediation, and expectations of high efficiency make mass production possible. Almost everything people need to feed themselves, in order to maintain their physical and mental productive powers with a minimum of investment, is provided in favor of productive cycles. In the pragmatic framework of the industrial age, this meant the *reproduction* of the productive forces of the worker in a context of permanency. The investment in education and training was to be recuperated over a lifetime of work. Nourishment contributed to the same pattern: the family adapted to the rhythms of the practical experience of industry related jobs.

At work, at home, in school, at church, and last but not least in nourishment, acceptance of authority together with the discipline of self-denial were at work. That literacy, through its own structural characteristics (hierarchy, authority, standardization) accentuated all these peculiarities should at this time be evident. On special occasions, accounted for in the overall efficiency of effort, nourishment became celebration. It was integrated in the calendar of events through which authority was acknowledged: Sabbath, religious holidays, and political celebrations were motives for a better, or at least different, menu. Other days were meant to raise the awareness of self-denial (fish on Friday, for instance).

The cook did not necessarily become a literate person, but he or she was a product of the literate environment of practical experiences of pre-industrial and industrial societies. The tools and the culture of spices, ingredients, matching food and dishes, of expressing social status in the dinnerware set out, and the meal, i.e., the structure of the entire statement which a meal constitutes were all subjected to literacy. Labor division made the cook necessary, while simultaneously generating an industrial culture of food. In the equation of the labor market in industrial society, with literacy as its underlying structure, eating equals maintenance of productive and reproductive power. It also means the reproduction of needs at an increasing scale, as well as their change from needs to desires triggering the expansion of industrial production.

In the expectations associated with food there is more than only the voice of hunger. Our system of values, as it was articulated in the literate use of language, is expressed in our hunger, and in our particular ways to satisfy it. Based on this observation, we acknowledge that all the forces at work in structuring democratic social relations also affect the socialization of our nourishment. Uniform quality, and access to this common denominator *quality*, are introduced in the market, and with them the possibility of stating and maintaining health standards. Within the boundaries of the civilization of literacy and its associated hygiene and health standards, there is little left that can be identified with the country home that cannot be industrialized and made uniformly available. Beyond these boundaries starts a new reality of expectations, of transcended needs, and of technological means to satisfy them within standards of quality that reinforce the notion of democracy.

It is the act of mixing ingredients, boiling or stir-frying them, and the preparation of everything, the testing of different proportions, of new ingredients, of new combinations that results in the food we care for so much. The awareness of the entire process during which humans distanced themselves from nature is reduced in our understanding to some simple facts: instead of devouring the hunted animal, humans cooked it, preserved some parts for other days, learned how to combine various sources of nutrition (animal and plant), noticed what was good for the body and the mind. What is generally not accounted for is the fact that the break from the direct source of food to the experience of *preparing* is simultaneous with the emergence and establishment of language. Consequent changes are the use of methods for preserving, the continuous expansion of the food *repertory* (sources of nourishment), the development of better artifacts for increasing the efficiency of production and preparation of foods, and industrial processing. These changes parallel differentiations in the status of language-based practical experiences: the appearance of writing, the emergence of education, progress in crafts, the pragmatic of industrial society.

With the experience of literacy, human awareness of food experienced as a necessity, and as an expression of human personality and identity, increases. Claude Lévi-Strauss, among others, forcefully dealt with this subject. The basic idea—of human dimensions expressed in nourishment—becomes more significant today. None of the many writers infatuated with the subject have noticed that once the limits of literacy, as limits of the pragmatics that made it necessary, are reached, we transcend the age of McDonald's, of synthetic nutritional substances, and of an infinity of prefabricated foods. This is also the age of endless variations and combinations. The human personality and identity are more difficult to characterize. It is expressed in our nourishment, as well as in how we dress—choosing from an infinity of available cloths—our sexual behavior—free to experiment in ever-expanding possibilities: patterns of family life, education, art, and communication. The infinity of choices available in the civilization of illiteracy eradicates any center, and to some extent undermines commonalty, even at the level of the species.

In this civilization, the *investment* in self is less community-related and more an act of individual choice. These choices are embodied in precise, customized diets based on individual requirements as defined by dietitians. Computer programs control personalized recipes and the production of any meal or menu. The balance of time and energy has changed totally. Experiences of work, free time, and fitness mix. The clear borderline between them is progressively blurred. It is not clear whether one burns more calories today in jogging than in working, but it is clear that discipline, in particular that of self-denial, is replaced by unpredictable self-indulgence. Consequently, to maintain the body's integrity, individual diet and exercise programs are generated, given a new focus through the transition from the economy of scarcity to that of consumption. Illiterate subjects accept that the market decide for them what and when and how to eat, as well as what to wear, with whom to pair, and how to feel. The appearance is that of self-determination. Independence and responsibility are not *instant-mix* experiences. Whether embodied in fast food chains, in microwave nourishment, in the television cooking shows, there is an illusion of self-determination, continuously reinforced in the seductive reality of a segmented world of competing partial literacies.

The appearance is that one can choose from many literacies, instead of being forced into one. The fact is that *we are chosen* in virtue of having our identity constituted and confirmed within the pragmatic context. Awareness of and interaction with nature, already affected in the previous age of industrial processing of basic foods, are further eroded. The immediate environment and the sources of nutrition it provides are assimilated in the picture of seasonless and context-free shelves at the supermarket. Space (where does the food come from?) and time (to which season does it correspond?) distinctions, accounted for so precisely in literacy, dissolve in a generic continuum. One does not need to be rich to have access to what used to be the food of those who could afford it. One does not need to be from a certain part of the world to enjoy what used to be the exotic quality of food. Time and space shrink for the traveler or TV viewer, as they shrink for the supermarket patron. They shrink even more for the increasing number of people shopping through the World Wide Web, according to formulas custom designed for them. With brand recognition, brands become more important than the food. The rhythms of nature and the rhythm of work and life are pulled further apart by the mediating mechanisms of marketing. The natural identity of food vanishes in the subsequent practical experience of artificial reality. There is little that distinguishes between a menu designed for the team of the space shuttle, for the military personnel in combat far from home, and the energy calculations for a machine. A little artificial taste of turkey for Thanksgiving, or the cleverly simulated smell of apple pie, makes the difference.

THE LANGUAGE OF EXPECTATIONS

Beasts of habit, people expect some reminders of taste and texture even when they know that what they eat or drink is the result of a formula, not of natural processes. This is why the almost fat-free hamburger, devised in laboratories for people in need of nourishment adapted to new conditions of life and work, will succeed or fail not on the basis of calories, but on the simulation of the taste of the *real thing*. This is how the *new Coke* failed. Non-alcoholic beer and wine, fat- and sugar-free ice cream, low cholesterol egg, vegetable ham, and all substitutes for milk, butter, and cream, to list a few, are in the same situation. In the fast lane of the civilization of illiteracy, we expect fast food: hamburgers, fish, chicken, pizza, and Chinese, Indian, Mexican, Thai, and other foods. The barriers of time and space are overcome through pre-processing, microwave ovens, and genetic engineering. But we do not necessarily accept the industrial model of mass production, reminiscent of literacy characteristics quite different from those of home cooking.

We cannot afford those long cooking cycles, consuming energy and especially time, that resulted in what some remember as the kitchen harmony of smell and taste, as well as in waste and dubious nutritional value, one should add: A McDonald's hamburger is close to the science fiction image of a world consuming only the energy source necessary for functioning. But the outlet reminds one of machines. It is still a manned operation, with live operators, geared to offer a uniform industrial quality. However, the *literate structure* gives way to more effective functioning. At intervals defined by a program continuously tracking consumption, the restaurant is stocked with the pre-processed items on the menu. None of the *cooks* needs to know how to write or read; food preparation is on-line, in real time. And if the requirements of the pragmatics of the civilization of illiteracy overcome the current industrial model, the new McDonald's will be able to meet individual expectations no less restricted than those of the Internet pizza providers. If this does not happen, McDonald's and its many imitators in the world will disappear, just as many of the mass production food manufacturers have already disappeared.

The mediating nature of the processes involved in nourishment is revealing. Between the natural and artificial sources of protein, fats, sugar, and other groups recommended for a balanced meal and the person eating them with the expectation of looking, feeling, and performing better, of living longer and healthier, there are many layers of processing, controlling, and measuring. Many formulas for preparation follow each other, or are applied in parallel cycles. After we made machines that resemble humans, we started treating ourselves as machines. The digital engine stands for the brain, pump for the heart, circuits for the nervous system. They are all subjected to maintenance cycles, clean sources of energy, self-cleaning mechanisms, diagnostic routines. The end product of food production—a customized pizza, taco, egg roll, hamburger, gefilte fish—resembles the "real thing," which is produced at the lowest possible cost in a market in which *literate* food is a matter of the past, a subject of reminiscence.

The new dynamics of change and the expectation of adaptability and permanence associated with the nourishment of the civilization of literacy collide at all levels involved in our need to eat and drink. What results from this conflict are the beautiful down-sized kitchens dominated by the microwave oven, the new cookware adapted to the fast food and efficient nourishment, the cooking instructions downloaded from the digital network into the kitchen. The interconnectedness of the world takes rather subtle aspects when it comes to food. Microwave ovens can perfectly be seen as peripheral devices connected to the *smart kitchens* of the post-industrial age, all set to feed us once we push the dials that will translate a desire, along with our health profile, into a code number. Three-quarters of all American households (*Barbie's* included) use a microwave oven. And many of them are bound to become an address on the Internet, as other appliances already are.

The conflict between literate and illiterate nourishment is also documented by the manner in which people write, draw, film, televise, and express themselves about cooking and related matters. This addresses the communication aspects of the practical experience of what and how we eat. The people who could go to their back yard for fresh onions or cabbage, get meat from animals they hunted or tended, or milk their own cow or goat, belong to a pragmatic framework different from that of people who buy produce, meat, cheese, and canned and frozen food in a small store or a supermarket. To communicate experiences that vanished because of their low efficiency is an exercise in history or fiction. To communicate current experiences in nourishment means to acknowledge mediation, distribution of tasks, networking, and open-endedness as they apply to communication and the way we feed ourselves or are fed by others. It also means to acknowledge a different quality.

Once upon a time, writing on food and dining was part of literature. Food authorities have been celebrated as writers. But with the advent of *nourishment strategies,* literate writing gave way to a prose of recipes almost as idiosyncratic as recipes for the mass production of soap, or *cookbooks* for programming. Some gourmets complained. Food experts suggested that precision was as good for cooking as temperature gauges. The understanding of how close the act of cooking is to writing about it, or, in our days to the tele-reality of the kitchen, or to the new interactive gadgets loaded with recipes for the virtual reality cooking game, is often missing. When conditions for exercising fantasy in the kitchen are no longer available, fantasy deserts the food pages and moves into the scripts of the national gourmet video programs and computer games—or on Web sites. Moreover, when predetermined formulas for bouillons, salad dressings, cakes, and puddings replace the art of selecting and preparing, the writing disappears behind the information added according to regulation, as vitamins are added to milk and cereals. A *super-cook* defines what is appropriate, and the efficient formula turns our kitchens into private processing plants ensuring the most efficient result. What is gained is the possibility to assemble meals in combinations of nutritional modules and to integrate elements from all over the world without the risk of more than a new experience for our taste buds. From the industrial age, we inherited processing techniques guaranteeing uniformity of flavor and standards of hygiene. The price we pay for this is the pleasure, the adventure, the unique experience. Food writing is based on the assumptions of uniformity. In contrast, cooking shows started exploring the worlds of technological progress, in which you don't cook because you are hungry or need to feed your family. You do it for competitive reasons, in order to achieve recognition for mastering new utensils and learning the names of new ingredients. In the post-industrial, the challenge is to break into the territory of innovation and ascertain practical experiences of cooking, presentation, and eating, freed from literate constraints.

Pragmatic frameworks are not chosen, like food from a menu or top-pings from a list. Practical experiences of human self-constitution within a pragmatic framework are the concrete embodiments of belonging to such a pragmatics. A new pragmatic framework negates the previous one, but does not eliminate it. Although these points were made in earlier chapters, there is a specific reason for dealing with them again here. As opposed to other experiences, nourishment is bound to involve more elements of continuity than science or the military. As we have already seen, literacy-based forms of preparing and eating food exist parallel to illiterate nourishment. This is the reason why some peculiar forms of social redistribution of food need to be discussed.

From self-nourishment to being fed
Humanized eating and drinking come with moral values attached to them, foremost the rule of sharing. Pragmatic rules regarding clean-liness, waste, and variation in diet are also part of the experience of nourishment. These associated elements—values, expectations, rules—are rarely perceived as constituting an extension of the prac-tical experience through which humanity distinguishes itself from sheer naturalness. Literacy appropriates the rules and expectations that acknowledge and support ideals and values. Once expressed in the literate text, however, they appear to be extraneous to the process. Changes in the condition of religion, civic education, family, and the legal code, as well as progress in biology, chemistry, and genetics, cre-ate the impression and expectation that we can attach to food what-ever best suits the situation morally or practically. The self-control and self-denial of previous pragmatic contexts are abandoned for instant gratification.

In the competitive context of the new pragmatics that renders lit-eracy useless, the sense of a *right* to affluence developed. Parallel to this, institutions, founded on literacy-based experiences, were set up to control equity and distribution. Against the background of high efficiency that the new pragmatics made possible, competition is replaced by controlled distribution, and the experience of self-nourishment is replaced by that of *being fed*. Absorbed by tax-supported social programs, the poor, as well as others who chose giving up responsibility for themselves, are freed from projecting their biological and cultural identity in the practical experience of taking care of their own needs. Thus part of the morality of eating and drinking is socialized, in the same manner that literacy is socialized. At the same time, people's illiteracy expands in the sphere of nourishment. Today, there are more people than ever who could not take care of themselves even if all the food in the world and all the appliances we know of were brought into their homes. Dependencies resulting from the new status of high efficiency and distribution of tasks free the human being in relative terms, while creating dependencies and expectations.

The problem is generally recognized in all advanced countries. But the answer cannot be so-called welfare reforms that result only in cutting benefits and tightening requirements. Such reforms are driven by short-sightedness and political opportunism. A different perspective is necessary, one that addresses motivation and the means for pursuing individual self-constitution as something other than the beneficiary of an inefficient system. The pragmatics that overrides the need for literacy is based on individual empowerment. As necessary as soup kitchens are under conditions of centralism and hierarchy, the dissemination of knowledge and skills that individuals need in order to be able to provide for themselves is much more important.

Run and feed the hungry
"Sponsorship for a charitable track event. Funds for Third World countries threatened by starvation sought. Register support through your donations." And on a nice sunny weekend, many kind-hearted

individuals will run miles around a city or swim laps in a pool in order to raise funds for organizations such as CARE, Oxfam, Action Hunger, or Feed the World. Hunger in this world of plenty, even in the USA and other prosperous countries, derives from the same dynamics that results in the civilization of illiteracy. The scale of humankind requires levels of efficiency for which practical experiences of survival based on limited resources are ill suited. Entire populations are subjected to hunger and disease due to social and economic inequities, to weather conditions or topological changes, or to political upheaval in the area where they live. Short of addressing inequities, aid usually alleviates extreme situations. But it establishes dependencies instead of encouraging the best response to the situation through new agricultural practices, where applicable, or alternative modes of producing food.

Seduced by our life of plenty and by the dynamics of change, we could end up ignoring starving and diseased populations, or we could try to understand our part in the equation. Living in an integrated world and partaking in the pragmatics of a global economy, people become prisoners of the here and now, discarding the very disconcerting reality of millions living in misery. But it is exactly the pragmatic framework leading to the civilization of illiteracy that also leads to the enormous disparities in today's world. Many forces are at work, and the danger of falling prey to the slogans of failed ideology, while trying to understand misery and hunger in today's world, cannot be overestimated. Starvation in Africa, South America, in some East European countries, and in parts of Asia needs to be questioned in light of the abundance of food in Japan, West Europe, and North America. Both extremes correspond to changes in human self-constitution under expectations of efficiency critical to the current scale of humankind.

If human activity had not changed and broadened its base of resources, the entire world would be subject to what Ethiopians, Sudanese, Somalis, Bangladeshis, and many others are facing. Extreme climatic conditions, as well as decreasing fertility of the land due usually to bad farming practices, can be overcome by new farming methods, progress in agricultural technology, biogenetics, and chemistry. Spectacular changes have come about in what is considered the most traditional practice through which humans constitute their identity. The change affected ways of working, family relations, use of local resources, social and political life, and even population growth. It resulted in a new set of dependencies among communities that had afforded autarchic modes of existence for thousands of years. The environment, too, has been affected probably as much by scientific and technological progress as by the new farming methods that take full advantage of new fertilizers, insecticides, and genetic engineering of new plants and animals.

Motivated by literacy-based ideals, some countries took it upon themselves to see that people in less developed lands be redeemed through benefits they did not expect and for which they were not prepared. At the global levels of humankind, when the necessity of literacy declines, dependencies characteristic of literacy-based interactions collide with forces of integration and competition. What results is a painful compromise. Hunger is acknowledged and tended to by enormous bureaucracies: churches, charities, international aid organizations, and institutions more concerned with themselves than with the task at hand. They maintain dependencies that originated within the pragmatics of the civilization of literacy. The activities they carry out are inherently inefficient. Where the new dynamics is one of differentiation and segmentation, the main characteristics of these experiences are those of literacy: establishment of a universal model, the attempt to reach homogeneity, tireless effort to disseminate modes of existence and work of a sequential, analytic, rationalistic, and deterministic nature. Consequently, where nourishment from the excess attained elsewhere is dispensed, a way of life alien to those in need is projected upon them.

Aid, even to the extent that it is necessary, re-shapes biology, the environment, the connection among people, and each individual. Diseases never before experienced, behavioral and mental changes, and new reliances are generated, even in the name of the best intentions. In some areas affected by starvation, tribal conflicts, religious intolerance, and moral turpitude add to natural conditions not propitious to life. These man-made conditions cannot and should not veil the fact that human creativity and inventiveness are prevented from unfolding, replaced by ready-made solutions, instead of being stimulated. Empowerment means to facilitate developments that maintain distinctions and result from differences, instead of uniformity.

Would all the populations facing hunger and disease actually jump from the illiteracy of the past—a result of no school system or limited access to education, as well as of a pragmatics that did not lead to literacy—to the pragmatically determined illiteracy of the future? The pragmatic framework of our new age corresponds to the need to acknowledge differences and derive from heterogeneity new sources of creativity. Each ton of wheat or corn airlifted to save mothers and children is part of the missionary praxis commenced long ago when religious organizations wanted to save the soul of the so-called savage. The answer to hunger and disease cannot be only charity, but the effort to expand networks of reciprocally significant work. The only meaningful pragmatics derives from practical experiences that acknowledge differences instead of trying to erase them. Access to resources for more effective activities is fundamentally different from access to surplus or to bureaucratic mechanisms for redistribution.

Where literacy never became a reality, no organization should take it upon itself to impose it as the key to survival and well being. Our literacy-based medicine, nourishment, social life, and especially values are not the panacea for the world, no matter how proud we are of some, and how blind to their limitations. Human beings have sufficient means today to afford tending to differences instead of doing away with them. In this process, we might learn about that part of nourishment that was rationalized away in the process of reaching higher levels of efficiency. And we might find new resources in other environments and in the peculiar self-constitution of peoples we consider deprived—resources that we could integrate into our pragmatics.

No truffles (yet) in the coop

Our civilization of illiterate nourishment is based on networks and distributed assignments. The change from self-reliance to affluence corresponds, first and foremost, to the change of the pragmatic context within which the human condition is defined. We project a physical reality—our body—that has changed over time due to modifications in our environment, and the transition from practical experiences of survival to the experience of abundance. The room for invention and spontaneity expands the more we discover and apply rules that guarantee efficiency or limit those preventing it. There might be several dozens of sauces one can select from, and no fewer cereals for breakfast, many types of bread, meat, fish, and very many preprocessed menus. It would probably be an exaggeration to say that all taste alike. But it would not necessarily be false to ascertain that behind diversity there are a limited number of changing formulas, some better adapted to succeed in the marketplace than others, and some better packaged than others.

Yes, people are nostalgic. More precisely, people are subjected to the nostalgia-triggering stimuli of mass media: the attraction of the homemade, homestyle, Mom's secret recipe. This is not because the majority of us know what these icons of the past are, but rather because we associate them with what is no longer possible: reassurance, calm, tradition, protection, permanence, care. We also hear the voices of those who demystify the literate cooking of yesteryear: women spent their lifetime slaving in their kitchens. They did so, the argument goes, to satisfy males, only too happy to be taken care of. Both voices, those idealizing and those demystifying the past, should be heard: We enslaved part of nature and took it upon ourselves to annihilate animals or, worse, change their genetic structure. In order to satisfy our appetites, we sacrificed the environment. And, giving in to gluttony, we effectively changed our genetic constitution. The truth, if there is any above and beyond the cultural and economic conditions of cooking, is that transitions from one scale of humankind to another subjected practical experiences of self-constitution to fundamental modifications. Trying to understand some of the patterns of life and work, as well as patterns of access to food or of preparing it, requires that we understand when and why such changes take place.

Language stored not only recipes, but also expectations that became part of our nourishment. The culture of food preparation and serving, the art of discovering new recipes and enjoying what we eat and drink, is more than language can convey. Truffles, the food of kings and nobles, and more recently of those who can afford them, bear a whole history, obviously expressed in language. Whether seen as the spit of witches, a more or less magic aphrodisiac, or a miraculous life-prolonging food, truffles gain in status because our experience, reflected in the language pertinent to cooking, led us to regard them from a perspective different from those who first discovered, by accident, their nutritive value. It is in the tradition of orality that fathers whispered to their sons the secret of places where truffles could be found. Practical experiences involving writing, and later literacy, raised the degree of expectancy associated with their consumption. They affected the shift regarding the eating of truffles from the sphere of the natural (the pigs that used to find them, and liked them probably as much as the gourmets, had to be replaced by specially trained dogs) to the realm of the cultural, where the interests of human beings prevail over anything else. Through language processes paralleled by the semiosis of high gastronomy, truffles enter the market as sign—of a discriminating palate, of snobbery, or of actually knowing why truffles are good.

Language and food interact. This interaction involves other sign systems, too: images, sounds, movements, texture, odor, taste. Through the influence of language and these other sign systems, the preparation of food and the appropriate drinks becomes an art. In the age of illiteracy, the languages of genetics, biology, and medicine make us aware of what it takes to avoid malnutrition, what it takes to maintain health and prolong one's life. Literacy was reinforced in the convention of how people eat, what, when, and how satisfaction or disappointment was expressed. In our new nutritional behavior and in our new values, literacy plays a marginal role (including interaction at the dining table). The artificial truffle is free of the mystique of origin, of the method for finding truffles, of secret formulas (except the trade secret). It is one item among many, cheap, illusory, and broadly available, as democratic as artificial caviar or, as Rousseau would have put it, government by representation.

Identical in so many ways, the cafeterias that extend an industrial model in a post-industrial context feed millions of people based on a formula of standardization. Hierarchies are wiped away. This is no place for truffles. One gets his tray and follows those who arrived before. There is no predetermined sequence. All that remains is the act of selection and the execution of the transaction—an exercise in assemblage not far removed from composing your own pizza on a computer monitor. When the language of available nourishment is standardized to the extent that it is in these *feeding environments*—elegant coops stocked with shining metal coffee, tea, and soda dispensers, refrigerated containers of sandwiches, cake, fruit—the language of expectations will not be much richer. The increased efficiency made possible this way accounts for the wide acceptance of this mediocre, illiterate mode of nourishing ourselves.

WE ARE WHAT WE EAT

If we were to analyze the language associated with what, how, when, where, and why we eat, we would easily notice that this language is tightly connected to the language of our identification. We are what, how, why, when, and where we eat. This identification changed when agriculture started and families of languages ascertained themselves.

It changed again when the pragmatic framework required writing, and so on until the identity of the literate person and the post-literate emerged from practical experiences characteristic of a new scale of human experiences. Today we are, for quite a broad range of our social life, an identification number of a sort, an address, and other information in a database (income, investment, wealth, debt history) that translates into what marketing models define as our individual expectations. Information brokers trade us whenever someone is interested in what we can do for him or her. Powerful networks of information processing can be used to precisely map each person to the shelf surface available in stores, to the menus of restaurants we visit on various occasions, and to the Internet sites of our journeys in cyberspace. Our indexical signs serve as indicators for various forms of filtering calories (how many do we really need?), fats (saturated or not), proteins, sugars, even the aesthetics of food presentation, in order to exactly match individual needs and desires. Scary or not, one can even imagine how we will get precisely what best suits our biological system, influenced by the intensity of the tennis game (virtual) we just finished, the TV program we watched for the last 30 *seconds,* or the work we are involved in. To make this happen is a task not so much different from receiving our customized newspaper or only the information we want through Point Cast, saving our monitors from excessive wear and saving us time from useless searches.

In the pragmatic framework where illiteracy replaces literacy, eating and drinking are freed from the deterministic chain of survival and reproduction. They are made part of a more encompassing practical experience. Each time we take a bite from a hot dog or sandwich, each time we enjoy ice cream, drink wine or beer or soda, take vitamins or add fiber to our diet, we participate in two processes: the first, of revising expectations, turning what used to be a necessity into luxury; the second, of continuous expansion of the global market present through what we eat and drink. Many transactions are embodied in our daily breakfast, business lunch, or TV dinner. With each bite and gulp (as with each other product consumed), we are incorporated into the dynamics of expanding the market. The so-called Florida orange juice contains frozen concentrate from Brazil. The fine Italian veal microwave dinner contains meat from Romania. The wildflower honey "Made in Germany" is from Hungarian or Polish beehives. Bread, butter, cheese, cold cuts, jams, and pasta could be marked with the flag of the United Nations if all the people involved in producing them were to be acknowledged. Meat, poultry, fruits, and vegetables, not unlike everything else traded in the global market, make for an integrated world in which the most efficient survives in the competition for pleasing if not our taste, at least our propensity to buy.

The efficiency reached in the pragmatic framework of illiteracy allows people to maintain, within the plurality of languages, a plurality of dietary experiences, some probably as exotic as the literacy of ancient Greek, Sanskrit, Aramaic, or cuneiform writing. Even the recipes of the Roman Empire can be enjoyed in exclusive settings (as in Saint-Bernard-de-Comminges in the Pyrénées) or as *haute*, ready-made cuisine (the Comptesse du Barry food company offers wild boar in spicy sauce, stuffed duck in ginger, and sea trout with wild leeks). The Japanese have their sushi prepared from resuscitated fish flown, in a state of anabiosis (organic rhythm slowed through refrigeration), from wherever the beloved delicacies are still available.

The multiplicity of food-related experiences in our time is representative of segmentation and heterogeneity in the civilization of illiteracy. It is also an expression of the subtle interdependencies of the many aspects of human self-constitution. The democracy of nourishment and the mediocrity of food are not necessarily a curse. Neither are the extravagant performances of artist-cooks that fetch a price equivalent to the average annual salary of a generic citizen of this integrated world. Difference makes a difference. Feminism, multiculturalism, political activism (from right to left)—all use arguments related to how and what we eat, as part of the broader how and why we live, to advance their causes. If nothing else, the civilization of illiteracy makes possible choices, including those pertinent to nourishment, for which we are ill prepared. The real challenge is still ahead of us. And no one knows how it tastes.

CHAPTER 6: THE PROFESSIONAL WINNER

The connections between sports and literacy are far from obvious. Watching sports events, as a spectator in the stadium, or in front of the television, does not require the literacy we associate with libraries, reading and writing, and school education. One does not need to read in order to see who is fastest, strongest, or jumps the farthest or highest, or throws or catches the best. And one does not really need to be literate in order to become a champion or to make it into a first-league team. Running, jumping, pushing, throwing, catching, and kicking are part of our physical repertory, related to our day-to-day existence, easy to associate with ways through which survival took place when scavenging, hunting, fishing, and foraging were the fundamental ways for primitive beings to feed themselves and to avoid being killed. Even the association of sports with mytho-magical ceremonies implying physical performance is easy to explain without reference to language, oral or written. Exceptional physical characteristics were, and still are in some parts of the world, celebrated as expressions of forces beyond immediate control and understanding. Gods were worshipped through exceptional physical feats performed by people worshipping them. In archaic cultures, athletes could even be sacrificed on the altar of gratitude, where the best were destined to please the gods. .

The initial phases of what was eventually called *sport* correspond to establishing those sign systems (gestures, sounds, shapes) which, in anticipation of language, made language possible and necessary. This was a phase of syncretism, during which the physical projection of the human being dominated the intellect. Running after an animal or from one, and running for play are different forms of human experience corresponding to different pragmatic contexts. They have different motivations and different outcomes. Probably 20,000 years separate these two experiences in time. In order to reach the level of generality and abstraction that a competition embodies, the human being had to undergo experiences of self-constitution within which the domination of physical over intellectual characteristics changed drastically. The qualifier *sport*—a word which seems to have ascended within the English language of the 19th century—probably came about in the framework of the division between secular and non-secular forms of human praxis. Both maintenance and improvement of the human biological endowment and mytho-magical practice were based on awareness of the role the body plays and the recognition of the practical need to disseminate this awareness. Efficiency was the governing aspect, not recognized as such, not conceptualized, but acknowledged in the cult of the body and the attempt to make it part of the shared culture. The contest (for which the Greeks used the words *athlos*) and the prize (*athlon*, which eventually led to the word *athlete*) embody generalizations of those practical situations through which survival and well-being came about.

As a complex experience, sports involves rational and irrational components. This is why approaching the relation between literacy and sports, one has to account for both dimensions. Sports is approached here from the perspective of the changes through which it became what it is today: a well defined form of relaxation, but probably more a competitive type of work acknowledged in the market like any other product of human practice.

The immediate connection between physical fitness and the outcome of practical experiences dominated by physical aspects was established within very limited, but strongly patterned, activity. It soon became the measure of survival success, and thus the rationality shared by the community experiencing the survival of the fittest is reflected in competition. Athletes competed in order to please gods; to conjure fertility, rain, or the extension of life; or to expel demons. The process is documented in a variety of petroglyphs (cave paintings, engravings on stone) and in carvings or etchings on animal horn and metal, as well as in the first written testimony, in which the role of the stronger, the faster, the more agile was evinced. Documents from all known cultures, regardless of their geographic coordinates, have in common the emphasis on the physical as it acquired a symbolic status.

To understand how some biological characteristics improved chances of survival means to understand the rationality of the body. Its embodiment in the culture of physical awareness facilitated practical experiences of human self-constitution that would result in sports professions. The irrational element has to do with the fact that although all males and all females are structurally the same, some individuals seem better endowed physically. As with many other aspects of the practical experience through which each person acknowledges his or her identity, what could not be clarified was placed in a domain of explanations where the rationality is lost. This is why expectations of rain, of longer life, of chasing away evil forces are associated with sports. The cult of the body, in particular of body parts, resulted from experiences leading to awareness of oneself. When the body, or parts of it, became a goal in itself, the rationality of physical fitness for survival is contradicted by the irrationality of fitness for reasons other than individual and communal well-being. Rituals, myths, religion, and politics appropriated the irrational component of physical activities. In ancient communities, in the context of a limited understanding of physical phenomena, attempts were made to infer from the immediate well-being of the body of competing athletes to the future well-being of the entire community.

When it comes to physical fitness in the context of survival of the fittest, can we suppose that a lone human being stands out, something like the lonely animals on their own until the time for pairing comes, competing with others, killing and being killed? Probably not. Scale defines the species as one that ascertains its self-constitution in cooperative efforts, no matter how primitive. Up to a certain scale, the only competition was for survival. It translated into food and off-spring. Only after the agricultural phase, which corresponds to a level of efficiency of more food than immediately necessary, the element of competition shifts from survival to ascertainment. Competition and expectations of performance correspond to the period of incipient writing, and were progressively acknowledged as part of the dynamics of communal life. Every other change in the role of humankind brought with it expectations of physical fitness corresponding to expected levels of efficiency.

SPORTS AND SELF-CONSTITUTION

Gymnastics is an expression of the cult of the body parallel to that of art. In order to realize its dimensions, it needs to be seen from this broader perspective, not as a random set of exercises. It has a physical and a metaphysical dimension, the latter related to the obsession with ideal proportions that eventually were expressed in philosophic terms. There are plenty of explanations to be considered for both the origin of the practical experience of sports and the forms this experience took over centuries. Alluding to some explanations, though not in order to endorse them, will help to show how diversity of sports experiences resulted in diversity of interpretations.

The basic assumption of this entire book, human self-constitution in practical experiences, translates into the statement that sports is not a reflective but a constitutive experience. Indeed, through running, jumping, wrestling, or otherwise participating in some game, human beings project themselves according to physical characteristics and mental coordination that facilitate physical performance in the reality of their existence. This projection is a direct way of identifying oneself and thus of becoming part of an interacting group of people. The majority of researchers studying the origins of sports identify these in the experience of survival, thus placing them in the Darwinian evolutionist frame. When survival skills, maintenance, and reproduction skills become distinct and relatively autonomous, they follow recurrent patterns on whose basis social practice takes place and new ideas are formulated.

From the perspective of today's jogger, running might seem an individual experience, and to a great extent it is. But fundamentally, running as a practical experience takes place among people sharing the notion of physical exercise and attaching to it social, cultural, economic, and medical meaning. We create ourselves not only when we write poetry, tend land, or manufacture machines, but also when we are involved in athletic experiences. There is in sports, as there is in any other form of practical experience, a natural, a cultural (what we learn from others and create with others), and a social (what is known as communication) dimension. The sports experience appears to us as the result of the coordination of all these elements. For someone attending a sports event, this coordination can become an object of description: this much is due to training, this much to natural attributes, and this much to social implications (pride, patriotism). This is why sports events sometimes appear to the spectator as having a predetermined meaning, not one resulting from the dynamics of the interaction characteristic of this human experience. In the mytho-magical stage of human dynamics, in which the ability of the body was celebrated, the meaning seemed to drive the entire event more than it occurs today in a game of hockey or football. Due to the syncretic nature of such events, rituals addressed existence in its perceived totality. The specialized nature of games such as hockey or football leads these to address only one aspect of existence—the experience of the particular sport. A game can degenerate from being a competition structured by rules to a confrontation of nerves, violence, or national pride, or into sheer exhibitionism, disconnected from the drive for victory.

Although the physical basis for the practical experience of sports is the same—human beings as they evolved in time—in different cultures, different recurrent patterns and different meanings attached to them can be noticed. This statement does not align itself with explanations of sports given in Freudian tradition, Marxist theory, or in Huizinga's model of the human being as *playful man* (*Homo Ludens*). It takes into consideration the contextual nature of any form of human practice and looks at sports, as it does at any human experience, from the perspective of a constitutional, not representational, act; in short, from the pragmatic perspective. When Japanese players kick a ball in the game called *kemari,* the recurrent pattern of interaction is not the familiar football or soccer game, although each player constitutes his identity in the performance. When the Zen archer tenses his bow, the pattern, associated with the search for unity with the universe, is quite different from the pattern of archery in Africa or of the archery competition at the Olympic games of the past. The ball games of the Mayans relied on a mythology which was itself a projection of the human being in quest of explaining and finding an answer to what distinguishes the sun from the moon and how their influence affects patterns of human practice. It is probably easier to look at the recurrent patterns of interaction of more recent sports experiences not rooted in the symbolism of the ancient, such as baseball, aquatic dancing, or ice skating, to understand what aspect of the human being is projected and what kind of experience results for the participants (athletes, sports fans, public, media). The surprising reality is the diversity. People never exhaust their imagination in devising new and newer forms of competition involving their physical aptitude. No less surprising is the pursuit of a standard experience, modeled in rules for the competition. Some are intrinsic to the effort (the rules of the game), others to the appearance (expected clothing, for instance). Parallel to the standard experience, there is also a deviant practice of sports (nonstandard), in forms of individual rules, *ad hoc* conventions, private competition. The social level of sports and the private level are loosely connected. To become a professional means, among other things, to accept the rules as they apply in the standard experience, within organizations or acknowledged competition. The language professional is pretty much in a similar situation. Literacy serves as the medium for encoding the rules.

But the subject here is not the similarity between sports and language, but rather their interrelation. The obvious entry point is to notice that we use language to describe the practical experience of sport and to assign meaning to it. As obvious as this is, it is also misleading in the sense that it suggests that sports would not be possible without language—an idea implicit in the ideal of literacy. In ages when written language emerged, sporting events become part of social life. Visual representations (such as petroglyphs and the later hieroglyphics), while not exactly a statement about the awareness of exercise, contain enough elements to confirm that not only immediate, purposeful physical activity (running after a wild animal, for instance) and the exercise and maintenance of the physical were, at least indirectly, acknowledged. Testimony to the effect that at a certain moment in time the community started providing for the physically talented—in the tombs of the Egyptian Pharaoh Beni Hasan the whole gamut of wrestling is documented in detail—helps us understand that labor division and increased efficiency are in a relation that goes far beyond cause and effect. The specialization, which probably started at that time, resulted not just from the availability of resources, but also from the willingness to allocate them in ways that make the sports experience possible because a certain necessity was acknowledged.

The pattern of kicking a ball in *kemari* and the pattern of language use in the same culture are not directly connected. Nevertheless, the game has a configurational nature: the aim is to maintain the ball in the air for as long as possible. Soccer, even football, are sequential: the aim is to score higher than the opposing team. In the first case, the field is marked by four different trees: willow, cherry, pine, and maple. In the second, it is marked by artificial boundaries outside of which the game rules become meaningless. The languages of the cultures in which such games appeared are characterized by different structures that correspond to very different practical experiences. The logic embodied in each language system affects, in turn, the logic of the sports experience. *Kemari* is not only non-predicative and configurational, but also infused by the principle of *amé,* in which things are seen as deeply interdependent. Soccer and football are analytical, games of planning, texts whose final point is the goal or the touchdown. No surprise then, that mentality, as a form of expressing the influence of practical experience in some patterned expectation, plays a role, too.

There are many extremely individualistic forms of competition, and others of collective effort. While in today's global market mentality plays a different role than in the past, it still affects sports in its non-standard form. These and other qualifiers are relevant to understanding how different practical experiences constitute different instances of human objectification, sports being one of these. Even when the sports instance is disconnected from the experience that made it necessary, it is still affected by all the structural elements that define the pragmatic context. Indeed, while there is a permanency to sports—involvement of the human body—there is also a large degree of variation corresponding to successive pragmatic circumstances.

Sport is also a means of expression. During the action, it externalizes physical capabilities, but also intellectual qualities: self-control, coordination, planning. Initially, physical performance complemented rudimentary language. Afterwards the two took different paths, without actually ever separating entirely (as the Greek Olympics fully document). When language reached some of its relative limits, expression through sports substituted for it: not even the highest literate expression could capture the drama of competition, the tragedy of failure, or the sublimity of victory. But more interesting is what language extracted from the experience of sports. Language captured characteristics of the sports experience and generalized them. Through language, they were submitted, in a new form, to experiences very different from sports: sports for warfare, athletics for instilling a sense of order, competitions as *circus* for the masses.

But primarily, people derived from sports the notion of competitiveness, accepted as a national characteristic, as well as a characteristic of education, of art, of the market.

Rationalized in language, the notion of competition introduces the experience of comparing, later of measuring, and thus opens the door to the bureaucracy of sports and the institutionalized aspects we today take for granted. Greeks cared for the winner. Time-keeping devices were applied to sports later, more precisely at the time when keeping records became relevant within the broader pragmatics of documentary ownership and inheritance. While playing does not require language, writing helped in establishing uniform rules that eventually defined games. The institution of playing, represented by organized competitions, is the result of the institution of literacy, and reflects pragmatic expectations pertinent to literacy.

In every sports experience, there is a romantic notion of nature and freedom, reminiscent of the experience of hunting, fishing, and foraging. But at the same time, sports experiences testify to changes in the condition of human beings as they relate to the natural environment, their natural condition, social environment, and the artificial world resulting from human practice. Target shooting, or, more recently, *Nintendo*-type aiming with laser beams, is at the other end of the gamut. The circumstances of human experience that made literacy necessary affected the status of the sports experience as well. The contest became a product with a particular status; the prize reflects the sign process through which competition is evaluated.

Allen Guttman distinguished several characteristics of modern sports: secularism, equality of opportunity, specialization of roles, rationalization, bureaucratic organization, quantification, and quest for records. What he failed to acknowledge is that such characteristics are not relevant unless considered in connection to the recurrent patterns of sports seen against the background of the general pragmatic framework. Once we make such connections, we notice that efficiency is more important than the so-called equality of opportunity, quantification, and bureaucratic organization. The quest for efficiency appropriate to the new scale of humankind is exactly what today affects literacy's degree of necessity.

The quest for efficiency in sports becomes evident when we compare the changes from the very sophisticated, indeed obscure, rules governing sports performances in ritualistic cultures (Indian, Chinese, Mayan, Apache) with the tendency to simplify these rules and make the sports experience as transparent as possible. When certain African tribes adopted the modern game of soccer, they placed it in the context of their rituals. The entire set of premises on which the game is based, and which pertain to a culture so different from that of the African tribes, was actually dismissed, and premises of a different nature were attached as a frame for the adopted game. Consequently, the *Inyanga* (witch-doctor) became responsible for the outcome; the team and supporters had to spend the night before the game together around a campfire; goats were sacrificed. In such instances, the ceremony, not the game, is the recurrent pattern; winning or losing is of secondary importance. Once such tribes entered literate civilization, the utilitarian aspect became dominant. If we take European soccer and extend it to the American game of football, we can understand how new patterns are established according to conditions of human practice of a different structural nature. This discussion cannot be limited to the symbolism of the two games, or of any other sport. The attached meaning corresponds to the interpreted practical experience and does not properly substitute for the recurrent patterns which actually constitute the experience as a projection of the humans involved.

What is of interest here is that literacy was a powerful instrument for structuring practical experiences, such as sports (among others), in the framework of a dynamics of interaction specific to industrial society. As the cradle of the industrial age, England is also the place where many sports and experiences associated with physical exercise started. But once the dynamics changed, some of the developments that the Industrial Revolution made necessary became obsolete. An example is national isolation. Literacy is an instrument of national distinction. By their nature, sports experiences are, or should be, above and beyond artificial national boundaries. Still, as past experiences show (the 1936 Olympics in Berlin was only the climax) and current experiences confirm (national obsession with medals in more recent Olympics), sports in the civilization of literacy, like many other practical experiences, is tainted by nationalism. Competition often degenerates into an adversarial relation and conflict. In the physical exercises of ancient Greece, China, or India, performance was not measured. The patterns were those of physical harmony, not of comparison; of aesthetics, not of functionality. In England, sports became an institution, and performance entered into the record books. Indeed, in England, the history of competitions was written to justify why sports were for the upper, educated classes, and should be kept for amateurs willing to enjoy victory as a reward.

Some games were invented in the environment of the civilization of literacy and meant to accomplish functions similar to those fulfilled by literacy. They changed as the conditions of the practice of literacy changed, and became more and more an expression of the new civilization of more languages of a limited domain. In the information age, where much of language is substituted by other means of expression, sports are an experience that results primarily in generating data. For someone attracted by the beauty of a tennis game, the speed of a serve is of secondary relevance. But after a while, one realizes that tennis has changed from its literate condition to a condition in which victory means obliteration of the game. A very strong and fast serve transforms the game into a ledger of hits and misses. Quite similar is the dynamics of baseball, football, basketball, and hockey, all generators of statistics in which the experts find more enjoyment than from the actual event. The dynamics of changes in the nature and purpose of sports is related to what makes the sports experience today another instance in the process of diversification of languages and the demotion of the necessity of literacy.

The dynamics of the change from the sports experience embodying the ideal of a harmoniously developed human being to that of high performance is basically the same as the dynamics of change behind any other form of human projection. Structurally, it consists of the transition from direct forms of interaction with the outside world to more and more mediated interrelations. Chasing an animal that will eventually be caught and eaten is a performance directly related to survival. In addition to the physical aspect, there are other elements that intervene in the relation hunter-hunted: how to mask the presence of one's odor from the prey; how to attract game (through noise or lure); how to minimize energy expended to succeed (where to hit the prey, and when). Ritual, magic, and superstition were added, but did not always enhance the outcome.

Running for the maintenance and improvement of physical qualities is immediate, but still less direct in relation to the outcome than in hunting. The activity displays an understanding of connections: What do muscle tone, heartbeat, resilience, and volition have to do with our life and work, with our health? It also testifies to our efforts to preserve a certain sense of time and space (lost in the artificial environments of our homes or workplaces) and projects sheer physical existence. Running for pleasure, as we suppose animals do when young and enjoying security (think about puppies!) is different from running with a purpose such as hunting an animal, catching someone (friend or foe), running after a ball, or against a record. Running for survival is not a specialized experience; running in a war game implies some specialization; becoming the world champion in field and track is a specialized effort for whose outcome many people work. In the first case, the reason is immediate; in the second, less direct; in the third, mediated in several ways: the notion of running to compete, the distance accepted by all involved (athletes, spectators, organizations), the value attached, the meaning assigned, the means used in training and diet, the running costume. Before specialization, which is exclusive commitment to a particular practical experience, socially acknowledged selection took place. Not everybody had the physical and mental qualities appropriate to high sports performance. In the background, the market continuously evaluates what becomes, to variable degrees, a marketable product: the champion. In the process, the human being undergoes alienation, sometimes evinced through pain, other times ignored—books never read don't hurt. People tend to remember the festive moments in a champion's life, forgetting what leads to victory: hard work, difficult choices, numerous sacrifices, and the hardship inflicted on the bodies and minds engaged in the effort of extracting the maximum from the athlete.

How literate should an athlete be? The question is not different from how literate a worker, farmer, engineer, ballerina, or scientist should be. Sports and literacy used to be tightly associated in a given context. The entire collegiate sports world (whose origin in 19th century Britain was already alluded to) embodies this ideal. *Mens sana in corpore sano*—a healthy mind in a healthy body—was understood along the line of the practical experience involving literacy as a rule for achieving high efficiency in sports. Some forms of sport are a projection from language and literacy to the physical experience. Tennis is one example, and possibly the best known. Such forms of sport were designed by literates and disseminated through the channels of literacy. *Collegiate sports* is their collective name. But once the necessity of literacy itself became less stringent, such sports started emancipating themselves from the confinements of language and developed their own languages. When winning became the aim, efficiency in specific sports terms became paramount and started being measured and recorded.

Literates are not necessarily the most efficient in sports where physical prowess or quick scoring are needed to win: football, basketball, or baseball, as compared to long-distance running, swimming, or even the exotic sport of archery. This statement might seem tainted by stereotype or prejudice to which one falls prey when generalizing from a distorted past practical experience (affected by all kinds of rules, including those of sex and race discrimination). What is discussed here is not the stereotypical illiterate athlete, or the no less stereotypical aristocrat handling Latin and his horse with the same elegance, but the environment of sports in general. People involved in the practical experience of sports are sometimes seen as exceptionally endowed physically, and less so intellectually. This does not have to be so; there is really nothing inherent in sports that would result in the intellect-physique dichotomy, one to the detriment of the other. Examples of athletes who also achieved a high level of intellectual development can be given: Dr. Roger Bannister, the runner who broke the four-minute mile barrier; William Bradley, the former basketball player who became a United States senator; Michael Reed, once defense lineman who is now a concert pianist; Jerry Lucas, now a writer; Michael Lenice, a wide receiver who became a Rhodes Scholar. They are, nevertheless, the exception, not because one kind of experience is counterproductive to the other, but because the expectations of efficiency make it very difficult for one and the same person to perform at comparable levels as athletes and as intellectuals. Specialization in sports, no less than in any human activity, requires a focus of energy and talent. Choices, too, come with a price tag.

While literacy does not result in higher performance in sports, a limited notion of sports literacy, i.e., control of the *language* of sports, allows for improved performance. It is relevant to analyze how today's sports experience requires the specialized language and the understanding of what makes higher performance, and thus higher efficiency, possible. Once sport is understood as a practical experience of human self-constitution, we can examine the type of knowledge and skill needed to reach the highest efficiency. Knowledge of the human body, nutrition, physics, chemistry, biology, and psychology is important. Information focused on reaching high performance has been accumulated for each form of physical exercise. As a result of the experience itself, as well as through import of pertinent knowledge from other domains of human activity, expertise becomes more and more focused. In some ways, the commonalty of the experience diminished while the specific aspect increased.

For instance, on the basketball court, as we see it in various neighborhoods, playing is the major goal. Rules are loosely respected; players exert themselves for the pleasure of the effort. One meets others, establishes friendships, finds a useful way of getting physical exercise. On the professional basketball team, various experts coordinated by a coach make possible an experience of efficiency predictable to a great extent, programmable within limits, original to some measure. The effort to coordinate is *facilitated* through natural language; but the expectation of efficiency in achieving a goal—winning the game—extends beyond the experience constituted in and communicated through language. Games are minutely diagrammed; the adversary's plays are analyzed from videotapes; new tactics are conceived, and new strategies followed. In the end, the language of the game itself becomes the medium for the new game objectives. In the last 30 seconds of a very tight game, each step is calculated, each pass evaluated, each fault (and the corresponding time) pre-programmed.

Technology mediates and supports sports performance in ways few would imagine when watching a volleyball team in action or a runner reaching the finish line. There are ways, not at all requiring the tools of literacy. To capture recurrent patterns characteristic of high efficiency performance and to emulate or improve them, adapt them to the type of sportsperson prepared for a certain contest, becomes part of the broader experience. Indeed, boundaries are often broken, rules are bent, and victories are achieved through means which do not exactly preserve the noble ideal of equal opportunity or of fairness.

Sports experiences were always at the borderline. A broken rule became the new rule. Extraneous elements (mystical, superstitious, medical, technological, psychological) were brought into the effort to maximize sports performance. The entire story of drugs and steroids used to enhance athletic prowess has to be seen from the same perspective of efficiency against the background of generalized illiteracy. The languages of stimuli, strategies, and technology are related, even if some appear less immoral or less dangerous. As drugs become more sophisticated, it is very difficult to assess which new record is the result of pure sports and which of biochemistry. And it is indeed sad to see sportsmen and sportswomen policed in their private functions in order to determine how much effort, how much talent, or how much steroid is embodied in a performance.

Stories of deception practiced within the former totalitarian states of Europe might scare through gruesome detail. People risked their lives for the illusion of victory and the privileges associated with it. But after the ideological level is removed, we face the illiterate attitude of means and methods intended to extract the maximum from the human being, even at the price of destroying the person. Whether a state encourages and supports these means, or a free market makes them available, is a question of responsibility in the final analysis. Facts remain facts, and as facts they testify to the commercial democracy in which one has access to means that bring victory and reward, just as they bring the desired cars, clothes, houses, alcohol, food, or art collections. Among the records broken at the Olympic games in Atlanta is the number of samples collected for doping control (amounting to almost 20 percent of the number of athletes).

American football is possibly the first *post-modern* game in that it appropriates from the old for use in a new age. Comparing American football with sports of different pragmatic frameworks—to tennis, volleyball, or rugby—one can notice the specialization, mediation, new dynamics, and language of the game. There are twenty-two positions and special formations for place kicks, kick-offs, and receiving. There are also support personnel for different functions: owners, managers, coaches, trainers, scouts, doctors, recruiters, and agents. The game is burdened with literacy-based assumptions: it is as totalitarian as any language, although its elementary repertory is quite reduced—running, blocking, tackling, catching, throwing, kicking.

Rules implicit in the civilization of literacy—all know the language and use it according to its rule, sequentiality, centralism—are observed. The word signal, snap numbers, color code, and play name are part of the semiosis. It is a minimal rule experience, which seems a comedy to someone who never watched it before. The players are dressed in ridiculous gear. They seem actors in a cheap show, and act according to plans shared through private code.

As opposed to many games that we can only sketchily retrace to someplace back in history, we know how all this came about in American football. The goal was no longer the game, as it was in its early history as a college sports, but winning. A more efficient game required more efficient football *machines*, specialized in a limited repertory, present only for the duration of their task. The game acquired a configurational aspect, takes place at many levels, requires distribution of tasks, and relies upon networks of communication for maintaining some sense of integration. Its violence, different from the staged buffoonery of wrestling, is in sync with the spirit of belligerence implicit in today's competitive environment: "We teach our boys to spear and gore.... We want them to plant that helmet right under a guy's chin." (Woody Hayes, legendary coach at Ohio State University, better known for its football team than its academic standards). There is physical involvement, injury, steroids, drugs, illicit money—and there are statistics. The spirit of the game is disseminated to other sports and other aspects of life (business, politics). In the case of baseball, the statistics are most important. They attach to each gesture on the field a meaning which otherwise would escape the mind of the viewer. In games of a more continuous flow (soccer, tennis, handball), the attraction is in the particular phase, not in the number of yards gained or the average (hits, home runs, strike-outs).

The general dynamics of existence and human interaction in the civilization of illiteracy also marked the dynamics of the practical experience of sports. Higher speed, shorter encounters, short action spans—these make the sports event more marketable in the environment of the new civilization. The more precise the experience, the less expressive. Almost no one watched the compulsory ice skating exercises at world championships, and so they were canceled, but millions enjoy the dramatics of dancing on ice that is becoming more and more a show watched around the world. The more extensive the effort, the less attractive to spectators. A twenty-five kilometer cross-country competition will never interest as many viewers as a fast, dangerous downhill race. These characteristics are definitive of the civilization of illiteracy. People do not want to learn how to perform at the same level; knowledge is irrelevant. Performance is what attracts, and it is the only thing which gains prizes that the winner of the ancient Olympics, who was also spoiled, never dreamed of. "Winner take all" is the final rule, and the result is that winning, more than competing, has become the goal.

The efficiency requirement leads not only to the relative illiteracy of those involved in sports, but also to a practice of discriminatory physical selection. In the USA, for instance, black African-Americans dominate football and basketball, which have become national obsessions. If equal opportunity were applied to professional sports as it is to other activities, the competitions would not be so attractive. The irony of this situation is that, in fact, black African-Americans are still entertainment providers in the USA. Regardless of how profitable professional sports are, the obsession with efficiency effectively consecrates an important segment of the population to entertaining the rest. Blacks are also playing in the most advanced major basketball leagues in the world. In what used to be the Soviet Union, chances were that the winter sports teams would be recruited from the Siberian population, where skiing is a way of life. All over Europe, soccer teams recruit from Spain, Italy, Africa, and South America. It is easier to attain maximum efficiency through those endowed with qualities required by the new goals of the games instead of creating a broad base of educated athletes.

The public, homogenized through the mediating action of television, is subjected to the language of the sports experience and is presented with performance and interpretation at the same time. Thus, even the mechanism of assigning meaning is rationalized, taken over by the market mechanism, freed from the constraints of literacy and reason, and rendered to human subjects without requiring that they think about it.

Blaming changes in sports, or for that matter in literacy, the condition of the family, the fast-food curse, television, increased greed, new technology, or lower levels of education, results in only partial explanations of the new condition of sports. Yes, the greatly celebrated champions are illiterate. No matter how good in their political game of finding excuses and alibis, colleges care for the high performances of physically gifted students, recruited only insofar as they add to the marketability of the institution, not to the academic entry requirements. Literacy is not a prerequisite for sports performance. It might actually interfere with it. In the world of competitions, sportsmen and sportswomen are either jetting around the globe or traveling from one exhibition game to another, barely able to breathe, never mind to take care of their literacy or their private lives. Their language is one of pitiful limitation, always inferior to the energy spent in the effort or externalized in frustration when the rules don't work in their favor. They don't read, they don't write. Even their checks are signed by others. The description might be somewhat extreme and sound harsh, and the attitude might seem impertinent, but after all, it is not because sportsmen and sportswomen know Shakespeare's sonnets by heart that people watch baseball, nor because they write novels (or even short stories) that the public applauds the ice skating dancers, and even less that they keep diaries, with minimal spelling errors and full sentences, that spectators die to be on the stand of the stadium where the drama of football starts in the fall and ends shortly before another sports takes over the media.

Sports are marketable work, of high intensities and no literate status. The efficiency of each sport is measured in the attraction it exercises over many people, and thus in the ability of a sport to transmit messages of public interest, insofar as public interest is part of the market process. Alienated from the expectation of integration, corresponding to the ideal of the complete human being, sport is as specialized as any other form of human praxis. Sports constituted their own domains of competence and performance, and generate expectations of partial sport literacies. That in the process, because they address physical attributes and intellectual functions, sports became a molding machine for the athletes, another *nature,* should not go without saying or understanding what it takes to succeed. All over the world, where efficiency reached levels corresponding to the new scale of humankind, football, basketball, soccer, and tennis players, swimmers, runners, and gymnasts are created almost from scratch. Experts select children, analyze their genetic history and current condition, devise training procedures, and control diet, psychology, and emotional life until the desired performer is ready to compete.

GENTLEMEN, PLACE YOUR BETS!

The investment in sports, as in the stock market, is supposed to return profit. Successful sportspeople need not testify to how high their own return is. That this return also means compromised physical or mental integrity is part of the cynical equation that the public enthusiastically validates. When players are traded and contracts are signed, the money they earn, disproportionate as it seems at times, corresponds, almost to the last digit, to the number of people who will watch them, some for the sake and pleasure of the performance, others making money from a team's victory or an athlete's record. In some states and countries, whether betting is legal or prohibited, it is by far the strongest sector of the economy. It takes very interesting forms, however. One is the direct bet: this horse, this player, this team.

Betting, with its partial literacy involving its own mediating elements that render reading and writing useless, is not a new institution. People were challenged by the odds down through history. But once the structural change that entailed means of networking, task distribution, and almost instant access to any event in the world was in place, the experience of betting totally took over that of competing. All our unfulfilled desires and drives are now embodied by those we choose to represent us, and for whose victory we not only root, but also invest in. There is an ideal stake—the successful player—and a mundane stake—the actual wager. Expectation of high figures is an extension of literate expectations. It embodies the naive assumption that cultivated minds and challenged bodies unite in a balanced personality of high integrity. The reason this model failed over and over need not be restated here. But the point needs to be made that the ideal stake and the trivial stake are not independent. This introduces to competition an element of obscurity in the form of motivations not intrinsic to sports. The indirect wager represents this element.

THE MESSAGE IS THE SNEAKER

The biggest indirect bet is made by marketing and advertising. On the never-ending table of Olympic records, the most spectacular performances are dollar signs preceding figures into the billions. Within the general shift from manufacturing to service economy characteristic of the civilization of illiteracy, sport becomes a form of entertainment. New media, replacing the printed word as the dominant means of communication, makes possible international viewing of competitions as they happen. In the past, we were satisfied with the image of the winner. Now we can own the tape of the game and can retrieve each moment of any event. More broadband, and soon we will download the running athlete directly onto our monitors. For a price, of course (as in pay per view).

People consume sports. They are able to fly to the Olympics, wherever the best bid takes them (Barcelona, Atlanta, or Sydney), even able to pay for forty-five minutes or a whole week of shaping up with the very best trainers. Facts in the world of sports, as much as in the rest of our activities, are less important than the image. The authority and self-discipline, on which physical education was built, are replaced by the freedom and opportunity to choose from among many sports events, and by an attitude of permissiveness and self-indulgence which many times results in considering the whole world as a sports show. Sports are used to further many causes and support many interest groups. On the stage of the events they sponsor, the world's largest companies compete with feminism, equal opportunity, AIDS, and various disabilities for the attention and dollars of the audience. Sponsorship is a highly selective experience. Nevertheless, it frequently contradicts the slogans it sets before the public. These are important because the indirect bet on sports takes into consideration the huge market of entertainment, and defines within this market the segments it will address.

Product endorsements, advertising, and public relations are the media through which marketing places its bets. No less than 500,000 brands were traded in Atlanta. Only to keep track of them was a major task, described officially as "protecting the integrity of the Olympic Games and the rights of official sponsors," but also "detecting attempts at parasitic marketing." Every square inch on the body of a tennis player or a track and field athlete can be rented. And is. The better the manager (not necessarily a player's game), the higher the endorsement contract. The minute detail picked up by the camera allows us to see the name of the maker on the watch, the manufacturer's logo on the socks, a sponsor company's name on the shirts and headgear, the brand of glucose or mineral water, the maker of ice or snow for winter games. It seems that the competition on the court and the competition among those who buy the space available on cyclists' ware, football players' uniforms, skiers, swimmers, runners, and chess players are feeding off one another. When the Canon company chose as its prime-time advertising actor a tennis player who did not make it beyond the preliminary games, the bet continued on the waves, on the screens, on the videotapes, and on any other imaginable display.

Marshall McLuhan plays year after year in the Superbowl. The world indeed becomes a village. Moreover, the world has almost decided that the outcome is less important than the new commercials, the new thirty-second drama, followed by the numbers telling us all how much more a second of prime time costs, and what benefits it might bring. But the message is actually lost. Here McLuhan was still somehow captive to literacy, believing there was a message, as we are used to when writing or reading a text. The message is the sneaker, or whatever will take over, for its own short turn in the glory of consumption, the world. The day the object is acknowledged, between New York and Zambia, Paris and the tribes in the Brazilian rain forests, Frankfurt and the starving populations of Africa or Asia, there will be a trade in the original and its many substitutes, reaching sheer madness. Sports entrusted with the marketing image are equalled in their persuasive power only by the entertainment stars, of similar illiterate condition, singing for the world's hungriest only in order to add one more marketing craze to their torment.

In these and in other characteristics mentioned, the unnatural aspect of sports takes over their original, natural component. It seems almost as though the sports experience is falling into itself, is imploding, leaving room for the many machines and gadgets we use at home in order to salvage our degenerating bodies. Now we still bicycle, ski, climb stairs, and row in the privacy of our rooms, with our eyes glued to the images of the very few who still do the real thing, but for reasons less and less connected with excellence. Soon we will swim in the pools and ski on the slopes of virtual reality. Some are already timing their performance. Little do they know that they are pioneering one of the many Olympic games of the future.

CHAPTER 7: SCIENCE AND PHILOSOPHY—MORE QUESTIONS THAN ANSWERS

> Words strain,
> Crack and sometimes break,
>   under the burden,
> Under the tension, slip, slide,
>   perish,
> Decay with imprecision, will
>   not stay in place,
> Will not stay still.
> T.S. Elliot, *Burnt Norton*

In some of the most advanced fields of scientific inquiry, research results are exchanged as soon as they become available. Obviously, the sluggish medium of print and the long cycles involved in the review process prior to academic publication do not come into the picture. On Web sites dedicated to research, the review process consists of acknowledging, challenging, and furthering breakthrough hypotheses. It is carried out by real peers, not by the geriatric or opportunistic hierarchies that have the publishing process in their firm grip. Frequently, research is carried out in and through the communication media. Images, data, and simulations are part of the work and part of the shared knowledge, already available in formats that can be inputted for further work or can be technologically tested.

Of course, there are many issues connected to the new dynamics of science, not the least of which is intellectual property and integrity. A totally new experience in research and knowledge dissemination is taking place. The majority of the researchers involved know that previous models, originating in the pragmatics of the civilization of literacy, will not provide answers. As beautiful as the science embodied in the technology of industrial society is, it will not, not even accidentally, contribute to the scientific progress in nanotechnology, in bioinformatics, in fluid dynamics, and in other frontier domains researched today. Gene expression and protein syntheses are many *working centuries*—the total of the years contributed by researchers to the advancement of their respective fields—ahead of everything that science has produced in the past. Add to these accomplishments in the ever-expanding list of modern sciences, and you get the feeling that humankind is literally reinventing itself in the civilization of illiteracy.

The list to follow is telling of the shift from the coarse level of scientific effort corresponding to the industrial operations of milling and grinding, to a level of atomic and sub-atomic re-ordering. The same components, differently ordered, can appear to us as graphite or diamonds, sand or silicon for chips. The list represents a reality of enormous consequence, confirmed in the daily commotion of a never-ending series of discoveries. Life on Mars, molecular self-assembly, protein folding, atomic resolution imaging, nano-structural materials with unprecedented properties, quantum devices, advances in neuro-medicine—the list is a shameless exercise in creating headlines, soon to be replaced by newer and more creative endeavors. This is why, in addressing issues of science and philosophy, I do not intend to offer a catalogue of current research, but to put the subject in a dynamic perspective. By all means, I want to avoid the danger of presenting science especially as the agent of change, as though its own motivations and means could give humankind its direction and purpose.

RATIONALITY, REASON, AND THE SCALE OF THINGS

The dynamics of change in scientific and philosophic thinking is not independent of the underlying structure of the pragmatics that leads to the civilization of illiteracy. Both involve rationality, which connects human practical experiences to consistent inferences (sometimes seen as logical conclusion) and to the ability to predict events (in nature or society), even to influence and control them. Rationality is connected to efficiency insofar as it is applied in the selection of means appropriate to accomplishing goals; or it serves as an instrument for evaluation of the premises leading to a selected course of action. In short, rationality is goal oriented. Reason, in turn, is value oriented; it guides practical experiences of human self-constitution in the direction of appropriateness. Rationality and reason are interconditioned. Right and wrong, good and bad, are the axes along which human action and emotion can be diagrammed in the matrix of living and working that they constituted under the guise of literacy.

The process through which human rationality and reason become characteristics of human self-constitution is long and tortuous. People defining themselves in different pragmatic contexts enter into a network of interdependency. At a very small scale of human existence and activity, rationality and reason were indistinguishable. They began to differentiate early on, already during hunting and gathering. But during the long experience of settlement and taking care of plants and animals, they grew aware of the distinction between what they were doing and how. With the culture of artifacts, to which tools belong, reason and rationality took separate paths. With the advent of science, in its most primitive forms, documented in ancient China, Egypt, India, and Greece, rationality and reason often conflicted. Things can be right, without being good at the same time. There is a rationality—goal oriented: how to get more goods, how to avoid losses—with the appearance of reason—actions to please forces supposed to control nature or matter. Parallel to science, magic manifested itself through alchemy, astrology, and numerology, all focused on the attempt to harmonize human beings, constituted in practical experiences focused on goodness, with the world housing them. In some cultures, rationality resulted in the propensity to face, change, and eventually dominate nature—that is, to submit the environment to a desired order. Reason aimed at finding practical grounds for harmony with nature.

After the phase of orality, writing served both of them equally. It made language a mold for new experiences, a container for storing knowledge, and an effective means for the practical experience of evaluation and self-evaluation. The overwhelming majority of human accomplishments leading to the possibility and necessity of literacy were connected to the experience of human self-constitution in writing. The science and philosophy upon which the scientific revolution and the revival of humanities (in particular philosophy) of the 16th and 17th centuries took place are deeply rooted in the pragmatics that made writing necessary. This revolution is usually summarized through three main accomplishments. First: a new picture of the universe, scientifically expressed in heliocentric astronomy and philosophically a turning point in understanding the role of the human being in this world. Second: the mathematical description of motion. Third: the new conceptual framework of mechanics. As impressive as they are, their meaning is revealed in the fact that the Industrial Revolution was actually triggered by the scientific and humanistic renewal embodied in these accomplishments. The change from an agrarian economy, appropriate to a relatively reduced scale of population and work, to industrial production changed efficiency by orders of magnitude corresponding to those of the critical mass reached by humankind. All the characteristics of this new pragmatics—sequentiality, linearity, centralism, determinism (mechanical in nature), clear-cut distinctions, interdependencies—contributed to the establishment of literacy.

A LOST BALANCE

Within the pragmatic framework of the industrial society, science progressively assumed the leading role over philosophy. In fact, science changed from an elitist practical experience strongly controlled by the guardians of literacy (i.e., religion) to an experience integrated in society. Philosophy followed an inverse path, from a generalized attitude of wonder to becoming the privilege of the few who could afford to contemplate the world. Generalized in technology, the rationality of science reached its peak in the civilization of literacy through standardization and mass production of processed food, means of transportation (cars, airplanes), home building, and the use of electricity as the efficient alternative energy source. But the real challenge was yet to come.

Einstein took a daring guess. "The tragedy of modern men...is that they created conditions of existence for which, from the perspective of their phylogenetic development, they are not adjusted." The lost balance between rationality and reason is reflected in the image of all the consequences of the Industrial Revolution that led to the runaway capitalism of the 19th and 20th centuries. Exhaustion of raw materials, air and water pollution, erosion of productive land, and mental and physical strain on humans are the concrete results of this imbalance.

But if these consequences were all people and society had to cope with, the dominance of literacy in science would still be defensible. The challenge comes from the new scale of humankind for which the Industrial Revolution model and literacy are no longer adequate. Efficiency expectations, of an order of magnitude incompatible with the underlying structure of the pragmatic framework based on literacy, result in the need for a new dynamics, for mediation, acknowledgment and use of non-linearity, vagueness, and non-determinism. Science, as well as the implicit philosophic component of this new science, already approached areas of knowledge beyond the borderline guarded by literacy. On the initial success of micro-physics, the first non-literacy-based technological challenge for more energy was met in the form of relatively rudimentary weapons. In the meanwhile, it became clear that a new physics and a new chemistry, and a new biology, along with many disciplines non-existent within literacy, of a systemic focus with quality and process is what we need. Some of the scientific themes mentioned already illustrate how science is evolving. They also illustrate how a new epistemological condition is established, one that is based on projecting explanatory models upon the world and testing them for appropriateness and coherence. In the lead are practical experiences of science driven by cognitive resources no longer constrained by observation. What is free of epistemological doubt is that almost all the science that has emerged has reclaimed interest in the living. These new sciences, which are philosophies at the same time, are computationally disclosed biophysics, biochemistry, molecular biology, genetics, medicine, and knowledge of the micro- and nano-universe.

Literacy, because of its inherent structural characteristics, is no longer the appropriate mold for such new experiences, the proper container for knowledge, or even an effective means of evaluation. Among many possible literacies, it maintains a domain of appropriateness, and within this domain it allows for local performance synchronized with the general expectation of efficiency. The shift from literacy to literacies—in fact, the shift to the pragmatic framework of the civilization of illiteracy—takes place against the background of conflict between means of restricted efficiency and new means for coping with larger populations, and with the newly acquired right to well-being, or even affluence. Almost all new sciences evolve in new technologies. We are already familiar with some, since we were told that from science programs (space exploration, genetic research, biophysics), products as trivial as calculators, thermal fabric, and new construction materials were made available at prices affordable in the global economy. We are getting used to others as they become available: intelligent materials able to alter their structure, and self-assembling materials.

One dominant inherited assumption is that thinking takes place only in language; that is, that language is the medium of thinking. This is a very difficult subject to deal with because, despite claims to the contrary, some people (Einstein is most quoted witness) maintain that they think in images, others in sounds, others in some combination of shapes, colors, textures, even odor and taste. Until now, no one could conclusively prove whether this is a way of speaking or a fact. But the same can be said of language. That we can express thoughts, sometimes frustratingly incomplete, in language does not necessarily mean that we think in language, or *only* in language. That language is a medium for explanation and interpretation, well adapted to support incomplete inductions or deductions, and sometimes hypothetical thinking (so-called abductions), is not necessarily the proof that it is the only one. Scientists think in the language of mathematical or logical formalism, or in some of the new programming languages, even if they do not carry on dialogue or try to write poetry or love letters in such languages.

Literacy, as a socially encompassing ideal, states that people should be literate because people think in language. Accordingly, proper use of language, as set forth in the rules of literacy, is a premise for successful thinking. Besides introducing circularity—the premise turns out to be the conclusion—this is a strong assumption, with too many implications for science and for philosophy to be left unchallenged. The assumption was never entirely proven; and it is probably impossible to prove, given the strong connection between *all* signs participating in thinking processes. Images call up words, but so do odors, flavors, textures, and sounds. Words recall or trigger images, music, etc. The *integrated* nature of thinking is probably affected by mechanisms of voluntary decision-making or by genetic mechanisms structured to accept a certain sign system (language, mathematical formalism, diagrams) as dominant, without precluding modes of thought different from those resulting from the premise of literacy.

If defining thinking as language processing resulted in human experiences possible only under this assumption, there are also other ways to define thinking which, in turn, may become, if they haven't yet, necessary and beneficial. In this respect, one question can be raised: Are thinking machines, i.e., programs able to autonomously perform operations we associate with human thinking, excluded from the discussion because they do not qualify as literate? Many scientific endeavors of our time would not have started if potential success were to be put to a literacy test. The area of new materials, able to fix themselves, and of machines resulting from self-assembly belong among our examples. Fortunately, science based on alternative practical human experiences, fairly independent of language and literacy, discovered that there are complementary ways to define thinking, and rationality, for that matter. Considering thinking together with other human traits, such as emotion, sense of humor, aesthetics, the ability to project ideas through various media, senses or languages will probably lead to even more daring scientific research.

Before considering alternative ways to define thinking and the relation between rationality and human reason, let us look at the characteristics of thinking in current praxis, science and philosophy included. The amount of language we need to function in the workplace and in social life has diminished in comparison to previous circumstances of human experience. If thinking took place only in language, that would mean that thinking itself has diminished. Very few people would be inclined to accept this conclusion. The small subset of language used in social life and in professional interaction is representative of the segmented nature of this life and of the interactions it supports. This small subset of language, the command of which does not require literacy skills, is composed of social stereotypes, but is not sufficient to constitute a medium for thinking. Parallel to the diminished subset of natural language, the languages of science and technology expanded as expectations of scientific and technological efficiency increased. Expressions in the small subset of natural language that people use in order to function are generated regardless of the requirement of variety and change in our reciprocal relations. As *canned* expressions of limited function, they are taken over from previous circumstances, and used independently of what once determined their need. Chances are that an illiterate neighbor will never be noticed since everything pertaining to the social status of such a neighbor is literacy independent: driving, washing clothes, cooking, banking, telephoning, watching television, connecting to the Internet. The trained illiterate can perform these tasks and those pertinent to work perfectly without ever displaying a literacy handicap. No doubt that the new machines, new materials, new foods, and new medicines that are more at the frontiers of science than in the mainstream of living and working will further affect the need and possibility of a civilization dominated by more than one of its means of expression and communication.

People can function as illiterates in societies of extreme specialization without being noticed as illiterates and without affecting the efficiency of the system to which they belong. Their own involvement in the functioning of the world in which they live is changing. Illiterate rationality is no less goal oriented than any other rationality. It is just expressed through other means. And it is no less concerned with predicting the behavior of systems driven by languages of extreme functionality, working regardless of the literacy of the operators. Scientific literacy is either stored in skills, through training, or in the systems operated by people who *know* less about their functioning than the machines themselves.

Symptoms such as misuse of words, sloppy language and grammar, use of stereotypes, the inability and even unwillingness to sustain dialogue might be telling something about thinking, too—for instance, that forms of thinking based on sign systems other than language are more effective, or more appropriate to what people do in our days; or even that appropriateness in one particular sign system does not translate into appropriateness and effectiveness in another practical experience. No wonder that science, in addition to reasons implicit in the nature of scientific inquiry, shies away from language, from its imprecision, ambiguity, and tendency to coalesce in stereotypes, or become stereotypes under circumstances of patterned use. Philosophy, by and large, follows the same tendency, although its alternatives are not comparable to those of science. The experience of science, and to a more limited degree that of philosophy, is simultaneously an experience in generating language capable of handling continuity, vagueness, and fuzzy relations. Spatial reasoning and replication of phenomena, usually associated with the living as aspects of common-sense knowledge, are also constitutive of the new science.

Extremely specialized human practical experiences are no longer predominantly experiences based on knowledge, but on constituting the person as *information integrator.* The continuous diminution of the need to think corresponds to the extreme segmentation of work and to the successful technological integration of various partial contributions resulting from this highly efficient segmented and mediated work. In one's individual life, in activities pertinent to self-maintenance (nourishment, rest, hygiene, enjoyment), the process is the same. Thinking is focused on selection: cooking one from many preprocessed meals at home, dressing in one from among many ready-made clothing items, living in pre-fabricated homes, washing objects in programmed machines. But the objects embody someone else's thinking. The *reified thinking* projected into gene manipulation, materials, and machines leads to a reduction of *live thinking.* People integrate themselves in the information network, and for a greater part of their existence they act as information processors: heat something until it pops; snap or zip to close; press a button that will adjust water temperature and wash cycle according to the type of clothes. More generally, people rely on the *living machine* that adapts to the user, re-assembles itself as requirements change, and/or fixes itself. Rationality is more and more integrated in the technology; thus it is rationalized away from the process of individual self-constitution. As tremendous as the consequences can be, they will be infinitely more dangerous if we do not start thinking about them.

Technology at this level uncouples the past from the present. Consequently, life and actual existence are alienated. Individuals do not have to think, they have to integrate themselves into the program embodying high efficiency rationality and reason. Today, knowledge of what goes into food, how preparation affects its qualities, what makes for a good shirt or sweater, what makes for a good house, what it means to wash, and how a material is affected by certain chemicals and water temperatures are rendered irrelevant. What matters is the result, not the process. What counts is efficiency, not individual know-how. Thinking is detached from thinking in the sense that all thinking, and thus rationality, is embodied outside the self-constituted human being. The appearance is that this *outside* thinking and this *outside* rationality have a life of their own. Memetic mechanisms are a testimony to the process.

In the civilization of illiteracy, we experience not only the benefits of high efficiency, but also the self-perpetuating drive of new pragmatic means. At times it appears that humans do not compete for achieving higher levels of creativity and productivity. Affluence appears as a given that takes over the need to match efficiency expectations characteristic of the global scale of humankind. To keep pace with technological progress and with scientific renewal becomes a rationale in itself, somehow disconnected from human reason. The confusing rationality of ever-increasing choices is matched by the frustrating realization that value options literally disappear, leaving no room for sensible reasoning. As a result, social and political aspects of human existence are short circuited, in particular those affecting the status of science and the condition of philosophy. Frequently, research is questioned as to whether its goals make sense at all. Only 15 years ago, half of the population in the USA suspected that science and the technology it fosters were the cause rather than the cure of many problems faced in the country, social problems included. The balance changed, but not the attitude of those captive to literacy's goals and values, who oppose science and the humanities instead of seeing them in their necessary, although contradictory, unity. Europe today, trailing badly in the new sciences, is even more reluctant to accept them. As healthy and necessary as skepticesm can be, it always comes at a price.

QUO VADIS SCIENCE?

Discovery and explanation

From among the many levels at which the issue of language in relation to science is relevant, two are critical: discovery and explanation. In all fairness, it should be said that literacy never claimed to be a way towards scientific discovery, or that language is the instrument making discovery possible. The main claim is that access to science, and thus the possibility to continue scientific work, is primarily through language. This assertion was correct in the past as long as scientific practice took place in a homogeneous cognitive context of shared representations of time and space. Once this context changed, the built-in language metrics of experience, what is called the *ratio*, the shared measure, started to get in the way of new discoveries and efficient explanations of previous discoveries. Among the many new codes scientists use today, *symbolic reasoning* (used in mathematics, logic, genetics, information science, etc.) is the most pervasive. All in all, a transition has been made from a centralized scientific practice to new experiences, which are quite often independent of each other and better adapted to the scale of the particular phenomenon of interest. This independence, as well as sensitivity to scale, results from different objects of specialized disciplines, from different perspectives, and from different sign systems structured as research tools or as medium for constituting efficient explanatory theories.

Plato would have barred entrance to the Academy to those who did not master mathematics: "Let no one enter who is not a mathematician." In today's world, the guardians of science would require logic, and others the mastery of artificial languages, such as programming languages, themselves subject to improved focus (as in object programming) and increased computational efficiency. In the time of Socrates, "the orator," language was ascertained to be constitutive of cities, laws, and the arts. In the time of the Roman poet Lucretius, physics was written in verse (7,000 lines of heroic hexameter were used to present Epicurus' atomic theory). Galileo preferred the dialogue, written in colloquial Italian, to share discoveries in physics and astronomy with his contemporaries. With Newton, equations started to replace words, and they became, almost to our time, the *vocabulary* of physics. Very similar developments took place in the evolution of science in China, India, the Middle East. The emergence of new visual or multimedia languages (of diagrams, systems of notation, visual representations, mixed data types) corresponds to the different nature of visual and multimedia experience. They are steps in the direction of deeper labor division, increased mediation, and new forms of human interaction—in particular, of a practice that is more intensional than extensional.

Time and space: freed hostages
The Encyclopedic tradition centered around the scientific human being (*l'homme scientifique*) who it defined through language. This tradition continued a line of progressive changes in humankind's scientific experience. We can learn about these changes by examining the language through which they are expressed. The syncretic stage of human activity was dominated by observations and short cycles of action-reaction. Incipient, rudimentary science was not independent of the human being's practical projection. Images and, later, names of plants, animals, mountains, and lakes pertained to the beginning. Only when the scope of observation broadened and, instead of the immediate connection, a series of connections was accounted for, did science become a praxis in itself.

Science was born together with the magical, and would continue to develop in this symbiosis. Eventually, it joined religion in opposing the magic. Observation and fear of the observed were one. Names of stars testify to changes in the language in which what we call astronomical science is embodied. Obviously there was little awareness of the *mechanics* of the cosmos during the time names changed. Mytho-magical terminology, followed by zodiac signs of magic origin (in both cases with reference to the practical activity of people during changing seasons), and by the *Christian* names (after the establishment of Christianity), is a line continued today in detailed catalogs encoding positions, dynamics, and interrelations in numeric form.

In the experience of observing the sky and in deriving the notion of duration (how long it took for celestial objects to change position), humans projected their biological and cognitive characteristics: seeing, association, comparison. Names were given and observations were made, of position mainly, but also of light intensity. With the emergent notion of time, generalized from the notion of duration, stars were no longer related to divinities. Still, astronomical observation was used to structure monastic life. Stars served as a nighttime clock. At a time of reduced scientific inquiry (Europe from the 5th century to the 10th), the observation of the skies, reflected in maps of various constellations, prepared for future progress in astronomy. Physical properties, such as intensity of light, color, and brilliancy, later suggested better names because the experience in which stars were recognized (navigation, in the first place) required identification for successful performance. Magic and science explained success in very different ways. This was the time when planets were identified through properties evident to all who *needed* the sky. The *magic* layer was projected as a result of associations people made between qualities characteristic of persons and the *behavior* of certain stars, i.e., the perceived influence they had on events pertinent to human existence. During the entire process, language served as an instrument of integration and observation, as well as a means for logical practice, such as deductions. Molding the experience of time perception, storing the acquired knowledge, and further shaping practical experiences of time, language acquired a very powerful position in the human being's self-constitution in time. This position would be strengthened by literacy, bound to generalize distinctions in language and introduce them as effective means of structuring new expectations. Only when time-dependent practical requirements, such as those of relativity, impossible to satisfy within literacy, became critical was time freed from the captivity of verbal language.

A giant cognitive step bridged the immediacy of the surroundings—where magic forces were rumored to exist, waiting for humans to free them—and the notion of space. Geometry—which literally means *to measure land*—is relevant as a practical experience of human self-constitution that unites the concrete task at hand (surveying, building, decorating, observing the sky) and the generalization of distance. Measuring land ends up not only in description of the land, but also in its reconstitution in the abstract category of space. Language was part of the process, and for as long as practical experiences in the immediate surrounding were direct, geometric conventions remained very close to their practical implications. Once distinctions beyond direct relations in space were made possible by the experience of navigation, by settled forms of social life (leading to future cities), and by strategies for successful securing and defense of land, the language of geometry changed. Internally motivated developments, as well as those rooted in forms of human praxis other than geometry, resulted in the constitution of many geometric languages.

The languages of the foundations of geometry and of algebraic, differential, or topological geometry are as different as the practical experiences from which they are derived. In many cases, literate language suffices for formulating geometric problems, but breaks down in supporting the practice of attempting solutions. Obviously enough, the intuitive visual aspect of geometry is quite often better adapted to subjects such as symmetry, higher order spaces, and convexity than is literacy. Rigid spaces and elastic spaces behave differently from spaces describable in language. Geometry frequently uses notations whose referent is rather abstract. The freeing of time and space from the captivity of language made an impact on the condition of rationality, where scientific praxis is rooted, and of reason, where philosophy originates.

Coherence and diversity

Science integrates the results of diversified experiences and expresses the perceived human need to maintain a coherent perspective of the whole. As a reaction to the establishment of a permanent and universal language embodied in the practice of literacy, partial languages of scientific focus emerged. Those who knew from their own self-constitution in scientific practice that global coherence, as preserved in language, and specialized knowledge conflict, gave up the effort to harmonize the general framework (of language) and the specialized perspective (of science). The understanding that the language of science is not simply a descriptive device, but a constitutive element of scientific practical experience, did not come easy, especially since language kept human awareness of space and time captive to its mechanism of representation. Seemingly, it was less difficult to notice how measuring some phenomena (especially in physics) changed the system observed than to understand how a scientific hypothesis expressed in language created a framework of *subjective* science. The subjectivity of the language description corresponds to a particular practical experience involving identification through language.

Particular developments in science are not identical in all scientific branches. Astronomy and geometry evolved differently from each other and from other sciences. As a result of the inherent dynamics of conflict between means and goals of sciences, a phase of liberation from language started. Once language itself reached its limits in literacy, in respect to the efficiency of the new human experiences that the current scale of humankind brought about, new languages were needed. Breaking the language barrier, with implicit emancipation from literacy, is a practical experience in itself. In this experience, two aspects of language come under scrutiny: the epistemological and the communicational. In the epistemological status, we evaluate how language is a medium for embodying science and shaping the perspective of scientific inquiry. The communicational status refers to language as a medium for sharing knowledge. The levels of problem formulation, of solutions, of interpretation, of experiment and validation, and of communication are quite different. They will continue to differentiate even more in order to be efficient. The rationality intrinsic to this new science is no longer reducible to finding the *logos* in things and phenomena, or to instill a *logos* into *techné*. This is why the legacy of Francis Bacon—the prophetic theoretician of experimental science—as well as of Descartes—whose rules for understanding dominated the literate phase of humankind's scientific practical experience—literally cease to be relevant once we move from language to languages, from literacy to illiteracy.

Computational science

Language is ambiguous, imprecise, and not neutral in respect to the phenomena observed and accounted for. For these and other reasons, researchers working within the informational paradigm needed to synthesize specialized languages designed in such ways to avoid ambiguity and make higher efficiency of automated processing possible. Many formal languages have become the new scientific *laboratories* of our time, preparing quite well for the new stage of computational disciplines. In parallel, new forms of scientific experimentation, which correspond to the complexity of the phenomena under observation and to their dynamics, were developed. These forms are known under the name *simulation* (sometimes *modeling*) and consist of observing not the behavior of the researched aspect of the world, but one or several of its descriptions.

To observe the explosion of a remote star, a time-span of data collection that extends well over the age of humankind is required. Instead of waiting (forever, so to speak), scientists model astrophysical phenomena and visualize them with the aid of sophisticated computable mathematical descriptions. These are better suited to the scale of the phenomena than all the equipment ever used for this purpose. Radio-astronomy is no longer about the stars seen through human eyes. It is not about the visible, and it is not burdened by all the history of star names. Radio-astronomy is about star systems, cosmic physics, dynamics, even about the notion, so often discarded, of the beginning of the universe. The geometry of higher (than three) space dimensions is not about the visible—the surveyed land, building, or ornament—never mind the magical spirits inhabiting it. Such geometries submit theoretical constructs supporting a practice of thinking, explaining, even acting, that is not possible without the generalization of space dimensions. Whether in the fiction of *Flatland* (Edwin Abbott's book about how different life is in lower-dimension space compared to life in what we take to be 3-dimensional reality), or in the computer graphics animated representation of the hypercube, or in the theories of higher dimension spaces (relating to Einstein's relativity theory), scientific languages, irreducible to the *general* language and non-translatable into it, are at work.

There are quite a number of similar subjects which make evident the border at which science can no longer rely on language. A non-language-based rationality—spatial reasoning, for instance—becomes necessary in this realm of inquiry. As sciences enter the age of computation, necessities become possibilities. There are subjects of research in which the brevity of a process makes impossible its direct observation and appropriate description in language. Indeed, the universe of extremely short interactions, of fast exchanges of energy, of high frequency patterns (which give the appearance of a continuum), among others, can be approached only with instruments of observation whose own inertia is lower than that of the phenomena scrutinized and with a conceptual framework for which language (of high inertia) is ill equipped.

Language preserves in its structure the experience that made it necessary; literacy does the same. This is why their sequentiality conflicts with subjects of configurational condition. This is also why linearity, inherent in the pragmatics that formed literacy, conflicts with the inherent non-linearity of the world. Many other conflicts are at work at the same time: centrality of work opposed to distribution of tasks; hierarchy and distributed networking; clear-cut distinctions and vagueness; deterministic experiences of limited scope opposed to self-configurational, chaotic processes of infinite adaptation to new circumstances; dualism as opposed to pluralism (in scientifically significant forms). At stake is the efficiency of the effort, as it approaches issues of recuperation mechanisms in nature and society, strategies of co-evolution (replacing strategies of dominance) with nature, and deploys holistic models made possible by both increased mediation and powerful integrative mechanisms. Idealizing all these possibilities would be as counterproductive as demonizing literacy-based practical experiences. Nevertheless, we need a better understanding of what no longer responds to requirements of human self-constitution under the new scale of humankind, as we need an image of the alternative practical experiences through which a new rationality is formed.

In the rapidly expanding context of parallel scientific endeavors and distributed tasks supported by speedy and reliable networks, scientific research is liberated from the industrial model. Instead of centralized institutions sharing in the use of expensive instruments, there is an increasing number of experiments taking place all over the world. Tele-presence is less expressive a name for what researchers actually perform thousands of miles away from each other, using expensive machines and various measuring and testing devices. The laboratories that once served as the place for scientific self-constitution are replaced by *collaboratories*, a combination of real instruments, which can be used more efficiently, and virtual places of research that allow for more creativity. Real-time interaction is fundamental to the context of focusing on nano-scale. Multidisciplinarity is no longer an illusion, but a practical requirement for the integration that scientific effort requires.

Explaining ourselves away
Systematic domains of human practical experiences are changing

fast. The science of the ever shorter and more intense phenomena in which the human being of this age is constituted consists of a body of expressive means in which language either plays a secondary function or is substituted with forms of expression other than language. Procedures to capture the coherence of the phenomena researched now need to be adapted to this reality. The coherence embodied in language reflects past experiences, but does not properly explain experiences characterized by new kinds of coherence. In recent years, a question has come up time and again: Is there some common element in language, in the possible messages exchanged in our universe by civilizations different from ours, in the messages exchanged at the genetic level of our existence or in the biochemical trails which we associate with the behavior of ant colonies or bee-hives? It would be premature to attempt an answer. As already mentioned, David Hirsch ascertains that 97% of human activity is concept free. Control mechanisms in charge of this form of activity are common not only to humans, but also to lower level biological entities (insects, for instance). Exploration of cosmic civilizations, genetics, biochemistry, not to mention memetics, is not necessarily helped by this answer. Having to explain abstract mathematical concepts or the behavior of complex systems (such as the human nervous system), some displaying learning capabilities or self-organization tendencies, raises the stakes quite high: Do we explain ourselves away in the effort to emulate the human being? Replication of ideas (scientific, philosophic, or of any other type) based on the genetic model inspired by evolutionary theory, contributes new angles to the subject. But even if we manage to establish methods for successful replication, have we captured the characteristics of human self-identification?

In the same vein, another question needs to be addressed: the mystique of science comes from the realization that the law of gravity applies everywhere, that electricity does not depend on the geographic coordinates of the place where people live, that computation is a universal calculus. Still, science is not value neutral; one model dominates others; one rationality wins over others. The truth of a scientific theory and its empirical adequacy are only loosely related. To accept one science over another is to the scientist an issue of rationality, while for those integrating it in their practical experiences, it becomes an issue of adequacy. This aspect constitutes more than a cultural or memetic issue. At stake is the fact that the natural condition of the human being is quite often rationalized away, regardless of the reason.

THE EFFICIENCY OF SCIENCE

In recent years language has changed probably more than in its entire history. Still, these changes are not of the depth and breadth of scientific and technological praxis. Computer science, as Dijkstra pointed out, deserves a better name, more in line with the fundamental change this practical experience brings about. ("Would anyone call surgery *knife science*"? he asked.) We don't have better names for many other fields of new human experience: artificial life, artificial intelligence, genetics, qualitative reasoning, and memetics. But we do have powerful new notation systems, new ways of reasoning (combining qualitative and quantitative aspects), and fresh methods of expression (interactive). Consequently, a new human condition resulting from the practice of science will probably emerge. This condition will reflect the changed premises of scientific experiment.

Experimentation joined logical analysis over 350 years ago. Simulation, the experiment of the civilization of illiteracy, is becoming the dominant scientific form of expression of the systematic search for the multitude of elements involved in new scientific theories and in their applications. A variety of simulators embody knowledge and doubt. This can be seen in a broader context. Through simulation, variability is accounted for, relations are scrutinized, functional dependencies are tested over a wide array of data critical to the performance of new systems, or over a wide array of the people involved with them. After heroically, and necessarily, separating from philosophy and establishing its own methods, science is rediscovering the need for the dimension covered by human reasoning. This is, after all, what the subject matter of artificial intelligence is and what it ultimately produces: simulations of our capability to reason. In the same vein, scientists are concerned with the *metaphysics* of the beginning of the universe, and the language of the mind (*lingua mentis*), evidently assumed to be different from language as we use it in the framework of community, cultural, and national existence.

To reflect upon the beginning of the universe or upon the mind means to constitute oneself, together with the appropriate language, in a pragmatic context different from community interaction, cultural values, or national characteristics. The focus is changed from obsession with quantity to preoccupation with quality. Qualities are pursued in the attempt to build a science of artificial reality. As a scientific artifact, this reality is endowed with characteristics of life, such as change and evolution over time, selection of the *fittest,* the best adapted to that world, and acquisition of knowledge, common sense, and eventually language. Focused on the model of life as a property of organization, artificial reality is intent on generating lifelike behavior: iterative optimization, learning, growth, adaptability, reproduction, and even self-identification. Whereas science followed strategies of standardization, artificial life is focused on generating conditions for diversity, which eventually foster adaptability. Allocation of resources within a system and strategies of co-evolution are seen as resources of incremental performance. Research starts from a premise that belongs to the realm of reasoning, not rationality: humans and the problem being solved are continuously changing.

EXPLORING THE VIRTUAL

Virtual realities are focused on almost everything that art pursues:

illusion of space, time, movement, projection of human emotions. Interacting with such a system means that the person becomes involved in the inside of images, sounds, and movements. All these are simulated, using animation as the new language of the science that the moving image embodies. In some ways, virtual reality becomes a general purpose simulator of a captivating variable reality, made possible by mediating elements such as computer graphics images, animation, digital sound, tracking devices, and quite a number of other elements. Inside this reality, virtual objects, tools, and actions open the possibility of practical experiences of self-constitution in a meta-knowledge world.

Quality in virtual reality is also pursued as scientists try to give a coherent image of the very first minutes of the universe. Physics, genetics, biophysics, biochemistry, geology, and all else integrated in this multi-mediated effort are turned from science into natural history or philosophic ontology. To explain why physicists needed an indestructible proton for explaining matter is not an issue of numbers, precision, or equations, but of common sense: If protons could decay, mountains, oceans, stars, and planets would crumble and turn back into neutrons and electrons, and a reversal of the Big Bang might occur. Is this predictive rationality? Is validation of this type of experimentation a subject of language? As a possible explanation, which facilitates a new array of experiments in computer simulation, particle accelerators, and radio-astronomic observations, virtual reality facilitates new forms of human praxis and is embodied in new theories of physics.

Obviously, the efficiency factor, one of the major elements in the transition from one dominant literacy to partial literacies, plays an important role in this endeavor. This generalized notion of efficiency has several components in the case of science. One is the efficiency of our attempts to make science productive. Compared to the efficiency of the lever and the pulley, the efficiency of the electric engine reaches a different scale of magnitude. The same applies to our new tools, but in more dramatic ways. So far, we have managed to make science the most expensive human endeavor. Its current development appears to be motivated by a self-perpetuating drive: knowledge for the sake of knowledge. Science generated technology, which dramatically affects the outcome of human effort.

The second component factor in the transition to the pragmatics of the civilization of illiteracy is the efficiency of our preparation for commanding these new tools, new forms of energy, and new forms of human interaction. Learning how to operate simple mechanical devices is different from learning how to program new tools capable of commanding sophisticated technology and of controlling tremendous amounts of energy. Although mediation has increased in human praxis, people do not yet know how to handle mediation, even less how to adapt education, their own and their children's, to shorter cycles of scientific and technological renewal.

Last among the factors at work in the change we are going through is the efficiency of invention, discovery, and explanation. Largely supported by society (states invest in science in order to pursue their goals, as do businesses and various interest groups), science is under the pressure of performance.

Markets confirm scientific results from the perspective of the return on investment they promise to deliver. Parallel to the most advanced and promising scientific endeavors, venture capital underwrites the industries of the near future. Insulation of any kind, even secrecy, no matter how stubbornly pursued and justified, is no longer possible within the economic dynamics of the present. No matter how hard companies try to impose secrecy, they fail when faced with the interactivity and integration of effort characteristic of the new dynamics. The expectation of change, of shorter cycles of investigation, and of shorter times for integration of results in the productive ability of technology is unavoidable. Still, in the USA and in Europe, there are conflicts between the new dynamics of scientific and technological progress and the bureaucracy of science. Driven by motivations characteristic of literate infatuation with national pride and security, this bureaucracy extends well beyond science and is hard at work to protect what is already *passé*. For science to advance, networks of activity, distributed tasks, and shared resources, all implying transparency and access, are essential.

The conflict between scientific goals and morality takes on its own characteristics in the civilization of illiteracy. Indeed, scientific results might be *right*, but not necessarily always *good* for humankind. They might support higher efficiency, but sometimes to the detriment of people obsessed with maintaining high standards of living. There are many activities—too many to list—in which humans can be entirely replaced by machines. Extreme effort, exposure to chemicals, radiation, and other unfriendly elements could be avoided. However, doing away with the living person whose identity is constituted in work experiences makes the activity itself questionable. It is no longer the case that we only talk about genetic control of populations, or about mind control, about creating machines endowed with extreme capabilities, including control of the people who made them. These are distinct possibilities, to which we are closer than many believe. Neither science nor technology, even less philosophy, can afford to ignore the conflict immanent in the situation, or the danger posed by giving in to solutions resulting from a limited perspective, or from our dedication to make real everything that is possible. After all, we can already destroy the planet, but we do not, or at least not so radically as it could be destroyed. Short of being paralyzed by all these dangers, science has to question its own condition. In view of this, it is far from accidental that sciences in the civilization of illiteracy rediscover philosophy, or they *re-philosophize* themselves.

QUO VADIS PHILOSOPHY?

The language of wisdom
Reflecting upon human beings and their relation to the outside world (nature, culture, society) constitutes a determined form of philo-

sophical experience. It involves awareness of oneself and others, and the ability to identify similarities and differences, to explain the changing dynamics of existence, and to project the acquired understanding into the practice of formulating new questions. Practical implications of philosophic systems are manifold. Such systems affect scientific, moral, political, cultural, and other human practical experiences of self-constitution. They accumulate wisdom more than knowledge. To this effect, we can say that the classic model of philosophy remains a science of sciences, or at least the *alma mater* of sciences. Philosophic systems are concerned with human values, not with skills or abilities involved in reaching goals defined by our rationality. Nevertheless, this status has been continuously challenged from inside and outside philosophy. The decline of respect for philosophy probably results from the perceived omniscient attitude philosophers have displayed and from their unwillingness to focus on aspects of human reason.

Philosophy has never been a domain for everyone. In our day, it has become a discourse expressed, if not in painfully contorted language, in a multitude of specialized languages addressed to a relatively small circle of interested parties, themselves philosophers for the most part. The change in the pragmatic condition of philosophy is reflected in its current linguistic equivocations. "My philosophy" is an expression used by anyone to express anything from a tactic in football to investments, drug use, diet, politics, religions, and much more.

Misunderstood cultural exigencies, originating in the civilization of literacy, and political opportunism maintain philosophy as a required subject in universities, no matter what is taught under its name, who teaches it, or how. Under communism in East Europe and the Soviet Union, where free choice was out of question, philosophy was obligatory because it was identified with the dominating ideology. In most liberal societies, philosophic abstraction is as much abhorred as lack of money. Philosophic illiteracy is a development in line with the deteriorating literacy manifested in our days. But what affects this change is the new pragmatic framework, not the decline in writing and reading proficiency.

The specialization of philosophic language, as well as the integration of logico-mathematical formalism in philosophical discourse, have not contributed to recuperating the prestige of philosophy, or of the philosopher, for that matter. Neither did it contribute to resolving topics specific to the discipline, in particular, to human experience and conscience. In fact, philosophy has disappeared in a number of *philosophies* practiced today: analytic, continental, feminist, Afro-American, among others. Each has constituted its own language and even perspective, pursuing goals frequently rooted in the philosophy of the civilization of literacy, or in its politics.

The relevance (or irrelevance) of philosophy cannot be ascertained outside the practice of questioning and answering, a practice that made philosophy necessary in the first place. Indeed, as a practice of positioning the human being in the universe of human experience, philosophy is as relevant as the practical results of this positioning. There are scientific theories, such as the theory of relativity in physics or gene theory in biology, that are as philosophically relevant as they are scientifically significant. And there are, as well, philosophic theories of extreme scientific significance. Many components of Leibniz's system, of Descartes' rationalism, and Peirce's *pragmaticism* can be mentioned. Each originates within a distinct pragmatic framework of practical experiences through which reason comes to expression and questions specific forms of rationality.

Philosophy, as we know it from the texts in which it was articulated, is a product molded through the experience that initially made writing possible (though not universally accepted) and, later, literacy necessary. Its fundamental distinctions—subject/object, rational/irrational, matter/spirit, form/content, analytic/synthetic, concrete/abstract, essence/phenomenon—correspond largely to human practical experiences in the framework of language. The traditional gnoseological approach reflects the same structure, as does formal logic, based on Aristotle's syllogistic theory. The fundamental linguistic distinction of subject/predicate marks—at least for Western civilization—the entire approach. Expectations of efficiency pertinent to the human scale leading to the Industrial Revolution affected the condition of philosophy. At this juncture, philosophers realized the practical aspect of the discipline. Marx thought that it would empower people and help them change the world: "Until now philosophers interpreted the world; it's time to change it." And change it did, but in ways different from what he and his followers anticipated. The hard grip of reified language turned the workers' paradise into a mental torture chamber.

Once the underlying structure (reflected in the requirements of literacy) changed, philosophy changed as well, also freeing itself from the categories of language that molded its speculative discourse. Nevertheless, its institutions (education, professional associations and conferences) continue to pursue goals and functions peculiar to literate expectations. This prompted a strong movement of philosophic dissidence (Feyerabend and Lakatos are the main representatives), attuned to the practical need of a philosophic praxis aware of the relative nature of its assertions.

Multi-valued logic, the logic of relations, fuzzy set theory, and computation in its algorithmic and non-algorithmic forms (based on neural networks) allow philosophers to free themselves from the various dualisms embedded in the language of philosophy. Significantly better answers to ontological, gnoseological, epistemological, and even historic questions have to reflect such and other cognitively relevant perspectives of knowledge. Philosophy undergoes a process of mathematization in order to gain access to science and improve its own efficiency. It has become logic oriented, more computational. It has adopted genetic schemes for explaining variation and selection, extending to the current memetic conversations and methods. It is not unusual for philosophers to abandon the pattern of rehashing older theories and views, and to attempt to understand pragmatic exigencies and their reason. The *scientification* of philosophy could not have happened under the scrutiny of language and the domination of literacy. Neither could we expect, within the literate framework, anything comparable to Plato's *Dialogues*, to the great philosophical systems of Leibniz, Kant, Hegel, and Marx, to the literary seduction of Heidegger, Sartre, or Martin Buber.

In scientific disguise

Developing, parallel to common language (which philosophers frequently call *natural language*), different types of sign systems, humans utilize the latter's mediating force in order to increase the efficiency of their action. "Give me a fixed point and I'll move the world" is the equivalent philosophical statement characteristic of the civilization of the lever and pulley. "When I use a word," Humpty Dumpty says in a scornful tone, "it means just what I choose it to mean, neither more nor less." "The question is," says Alice, "whether you can make words mean so many different things." Reading the dialogue from Lewis Carroll's *Through the Looking Glass*, with the magnificent works of great philosophers (from Plato to Leibniz, Kant, and Hegel, Peirce and many more) in mind, one understands Alice's trouble. With the exception of Wittgenstein, nobody really seems to have been bothered by the ability people have to make words mean many things.

Today, we could be directed to a philosophical paraphrase in which, instead of a fixed point, the need for a sign system (a language) is spelled out. Adapted to the scope of the conceived practical experience, such a sign system, when put into practice, will change the world, will "move" it. Diagrammatic thinking, the powerful cognitive model Peirce advanced, exemplifies the idea. Cybernetics, biogenetics, computers, and research in artificial intelligence and artificial life, as well as political, social, aesthetic, or religious concepts are examples of domains where such sign systems have been devised. They have facilitated forms of human self-constitution that contribute to the contradictory image of today's world. Such languages reflect the fundamental process of progressive mediation, participate in the diversification of the languages used, and affect the status and value system of the ideal of literacy. They serve as the scientific disguise of philosophy. Clarity (difficult to achieve in natural language), evidence, and certainty seem guaranteed in the language of science. In addition, objectivity and the ever seductive truth, for which philosophy was never known, are also apparently within reach.

There is to philosophic discourse an internal reason for its continuous unfolding: People constituting themselves as philosophers change as the world they live in changes. Human reasoning is part of the world; the ability and, moreover, the desire to think of new questions, attempt answers, and doubt our own ability to reach the right answer are part of what defines the human being. The consequences of mediation in philosophy should not be ignored. Mediation implies, on one hand, a high degree of integration of human praxis (to the extent of making individual contribution anonymous), and on the other, a no less high degree of the subject's independence in respect to the object of work or reasoning, or the object represented by the other participants in human praxis. While it seems appropriate for science to know more and more about a narrower range of subjects, it contradicts the image of philosophy as it is formed in language and embodied in the ideal of literacy. Due to this metaphorically defined deepening of knowledge, each philosopher is more independent of the other, but more intensely integrated than ever before due to the necessary interconnection of this knowledge. The meaning of this paradoxical situation is not easy to clarify. The overall process has followed two qualitatively contrary directions: 1) concentration on a precisely delineated aspect of knowledge or action in order to understand and control it; 2) abandoning interest in the whole as a consequence of the assumption that the parts will finally be reunited in the social integrating mechanism of the market, whether we want it or not. We now have particular philosophies—of law, ethics, science, sport, recreation, feminism, Afro-Centrism—but no longer a comprehensive philosophy of existence.

The scientific disguise of philosophy contributes to its renewed struggle for legitimacy. It adopts concepts and methods pertinent to rationality. In order to deal with reason, or to do away altogether with questions of reasoning, it unfolds in science and technology. Durkheim tried to apply Darwin's natural selection model to explain labor division. At present, philosophers have become *memeticians,* and examine computational simulations of Darwinian principles in order to see how ideas survive and advance. Spencer believed that the increase of the productive power of work increases happiness. Present-day philosophers are eager to diagram the relation between work satisfaction and personality. Some even try to revive Compte's positivist philosophy, to improve upon past Utopian schemes, or to invent a calculus of intellectual well-being. Short of a philosophic inquiry, everything becomes a subject waiting for a philosopher who does not want to stay within the boundaries of the history of philosophy.

Once new movements, some better justified than others, and all reflecting the shift from the authority-based civilization of literacy to the endless freedom of choice of the illiterate context, needed a powerful instrument to further their programs, they chose, or were chosen by, philosophy. Secularism and pluralism meet within philosophic concerns with the gay movement, feminism, multi-culturalism, integration of new technology, implications of aging, the new holisms, popular philosophy, sexual emancipation, virtuality, and more along this line. In a way, this reflects the new awareness of efficiency that permeates philosophic activity, but also its struggle to maintain its relations to literacy. Legitimate doubt is generated by the choice of subjects that seem to attract philosophers, and by the apparent lack of philosophic matter. When the language is not obscure, the philosopher seems to discuss matters, not really question reasons, and even less advance ideas or explanatory models. Wholesale generalizations do not help, but one can really not escape the feeling that the process through which philosophy liberates itself from literacy has been less productive than the similar process of science's emancipation from language.

A journey through the many philosophically oriented Web sites reveals very quickly that even when philosophy opts out of the print medium, it carries over many of the limitations of literacy. The ability to open philosophic discourse, to adopt non-linearity, and to encourage dialogue free of the pressure of tradition is often signaled, but rarely accomplished. The medium is resisted, not enjoyed as an alternative to classic philosophical discourse. Such observations have prompted the opinion that scientists are becoming the most appropriate philosophers of their own contributions.

Who needs philosophy? And what for?
At this point, one question naturally arises: Is philosophy relevant after all? Moreover, is it even possible without the participation of natural language, or at least without this intermediary between philosophers and their public? In blunter terms, can we live without it? In the context in which efficiency expectations translate into a practical experience of an unprecedented degree of specialization, will philosophy turn into another mediating activity among people? Or will it be, as it was considered in the culture of a Romantic ideal, humanity's self-consciousness, as expressed in Hegel's philosophy? If indeed philosophy is absorbed into science, what can its purpose be?

As with literacy, the inclination is to suggest that, regardless of the new condition of language, philosophy remains possible and is indeed relevant. As far as its functions are concerned—mediating activity, humanity's self-consciousness, corpus of interpretive discourse about humanity and nature—they remain to be defined in the pragmatic context. It is needless to reiterate that within each scale of humankind, philosophy pursued different interests as these proved pertinent to efficiency expectations. Philosophers never contributed bread to the table nor artifacts. Their skill was to formulate questions, especially the very probing questions—"What is what?" and "Why?"—in their attempt to address the origins of things. Deciphering the reason of things and actions—in other words, understanding the world and its apparent order (what the Greeks called *eunomia*)—made them simultaneously philosophers and interpreters of science. "How can we know?" and "How can we explain?" are subsequent questions, pursued more stringently by people in search of scientific rationality than by philosophers *per se.*

No historic account, no matter how detailed, can do justice to the definition of philosophy. Its subject changes as human beings change in the process of their practical self-constitution. From philosophy, science and all the humanities (ethics, aesthetics, politics, sociology, law) evolved. Even our concern with language is of a philosophic nature. It seems that philosophy is, in the final analysis, the only authentic domain of abstraction. Its interest is not the individual, the concrete, the immediate, not even the idea, but the abstraction of these. Where other domains, such as mathematics, logic, linguistics, and physics are intent on understanding the abstract notions around which their domains are built, on giving them life in the context of practical experiences, philosophy seems driven by the quest for reaching the next level of abstraction, the abstraction of abstractions, and so on. Science uses abstraction as an instrument for reaching concreteness; philosophy follows the inverse path. There is always to the philosophic attempt a call for the next step, into the infinite. Each accomplishment is provisional. To experiment philosophically means not so much to search systematically for causes as to never end the inquiry. There are no right or wrong philosophic theories. Philosophy is cumulative and self-devouring.

That people will never stop wondering *what is what,* the more their own activity will multiply the domain of existing entities, goes almost without saying. That they will ask again and again how they can know, how they can be sure that what they know is true, or at least relevant, is also evident. The species is characterized by its ability to think, produce and master tools, acknowledge value, and constitute itself as a community of shared concern and resources, through its playfulness and other characteristics (alluded to in terms such as *Homo economicus, Zoon semiotikon, Zoon politikon, Homo ludens*). Probably more than all these partial qualifiers, the species is the only one known to question everything. As language experience marked the genetic condition of the human being, questioning marked it too, probably through language mechanisms in the first place. When the child articulates the first question, the entire genetic endowment is at work.

We are who and what we are in our inquisitive interaction with others. Our minds exist only through this interaction. This statement says in effect that to philosophize became part of the process of human self-constitution and identification. The only referent of philosophy is the human being constituted in practical experiences. Together with other surviving literacies, philosophic literacy will be one of many. The philosophy of the civilization of illiteracy will reflect the circumstances of work and life characteristic of the pragmatic framework. It will also be subjected to the severe test of market exigencies as these reflect efficiency expectations characteristic of the new scale of humankind. Science can justify itself by the return in investment in new explanatory models. It also leads to new technologies and to higher levels of efficiency in human practical experiences. Philosophy certainly has a different justification. Philosophic necessity is *evasive*. Short of living off the past, as literacy, religion, and art do, it needs to refocus on reason as the compass of human activity. Focusing on alternative practical experiences, philosophy can practically help people to free themselves from the obsession with progress—seen as a sequence of ever-escalating records (of production, distribution, expectation)—and moreover, from the fear of all its consequences. It can also focus people's attention on alternatives to everything that affects the integrity of the species and its sense of quality, including the relation to their environment. When past, present, and future collapse into the illiterate frenzy of the instant, philosophy owes to those who question its articulations an honest approach to the question, "Is there a future?" But as this future takes shape in the presence of humans partaking in the open world of networked interactions, banalities will not do.

CHAPTER 8: ART(IFACTS) AND AESTHETIC PROCESSES

Confusing as it is, a snapshot of everything that today goes under the names *art* and *literature* conveys at least a sense of variety. Forget the never-ending discussions of what qualifies as art and what does not. And forget the irreconcilable disputes over taste. What counts are practical experiences of self-identification as artist or writer, as well as involvement with artifacts eventually acknowledged within the experience as art or as literature, i.e., experiences through which the art public and readership are constituted.

What comes to mind when we think about the art and literature of the civilization of illiteracy are not illiterate writers—although they exist—and not illiterate painters, composers, pianists, dancers, sculptors, or computer artists of all kinds. Rather, disparate examples of works, each remarkable in its own way (or altogether unremarkable), but above all marked by characteristics that distinctly disconnect them from the literate experience of art and literature capture our memory. Cautionary note ended. Here are the examples: surviving Auschwitz translated into a comic book parable populated by cats (depicting the Nazis) and mice (depicting their victims); a Grammy Award returned by a famous singing group because someone else was doing the singing for them; the tear-jerkers from Disney Studios (a company whose audience is the world), classic stories or history turned into feminist or politically correct musicals; paintings by a controversial artist (self-made or made by the market?), fetching prices as high as overvalued shares of a new Internet company, after he died of AIDS at an early age; the never-ending parade of computer animation miracles; the Web sites of uninterrupted aesthetic frenzy that would have delighted Andy Warhol, one of the authentic founders of art in the civilization of illiteracy, if anyone could pinpoint the beginning of this civilization.

These are examples. Period. Originality, aesthetic integrity, homogeneity, and artfulness are the exception. The process through which these examples were produced begs qualifiers different from art produced under the aegis of literate expectations. Today, art is produced much faster, embodied—or disembodied—in and disseminated through more media, and exhausted in a shorter time—sometimes even before it comes into being! Cycles of artistic style are abridged to the extreme of being impossible to define. Artistic standards are leveled as the democracy of unlimited access to art and literature expands their public, without effecting a deep rapport, a long-lasting relation, or a heightened aesthetic expectation.

Never before has more kitsch been produced and more money spent to satisfy the obsession with celebrity that is the hallmark of this time. Museums became the new palaces and the new shopping malls, opening branches all over the world, not unlike MacDonalds and fashion retail stores. And never before were more technological and scientific means involved in the practical experience of art, always on the cutting edge, not only because art is traditionally associated with innovation. These new experiences make possible the transition from an individual, private, almost mystical, experience to a very public activity. Open a virtual studio on the Web, and chances are that many people will exercise their calling (or curiosity) on the digital canvas. Not infrequently, this activity is carried on at the scale of the integrated world: major concerts viewed on several continents, attempts to integrate art from all nations into a super-work, the melange of literatures fused into new writing workshops, distributed, interactive installations united in the experience of digital networks. Good taste and bad co-exist; pornography resides as bits and bytes in formats not different from those of the most suave examples from art history. The Internet is the one and only uncensored place left on the earth. All these phenomena deserve to be understood as testimony to the change of the condition of human experience, and in the context of change from a literacy-dominated art to an art of many partial literacies, of mediations, and of relatively vague notions of value and significance.

MAKING AND PERCEIVING

Nature and culture meet in artistic practical experiences of human self-constitution, as they meet in any other human experience. What makes their meeting extraordinary is the fact that what we see, or hear, or listen to is the expression of their intersecting. Through art, humans project sensorial, as well as cognitive, characteristics. The experience of structuring a category of artifacts, defined through their aesthetic condition, and the complementary experience of self-definition through aesthetically relevant actions constitute the realm of the artistic. In their interaction with objects and actions resulting from such experiences, individuals conjure meaning as they define themselves in respect to the experiences in a given context. Like any other practical experience, the production of art belongs to the pragmatic framework. We are what we do: hunting, running, singing, drawing, telling stories, creating rhymes, performing a play. In their respective *doings*, artists identify themselves through particular aptitudes and skills: rhythm, movement, voice, sense of color, harmony, synchronism, contrast. The emergence of language and the consecutive experience of recording led to the association of skills with the *writing* of the language, that is, *drawing* and *reading* it to others, performing it in rituals.

The domain of art seems to be characteristic only of the human species. Since the practical experience of art is so close to our biogenetic structural reality, while at the same time constitutive of a non-existential domain, the making of art and the cultural appropriation of art are perceived as similar experiences. Nevertheless, language exercised coordination for the simple reason that successive motivations of the art experience—such as the mytho-magical, practical, ritual, sexual, gnoseologic, political, or economic—and the underlying structure of art belong to different domains. The underlying structure of art defines its aesthetics. The underlying structure of magic, ritual, or the sexual defines their respective condition, as it expresses human understanding of the unknown, or the many aspects of sexuality.

The interaction between artist and society, once markets emerged and art was acknowledged as a product with its own identity, resulted in specific forms of recurrence: recognition of the uniqueness of the work, of the artist, and of interpretive patterns. Once the framework for recognizing artworks as merchandise was established, transactions in artworks became transactions in the artist-society relation, with a lot of give-and-take that was difficult, if not impossible, to encode. The nature of the relations can be partially understood by examining behaviors of artists, who are almost always seen as eccentric, a little off the middle of the road, and behaviors of the public. There is much instinctive interaction, and even more learned behavior, mediated through an experience constituted in and communicated through language.

Looking at a painting—once painting is acknowledged as artifact—is more than acknowledging its physical reality: the optical, and sometimes the textual, appearance, or the context of contemplation. The action of painting, sculpting, dancing, performing, or writing poetry or a novel is simultaneously an action of constituting oneself as artist or writer and projecting this self, as it results from the practical experience characteristic of such an endeavor, into the social space of interactions. This is why art is in the first place expression, and only secondly communication. This is also why looking at a work is to constitute the individual experience of context, in the first place, and only secondly to conjure and assign meaning. In both the action of painting and looking at a painting, biologically inherited characteristics, together with learned elements (skills), participate in the process of constituting the being (the painter and the onlooker, for instance) as both individual and member of the community.

The natural and the acquired, or learned, interact. And in the course of time, the natural is *educated,* made aware of characteristics connected to culture rather than nature. Two simultaneous processes take place: 1) the recurrent interaction of those making art and those acknowledging it in their practical life; 2) establishment of patterns of interpretation as patterns of interaction mediated by the artwork. Language experiences take place in both processes. Consequently, artistic knowledge is accumulated, and art-related communication becomes a well defined practical experience, leading to self-identification such as *art historian, art theoretician, art critic,* and the like. The nature and characteristics of the practical experience of art-related language ought to be examined so that we can reach an understanding of the circumstances under which they might change.

ART AND LANGUAGE

Language is a multi-dimensional practical experience. In the interaction between individuals who *produce* something (in this case, works of art) and those who consume them, self-constitution through language makes coordination possible. Production and consumption are other instances of human self-constitution. Frequently, integration takes place in the process of exchanging goods or, at a more general level, values.

Drawing something, real or imaginary, and looking at the drawing, i.e., trying to recognize the drawn object, are structurally different experiences. These two practical experiences can be related in many ways: display the drawing and the object drawn side-by-side; explain the drawing to the onlookers; attach a description. Here is where difficulties start to accumulate. The artifact and the experience leading to it appear as different entities. Descriptions (what is on paper or on canvas) lead to identification, but not to interaction, the only reason behind the artistic experience. Language substitutes its own condition for the entire physical-biogenetic level of interaction. It overplays the cultural, which is consequently made to represent the entire experience.

People speak about works of art, write about art, and read writings about art as though art had no *phylogenetic* dimension, only a *phylocultural* reality. Language's coordinative function is relied upon because of the dissimilarity between the practical experiences of making art and of appropriating it in the cultural environment. Through cultural experiences, the coordinating function of language extends to facilitating new forms of practical experiences associated with making art: instruction, use of technology, and cooperation peculiar to artmaking. It also facilitates experiences of appropriation in the art market, the constitution of institutions dedicated to supporting education in art, the politics of art, and forms of public evaluation. Art implicitly expresses awareness, on the part of artists and public, of how persons interacting through artistic expression are changed through the interactions.

Language, especially in forms associated with literacy, makes this awareness of reciprocal influence explicit. In the civilization of illiteracy, all non-literate means of information, communication, and marketing (e.g., songs, film, video, interactive multimedia) take it upon themselves to reposition art as yet another practical experience of the pragmatics of high efficiency peculiar to a humankind that reached yet another critical mass. It was not unusual for an artist in the literacy-dominated past to go through very long cycles in preparing for the work, and for the work itself to unfold after years of effort. It is quite the contrary in the case of the instantaneous gratification of a video work, of an installation, or of gestural art. Within the pragmatics of an underlying structure reflected in literacy, art was as confined as the experience of language, which represented its underpinning. The pragmatics of the civilization of illiteracy makes the experience of art part of the global experience.

Many people wonder whether the basic, though changing, relation between art and language, in particular art and literacy, is unavoidable—furthermore, whether coordination can be assumed by a sign system other than literate language. In prelude to answering this question, I would like to point out that the influence of language on the arts, and even on the language arts (poetry, drama, fiction), was hailed by as many as deplored it. To account for attitudes in favor of or against an art connected to, or resulting from, high levels of literacy, i.e., of favoring an art emancipated from the domination of language, means to account for the change of art and its perceived meaning. The entire artistic effort to transcend the figurative and the narrative, to explore the abstract and the gestural, to explore its own reality, and to establish new languages testifies to this striving towards emancipation. Ascertaining that the art-language relation is not inescapable does not purport the invention of a new relation as an alternative to what culture acknowledges as the relatively necessary dependence of the two. As with the case of other forms of practical experiences discussed against the background of literacy, examination of directions of change and the attempt to conjure their meaning is required.

Human beings are agents of change and, at the same time, outside observers of the process of change. An observer can distinguish between the recurrent influence of the human biogenetic structure and the interactions based on this structure. An observer can also account for the role of the phylocultural, in particular the interactions this triggers. Restricted to the literate means of communication that I chose for presenting my arguments, I want to show that art and its interpretation are no longer the exclusive domain of literate language. Alternative domains of creation and interpretation are continuously structured as we project ourselves in new practical experiences. Moreover, the eternal conflict inherent in art experiences, between what is and what unfolds, best expressed in the quest for innovation, integrates aspects of the conflict between literacy-dominated pragmatics and pragmatics dominated by illiteracy. Were I an artist, and were we all visually attuned, this topic could have been explained through one or several artworks, or through the *process* leading to an artwork. The role of processing current practical experiences of art needs to be properly highlighted. Exacerbated in the self-consciousness of art in the age of illiteracy, artistic processes take precedence over artifacts; the *making* of art becomes more important than the result. Artists would say that we exist not only in the environment of our language projections, but probably just as much (if not more) in the environment of our art projections.

IMPATIENCE AND AUTARCHY

The prophets of the end of the arts (Hegel was their most convincing, but most misunderstood, representative) were so confused by changes in the arts that, instead of approaching the dynamics of the process, they concentrated on the logical possibility that artistic practice is self-devouring and self-destructive. The initial end-of-the-arts prophecies were delivered during a time of relatively mild change in the status of the aesthetic appropriation of reality. Recent prophecies occurred in a very different context. It was only after World War I that aesthetic experiences really difficult to connect and integrate in an accepted explanation changed our notion and expectations of art. With the experience of disposable language, which the Dadaist movement submitted to a community already skeptical of language, came the experience of disposable art.

While literacy supplied a framework for (almost) consistent representations of values and norms, human practice at the border between literacy and a-literacy introduced and fostered inconsistency, believed to be the last resort of individual freedom. Eclecticism and consumption joined in this experience, since mixing without system or justification of any kind is like stating that everything is worth whatever people make of it, and therefore they want to have it. Re-evaluation of available art, good or bad, aesthetically relevant or kitsch, significant or insignificant, is part of this change. Once re-evaluation started, the processes of artmaking and aesthetic appropriation grew relatively disconnected. Where language, through literacy as a generalized medium of interaction, maintained cultural distinctions, such as the ones embodied in our notions of perspective, resemblance, and narration, the new art experience introduced distinctions at the *natural* level, such as instinct, energy, choice, and change. For as long as literacy maintained control and integration, viewers, irritated by conventions foreign to them, physically attacked works (such as Impressionist paintings) resulting from artistic practices different from those congruent to the practice of language and to the associated expectations of seeing.

Art under the scrutiny of literacy is always model driven. Once the necessity of literacy as the only integrating mechanism was challenged by the need to maintain levels of efficiency for which language is not well equipped, new forms of artistic appropriation of reality and a new notion of reality itself became possible. Model was replaced by iconoclasm. Walter Benjamin captured some of these changes in the formula of "art in the age of its mechanical reproduction." The end of the aura, as Benjamin has it, is actually the aura's shift from the *artifact* to the *process* and the *artist*. It corresponds not to the end of art's uniqueness, but to the artist's determination to get rid of all restrictions (of subject matter, material, technique) and to ascertain artistic freedom as the goal of artistic experience. But there are yet more possibilities for the emancipation of artists and their work.

As we enter the age of electronic reproduction, massive communication that supports interactive multimedia, and information integration through networks (adapted for pipelining data and all kinds of images), we encounter such possibilities. We are also subjected to new experiences—for instance, simultaneous transmission of art and interpretation, moreover the possibility to contribute our own interpretation, to become co-makers of whatever is presented to us through the very malleable digital media. Technology and change of aesthetic goals affect the scale of artistic experience, as well as the relation between artists and the world. Projects such as Walter de Maria's *Lightening Field* and Christo's *Umbrella* project (extended over California and Japan) are examples of both the change of scale and of new interpretation processes. They are also vivid proof that globality permeates art at each level. So does the sense of rapid change, the acknowledgment and fear of perishability, and the open-endedness of the practical experience of making art. I doubt that anyone could have captured this sense as well as the Web site on which millions of viewers could experience the wrapping and unwrapping of the Reichstag in Berlin. Christo and Jeanne-Claude might remain the authors of record, but the event grew beyond the notion of authorship.

The artistic experience of the civilization of illiteracy is also characterized by impatience and autarchy. Things happen fast and relatively independent from one another. Artistic experiment always embodied characteristics of the practical experience of human self-constitution. From petroglyphic expression to the art of our age, this happens again and again, obviously in context-dependent forms. The Dutch and Flemish Baroque artists celebrated results of industriousness through mythological themes. Before that, religion dominated up to and through the Renaissance. In the context of African, Asian, and South American art, the forms were different, but the pragmatic stamp is faultlessly evident. No wonder that in the settled age of literacy, art had a structure similar to that of the practical experience of literate language, regardless of the richness of its forms. It even called for experimental settings reminiscent of industry, or of the university context, as we know from art history. And it was sanctioned on the same pragmatic criteria as any other literate experiment: success (it was useful), or failure (it was discarded). Accordingly, it implied sequential development and a rather settled succession of operations. As artistic experimentation took place in line with all other experiments characteristic of the pragmatic context of literacy, it even resulted in an industrial model based on modularity, which the Bauhaus enthusiastically promoted. A number of shops produced thousands of ready-made artistic objects with a clear goal in mind: value through usefulness, function over form, functionality as aesthetics at work. Artistic practice and appropriation were coordinated through the still literate language of the market.

Art in the civilization of illiteracy is less a matter of invention and discovery, as it was in the civilization of literacy, and more one of selection, framing, and endless variation. Since the end of the last century, artists started breaking away from some of the characteristics implicit in the literate experience, such as hierarchy, centralism, and nationalism. This is not a time for rules and laws, unless they are taken from the books of the past, relativized and integrated in the tools needed in artistic practice, made into underlying principles. Appropriation is not of the object, but of the method, process, and context. The tools of this civilization are endowed with the *literacy* required for certain partial experiences. Artists, instead of acquiring skills, are trained to master such tools. In his series of ready-mades, Marcel Duchamp anticipated much more than a style. He anticipated a new kind of artistic practice and a different interrelation among the individuals involved in producing—literally selecting from the infinite repertory of ready-mades and framing—and the individuals who appropriate the artifact for whatever reason (aesthetic satisfaction, status, investment, irrational drive to collect).

Today, artists are more dependent on others involved in the pragmatic framework of the time. This dependency is the result of the more integrated nature of human effort. Everything that is eventually built into the work, regardless of whether this work is an object, an action, or a process, results from other human practical experiences. The time of the artist's inventing his own pigments, making his own canvasses and frames, that is, the time of the artist's integral ownership and quasi-independence, was already over with the advent of industrial production. In the context of mediation and task distribution, new levels of dependencies are established and reflected in the work. Video art, photography, film, computer-based installations, and much of the computer music, interactive multimedia, and virtual art experiences are examples of such dependencies. Simultaneously they are examples of the new forms of conflict and tension that mark the artistic experience. Artistic freedom and self-determination are only apparent. The limits of the many elements involved in an artistic experience affect choice and artistic integrity. Free choice, a romantic notion, is a delusion under these new circumstances. There is no censorship on the Internet, but that does not make the medium totally free.

The forms of integration in the guise of new science and technology are probably less troublesome than integration through language. They are, however, much more constricting and restrictive because they derive from elements over which the artist has little, if any, control. The growth of non-verbal modes of human expression, communication, and interaction introduces elements of mediation. These can be seen as intermediaries, such as images to be integrated, sounds, political actions (a sit-in is the best known example) that are involved in the practical experience of art in all its phases. Formulation of aesthetic goals, in the form of video improvisations, diagrams, multimedia installations, computer-generated simulations, interpretation of an artwork (animation of a painting or sculpture, for example), and processes of meaning realization and valuation (represented by market transactions, insurance estimates, political relevance, ideological tendency, cultural significance) use mediating elements. None of Christo's elaborate and very comprehensive projects could have been carried through without such means. Keijo Yamamoto's widely celebrated virtual performance could not come into being without an understanding of all that it takes to establish a *Worldwide Network Art*.

Art, as a human experience, emphasizes its own transitory nature and becomes less permanent than in previous stages of artistic practice, but far more pervasive. Still, to qualify this process as mere democratization of the arts would be misleading. That supermarkets are full of meat, oranges, cheese, and all kinds of graphic signs should not be interpreted as the democratization of meat, oranges, cheese, or graphic signs. The majority of artists still strive for recognition. To the extent that their own recognition as *different* means that there are people who do not qualify for the same recognition and reward, there is no equality in the realm of art. On the other hand, the pressures of leveling and the iconoclastic component of artistic experience reduce the passion that drove artists in the past, or at least changes the focus of this passion. Although the artistic process has changed in line with other changes in the systematic domain of human experience in general, it still resists doing away with the terms for artistic recognition. The uncertainty (including that of recognition, but not limited to it) projected in the work qualifies it as an expression of individualism. The heuristic attempt to establish new patterns of human interaction through art reflects the uncertainty. To own art that is stored in units of information and in invisible processing instructions means something totally different from being in possession of unique artifacts embodied in matter, regardless of how much they are affected by the passing of time.

The recurrent phylogenetic and phylocultural structure, on which the artist-public interaction was built in the pragmatic framework fostering literacy, is questioned from within artistic practice. Art is only indirectly affected by the new scale of humankind, as it tries to acknowledge this scale. But the efficiency that this scale requires is reflected in the means available to support experiences of human self-constitution as artist. Related to scale are the notions of survival and well being. People do not need art to survive, and the majority of people on Earth are living proof of this assertion. But in a broader sense, life that does not have an artistic dimension is not human. That is what we have learned or what we want to believe.

To express oneself in forms involving an artistic element is part of self-constitution as a human being, distinct from the rest of the natural realm. Moreover, to have access to the richness of other expressive forms—rhythms, colors, shapes, movements, metaphors, sounds, textures—is to reascertain a sense of belonging. In this vein, the right to affluence implicit in the civilization of illiteracy extends well into the domain of the aesthetic. New artistic structures and means are continuously submitted and consumed. Some end up in oblivion; others suggest dynamic patterns. Freed from the constraints of a dominant literacy, artistic practice is becoming more and more like any other form of human experience, emancipated from the obsession of universality and eternity (embodied in museums and art collections), from centralism (expressed in such elements as the vanishing point, the tonal center of music, the architectural keystone). True, a great deal of narcissism has come to the forefront. And there is a tendency to break rules for the sake of breaking them, and to make the *act* of breaking the rule the object of artistic interest. In transcending old media boundaries, production and appropriation come closer together. The person making the artwork already integrates the appropriation in the making. Thus a complicity beyond and above language is established in defiance of time, space, and the universal. Nevertheless, artists still want to be eternal!

Art establishes itself on a plurality of levels of interaction. This is its main characteristic, since the cultural level supported by literacy is breaking the bonds of a generic, pervasive literacy. Several specialized languages mediate at various levels. The language of art history addresses professionals at one level, and laymen at another, through an array of journals and magazines. Art theory speaks to experts and, in a different tone, to neophytes who themselves will judge or produce artworks. The language of materials and techniques delves into particulars beyond oil, canvas, melody, beat, and rhythm that a generally literate onlooker or listener would not readily comprehend.

The art of the civilization of illiteracy partly reprocesses previous artistic experience. By no accident, the entire modern movement looked back at ancient art forms and exotic art and appropriated their themes and structural components. In this experience, cultural conventions expressed through literacy (such as the recurrent linear perspective, illusory space, or color symbolism) are of secondary import. The goal is to account for the tension between motives (the magical, the sacred, or the mythic), the realistic image, and abstract extensions. The experience, which language inadequately reported, but could not substitute, is the subject of artistic investigation. African and Chinese masks, Russian icons, Mayan artifacts, Arabic decorative motifs, and Japanese syllabaries are invoked with the intention of arousing awareness of their specific pragmatic context, which in turn will influence new artistic practical experiences. This is art after art. Evidently, Russian avant-garde, French cubism, American conceptualism, and all the other-*isms* cannot be seen as ordinary extensions to experiences alien to tradition, or as attempts to loosen the ties between art and literacy in conscious preparation for relative emancipation from language. This phase has its own, new, recurring interactions. The post-modern is probably the closest we have come to the expression of awareness and values about art in art, a generic hall of mirrors.

Artistic practice led to a change in the structure of the domain: art assumes a self-referential function and submits the results to the public at large (literate or not). To look at post-modern art and architecture as only illustrative of cultural quotes, and possible self-irony, would mean to miss the nature of the experience projected in making the new artifacts. It is an undoing of the past in order to achieve a new freedom (from norm, ideal, value, morality, even aesthetics). The concept of art, resulting from the theoretic practice focused on accumulated artistic experience in its broadest sense, is subjected to change. Artifacts resulting from the practical experience of artists constitute a domain congruent to the aesthetic dimension of human interaction in the social environment. This art is illiterate in the sense that it refuses previous norms and values, comments upon them from within, and projects a very *individual* language, with many *ad hoc* rules, and a vocabulary in continuous change. Think about how, in the post-modern, the condition and function of drawing change. Drawing no longer serves as an underlying element of painting, architecture, or sculpture. Rather, drawing ascertains its own aesthetic condition. In a broader sense, it is as though art continuously generates its definition and redefinition, and allows those involved in artistic practice to constitute themselves as entities of change more than as manufacturers of aesthetically relevant objects. In a similar way, harmony is re-evaluated in the experience of music.

The specializations within artistic practice (e.g., drawing, harmony, composition) correspond to an incredible diversification of skills and techniques, to the creation and adoption of new tools (digital devices included), and awareness of the market. Those who know the *language* of an artifact, or of a series of relatively similar artifacts, are not necessarily those who will appropriate and interpret the artifact. In this age, aesthetic expression becomes an issue of information processing resulting from the systematic deconstruction of the aesthetic practice of the age dominated by literacy. Images and sounds are derived from various experiences (photographic, mechanical, electronic). Spontaneity is complemented by elaboration. Previous stylistic characteristics—spontaneity is only the most evident—are reified and framed in new settings together with the interpretation. They are also reified in artistic expression as the gesture of *making* the work and the act of submitting it to the public with the aim of pleasing, provoking, criticizing, ridiculing, confounding, challenging, uplifting, or degrading (intentionally or not).

Post-modern artistic practice results from the display of broken conventions and rules, or of disparate and sometimes antagonistic characteristics. Suffice it to point out how the private (the personal side of art, layout strategies, art of proportions, drawing, symbolism, harmony, and musical or architectural composition) becomes public. *Real Life*, an MTV series, is the personal drama of five young people trying to make it in New York City. The script was their day-to-day existence, the attempt to harmonize their conflicting lifestyles in the elegant loft that MTV provided. When the director fell in love with one of the characters, he was brought in front of the camera's merciless eye. Likewise, the artist—painter, composer, sculptor, dancer, or film director—submits the *secrets* of his experience to the viewer, the listener, and the spectator. The artifact comes to the market delivered with its self-criticism, even with a *time bomb* set for the hour after which the work has become valueless. The making of art made public is at the same time its unmaking.

Appropriation, one of the preferred methods of the art experience, is based on a notion of aesthetic or cultural complicity. The *illiterate* public accepts a game of allusions. The alluded must be present in the work, because in the absence of a unifying literacy, there is no shared background one can count on. Insinuations, innuendo, and provocation are practiced parallel to the quote around which the work establishes its own identity.

Art is infinitely fragmented today. No direction dominates, or at least no longer than the *15 minutes* of fame that Warhol prophesied. There is a real sense of artistic glut and a feeling of ethical confusion: Is anything authentic? The public is lured into the work, sometimes in ridiculous forms (a painting with live characters touching the viewers, pinching them, reaching for pocketbooks, or spitting chewing gum); other times in naive ways (through mirrors, interactive dialogue on computer screens, live installations in a zoo, live keyboards in a music hall). Art is delivered unfinished, as a point of entry, and as an open challenge to change. To copyright openness and sign it is as absurd, or sublime, as delivering beautiful empty bars of music to serve as a score for symphonic interpretation or a multimedia event.

THE COPY IS BETTER THAN THE ORIGINAL

Within artistic practice, as much as within any other practical form of human projection, we notice the transition from a centralized system of reference and values to a system of parallel values. In the continuum generically qualified in the market as art—and what cannot be declared art today?—there is a noticeable need for intrinsic relations of patterns: what belongs together, and how commonalties are brought about. And there is a need for disparity and distinction: How do we distinguish among the plenty accumulated in a never-ending series of shows when all that changes is the name on the canvas? The same applies to photography, video art, theater, dance, minimalist music, and the architecture of deconstruction. An evident tension results, not different from the one we perceive in the market of stocks and options. The dilemma is obvious: where to invest, if at all, unless someone has insider information (*What is hot?*). This is not an expression of an ideal, as the values of literacy marked art to be, but of alternatives delivered together with the uncertainty that characterizes the new artistic experience as one of obsession with recognition in an environment of competition that often becomes adversarial. The umbrellas that the Parisians used to attack Impressionist canvases at the turn of the century are children's toys in comparison to the means of aesthetic annihilation used in our time.

Becoming a practical experience focused on its own condition and history, this kind of art affects the appropriation of its products in the sense of increasing artificiality—the shared phylocultural component—and decreasing naturalness. Accordingly, interpretive practice is focused on establishing distinctions (often hair-splitting), more and more within the artistic domain, in disregard of message, form, ethical considerations, and even skill. This is the type of art whose photographic reproduction is always better than the original. This is the music that always sounds crisper on a compact disk. This is the art whose simuli of the show, performance, dance, or concert on television are even better than the production. Meaning comes about in an individual experience of relating distinctions, not common experiences.

The specialization of art, no less than the specialization of sciences and humanities, results in the formation of numerous networks of recurrent or non-recurrent interaction. Examples of this are layering, tracing from photo-projection, expanding the strategies of collage (to include heterogeneous sources), mixing the elaborate and the spontaneous (in dance, performance, video, even architecture). The pencil and brush are replaced by the scanner and by memes of operations favoring minute detail over meaningful wholes. Music is generated by means of sampling and synthesizing. We deal with a phenomenon of massive decentralization—each is potentially an artist—and generalized integration through networks of interaction, within which museums, galleries, and auction houses represent major nodes. It is not unusual to see the walls of a museum become the support for a work whose life ends with the end of the show, if not earlier. Many musical compositions never make it to paper, forever sentenced to tape or compact disk. Composers who do not know how to read or write music rely on the musical knowledge integrated in their digital instruments.

With the advent of technological means for the production and dissemination of images, sounds, and performances begins an age of a *sui generis* artistic environment of life that is easy to adapt to individual preference, easy to change as the preference changes. The new artistic practice results in the demythification of artists and their art. Art itself is demythified at the same time. As a consequence of electronic reproducibility and infinite manipulation, art forms a new library of images with memory devices loaded with scanned art, but with no books. Sound samples are the *library* of the composer active in the civilization of illiteracy. Using networking as a matter of practicability, people could display, in places of living or work, images from any collection, or listen to music from any ongoing concert around the globe. They could also change the selection without touching the display. They could redo each artwork as they please, painting over its digital double in the act of appropriating it, probably beyond what any artist of the past would ever accept, or any artist of the present would care for. Music could be subjected to similar appropriations. As a matter of fact, televised images are already manipulated and *re-written*. DVD—three letters standing for Digital Video Data—yet to make it into the everyday jargon reflecting our involvement with new media, will probably replace the majority of televised images. With the advent of digital video delivered via the familiar compact disk format, a tool as powerful as any TV production facility will support artistic innovation that we still associate with high budgets and glamorous Hollywood events.

Art, as much as any other form of human interaction in the civilization of illiteracy, involves shorter cycles of exchange and contact at each of its levels: meaning constitution, symbolism, education, merchandise. The *eternity* and *transcendence* of art, notions and expectations associated with the literate experience, become nostalgic references of a past pragmatics. Viewers consume art almost at the rhythm at which they consume everything else. Art consumes itself, exhausting a model even before it can be publicly acknowledged as one. In its new manifestations, not all necessarily in digital format, but many in the transitory existence of networks, it either comes in an abundance, which contradicts the literacy-based ideal of uniqueness, or in short-lived singular modes, which contradicts the ideal of permanency. Strategies of over-writing, over-dancing, over-sounding, and over-impression are applied with frenzy. Grid structures made visible become containers for very fluid forms of expression, bringing to mind the fluidity of Chinese calligraphy. Afro-American street dancers, West European ballet groups, and theaters in which the human body is integrated into the more comprehensive body of the show, practice these strategies for different purposes and with different aesthetic goals. There is also a lot of parody, and fervor, in expanding one medium into another: music becomes painting or sculpture; dance becomes image; sculpture lends its volume to theatrical projects or to 3D renditions, virtual or real events that integrate the natural and the artificial.

In this vast effort of exploration, authenticity is rarely secured. Photography, especially in its digital forms, would be impossible without the industry it created; nor would painting, sculpture, music, or computer-based interactive art (cyberart, another name for virtual reality) without the industries they stimulated. The legitimate market of *fakes* and the illegitimate market of *originals* meet in the illiterate obsession with celebrity, probably the most fleeting of all experiences. The extension of *art as practice* to *art as object,* resulting from the aesthetic experience in the space of reproductions better than originals, is challenged by the intensions of the act (process). Intensity is accepted more and more as the essence of the artistic practical experience, impossible to emulate in a reproduction, and actually excluded in the perfection of a concert transposed onto a compact disk, for example, or of images on CD-ROM and DVD disks.

When each of us can turn into a gazelle, a lobster, a stone, a tree, a pianist, a dancer, an oboe, or even an abstract thought by donning gloves and goggles, we are projected in a space of personal fantasy. Creativity in virtual reality, including creativity of interaction on the Internet, invites play. It can be in someone's private theater, sex parlor, or drug experience. As an interactive medium, virtual reality can be turned into an instrument for knowing others as they unfold their creativity in the virtual space shared. As opposed to art in its conventional form, virtual reality supports real-time interactions. The artist and the work can each have its own life. Or the artist can decide to become the work and experience the perception of others. No Rembrandt or Cézanne, not even the illiterate graffiti artists in the New York subway system could experience such things.

Surprisingly, this experience is not limited only to non-language based experiences, but also to the art of writing and reading. Embodied in avatars, many would-be writers contribute their images or lines to ongoing fictional situations on chat sites on the World Wide Web. While art is freeing itself from literacy, literature does not seem to have the same possibility. Or is this another prejudice we carry with us from the pragmatic framework of literacy-defined self-constitution? The borderline, if any, between art and writing is becoming fuzzier by the hour.

The art of the word, of language, as exemplified in poetry, novels, short stories, plays, and movie scripts, takes place in a very strange domain of our existence. Why strange? The languages of poetry and of our routine conversations differ drastically. How they are different is not easy to explain. Many a writer and interpreter of poetry, plays, and stories (short or long) used their wisdom to explain that Gertrude Stein's "A rose is a rose is a rose," (or for that matter, Shakespeare's "A rose by any other name...") is not exactly the same as "A nose is a nose is a nose..." (or "A nose by any other name..."). Although the similarities between the two are so evident that, without a certain shared experience of poetry, some of us would qualify both as identically silly or identically strange, there is a literary quality that distinguishes them.

The *art* of written words, usually called literature, involves using language for practical purposes other than projecting our common experiences and sharing them on a social level. Nabokov once told his students that literature was not born on the day someone cried "Wolf! Wolf!" out of the Neander Valley as a wolf ran after him (or her). Literature was born when no wolf chased that person. "Between the wolf in the tall grass and the wolf in the tall story, there is a shimmering go-between. That go-between, that prism [Nabokov qualified Proust as a prism] is the art of literature." This is not the place to discuss the definition of literature, or to set one forth. It is clear, nevertheless, that literature is not the mere use of language. By a definition still to be challenged, there is no literature outside *written* language. (The term *oral literature* is regarded as a sad oxymoron by linguists who specialize in oral cultures.) Furthermore, there is no appropriation of the art of language, of its aesthetic expressiveness, without understanding language, a necessary but still insufficient condition. (It is insufficient because to understand language is not equal to using language creatively). Partisans of literacy will say that there is no literature *without literacy*. However, language use in literature is not the same as language use in daily life, in the self-constitutive experience of living and surviving.

When human experience is projected in language and language becomes a medium for new experiences, there is no distinction in the experience. The syncretic character of language as it is formed in a particular pragmatic framework corresponds to the syncretic character of human activity in its very early stages. Distinctions in language are introduced once this experience of self-constitution is segmented and various forms of labor division are brought about by expectations of efficiency. The scale of humankind, whatever it might be at a given moment, is reflected in distinctions in the pragmatic framework, which, in turn, determines distinctions in human expression and communication through language. Survival becomes a form of human practice, losing its primeval condition when it implies the experience of cooperation, and the realization, though limited, of what transcends immediacy. Killing an animal to satisfy hunger does not require awareness of needs and the means to fulfill them, as much as it requires natural qualities such as instinct, speed, and strength. Noticing that the flesh of an animal hit by lightening does not rot like the flesh of slaughtered animals requires a different awareness. The first reports about the immediate sequence of cause and effect; the second, about the ability to infer from one practical domain to another. So does the perceived need to share and expand experience.

In the oral phase, and in oral cultures still extant, the immediate and the remote (fear, for example, and the magical addressed with the hope of help) are addressed in the same language. The poetry of myths, or what is made of them as examples of poetry, is actually the poetry of the pragmatics pertinent to efficiency expectations of a small scale of humanity conveyed in myth. Rules for successful action were conveyed orally from one generation to another. Only much later in time, and due to demand for higher efficiency and the expanding scale, do different forms of practical experience separate, but not yet radically. Wolf is wolf, whether it is running after someone, or it is only a product of someone's imagination, or it is displayed in a cage in the zoo, or it is in the process of becoming extinct. Behind each of these situations lies an experience of conflict, on whose basis symbolism (rooted in zoomorphic, anthropomorphic, geometric, astrologic, or religious forms) is established. The use of language symbols is structurally identical to the use of astronomic, mathematical, or mytho-magical symbols in that it uses the conventional nature of the representation in sign processes (generation of new symbols, associations among symbols, symbolic inferences, etc.).

CRYING WOLF STARTED EARLY

Literature results from the perceived need to transcend the immediate and to make possible an experience in a time and space of choice, or in the space and time of language itself. Naming a place *Florence, Brugges, Xanadu, Bombay, Paris, Damascus, Rio de Janeiro,* or *Beijing* in a story derives from a motivation different from how names were given to real cities, to rivers, to mountains, even to human beings. Names are usually identifiers resulting from the pragmatic context. They become part of our environment, constituting the markers for the context, the stones and barbwire fence of the borders of the experiences from which they result. In each name of a person, place, or animal in what is called real life, as well as in fiction (poetry, plays, novels), the practical experience of human self-constitution creeps in.

When readers of a novel, audiences at a play, or listeners at a poetry recitation say that they learn something about the place, characters, or subject, they mean that they learn something (however limited) about the practical experience involved in constituting that novel, performance, or poem. Whether they really know about something, or whether they care to know it, is a different question. Usually, they do not know or care to know because, being born in a language, moreover being subjected to literacy, they believe that things are real because they are in language. They take the world for granted because words describe it. With such a frame of mind, things become even more real when they are written about. Some people are educated to accept some things as more real than others: historical accounts, geographic accounts, biographies, diaries, books, images on a screen. More often than not, people walk through Verona in order to see where Shakespeare's famous pair of enamored adolescent lovers swore undying love to each other. They wind up in front of some ridiculous plaque identifying *the place.* And because the incident has gone down in writing, they accept the place as real. A picture taken there seems to extend the *reality* of Romeo and Juliet into their lives. The same can be said of Bran Castle and the fictional Dracula; likewise for the so-called holy places in Jerusalem, reputed cafés in Paris, or sites associated with the name of Al Capone. Real life eventually makes the distinction between fiction, the fiction of fiction, the tourism of the fiction of fiction, and reality.

There is a borderline between the practice of writing (fiction or not) and the appropriation of literature by critics, historians of literature, linguists, tourist organizations, and readers. In the experience of writing, authors constitute themselves by projecting, in selected words and sentences, the ability to map between the world they live in and the world of language. In the experience of reading, one projects the ability to understand language and recreate a world in a text, not necessarily the same world in which writers constitute their identity. The process comprises a reduction, from the infinity of situations, words, ideas, characters, stylistic choices, and rhythms, to the uniqueness of the text, and the extension from one text to an infinity of understandings of the many components of a printed book or performed play. In this process, new reductions are made possible. The history of literature and language is well known for the stereotypes of systematic scholarly exposition. Literary critics proceed with a different strategy of reduction; book marketers end up summarizing a novel in a catch-phrase. What we learn from this is that there are several ways to encode, decode, and then encode again thoughts, emotions, reactions, and whatever else is involved in the experience of writing and reading.

The history of literature is connected to the diversification of language in more ways than traditional historic accounts lead us to believe. Even the emergence of genres and subgenres can be better understood if we consider the practice of literature in relation to the many forms of human practice. My intention is not to endorse the convention of realism, one of the weak explanatory models that theoreticians and historians of art and literature have used for a long time. The goal is to explain and document that various relations between spoken and written language and the language of literature lead to various writing conventions. In the syncretic phase of human practice, the relation was based on identity. In other words, the two forms of language were not distinguishable. Language was one. Distinctions in practical experiences resulted in distinctions in the self-constitution of the human being through a language that captured similarities and differences, and became a medium for conventions. These eventually led to symbols. Symbolism was acknowledged in writing, itself an expression of conventions.

The language of astronomy, agriculture, and alchemy (to refer here to incipient science, technology, and magic) was only as remote from *normal* language as normalcy was from observing stars, cultivating soil, or trying to turn lead into gold, conjuring the benevolence of magic forces. Reading today whatever survived or was reconstituted from these writings is an experience in poetry and literature. Unless the reader has a specific interest in the subject matter (as a scientist, philosopher, historian, or linguist), these writings no longer recall the *wolf,* but the art of expression in language. They are considered poetry or literature, not because they contain wrong ideas or false scientific hypotheses—their practical experience is in a pragmatic context to which we have difficulty connecting—but because their language testifies to an experience of transcending the borders between human practice and establishing a systematic, encompassing domain which now seems grounded in a fictional world. Religious writings (the *Old Testament, Tao*) are also examples.

The same happens to the child who *saw* a wolf (the child did not really see a wolf, he was bored and wanted attention), started crying wolf, and when finally adults show up, there is no wolf. "Oh, he likes to tell stories," or "She has a wild imagination. She will probably become a writer." In some cases, elves, ghosts, or witches are blamed for a sudden wind, changes in weather, or trees creaking in a storm or under the weight of snow, and this is reported as private fiction. Artistic writing and appropriation form a domain of recurrences at least as much as painting, dancing, observing stars, solving mathematical equations, or designing new machines do. Literature involves a convention of complicity, something along the line of "Let us not confuse our lives with descriptions of them," although we may decide to live in the fiction. As with any convention, people do not accept it in the letter, spirit, or both, and wind up crying with the unhappy hero, laughing with the comic character or at somebody. In other words, people live the fiction or derive some lesson from it, or identify with characters, in effect, rewriting them in the ink or blood of their own lives.

META-LITERATURE

The recurring interaction between a writer (indirectly present) and a reader takes place through writing and reading. It is proof of the practicality of the literary experience and an expression of its degree of necessity. The extent of the interaction is thus the expression of the part of the practical experience that is shared, and for what purpose. This is illustrated by the uses we give to literature: education, indoctrination, moral edification, illustration, or entertainment. Becoming who they are, the writer and reader project themselves in the reading through a process of dual reciprocal constitution, changing when circumstances change, objectified in the forms through which literature is acknowledged. It has a definite learned quality, in contrast to the arts of images, sounds, and movements, in which the natural component (as in seeing, hearing, moving) made the art possible. Accordingly, artistic writing has an instrumental characteristic and exercises virtual coordination of the experience of assigning meaning. In some ways, this instrumental characteristic begs association to music. To someone watching how the process unfolds, it seems that the recurrent interaction is triggered less by the dynamics of writing and reading, and more decisively by what comprises the act of instilling meaning of the objectified practice of the poem, play, script, novel, or short story. The fact is that language, more than *natural* systems of signs, pertains to an acquired structure of interactions, as humans progress from one scale to another, within which meaning is conjured. Language is influenced by the conditions of existence (human biology), but not entirely reducible to them. It constitutes as many domains of interaction as there are experiences requiring language, a subset of language, or artifacts similar to language.

The claim made from the perspective of literacy was, and still goes strong, that the universality of language is reflected in the universality of literature, and thus the universality of conveying meaning. Actually, to write literature means to *un-write* the language of everyday use, to empty it of the reference to behavior, and to structure it as an instrument of a different projection of the human being. It means understanding the process through which meaning is conjured as human self-constitution takes place. While it is true that when someone reads a text for the first time, the only reading is one that refers to the language of that particular reader's experience (what is loosely called *knowledge of language*); once the convention is uncovered, personal experience takes second place, and a new experience, deriving from the interaction, begins. The *acquaintance* makes the interaction possible; but it might as well stand in the way of its characteristic unfolding as a literary experience. Sometimes, the language of artistic wording establishes a self-contained universe of self-reference and becomes not only the message, but also the context. The practical experience of writing is discovery of universes with such qualities. The practical experience of reading is populating such a universe through personal projection that will test its human validity. Both writer and reader create themselves and ascertain their identities in the interaction established through the text.

It goes without saying that while literature is not a copy (mimesis) of the world, neither does it literally constitute something in opposition to it. In a larger framework, literature is but one among many means of practical human experiences resulting, like any other form of objectification, in the alienating process of writing, reading, criticizing, interpreting, and rewriting. Alienation comes from *giving life* to entities that, once expressed, start their own existence, no longer under the control of the writer or reader. For as long as language dominated human praxis according to the prescriptions of literacy, we could not understand how writing could be an experience in something other than language, or how it could be performed independent of language-based assumptions. Since the turn of the century, this situation has changed. Initially, there was a reaction to language: *Dada* was born when a knife was used to select a word from a Larousse dictionary. Between the action and its successive interpretations, many layers of practical experiences with language accumulated. The literature of the absurd went further and suggested situations only vaguely defined with the aid of language, actually defined in defiance of language conventions. There is more silence in the plays of Beckett and Ionesco than there are words.

Before becoming what many readers have regarded as only the expression of the poetics of self-reference, the experience of concrete poetry attempted to make poetry visual, musical, or even tactile. *Happening* was based on structuring a situation, with the implicit assumption that our domains of interactions are not defined only through language. The modern renewal of dance, emancipated from the condition of illustration and narration, and from the stifling conventions of classic ballet; the new conventions of film facilitated by understanding the implicit characteristics of the medium; and the expressive means of electronic performances only add to the list of examples characteristic of a literature trying to free itself from language and its literate rules. Or, in order to avoid the animistic connotation (literature as a living entity trying to do something), we should see the phenomena just mentioned as examples of new human experiences: constitution of the literary work as its own language, with the assumption that the process of appropriation would result in the *realization* of that particular language.

A realization, in literature as much as in science, is a description of a system which would behave as though it had this description. Accordingly, the day described in Joyce's *Ulysses* (Thursday, June 16, 1904) was not a sequential description, but a mosaic in which rules of language were continuously broken and new rules introduced. There is no character by the name of *Ulysses* in the book. The title and the chapter subtitles were meant to enforce the suggestion of a parallel to Homer's *Odyssey*. ("A beautiful title," wrote Furetière almost 300 years ago, "is the real pimp of the book.") Language—rather, the appearance of language—provided the geometry of the mosaic. For Joyce, writing turned out to be a practical experience in segmenting space and time in order to extract relations (hopeless past, ridiculous tragic present, pathetic future), an aesthetic goal for which the common use of language is ill equipped. The allusion to the *Odyssey* is part of the strategy, shared in advance with the critics, a para-text, following the text as a context for interpretation. But before him, Kafka and others, following a tradition that claims Cervantes' *Don Quixote* as a model, seemed no less challenged by the experience of designing their own language, ascertaining characters who transcend the conflict put in words, of using the power of para-text. Dos Passos, Laurence Sterne, and Hermann Hesse are examples from the same tradition. Gertrude Stein was a milestone in this development. In poetry, designing a language of one's own is strikingly evident, although more difficult to discuss in passing (as I know I am doing with some of the examples I give). Many poets—Burns comes easily to mind—invented their own language, with new words and new rules for using them. Others—and for some reason Vladimir Brodsky comes first to mind—wrote splendid para-texts (political articles, interviews, memoirs) that very effectively framed their poetry and put it in a perspective otherwise not so evident.

The experience of artistic writing does not happen in a vacuum. It takes place in a broader frame. To realize and to understand that there is a connection between the cubist perspective, Joyce's writing, and the scientific language of relativity theory will probably not increase reading pleasure. It will change the perspective of interpretation, though. The connection between genetics, computational models, and post-modern architecture, fiction, and political discourse is even more relevant to our current concern for literature. Recurrences of interactions come in varieties, and each variety is a projection of the individual at a precise juncture of the human practical experience of self-constitution as a writer or reader. Language split, and continues to split, into languages and sub-languages. *Rap* frequently subjects the listener of its rhythmic stanzas to slang. Gramsci, the Sardinian leftist philosopher, suggested the need for a language of the proletariat. Pier Paolo Pasolini, an admirer of Gramsci and a very sophisticated artist, wrote some of his works in the Friaul dialect and in the argot used by the poor youngsters of the streets of Rome. His argument was aesthetic and moral: corrupted by commercial democracy, language loses its edge, and people living in such a deprived language environment undergo anthropological mutation. Art, in particular literature, can become a form of resistance. A new language, reconnected to the authentic being, becomes an instrument for new literacy experiences. Tolkien wrote poems in *Elvish;* Anthony Burgess made up a language by combining exotic languages (Gypsy, Malay, Cockney) and less exotic languages (English, Russian, French, Dutch). An entire magazine (*Jatmey*) publishes fiction and poetry written in *Klingon.*

In a broader perspective, it is clear that in order to effectively create literary domains, people need instruments and media for new experiences. Meta-fiction is such an experience. It unites special types of illustrated novels, photographic fiction (which proliferates in South America and the Far East), and comic books. In *Further Inquiry,* Ken Kesey offers a documented journey in order to recapture the spirit of the sixties. Images (including some from Allen Ginsberg's collection) make the book almost a collective *oeuvre.* Using similar strategies, a text of meta-fiction first establishes the convention of the text as a distinct human construct made up of words, but which behave differently from informative, descriptive, or normative sentences that we use in interhuman communication. The strategy is to place the domain of the referent in the writings. The writer thus ensures that the potential reader will have no reason to look for references in empirical reality. This act of preempting the practice of reading, based on reflex associations in a different systematic domain, is not necessarily a warranty that such associations will not be made.

There are many people who, either due to their cognitive condition, or to their relative illiteracy, take metaphors literally. However, the writer makes the effort to establish new kinds of recurrent, intertextual, and self-referential relations that signal the convention pursued. When the act of writing becomes, overtly or subvertly, the object of the writing experience, writers, and possible readers with them, move from the object domain to the *meta* domain. The writer knows that in the space of fiction, as much as in the space of the empirical world, people write on paper, tables are used to set dinner on, flowers have a scent, subways don't fly. But artistic writing is not so much reporting about the state of the world as it is constituting a different world, along with a context for interactions in this world. The validity and coherence of such worlds stems from qualities different from those that result from applying correct grammar, formal structure of arguments, syntactic integrity, and other requirements specific to the practice of language within the convention of literacy.

WRITING AS CO-WRITING (PAINTING AS CO-PAINTING, COMPOSING AS CO-COMPOSING...)

The post-modern practice of creative writing involves the intention of interaction in ways not experienced in the civilization of literacy. The written is no longer the *monument* that must not be altered or questioned, continued, or summarized. Reading, seen in part as the effort to extract the truth from the text, takes on the function of projecting truth in the context of text interpretation. Actually, the assumption of this practical experience of co-creation (literary, musical, or artistic) has to do with different languages in the practice of writing and reading (painting and viewing, composing and listening, etc.), and even of co-writing (co-painting, co-composing, etc.).

Recent literary work in the medium of hypertext—a structure within which non-linear connections are possible—shows how far this assumption extends. A structure and core of characters are given. The *reading* involves the determination of events through determination of contexts. In turn, these affect the behavior of characters in the fictional world. This can unfold as a literary work conceived as a game, whose *reading* is actually the playing: The *reader* defines the attributes of the characters, inserts herself or himself in the plot, and the simulation starts. Neither the writer nor reader needs to know what programs stand behind the ongoing *writing*, and even less to understand how they work. The product is, in all of these cases, an infinite series of co-writing. The reader changes dialogues, time and space coordinates, names and characteristics of participants in the literary event. No two works are alike. Characteristics of self-ordering and self-informing—such as "X knows such and such about Y's peculiarities," or "Group Z is aware of its collective behavior and possible deviations from the expected"—allow for the constitution of an entirely artificial domain of fiction, with rules as interesting to discover as is the mystery behind a suicide, the complexities of a character's philosophy, or the existence of yet unknown universes.

This extreme case of the literature of *personal* language—of languages as they are formed in the practice of creative co-writing—was anticipated in the various forms of fantastic literature. Voyages (anticipated in Homer's epics), explorations of future worlds, and science fiction have paved the way for the writing of meta-fiction. This probably explains how Jorge Luis Borges constituted a meta-language (of the quotes of quotes of quotes) for allegories whose *object* are fictions, not realities. There is no need to be literate to effectively appropriate this kind of writing, although at some level of reading the literate allusion awaits the literate reader (at least to tickle his or her fancy). To a certain extent, it is almost better not to have read *Madame Bovary*, with its melodramatic account, because the constitution of Borges' universe takes place at a different level of human practice, and in a context of disconnected forms of praxis.

Co-writing also takes the form of using shared code as a strategy of literary expression. The many specialized languages of literary criticism and interpretation—such as comparative studies, phenomenological analysis, structuralism, semiotic interpretation, deconstructionism—as difficult and opaque to the average literate reader as scientific and philosophic languages, are duplicated in the *specialized language* of creative post-modern writing. Reading requires a great deal of preparation for some of those works, or at least the assumed shared understanding of the particular language. The writings of Donald Barthelme, Kurt Vonnegut, and John Barthe are not casual reading, for sheer enjoyment or excitement. Mastery of the language, moreover of the language code, as part of the practical experience it facilitates, does not come from studying English in high school or college, rather from decoding the narrative strategy and understanding that the purpose of this writing is knowledge about writing and reading. The epistemological made into a subject of fiction—how do we know what we know?—makes for very dense prose. This is why in this new stage, it is possible to have readers of a one and only book (I am not referring to the *Bible* or *Koran*), which becomes the language of that reader. *Alice in Wonderland* is such a book for quite a few; so is

Ulysses; so are the two novels of William H. Gass. In the civilization of illiteracy, we experience the emergence of micro-readership attracted to non-standard writing. Efficiency considerations are such that the non-standard practical experience of writing is met by a non-standard experience of reading books, and other media (including CD-ROM) that address a small number of people.

The effort to recycle (art or literature) is part of the same co-writing strategy. The co-writers are authors (recycled) and readers whose past readings (real or imaginary) are integrated in the new experience. Recycling (names, actions, narratives, etc.) corresponds to, among other things, the attempt to counteract the sequentiality of writing, even the literate expectation of originality. Taking a piece from a literary work and using it in its entirety means to almost transform the language sequence into a configuration. That piece resembles a painting hung in the middle of a page, or, to force the image, between the parts of a sonata. It entails its own history and interpretation, and triggers a mechanism of rejection not dissimilar to that triggered by organ transplants. The convention of reading is broken; the text is manipulated like an image and offered as a collage to the reader. The seams of different parts sewn together are not hidden; to the contrary, a spotlight is focused on them. Gertrude Stein best exemplifies the tendency, and probably how well it synchronized with similar developments in art (cubism foremost). W. H. Gass masterfully wrote about words standing for characters, object, and actions; he invented new worlds where the writer can define rules for their behavior. Concrete poetry, too, in many ways anticipated this type of writing, which comes from visual experiences and from the experiments in music triggered by the dodecaphonic composers. In concrete poetry, one can even discover the expression of jealousy between those interacting in the systematic domain of abstract phonetic languages, and those in the domain of ideograms. Japanese writers of concrete poetry seem equally eager to experience the sequential! The effort to recycle, interpret, visualize, to *read* and *explain* for the reader, and to *compress* (action, description, analysis) corresponds to the ever faster interactions of humans and to the shorter duration of such interactions. The reader is presented with *pieces* already known, or with easily understandable images that summarize the action or the characters. Why imagine, as writers always expected their readers to do, if one can see—this seems to be the temptation.

THE END OF THE GREAT NOVEL

The ideal of the great novel was an ideal of a monument in literacy. Despite the technology for writing, such as word processing machines and the hypertext programs for interactive, collaborative authoring, writing the great novel is not only impossible, but irrelevant. Expectations associated with the great novel are expectations of unity, homogeneity, universality. Such a novel would address everyone, as the great novels of the civilization of literacy tended to do. The extreme segmentation of the world, its heterogeneity, the new rhythms of change and of human experiences, the continuous decline of the ideal embodied in literacy, education included, are arguments against the possibility of such a novel. An all-encompassing language, which the practical experience of writing such a novel implies, is simply no longer possible. We live in a civilization of partial languages, with their corresponding creative, non-standard writing experiences, in a disembodied domain of expression, communication, and signification. If, *ad absurdum,* various literary works could talk to each other (as their authors can and do), they would soon conclude that the shared background is so limited that, beyond the phrases of socializing and some political statements (more circumstantial than substantial), little else could be said.

Furthermore, writing itself has changed. And since there is a consubstantiality among all elements involved in the experience, the change affects the self-constitution of the writer, and subsequently that of the reader. Technology takes care of spelling and even syntax; more recently it even prompts semantic choices. This use of technology in creative writing is far from being neutral. Different rhythms and patterns of association, as embodied in our practice with interface language—the language mediating between us and the machine—are projected *volens-nolens* into the realm of literature. Moreover, different kinds of reading, corresponding to the new kinds of human interaction, become possible. One can already have a novel delivered on tape, to be listened to while driving to work. The age of the electronic book brings other reading possibilities to the public. An animated host can introduce a short story; a hand-held scanner can pick up words the reader does not know and activate a synthetic voice to read their definitions from the on-line dictionary. And this is not all!

Language used to be the medium for bridging between generations in the framework of homogeneous practical experiences. Edmund Carpenter correctly pointed out that for the civilization of literacy, the book—and what, if not the literary book, best embodies the notion of a book?—"became the organizing principle for all existence." Yes, the book seemed almost the projection of our own reality: beginning (we are all born), middle, and end (at which moment we become memory, the book itself being a form of memory), followed by new books. Carpenter went on to say, "Even as written manuscript, the book served as a model for both machine and bureaucracy. It encouraged a habit of thought that divided experience into specialized units and organized these serially and causally. Translated into gears and levers, the book became machine. Translated into people, it became army, chain of command, assembly line, etc." Handwriting, typing, dictation, and word-processing define a context for the practical experience of self-identification as novelist, poet, playwright, screenplay author, and scriptwriter. Interaction with word-processing programs produces a fluidity of writing that testifies to endless self-correction, and to rewriting driven by association. Word-processing is cognitively a different effort from writing with a pen or typewriter. And no one should be surprised that what is written with the new media cannot be the same as the works of Shakespeare, Balzac, and Tolstoi, entrusted by hand to paper. A distributed narrative effort of many people, via network interaction, is a practical experience above and beyond anything we could have had in the framework of literacy.

The first comic strip in America (1896) announced the age of complementary expression (text and drawing). Nobody really understood how far the genre would go, or how many literacy-based conventions would be undone in the process. Comic-strip characters occupied a large part of the memory of those who grew up with the names of characters from books. The influence of new media (film, in particular) on the narrative of the strip opened avenues of experiments in writing. When classics of literature (even the Bible) were presented in comic-strip form, and when comic strips were united under the cover of books, the book itself changed. Structural characteristics of the strip (fast, dense, focused, short, expressive) correspond to those of the pragmatic framework of the civilization of illiteracy.

Does the civilization of illiteracy herald the end of the book? As far as the practice of creative writing goes, it might as well, since writing does not necessarily have to take a book format. Narrative, as we know from oral tradition, can take forms other than the book. My opinion in regard to books should not be understood as prophecy. Pointing to alternatives (such as digital books, electronic publications distributed on networks and stored on disks), some perhaps not thought through as yet, keeps the influence of our own framework of reference at a distance. A video format, as poor and unsatisfying a substitute as it might seem to someone raised with the book, is a candidate everyone can name. After all, the majority of the books studied a generation ago are known to the students of this time mainly through television and movie adaptations. The majority of today's children's books are released together with their video simuli. Computer-supported artifacts, endowed or not with literary intelligence, are another candidate for replacing the book. What we know is that paper can be handled only so much and preserved only so long (even if it is non-acid paper). Furthermore, it becomes more and more an issue of efficiency whether we can afford transforming our forests into books, which humankind, faced with many challenges, may no longer be able to afford, or which are so disconnected from current pragmatics that they have lost their relevance.

Today, while still entirely devoted to the ideal of literacy, societies subsidize literary practical experiences which are only peripherally relevant to human experience. A large number of grants go to writers who will probably never be read; many more to contests (themselves anchored in the obsession with hierarchy peculiar to literacy) open to students lost in the labyrinth of an illusion; and even more to schools and seminars of marginal or very narrow interest, or to publications that barely justify the effort and expense of their endeavor. From the perspective of the beneficiaries, awarding such grants is the right thing to do. In the long run, this altruism will not save more of the literacy-based literature than highly specialized contemporary society perceives as necessary in respect to efficiency requirements facing the world at the current scale. In labor division, the literate writer and reader constitute their systematic domain of interaction.

The book will no doubt remain in some form or another (words on paper or dots on an electronic page of a portable reading device) as long as people derive pleasure or profit from the printed word. But as opposed to the past, this is only one among many literary and non-literary domains of interaction. It is, for example, very difficult to say whether the artists of the graffiti movement were writers, using an alphabet reminiscent of Egyptian hieroglyphs, or painters with words, or both. Keith Haring, their best known representative, covered every available square inch—*horror vacui*—with expressions that constituted a new systematic domain of interaction among people, as well as a new space for his own self-constitution as a different type of artist.

Instead of decrying the end of an ideal, we should celebrate the victory of diversity. Those who really feel that their destiny relies on the ideal of literature might choose to give up some of their expectations, stimulated by the literate model, in order to preserve the structure within which literacy is possible and necessary. The demand for more at the lowest price that heralds the multi-headed creature called the civilization of illiteracy affects more than the production of clothes and dishes, or of cars and an insatiable appetite for travel. It affects our ways of writing, reading, painting, singing, dancing, composing, interpreting, and acting—our entire *aesthetic experience.*

CHAPTER 9: LIBRARIES, BOOKS, READERS

Carlyle believed that "The true university is a collection of books." If books truly represent the spirit and letter of the civilization of literacy, a description of their current condition can be instructive. Obviously, one has to accept the possibility that the civilization of literacy will continue in some form, or in more than one, that will extend the experience of the book, as we know it today through its physical form. Or the civilization of literacy may continue in a totally new form that responds to the human desire for efficiency. Addressing the International Publishers Association Congress in June, 1988, George Steiner tried to identify the "interlocking factors" that led to the establishment of book culture. The technology of printing, paper production, and advances in typography that are associated with the "private ownership of space, of silence, and of books themselves" are among factors affecting the process. Another important factor is book aesthetics, the underlying formal quality of a medium that had to compete with vivid images, with powerful traditions of orality, and with patterns of behavior established within practical experiences different from those of book culture.

Near the end of the 15th century, Aldus Manutius understood that the new technology of printing could be, and should be, more than the mere continuation of the tradition of manuscripts. The artifact of the book, close to what we know today, is mainly his contribution to the civilization of literacy. Manutius applied aesthetic and functional criteria that led to the smaller-sized books we are familiar with. He worked with covers; the hard cover in thicker cardboard replaced the covers of pinewood used to protect manuscripts and early printed texts. The understanding of aesthetics and of the experience of reading led him to define better layouts and a new typography. His concern with portability (a quality obsessing contemporary computer designers), with readability (of no less interest to computer display experts), and with a balanced visual appearance make him the real saint of the *order of the book*.

The book also entails conventions of intellectual ownership. In their effort to stop the dissemination of heretical books through print, Philip and Mary, in 1557, limited the right of printing to the members of the Stationers' Company. In 1585, copyright for members was introduced; and in 1709, copyright for authors. From that time on, the book expanded the notion of property, different from the notion of ownership of land, animals, and buildings, especially in view of the desire, implicit in literacy, to literally *spread the word*. Now that desktop capabilities and technologies that facilitate print on demand affordably reproduce print, old notions of property and ownership need to be redefined. Our understanding of books and the people who read them, too, needs to be redefined as well.

Today, books can be stored on media other than sheets of paper, on which words are printed and which are bound between hard or soft covers. One hundred optical disks can store the entire contents of the Library of Congress. This means, among other things, that works of incredible significance cost five cents per book *printed* digitally. Another result is that the notion of intellectual ownership becomes fuzzy. Actually, the word *book* is not the proper one to use in the case of digital storage. The new pragmatics makes it crisply clear that the book is merely a medium for the storage and transmission of data, knowledge, and wisdom, as well as a lot of stupidity and vulgarity.

For people who prefer the book format, high-performance printing presses are able to efficiently provide runs for very precisely defined segments of the population just waiting for the *Great American Novel* that is custom written and produced for one reader at a time. "Personalized Story Books Starring Your Child," screams an advertisement. It promises "Hard cover, full color illustration, exciting stories with positive image building storylines." All that must be provided is the child's name, age, city of residence, and the names of three friends or relatives. The rest is permutation (and an order form). Grandma did a better job with her photo and keepsake album, but the framework of mediation replaced her long ago. Paper is available in all imaginable quantities and qualities; the technologies of typesetting, layout, image reproduction, and binding are all in place.

Nowadays, there is enough private space. The wash of noise is not a serious obstacle to people who want to read, even if they do not wear noise cancellation headphones. And never were books published at more affordable prices than today. Some books reside on the *shelves* of the Internet or are integrated in broader hyper-books on the World Wide Web. A word from one book—let's say a new concept built upon earlier language experiences—connects the interested reader to other books and articles, as well as to voices that read texts, to songs, and to images. The book is no longer a self-sufficient entity, but a medium for possible interaction.

At the threshold of the civilization of illiteracy, how many books are printed? In which medium? How many are sold? Are they read? How? By whom? These are only some of the questions to be posed when approaching the subject of books. Even more important is the "Why?"—in particular, "Why read books?"—the real test of the book's legitimacy, and ergo, the legitimacy of the civilization which the book emblemizes. The broader issue is actually reading and writing, or to be more precise, the means through which an author can address many readers.

The fine balance of factors involved in the publishing and success of a book is extremely difficult to describe. The general trend in publishing can be described as more and more titles in smaller and smaller editions. Ideally, a good manuscript (of a novel, book of poetry, plays, essays, scientific or philosophic writings) should become a successful book, i.e., one that sells. In the reality of the book business, many mediating elements determine the destiny of a manuscript. Most of these elements are totally unrelated to the quality of writing or to the satisfaction of reading. They reflect market processes of valuation.

These elements are symptomatic of the book's condition in the civilization that moves towards the pragmatics of many competing literacies, almost all contradicting the intrinsic characteristics of literacy embodied in the book. The life of books is shorter (despite their being printed on acid-free paper). Books have a decreasing degree of universality; more books address limited groups of readers as opposed to a large general market, not to mention the whole of humankind, as was once the book's purpose. Books use specialized languages, depending on their topics. The distinct ways these languages convey contents frequently contradict the culturally acknowledged condition of the book, and are a cause of concern to people who are the products of (or adherents to) a civilization based on books. More and more books end up as collections of images with minimal commentary. Some are already delivered together with a tape cassette or compact disk, to be heard rather than read, to be seen rather than to engage the reader's mind. *Road Reading* is a billboard trademark for recorded books. Narrated by voices appropriate to the subject (a southern drawl for a story like *To Kill a Mockingbird*; a cultivated voice for Charles Dickens's *A Tale of Two Cities*), the books compete with red lights, landscapes, and other signs along the road. Many books written in our day contain vulgar language and elevate slang to the qualitative standard of fiction. There are books that promise the excitement of a game (find the object or the criminal). A reward, effectively replacing the satisfaction of reading, will be handed to the lucky finder. The subject of reading has also changed since the time the Bible and other religious texts, dramas and poetry, philosophic and scientific writings were entrusted to the printing press. Melodramatic fiction, at least 200 years old, paved the way for pulp fiction and today's surefire bestsellers based on gossip and escapism.

Our goal is to understand the nature of change in the book's condition, why this change is a cause for concern, as well as our own relation to books. To do this, we should examine the transition that defines the identity and role of the writer and reader in the new pragmatic context.

WHY DON'T PEOPLE READ BOOKS?

"Do you ever read any of the books you burn?" Clarisse McClellan asks in *Fahrenheit 451*. (This book is also available in video format and as a computer game.) Guy Montag, the fireman, answers, "That is against the law." This conversation defines a context: The group that still reads is able to pass the benefits of their experience to people who are not allowed to read books. In our days, no fireman is paid to set books ablaze. To the contrary, many people are employed to save deteriorating books printed in the past. But the question of whether people read any of the books they buy or receive, or even save from destruction, cannot be dismissed.

The majority of the books changing hands and actually read are reference publications. The home contains an increasing number of radios, television sets, CD players, electronic games, video cassette recorders, and computers. The shelf space for books is being taken up by other media. Instead of the personal library, people consecrate space in their homes for *media centers* that consume a great deal of their free time. Instead of the permanence of the printed text, they prefer the variability of continually changing programs, of scanning and sampling, and of surfing the Internet. The digital highway supplies an enormous amount of reference material. This material is, moreover, kept up to date, something that is not so easy to accomplish with bound sets of encyclopedias or even with the telephone book.

Books are not burned, but neither are they read with much commitment. Scanning through a story or reading the summary on the flip jacket, filling one's time during a commute or at the airport is all that happens in most cases. A variety of books are written for such purposes. Required reading for classes, according to teachers, cannot exceed the attention span of their pupils. Growing up under the formative influence of short cycles and the expectation of quick conclusions to their acts, youngsters oppose any reading that is not to the point (as they see it). In most cases, outlines provide whatever knowledge (information is probably a better word) is needed for a class or for a final examination. The real filter of reading is the multiple choice grid, not the satisfaction of immersion in a world brought to life by words.

All this is almost the end of the story, not the substance of its arguments. The arguments are manifold and all related to characteristics of literacy. In the first place, publishers simply discard the traditional reverence for books. They realize that a book placed somewhere on the pedestal of adulation, extended from the religious Book to books in general, keeps readers away or makes them captive to interpretive prejudices.

How can one be involved in the practice of democracy without extending it to books, thus giving Cervantes and Whitman a place equal to that of the cheap, mass-produced pulp literature and even the videotape? The experience of the book reveals a double-edged sword, deriving mainly from the perception that the book, as a vessel, sanctifies whatever it carries. Hitler's *Mein Kampf* was such a book in Nazi Germany, and still is for Nazi revivalists. In the former communist countries, the books of Marx and Engels were sanctified, printed without end (after careful editing), and forced upon readers of all age groups, especially the young. Nobody could argue against even trivial factual errors that slipped into their writings, into translations, or into selective editions. Mao's little *Red Book* was distributed free to everyone in China. In our day, Hitler and other authors of the same bent are published. These very few examples follow a long line of books dealing in indoctrination (religious, ideological, economic), misrepresentation, and bigotry. As insidious attempts to seduce for disreputable, if not frankly criminal causes, they have inflicted damage on humanistic expectations and on the practice of human-based values. Champions of literacy point to the classics of history and enlightenment and to the great writers of poetry, fiction, and drama as the authentic heritage of the book. How much space do they occupy on the shelves of bookstores, libraries, and homes? In good faith and without exaggerating, one can easily conclude that from all the books stored in homes and places of public access, the majority should probably have never been written, never mind printed or read. If these books and periodicals were only repetitive of what had been said and thought previously, they would not deserve such strong condemnation. The judgment expressed above refers to words and thoughts whose shallowness and deceit are consecrated through the associations that the printed word entails.

Hard facts about books in the new pragmatic context confirm that people, either due to illiteracy or a-literacy, read less and use books less and less for their practical experiences. Titles make it onto the bestseller lists only because they are sold, not read. Intrinsic qualities—of writing, aesthetics, the ideas set forth—are rarely taken into consideration, unless they confirm the prejudices of their consumers. Books often make it onto the bookshelf as a status symbol. In the early eighties, everyone in Italy, Germany, and the USA wanted to display *The Name of the Rose*. Or they become a subject of conversation—"It will be made into a movie." But even such books remain unread to the last page 70% of the time. Today, by virtue of faster writing and printing, books compete with the newspaper in capturing the sensational. The unholy alliance between the film industry, television, and publishing houses is very adept at squeezing the last possible drop of sleaze from an event of public interest in order to catch one more viewer or purchaser of cheaply manufactured books.

Because of a combination of many factors—long production cycles, high cost of publishing and marketing, low transparency, rapid acquisition of knowledge that makes high quality books obsolete in one or two years, to name a few factors—the book has ceased to be the major instrument for the dissemination of knowledge related to practical experiences. First among the factors affecting the book's role is that the rhythm of renewal and conversion requires a medium that can keep pace with change. Prior to the breakdown of the former Soviet Union and the Eastern Block, the majority of books on politics, sociology, economics, and culture pertinent to that part of the world became useless from one day to the next as events and whims rendered their content meaningless. Once the Eastern Block started to unravel, even periodicals could not keep pace with events. All around the world, strikes, various forms of social activism, political debates, successive reorganizations, new borders, and new leaders contradicted the image of stability settled in the books of scholars and even in the evaluations issued by intelligence agencies.

Not only politics required rewriting. Books on physics, chemistry, mathematics, computing, genetics, and mind and brain theory have to be rewritten as new discoveries and technologies render obsolete facts associated with past observations published as eternal truth. In some cases, the books were rewritten on tape, as visual presentations impossible to fit in sentences or between book covers, or on CD-ROM. More recently, books are being rewritten as Internet publications or full-fledged Web sites that can easily be kept current. Photocopies of selected pages and articles already substitute for the book on the desks of students, professors, scholars, and researchers. College students, who are obliged to buy books, don't like to invest in items that they know will be outdated and useless within a year. The book will appear in a new edition, either because the information has been updated or because the publisher wants to make more money. Students prefer the videotape, so much closer to tele-viewing, an experience that ultimately forms cognitive characteristics different from those of reading and writing. Or they prefer to find material on-line, again a cognitive experience of a dynamic condition incompatible with the book.

The complexity of human practical experiences is as important as the dynamics. The pragmatic framework that made literacy and the book necessary was relatively homogeneous. Heterogeneity entails a state of affairs for which books can only serve after the experience, as a repository medium. Even in this documentary or historic function, books capture less than what other media, better adapted to sign processes irreducible to literacy, could. For the experience as such, books become irrelevant, whether we like it or not. The facts relating to the consequences of the increased complexity of current pragmatics have yet to be realized, much less recorded. What is available is the accumulated human experience with alternate media, not necessarily cheaper than books, but certainly better adapted to instances of parallelism and distributed activities.

Books do justice to simultaneous temporal phenomena only at the expense of capturing their essence. The nature of human praxis is so radically disconnected from the nature of literacy embodied in the book that one can no longer rely on it without affecting the outcome. Practical experiences in which time is of the essence, and activities that require synchronization or are based on a configurational paradigm are different in nature from writing and reading. To open a book, to look for the appropriate page, and to read and understand the information slows down (or stops) the process. The sequential nature of literacy misses the requirement of synchronism and might not even lead to solutions to questions related to non-sequential connections.

In addition to these major factors, there is the broader background: Access to knowledge conveyed through literacy implies a shared literate experience. Shared experience, especially in open, dynamic societies, can no longer be assumed as a given. There are cultural as well as physical differences to be accounted for among all the human beings in the developed world. There are the visually impaired and physically handicapped who cannot use books. There are people with conditions that do not allow for the deciphering of printed letters and words. These individuals must rely on devices that *read* for them, on senses other than sight, and on a good memory.

The decreased interest in books is indicative of a fundamentally different human practical experience of self-constitution. In line with the shift from manufacturing to service, books perform mainly functions of incidental information (when not replaced by a database), amusement, and filling time. Even if the great novel, or great epic poem, or great drama were written, it would go unnoticed in the loud concert of competing messages. It might be that literature today is passionless, or it might be that the seduction of commercial success brings everything to the common denominator of return on an investment, regardless of cultural reward. Books written to please, books published to satisfy vanity, and books of impenetrable obscurity did not exactly trigger reader interest. All in all, good and bad considered, the general evolution does not testify to less literary talent. The issue of quality is open to controversy, as it always has been. Many books reflect a level of literacy that is not exactly encouraging. Still, literature does not fail on its merits (or lack thereof). It fails, rather, on the context of its perception. Like anything else in the civilization of illiteracy, the multiplication of choices resulted in the annihilation of a sense of value and of effective criteria for differentiation within the continuum of writing.

The overall development towards the civilization of illiteracy suggests that the age of the book is being followed by an age of alternative media. The promoters of literacy are doing their best to resist this change. Their motto is "Read anything, as long as you read." They effectively discount any and all other means of acquiring knowledge, and totally disenfranchise individuals who cannot read. There are many avenues to self-constitution: all our senses—including common sense—repetition and memory. Some of these avenues are more efficient than the medium of the book. If they were not, they would not be succeeding as they do. The champions of literacy also imply that anything acquired through reading is good. The harm that can be transmitted through the book medium can be recorded in volumes. On the collective level, it has led to persecution and violence, even mass destruction. On the individual level, it can lead to imbalance. The child who is forced to read at age three is being deprived of time for developing other skills essential to his or her physical and mental well-being. The cognitive repertory of these children is being stunted by well meaning but misguided parents. It is being stunted, too, by the market that sells literacy as though there were no tomorrow despite the fact that literacy has lost its dominant position in our lives.

TOPOS URANIKOS DISTRIBUTED

This book began by contrasting the readers of the past to today's typical literate: Zizi the hairdresser and her boyfriend, the taxi driver with the college degree in political science. The underlying structure of human practical experiences through which average persons like Zizi and Bruno G., as well as the Nobel prize winner in genetics, artists, sportsmen and sportswomen, writers, TV producers, and computer hackers (and many other professionals), constitute themselves is characterized by a new type of relations among parts. These relations are in flux. Whereas many functions associated with human experiences can be rationalized, levels of efficiency beyond individual capabilities can be achieved. Thus, one of the main goals is to harmonize the relation between human experience and the functioning of devices emulating human activities. This raises the issue of the altered human condition. In this context, the relevance of knowledge has changed to the extent that, in order to function in a world of arbitrary bureaucratic rules designed to blindly implement a democracy of mediocrity, one has to know the trivia of prices in the supermarket. Someone has to know how to access them when they are stored in a memory device, and how to charge the bill to a credit card number. But no one has to know the history of cultural values. It actually helps to ignore value altogether.

The roots of almost everything involved in current practical experiences are no longer effectively anchored in tradition, but in the memory of facts and actions extracted from tradition. At a time when books are merely an interior designer's concept of decoration, beautifully crafted editions fill the necessary bookcase. Humanity has reached a new stage: We are less grounded in nature and tradition. This condition takes some of the wind out of the sails of memetics. Practical experiences of human self-constitution extended the human phenotype beyond that of any other known species. But this extension is not the sum total of genetic and cultural evolution. It is of a different quality that neither genetic nor memetic replication suggests, let alone explains. Our obsession is to surpass the limitations of the past, cultural as well as natural. That makes us like the many things we generated in the attempt to reach levels of efficiency which neither nature nor tradition can support. The hydroponic tomato, the genetically engineered low-fat egg, the digital book, and the human being of the civilization of illiteracy have more in common than one thinks at the mere mention of this opinion.

The life of books, good or bad, useful or destructive, entertaining or boring, is the life of those who read them. Free to constitute ourselves in a framework of human experiences opened to much more than books, we have the chance of exploring new territories of human expression and communication, and of achieving levels of significance. Individual performance in the civilization of literacy could not reach such levels. But this formulation is suspect of cheap rhetoric. It begs the question "Why don't we?" (accomplish all these potentialities). We are so many, we are so talented, we are so well informed. The civilization of illiteracy is not a promised land. Interactive education centers, distributed tasks, cooperative efforts, and cultivation and use of all senses do not just happen. Understanding new necessities, in particular the relation between the new scale of humankind and the levels of efficiency to be reached in order to effectively address higher expectations of well being, does not come through divine inspiration, high-tech proselytizing, or political speeches. It results from the experience of self-constitution itself, in the sense that each experience becomes a locus of interactions, which transcends the individual.

The realization of potential is probably less direct than the realization of dangers and risks. We are still singing the sirens' song instead of articulating goals appropriate to our new condition. One area in which goals have been articulated and are being pursued is the transfer of the contents of books from various libraries to new media allowing for storage of information, more access to it, and creative interaction. The library, perceived as a form of trans-human memory, a space of *topos uranikos* filled with eternal information, was the collection of ideas and forms that one referred to when in need of guidance. Robert de Sorbon gave his books to the University of Paris almost 750 years ago. Little did he know what this gesture would mean to the few scholars who had access to this collection. By 1302 (only 25 years after his donation), one of the readers would jot down the observation that he would need ten years to read the just under 1,000 books in the library. One hundred years later, Pembroke College of Cambridge University and Merton College of Oxford obtained their libraries. The Charles University in Prague, the universities in Krakow (Poland), Coimbra (Portugal), Salamanca (Spain), Heidelberg and Cologne (the future Germany), Basle (Switzerland), and Copenhagen (Denmark) followed suit. Libraries grew into national cultural monuments. Museums grew within them and then became entities in their own right. Today, billions of books are housed in libraries all over the world. Books are in our homes, in town and city libraries, in research institutions, in religious centers, in national and international organizations. Under the guise of literacy, we are happy to be able to access, regardless of the conditions (as borrowers or subscribers), this enormous wealth of knowledge. The library represented the permanent central storehouse of knowledge.

But the pragmatic framework of human self-constitution moved beyond the characteristics embodied by both library and book. Therefore, a new library, representative of many literacies—visual, aural, and tactile, relying on multimedia, and models and simulations—and able to cope with fast change had to come about. This library, to which we shall return, now resides in a distributed world, accessible from many directions and in many ways, continuously open, and freed from the anxiety that books might catch fire or turn into dust. True, the image of the world limited almost exclusively to reference books does not speak in favor of the enormous investment in time, money, and talent for taking the new routes opened by non-linear means of access to information, rich sensorial content, and interactivity. Still, in many ways Noah Webster's experience in publishing his dictionary—a reference for America as the *Larousse* is for France and the *Duden* for Germany—can be retraced in the multimedia encyclopedias of our day, moreover in the emergence of the virtual library.

In 1945, Vannevar Bush wrote his prophetic article in the *Atlantic Monthly*. He announced, "Wholly new forms of encyclopedias will appear, ready-made with a mesh of associative trails running through them." He went on to illustrate how the lawyer will have "at his touch the associated opinions and decision of his whole experience." The patent attorney could call "the millions of issued patents, with familiar trails to every point of his client's interest." The physician, the chemist, the historian will use Bush's modestly named *Memex* to retrieve information. The conclusion, in a well subdued tone, was "Presumably man's spirit should be elevated if he can better review his shoddy past and analyze more completely and objectively his present problems."

Written immediately after World War II, Bush's article was concerned with applying the benefits of scientific research for warfare in the new context of peace. What he suggested as a rather independent application is now the reality of on-line communities of people working on related topics or complementing each other's work. The benefits of electronic mail, of shared files, of shared computing power are not what interest us here. Ted Nelson, whose name is connected to Project Xanadu, acknowledged the benefits deriving from Bush's vision, but he is mainly concerned with the power of linking.

Nelson learned from literacy that one can link text to a footnote (the *jump-link*), to a quote (the *quote-link*), and to a marginal note (the *correlink*, as he calls it). He designed his project as a distributed library of ever new texts and images open to everyone, a medium for authoring thoughts, for linking to others, for altering texts and images. Multiplicity of interpretations, open to everyone else, ensures efficiency at the global level, and integrity at the individual level. He called his concept a *thinker-toy*, an environment that supports dedicated work without taking away the fun. Generalized beyond his initial scheme, the medium allows people to make notes, by either writing them, dictating them, or drawing diagrams. Text can be heard, images animated. Visualization increases expressivity. Participation of many *readers* enlarges the library while simultaneously allowing others to see only what they want to see. Privacy can be maintained according to one's wishes; interaction is under the control of each individual. In this generalized medium, videotapes, films, images from museums, and live performances are brought together. The rule is simple: "Accessibility and free linking make a two-sided coin." In translation: If someone wants or needs to connect to something, i.e., to use a resource created by someone else, the connection becomes available to all those to whom it might be relevant. Relinquishing the right to control links, established in the first place because one needed them, is part of the Xanadu agreement. It is part of the living library, without walls and bookshelves, called the World Wide Web.

Roads paved with good intentions are notorious for leading where we don't want to wind up. For everyone who has searched for knowledge in the Web's virtual library, it becomes clear very soon that no known search engine and no intelligent agent can effectively distinguish between the trivial and the meaningful. We have co-evolved with the results of our practical experiences. Selection neither increases the chances of the fittest, nor eliminates the biologically unfit. Cultural artifacts, books included, or for that matter, the zeroes and ones that are the making of digital texts of all kinds and all contents, illustrate the thesis no less than the increasing number of people kept alive who, under Darwin's law, would have died. These individuals are able to constitute their practical experiences through means, among which books and libraries do not present themselves as alternatives. Global networks are not a habitat for the human mind, but they are an effective medium for mind interactions of individuals who are physically far from being equal. Custom access to knowledge available in the virtual library is the main characteristic, more so than the wealth of data types and retrieval procedures.

The question posed at the beginning of this section, "Why don't we?" referring to the creative use of new means, finds one answer here. As more and more people, within their realms of needs and interests, become linked to what is pertinent to their existence and experience, they also enter an agreement of exchange that makes their linking part of the distributed space of human memory and creativity. The naked need to enter the agreement is part of the dynamics of the civilization of illiteracy. Reading and enjoying a book implied an eventual return of money to the publisher and the writer. It might also have affected the reader in ways difficult to evaluate: Some people believe that good books make better people. Distributed environments of knowledge, expression, and information change the relation. From the world of orality—"Tell me and I will forget"—to that of literacy—"Let me read, but I might not remember"—a cognitive change, still evident today, took place. The next—"Involve me and I will understand"—began. The line of thought continues: Involvement returns value to others.

CHAPTER 10: THE SENSE OF DESIGN

To design means to literally involve oneself in a practical experience with signs. *To design* means to express, in various signs, thoughts, feelings, and intentions pertinent to human communication, as well as to project oneself in artifacts appropriate to human practical experiences. In the remote age of direct practical experiences, there was no design. The practice of signs entails the possibility to transcend the present. In nature, future means insemination; in culture, future is *insignation:* putting into sign, i.e., design. In its broadest definition, design is the self-constitution of the human being as an agent of change. This change covers the environment. conceiving artifacts (tools included), shelter, clothing, rituals, religious ceremonies, events, messages, interpretive contexts, interactions, and more recently, new materials and virtual realities. Shakespeare, who would have enjoyed the intense fervor of our age, gave a beautiful description of design: "...imagination bodies forth/The forms of things unknown" (*Midsummer Night's Dream*). Although design contains elements ensuing from experiences involving language, design is essentially a non-verbal human activity. Its means of expression and communication are grounded in the visual, but extend to sound, texture, odor, taste, and combinations of these (synaesthesia), including rhythm, color, and movement.

To the human being involved in practical experiences of self-constitution, the realm of nature appears as given. In counter-distinction and in retrospect, human nature appears as designed. In some cases, design is an act of *selection:* something is picked up from the environment—a stick, stone, plant—and assigned an a-natural function through implementation: mark territory, aid an activity, support a structure or the human body, trap animals or humans, attack or defend against attack, color skin or clothing. In other cases, selection is followed by some form of *framing,* such as the *frame* of the ritual around a totem pole, animal sacrifice, mourning, and celebrations of fecundity and victory. Selection and framing are related to efficiency expectations. They embody the hope for help from magic forces and express willingness to pursue goals that support the individual, family, and community. Between the present of any experience and the future, the experience of design bridges in the form of new patterns of interaction (through tools, artifacts, messages), recurrences, and extensions of consequences of human activity from the immediate to the future.

The projection of biology into an experience of long-lasting consequences implies elements of planning, no matter how rudimentary, and expectations of outcome. It also leads to new human relations in family-based interactions, education, shared values, and patterns of reciprocal responsibility. Random sexual encounters that reflect natural drives are not designs. Awareness of reciprocal attraction, shared feelings, and commitments extending well beyond the physical encounter can be identified as a design component present even in sexuality. Between the design component of sexual consequence of the evolving human being and the *design* of offspring by selection of a partner, by selection of genetic traits catalogued in semen banks, by genetic splicing and mutation, and by all that is yet to come upon us, there is a difference that reflects the altered human pragmatic condition.

Of real interest here is how the future is captured in design. Moreover, we want to know how it unfolds in practical experiences of design by which human beings extend their reality from here and now to then and there. In ways different from language, design gives the human being another experience of time and space. This experience is for the most part coherent with that of language. But it can also make individuals constituting themselves through design work aware of aspects of time that the language experience misses altogether or makes impossible. Designs are expressed in drawings and eventually complemented by models testifying to the experiences of volume, texture, and motion. The anticipated time dimension is eventually added in simulations. Design liberates the human being from total conditioning through language.

Within the convention of design, signs are endowed with a life of their own, supported by the energy of the persons entering the convention. This is how human symbolism, of confirmed vitality and efficiency, is factually established. Symbols integrated in human experience are given the *life of the experience*. The entire heritage of rituals testifies to this. Today the word *ritual* is used indiscriminately for any habitual preparation, from bathing to watching TV to after-game celebrations. Initially, rituals appeared as dynamic designs centered around episodes of life and death. Their motivation lay in the practical experience; their unfolding in connected interactions acquired an aesthetic quality from the underlying design.

From the earliest known experiences, the implicit aesthetic component is the optimizing element of the experience. This aesthetic component extends perceived formal qualities found in nature to the aesthetics of objects and activities in the realm of human nature. The language of design expresses awareness of these formal characteristics. Practical experiences display a repetitive pattern: the optimal choice (of shapes, colors, rhythms, sounds, movement) is always pleasing. The quality through which pleasure is experienced is not reducible to the elements involved, but it is impossible without them. Selection is motivated by practical expectations, but guided by formal criteria. Individuals involved in the earliest pragmatic framework were aware of this. Other formal criteria make up a generic background. One of the recurrent patterns of the practical experience of design is to appropriate the formal quality associated with what is pleasing in nature and to integrate it in the optimal shaping of the future. This is how the aesthetic dimension of human practical experiences resulted within such experiences.

Notation systems (e.g., the *quipu*, representational drawings on stone or on the ground, or hieroglyphics) that eventually became writing can be classified as design, not lastly in view of their aesthetic coherence. Only when rules and expectations defined by verbal language take over notation does writing separate from design and become part of the broader experience of language. We can now understand why changes in verbal language, as it constituted a framework for time and spatial experiences, were not necessarily reflected in changes in design. By the time literacy became possible, the underlying structure that led to it was embodied in the use of language. This is not true, to the same extent, in the practice of design. It is at this juncture that design is ascertained as a profession, i.e., as a practical domain with its own dynamics and goals. By no coincidence, engineering design emerged in the context of the pragmatics that began with building pyramids, ziggurats, and temples, and culminated in the Industrial Revolution in the design of machines. The broad premise of the Industrial Age is that everything is a machine: the house, the carriage, stoves, the contraptions used in literate education, schools, colleges, institutions, art studios, even nature.

From a relatively focused and homogeneous field of practical experiences within industrial society, design evolved, in the civilization of illiteracy, as an overriding concern that extended to many specialized applications: tool design, building and interior design (architecture), jewelry design, apparel design, textile design, product design, graphic design, and to the many fields of engineering (including computer-aided design), interactive media and virtual reality, as well as genetic engineering, new materials design, event design (applied to politics and various commodities), networking, and education. Technologies, from primitive to sophisticated, supporting visual languages made possible complexities for which the intuitive use of visual expression is not the most effective. Consequently, the scope of design-oriented practical experiences changed. Design now affords more integrative projects of higher levels of synaesthesia, as well as experiences involving variable designs—that is, designs that *grow* together with the human being self-constituted in practical interactions with the designed world.

In the pragmatic framework based on the digital, design replaced literacy more than any other practical experience has. The results of design are different in nature from those of literacy. As optimistic as one can become about a future not bound to the constraints of literacy, it takes more to comprehend the sense of design at a time when evolutionary progress is paralleled by revolutionary change.

DRAWING THE FUTURE

Drawing starts with seeing and leads to a way of envisioning and understanding the world different from the understanding filtered through language. From a cognitive viewpoint, drawing implies that persons constituting their identity in the act of drawing know the inside and the outside of what they render. To draw requires that things grow from their inside and take shape as active entities. Visible and invisible parts interact in drawing, surface and volume intersect, voids and fills extend in the visual expression, dynamically complementing each other. Each line of a drawing makes sense only in relation to the others. In contrast to words and sentences, elements of a drawing conjure understanding only through the drawing. Visual representation, as opposed to language expression, attains coherence as a whole, and the whole is configurational. One can write the word *table* without ever experiencing the object denominated. Extracted from direct or mediated experiences, knowledge about the object and its functions is a prerequisite for drawing an old table or conceiving a new one. To design means to express in a language that involves rendering. It also involves understanding that practical expectations are connected to the projected object. Consequently, to design means to experience the *table* in advance of its physical embodiment. Thus designing is the *virtual* practical experience, at the borderline between *what is* and what new experiences of self-constitution require.

In designing, people virtually project their own biological and cultural characteristics in whatever they conceive. This corresponds to the reality that design is derived from practical experiences, extending what is possible to what is desirable. Functionality expresses this condition, though only partially. With the emergence of conditions embodied in the underlying structure reflected in literacy, image and literate renditions—statements of goal and purpose, descriptions of means, procedures for evaluation—met. Literacy then effected changes in the condition of design. These are reflected as general expectations of permanence, universality, dualism, centralism, and hierarchy. *International style*—an expression that really covers more than the name of a style—reflects these literate expectations from design.

Is drawing natural? The meaning of such a question can be conjured only if articulated with its pendant: Is literacy unnatural or artificial? Everything already stated about drawing implies that it is not natural, though it is closer to what it represents than words are. Except for metaphoric qualifications, there is no such thing as drawing an abstraction of drawing, although there is *abstract drawing*. Through drawing, persons constitute themselves as having the ability to see, to understand (for instance, the invisible part of objects, how light affects an image, how color or texture makes an object seem lighter or rounder), to relate to the pragmatic context as definitory of the meaning of both the object—real or imagined—and the drawing. Different contexts make different ways of drawing possible. Disconnected from the context, drawing is almost like the babble of a child, or like a fragmented, unfinished expression. Vitruvius had a culture of drawing very different from that of the many architects who followed him. Critics who compared him to Le Corbusier and his architectural renditions, to the architects of post-structuralism, and to the deconstructivists and deconstructivist designers declared the drawings of these architects to be ugly, bad, or inappropriate (Tom Wolfe went on record with this). At this instance, drawing ceases to be an adjunct to art; it petitions its own legitimacy.

If we ignore the pragmatic context and the major transition from a design initially influenced by language—Vitruvius wrote a monumental work on architecture—the statement stands. But what we face here is a process in time: from design influenced by the pragmatics embodied in Vitruvius' work, to design subordinated to literacy, and finally to design struggling for emancipation as a new language, in which the critical component is as present as the constructive impulse to change the world.

Design carries over many formal requirements from practical experiences subordinated to literacy. But there is also an underlying conflict between design and language, moreover between design and literacy. This conflict was never resolved inside the experience of designing. In society, literacy imposed its formative structure on education, and what resulted was design education with a strong liberal arts component. Needless to say, designers, whether professionals in the field or students (designers-to-be), resented and resent the assumption that their trade needs to be elevated to the pedestal of the eternal values embodied in literacy. Instead of being stimulated to discover the need for literacy-based values in concrete contexts, design and design education are subjected to the traditional smorgasbord of history, language, philosophy, a little science, and many free choices. Its own theoretic level, or at least the quest for a theory, is discarded as frivolous. Moreover, the elements grouped under *intuition* are systematically explained away, instead of being stimulated.

Whereas the context of education allows for the artificial maintenance of literacy-based training programs in design, the broader context of pragmatic experiences confirms the dynamic changes design brought about since the profession ascertained its identity. The conflict between training and engaging prompted efforts to free design from constraints that affect its very nature: How do we get rid of the mechanical components of design (paste-up, rendering, model making)? These efforts came from outside the educational framework and were stimulated by the general dynamics of change from the pragmatics of literacy to the pragmatics of the civilization of illiteracy. The change brought about the emergence of new design tools that open fresh perspectives for the expression of design: animation, interactivity, and simulation. It also encouraged designers to research within the realm of their domain, to inquire into the many aspects of their concern, and to express their findings in new designs. The computer desktop and various rapid prototyping tools brought execution closer to designers. It also introduced new mediating layers in the design process.

BREAKAWAY

The majority of all artifacts in use today are either the result of the *design revolution* at the beginning of the 20th century, or of efforts to redesign everyday objects for use in new contexts of practical experiences. From the telephone to the television set, from the automobile to the airplane and helicopter, from the lead pencil to the fountain pen and disposable ball-point pen, from the typewriter to the word processor, from cash registers to laser readers, from stoves to microwave ovens—the list can go on and on—a new world has been designed and manufactured. The next world is already knocking at the door with robots, voice commanded machines, and even interconnected intelligent systems that we might use, or that might use us, in some form. The steam and pneumatic engines fired by coal, oil, or gas are being replaced by highly efficient, compact, electric or magneto-electric engines integrated in the machines they drive, controlled by sophisticated electronic devices.

There is almost nothing stemming from the age that made literacy necessary that will not be replaced by higher efficiency alternatives, by structurally different means. What about the technology of literacy? One can only repeat what once was a good advertisement line: "The typewriter is to the pen what the sewing machine (Remember the machine driven by foot power?) is to the needle." Remington produced the beautiful *Sholes and Glidden* typewriter in the 1870's. It was difficult to decide whether the ornate object, displaying hand-stenciled polychrome flowers, belonged in the office or in a Victorian study. Now it is a museum piece. Compare it to the word processor of today. Its casing might survive the renewal cycle of two to three years that hardware goes through. The chip's processing abilities will double every eighteen months, in accordance with *Moore's Law.* The software, the *heart and mind* of the machine, is improved almost continuously. Now it provides for checking spelling, contains dictionaries, checks syntax and suggests stylistic changes. Soon it will take dictation. Then it will probably disappear; first, because the computer can reside on the network and be used as needed, and second, the written message will no longer be appropriate in the new context. Those who question this rather pedestrian prediction might want to ask themselves some other questions: Where is the ornamental ink stand, the beautiful designs by Fabergé and Tiffany? Where are the fountain pens, the Gestetner machines? Carbon paper? Are they replaced by miniature tape recorders or pocket computers, by integrated miniature machines that themselves integrate the wireless telephone? Are they replaced by the computer, the Internet browser, and digital television? Edward Bulwer-Lytton gave us the slogan "The pen is mightier than the sword." Today, the function of each is different from what it was when he referred to them. They became collectibles. The disposable pen is symptomatic of a civilization that discards not only the pen, but also writing.

The breakaway of design occurs first of all at structural levels. It is one thing to write a letter, manuscript, or business plan with a pencil, quite another to do the same on a typewriter, and even more different to use a word processor for these purposes, or to rely on the Internet. The cognitive implications of the experience—what kinds of processes take place in the mind—cause the output to be different in each case. No medium is passive. In each medium, previous experiences and patterns of interaction are accumulated. The more interaction there is to a process, and sometimes to a collaborative effort, the more the condition of writing itself changes. We can think of messages addressed to many people at once. Think of the Mullah chanting evening prayers at the top of a minaret; or of the priest addressing a congregation; of the president of a nation using the powerful means of television, or of a *spammer* on the Internet, distributing messages to millions of e-mail addresses. Each communication is framed in a context constituting its parameters of pre-understanding. To the majority, *spam* means no more than chopped meat in a can. Even today, over 50% of the world's people have never used a telephone. And with some 50 million people on the Internet, *Netizenship* is more vision than reality.

Design as a semiotic integrative practical experience is a matter of both communication and context. The possibility to customize a message so that it is addressed not to an anonymous group (the believers gathered for the occasion, or members of society eager to learn about political decisions affecting their lives), but to each individual, reflecting concern for each one's individual condition and respect for his or her contribution in a system of distributed tasks, was opened by design. The semiosis of group and mass communication is very different from the semiosis of pointcasting. Technologically, everything is available for this individualized communication. However, it does not occur because of the implicit literate expectation in the functioning of church, state, education, commerce and other institutions. Design experiences submit the centrality of the writer to reassessment. One relates to the literate model of one-to-many communication. This model is based on the assumption of hierarchy, within a context of sequential interaction (the word is uttered, the listener understands it, reacts, etc.). In the industrial pragmatic framework, this was an efficient model. Perfected through the experience of television, it reached globality. But scale is not only sheer numbers. More important are interactions, intensities, the efficient matching of each individual's needs and expectations. Thus, efficiency no longer means how many individuals are at the receiving end of the communication channel, but how many channels are necessary to effectively reach everyone. A different design can change the structure of communication and introduce participatory elements. For those still captive to literacy, the alternative is the ubiquitous word-processed letter matched to a list in a database. For those able to re-think and reformulate their goals, effectiveness means transcending the literate structure.

The challenge begins at knowing the *language* of the individuals, mapping their characteristics (cognitive, emotional, physical), and addressing them specifically. The result of this effort is represented by individualized messages, addressing in parallel people who are concerned about similar issues (environment, education, the role of the family). Moreover, it is possible to have many people write together, or to combine one person's text with someone else's image, with animation, spoken words, or music. In the design effort that takes the lead here, hierarchies are abolished, and new interactions among people are stimulated. The design that leads to such patterns of human experiences must free itself from the constraints of sequentiality. Such design can no longer be subject to the duality of good or bad, as frequently related to form (in particular, typography, layout, coherence). Rather, it covers a continuum between *less appropriate* to *very well adapted* to the scope of the activity. No longer cast in metal, wood, or stone, but left in a soft condition (as software or as a variable, self-adaptive set of rules), the design can improve, change, and reach its optimum through many contributions from those who effectively constitute their identity interacting with it. The user can effectively finish the design by choosing identifiers and modifying, within given limits, the shape, color, texture, feel, and even function of the artifact.

There is also a deeper level of knowing the language of the individuals addressed. At this level, to know the language means to *know the experience*. Henceforth, the new design no longer takes place at a syntactic or a semantic level, but is pragmatically driven. To reach every individual means to constitute a context for a significant practical experience: learning, participation in political decisions, making art, and many others. But let us be realistic as we experience the urge to convey a sense of optimism: the common practical experience involves partaking in the distribution of the wealth and prosperity generated in this extremely efficient pragmatic framework. As discouraging as this might sound, in the last analysis, consumption, extremely individualized, constitutes the most engaging opportunity for efficient pointcasting. The questions entertained today by visionaries, innovators, and venture capitalists placing their bets on the Internet might not always make this conclusion clear.

CONVERGENCE AND DIVERGENCE

Telecommunications, media, and computation converge. What makes the convergence possible and necessary is a combination of factors united in the necessity to reach efficiency appropriate to human practical experiences at the global scale of existence and work. It is within this broad dynamics and inner dynamics that design ascertains itself as a force for change from the civilization of literacy to the civilization of many, sometimes contradictory, literacies. A shirt used to be mere clothing; the T-shirt became, in view of many concurrent forces, a new icon, a *sui generis* medium of communication. The commercial aspect is obvious. For example, each university of certain renown has licensing arrangements with some manufacturer who advertises the name on the *walking billboards* of chests, backs, and bellies. The T-shirt effectively replaces wordy press statements and becomes an instance of live news. Before Operation Desert Storm got into full swing, the T-shirt already signaled love for the troops or, alternatively, anti-war sentiment. Magic Johnson's admission that he had tested HIV positive was followed, less than two days later, by the "We still love you" T-shirts in Los Angeles.

The quasi-instantaneous annotation of events is in keeping with the fast change of attitudes and expectations. Institutions have inertia; they cannot keep up with the rhythm of the times. The news, formed and conveyed outside the institution of media, reads as a manifesto of immediacy, but also as a testimony to ephemerality. We actually lose our shirts on the immediate, not on the permanent. Design projects this sense of immediacy and ephemerality not only through T-shirts or the Internet. The house, clothes, cars, the Walkman, everything is part of this cycle. Is design the cause of this, or is it something else, expressed through design, or to which designers become accomplice? The shorter fashion cycles, the permanent renewal of design forms, the 30-second drama or comedy of advertisement—more appropriate to the rhythms of existence than never-ending soap-operas—the new VLSI board, the craze for designer non-alcoholic beer or low-fat pork—all testify to a renewal speed met by what seems an inexhaustible appetite on the side of our current commercial democracy. The refresh rate of images on our TV sets and computer monitors, predicated by the intrinsic characteristics of technology and human biology, is probably the extreme at which cycles of change can settle.

To take all this with enthusiasm or trepidation, without understanding why and how it happens, would contradict the basic assumption pursued in this book. The pragmatic context of high efficiency is also one of generalized democracy, extended from production to consumption. The ubiquitous engine driving the process is the possibility, indeed necessity, of human emancipation from all possible constraints. The experience of design acknowledges that emancipation from constraints does not ultimately result in some kind of anarchic paradise. The right to partake in what human experiences generate often takes the form of taste that is equalized and rendered uniform, and of ever-expanding choices that ultimately turn out be mediocre.

As a reaction to the implicit system of values of literacy, related to limited choices, illiterate design expression does not impose upon the user in design, but involves the user in choices to be made. In this way, design becomes an indicator of the state of public intelligence, taste, and interest. It also points to a new condition of values. The indicator might not always show a pretty picture of who we are, and what our priorities are. The honest interpretation of such an indicator can open avenues to understanding why the *Walkman*—which seems to seduce people by an ideal of insulation from others—has the success it has, why some fashion designs catch on and others don't, why some car models find acceptance, why movies on significant themes fail, and why, on a more general level, quality does not necessarily improve under circumstances of expectations in continuous expansion. New thresholds are set by each new design attempt. The wearable computer is yet another gadget in the open-ended development that unites evolution and revolution.

The need to achieve high levels of efficiency corresponding to the current human scale is probably the aspect most ignored. Efficiency, pre-programmed through design, confirms that human involvement is expensive (*do-it-yourself* dominates at all levels of design), and service more profitable than manufacturing in developed countries. None of these solutions can be taken lightheartedly. After all, design bridges to the future, and to bridge to a world of depleted resources, destroyed ecology, and a mediocre human condition is not necessarily a good reason for optimism. The goal of reducing human involvement, especially when the human is forced into exhausting and dangerous experiences, is very attractive, but also misleading. To reduce human involvement, energies different from those of an individual involved in experiences of self-constitution as a user need to be provided. Faced with the challenge posed by the dualistic choice *expectations vs. resources,* designers often fail to free themselves from the literate ideology of dominating nature. Fortunately, design based on co-evolution with nature is gaining momentum. So is the design of materials endowed with characteristics usually associated with human intelligence.

The inherent opposition between means and goals explains the dynamics of design in our time. Extremely efficient methods of communication lead to information saturation. New methods for designing result in an apparent overabundance of artifacts and other products of design. It seems that the driving force is the possibility to practically meet individual expectations at levels of productivity higher than those of literacy-based mass production, and at costs well below those of mass production. The challenge—how to maintain quality and integrity—is real and involves more than professional standards. Market-specific processes, probably well reflected in the notion of profit, affect design decisions to the extent that often human practical experiences in the market result in under-designing or over-designing negotiated items. Changing expectations, as a consequence of rapidly changing contexts of human experiences, affect the design cycle even more than the production cycle. The ability to meet such changes by a built-in design variability is, however, not only a test of design, but also of its implicit economic equation.

Enormous segments of the world population are addressed by design. This fact gives the design experience, taken in its entirety, a new social dimension. Against the background of the opportunity to fine-tune designs to each individual without the need to build on expected literacy, the responsibility of such an activity is probably unprecedented. Whether designers are aware of it, and able to work within the boundaries of such an experience, is a different question.

THE NEW DESIGNER

Designs mediate between requirements resulting from human practical experiences and possibilities (Gibson defined them as affordances) in nature and society. They embody expectations and plans for change; and they need to interface between *the given* and *the desired* or *the expected*. The language of design has an implicit set of anticipations and a projected endurance. Aesthetic structuring, culturally rooted and technologically supported, affects the efficiency of designed items. The explicit set of expectations is measured against this implicit set of anticipations. It translates from the many languages of human practical experiences to the language of design, and from here to the ways and means of embodying design in a product, event, message, material, or interaction.

It is interesting to consider the process of designing from as many perspectives as possible. From the thumbnail sketch to the many variations of a conceptual scheme, one eliminating the other, many decisions are arrived at. Design resembles a natural selection process: one solution eliminates the other, and so on until a relatively appropriate design emerges. This is the memetic scheme, successfully translated into design software programs based on genetic algorithms. In the absence of rules, such as those guiding literacy, and freed from dualistic thinking (the clear-cut good vs. bad), the designer explores a continuum of answers to questions that arise during the design process. The fact that various solutions compete with each other confers a certain drama on design. Its open-endedness projects a sense of change. Its mediating nature explains much of its engaging aspect. There is an obvious difference between the design experience within a context of assuming identity between the body and machines, and the new context of digital cloning of the human being. Designs in the area of neurobionics, robotic prosthetics, and even the cyberbody could not have emerged from any other pragmatic context but the one on which the civilization of illiteracy is established.

Still, if someone had to choose between the *Greek Temple* typewriter of 1890 and today's word processor, thoughtlessly designed and encased in cheap plastic, the choice would be difficult. One is an object of distinct beauty, reflecting an ideal we can no longer support. Its distinction made it unavailable to many people who needed such an instrument. Behind or inside the word processor, as behind any digital processing machine, are standardized components. The entire machine is a highly modular ensemble. One program is the archetype for all the word processing that ever existed. The rest is bells and whistles. Here is indeed the crux of the matter: The ability to achieve maximum efficiency based on the recognition that raw materials and energy mean nothing unless the creative mind, applied to tasks relevant to human experiences of self-constitution, makes something out of them.

In the line of the argument followed, design sometimes seems demonized for what we all experience as waste and disdain for the environment, or lack of commitment to the people replaced by new machines. That people eventually become addicted to the products of design—television sets, electronic gadgets, designer fashion, designer drugs—is an irony soon forgotten. At other times, design seems idealized for finding a way to maximize the efficiency of human practical experiences, or for projecting a challenging sense of quality against the background of our obsession with more at the lowest price. But it is not so much the *activity* as the *people who are the activity* that make either the criticism or glorification of design meaningful. This brings up the identity of the designer in the civilization of illiteracy.

Designers master certain parts of the vast realm of the visual. Some are exquisite in visualizing language: type designers, graphic artists, bookmakers; others, in realizing 3-dimensional space either as product designers, architects, or engineers. Some see design dynamically—clothes live the life of the wearer; gardens change from season to season, year to year; toys are played with; and animation is design with its own heart (*anima*). The variety of design experiences is only marginally controlled by design principles. There is integrity to design, consistence and pertinence, and there are aesthetic qualities. But if anyone would like to study design in its generality, the first lesson would be that there is no *alphabet* or *rule* for correct design, and no generally accepted criteria for evaluation. Literacy operates from top (vocabulary, grammar rules, and phonetics are given in advance) to bottom. Design operates the opposite way, from the particular context to new answers, continuously adding to a body of experience that seems inexhaustible.

People expect their environment to be designed (clothes, shoes, furniture, jewelry, perfume, home interiors, games, landscape) in order to harmonize with their own *design*. There are models, just as in the design process, mainly celebrities, themselves designed for public consumption. And there is the attempt to live life as a continuum of designed events: birth, baptism, communion, graduations (at different moments in the cycle of *designed* education), engagement, marriage, anniversaries, promotions, retirement, estate planning, funerals, estate execution, and wars. As a designed practical experience involving a variety of mediations, life can be very efficient, but probably not rewarding (in terms of quality) at the same time. The conclusion applies to the result of all design activities—products, materials, events. They make possible new levels of convenience, but they also remove some of the challenges people face and through which human personality emerges.

The relation between challenges—of satisfying needs or meeting higher and higher expectations—and the emergence of personality is quite intricate. Every practical experience expresses new aspects of the individual. Personality integrates these aspects over time and is projected, together with biological and cultural characteristics, in the never-ending succession of encounters of new situations, and consequently new people. The civilization of illiteracy shifts focus from the exceptional to the average, generating expectations affordable to everyone. The space of choices thus opened is appropriate to the endless quest for novelty, but not necessarily for the affirmation of the extraordinary. In most cases, the designer disappears (including his or her name) in the designed product, material, or event. Nobody ever cared to know who designed the *Walkman*, computers, earth stations, or new materials, or who designs *designer* jeans, dresses, glasses, and sneakers, tour packages, and Olympic games. No one even cares who designs Web sites, regardless of whether they attract many interactions or turn out to be only ego trips. Names are sold and applied on labels for their recognition value alone. No one cares whether there is a real person behind the name as long as the name trades well on the market in which the very same bag, watch, sneakers, or frames for glasses, sells under different identifiers.

This has to be seen in the broader picture of the general disconnectedness among people. Very few care to know who their neighbors or colleagues are, even less who the other people are who namelessly participate in expected abundance or in ecological self-destruction. Illiteracy indeed does away with the opaqueness of literacy-based human relations. All the means through which new practical experiences take place make each of us subject to the transparency of illiteracy. The result is even deeper integration of the individual in the shared databank of information through which our profile of commercial democracy is drawn. Design endlessly interprets information. Each time we step out of the private sphere—to visit a doctor or lawyer, to buy a pair of shoes, to build a house, to take a trip, to search for information on the Internet—we become more and more transparent, more and more part of the public domain. But transparency, sometimes savage in competitive life (economy, politics, intelligence), does not bring people closer. As we celebrate new opportunities, we should not lose sight of what is lost in the process.

DESIGNING THE VIRTUAL

The experience of design is one of signs and their infinite manipulation. It takes place in an experiential context that moved away from the object, away from immediacy and from co-presence. Some people would say it moved from the real, without thinking that signs are as real as anything else. When pushing this experience to its limits, the designer lands in imaginary territories of extreme richness. One can imagine a city built underwater, or a spherical house that can be rolled from location to location, devices of all kinds, clothing as thin as someone's thought, or as thick as tree bark or a rubber tire. One can imagine the wearable computer, new intelligent materials, even new human beings. Once the imagination is opened to fresh human endeavors—live in an underwater city, wear the lightest or heaviest clothing, interconnect with the world through what you wear, interact with new, genetically engineered humans—virtual space is opened for investigation. Regardless of how a virtual experience is made possible—drawings, diagrams, combinations of images and sounds, triggered dreams, happenings, or the digital embodiment of virtual reality—it escapes literacy-based constraints and embodies new languages, especially synaesthetic languages. In fact, if design is a sign focused on the practical experience, the design of virtual space is one level beyond, i.e., it is in the meta-sign domain. This observation defines a realm where the person frees himself from the structures characteristic of literacy.

In virtuality, the sequentiality of written language is overwritten by the very configurational nature of the context. Reciprocal relations among objects are not necessarily linear because their descriptions are no longer based on the reductionist approach. This is a universe designed as vague and allowing for the logic of vagueness. Within virtual space, self-constitution, hence identification, no longer regards cultural reference, which is literacy-based, but a changing self-reference. All attempts to see how a human being would develop in the absence of language could finally be embodied in the individual experience of a being whose mind reaches a state of *tabula rasa* (clean slate) in the virtual. That such an experience turns out to be a design experience, not a biological accident (e.g., a child who grew up among animals, whose language fails to develop and whose behavior is uncouth), is relevant insofar as freedom from language can be investigated only in relation to its consequences pertaining to human practical experiences.

Virtuality is actually the generic reality of all and any design practical experience. From among the very many designs in a state of virtuality, only a small number will become real. What gives one or another design a chance to transcend virtuality are contextual dependencies within any defined pragmatic framework. Designers do not simply look at birds flying and come up with airplanes, or at fish swimming and come up with boats or submarines. There are many design experiences that are based on knowledge resulting from our interaction with nature. But there are many more that originate in the realm of humanity. There is nothing to imitate in nature that will lead to the computer, and even less that will lead to designing molecules, materials, and machines endowed with characteristics that allow for self-repair and virtual environments for learning difficult skills. Design in the civilization of illiteracy relies foremost on human cognitive resources. Experience, like most of the practical endeavors of this pragmatic framework, becomes predominantly computational and disseminates computational means.

Design human praxis, as the dominant factor of change from the pragmatics embodied in manufacturing to the new experiences of service economy, effected differentiations in respect to means of expression and communication, in respect to the role of representation, and to our position in regard to values. The electronic data storage and retrieval that complements the role of print, and progressively replaces it, results from the experience of design supported by fast and versatile digital data processing. When, at the social level, representation is replaced by individual activism, and by the militancy of interest groups, we also experience a diffusion of politics into the private, and to a certain extent, its appropriation by interest groups assembled around causes of short-term impact that keep changing. This change effects a shift from the expectation of authority, connected to literacy-based human experiences, to the slippery authority of individual choice.

The designed world of artifacts, environments, materials, messages, and images (including the image of the individual) is a world of many choices, but of little concern for value. Its life results from the exercise of freedom to choose and freedom to re-design *ad infinitum*. Almost everything designed under these new pragmatic conditions embodies expectations associated with illiteracy. The object no longer dominates. The impressive mechanical contraptions, the engines, the shift systems, articulations, precious finish—they all belong among the collectibles. Quite to the contrary, the new object is designed to be idiot-proof (the gentler name is *user friendly*), reflecting a generalized notion of permissiveness that replaces discipline and self-control in our interaction with artifacts.

Design also affects change in our conception of fact and reality, stimulating the exploration of the imaginary, the virtual, and the meta-sign. Facts are replaced by their representations and by representations of representations, and so on until the reference fades into oblivion. Henceforth, the positivist expectations ingrained in the experiences of the civilization of literacy are reconstituted as a frame of relativist interactions, dominated by images, seconded by sounds (noise included). Imaging technologies make drawing available to everyone, exactly as writing was available to those processed as literates. The photographic camera—drawing with light on film—the electronic camera, the television camera, the scanner, and the digitizer are, effectively, means for drawing and for processing the image in full control of all its components. A sound level can easily be added, and indeed sound augments the expressive power of images. Interactivity, involved in the design process, adds the dimension of change. That literacy, as one of the many languages of the civilization of illiteracy, uses design in its various forms to further its own program is clear. Probably less clear is that the literate experience is itself changed through such instances. After all, literacy is the civilization that started with the conventions of writing and grew to the one Book open to all possible interpretations, as these were generated in the attempt to effectively conjure its meaning in new pragmatic contexts. Literacy subjected to all the means that become possible in the civilization of illiteracy, in particular to those that design affords, results in the infinity of books, printed for the potential individual reader (or the very limited readership that a title or journal tends to have) who might finally give it one interpretation (equal to none) by placing it, unopened and unread, on a bookshelf. The radical description given above might still be far away from today's reality, but the dynamics of change points in this direction.

On the Internet, we come closer to what emerges as a qualitatively new form of human interaction. Design is integrated in the networked world in a number of ways: communication protocols, hypertext, document and image layout, structure of interactive multimedia. But no one designer, and no one company (not even the institution of defense, which supports networking) can claim that it *designed* this new medium of human practical experiences. Many individuals contributed, mostly unaware that their particular designs would fit in an evolving whole whose appearance and function (or breakdown) no one could predict. These kept changing by the year and hour, and will continue to change for the foreseeable and unforeseeable future.

Consider the design of communication protocols. This defies all there is to literacy. A word spelled correctly is disassembled, turned into *packages* that carry one letter at a time (or a portion of a letter), and given indications where they should arrive, but not through which route. Eventually, they are reassembled, after each package travels its own path. But in order to become a word again, they are further processed according to their condition. Such communication protocols negate the centrality and sequentiality of literacy and treat all that is information in the same way: images, sounds, movements. Many other characteristics of literacy-dominated pragmatics are overridden in the dynamic world of interconnections: formal rules of language, determinism, dualistic distinctions. Distributed resources support distributed activities. Tremendous parallelism ensures the vitality of the exponentially increasing number and types of transactions. Design itself, in line with almost any conceivable form of practical experience, becomes global.

Enthusiasm aside, all this is still very much a beginning. Networks, for transportation (trains, buses, airplanes, highways), for communication (telephone, telegraph, television), for energy distribution (electric wires, gas pipelines) were designed long before we knew of computers and digital processing. In the context in which human cognitive resources take precedence over any other resources, as we face efficiency requirements of the global scale of humankind, connecting minds is not an evolutionary aspect of design, but a revolutionary step. All the networks mentioned above can participate in the emergence of humankind's integrated network. Their potential as more than carriers of voice messages, electricity, gas, or railway passengers is far from being used in the ways it can and should be. Design experiences of integration will make the slogan of convergence, applied to the integration of telecommunication, media, and computing, a reality that extends beyond these components. In some curious ways, the Netizen—the citizen of the digitally integrated world—is a consequence of our self-identification in practical activities based on a qualitatively new understanding of design.

CHAPTER II: POLITICS: THERE WAS NEVER SO MUCH BEGINNING

Hölderlin's verse, "There was never so much beginning" (So viel Anfang war noch nie) captures the spirit of our time. It applies to many beginnings: of new paradigms in science, of technological directions, of art and literature. It is probably most applicable to the beginnings in political life. The political map of the world has changed more rapidly than we can remember from anything that books have told us. It is dangerous to generalize from events not really settled. But it is impossible to ignore them, especially when they appear to confirm the transition from the civilization of literacy to the civilization of illiteracy.

People who deal with the development and behavior of the human species believe that cooperative effort explains the development of language, if not its emergence. Cooperative effort is also the root of human self-constitution as political animals. The social dimension, starting with awareness of kinship and followed by commitments to non-kin is, in addition to tool-making, the driving force of human intellectual growth. Simply put, the qualifiers *political animal* (*zoon politikon*) and *speaking animal* (*zoon phonanta*) are tightly connected. But this relationship does not fully address the nature of political human experiences.

Different types of animals also develop patterns of interaction that could be qualified as social, without reaching the cognitive sophistication of the species *Homo Habilis*. They also exchange information, mainly through gestures, noises, and biochemical signals. Tracking food, signaling danger, and entrance into cooperative effort are documented aspects of animal life. None of these qualifies them as political animals; neither do the means involved qualify as language. Politics, in its incipient forms or in today's sophisticated manifestations, is a distinct set of interhuman relationships made necessary by the conscious need to optimize practical experiences of human self-constitution. Politics is not equivalent to the formation of a pack of wolves, to the herding tendency of deer, nor to the complex relations within a beehive. Moreover, politics is not reducible to sheer survival strategies, no matter how sophisticated, which are characteristic of some primates, and probably other animals.

The underlying structure of the activities through which humans identify themselves is embodied in human acts, be they of the nature of tool-making, sharing immediate or remote goals, and establishing reciprocal obligations of a material or spiritual nature. Changes in the circumstances of practical experiences effect changes in the way humans relate to each other. That the scale of *human worlds*, and thus the scale of human practical experience, is changing corresponds to the dynamics of the species' constitution. Incipient agricultural activity and the formation of the many families of languages correspond to a time when a critical mass was reached. At this threshold, syncretic human interaction was already rooted in well defined patterns of practical experience. The pragmatic framework shaped the incipient political life, and was in turn stimulated by it. Politics emerged once the complexity of human interactions increased. Political practical experiences are related to work, to beliefs, to natural and cultural distinctions, even to geography, to the extent to which the environment makes some forms of human experiences possible. This is why, from a historic perspective, politics is never disassociated from economic life, religion, racial or ethnic identity, geography, art, or science.

The underlying structure of human praxis that determined the need for literacy also determined the need for appropriate means of expression, communication, and signification. This becomes even more obvious in politics, which is embedded in literacy-based pragmatics. Consequently, once the particular pragmatic circumstances change, the nature, the means, and the goals of politics should change as well.

THE COMMERCIAL DEMOCRACY OF PERMISSIVENESS

The condition of politics in a pragmatic framework of non-sequentiality, non-linear functional dependencies, non-determinism, decentralized, non-hierarchic modes of interaction or accelerated dynamics, extreme competitive pressure—that is, in the framework of the civilization of illiteracy—currently escapes definition. *State of flux* appropriately describes what such a political experience can be. What we have today, however, is a conflict between politics anchored in the pragmatics that is still based on literacy and politics shaped by forces representing the pragmatic need to transcend literacy. The conflict affects the condition of politics and the nature of contemporary political action. It affects everything related to the social contract and its implementation: education, exercise of democracy, practice of law, defense, social policies, and international affairs.

Changes affecting current political experiences are part of a sweeping dynamics. These changes range from the acknowledged transition from an industrially based national economy to an information processing global economy focused on service. Part of the change is reflected in the transition from national economies of scarcity (usually complemented by patterns of preserving and saving) to large, integrated commercial economies of access, even right, to consumption and affluence. Established in the context of political movements that focused on individuality, these integrated economies affect, in turn, the condition of the individual, who no longer sees the need for self-restraint or self-denial, and indulges in the commercial democracy of permissiveness. Consequently, political trials are met, or avoided, with an Epicurean response: withdrawal from public life for the pleasures of buying, entertainment, travel, and sport, which in a not-so-distant past only the rich and powerful could enjoy. Politics itself, as Huxley prophesied in his description of the *brave, new world*, becomes a form of entertainment, or yet another competitive instant, not far from the spirit and letter of the stock market, of the auction house, or the gambling casino.

Political involvement in a democracy of permissiveness is channeled into various forms of activism, all expressions of the shift from the politics of authority to that of expanding freedom of choice. The new experience of increasingly interactive electronic media is probably correlated to the shift from the *positivist* test of facts, as it originated in science and expanded into social and political life, to the rather *relativist* expectation of successful representations, in public opinion polls, in staged political ceremonies, in the image we have of ourselves and others. Albeit, the power of the media has already surpassed that of politics.

All these considerations do not exhaust the process under discussion. They explain how particular types of activism—from emancipatory movements (feminist, racial, sexual) to the new action of groups identified through ethnic origin, lifestyle, concern for nature—use politics in its newer and older forms to further their own programs. Openness, tolerance, the right to experiment, individualism, relativism, as well as attitudinally motivated movements are all illiterate in nature in the sense that they defy the structural characteristics of literacy and became possible only in post-literate contexts. Some of these movements are still vaguely defined, but have become part of the political agenda of this period of fervor and upheaval. Literacy, in search of arguments for its own survival, frequently embraces causes stemming from experiences that negate it.

The impact of new self-constitutive practical experiences and definition on digital networks already qualifies these experiences as alternatives, regardless of how limited an individual's involvement with them is. Within the realm of human interaction in the only uncensored medium known, a different political experience is taking shape. What counts in this new experience are not anonymous voters lumped into ineffective majorities, but individuals willing to partake in concrete decisions that affect their lives in the virtual communities of choice that they establish. While the mass media, still connected to the literate nest in which they were hatched, partake in the functioning of political machines that produce the next meaningless president, a different political dynamics, focused on the individual, is leading to more efficient forms of political practical experiences. There is nothing miraculous to report in this respect. Notwithstanding, the Internet can be credited for the defeat of the attempt in 1991 to turn back the political clock in Russia, as well as for the way it is influencing events in China, East Europe, and South America.

HOW DID WE GET HERE?

Human relations can be characterized, in retrospect, by recurrences. Distinctions within self-constitutive experiences occur under the pressure of the realized need to achieve higher levels of efficiency. Relations, which include a political component pertinent to cooperative efforts and the need to share the outcome, have been evinced since the syncretic phase of human activity. There is no distinct political dimension in the syncretic pragmatics of immediacy. Incipient political identity, as any other kind of human self-identification, is foremostly natural: the strongest, the swiftest, those with the most acute senses are acknowledged as leaders. The most powerful are successful on their own account. And this success translates into survival: more food, more offspring, resilience, ability to escape danger. Once the natural is *humanized,* the qualities that make some individuals better than others were acknowledged in the realms of nature and human nature. Whether as tribal leaders, spiritual animators, or priests, they all accomplished political functions and continuously reaffirmed the reasons for their perceived authority. Over time, natural qualities lost their determinant role. Characteristics based on human nature, in particular intellectual qualities such as communica-

Civilization of Illiteracy: Book IV

tion skills and management and planning abilities, progressively tipped the balance. Current textbooks defining politics do not even mention natural abilities, focusing instead on the art or science of governing, shrewdness in promoting a policy, and contrivance.

From participatory forms of political life, in which solidarity is more important than differences among people, to the forms characteristic of our time of personal and political shift away from each other, changes have taken place because human practice made them necessary. Politics was not and is not a passive result of these changes, some of which it stimulated, others of which it opposed. The survival drive behind participatory forms was continuously redefined and became a different kind of assertion: not just better than other species, but better than those before us, better than others. Competition shifted from the realm of nature—man against nature—to the realm of humanity. Once the element of comparison to the other, or judgment by others, was introduced, hierarchy was established. Hierarchy put on record became, with the advent of notation, and more so with the advent of writing, a component of experience, one of its structuring elements. It is no longer a *here-and-now* defined action of immediacy, but action expanded as progression over generations and societies, and among various societies. Accordingly, while solidarity, though permanently subject to redefinition, was still in the background, the driving forces were quite different. They resulted from the need to establish a political practice of efficiency pertinent to the pragmatic framework, henceforth to the needs of the community.

For as long as human activity was relatively homogeneous, there was no need for political delegation or for reifying political goals into rules or organizations. Once diversification became possible, the task of integration, to which rituals, myths, religion, assignment distribution, and leadership contributed, changed. Not only did people involve more of their past in new practical experiences, but they also started to keep records and to measure the adequacy of effort, and thus the appropriateness of their own policies. Attention to their past, present, and future also allowed them to become aware of the means that distinguished political practical experiences from all other experiences (magic, myth, religion). It was a difficult undertaking, especially under the provisions of centralized, syncretic authority. The natural, the magical, the religious, the logical, the economical, and the political mingled. The critical element proved to be represented by practical expectations. To implore unknown forces for rain, a successful hunt, or fertility was very different from articulating expectations related to what needs to be done to maintain the integrity of work and life. Initially, these expectations were mixed. They progressively became more focused, and a sense of accountability, based on tangible results, embodied in comparisons, was introduced.

While self-constitution is the projection of individual characteristics (biological, cultural) in a given practical experience, political practice is to a great extent a projection of expectations. At each juncture in humankind's practical experience, the previous expectation is carried over as new expectations appear. Accordingly, it is expected that a political leader embodies, in fact or through the symbolism of authority, natural qualities, cognitive abilities, and communication skills (rhetoric included), among other attributes. When these expectations are embodied in specific functions (tribal chief, judge, army commander, elected legislator, or selected member of the executive body) and in political institutions, the projection is no longer that of individuals, but of the society committed to the goals and means expressed, to its acknowledged values. Whether indeed each tribal leader was the fastest, or each judge the most impartial in ascertaining the damage done by a person who defied rules of life and work, whether the military leader was the bravest, or the legislator the wisest, became almost irrelevant after their political recognition. Expectation overcame reality. This aspect becomes very significant in the context of literacy. Moreover, it becomes critical in the transition from the pragmatics on which literacy is based to a pragmatic framework in respect to which literacy requirements only hinder.

Political institutions firmly grounded in the assumptions of litera-cy still debate whether tele-commuting is acceptable, tele-commerce secure, or tele-banking in the national interest. While the debates are going on, and antiquated tax laws applied, these new practical experi-ences are taking hold in the global economy. Networks, in full expan-sion, are altering the nature of human transactions to the extent that fewer and fewer people participate in elections because they know that the function of these elections—to present choice—is no longer politically relevant. There is a need to bring politics closer to individ-uals; and this need can be acknowledged only within structures of individual empowerment, as opposed to empty representation.

Political activity resulted in norms, institutions, values, and a con-sciousness of belonging to society. Not by any stretch of the imagi-nation is politics a harmonizing activity, because to live with others, to enter a contract and pursue one's individual goals within its limita-tions, means to accept a condition of a *sui generis* trade-off. Political experiences involve, in various degrees, skills and knowledge for giv-ing life and legitimacy to trade-offs. Language is the blood that flows through the arteries of the political animal. When tamed by literacy, this language defines a very precise realm of political life. The heart-beat of the literate political animal corresponds to a rhythm of life and work controlled by literacy. The accelerated rhythm that became necessary under a new scale of experiences requires the liberation of political language from the control of literacy, and the participation of many languages in political experiences.

It should come as no surprise that the expectation of language skills, even when language changes, in people involved in the practi-cal experience of politics is carried over from one generation to another. Regardless of the level of sophistication reached by a par-ticular language, and of the specific form of political practice, effec-tive use of powerful means of expression and communication is required. Even when they did not know how to write, kings and emperors were regarded as being better writers than those who could. They would dictate to the scribe, who created the perception that they probably *translated* what higher authorities whispered into their ears. Even when their rhetoric was weak, the masters of persuasion they used were seen as ónly agents of power. Books were attributed to political leaders; victory in war was credited to them, as well as to military commanders. Law codes were associated with their names, and even miracles, when politics joined the forces of magic and religion (often playing one against the other). All this and more represent the projection of expectations.

The particular expectations of literacy confirm values associated with its characteristics. Politics and the ideals embodied in the Enlightenment—it carried into action political aspirations originating in religion—and the Industrial Revolution cannot be separated. Expectations of permanency, universality, reason, democracy, and stability were all embodied in the political experience. New forms of political activism were encouraged by literacy and new institutions emerged. Awareness of boundaries among cultures and languages increased. Centralism was instituted, and hierarchies, some very subtle, others insidious, were promoted with the help of the very powerful instrument of language. Within this context, the practical experience of politics established its own domain and its own criteria for effectiveness, very different from those in the ancient city-state or in the pragmatics of feudalism. Identification of the professional politician, different from the heir to power, was part of this process. Politics opened to the public and affirmed tolerance, respect for the individual, and equality of all people before the law. Political functions were defined and political institutions formed. Rules for their proper operation were encoded through literate means. The alliance between politics and literacy would eventually turn into an incestuous love, but before that happened, emancipation of human political experiences would reach a historic climax in the revolutions that took place during this time.

To celebrate all these accomplishments, while remaining aware of the many shadows cast upon them by prejudices carried over from previous political experiences (in regard to sex, race, religion, ownership), was a task of monumental dimensions. We can and must acknowledge that human political experiences played a more important role than in previous social contexts in maximizing efficiency in the pragmatic framework that made literacy necessary. It was at this time that the role of education, and especially the significance of access to it, were politically defined and pursued according to the efficiency expectations that led to the Industrial Revolution. The process was far from being universal. The western part of the world took the lead. Its political institutions encouraged investment, and education was such an investment.

Political institutions reflect the pragmatic condition of the citizen and, in turn, effect changes in the experience of people's life and work. While the word *illiteracy* probably first appeared print in 1876 in an English publication, in 1880 illiteracy in Germany was only one per cent of the population: "Heil dem König, Heil dem Staat/ Wo man gute Schulen hat!" went the slogan hailing the king and state where good schools were the rule. This was the time when Thomas Alva Edison invented the incandescent light bulb (1879); Alexander Graham Bell, the telephone (patented in 1876); Nicklaus Otto, the four-stroke gas engine (1876); Nikola Tesla, the electric alternator (1884). Nevertheless, before Leo Tolstoy wrote *War and Peace*, he learned that only one per cent of all Russians were literate. In many other parts of the world, the situation was not much better. In addition, this was also a time when literacy was *literally* an instrument of political discrimination. Those not literate were looked down on, as were women (some held back from literacy and study), as were nations considered ignorant and of inferior morals (Russia being one of them).

Reflected in the ability to dominate nature, the growth of science and the use of effective technological means influenced the political nature of states, as well as the relation among nations. Rationality formed the foundation of legality; the state ascertained priority over individuals—a very direct reflection of its literate nature. Rules were applied to everyone equally (which later translated into an effective "all are equal," quite different from the empty slogans of populist movements). The rationality in place derived from literacy. To be effective meant to dominate those who were less effective (citizens, communities, nations).

Far from being a historic account, these observations suggest that the literate political animal pursues political goals in line with the sequential nature of literacy in a context of centralized power, acknowledged hierarchies, and deterministic expectations. The political institution is a machine, one among many of the pragmatics of the Industrial Revolution. It did one thing at a time, and one part of the machine did not have to *know* what the other was doing. Energy was used between input and output, and what resulted—political decisions, social policies, regulations—was mass production of whatever the society could negotiate: *lubrication diminished friction.* Parties were formed, political programs articulated, and access to power opened to many. Two premises were implicit in the literate discourse: people should be able to express opinions on issues of public interest; and they should be able to oversee the political process, assuming responsibility for the way they exercise their political rights. These two premises introduced an operational definition of democracy and freedom, eventually encoded in the doctrine of liberal democracy. They also confirmed the literate expectation that democracy and freedom, like literacy, are universal and eternal.

The failure of literacy-based politics takes place on its own terms. Dictatorships (left-wing and right-wing), nationalism, racism, colonialism, and the politics of disastrous wars and of the leveling of aspirations that leads to the mediocrity embodied in bureaucracy have brought the high hopes, raised during the climax of literate political action, to the low of indifference and cynicism we face in our day. Instead of the people's broader participation in the political process, a hope raised by progress in making equality and freedom effectively possible, society faces the effects of the ubiquitous dedication to enjoyment in corrupted welfare states unable to meet the obligations they assumed, rightly or not. At times, it seems that the complexity of political experience prevents even the people's symbolic participation in government. Volunteering and voting, a right for which people fought with a passion matched only by their current indifference, have lost their meaning. There is no proper feedback to reinforce the will and dedication to participate. It also seems that in advocating equality and freedom, a common denominator so low was established that politics can only administer mediocrity, but not stimulate excellence. From among all its functions, nationhood, as the embodiment of the experience of political self-constitution, seems to maintain only the function of redistribution.

Individual liberty, hard fought for under the many signs of literacy, appears to be conformistic at best, and opportunistic. To many citizens, it is questionable whether the lost sense of community is a fair trade-off for the acquired right to individualism. The hundreds of millions again and again seduced by the political discourse of hatred (in fascism, communism, nationalism, racism, fanaticism) wasted their hard-won rights in order to take away from others property, freedom of expression and religion, liberty, dignity, and eventually life. Politics after Auschwitz was not meant to become yet another instance of pettifogging. But it did, and we all are aware of the opportunistic appropriation of tragedy (hunger, oppression, disease, ecological disaster) in current political entertainment.

The efficiency expected from political action under the assumptions of literacy is characteristic of the scale at which people constitute themselves. The nation is the world, or the only thing that counts in this world of opportunity and risk. The rest is, relatively speaking, superfluous. Nations, even those that acknowledge the need to integrate, try to secure functioning as autonomous entities. National borders may be less guarded, but they are maintained as borders of literacy translated into economic opportunity. When the goal of autonomous existence is no longer attainable, expansion is the answer. Ideological, racial, economic and other types of arguments are articulated in order to justify the extension of politics in the experience of battle. The two World Wars brought literate politics to its climax, and the Cold War (the first global battle) to its final crisis, but not yet to its end, even though the enemy vanished like a humorless ghost.

A closer look at the systematic aspects of the political experience of human self-constitution should prepare us for approaching the current political condition. This should at least provide elements for understanding all those accumulated expectations that people have with respect to politics, politicians, and the institutions through which political goals are pursued. Political goals are always practical goals, regardless of the language in which they are expressed or the rituals attached. As recurrent patterns of human relationships, political experiences appear to have a life of their own. This creates the impression that agreements dictated by practical reasons originate outside the experience, at the initiative of politicians, due to a certain event, or as the result of random choice.

POLITICAL TONGUES

Language is the instrument through which political practical experience takes place. To reconstitute past succeeding political experiences therefore means to reconstitute their language(s). The task is overwhelming because politics is mingled with every aspect of human life: work, property, family, sex, religion, education, ethics, and art. It is present even in the interrelations of these aspects because politics is also self-reflective. That is, the identity of one entity is related to the identity of others in relation to which self-identification takes place. The variety of political experiences corresponds to the variety of pragmatic circumstances within which humans project their identity.

Individual existence resulting from interaction with others extends to the realm of politics and is embodied in the recurrent patterns that make up expectations, goals, institutions, norms, conflicts, and power relations. The individual is concealed in all these. In some ways, politics is a social-educational practice resulting in the integration of instinctive actions (a-political) and learned modes of practice with social impact. What constitutes politics is the dynamics of relations as they become possible and as they unfold as openings towards new relations. One of the concrete forms of such relations is the propensity to coalition building. Politics is contingent upon subjects interacting. Their past (ontogeny) and present (pragmatics) are involved in these interactions. To a certain extent, it is a learned form of practice requiring means for interaction, among which language has been the most important. It is also a practice of investigation, discovery, and social testing.

The manifold of political languages corresponds to the manifold of practical experiences. There are probably as many political tongues as there are circumstances of self-identification within a society. But against the background of this variety is the expectation that word and deed coincide, or at least that they do not stray too far from each other.

The advent of writing changed politics because it attached written testimony to it, which became a referential element. As Socrates and Plato noticed, this was a blessing in disguise. Since the time writing entered the political sphere, the practical argument shifted from the fact, argued and eventually settled, to the record. It became itself a practical experience of records (of property, law, order, agreements, negotiations, and allocations for the good of society). The institutions that emerged after the practical experience of writing operated within the structure of and in accordance with the expectations brought about by writing. And soon, as relative as soon can be, political self-consciousness was established parallel to political action and pursued as yet another practical experience.

The many languages of political experience multiply once more in the new languages of political awareness. Where values were the final goal of politics, the value of the political experience itself became a subject of concern. Many political projects were pursued at this self-reflective level: conceiving new forms of human cooperation and political organization, advancement of ideas concerning education, prejudices, emancipation, and law. This explains, too, why in the sequence of political practical experiences, expectations did not nullify each other. They accumulated as an expression of an ideal, forever moving away from the last goal attained. Without a good understanding of the process, nobody could account for the inner dynamics of political change. The same applies to accounting for the role played by political leaders, philosophers, and political organizations involved, by virtue of their own goals and functions, in political life.

Politics in the civilization of illiteracy is not politics out of the blue sky. Along the continuum of political practical experiences, it entails expectations generated under different pragmatic circumstances. And it faces challenges—the major challenge being the efficiency expected in the new scale of human experience—for which its traditional means and its inherited structure are simply not adequate. Political discontinuity is always more difficult to accept, even understand. Revolutions are celebrated only after they take place, and especially after they successfully establish a semblance of stability.

CAN LITERACY LEAD POLITICS TO FAILURE?

In our time, much is said regarding the perception that the language of politics and the political practice it seems to coordinate are very far apart. People's mistrust of politics appears to reach new heights. The role and importance of political leaders and institutions apparently have changed. The most able are not necessarily involved in politics. Their self-constitution takes place in practical experiences more rewarding and more challenging than political activism. Political institutions no longer represent the participants in the political contract, but pursue their own goals, survival included. Law takes on a life of its own, more concerned, so the public perceives, with protecting the criminal, in the name of preserving civil rights, than upholding justice. Taxes support extravagant governments and forms of social redistribution of wealth, more often reflecting a guilt complex over past inequities than authentic social solidarity. Instead of promoting meaningful human relationships and addressing the future, they keep fixing the past. Everyone complains, probably a phenomenon as old as any relation among people involved in a *sui generis* give-and-take interaction. But fewer and fewer are willing to do something because individual participation and effort appear useless in the given political structure.

The majority of people look back to some prior political experience and interpret the past in the light of books they have read. They fail to realize that the complexity of today's human experience cannot be met by yesterday's solutions. They are convinced that if we are faithful to our political heritage, all problems, credibility and corruption included, will be solved. They also believe religious systems and their great books contain all that is needed to meet all imaginable present and future challenges. Even the very honorable conviction that the founders of modern democracies prepared citizens to cope with this unprecedented present cannot go unchallenged. The Constitution of the United States (1787) as well as the Declaration of the Rights of Man and the Citizen in France (1789) reflect the thinking and the prose of the civilization of literacy. Similar documents are on record in Latin America, Europe, India, and Japan. They are as useless as history can be when new circumstances of human self-constitution are totally different from the experiences that gave birth to these documents. Revisionism will not do. The new context requires not a static collection of admirable principles, but dynamic political structures and procedures of the same nature as the pragmatics of shorter cycles of change, non-determinism, high efficiency, decentralization, and non-hierarchical modes of operation. As the world reinvents itself as interwoven, it breaks loose from prescriptions of local significance and traditional import.

Although the number of emerging nations has increased—and nobody knows how many more will emerge—we know of no political documents similar to those articulated in 1776, 1789, 1848, or even 1870. Nothing comparable to the *Declaration of Independence*, the *Declaration of the Rights of Man and Citizen*, even the *Communist Manifesto* (no matter how discredited it is at present), whether in substance or style, has accompanied current political movements. The reason why no such document can emerge can be connected to the inadequacies of literacy-based politics. This civilization is no longer one of ideas, religious or secular. It is characterized by processes, methodologies, and inventions expressed in various sign systems that have a dynamics different from that of language and literacy. The ideas of the civilization of literacy address the mind, soul, and spirit.

The most one can expect in our time of upheaval and change are provisions for establishing conditions for unhampered human interactions in the market and in other domains of human self-constitution (religion, education, family). Steady globalization means that the health of national economies, education, sports, or art matters just as little as national borders and the theatrics of diplomacy and international relations. One can hear Dostoyevsky's prophetic line: "If it's otherwise not possible, make us your servants, but make us full." It hurts to repeat it, but it will hurt more to ignore it at a time when nothing grows faster than the urge of millions of people to emigrate to any developed country willing to take them, even as second-class citizens, so long as they escape their current abysmal condition.

The dynamics of change in the world is characterized by the acknowledged need of many countries to be integrated in the global economy while preserving or requiring a token of national identity. State sovereignty is self-delusive in the context of commercial, financial, or industrial autonomy that is impossible to achieve. Self-determination, always to the detriment of some other ethnic group, echoes those tribal instincts that make the ideal of constitutional government an exercise in futility. The underlying structure of literacy is reflected in national movements and their dualistic system of values. The logic of the good and the bad, more difficult to define in a context of vagueness, but still pursued blindly, controls the way coalitions are established, migration of populations is handled, and national interests defended, while these very nations argue for integration and free market.

Nevertheless, the language of today's politics is, in the final analysis, shaped by the pragmatic framework. Its sentences are written in the language of ledgers; the freedom it purports to establish is that of commercial democracy, of equal access to consumption, which happens to be the main political achievement of recent history. The fact that the nations forming the European Community gave up sovereignty with respect to the market proves the point. That they still preserve diplomatic representation, defense functions, and immigration policies only attests to the conflict between the politics of the civilization of literacy and the politics of the civilization of illiteracy.

The great documents of the literate past perpetuate the rhetoric of the time of their writing. All the structural characteristics of literacy, valid for the pragmatic framework that justifies them, deeply mark the letter and spirit of these documents. They ascertain politics as sequential, linear, and deterministic. They rejoice in promulgating ideals that correspond to the scale of humankind in which they guarantee the means that result in the efficiency of industrial and productive society. *Liberté, egalité, fraternité* are shorthand for rights of conscience, ownership, and individual legal status. They are an expression of accepted hierarchy and centralism to the degree that these could be rendered relative as need required. Expectations of permanency and universality were carried over from earlier political experiences, or from religion, even though separation of Church and State was emphatically proclaimed during the French Revolution, and in revolutions that took place afterwards. Amendments required by altered circumstances of human self-constitution in practical experiences not anticipated in the documents render their spirit relative and solve some of the problems caused by the limitations mentioned.

Political documents, such as the ones mentioned above, are still perceived as sacrosanct, regardless of their obvious inadequacy in the pragmatic context of the civilization of illiteracy. It is one thing to establish the sanctity of property in a framework of agricultural praxis, whose politics was inspired by a shared expectation of cycles parallel to natural cycles. Jefferson envisioned the land as a vast agrarian state: "We are a people of farmers. Those who work the fields are the chosen people of God, if He had a chosen people. In their heart He planted the real virtue." It is quite another thing to live in a pragmatic context of new forms of property, some reflecting a notion of sequential accumulation, others an experience of work with machines, of humans seen as commodity. It is a new reality to live in today's integrated world of property as elusive as new designs, software, information, and ways to process it. To apply to this context political principles inspired by a movement that sought independence from England while using slaves brought from Africa is questionable, at least.

Equality of natural rights, deriving from nature-based cycles, is quite different from equality of political rights and responsibilities deriving from a machine-inspired model for progress. Both of these sources are different from the political status of people involved in a pragmatics of global networking and extreme task distribution. One can cautiously make the case that the major political documents of the past were conceived in *reaction* to an intolerable state of affairs and events, not proactively, in anticipation of new situations and expectations. These documents are the expression of the need to unify, homogenize, and integrate forces in a world of relatively autonomous entities—national states—competing more for resources and productive forces than for markets. The values reflected therein correspond to the values on which literacy is founded and for which literacy-inspired ideologies fought.

But maybe these political documents are exemplary in another way, let's say as an expression of moral standards that we apparently lost in the course of 200 years; or of cultural standards for both society and politicians, standards that can only rarely be acknowledged today, if at all. If this is the case, which is difficult to prove, what this seems to suggest is that the price paid for higher political efficiency is the lost ethics of politics, or its current deplorable intellectual condition. The lack of correlation between political practice and language results from the pragmatic context reflected in the condition of language itself. While in real life, many literacies are at work, *Literacy* (with a capital L) still dominates the structure of politics. Its rules are applied to forms of human interaction and evaluation that are not reducible to self-constitution in language.

Political activity by and large follows patterns characteristic of the civilization of literacy, despite its own indulgence in non-linguistic semioses: the use of images, film, and video, or the adoption of new networking technologies focused on information exchange. Former expectations that politicians adhere to standards of the civilization of literacy are carried over in new political and practical experiences. The expectation that their literacy should match that of political documents belonging to the political tradition (the Constitution of the United States of America, for instance) is paradoxical, though, since the majority of Americans cannot recall what these political documents state. And they see no reason to find out. Their own practical experience takes place in domains for which the past is of little consequence to their well-being. As things stand now, the political principles required by the dynamics of industrial society are embodied in institutions and laws dedicated to their own preservation.

Free of concern for their own freedom, politically rooted in a prior pragmatic framework, citizens take freedom for granted in their new practical experiences and end up evading the associated civic responsibility. They expect their politicians to be literate for them. We deal here with a strange mixture of assumptions: on the one hand, a notion of political life corresponding to a context of homogeneity and a deterministic view of the social world; on the other, a realization that today's world requires specialized political practical experience, means and methods characteristic of heterogeneous and non-deterministic political processes. The simmering conflict is met with the type of thinking that will not solve the problem because it *is* the problem.

The coordination of political action through literacy-based language and methods and the dynamics of a new political practice, based on the characteristics of the civilization of illiteracy, simply diverge. As in many other domains of literate condition, it is as though institutions, norms, and regulations take on lives of their own, as literate language does, perpetuating their own values and expectations. They develop as networks of interaction with an autonomous dynamics, uncoupled from the dynamics of political life, even from the new pragmatic context. The tremendous amount of written language (speeches, articles, forms, contracts, regulations, laws, treatises) stands in contrast to the very fast changes that make almost every political text superfluous even before it is cast in the fast eroding medium of print or in the elusive bits and bytes of electronic processing.

Many economies have undergone, or realize they must undergo, profound restructuring. Massive down-sizing, paralleled by flatter hierarchies and smoother quality control, have affected economic performance. But very little of this has touched the sacrosanct centralized state institutions. In the USA alone, 14 departments, 135 federal agencies employing more than 2.1 million civilians and 1.9 million military personnel account for $1.5 trillion in yearly expenditure. Only the cost of implementing regulations reaches well over 250 billion dollars a year. To comply with the tax code, companies and individuals must annually spend an almost equal amount of money. If the economy were as inefficient as political activity is, we would face a crisis of global proportion and consequences that are impossible to anticipate. The fact that European countries spend even more is no justification for the state of affairs in the USA.

This is why today, some citizens would write a Declaration of Independence that begins with the following line: "We're mad as hell and we're not going to take it anymore." But this would not mean that they would vote. When five times more people watch *Married with Children* than vote in primaries, one understands that the morality and intellectual quality of the politician and citizen correspond closely. Cynical or not, this observation simply states that in the civilization of illiteracy, political action and criteria for evaluating politics do not follow the patterns of political practical experiences peculiar to the civilization of literacy. Multiplied to infinity, choices no longer undergird values, but options that are equally mediocre.

The issue of literacy from the perspective of politics is the issue of the means through which political practice takes place. A democracy resting solely upon the contribution to political life in and through literate language is at the same time captive to language. The experience of language resulted from developments not necessarily democratic in nature. Embedded in literacy, past practical experiences pertinent to a pragmatic context appropriate to a different scale of humankind are often an obstacle to new experiences. So are our distinctions of sex, race, social status, space, time, religion, art, and sport. Once in language, such distinctions simply live off the body of any new design for political action. Language is not politically neutral, and even less so is the literate practice of language. Various minority groups made a very valid point in stating this. Power relations, established in political practice, often become relations in the literate use of language and of other means, as long as they are used according to literacy expectations. It is not that literacy prevents change; literacy allows for change within the systematic domain of practices relying on the literate practical experiences of language. But when literacy itself is challenged, as it is more and more in our day, it ends up opposing change.

Discrepancies between the language and actions of politics, politicians, and political institutions and programs result from the conflict between the horizon of literacy and the dynamics for which the literate use of language is ill equipped. If the formula *deterioration of moral standards* corresponds to the failure of politics to meet its constituency's expectations, the most pessimistic views about the future would be justified, because politicians are not better or worse than their constituency. But as with everything else in the new pragmatic context, it is no longer individual performance that ensures the success or failure of an activity. Integrating procedures ascertain a different form of cooperation and competition. Such processes are made possible by means characteristic of high efficiency pragmatics, that is, task distribution, parallelism and reciprocal testing, cooperation through networking, and automated procedures for planning and management. They are meaningful only in conjunction with motivations characteristic of this age. If, on the other hand, the romantic notion that the best become leaders were true of today's political experience, we would have cause to wonder at our own stupidity. In fact, it does not matter which person leads.

Political processes are so complex that the industrial model of successful stewardship no longer makes sense. Political life in society does not depend on political competence, people's generosity, or self-motivation that escapes institutional, religious, or ideological coercion. The degree of efficiency, along with the right ascribed to people to partake in affluence, speaks in favor of political experiences driven by pragmatic forces. Such forces are at work *locally* and make sense only within a context of direct effectiveness. But short of taking these forces for granted, we cannot escape the need to understand how they work and how their course can be controlled.

CRABS LEARNED HOW TO WHISTLE

Some of today's political systems are identified as democracies, and others claim to be. Some are identified as dictatorships of some sort, which almost none would accept as a qualifier. But no matter which label is applied, there is an obsession with literacy in all these systems. "We need literacy for democracy to survive," says the literacy special interest group. But how do dictatorships come about in literate populations? The biggest dictatorship (the Soviet block) was proud of its high literacy rate, acknowledged by the western world as an accomplishment impossible to overlook. It fell because the underlying structural characteristics reflected in literacy collided with other requirements, mainly pragmatic.

An empire, the fourth in the modern historic succession that started with the Turkish Empire and continued with the Austro-Hungarian and British Empires, crumbled. What makes the fall of the Soviet Empire significant is its own underlying structure. The former members of COMECON, those East European countries that, along with the Soviet Union, once formed the communist block, represent a good case study for the forces involved in the dynamics of illiteracy. While writing this book, I benefited from an experiment probably impossible to duplicate. A rigid structure of human activity, basically captive to a slightly amended paradigm of the Industrial Revolution, hailing itself as the workers' paradise, and laboring under the illusion of messianic collectivism, maintained literacy as its cultural foundation.

Even the harshest and blindest critics of the system had to agree that if anything of historic significance could be attributed to communism, it was its literacy program. Large segments of the population, illiterate prior to communism, were taught to read and write. The school system, deficient in many ways, provided free and obligatory education, much better than its free medical system. This effort at education was intended to prepare the new generations for productive tasks, but also to subject each person to a program of indoctrination channeled through the powerful medium of literacy. Questioned about his own ideas for the reform of the orthodox communist system, Nikita Khruschchev, the maverick leader of the post-Stalin era, declared: "He who believes that we will give up the teachings of Marx, Engels, and Lenin deludes himself tremendously. Those who are waiting for this to happen will have to wait until crabs learn how to whistle." When, throughout Russia, statues of Lenin started falling and Marx's name became synonymous with the failure of communism, people probably started hearing strange sounds from crustaceans.

The abrupt and unexpected failure of the communist system—an event hailed as victory in a war as cold as the market can be—makes for unexpected proof of this book's major thesis. The breakdown of the Soviet system can be seen as the failure of a structure that kept literacy as its major educational and instrumental medium, and relied on it for the dissemination of its ideological goals inside and outside the block. Literacy, as such, did not fail, but the structures that literacy entails: limited efficiency, sequential practical experiences of human self-constitution in a hierarchic and centralized economy; deterministic (thus implicitly dualistic) working relations, a level of efficiency based on the industrial model of labor division, mediation subjected to central planning without choice as to the mediating elements; opaqueness expressed in an obsession with secrecy, and last but not least, failure to acknowledge the new scale of humankind—in short, a pragmatic framework whose characteristics are reflected in literacy—all led to the final result. Indeed, the system acted to counter integration and globality. It maintained rigid national and political boundaries under the false assumption that insularity would allow a controlled and orderly exchange of goods and ideas, perpetuation and dissemination of an ideology of proletarian dictatorship, and eventually coexistence with the rest of the world under the assumption of its progressive conversion to communist values.

In the doctrine of Marx and Engels, the proletariat appears endowed with all the qualities associated with Divinity in the prototypic Book (the Old Testament): omniscience, omnipotence, and right almost all the time. There is a self-creative moment in the historic process they described, resulting from political activism and commitment to change in the world. No one should lightly discard the utopian core or the ideal embodied in the doctrine. After all, nobody could argue against a world of freedom where each person participates with the best one has to offer, and is rewarded with everything one needs. Free education, free medical care, access to art and liberty in a context of limitless unfolding of talent and harmony with nature, of shared wealth and emancipation from all prejudices—all this is paradise on Earth (minus religion).

It should be pointed out that, within the system, the entire practical human experience related to literacy—and the accomplishments listed above are literacy-based—was subsidized. In no other part of the world, and under no other regime, were so many people subjected to literacy. That the system failed should not lead anyone to ignore some of the achievements of the people regimented under a flag they did not care for: fascinating art, interesting poetry and music, the massive collection and preservation of folklore, spectacular mathematics, physics, and chemistry arose from beneath terror and censorship. To survive as an artist, writer, or scientist meant to force creativity where almost no room for it was left. Under no other regime on Earth did people read so much, listen to music more intensely, visit museums with more passion, and care for each other as family, friends, or as human beings, episodes of brutality notwithstanding. It is too simplistic to accept the line that people read more in East Europe and the Soviet Union because they had nothing else to do. The pragmatic framework was set up under the assumption of permanence, stability, centrality, and universality founded on literacy.

It goes without saying that the misuse of language (in political discourse and in social life) played its role in the quasi-unanimous silent rejection of the system, even more in silent, cowardly complicity with it. When the literate machine of spying on the individual fell apart, people saw themselves in the merciless mirror of opportunistic self-betrayal. The records will stand as a testimony that writing does not lead only to Solzhenitsyn's novels, Yevtushenko's poetry, Shoshtakovich's music, and the romantic *Samizdat,* but also to putrid words about others, kin included. The opaqueness of literacy partially explains why this is possible. Something other than the opaqueness granted by literacy (i.e., complicity established in society) explains how it became a necessary aspect of that society. Germans were not better, exceptions granted, than their fascist leaders; the peoples in the Soviet block were not better, exceptions granted again, than the leaders they accepted for such a long time.

But what went relatively unnoticed by experts in East European and Soviet studies, as well as by governments fighting the Cold War, is the dynamics of change. The system was economically broke, but still militarily viable (though overrated) and over-engaged in security activities—tight control of the population, economic and political espionage, active attempts to export its ideology. The structure within which people were to realize their potential—one of the ideals of communism—had few incentives. But all this, despite the impact of the yet unfinished revolution, is only the tip of the iceberg, the visible side when one looks from the riverbank of the free world where incentives lead to self-sufficiency and complacency. The major aspect is that the dynamics of the system was severely affected by artificially maintaining a pragmatic framework and a system of values not suited to change. This applies especially to the major shift—from the industrial model to post-industrial society, to a context of practical experiences of human self-constitution freed from the restrictions carried over from the politics of mind and body control—experienced by the rest of the western world.

Levels of expectation beyond the satisfaction of immediate needs (food, clothing, shelter), and of literacy-associated expectations (education, access to art and literature, travel), could not be satisfied unless and until levels of efficiency impossible to reach in the pragmatic context of industrial societies were made possible by a new pragmatics. Despite the fact that more writers, more publishing houses, more libraries, as well as more artists, theaters, opera houses, symphonic orchestras, research institutes, and more museums than in the rest of the world were politically and economically supported in the Eastern Block (almost to the extent that the secret police was), activities related to literacy had only a short-term impact on the individuals subjected to or taking advantage of them. This was proven dramatically by the proliferation of commercially motivated newspapers and publications (pornography among them) following the breakdown of the power structure in various countries of the Block, and followed by an even faster focus on entertainment television and obsession with consumption.

The main events leading to the breakdown—each country had its own drama, once the major puppeteer was caught off-guard by events in the Soviet Union—took place with the nation staring at the TV screens, seduced by the dynamics of the live transmission for which literacy and prior literate use of the medium were never well equipped. The live drama of the hunt for Ceausescu in Romania, the climax of the fall of the Berlin Wall, the events in Prague, Sofia, and Tirana continued the spirit of the Polish tele-drama in the shipyards. It then took another turn, during the attempted coup in the Soviet Union, practically denying the literate media any role but that of late chroniclers. The initial lessons in democracy took place via videotape. Various networks, from WTN (World-Wide Television News) to CNN, but primarily the backward technology of the fax machine, which absorbed essential literacy into a focused distribution of individual messages, provided the rest. As primitive as digital networks were, and still are in that part of the world, they played an important role. Not political manifestos or sophisticated ideological documents were disseminated, but images, diagrams, and live sequences. In the meanwhile, entertainment took over almost all available bandwidth. What the rest of the world consumed in the last fifteen years (along with fashion, fast food chains, soft drinks, and consumer electronics) penetrated the lives of those whose revolt took place under the banner of the right to consume. Here, as in the rest of the world, the spiritual and the political split for good. The spiritual gets alimony; the political becomes the executor of the trust.

What failed the system was the lack of understanding of all the factors leading to new productive experiences: the framework for optimal interaction of people, circumstances of progressive mediation and further specialized human self-constitution, a practical context of networking and coordination based on individual freedom and constraints assumed by individuals as they define their expectations. Parallel to the literate structure of a politics that failed is the experience of churches in the Soviet Block. In a show of defiance towards the political dictatorship, people attended church, itself a mainstay of literate praxis (independent of the book or books they adopt for their basic program). Once religion was able to assert its literate characteristics through the imposition of constraints—so like those of the political system just overthrown—churches began to experience the low attendance that the rest of the world is already familiar with.

No matter how much more quickly events take place in our age, it is probably still too early to understand all the implications of the major political event represented by the fall of the Soviet empire. For instance, in a context of global economy, how can one correctly evaluate the emergence of new national states and forceful national movements when the post-national state and the trans-national world are already a reality? The question is political in nature. Its focus is on identity. Identity reflects all the relations through which people constituted themselves as part of a larger entity—tribe, city, region, nation—defined by biological and cultural characteristics, shared values, religion, a sense of common space and time, and a sense of future.

A WORLD OF WORLDS

"We have made Italy, now we have to make Italians," declared Massimo d'Azeglio during the first meeting of the Italian Parliament. A little over 100 years old, the nation-state was the most tangible product of the political practical experience in the pragmatic context whose underlying structure is so well reflected in literacy. Together with the nation-state, the modern notion of nationality was defined and became a major force of political life. As part of the political

consciousness in the age of industrial production, national consciousness played a very precisĕ role, ultimately expressed in all
forms of nationalism. It unified all those whose similarities in biological characteristics, language, lore, and practical experiences were
constituted in a framework of shared resources and political goals.
Germany came into existence through a unifying language (hoch
Deutsch) and was consolidated through its literacy. Italy went
through a similar process. In other instances, nations were born as a
result of voluntary political acts: the United States, the nations
declared independent after the fall of the Soviet Union, Croatia,
Macedonia, some of the Arab countries, and a number of African
nation-states, once colonial powers could no longer afford to resist
the force of change. As with everything pertaining to politics, national politics entails expectations corresponding to past phases (the basic
passions that once made up tribal solidarity), to instances of human
interaction well overhauled by the new realities of the integrated
world.

What, if any, explanation can one find in the dissolution of
Yugoslavia? Against the background of conflict in Bosnia-Herzegovina, this question has divided many well intentioned intellectuals (not
only in France) inclined to solve an absurd situation of genocide.
Intellectuals questioned what appeared to be irreducible religious
contradictions between Catholic and Orthodox Christians, or
between Christians and Moslems. The old conflict between the pro-
fascist Croatian Ustash and the Serbian Chetniks dedicated to the
vain goal of a greater Serbia was also on their minds. They also wondered what the chances of the new nation-states of Estonia, Lithua-
nia, and Latvia, and many of the autonomous regions and republics
of the former Soviet Union were. How will the Commonwealth of
Independent States function once goals and purposes of nation-
states take over those assumed in a nebulously defined commonwealth? And how can one explain the enormous discrepancy between
the attempt to constitute a broad European Community (actually, the
United Markets of Europe), while other parts of Europe break into

small nation-states? How much of the underlying tribalism, or provincialism, or religious adherence, or how much of the functions of literacy at work can be read in the political fervor of nationalistic activism of our day? In Serbia, Hungary, Slovakia, the Czech Republik, Crete, Macedonia, Ukraine, Chechenya, and in many other newly formed lands, this question is far from being merely rhetorical. One answer, no matter how encouraging, cannot address a full paragraph of questions. These questions suggest that the politics of nations is so multifaceted that understanding it requires not so much rehashing the past but focusing on the broad picture of its dynamics.

Between the old city-state, the early empire (Roman, Byzantine), the medieval world of local attachments (pertaining to shared space used mainly for agriculture, and under the firm grip of the Papacy), and today's world of mass immigration and human displacement (for political, economic, religious, or psychological reasons), we find inserted the settled universe of nation-states and their respective literacies. In this universe, literacy and religion undergird the legal system. Politics defines national identity, subsuming language, ethnicity, ways of working, culture, superstitions, prejudice, art, and science. Within the nation-state's borders, citizens are subjected to a political practical experience of homogeneity, centralism, and uniformity, required by the efficiency expectations of the Industrial Revolution. The ideal of *cosmopolis,* the all-embracing empire of reason declared by the Stoics, runs counter to the ideal of the nation-state, which celebrates national reason and willingness to compete with others.

When the pragmatic circumstances leading to today's global economy started exercising their action, an all-embracing empire of a different nature resulted. The new statement says that Christians, Moslems, Jews, Buddhists, animists, even atheists, although bearing a national identity, are part of the global economy. Not surprisingly, political action and economic integration each run its own course. Commerce, with all its imbalances and unfairness, the almost uncontrollable financial dynamics, and migration of industries take more and more frequently what appears as the necessary path of globality.

Politics, even when it acknowledges globality, focuses on national definitions. To an outside observer, a nation's politics appears insignificant, powerless in comparison to economic forces, although it claims to control these forces through monetary policies, labor laws, and trade regulations. The trans-national world has its own impetus. It continues to evade political constraints, ascertaining its own life. It was described from the perspective of its financial and economic condition as *The Borderless World* (the title of Kenichi Ohmae's book), within which nationality counts only marginally. This is yet another reason for the low interest in public life on the part of the wealthy in our days.

When the new southern republics freed by the breakdown of the Soviet Union debate which form of writing they should adopt—Arabic, Cyrillic, or Roman—and how to define their respective nations, they still look for national identifiers. Turkmanis and Uzbekistanis, Latvians and Estonians, Ukrainians and Georgians, Hungarians and Romanians, and enterprising Poles comb their territories in search of business opportunities. The same takes place in many other countries, whose citizens are obsessed more with prosperity than with sovereignty, with access to financial means more than with self-determination, and with cooperative effort, even involving traditional enemies, more than with a constitutional foundation or universal protection of human rights. Interestingly enough, while national identity is more and more superseded by people's a-nationality, many new countries, emerging as a result of the asserted right to self-determination, face as their first task not the future but the past: definition of their national identity. Nevertheless, the civilization of illiteracy does not promise that *Italians* can be made for all these new countries. Rather, these nations will become, in not necessarily satisfying ways, the provisional home of a-nationals, citizens of the world economy. Many of them will make up the new immigrant populations settled in ethnic neighborhoods where access to consumption will arouse a nostalgia for some remote homeland.

No one can or should generalize. Many prejudices still heat the furnaces of hatred and intolerance. Enough citadels from the past pragmatic framework maintain hopes for expansion and cultivate a politics appropriate to ages long passed. But regardless of such unsettling developments, the nation-state enters an age of *denationalization,* absorbed into a world of economic globality, less and less dependent on the individual and thus less and less subject to political dogma.

OF TRIBAL CHIEFS, KINGS, AND PRESIDENTS

Changes in the condition of human practical experiences effect changes in the self-identification of the individual and of groups of people. Emphasis is less and less on nature and shared living space, and more on connections free of arbitrary borders, even of elements pertaining to culture and history. New political experiences, still subjected to expectations carried over from the past, do not actually continue the past. Accordingly, the nature of political experiences changes. Assumptions regarding leadership, organization, planning, and legality are redefined. Tribal chiefs might well have turned, through the centuries, into the kings of the Middle Ages, and, with the advent of a new society, into presidents. There is, nevertheless, no reason to believe that in a universe of distributed tasks and massive parallelism, a need for political centralism and hierarchy will remain. The president, for instance, is the king of the civilization of literacy; and his wife becomes the queen, in defiance of all the literate documents that justify presidency. Executive power, in conjunction with the legislative and judicial branches, implements ideals of liberal political democracy as these became essential to the pragmatics of industrial society. But once new circumstances emerge, the underlying structure reflected in the power structure undergoes change as well.

In the spirit of the dynamics of change, one should notice that, in a framework of non-hierarchic structures, there is no legitimate need for the presidency. Theoretic arguments, no matter how rigorous, are after all irrelevant if not based on related facts. New circumstances already made the function of president strictly ceremonial in many countries. In other countries, a president's ability to exercise power is impeded by laws that make this power irrelevant. Economic cycles, affecting integrated economies, turn even the most visionary heads of states (when they happen to be visionary) into witnesses to events beyond their control. Politics does not happen at levels so remote from the individual that individuals disconnect themselves from the political ceremonial. It happens closer and closer to where ideals and interest crystallize in the form of new human interactions.

Who would represent the country if the function of head of state were abolished? How can a country have a consistent political system? Who would be responsible for implementing laws? Such questions originate, without exception, within literacy's system of expectations. The extreme decentralization that is made possible by the new means of the civilization of illiteracy requires, and indeed stimulates, different political structures. Instead of the self-delusion and demagoguery triggered by an idealized image of the politically concerned citizen, we should see the reality of citizens pursuing goals that integrate political elements. Literacy resulted in a politics of representation that ended up in effectively excluding the citizen from political decision-making. Rationalized in the structures of democracy, political ideals are now a matter of efficient human interaction. A president's performance is totally irrelevant to the exchange of information on networks of human cooperative effort. Agreements relevant to the people involved, executed in view of reciprocal needs and future developments, result more and more outside political institutions, for reasons having little to do with them.

The majority of political functions, as they apply to presidents, congresses, or other political institutions, still originate in forms characteristic of past political experiences. They are based on allegiances and commitments contradicted by the pragmatics of today's world. The fact that heads of states are also heads of the military (commander-in-chief) comes from the time when the strongest man became the leader. But in the modern world of growing emancipation, women are valid candidates as heads-of-state all over the world. However, sexual bias has kept women from gaining the military competence that a commander-in-chief is expected to have. Another example: What is the reason for a president to be at the funeral of a deceased head-of-state? Blood ties used to bond kings and nobility more strongly than political arguments, long before fast transportation could carry a monarch to the deceased in less time than it took for decay to set in. A *farewell* wished today at the funeral of a Japanese emperor, a Moslem ruler, or an atheistic president belongs to the spectacle of politics, not to its substance. The expensive, and delusive, literate performance of state funerals, oath-taking, inauguration, parades, and state visits is more often than not an exercise in hypocrisy. These spectacles please only through their cynical pandering to the people's desire for circus. Pragmatically relevant commitments are no longer the privilege of state bureaucracies. When the historic necessity of states winds up to be no more than the expression of remote tribal instincts, the literate institution of state becomes superfluous.

Political idolatry, commercial nationalism, and ethnic vanity affect politics at many levels. Nationalism, emerging as a form of collective pride and psychological compensation for repressed instincts, celebrates gold medals at Olympic games, the number of Nobel Prize laureates, and achievements in the arts and sciences with a fervor worth a better cause. Borders of pride and prejudice are maintained even where they have *de facto* ceased to exist. No scientist who achieved results in his or her field worked in isolation from colleagues living all over the world. The Internet supports the integration of creative effort and ideas, beyond borders and beyond national fixations, often expressed as military priorities rather than as cooperation and integration. Art is internationally nurtured and exchanged.

648

Political programs, very much like hamburgers, cars, alcohol, sports events, artworks, and financial services, are marketed. Success in politics is valued in market terms rather than in the increasingly elusive political impact. The expression "People vote their pocketbooks" bluntly expresses this fact. But are they voting? Poll after poll reveals that they are not. Illiterates used to be excluded from voting, along with women, Blacks in America and South Africa, and foreigners in a large number of European countries.

In an ideal world, the best qualified would compete for a political position, all would vote, and the result would make everyone happy. How would such an ideal world function? Words would correspond to facts. The reward of political practical experience would be the experience itself, satisfying the need to best serve others, and thus oneself as a member of the larger social family. This is a utopian world of perfect citizens whose reason, expressed in the language of literacy, i.e., made available to everyone and implicitly guaranteed to be a permanent medium for interaction, is the guardian of politics. We see here how authority, of the thinking human being, is established and almost automatically equated with freedom. Indeed, the doctrine of individual conformity to rational necessity was expressed in many pragmatic contexts, but never as forcefully as in the context that appropriated literacy as one of its guiding forces.

In the horizon of literacy, the expectation is that the experience of self-constitution as literate makes people submit their own nature to the rationale of literacy and thereby find fulfillment. In short, the belief that to be literate makes one respect his word, respect others, understand political expectations, and articulate one's ideas is more of an illusion. Moreover, if political action could result in having everyone accept the values of literacy and embody them as their second nature, conflicts would vanish, people would all share in wealth and, moreover, would be able to abide by the standards of democracy. It even follows that the literate need to feel the obligation of inculcating literacy in others, thus creating the possibility of changing patterns of human experiences so that they reflect the demands of reason associated with literacy. Isaiah Berlin, among others, noted that the belief in a single encompassing answer to all social questions is indefensible. Rather, conflict is an overriding feature of the human condition. This conflict develops between the propensity to diversity (all the ends pursued) and the almost irrational expectation that there is one answer—a good way of life—worth pursuing and which can be attained if the political animal acknowledges the primacy of reason over passion, and freely chooses conformity to widely shared values over chaotic individualism.

Under the pragmatic circumstances of the civilization of illiteracy, the literate expectation of unanimous or even majority vote is less than significant. Voting results are as good an indicator of a society's condition as seismographs are of the danger of an earthquake. On election days, the results are known after the first representative sample makes it through the voting mechanism. Actually, the results are already at hand days before the election takes place. The means within our reach are such that it would suffice to commit a short interval of telephone time so that people who want to vote—and who know why they vote— can, and without having to go our of their way. Any other connection, such as the generalized cable infrastructure, connected to a central data processing unit outfitted for the event, would do as well. Such a strategy would answer only one part of the question: making it easy for people to vote. The second part regards what they are asked to vote for. The political process is removed from the exciting practice of offering authentic choice. Literacy-based political action is opaque, almost inscrutable. Accordingly, the citizen has no motivation for commitment and no need to express it through voting. There is a third part: the assumption that voting is a form of participating in the power of democracy. No one aware of the dynamics of work and life today can equate the notion of *majority* with democracy. More often than not, efficiency is achieved through procedures of exception.

Under the circumstances of a global economy of fast change and parallel practical experiences, no president of a country, no matter how powerful, and no central political power can effectively influence events significant to the citizen. The civilization of illiteracy requires alternatives to centralism, hierarchy, sequentiality, and determinism in politics. It especially entails alternatives to dualism, whether embodied in the two-party system, the legislative and executive opposition, and lawfulness vs. illegality, for example. This implies a broad distribution of political tasks, in conjunction with a politics that takes advantage of parallel modes of activism, networking, open-ended policies, and *self-determination* at meaningful levels of political life. Political fear of vagueness can only be compared to the fear of a vacuum that once upon a time branded physics and political doctrines. Faster rhythms of existence and the acknowledged need to adapt to circumstances of action never before experienced—scale of politics, globality, scale of humankind—speak against many of the literate expectations of politics as a stabilizing form of human practice. Politics, if true to its call, should contribute to speeding up processes and creating circumstances for better negotiations among people who have lost their sense of political adherence, or even lost their faith in law and order.

In this global world, where scale is of major importance, politics is supposed to mediate among the many levels at which people involved in parallel, extremely distributed activities, partake in globality. Apportionment of goods, as much as the apportionment of rights pertaining to creative aspects of human practical experiences, on a scheme similar to auctioning, follow the dynamics of the market more closely than rigid regulations. Awareness of this apportionment is a political matter and can be submitted to the concerned parties in forms of evolving opinions. Politics has also to address the new forms of property and their impact on political values in the new pragmatic framework. For instance, the real power of information processing is in the interaction of those able to access it. One should not be forced to apply rules originating from the feudal ownership of language, or from the industrial ownership of machines, to the free access to information, or to networks facilitating creative cooperative efforts. The challenge is to provide the most transparent environment, without affecting the integrity of interaction. A specific example in this regard is legislation against computer hackers. Such legislation, as well as the much publicized Communication Decency Act, only shifts attention from the new pragmatic context—unprecedented challenges arising from very powerful technologies—to one of routine law enforcement. Administrative reaction is the consequence of the built-in dualism, based on the clear-cut distinction between good and bad, characteristic of literacy-based politics.

A positive course of events can originate only from political experiences of individual empowerment. Wider choice and broader possibilities involve specific risks. Hacking is by no means an experience without precedent in past pragmatics. The German war code was hacked, and nations are very eager to confer honor upon other hackers of distinction: scientists who break the secrets of genetic codes, or spies who discover the secrets of the enemy. Examined from a literate political perspective, hacking, as a peculiar form of individual self-constitution, can appear as criminal. In a political experience coherent with the pragmatics leading to the civilization of illiteracy, hacking appears on a continuum joining creativity, protest, invention, and non-conformity, as well as criminal intention. The answer to hackers is not a code of punishment of medieval or industrial inspiration, but transparency that will, in the long run, undermine possible criminal motivations. A society that punishes creativity, even when relatively misdirected, through its policies and laws punishes itself in the long run. Someone who works at his terminal for a company producing goods all over the world, and pursuing social and economic programs that effectively touch citizens of many cultures, different faiths, race, political creed, sexual preference, different history and different expectations, participates in the politics of the world more than the institutions and the bureaucrats paid for functions that they *cannot* effectively fulfill. It is again pragmatics that makes us citizens of our small village or town, that integrates all of us, *Netizens* included, in the global world.

This short parenthesis in the discussion of politics can be justified by the fact that justice is the object of both politics and law. The practice of law is the practice of politics on a smaller stage. Political action, involving a new concept of law and justice, closer to the environment of industrial work, established not only that all (or almost all) were equal in respect to the law, but also that justice would take its own course. In the course of history, the various moments of change in the pragmatic framework were also moments of change in regard to the justice system. In incipient political praxis, rulers administered the law. Even today, a governor or president is the court of last resort in some legal cases. And law, like politics, relies on rhetoric, on language as the mediating mechanism of concepts.

In the course of history, the various moments of change in the pragmatic framework were also moments of change in regard to what today we call justice. The more powerful applied their own ideas of law under circumstances of incipient human practical experiences. It was the role of the appointed leader, whether in the magic of ritual, in tribes, in religion, in forms of settlement, to judge matters under dispute. Law focused on agreements, commitments, and integrity of the human body, of property, of goods, and of exchange. In time, the distance between what was done, affecting the balance of people's rights and obligation, and the reaction to it increased. A whole body of mediating elements, religion included, governed action and reaction. Just as myth and ritual did in their ways, major religious texts testify to how rules of living together and preserving life were established and implemented. The scale of society, reflected in the nature of the pragmatic context, played a crucial role in the process in respect to what was considered a crime, the type of punishment, and the swiftness of punishment.

What is of concern here is the change from the legal code elaborated in the framework of literacy and legal experience in the civilization of illiteracy. The institution of law and the professions involved in it embody expectations of justice under assumptions of efficiency pertinent to human practical experiences. New lands were discovered, new property was created, and machines and people made higher productivity possible. Rights were fought for, access to education opened, and the world became a place of new transactions for which the law of the land, inspired by natural right, no longer sufficed. It was in this context that literacy stimulated both the practice of legality and the inquiry into the nature of human rights and obligations. But it is also in this context that the language of legal practical experiences commenced its journey into today's *legalese* that no ordinary person can understand. Raskolnikov, in Dostoyevsky's *Crime and Punishment*, criticized the "legal style" of those educated as lawyers. "They still write legal papers that way." Though he remarks that the writing had "a kind of flourish to it..., yet look how illiterate his writing is." The criticism could be glossed over, due to its context, if it were not for an interesting remark: "It's expressed in legal language and if you use legal language, you can't write any other way." Trying to cope with ambiguity in language forces the lawyer to look for precision.

The equivocal condition of the practice of justice is that law originates in the realm of political experiences, but needs to be implemented free of politics, i.e., regardless of who is in power. The blindfolded goddess holding the scales of justice is expected to be objective and fair. The separation between judicial and governing entities is probably the highest achievement of the political system based on literacy. But it is also the area where, under circumstances of practical experiences different from those based on the underlying structure of literacy, the need to change is critical. This applies to new means of maintaining a just system for people less affected by the subjectivity of those holding the balance of power, and more by the ability to process information relevant to any object of dispute. The blindfolded goddess already uses X-ray vision in order to substantiate claims and counterclaims. Modeling, simulation, expert genetic testimony, and much more became part of the justice routine. Each party in a trial knows in advance what type of jury best serves its interests. The context for all these changes sheds light on their political meaning. If the practical experience of politics and justice are disconnected, the effectiveness of both suffers.

Politics stimulated change in respect to the perception of democracy, civil rights, political authority, and welfare. It demystified the origin, function, and role of property, and introduced a generalized level of relativity and uniform value. Law, on the other hand, supposed to protect the individual, should therefore be less inclined to trade off fairness for the lowest common denominator. Comparing this ideal to real legal practice is an exercise in masochism. The ever increasing, and fast increasing, human interaction via market mechanisms was followed by instances of conflict and expectations of negotiation. Without any doubt, the most pervasive mediating role is played in our day by legal professionals.

Due to its own self-interested dynamics, the legal profession insinuates itself in every type of practical experience, from multinational business to relations between individuals. Lately, it is involved in finding a place for itself in the world of new media, involving copyright laws and private rights versus public access. So one cannot say that law, as opposed to politics, is not proactive. The problem is that it is so in a context bound to literacy, and in such a way that style transcends substance. Latin, reflecting the origin of the western legal experience, used to be the language of law. Today, few lawyers know Latin. But they are well versed in their own language.

Legalese is justified by the attempt to avoid ambiguity in a given situation. There is nothing wrong with this. What is wrong is when legal language and the procedures encoded in legal language do not meet the pragmatic expectation, which is justice. Law and justice are not the same thing. A good case in point is the recent case of the State of California vs. O. J. Simpson. The spectacle of the legal procedure showed how a literate practice ended up convoluting justice. In fact, literate law is not meant to serve justice. Its purpose is to use the law to acquit a client. Allan Derschowitz claimed that the lawyer's duty is to his or her client, not to justice. This statement is far from the expectation that each member of society has. Therefore law loses its credibility because it undermines the notion of the social contract.

Some might say that this state of affairs is nothing new. Even Shakespeare criticized lawyers. Far from being a wholesale attack on the profession, the description I have given deserves to be contrasted to the possibility of effective judicial mediations in the civilization of illiteracy. Since changes occur so rapidly, the law of yesterday rarely applies to new circumstances created today. It used to be, people often find themselves reminiscing, that laws and rules (the Ten Commandments, at least) were expected to last and be respected, in their letter—which was carved in stone—and spirit, forever. No one will argue that justice is not an eternal desideratum. But achieving it does not necessarily mean that laws and the methods of lawyers are eternal. Some actions that society once accepted—child abuse, sexual harassment, racial discrimination—are now considered illegal, as well as unjust. Other *crimes* (whistling on Sundays, kissing one's spouse in public, working or operating a business on Sunday) might still be in some legal books and locally observed, but they are no longer considered instances of law-breaking. The result of changes brought about by changing pragmatics is the realization people have that there is no stable frame of reference, either for morality (as it is subject to law and law enforcement) or for legality.

Did lawyers create this situation? Are they a product of new human relations required by the new pragmatics? Who judges the legal system in order to determine that its activity meets expectations? There is no simple answer to any of these questions. If justice is to affect human practical experiences, it has to reflect their nature and participate in defining its own perspective in respect to the rights

656

that people integrate in new practical experiences of self-definition. It is all well and good for the legal system to use non-literate means, such as DNA evidence, videotapes, and access to legal information from around the world via Internet. But if they are then subjected to literate pettifogging, all this effort is to no avail.

THE PROGRAMMED PARLIAMENT

Politics in action means not elections but the daily routine of hard work on matters of interest to the people represented. Party affiliation aside, in the end the common good is supposed to be maintained or improved. Legislative political work continues a tradition that goes well beyond literacy. Nevertheless, effective legislation became possible only within the pragmatic framework that made literacy necessary. Once literacy itself reached its potential, new means for the political legislative practical experience became necessary. The driving force is the expectation that the legislative process should reflect practical needs emerging in a context of rapid change over shorter patterns of recurrence. As within the entire political practical experience, forces at work continuously collide.

Although literacy-based perspectives and methods for political legislation are no longer appropriate in handling issues and concerns stemming from a pragmatics that invalidates the literate model, politicians seem to be unwilling to realize the need for change. They find it more useful, and easier to defend, to legislate improved literacy-based education, for example, instead of rethinking education in the context of its necessity. They accept the mediating power of specialized knowledge, the generalized network of information, use all means for disseminating their own programs, but work within constraints originating in the literate practice of politics. It is hard to believe that in an age of limitless communication, speakers, mainly in the USA, arguing for the most intricate programs, will perform before an empty room in Congress. It is also hard to believe that a language rooted in experiences established a long time ago, and many times proved ineffective, is maintained. Procedures, testifying more to the past than the present, govern the activity of many legislative bodies (not only in Great Britain, where this legacy translates into a dress code as outmoded as the British monarchy). As with the executive political experience and the infatuation of justice, symbolism overtakes substance.

Nevertheless, under the pressure for higher efficiency, major changes are taking place. Legislative practical experiences, as disconnected as they are from new human practical experiences, are less and less an exercise in convincing writing or in formal logic. They increasingly reflect the expectations of globality and often apply mediation, task distribution, and interactivity. Electronic modeling is applied, simulation methods are tried out. The new methods of accessing information free the legislative politician from the time-consuming task of accumulating data. Consultants and staff members make use of powerful knowledge filters in order to involve in the political process only information pertinent to the subject. Politicians know that knowledge, at the right time and in the right context, is power. Their new experience, as members of computerized parliaments of many countries can testify, is that everyone has the data, but only few know how to process it effectively. In fact, political parties develop competitive processing programs that will give politicians pursuing their goals more convincing arguments in a public debate, or in discussions leading to legislative vote. The transparency brought about by means in the civilization of illiteracy ensures public access to the debate. The competitive edge is provided by the intelligent use of data. Power, that elusive aspect of any political activity, comes from the ability to process, not from the amount of information stored.

All this, kept at a minimum in this presentation, might sound like anticipation, or dreams for the politician of the future. It is not. The process is probably still at the beginning, but unavoidable. It will sooner or later affect such components as time in office—permanence of a representative reflects literacy-based expectations—procedures for public evaluation, candidacy, and voting. It will also require a rethinking of the relation between politicians and constituents. Rethinking the motivations and methods of legislation, even its legitimacy, are goals worthy of being pursued. Increased mediation affects the connection between facts and political action. Unless balanced by the use of the new means of communication that allow personal interaction with each voter, it will continue to alienate politics from the public. Mass-media politics is already a thing of the past—not because television is overridden by the Internet, but because of the need to create a framework for individual motivation for political action. Political efficiency is based on human interaction. What counts is not the medium, as this will continue to change, but what is accomplished through the medium.

To create a legislative framework that reflects the new nature of human relations and is appropriate to the pragmatic context means to understand the nature of the processes leading to the civilization of illiteracy. Consolidation of bureaucracy is as counter-indicative of this understanding as is the continuation of the monarchy and the House of Lords in Great Britain. Both these phenomena are as convincing as the mass generation of electoral letters that report on how the political representative best served his or her constituency. A sense of the process, as it involves the need to overcome models based on sequentiality, dualism, and deterministic reaction, can be realized only when the political process itself is synchronized with the prevalent pragmatics.

A BATTLE TO BE WON

As a practice of building, changing, and destroying coalitions, politics today is a summation of human practice. Professional politicians design strategies for coalition implementation and identify the most effective interactions for a certain policy. They develop their own

language and criteria for evaluating the efficiency of their specialized practice and of their mediating function in a society of many
and varied forms of mediation.

The obsession with efficiency, whether applied to politics or not, is
not imposed by forces outside ourselves. The tendency to transfer
responsibility does not result in some curse spoken by a disappointed
politician, philosopher, or educator. The shorter political cycles that
we encounter correspond to the dynamics of a human practical
experience focused on the immediate within the framework of a
global existence. It seems that the transition is from the small communal life striving for continuity and permanence, to a global community of interacting individuals, whose identity itself is variable,
prepared to experience discontinuity and change. Coordinations of
actions in this universe are no longer possible through large integrative mechanisms, such as language and bureaucratic institutions.
Small differentiating operations, in the nature of coalitions tested
through polling or electronic balloting, and modified in accordance
with the rapid change of political roles, represent an alternative.

Monarchies embodied the eternity of rule; treaties among mon-
archs were supposed to outlast the monarch. The 15-minute access to
political power, far from being a metaphor in some parts of the
world, is as relevant as any other form of celebrity (Warhol's included), since political processes and power relations are more and more
uncoupled from each other and disconnected from the obsession
with universality and timelessness. A 15-minute coalition is as critical
as access to power, and as useful as the new principles accepted by
the people involved. Instead of the top-down model of politics, we
can experience a combination of bottom-up and top-down procedures. Under these circumstances, the making and unmaking of
coalitions remains one among very few valid political functions. The
centers of political power—economics, law, interest groups—constitute poles around which such coalitions are established or abandoned.

One should ask whether such coalitions do not come into being in the *universal* language of literacy. Literacy is defended with the argument that it is some kind of common denominator. What is not accounted for is the fact that coalitions are not independent of the medium of their expression. Literacy-based coalitions pursue and further goals and actions consistent with the pragmatic framework that requires them. Needs characteristic of a pragmatic context incompatible with the structures imposed by literacy-based practical experiences require other means for establishing coalitions. When the leaders of the most advanced industrial states agree on indexing the value of their currency, or when friend and foe establish a political coalition against an invasion that could set a precedent and trigger consequences for the global economy, the means in place might take the appearance of literacy. In fact, these means are freed from words and literate articulations. They emerge from data processing and simulation of behavior in financial markets, virtual reality scenarios turned into actions for which no script could provide a description in advance. While politicians might still perform their script in a literate manner, the centers of power choose the most efficient means for evaluating each new coalition. As a consequence, and this is a distinguishing element, there is little connection between the authority of political institutions, as it results from their literate premise, and the dynamics of coalitions, reflecting the pragmatics of the civilization of illiteracy.

The sense of beginning experienced in our day goes well beyond the new states, new political means, beyond the science (or art) of coalition making. It is basically a beginning for the new *zoon politikon*, for a political animal that has lost most of its natural roots and whose human nature is probably better defined in terms of political instincts than cultural accomplishments. Culture is by and large discarded. People simply cannot carry culture with them, but neither can they negotiate their existence without political means appropriate to a social condition structurally different from that experienced in the past. The self-centered individual cannot escape relating to others and defining himself in reference to them. "We Am a Virtual Community" is not merely a suggestive title (conceived by Earl Babble) for an article on Internet interaction, but a good description of today's political world. The specific forms of relations, the *We Am* faction among them, are subject to many factors, not least to the biological and cognitive redefinition of the human being. When everything, literally everything, is possible and indeed acceptable, the political animal has to find new ways to make choices and pursue goals without facing the risk of losing identity. This is probably the decisive political battle that the humans have yet to win.

CHAPTER 12: "THEIRS NOT TO REASON WHY"

High precision electronic eyes placed on orbiting satellites picked up the firing of the rocket and the launch parameters. Data was transmitted to a computer center for information processing. The computed information, specifying angles, firing time, and trajectory, was relayed to antirocket missiles programmed to intercept enemy attack. The system—consisting of a vast, distributed, highly interconnected configuration—incorporates expertise from electronic vision devices, knowledge encoded in software designed to calculate rocket orbits (based on launch time, position, angle, speed, weight, meteorological conditions), fast transmission networks, and automated positioning and triggering devices.

This integrated system has replaced literacy-based modes of practical experiences pertinent to war. Instead of manuals describing the many parameters and operations that military personnel need to consider, information is contained in computer programs. These also eliminate the need for long training cycles, expensive practical exercises, and the continuous revision of manuals containing the latest information. Distributed knowledge and interconnectedness have replaced the structure of top-down command. The system described above contains many mediating components that allow for highly efficient wars.

Examples similar to the relative annihilation of the infamous (and ineffective) Scud missiles can be given from other episodes of the Gulf War, including the 100 hours of the so-called ground battle. This battle displayed the deadly force of artillery and tanks, the power of modeling and simulation, and major planning and testing methods independent of literacy-based military strategy and tactics.

The enemy consisted of an army structured on the principles derived from the pragmatic framework of literacy: centralized line of command, rigid hierarchy, modern military equipment integrated in a war plan that was essentially sequential and deterministic, and based on a logic of long-term encounters.

THE FIRST WAR OF THE CIVILIZATION OF ILLITERACY

An earlier draft of this chapter—introductory lines excepted—was written when no one anticipated a conflict involving American troops in the Arabian Gulf. During this war, theoretic arguments regarding the institution of the military in the civilization of illiteracy were tested in the flesh and blood of confrontation, probably well beyond my, or anybody's, expectations or wishes. The Gulf War reported by the media resembled a computer game or a television show. As I watched, I felt as though someone had lifted part of my text and sent it through the news wires. The story made for great headlines; but out of context, or in the context of a reality reduced to the TV screen, its overall meaning was obscured. In many ways, the armed conflict ended up trivialized, another soap opera or spectator sport. Other reports related the frustration of the troops with the limited number of phone lines. The reports also commented on the replacement of the traditional letter by videotape as the preferred method of communication. We also heard about an almost magical device, called CNX, used to help orient each person involved in the vast desert theater of war. And we saw or heard about the exotically named preprocessed and prepackaged food, about the pastimes of the troops.

The context started coming into focus. This was to become the first war of the civilization of illiteracy: a highly efficient (the word takes on an unintended cynical connotation here) activity that involved non-sequential, massively parallel practical experiences. These required precise synchronization (each failure resulted in victims to what was euphemistically called "friendly fire"), distributed decision-making, intense mediation, advanced specialization, and task distribution. These characteristics embodied an ideology of relative value disengaged from political discourse, and even more from moral precepts. Nobody expected this war to reinvent the bow and arrow (documented shortly after human self-constitutive experiences in language), or even the wheel (originating in the practical experience of populations whose home was the territory where the fighting took place). It is possible that some of the military personnel had heard about the book entitled *The Art of War* (written by Sun Tzu in 325 BCE or earlier), or about the books, some of undisputed notoriety, filling the libraries of military academies and the better research libraries. But this was not a war fought for the Book, in the spirit of the Book (*Koran* or *Bible*), or in the way books describe wars. In a way, the Gulf War was truly the "mother of all battles" in that it *rewrote* the rules on war—or did away with them.

All the characteristics of the civilization of illiteracy are retraceable in the practical experience of today's military: highly mediated praxis through electronic information storage and retrieval; transition from an economy of wartime scarcity to a war of affluent means of defense and destruction; shift from war based on the positivist notion of facts (many requiring incursions into enemy territory) to a relativistic notion of image, and the corresponding technology of image processing; shift from a hierarchical structure of rigid lines of authority and command to a relatively loose line of context dependent on freedom of choice extended almost to the individual soldier; a discipline of austerity and isolation from the non-military (conditions accepted in the past as part of a military career) replaced by expectations of relaxation and enjoyment, derived from the permissiveness and drive for self-satisfaction of society at large. That some of these expectations could not be fulfilled was criticized, but not really understood. The hosts of the American army live by different standards. Muslim law prohibits alcohol consumption and certain forms of entertainment, as well as burial of dead infidels in a land claiming to be holy.

The Gulf War, on its various fronts, was not a conflict of irreducible or irreconcilable religions, morals, or cultures. It was a conflict between an artificially maintained civilization of literacy, in which rich reserves of oil serve as a buffer from efficiency requirements in all aspects of life, and another civilization, one that entails the illiteracy of a society and an energy-hungry, global economy that reflects a dynamics of high efficiency.

It might well be that the final attack reminded experts in war history, military strategy, or evolution of tactics of the surprising maneuver tried by Epaminondas, the Theban commander (371 BCE) in the battle of Leuctra: instead of a frontal assault, an attack on one flank. General Schwartzkopf is not Epaminondas. He succeeded in his mission by allowing for task distribution in an international army—more of a pain than a blessing—that resulted in many flanks. Helmuth von Moltke, in the exhausting Franco-Prussian War (1870-1871), changed the relation to his subordinate commanders by letting them operate under broad directives. The generals and commanders of the many armies involved in the Gulf War took advantage of the power of networking in order to orchestrate an attack that tested extremely efficient, and costly, annihilation technology under a plan that today's computers have simulated many a time over.

But once I confessed that I wrote much of this chapter three years before the Gulf War, the reader might question whether I looked at the war through the spectacles of my hypothesis, seeing what I wanted to see, understanding events as they fit my explanatory model. I asked myself the same questions and concluded that presenting the argument as it stood before the war would shed light on the question and ultimately qualify the answer.

"War is a sheer continuation of politics with other means," wrote Carl von Clausewitz (*On War*, 1818). It is difficult to argue against this; but a paraphrase, intended to put the line in historic perspective, might be appropriate: War is the continuation of the practical experience of survival in the context of a society trying to control and adjudicate resources. Accordingly, combat follows the line of other practical experiences. The practical experience of hunting—formerly combat with non-human adversaries—required the weapons eventually associated with war. These were the tools that primitive humans used to wrest food for their survival and the survival of their community. Future aspects of these activities, and the associated moral values, make us sometimes forget that the syncretic nature of human beings, i.e., projection of their natural endowment in the practical act, is expressed in the syncretism of the tools used. This syncretic condition evolved under the need for labor division, and one of the main early demands of labor division resulted in the establishment of the semi-professional and professional warrior.

As the tools of the martial profession diversified more and more from working tools, a conceptual component (tactics and strategy) became part of the praxis. The conceptual component set forth a sequence to be followed, a logic to be used, and a method for counteracting enemy maneuvers in order to achieve victory. Von Clausewitz was the first to explicitly point out that war continues politics, while other writers on the subject, living centuries before he did, perceived war as a practical effort. Two Byzantine emperors, Maurice (539-602) and Leo, called the Wise (886-911), tried to formulate military strategy and tactics based on the pragmatic premise. They stipulated that the pragmatic framework defined the nature of the conflict and the actual condition of the battle, weapons included. Indeed, every known change in military materiel in a society has been synchronized to changes in the status of its practical experience. The invention of the stirrup by the Chinese (600) improved the ability of men riding horseback. It opened the avenue to wars where the backbone of battle formation was no longer composed of foot soldiers but of warriors on horses. Mechanical contraptions (e.g., the *Trebuchet*, acknowledged at 1100, based on releasing a heavy counterweight) for throwing large stones or missiles, opened the way to what would shift superior defensive capabilities (through fortifications, city walls, castles built before the 14th century) to superior offensive power. This was also the case with the cannons that the Turks used to conquer Constantinople (1453). But it is not military practice *per se* that concerns us here, but rather the implications of language, in particular literacy.

At a very small scale of human activity, with many autarchic groups composed of few people, there was little need for organized combat or specially trained warriors. Incipient, rudimentary military practical experience, in its basic functions of aggression and defense, became desirable at a larger scale of human activity. This experience was simultaneous with the establishment of language, especially writing. Sun Tzu's book, as well as many earlier testimonies to battles (mythology, religious writings, epic poetry, and philosophy), can be mentioned here. This military practice integrated the means and skills of survival, such as hunting and safeguarding the territory from which food was obtained.

Awareness of resources corresponded to awareness of scale. The scale of human activity in which the constitution of community member-warrior took place corresponded to increased settlement of populations, increased demand for resources, higher productivity, and accumulation of property—all reflected in the need to expand the practical experience of language beyond the immediate characteristic of orality. The efficiency of work and combat was at about an equal level. In a sense, wars lasted forever; peace was merely respite between conflicts. The notion of prisoner (usually sold into slavery) confirmed the importance of human labor and skill for consolidating a community, producing wealth for those in power, and subsistence for everyone else. The social constitution of the military was not excepted from pragmatic requirements of efficiency and mediation, i.e., of ensuring the highest efficiency within the given scale of human experience, as needs and expectations corresponding to this scale were manifested. While it is true that combat efficiency was spelled out in units of intentional destruction or preservation (of life and various artifacts relevant to human self-constitution), combat efficiency also referred to defenders whose goal was to make destruction by the enemy less possible (even impossible).

While individual conflicts did not require the intervention of language more than orality could provide, conflicts between larger groups made the need for a coordinating instrument clear. Human language, through new words and constructs, testified to the experience of conflicts and the associated mytho-magical manifestations. Through language, this experience was projected against the background of many different forms of human praxis. As a general rule, armies of all types, under every type of government, acquired a special status in society due to the function they fulfilled. Written language did not generate armies; but it served as a prerequisite (even in its most rudimentary notation forms) for the institution of the military. Writing introduced many elements that influenced the combat experience: a record of means and people, a record of actions, an instrument for planning, a record of consequences. All the components of the military institution objectify the purpose of war at a particular time. They also objectify the relations between a society at war and, during times of peace, between society and its warriors. Language is the medium through which objectification takes place. The sequentiality of writing and the need to express sequences pertinent to conflicts are consubstantial. Von Clausewitz's line encompasses the extension in language of the many aspects of wars.

"Did Gideon know how to read Hebrew? Did Deborah?" some people might ask, referring to leaders of decisive battles documented in the Old Testament. Others would refer to examples from the same time that are accounted for in Greek epics and the chronicles of the Middle East. Roman mythology and the testimony of Islam do not tell us whether all their warriors wrote or read. These documents do inform us of the pragmatic circumstances that led to the institution of the army as a body constituted in continuation of syncretic practical experiences, progressively constituting its own domain of existence and its own reason for being.

From face-to-face conflicts that required almost no language, and which resulted in the victory of the stronger, to the conflicts between humans in which much technology—requiring little language—was also involved, changes parallel to the levels of literacy occurred. Under the circumstances of wars fought by armies facing each other, language was the medium for constituting armies and coordinating action. In order to define goals, to share plans for achieving victory, and to modify plans in response to changing conditions, language was as important as the number of horses, quality of swords and shields, and quality of ammunition. The profession of warrior, as much as the profession of hunter, was based on the ability to attack and defend, and on the skills needed to adapt means to goals within a changing balance of power. The first wars, and probably the majority of them, were fought before generalized literacy. The major warriors—the Egyptian pharaohs Tuthmose III in the battle for Meggido (1479 BCE), Ramses II battling the Hittites at Kadesh (1296 BCE), Nebuchadnezzar and Darius, the Spartans under Leonidas (480 BCE), Alexander the Great (conquering Babylon in 330 BCE), Julius Caesar (49-46 BCE) and Octavian (31 BCE), and the many Chinese warriors of this period and later—did not need literacy for their battles as much as for their politics. Their strategies resulted from the same expectations and pragmatic requirements that gave rise to the experience of written language.

Wars were fought on terrain well chosen, by armies composed of men who carried out orders selected from a limited set of possibilities. To paraphrase the terminology of generative grammars, it was a limited *war language*, with not too many possible *war sentences*. Once improved means of work and production became the means of carrying on war, those in command could *write* more *war texts*, more scripts. As *war efficiency* increased, so did the possibility of a break-down of the effort due to lack of integration and coordination. The military structure reflected the characteristics of the human praxis that fostered written language and, much later, literacy: relatively limited dynamics, centralized, hierarchical organization, low level of adaptability, a strictly sequential course of action, a deterministic mentality. David Oliver convincingly described the process: "Mechanics is the vehicle of all physical theory. Mechanics is the vehicle of war. The two have been inseparable." He refers to the practical demands of warfare in the context that led to the science of mechanics and eventually to the beginnings of projectile ballistics. By 1531, Nicolo Tartaglia of Brescia overcame his disdain for war and devised the gunner's square, which was perfected 100 years later by none other than Galileo. In 1688, the French introduced the socket bayonet on their muskets, which occurred simultaneous to changes in tools used at the time, i.e., the tools that allowed for manufacturing the bayonet.

The framework that created conditions for the ideal of literacy affected the pursuit of war not only in technology, but also in the way wars were played out. The advancing line of exposed troops were involved in a dynamics of confrontation that reflected linearity, a characteristic prevalent in the practical experience of civilian life. Destructive power was added until the enemy was destroyed. Row by row, soldiers stopped to fire platoon volleys, then continued onto the decisive bayonet charge. The structure of writing (sequences, hierarchy, accumulation, closure) and the structure of this particular military engagement were similar. Literacy as such was registered rather late as a qualifier of the warrior. But once integrated in the practical experience of military self-constitution, literacy changed the nature of making war and enabled higher levels of efficiency corresponding to the new scale of war. These were no longer skirmishes among feudal warlords, but major conflicts between nations. These conflicts diminished in number but grew in intensity. Their duration corresponded to the relatively long cycles of production, distribution, and consumption characteristic of literacy-based practical experiences.

Under the pressure of many types of necessity embodied in human pragmatics, war was submitted to rules. It was *civilized*, at least in some of its aspects. The Catholic Church, preserver of literacy during the Dark Ages, when many *little* wars between feudal lords were carried on, took the lead in this direction. In order to avoid destruction of crops and lives in the barbarian societies of Europe after the fall of the Roman Empire, the only viable hierarchy tried to tame warriors with the literate rules that the Church preserved. With their own pragmatic considerations in mind, rulers accepted these prescriptions. It took a millennium for people to discover that wars never have final results. But they also learned that the experience of war creates knowledge—for example, of means used, weather patterns, territory, characteristics of the enemy—and creativity—what is called *the art of war*. Resulting in death and destruction, wars are also instances of self-education in one of life's most unforgiving schools.

THE INSTITUTION OF THE MILITARY

"The draft is the legitimate child of democracy," as Theodor Heuss defined it. Obligatory military service was introduced during one of the first modern revolutions—the French *levée en masse* (conscription) of 1793. The citizen-soldier replaced mercenaries and professional soldiers. The call "Aux armes, mes citoyens" that became a stanza of the French national anthem, glorified the expectations of the moment. Prussia followed suit almost immediately, motivated by economic reasons: cheap manpower for war. During the prolonged process of becoming an institution, the military enlisted the support of the state it defended or of those private establishments (church, landowners, merchants) that needed its services.

Feeding off the means generated by society, the military institution integrated the practical experience of the people in its structure and actively pursued courses of action meant to increase its efficiency. At every juncture of humankind's continuous change, the military had to prove levels of efficiency that justified its own existence as a factor in the active defense of resources. When it was no longer efficient and weighed too heavily on the socio-economic foundation, it was eventually overthrown, or the society supporting it stagnated, as we see happening time and again in military dictatorships.

As one of the many highly structured environments for human interaction, the military identified itself, as did all other social mechanisms, through repetitive actions. Each action could be further seen as a set of tasks, or orders, connected to motivations or justifications, which anticipate or follow practical experiences specific to the military. Some were connected to life within the organization, such as the possibility to advance in the hierarchy and affect future activity. These were internal in the sense that they were affected by the implicit rules adopted by the institution. Others were external, expressed in the nature of the relation between the military and society: symbolic status, participation in power, expectations of recognition.

Evolution of the military resulted in changes in the language involved in defining and modifying the interactions characteristic of military practical experience. This language became progressively more adapted to the goal—win the war—and less coordinated with civilian language, in which the discourse of motivations leading to the conflict occurred. Correspondingly, relations with the outside world—future members of the military, social and political institutions, cultural establishments, the church—took place in what appeared to be a different language.

Changes in the structure of the practical experience of human self-constitution, as well as changes resulting from a growing scale, had an influence both inside and outside the military. When the individuals making up the world constituted themselves as literate, the functioning of the military assumed the expectations and characteristics of literacy. What would emerge as military academies were probably established at this time. Von Moltke's ideas of changing the nature of relations with subordinates just predated the many modern advances in war technology: the use of steam-powered warships (by the Japanese in their war against the Russians in 1905); the introduction of radio, telephone, and automotive transportation (all tested in Word War I); and even the articulation of the concept of total war (by Erich Lindendorf). All these correspond to a pragmatic framework within which literacy was necessary, and literacy's characteristic reflected upon new practical experiences. The total war is of the same nature as the expectation of universal literacy: one literacy replaces all others. There is to the military institution of the civilization of literacy an expectation of permanency, embodied in rules and regulations, in hierarchies, and centralized structure, similar to that of state, industry, religion, education, science, art, and literature. There is also an expectation of centralism, and thus hierarchy and discipline. These characteristics explain why almost all armies adopt similar literacy-based structures. Guerrilla wars, in their early manifestations (skirmishes during the American Revolution) and in their current forms in South America, for example, are illiterate in that they are not based on the conventions of literacy. They unfold in a decentralized manner, and are based on the dynamics of self-organizing nucleii. This is why military strategists consider them so dangerous today.

Patterns of military action and the language recurrences associated with these patterns express attitudes and values pertinent to the pragmatic framework. England, at the height of its literate experience, had a highly structured, almost ritualized way of carrying out war. One of the main complaints during the American Revolution was that the colonials did not fight according to the rules that literate West Europe had established over the centuries. Under circumstances of change, as those leading to the end of the need for a generalized, all-encompassing literacy, these attitudes and values, expressed in language and in patterns of military activity, are exhausted, except where they are carried over to other forms of praxis, especially to politics and sports.

As is the case with many literacy-based institutions, the military became a goal in itself, imposing rules on social and political circumstances, instead of adapting to them. Following World Wars I and II, the military took control of many countries under the guise of various political and ideological justifications. Military, or military-supported, dictatorships, displaying the same characteristics of centralized rule as monarchy and democracy under presidents, sprang up where other modes of government proved ineffective. This happens today in many parts of the world that are still dedicated to economic and political models of the past, such as in South America, the Middle East, and Africa, for example.

FROM THE LITERATE TO THE ILLITERATE WAR

The last war fought under the sign of literacy was probably World War II. The very fact that the last world war came to its final end after the atomic bomb was deployed is indicative of the fact that once one aspect of human practical experience is affected by a change of scale, others are affected as well. While the millions of victims (the majority of whom were raised in the expectations of the civilization of literacy) might make us reluctant to mention literacy, in fact, war's systematic cruelty and extermination power are the result of literacy characteristics implicit in the effective functioning of the war machine and in the articulation of war goals. In the history of World War II, the chapter about language is probably as enlightening as the chapters devoted to the new weapons it brought about: the precursors of modern rocket systems, in addition to the atomic bomb. Each of the powers involved in this large-scale war understood that without the integrating force of literacy, exercised in and around the conflict, the enemy could not succeed. Many books were written about the escalation of hostility through the language of political and ideological discourse. Many prejudices associated with this war were expressed in exquisitely literate works, supported by formally perfect, logical arguments. On the other hand, some writers pointed out the weaknesses of literacy. Roland Barthes, for example, studied its fascist nature. Others mentioned the inadequacy of a medium bound to fail because it was so opaque that it covered thoughts instead of revealing them, validated false values instead of exposing them for what they were.

The language of politics extended truly into the language of the conflict. Thanks to radio and newspapers, as well as the rhetoric of rallies, it was able to address entire nations. The industrial establishment, upon which the war machine was built, still embodied the characteristics of the pragmatic framework of literacy. It was based on the industrial model of intense manufacturing. Millions of people had to be moved, fed, and logistically supported on many fronts. The war involved elements of an economy in crisis, affording much less than abundance. Germany and its allies, having planned for a *Blitzkrieg*, threw all their limited resources into the preparation and execution of the war. Europe was coming out of the depression resulting from World War I. The people were promised that victory would bring the well deserved recompense that had eluded them the first time around. Against this background, literacy was mobilized in all the areas where it could make a difference: education, propaganda, religious and national indoctrination, in the racist discourse of justifications and in articulating war goals. Ideological purposes and military goals, expressed in literate discourse, addressed equally those on the front lines and their families. Literacy actively supported self-discipline and restraint, the acceptance of centralism and hierarchy, as well as the understanding of extended production cycles of intense labor and relatively stable, although not necessarily fair, working relations.

All these characteristics, as well as a self-induced sense of superiority, were reflected in the war. Advanced levels of labor division and improved forms of coordination of the parties involved in the large scale experience of factory labor marked the military experience. The war entailed confrontations of huge armies that practically engaged entire societies. It combined strategies of exhaustion (blockades, crop destruction, interruption of any vital activities) and annihilation. Millions of people were exterminated. The structure of the army embodied the structure of the pragmatic framework. Its functioning was reflective of industrial systems designed to process huge quantities of raw material in order to mass-manufacture products of uniform quality.

What made literate language use essential in work and market transactions made it essential, in forms appropriate to the goal, to the prosecution of the war. From this perspective, it should become clear why major efforts were made to understand this language. Efforts were also made to get information about tactics and strategy embodied in it, as much ahead of time as possible, and to use this *literate* knowledge to devise surprise or counter-strategies. This is why language became a main field of operation. Enemies went after military code (not a different language, but a means of maintaining secrecy) and did not spare money, intelligence, or human life in their efforts to understand how the opposing forces encoded their plans. The brightest minds were used, and strategies of deceit were developed and applied, because knowing the language of the enemy was almost like reading the enemy's mind.

At the risk of dealing with the obvious, I should state here clearly that the language of war is not the same as everyday language; but it originates in this language and is conceived and communicated in it. Both are structurally equivalent and embodied in literacy. To dispose of the enemy's use of language means to know what the enemy wants to do and how and when. In short, it means to be able to understand the pragmatics of the enemy as defined under the circumstances of war, as these extended the circumstances of life and work. Since language projects our time and space experience, and since wars are related to our universe of existence, understanding the language of the enemy is actually integrated in the combat plan and in a society's general war effort. Climbing hills to establish a good offensive position, crossing rivers in a defensive move, parachuting troops behind enemy lines in a surprise maneuver are human experiences characteristic of the pragmatic context of literacy, impossible to relate to the goal pursued without the shared conventions implicit in language. Some people still believe that the master coup of World War II was the breaking of the ciphers of the *Enigma* machines used by the Germans, thus making the function of language, in such an effort of millions of people, the center of the war effort. Polish cryptoanalysts and the British operation, in which Alan Turing (the father of modern computing) participated, succeeded in deciphering, reconstructing, and translating messages that, re-enciphered in Allied codes (the ULTRA material), decisively aided the war effort.

By the end of the war, the world was already a different place. But within the framework of war, and in direct connection to the changes in practical human self-constitution, a structural shift to a different dynamics of life and work had started. Various aspects related to the determinism that eventually resulted in the war started to be questioned through new practical experiences: the need to overcome national interests; the need to transcend boundaries, those boundaries of hate and destruction expressed in the war; the need to share and exchange resources. Visionaries also realized that the incremental increase in world population, despite the enormous number of deaths, would result in a new scale of human experiences that could not be handled within a rigid system with few degrees of liberty.

The recent illiterate war in the Arabian Gulf, and the never-ending terrorist attacks all over the world, can be seen, in retrospect, as the progeny of the war that brought down the civilization of literacy. The concept of *Blitzkrieg* and the dropping of the A-bomb at Hiroshima and Nagasaki were a foretaste of the quick, efficient, illiterate war. Its newest extentions are sophisticated genetic scripts and nanotechnology that seem to come out of science fiction.

Military all over the world disposes of the highest technology. Even countries that can afford to maintain outmoded large armies—because of population density, relatively low salaries, and the ability to draft the entire population—seek the latest weapons that scientific discovery and technological progress can offer. The weapons market is probably the most pervasive of all markets. Among the numerous implications of this state of affairs, none is more disconcerting than the fact that human genius serves the cause of death and destruction. In some countries, food reserves barely cover needs beyond a season or two; but the military has supplies to cover years of engagement.

Today the military is in control of the most sophisticated technology ever created. It is also becoming an institution of a rather low level of literacy, publicly deplored and politically questioned. This assertion applies less (but it still applies) to the command level, and more to its enlisted men and women. Addressing the topic of language proficiency, Darell Bott provides an interesting portrait of a person who joins the military intelligence unit of the National Guard as a linguist. After training in the Defense Language Institute, the individual loses 25 percent of his language skills and fails to meet language proficiency standards. Every effort is made to change this situation, even before understanding it. Darell Bott's description does not refer to an accidental, individual failure, but to the implicit dynamics of military practical experiences in the civilization of illiteracy. A linguist, of all professionals, does not choose to lose literate language proficiency. This proficiency is just not necessary for attaining the efficiency called for in the military. Not really understanding this structural condition, armies introduce their recruits to weaponry—the majority designed for the illiterate warrior—and to the skills of reading and writing. These skills dispense ideology, religion, history, geography, psychology, and sex education in concentrated doses. The situation is paradoxical: what defines the practical experience of the military today—high technology, division of tasks, networking, distributed responsibilities—conflicts with the traditional expectations of clear lines of command, hierarchy, authority, and discipline. The means that render useless the characteristics stemming from literacy-based pragmatics are welcome, but the human condition associated with them is frightening.

Yes, a literate soldier can be better indoctrinated, subjected to the inherent arguments of literacy, of rules and authorities to be obeyed. But the nature of the pragmatics of war has changed: faster action makes reading—of instructions, commands, messages—inappropriate, if not dangerous. For focusing on targets moving at a speed far higher than that afforded by literacy-based training, one needs the mediation of the digital eye. Conflicts are as segmented as the world itself, since clear-cut distinctions between good and bad no longer function effectively. Centralized military experiences based on structures of authority and hierarchy are counterproductive in actual conflicts of complex dynamics.

The war in Vietnam is a good example of this. During this war, instructions were transmitted from the top of the hierarchy down to the platoons through commanders not adept at the type of war Vietnam represented. Even the President of the USA was effectively involved, more often than not through decisions that proved detrimental to the war effort. The USA forgot the lesson of its own pragmatic foundation in imitating, as it did in Vietnam, the literate wars of Europe in a context of confrontation characteristic of the civilization of illiteracy. Memoirs, published too late (Robert MacNamara's is but one example), reveal how the literate paradigm embodied in the government and the military kept from the public essential information that, in retrospect, rendered the loss of so many human lives meaningless.

The luxury of a standing army and the cost of subjecting soldiers to long cycles of training, literacy included, belong to the previous pragmatic framework. The time of the life-long warrior is over. The experience of war changes as quickly as new weapons are invented. The new scale of humankind requires global levels of efficiency impossible to attain if productive forces are withdrawn from productive experiences. Once upon a time, the military distinguished itself as a separate body in the social texture. The civilization of illiteracy reintegrated the military in the network of assignments and purposeful functions of the pragmatics of high efficiency. From the complete suit of armor worn in medieval Europe (before firearms rendered it ineffective) to the plain-clothes military of today—many of them educated in science and technology—not only have over 500 years gone by, but, more important, new forms of self-constitution, and hence identification, became necessary and real. Sulfur fumes used over 2,000 years ago in the battle at Delium and the threat of chemical and biological weapons in the Gulf War are superficially related. The same knowledge that goes into producing new chemical and biological means used in high efficiency agriculture and in food preparation goes into chemical and biological weapons of mass destruction. Genetics is the new frontier, and so are extremly complex digital means and methods.

This is not a discourse in favor of efficient armies which are of great help during natural disasters, nor is it a discourse in favor of destructive wars, no matter who justifies them. If it sounds like one, it is because the literate description of the structural background against which, whether we like it or not, the practical experience of the military takes place, bears the stamp of literate praxis. In the civilization of illiteracy, the military has come to acknowledge that there is little that can, or should, be done to restore literacy as its coordinating mechanism. Literacy is not necessarily the best system for achieving optimal military performance at the level facilitated by new technologies. Neither is it, as some would like to believe, a means of avoiding war. The literate human being proved to be a war beast equal, if not superior, to the illiterate who was subjected to impression and conscription, or who enlisted as a mercenary.

Current military research attempts to remove human beings from the direct confrontation that war used to entail. Nothing affects public support for military action more than body-bags. These spoil the fun and games that expensive missiles provide, the reason for which the Gulf War was nicknamed "the Nintendo War." And missiles fare better among the Netizens, despite their reluctance to embrace belligerence for settling disputes. Highly efficient, sophisticated digitally programmed systems do not relate to space and time the way humans do. This aspect gives the digital machines and genetic weapons an edge in respect to the implicit coordination expected in war. The kinds of interaction that military praxis requires makes literacy inadequate for coordinating the humans who constitute today's armies. Time is segmented beyond human perception and control; space expands beyond what a person can conceive and control. Major components of a war machine are placed in outer space and synchronized by extremely time-sensitive devices. The Strategic Defense Initiative (dubbed *Star Wars*) was the most advertised example. More trivial systems, like those used in orienting troops in the desert, are a matter of routine. The expressive power required for increasing motivation, and for projecting a rational image of irrationality, collides with the requirement for speed and precision essential to accomplishing complex tactical and strategic plans. Coordination of sophisticated information systems machines does not have to rely on a language frequently not precise enough, or fast enough, to accommodate very dynamic processes. At speeds beyond that of sound at which battles are fought with airplanes, rockets, satellites, and missiles, a soldier observing a target would be late in pressing a trigger, not to mention waiting for the command to fire.

The complexity of war machines is such that even their maintenance and repair requires means independent of the language that functions according to the rules of literacy. It should come as no surprise that the electronic book has already appeared in the military sphere of human experience. This *book* is the digitally stored description of a device, not the printed book that was once the manual describing it. If the device is an airplane, or gun system on the airplane, or equipment on a ship, the weight of manuals needed to explain its functioning, or to support maintenance and troubleshooting, would keep the airplane grounded. Any change in such a complex system would require reprinting of thousands of pages. In its electronic version, the book is a collection of data manipulated by a computer, displayed in visual form when necessary, and programmed to make recognition of the problem and its solution as simple as possible—idiot-proof, in fact. It is not a sequential collection of pages indexed in a table of contents and requiring a linear reading strategy. The electronic book opens to the appropriate *page,* and every page is generated only as necessary, according to the maintenance or repair requirements of the case. Obviously, the readers addressed by the electronic book are different from the literate. They are at least partially visual literates who know how to look at an image and follow pictographic prompts. Instead of reading, the human operators carry out the required operation, supervised by the system, counting only on the feedback from the machine. Under these circumstances, efficiency expectations make the use of the human being almost a luxury. The paradigm of self-servicing machines, of circuits that can fix themselves (von Neumann's genius at work) is already a reality.

The electronic book—here presented in an application of military relevance, although there is more to it than that—is one example from the many that can be given regarding how our good old verbal literacy is becoming obsolete. Electronic books constituted over networks (wired or wireless) support a wide range of collaborative activities. By their nature, military experiences utilize such activities. Access to resources and to an unlimited array of possible interactions is essential to collaboration. Literate expression cannot fulfill these requirements. Digital formats used in electronic books serve as a medium for sharing and understanding goals. The subsumation of individuality to the goal is probably the only specifically military component that carries over from previous experiences of war. Nevertheless, this subsumation does not follow the patterns of centralism and the hierarchy of literacy. The methods are different in that more initiative than ever before is required from the soldiers. This initiative is embodied in alternate means of expression and communication.

In electronically synchronized instruments, programs of distributed tasks and massive parallel computation replace literacy and literacy-based actions. Today's technology permits flying at low altitude and high speed, but limitations of the human biological system make this dangerous for the pilot. When reaching a certain speed, the human can no longer coordinate movements without which low altitude flying becomes suicidal. But suicide is no alternative to avoiding enemy radar, since there are no words capable of alerting a pilot to the heat detector guided missile. Accordingly, *languages* addressing machines and vision systems with detection capabilities change the nature of human involvement in military situations. Again, these languages make the participation of literate language less and less significant.

Literacy-based means cannot provide for the expected coordination. Mediation takes place among many distributed, loosely interconnected devices; efficiency increases due to the many resources integrated in such powerful and ubiquitous systems. I give these examples—rudimentary in comparison to the *Nintendo* war we watched on our television screens a few years ago—from the viewpoint of someone who believes in life, peace, and human understanding, but also as one who sees a progressive discarding of literacy from one of the most language-dependent forms of human interaction and coordination. As with everything liberated from language and literacy, military practice was dehumanized. This consequence is likely to be welcomed in its more general significance: Let machines kill machines. Let the war be one of genes and genetic manipulation, of neural networks and machine learning, of intelligent database management and networked distributed tasks. Just as in factories and offices, the human being is replaced by programs endowed with knowledge mediated by something other than literacy. What changes the structure of military activity, and language's participation in it, are the new languages embodied in the technology. That computer-game simulations of flight or target-shooting are basically equivalent to the systems of precision and destruction used in the Gulf War need not be repeated. But that players of computer games grow up with skills expected from jet pilots and from operators of extremely productive technology deserves attention and thought.

Do weapons speak and write and read? Do they understand the language of the officer who decides when they are to be fired? Is an *intelligent* weapon system capable of interpreting whether a legitimate target should indeed be wiped out, even if at the time of its use, circumstances would speak against destroying it on moral grounds? Do genetic methods of enemy annihilation withstand moral criteria? I ask these questions—which can only be answered with a "No"—on purpose. The literate attitude, according to which military praxis is one of command and execution requiring language, presents us with a contradiction. Non-military practical experience is more and more mediated by many languages and synchronized in a vast network of distributed assignments. If military experiences were to remain literacy-based, this would be equal to maintaining different pragmatic structures and pursuing goals of disparate efficiency. It is true that the literacy still involved in the military is reflected in structures of hierarchy, a relative expectation of centralism (in the USA, as in many other countries, the President is the commander-in-chief), and dependency on deterministic models. Nevertheless, the expectation of efficiency makes critical the need to adopt essentially non-hierarchic, self-management structures promoting coordination and cooperative efforts within a distributed network of different assignments. In the partial literacy of the military, a redefinition of the process of goal-setting and the pursuit of assignments other than destruction, such as relocation of refugees or aiding vast populations subjected to natural disasters, continuously takes place. Security is another area of self-constitution that derives benefits from military praxis. The smaller and more distributed wars through which terrorism seeks to accomplish its goals have resulted in small armies of highly trained security personnel to protect the civilian public. Combat is truly global. But as opposed to the small war of the Middle Ages, the illiterate terrorist respects no rules and recognizes no higher authority.

No army could have changed the world more than the new system of human relations geared toward achieving levels of efficiency corresponding to numbers of people in pursuit of satisfying their needs, and of others achieving levels of prosperity never before experienced. Armies, as much as schools and universities, as much as the nations they are supposed to defend, as much as the nuclear family, and all the activities related to them and all the products they generate, correspond to the structure of praxis of a loosely connected world with patterns of human practical experiences marked by individual success and dependent on personal performance.

THE LOOK THAT KILLS

Smaller, more deployable, as efficient as possible—this description sums up the characteristics of new weapons on the wish-list of almost any army in the world. On a more specific basis, defense officials have sketched some research and development objectives. Here are some, obviously all subject to obsolescence:

- Worldwide all-weather forces for limited warfare, which do not require main operating bases, including a force that is logistically independent for 30 days
- Tracking of strategically relocatable targets
- Global command control, communications, and intelligence (C^3I) capabilities to include on-demand surveillance of selected geographical areas and real-time information transfer to command authorities
- Weapon systems that deny enemy targeting and allow penetration of enemy defenses by managing signatures and electronic warfare
- Air defense systems to overmatch threat systems

686

- Weapons that autonomously acquire, classify, track, and destroy targets
- Reduction of operations and support resources requirement by 50% without impairing combat capability.

Expected are a force powered by electricity (ecological concerns), robotic tanks and aerial vehicles, and—this is not science fiction—bionically enhanced soldiers with embedded chips, able to sleep when commanded, and an exoskeleton system allowing individuals to carry 400 pounds around the battlefield (compared to the mere 100 they carry now). General Jerry C. Harrison even formulated the following order: "Okay guys, let's shoot number 49. Tune in your goggles to see but not be seen." The look that kills (the proud accomplishment of university-based research) becomes reality, together with genetic targeting.

The only comment that can follow such a description is that all the characteristics of the civilization of illiteracy are embodied in the expectations of military efficiency. Globality, interconnectedness, open-ended goals and motivations, reduced human involvement, and many partial literacies are all here, presented in specific expectations. The questionable aspect is the implicit theme of the permanence of the institution of the military, probably the most resilient legacy of the civilization of literacy. What the technology of the civilization of illiteracy requires is the command of the abstractions (the *language*, the genetic code) driving it, the partial literacy associated with this language, pertinent to military or any other use. As one of the partial literacies of this time, military literacy defines the domain of action and the interpretation of such actions. It is relevant, for instance, that disarmament treaties not be formulated without military language, i.e., without the military experts, the ones we want to release from their functions. Each such treaty either discards a part of the language of weapons and associated technologies, or makes it less relevant, as it opens new avenues for increased military efficiency.

The new organization of the military is one of confronting technologies and associated military literacy. Accordingly, to talk about orders given by an officer, whether a weapon understands such orders, and all similar logocentric examples, means to still look at the military from the perspective of a civilization from which it continuously distances itself. Artificial eyes (radar, vision systems), odor detectors, touch-sensitive devices, speed sensors, and many other digital devices free the human being from confrontation and progressively eliminate death from the equation of war. Those who compare the photographic images of previous wars to animation on computer game terminals compare a condition of direct confrontation, of our own nature, and of the realization of the limited condition of life to that of mediated experiences. The night sky lit up by tracers, the eerie video-game-like actions, the targets seen through remote cameras are of a realm different from that of destruction and blood, where moral concern is triggered. The expectation is pragmatic, the test is efficiency.

The survival of the military institution in its literate structure and the lack of understanding of just what makes literacy unnecessary in the pragmatic framework of today's global world are not the same thing. The first aspect refers to the immense inertia of a huge mechanism; the second involves the difficult task of freeing ourselves, as products of literate education, from ourselves. Recognition of such a fundamental change does not come easy. Universities, bastions of literacy, producing the illiterate technology of war, are caught in the dilemma of negating their own identity, or becoming agents of illiterate action. We hang on to the ideal of literacy, as well as to the so-called necessity of strong defense—which reflects literacy-based values such as national borders in a global world—because we are not yet ready to cope with a new dynamics of change that is not militarily determined, but which results from structural necessities of a socio-economic nature. The political map of the world changed drastically in recent years because factors affecting the pragmatic framework of human practical experience, at the scale we reached today, are at work. Globality is not a dream, a political goal, a utopian project, but a necessity resulting from this new scale.

BOOK V.

CHAPTER I: THE INTERACTIVE FUTURE: INDIVIDUAL, COMMUNITY, AND SOCIETY IN THE AGE OF THE WEB

Collapse and catastrophe as opposed to hope and unprecedented possibilities—these are the party lines in the heated discussions centered on the dynamics of ongoing changes in which the whole world is involved. Paul Virilio is quite expressive in his formulation of the problem:

> An accompanying evil...is the end of writing, as it unfolds through image technology, cinema/film, and television screen. [...] We don't read anymore, we hardly write each other, since we can call each other on the phone. Next, we will no longer speak! I'd really like to say: this will indeed be the silence of the lambs!

No less powerful in their assertions are those who see chances for social renewal in interactions not embodied in the rules of literacy. The electronic forum of the European Commission, involved in *Project Information Society*, lists *Ten Bones of Contentions* from which I chose the following:

> The system we are stuck with and frantically trying to fix comes from another time and an entirely different set of circumstances. It is changing massively in front of our noses and needs to be completely rethought and radically overhauled.

The statement is less expressive than Virilio's, but no less intolerant.

As discussions continue to bring up extremely important aspects of the conflict marking this time of discontinuity, the billions of people populating our world today constitute themselves through a broad variety of practical experiences. A list of these experiences—

from primitive patterns of hunting and gathering food to eye movement command of remote systems and applications driven by voice recognition in the world of nanotechnological synthesis—would only augment the confusion. Given this broad pragmatic spectrum, no one could seriously project the future as one of virtual communities, or of an electronic democracy, without sounding overly naive or directly stupid. We know how far we have come, but we do not really know where we are.

In advancing a comprehensive pragmatic perspective, I chose to undertake an elaboration well beyond the short-breathed argumentation peculiar to this moment in time. The advantage of this approach deserves to be shared. Endorsing one perspective or another, such as the California Ideology—defined by its critics as "global orthodoxy concerning the relation between society, technology, and politics"— or alternatives—the so-called European model, or the transactional structure, or neo-Marxian solutions, to name a few—is not an option. Indeed, the argument of this book is that answers cannot result from infatuation with technology, cultural self-replication, models based on biological mechanisms, unfocused bionomic elaborations, or incessant criticism of capitalism. Affirmations of a deep nature, above and beyond the rhetoric of intellectual controversy and political discourse, must originate from those *affirmative* actions through which our identity as individuals, communities, and society are established. The metaphor of the interactive future is the expression of a simple thesis: At the global scale, human interaction, as the concrete form of engaging infinitely diverse cognitive resources, is the last available resource on which the future of the species can depend.

TRANSCENDING LITERACY

Transcending literacy takes place in the practical experiences of the pragmatics of high efficiency corresponding to the global scale of humankind. This scale affects the constitution of human communities and the interaction between individuals and community. As has already been mentioned, Bedouins in the Sahara Desert and Indians in the Andes Mountains are no less hooked up to television than people living in technologically highly developed countries. More important, the identities of peoples in less developed societies on the global map of economic and political interdependencies are already subject to the most advanced processing techniques. In the ledgers of the global economy, their existence is meticulously entered with respect to what they can contribute and through what they need and can afford. People constituting virtual communities, in Silicon Valley, Japan, France, Israel, and any other place on this globe, are subject to integration in the global scale through different means and methods.

The expansion of non-literacy based human practical experiences of self-constitution raises legitimate concern regarding the social status of the individual and the nature of community interdependencies. Children, for example, are subjected to more images than language. They have the tendency to perceive time as a continuous present and expect gratification to be as instantaneous as it appears on television, or as easy to achieve as connecting to exciting Web sites. They wind up experts in interactive games and in controlling extremely fast processes. Disconnected from culture and tradition, they are extremely adaptable to new circumstances and in a hurry to ascertain their version of independence. Sex, drugs, rap music, and membership in cults or gangs are part of their contradictory profile. These adolescents are the pilots of the Nintendo wars, but also the future explorers of outer space, the physicists, biologists, and geneticists who create new materials and subject machines of breathtaking complexity to tasks in which every millionth of a second is essential to the outcome. They are also the future artists and record-breaking athletes; they are computer programmers and designers of the future. And they will be the service providers in an economy where change, predicated by the need to swiftly match outcome to ever-increasing demand, cannot be met by means burdened by the inertia and heavy-handedness of literacy.

As data make clear, such individuals are bound to be less involved in community life and less committed to the ethics of the past. Moral absolutes and concern for others do not play a major role in their lives, which are shaped by practical experiences tending towards self-sufficiency, sometimes confused with independence. In view of all these characteristics, which reflect the decreasing role of literacy-based human experiences, the question often asked is how will the relation between the community and extremely efficient individuals, constituted in relatively insular experience, be shaped? Moreover, what will the status of community be? In this respect, it is important to know what forces are at work, and to what extent our own awareness can become a factor in the process.

In our day, many people and organizations deplore the state of urban life (in the USA and around the world), high unemployment, the feeling of disenfranchisement that individuals, and sometimes whole communities, have. Immigrants of all the countries they landed in; guest workers in the European Community; the young generation in Asia, Africa, and the countries that once made up the Eastern Block; the minorities in the USA; the unemployed around the world—each of these groups faces problems reflecting the relation between them as a *different* entity and the society as a whole. Immigrants are not necessarily welcome, and when accepted, they are expected to integrate. Guest workers are required to work at tasks with which citizens of the host country do not want to dirty their hands. The young generation is expected to follow in their parents' footsteps. One minority group will have problems with another, and with society at large, in which they are supposed to integrate. The unemployed are expected to earn their benefits and eventually to accept whatever job is available. Literacy implied expectations of homogeneity. Immigrants were taught the language of their new homeland so they could become like any other citizen. Guest workers, defined by their status in the labor market, were expected to gradually become unnecessary and to peacefully return to their native countries. Young people, processed through education, and the unemployed, after being offered some short retraining, would be absorbed in the machine called national economy.

In respect to community, the historic sequence can be summarized as follows: individuals loosely connected to their peers; individuals constituting viable entities for survival; transfer of individual attributes (self-determination, choice) to the community; integration in centralized community; distribution of tasks; decentralization. Each step is defined by the extent of an individual's optimal performance: from very high individual performance, essential to survival, to distributed responsibility, until society takes over individual responsibility. Liberal democracy celebrates the paradox of socialized individualism. In this respect, it ends the age of political battles (and, as we hear, the age of history), but opens the age of increased access to abundance. Commercial democracy is neither the result of political action nor the expression of any ideology. Within its sphere of action, the boundaries between the individual and the very unsettled community represent the territory of conflict. Moral individualism succeeds or fails within a framework of adversarial human relations. Since moral individualism is actually the underpinning of liberalism—"Do what's best for yourself"—the liberty it advances is that of competitive access to abundance. Socialized individualism accepts the state only as purveyor of rights and possibilities (when the Hegelian notion of the priority of the state over the individual is accepted *de facto*), not as moral instance.

The transition to a pragmatics in which individual performance becomes marginal, in view of the many coordinating mechanisms ensuring redundancies that obliterate personal participation, is definitive of this process. The relative significance of malfunctions—breakdown in the legal and social system, for example—as instances of self-awareness and new beginnings, prompted by the need to remedy past practices, is different in each of the stages mentioned. So is the possibility of change and renewal. Creativity in current pragmatics is less and less an issue of the individual and more the result of orchestrated efforts in a large network of interactions. The underlying structure of the civilization of illiteracy supports a pragmatics of heterogeneity, distributed tasks, and networking. Human practical experiences of self-constitution no longer generate uniformity, but diversity. There is no promise of permanency, even less of stable hierarchies and centralism. We face new problems. Their formulation in literate form is deceptive; their challenge in the context of illiteracy, in which they emerge, is unprecedented. This is what prompts concerns about the civilization of illiteracy.

BEING IN LANGUAGE

The two aspects of human self-constitution through language—individual and community (society)—derive from the basic issue of social interrelationships. One's language is not independent of the language of the society, despite the fact that, in a given society, people identify themselves through noticeable peculiarities in the way they speak, write, read, and carry on dialogue. Elements pertaining to language are integrated in the human's biological structure. Still, language does not emerge, as the senses do, but is progressively acquired. The process of language acquisition is at the same time a process of projecting human abilities related to language's emerging characteristics. Regardless of the level of language acquired, language *overwrites* the senses. It projects integrated human beings—a unity of nature and language—prone to identify themselves in the culture that they continuously shape.

While nature is a relatively stable system of reference, culture changes as humans change in the process of their various activities. To be within a language, as all human beings are, and in a community means to participate in processes of *individual integration* and *social coordination*. Individual language use and social use of language are not identical. Individuals constitute themselves differently than communities do. That in each community there are elements common to the individuals constituting it only says that the sum total of individual practical experiences of language is different from the language characteristic of the social experience. The difference between the language of the individual and the language of a community is indicative of social relationships. A more general thesis deserves to be entertained: The nature and variety of human interactions, within practical experiences of self-constitution in language, describe the complexity of the pragmatic framework. These interactions are part of the continuous process of identification as individuals and groups in the course of ascertaining their identity as a particular species.

Acknowledged forms of relationships in work, family life, magic, ritual, myth, religion, art, science, or education are evinced through their respective patterns. Such patterns, circumscribed by human self-constitution in the natural and cultural context, are significant only retroactively. They testify to the human being's social condition and express what part of *nature* and what part of *culture* is involved in this condition. The primordial significance of these two phenomena lies in the expression of practical experiences followed, not preceded, by cognition. Active participation of individuals in practical experiences of language acknowledges their need to identify themselves in the patterns of interrelation mentioned. People do not get involved with other people because either party may be nice. Involvement is part of the continuous definition of the individual in contexts of conflict and cooperation, of acknowledging similarity and difference. Any dynamics, in biology or in culture, is due to differences.

People take language for granted and never question its conventions. As a *natural,* inherited (in Chomsky's view) attribute, rather like the human senses, language is not reinvented each time practical experiences of constitution through language take place. Neither is its usefulness questioned—as happens with artifacts (tools in particular)—each time our practical experience reaches the limits of language. The breakdown of an artifact—i.e., its inappropriateness to the task at hand—suggests the possible experience of crafting another. The breakdown of language points to limits in the human experience, not in its accessories. Malfunctioning of language points to the biological endowment and the ways this is projected in reality through everything people do. This is not true in respect to other, *less natural,* sign systems: symbols, artificial languages, meta-languages.

What changes from one scale of humankind, i.e., from one situation of matching needs to means for satisfying them, to another is the coefficient of the linear equation, not the linearity as such. A small group of people can survive by combining hunting, fruit gathering, and farming. The effort to satisfy a relatively bigger group increases only in proportion to the size of the group. In the known moments when a critical mass, or threshold, was reached (language acquisition, agriculture, writing, industrial production, and now the post-industrial), the expectation of higher efficiency corresponding to each scale of human experiences triggered changes in the pragmatic framework. The awareness of language's failure derives from practical experiences for which new languages become necessary.

Miscommunication is an instance of language not suitable to the experience. Lack of communication points to limitations of the humans involved in an activity. Miscommunication makes people question (themselves, others) about what went wrong, why, and what, if anything, can be done to avoid practical consequences affecting the efficiency of their activity. Other forms of language malfunction can affect people as individuals or as members of a community in ways different from those peculiar to communication. The failure of political systems, ideologies, religion(s), markets, ethics, or family is expressed in the breakdown of patterns of human relations. We keep alive the language of those political systems, ideologies, religions, and markets even after noticing their failure, not by accident or through oversight but because all those languages are us, as we constitute ourselves as participants in a political process, subjects of ideological indoctrination, religious believers, commodities in the market, family members, and ethical citizens. The inefficiency of these experiences reflects our own inefficiency, more difficult to overcome than poor spelling, etymological ignorance, or phonetic deafness.

An appropriate example of the solidarity between language experience and the individual constituted in language is provided by the breakdown of the East European block, and even more pointedly by the breakdown of the Soviet Union. Nobody really suspected that once the infamous Berlin Wall came down, the people who lived to the east of it, trained and educated in and for a pragmatic framework whose underlying structure was reflected in their high degree of literacy, would remain captive to it as their legal, social, and economic conditions changed. Despite the common language—German is the language through which national unity was ascertained—East Germans are prisoners of the structural characteristics of the society projected on them through literacy: centralism, clear-cut distinctions, determinism, strong hierarchical structures, and limited choice. The invisible but powerful inner conditioning of the East Germans' literacy—categorically superior to that of their Western brothers and sisters—is not adequate to the new pragmatics attained in West Germany and raises obstacles to East Germany's integration in a dynamic society. The illiterate pragmatics of high efficiency, associated with high expectations that seem to outpace actual performance, was foisted on East Germans by the well intentioned, though politically opportunistic, government from across a border that should never have existed.

Things are not different in other parts of the world—Korea, Hungary, Romania, the Czech Republic, Slovakia, Poland, Croatia, Serbia, etc., where the rhythms of pragmatic developments and social, political, economic, national, and cultural developments are totally desynchronized. The best poetry was written in East Europe; most of the books ever written were read by its people. It is impossible to ignore that the best theater in the world, the most elaborate cinematography, the best choirs and dance ensembles, and even the highest level of mathematical theory, physics, and biology became possible in a context of restriction, oppression, and disregard of individuals and their creativity. It is also impossible not to finally realize that the strength built on literacy-based structures was deceiving and self-deceiving.

In the not-too-distant past, the people of these countries read books, attended concerts and operas, and visited museums. Now, if they are not in misery, they are as obsessed with indulging in everything they could not have before, even if this means giving up their spiritual achievements. Consumption is the new language, even before a basis for efficient practical experiences is put in place, and sometimes instead of it. The old relation between the language of the individual and the language of society displayed patterns of deception and cowardice. The new emergent relation expresses patterns of expectation well beyond the efficiency achieved, or hoped for, in this integrated world of extreme competitive impact. The wall behind the Wall is embodied in extremely resistant patterns of human interaction originating in the context of literacy-based pragmatics. With this example in mind, it is critical to question whether there are alternatives to the means of expression people use and to the social program they are committed to—democracy. The experience of language today is very different from that of the time when the Jacobins asserted a notion of democracy as the general will (1798), under the assumption of a literate background shared by all people.

THE MESSAGE IS THE MEDIUM

Language is a form of social memory. When saying something or listening to some utterance, we assume a uniform use of words and of higher level linguistic entities. As stored testimony to similar practical experiences, language, stabilized in literacy, became a medium for *averaging* them. The patterns of human relations captured in language make people aware, in retrospect, of the relevance of these patterns to human efficiency. So it seems that we constitute ourselves as our own observations about how we interact. These observations are identified as *cognition*, because it is through interaction that we know each other and know how, what, and when our immediate and less immediate needs are satisfied. The paradigm of literacy asserts that human self-constitution takes place in language, moreover that it could effectively happen *only* in language, expressed in written forms and made available through reading. Indeed, knowledge was derived from praxis implying human interaction that integrated language-based exchanges of information. This knowledge shaped political, ideological, religious, and economic experiences, as well as efforts to improve the technology used, and even broaden the scientific perspective. The dimension of *future* is intrinsic to life, from where it extends to language and literacy, as it extends to artifacts, work, and pragmatic expectations.

The practical experience of language, as any other semiotic practical experience, embodies agreements regarding the nature and condition of whatever is constituted in language, human identity included. The projection of the biological and cultural characteristics on the world of our life and action establishes elements of reference. The ability to see, hear, and smell, and the ability to use tools are acknowledged as humans interact. Ability and performance differ widely. Self-evaluation and evaluation by others in the process of defining and achieving goals of common interest are quite distinct. Language mediates, hence it makes commitments part of the experience. When these are not carried through, language can become a substitute medium for confrontation.

Experiences of agreement and experiences of confrontation are part of the patterns of interrelationship that define how the language of individuals and the language of the community are related. Socialization of language leads to paradoxical situations: humans self-constituted in the language experience perceive their own language as though confrontation is not among themselves, but among their languages. Only a few years ago, we heard about how much Americans and Russians liked each other, although the language of politics and ideology was one of conflict. Now we hear how *Ossies* (East Germans) and *Wessies* (West Germans) have strong feelings about each other (one side is described as lazy, the other as arrogant; one side as cultivated, the other as ignoramuses; some as honest, the others as corrupt) although the language they both share is the same (though not quite). Iranians and Arabs, Armenians and Georgians, Serbs and Croats, Romanians and Hungarians, Czechs and Slovaks, Canadians and United States citizens, or United States citizens and Mexicans, could add to this subject more than we want to know about the language of prejudice.

Shortly before Malthus issued his equation of population growth in relation to the growth of subsistence means, Rousseau stated a law of the inverse proportion between size of population and political freedom. Rousseau ascertained that the strength of those exercising power over others increases as the number of those subjected to power increases. The inverse proportion has to do with the influence each individual has in the political process—the more people, the weaker each voice. Scale is critical, but so is understanding the relation between the underlying structure of the pragmatics that defines the role of language and how this role is carried out. Practical experiences of power concentration are supported by literacy, whose implicit structure and expectation is centralism and representation. Literacy generates instances of conflict as well as institutions that regulate the nature of agreements and disagreements. Bureaucracy, the expression of these institutions, is the offspring of the incestuous relation between literacy and democracy.

A new scale of humankind, for which literacy-based practical experiences are not adequate, and within which democracy—the power of the people—can no longer be exercised (as Rousseau pointed out), poses many challenges. Among them: What, if anything, should replace literacy? What could replace democracy? How do we free ourselves from the choking grip of bureaucracy? Even before attempting an answer, the notion that the cultural experience of literacy and the social experience of democracy have reached their potential and are due for replacements has to be understood.

In a different vein, the understanding that literacy participates in power, of which people become aware in a given cultural and social context, triggers another reaction: means of expression and communication different from those originating under the aegis of literacy participate in pragmatic processes that result in access to power. It is not what a political leader says, but how. Powerful images, sophisticated directing, and inspired stage design or selection of backdrops become the message itself. This is why "The message is the medium," a not irreverent reversal of McLuhan's famous formula, phrases the altered nature of the relation between language and the world. Interactions in the networked world exemplify this rephrasing even better. The redefined relationship between the many languages of our new practical experiences and reality is expressed in the means and values of the civilization of illiteracy.

Written into the pompous architecture of Mitterand's palaces and monuments in Paris, and into the "new" Berlin reflecting the medieval notion of centralized power—to the tune of hundreds of billions of dollars—the message of literacy is turned into the medium of brick-and-mortar. In an age of task distribution and decentralization, the appropriate alternative is virtual environments and an advanced infrastructure for access to cognition. "The message is the medium" translates into the requirement of overcoming infatuation with the past, never mind trying to reinvent it. The statement demands that we create alternative media that support the empowerment of individuals, not the further consolidation of power structures that were relevant in the past but which prevent the unfolding of the future.

Democracy is a domain of expectations. Humans constitute themselves as members of a democracy to the extent that their practical experiences acknowledge equality, freedom, and self-determination. The concept of democracy has varied enormously over time. In ancient societies, it acknowledged equality of the *demos,* and that free men—not slaves, not women—were entitled to vote. Subject to many emancipations, democracy denotes the right of people to elect their government (based on the general will set forth by the Jacobins, as mentioned above). How this self-government actually works— through direct or indirect representation, in forms of government based on the division of power between the executive and legislative, or under monarchies—is itself a matter of practical experiences pertinent to democracy. The democracy of human misery and neglect is quite different from the democracy of affluence. Equal access to work, education, health care, and art, and equal access to drugs, murder, joblessness, ignorance, and disease are far from being similar. A small town-meeting in Vermont or one in a Swiss canton, effectively governing life in town, is quite different from the forms of political self-governance in countries where the central power effectively overrides any self-governance. The same can be said of the overriding power of other factors—the economy, for instance.

Democracy is a major form of social and political experience. The power of the majority, expressed in votes, is only one of its possible manifestations. When only a minority of the population votes, the so-called majority ceases to be representative, no matter what the formal rules say. We live by democratic practices of delusion, and multiply, enthusiastically, their effect through the literate discourse of democracy. As a domain of expectations, mirroring hope implicit in literacy, democracy conjures meaning only if it is paralleled by democratic participation in social and political experiences. When one of the two terms of this critical equation diminishes—as is the case with *participation*—democracy diminishes in the same proportion. There are many reasons for decreasing participation. In countries where effective democracy was replaced by democratic demagoguery, changes, such as those brought about by revolutions, revolts, and reforms, initially mobilize the people, almost to the last citizen. We are still observing a phenomenon symptomatic of democracy in East Europe and the republics of the former Soviet Union. From the almost unanimous enthusiasm over renewal, leading to formal conditions for democracy, individual participation in government is slowly diminishing. What are the causes of this phenomenon, which is paralleled by diminishing interest in religion, art, and solidarity?

Many answers are given, and even more hypotheses are advanced: psychological fatigue, lack of democratic tradition, egotism, desire to catch up with affluent societies. From the perspective of the relationships characteristic of an individual's literate language and literacy programs of societies claiming to be democratic, the answer should be sought in the conflict between literacy-based values and the expectations of efficiency characteristic of the new scale of humankind. Efficiency made possible by a pragmatics emancipated from the structural characteristics reified in literacy converted democracy into commercial democracy. People can buy and sell whatever they want. Their equality is one of access to the market of affluence; their freedom is sealed in the mutually acknowledged right to plenty. Democratization, which people believe is taking place all over the world, is a process of absorbing newer and newer groups of people into prosperity, into the superficial culture of entertainment (including sports competition), and into a government that guarantees the right to wealth and consumption.

This description can easily become suspect of moralizing instead of tight analysis. Literacy embodies certain expectations from democratic institutions. Like other institutions, this type is also subjected to the test of efficiency. When the institutions of democracy fail this test, they are, in the language of democracy, diverted to consolidating not democracy, as a practical experience of the people, but the institution. Bureaucracies are generated as a diversion of democracy from its social and political focus in an incestuous love with the language in which its principles are enunciated. Mediation insinuates itself between the people and the institutions of democracy.

Media generalize the role of the literate system of checks and balances and, as mass-media, becomes a participant in the equation of power. Taking full advantage of means that characterize the civilization of illiteracy—the power of images, instantaneous access to events, the power of networking, communicative resources of new technologies—the media play a double role: representative of the people and representative of power. Since their own domain of experiences is representation, the media depend on the efficiency of the practical experiences of people's self-constitution in productive activities. Mass media activity is carried not by its own motivations, but by those of the market, whose locus it becomes. Consequently, the equation of democracy becomes the equation of competition and economic success. The media select and endorse causes and personalities appropriate to the process of marketing democracy. Instead of government, and the responsibilities associated with it, democracy becomes the people's right to buy, among other things, their government and the luxury of transferring their democratic responsibilities to its institutions.

Media bashing is a favorite sport of politicians whenever things don't work the way they expect. It is also practiced by the public, especially in times of economic uncertainty or during political developments that seem out of control (wars, violent mass demonstrations, elections). Bashing or not, criticism of the media reflects the fact that media expanded their participation in power. The practical experience of public relations, an outgrowth of media participation in power, uses the methods of the media to promote causes and personalities as products best suited for a certain need: support hungry children, elect a sheriff, endorse a tax hike or reduction, etc., etc. The domains of competence and ability are effectively disconnected from the domain of representation. Literacy-based methods of establishing hierarchies and influencing choices are enforced by new technologies for reaching targets, even in the most saturated contexts of information dissemination. Advisers committed only to the success of their endeavors use the discriminating tools of the market in order to adapt the message to all those who care to play the muddled game of democracy.

Information brokerage, feedback strategies, symbolic social engineering, mass media, psychology, and event design form an eclectic practical experience. Calling it by a certain name—*media-ocracy*—is probably tendentious. But the shoe seems to fit. From all we know, the effort of this activity does not go towards promoting excellence or persuading communities that democracy entails quality and defending self-government from corruption. It rather focuses on what it takes to convince that mediocrity adequately reflects the quest for equality, and is the most people can expect if they are not dedicated to the exercise of their rights. The literate and illiterate means used to defend democracy, and the entire political system built on the democratic premise, make it only more evident that democracy, an offspring of language-based practical experiences, is far from being the eternal and universal answer, the climax of history. Indeed, the scale of humankind renders impossible participation in power through the definition of ideals and goals, as well as awareness of the consequences of human actions. Alternative forms of participating in democracy need to be found in the characteristics of the pragmatics corresponding to the new scale. Such alternatives have to embody the distributed nature of work, better understanding of the connection (or lack thereof) between the individual and the community, awareness of change as the only permanence, and strategies of co-evolution, regarding equally all other people and the nature to which humans still belong. Democracy is the offspring of human experiences based on the postulate of sameness. The alternatives derive from the dynamics of difference.

Time, energy, equipment, and intellect have been invested in the research of artificial life. Knowledge derived from this research can be used to advance models of individual and social life. This knowledge tells us that diversity and self-organization, for instance, prompted by structural characteristics and externalized through emerging functions, maintain the impetus of evolution in a living system. Obviously, humans belong to such a system. In the past, we used to focus on social forms of variable organization. Within such forms, iterative optimization and learning take place as an expression of internal necessities, not as a result of adopted or imposed rules of functioning.

The entire dynamics of reproduction that marks today's states and organizations in the business of population control, needs to be reconnected to the pragmatic context. As a result, we can expect that communities structured on such principles are endowed with the equivalent of *social immune systems,* able to recognize and to counteract social disease. Reconnection to the pragmatic context needs to be understood primarily as a change of strategy from telling people what has to be done to engaging them in the action. All the promises connected to the fast-growing network of networks are based on this fundamental assumption. A social immune system ought to be understood as a mechanism for preventing actions detrimental to the effective functioning of each and every member of the community. Social disease entails connotations characteristic of a system of good and bad, right and wrong. What is meant here is the possibility that individual effort and pragmatic focus become disconnected. Reconnection mechanisms are based on recognition of diversity and definition of unity, means, goals, and ideals.

Adaptability results from diversity; so does the ability to allocate resources within the dynamic community. More than in the past, and more than today, individuals will partake in more than one community. This is made possible by means of interaction and by shared resources. Today's telecommuting is only a beginning when we think of the numbers of people involved and the still limited scope of their involvement. The old notion of community, associated mainly with location, will continue to give way to communities of interests and goals. Virtual communities on the Internet already exemplify such possibilities. The major characteristic of such self-organizing social and cultural cells is their pattern of improvement in the course of co-evolution, which reflects the understanding that political and social aspects of human interaction change as each person changes.

The model described, inspired by the effort to understand life and simulate properties pertinent to life through simulations, applies just as much to the natural as to the artificial. Global economy, global political concerns, global responsibility for the support system, global vested interests in communication and transportation networks, and global concern for the meaningful use of energy should not lead to a world state—not even Boorstin's *Republic of Technology* will do—but to a state of *many worlds*. Complexities resulting from such a scale of political practical experiences are such that self-destruction, through social implosion, is probably what might happen if we continue to play the game of world institutions. The alternative corresponds to decentralization, powerful networking associated with extreme distributions of tasks, and effective integrating procedures.

In more concrete terms, this means that individuals will constitute their identity in experiences through which their particular contribution might be integrated in different actions or products. They will share resources and use communication means to optimize their work. Access to one another's knowledge through means that are simultaneously open to many inquiries is part of the global contract that individuals will enter, once they acknowledge the benefits of accessing the shared body of information and the tools residing on networks. Self-organizing human nuclei of diverse practical experiences will allow for the multiplicity of languages of the civilization of illiteracy, freedom from bureaucracy, and more direct co-participation in the life of each social cell thus constituted.

Advanced specialized knowledge, empowering people to pursue their practical goals with the help of new languages (mathematical notation, visualization, diagramming, etc.), usually insulates the expert from the world. If circumstances are created to meaningfully connect practical experiences that are relevant to each other, fragmentation and synthesis can be pursued together. We are very good at fragmentation—it defines our narrow specialties. But we are far less successful in pursuing synthesis. The challenge lies in the domain of integration.

Since human activity reflects the human being's multi-dimensionality, it is clear that nuclei of overlapping experiences, involving different perspectives, will develop in environments where resources are shared and results constitute the starting point for new experiences. The identity of people constituting themselves in the framework of a pragmatics that ensures efficiency and diversity reflects experiences through many literacies, and survival skills geared towards co-evolution, not domination. Co-evolving technology is only an example. From the relatively simple bulletin boards of the early 1960's to the Internet and Web of our day, co-evolution has been a concrete practical instance of the constitution of the *Netizen*. Michael Hauben, who coined the term, wanted to describe the individuals working towards building a cooperative and collective activity that would benefit the world at large. Conflicts are not erased. The Net community is not one of perfection but of anticipated and desired diversity, in which imperfection is not a handicap. Its dynamics is based on differences in quantity and quality, and its efficiency is expressed in how much more diversity it can generate.

THE SOLUTION IS THE PROBLEM. OR IS THE PROBLEM THE SOLUTION?

The inadequacy of literacy and natural language, undoubtedly the main sign system of the human species, is brought more forcefully to light against the background of new forms of practical experiences leading to human self-constitution through many sign systems. Extremely complex pragmatic circumstances, predicated by needs that long ago surpassed those of survival, make the limits of literacy-based language experiences stand out. This new pragmatics demands that literacy be complemented with alternative means of expression, communication, and signification. The analysis of various forms of human activity and creativity can lead to only one conclusion: the patterns of human relationships and the tools created on the foundation of literacy no longer optimally respond to the requirements of a higher dynamics of human existence.

Misled by the hope that once we capture extensions in language—everything people do in the act of their practical self-identification—we could infer from these to intensions—how a particular component unfolds—we have failed to perceive the intensional aspects of human actions themselves. For instance, we know of the diverse components of the practical experience of mathematics—analytic effort, rationality, symbolism, intuition, aesthetics. But we know almost nothing about each component. Some simply cannot be expressed in language; others are only reduced to stereotype through literate discourse. Does the power of a mathematical expression rely on mathematical notation, or on aesthetic quality? How are these two aspects integrated? Where and how does intuition affect mathematical thinking?

The same criteria apply, but more critically, to social activities. Interactions among people involve their physical presence; their appearance as beautiful, or fit, or appropriate; their capability to articulate thoughts; their power of persuasion; and much more. Each component is important, but we know very little about the specific impact each one has. Surprised at how dictators come to power, and even more by mass delusion, with or without television as part of the political performance, we still fail to focus on what motivates people in their manifestations as racists, warmongers, hypocrites, or, for that matter, as honest participants in the well-being of their fellow humans. When the argument is rotten but the mass follows, there is more at work than words, appearance, and psychology. Language has projected the experience involved in our cultural practice, but has failed to project anything particularly relevant to our natural existence. Thus patterns of cultural behavior expressed in language seem quite independent of the patterns of our biological life, or at least appear to have acquired a strange, or difficult to explain, independence.

We must give serious thought to our obsession with invulnerability, easy to conceptualize and express in language. It is, for instance, embodied in the medicine of the civilization of literacy. The abrupt revelation of AIDS, marking the end of the euphoria of invulnerability, might help us understand the ramifications of the uncoupling of our life in the domain of culture—where human sexuality belongs—and our life in the domain of nature—where reproduction belongs. Magic reflected the attempt to maintain a harmonious relation with the outside world. It has not yet been decided whether it is medicine—the reified experience of determinism applied in the realm of individual well-being—or a parent's embrace that calms a baby's colic; or whether the psychosomatic nature of modern disease is addressed by the technology of healthcare in our days. What we already know is that populations were decimated once new patterns of nourishment and hygiene were imposed on them. When an attained balance was expelled by a foreign form of balance, life patterns were affected. This happened not only to populations in Asia, Africa, Australia, and New Zealand, but also in the native populations of the American continents. Medical concepts resulting from analytic practical experiences of self-constitution—many reified in the medicine of the civilization of literacy—defy the variety of possible balances and embody the suspicion that "The solution is the problem."

Literacy, when applicable, works very well, but it is not the universal answer to humankind's increasingly complex pragmatics. In the fortunate position of not having totally abandoned experiences with sign systems other than language, people have been able to change the patterns of training, instruction, industrial production, modern farming, and healthcare. Patterns of practical understanding of domains which for a very long time were concealed by literacy are also affected: pattern recognition, image manipulation, design. As a result, new methods for tackling new areas of human experience are becoming possible. Instead of describing images through words, and defining a course of action or a goal through a text, and then having the text control the use of visual elements, people use the mediating power of design systems with integrated planning and management facilities. A new product, a new building, and concepts in urban planning are generated while the pertinent computer program processes data pertinent to cost, ecological impact, social implications, and interpersonal communication. The practice of transcending literacy, while still involving literacy, also resulted in the development of new skills: visual awareness, information processing, networking, and new forms of human integration, far less rigid than those characteristic of integration exclusively through verbal language.

There is no need to eliminate literacy, as there is no need to reduce everything to literacy. Where it is still applicable, literacy is alive and well. On the Internet and World Wide Web, it complements the repertory of means of human interaction characteristic of computer-mediated communication. Television holds a large audience captive in one-way communication. The ambition of the World Wide Web is to enable meaningful one-to-one and one-to-many interactions.

The civilization of illiteracy is one of diversity and relies on the dynamics of self-organization. But in order to succeed, several conditions need to be met. For instance, we have not yet developed in appropriate practical experiences of human self-constitution the ability to think *in* media other than natural language. Like many beginners in a new language, people still translate from one language to another. When this does not work, they look for help in the language they know, instead of formulating questions in the alternative language in which they suspect they can be answered. After intuition was eliminated by rationality and system, only minor effort is made towards understanding how intuition comes about, whether in mathematics, medicine, sports, the arts, market transactions, war skills, food preparation, and social activities.

In the civilization of literacy, people were, and to a great extent still are, able to ignore some forms of human relationships without affecting the general outcome of human practice. Within the new scale and dynamics, human civilization relies on the interplay of more elements. The timing involved in integrating this diversity is much more difficult to accomplish through literacy-based methods, even though timing is critical to the outcome. Literacy captures the rough and linear level of relations. New practical experiences of higher efficiency require finer levels and tools adequate to non-linear phenomena for dealing with the parallel processes involved in the self-constitution of individuals and of society.

FROM POSSIBILITIES TO CHOICES

If the multiplication of possibilities were not to be met by effective ways of making choices, we would be sucked into the whirlwind of entropy. In practice, this translates into an obvious course of events: allowing for new possibilities, which sometimes take the appearance of alternatives, means to disallow certain known and practiced options of confirmed output. For example, where democracy is taken over by bureaucracy, the town meeting fulfills only a decorative function. There is nothing of consequence in the American President's State of the Union address, or in the conventions where political parties nominate candidates for the Presidency. With the choice of local and national political representation, the possibility to directly participate in power is precluded.

The possibility of using sign systems other than language is far from being a novelty. Even the possibility of achieving some form of syncretism is not new by any means. What is new is the awareness of their potential malfunctioning and of the potential for losing control over forms of praxis that become highly complex. From among the many ways the relation between the individual and the community is manifested, the condition of the legal system is probably the best example. Whether independent, constituting a domain of regulations and checks with its own motivations, or part of other components of social and political life, the institution of justice encodes its typologies, classifications, and rules in laws. This domain parallels one of human interactions where expected values are permanently subjected to the scrutiny of the pragmatic activity. Integrity of the individual and his lawfully acquired goods, the binding nature of commitments, and prohibition of misrepresentation or of rules essential to the well-being of the community are rules on which legal experience developed. Right and wrong, once identified under circumstances of direct practical experience through consequences for the community's well being, are now constituted in a domain with a life and rules of its own. Killing, stealing, and misrepresentation are actions well defined in the written texts of the law. But the law itself, anchored in literacy, consequently detached itself from the real world and now constitutes its own reality and motivations. Since this is the case, it is no surprise that legal practice turns out to be nothing more than interpretations of texts and attempts to use language to bring about an outcome based on chimera, not reality.

The legal system reacts to innovation by forcing rules originating in other pragmatic frameworks—the strong evidence of DNA analysis is only one example—to fit its own criteria of evaluation. Instead of constituting a proactive context for the unfolding of the human genius, legal praxis ends up defending only its own interests. The jury system in the USA might appear to many people as an expression of democracy. In the pragmatic context in which the jury system originated, the notion of peer made sense, since it applied to a reduced and relatively homogeneous community. Today, the jury has become part of the odious equation of the dispute between lawyers. The jury is selected to reflect the lowest common denominator so that its members, mostly incompetent, can be manipulated in the adversarial game of the performance produced under the generic label of justice.

As an extension of literate language, the experience of legal language builds on its own rules for efficient functioning and establishes criteria for success that corrupt the process of justice. It is a typical example of malfunctioning, probably as vivid as the language of politics. Judicial and political praxes document, from another angle, how democracy fails once it reaches the symbolic phase manifested in the bureaucracy of the legal system and of reified power relations.

COPING WITH CHOICE

Self-definition implies the ability to establish a domain of possibilities. But possibilities do not present themselves alone. In the transition from the civilization of literacy to the new civilization of illiteracy, the global domain of possibilities expands dramatically, but the local, individual domains probably narrow in the same proportion. This happens because what at the global level looks like a multiplication of choices, at the level of the individual appears as a matter of effective selection procedures. As long as there is little to choose from, selection is not a problem.

The primitive family had few choices regarding nourishment, self-reproduction, and health. Choices increased as the practical experiences of self-constitution diversified. Migrating populations chose from among selections different from those available to settled human beings. The first known cities embodied a structure of relations for which written language was appropriate. The megalopolis of our day embodies a universe of choices on a different scale. Within such a domain of possibilities, there are no effective selection procedures. Reduction from practically infinite choices to a finite number of realizations is at best a matter of randomness and exposure.

Inversely, the slogan "Act locally, think globally" can easily lead to failure. Many accomplishments that are successful on a local scale would fail if applied globally if they do not integrate awareness of globality from the beginning.

Within literacy, the expectation that literate people receive, by virtue of knowledge of language, good selection procedures—considered as universal and permanent as literacy itself—was part of its multi-layered self-motivation. In the civilization of illiteracy, this expectation gives way to pursuing consecutive choices, all short-term, all of limited scope and value-free, which even seem to eliminate one's own decision. It appears that choices grab individuals. This explains why one of the main drives in the world today is towards greater numbers of people seeking to live in cities. Once a choice is exhausted, the next follows as a consequence of the scale, not as a result of searching for an alternative. This applies as well to professional life, itself subject to the shorter cycles of renewal and change.

The powerful mechanism of social segmentation, the result of the many mediating mechanisms in place, makes the problem of coping with choice look like another instance of democracy at work. Let's consider some of these choices: to distribute, or not to distribute, condoms to high school and junior high school students; to confirm or deny the right to end one's life (pro-choice or pro-life); to expand heterosexual family privileges to homosexual cohabitation; to introduce uniform standards of testing in education. These examples are removed from the broader context of human self-constitution and submitted, through the mechanism of *media-ocracy*, more to market validation than to a responsible exercise of civic responsibility.

Mediation mechanisms characteristic of the civilization of illiteracy cause the choices that a community faces to become almost irrelevant on the individual level. In the new universe of possibilities, expanding as we speak, human beings are giving up autonomy and self-determination, as they participate in several different communities. They share in the apparent choices of society insofar as these match their own possibilities and expectations. But they often have the means to live outside a society when their choices (regarding peace, war, individual freedom, lifestyle, etc.) are different from those pursued by states. Citizens of the trans-national world partake in the dynamics of change to a much higher degree than do people dedicated to the literate ideals of nationalism and ethnicity.

We can fly to the moon (and people will, either as participants in the space program or as paying passengers). We can afford partaking in unique events—concerts, contests, auctions—some in person, others through the electronic means they can afford. Each individual can become president or member of some legislative body; but only some can afford applying for these positions. Whether through wealth, intelligence, sensitivity, race, gender, age, or religion, we are not equal in our possibilities, although we are equal in our rights. Coping with choice involves matching goals and means of achieving them. Literacy is a poor medium for this operation, which takes place between individuals and the many communities to which they belong. The various languages of the pragmatic identification of all those involved in coping with choice operate more effectively.

The network of interrelations that constitute our practical existence and the patterns of these relations will continue to change and become globally more complex and locally more confined. While we gain global freedom, we lose local dynamics. At the particular level at which we input our mediating performance, we are in almost total control of our own efficiency. Each of the many service providers for industry, physicians, lawyers, or writers is an example of local choices reflected in the increased productivity of those they service and of their own output. At higher levels, where these services are integrated—regardless of whether they provide rust control, X-ray processing, graphic design, or accounting—choices become more limited. Consequently, coordination becomes critical. The strategy of outsourcing is based on the notion that maximum efficiency requires specialization that companies cannot achieve. If the process continues in the same direction, coordination will soon be the most difficult problem of practical experience. This is due to the complexity that integration entails, and to the fact that there are no effective procedures for simplifying it. The simpler each task, the more complex the integration. Short of submitting a law that reflects this situation, another thesis can be formulated: Overall complexity is preserved regardless of how systems are subdivided, or tasks distributed. As tasks are devided in order to be efficiently carried out, complexity is transferred from the task to the integration.

TRADE-OFF

Awareness of possibilities is more direct than that of complexities. Trading choice and self-determination for less concern and higher rewards in terms of satisfying needs and desires is not an exciting alternative. Language has not brought the promised awareness of the world, but has made possible a strategy of confinement. The loss of language seems to trouble mainly people who work at language dissemination, maintenance, and awareness. However, after taking language for granted for a long time, people notice those instances when, in need of a word or trying to function in a world of language conventions, language is not up to the task. Faced with unprecedented experiences in scientific experimentation, large-scale communication, radical political change, and terrorism, people observe that they do not have the language for these phenomena. They look for words and ultimately realize that those words, assumed to exist, cannot be found because the pragmatic framework requires something other than language. In contrast to tools, like the ones we keep around the house or see mechanics and plumbers using, language is not taken away or lost because *we are our language*. What is lost from language is a certain dimension of human being and acting, of appropriating reality and producing and exchanging goods, of acknowledging our experience and sharing it with others.

Cultural, historical, economic, social, and other developments contribute to our notion of literacy. Its crisis is symptomatic of everything that made literacy necessary and is based on the particular ways in which literate societies function. This statement does not suggest that the crisis of literacy implies a cultural or economic crisis. For instance, women's emancipation did not start with the emancipation of language. In Japanese, in which the man-woman distinction goes so far as to require that women use a different vocabulary than men, women's emancipation could hardly be considered. As an expression of a specific type of social relations, this distinction in language maintains a status against which women might feel entitled to react.

Many other patterns of human interaction, which prompt practical action for change, are deeply seated in language. Watching our children, upon whom we impose literacy, grow, we almost always count the words they learn and evaluate their progress in articulating desires, opinions, and questions. What we neglect to ask is what kind of world does language bring to them in the process of learning language? What kind of practical experiences does language make possible? When children break loose of our language, it is almost too late to understand the problem. Language use seems so natural that its syntactic and value-loaded conventions are not questioned. We accept language as it is projected on us. It comes with gods or God, goodness, right, truth, beauty, and other values, as well as distinctions (sexual, racial, generational) that are held to be as eternal as we were taught that language itself is. We project language on our children only in order to be challenged by them through their own language, pretty much attuned to their different pragmatic frame of reference.

As a framework within which parents, and ultimately society, want children to think, communicate, and act, language appears to have two contradictory characteristics: liberty and constraint. The all-encompassing change we are witnessing concerns both. In order to function effectively in a society of very specialized patterns of interaction, people realize that a trade-off between liberties and constraints is inescapable. On the level of social and cultural life, people realize that constraints, represented by accepted prejudices and ideologies, impinge upon their limited space of decision-making and infringe upon individual integrity. Language turned out to be not only the medium for expressing liberating ideals, but also a stubborn embodiment of old and new prejudices. It is also the instrument of deception, and bears in its ideal of literacy the most evident deception of all—literacy as a panacea for every problem the human species faces, from poverty, inequity, and ignorance to military conflict, disease, starvation, and even the inability to cope with new developments in science and technology. Interestingly enough, Netizens believe the same thing regarding the Internet! In their campaign for free choice of literacy, they are just as dogmatic about their type of literacy as, for example, the Modern Language Association, and its equivalent organizations in other countries, is about the old-fashioned kind.

We can accept that this world of enormously diversified forms of human practice (corresponding to the diversity of human beings) requires more than one type of literacy. But this is not yet sufficient condition for changing the current premise of education if the avenues of gaining knowledge are not developed. The assumption that language is a higher level system of signs is probably correct, but not necessarily significant for the inference that in order to function in a society, each member has to master this language. To free ourselves of this inference will take more than the argument founded on the efficiency of illiterate and aliterate individuals who constitute their identity in realms where literacy does not dominate, or ceased being entirely necessary.

LEARNING FROM THE EXPERIENCE OF INTERFACE

The exciting adventure of artificially replicating human characteristics and functions is probably as old as the awareness of self and others. Harnessing tools and machines in order to maximize the efficiency of praxis was always an experience in language use and craftsmanship. So far, the most challenging experience has been the use of computers to replicate the ability to calculate, process words and images, control production lines, interpret very complex data, and even to simulate aspects of human thinking.

Programming languages serve as mediating entities. Using a limited vocabulary and very precise logic, they translate sequences of operations that programmers assume need to be executed in order to successfully compute numbers, process words, operate on images, and even carry out the logical operations for playing chess and beating a human opponent at the game. A programming language is a translation of a goal into a description of the logical processes through which the goal can be achieved. Computer users do not deal with the programming language; they address the computer through the language of interface: words in plain English (or any other language for which interface is designed), or images standing for desired goals or operations. The entire machine does not *speak* or *understand* an interface's high-level language. The interaction of the user with the machine is *translated* by interface programs into whatever a machine can process. Providing efficient interfaces is probably as important as designing high level abstract programming languages and writing programs in those languages. Without such interfaces, only a limited number of people could involve themselves in computing. The experience of interface design can help us understand the direction of change to which the new pragmatics commits us. At the end of the road, the computer should physically disappear from our desks. All that will be needed is access to digital processing, not to the digital engine. The same was true of electricity. Once upon a time it was generated at the homes or workplaces where the people who needed it could use it. Now it is made available through distribution networks.

Natural language accomplished the function of interface long before the notion came into existence. Literacy was to be the permanent interface of human practical experiences, a unifying factor in the relation between the individual and society. Ideally, interface should not affect the way people constitute themselves; that is, it should be neutral in respect to their identity. This means that people can change and tasks can vary. The interface would account for the change and would accommodate new goals. Even in their wildest dreams, computer scientists and researchers in cognitive science and artificial intelligence, who work with intelligent interfaces, do not anticipate such a *living* interface. Interfaces affect the nature of practical experiences in computing. As these become more complex, a breakdown occurs because interfaces do not scale up. Instead of supporting better interactions, an interface can hamper them and affect the outcome of computing. Language has performed quite well under the pressure of scaling up. It grows with each new human practical experience and can adapt to a variety of tasks because the people constituted in language adapt. In the intimate relation between humans and their language, language limits new experiences by subjecting them to expectations of coherence. Language's expressive and communicative potential reaches its climax as the pragmatics that made it possible and necessary exhausts its own potential for efficiency. Literate language no longer enhances human abilities in practical experiences outside its pragmatic domain. Literacy only ends up limiting the scope of the experience to its own, and limits human growth.

Many impressive human accomplishments, probably the majority of them, are testimony to the powerful interface that literate language is. But these accomplishments are equal testimony to what occurs when the interface constitutes its own domain of motivations, or is applied as an instrument for pursuing goals that result in a forced uniformity of experiences. If literacy had been a neutral mediating entity, it would have *scaled up* to the new scale of humankind and the corresponding efficiency expectations, once the threshold was reached. Successive forms of religious, scientific, ideological, political, and economic domination are examples of powerful interface mechanisms. To understand this predicament, we can compare the sequence of interfaces connected to the experience of religion to the sequence of computer-user interfaces. Notwithstanding the fundamental differences between these two domains of practical experience, a striking similarity has to be acknowledged. Both start as limited experiences, open to the initiated few, and expand from a reduced sign system on interactions to very rich multimedia environments. From a limited secretive domain to the wide opening afforded by a trivial vocabulary, both evolve as double-headed entities: the language of the initiated individuals interfaced with the language of the individuals progressively integrated in the experience. No one should misconstrue this comparison, meant only to illustrate the constitutive nature of the experience of interfacing. We could as well focus on the experiences of economics, politics, ideology, science, fashion, or, even better, art.

The experience of literacy resulted in some consistency, but also in lost variety. Every language of interaction (interface) that disappeared took with it into oblivion experiences impossible to resuscitate. The relation between the individual and community, once very rich at various levels, grew weaker the more literacy took over. Literacy norms this relation, shaping it into a multiple-choice quiz. Information processing techniques applied on literacy-controlled forms of social interaction require even further standardization in order to be efficient. As a result, the individual is rationalized away, and the community becomes a locus for data management instead of a place for human interaction. The process exemplifies what happens when interface takes over and interacts with itself.

The various concerns raised so far only reiterate how important it is to understand the nature of interface processes. But experience gained in computational research of knowledge points to other aspects critical to the relation between the individual and society. Humans constitute themselves in a variety of practical experiences that require alternatives to language. Powerful mathematical notations, diagrams, visualization techniques, acoustics, holography, and virtual space are such alternative means. Non-linear association and cognitive paths, until now embodied in hypertext structures that we experience on the World Wide Web, belong to this category, too. Processing language is not equivalent to integrating these alternative means.

Cognitive requirements put severe restrictions on experiences grounded in means different from language, on account of the intensity and nature of cognitive processes, as well as of memory requirements. The genetic endowment formed in language-based practical experiences of self-constitution is not necessarily adapted to fundamentally different means of expression. Communication requires a shared substratum, which is established in an acculturation process that takes many generations. Enhanced by the new media, communication does not become more precise. Programs are conceived to enable the understanding of language. Everything ever written is scanned and stored for character recognition. Images are translated into short descriptions. A semantic component is attached to everything people compute. Hopes are high for using such means on a routine basis, though the compass might be set on some elusive direction. Even when machines will understand what we ask them to do—that is, when they integrate speech and handwriting recognition functions in the operating system—*we* will still have to articulate our goals. A technology capable of automating many operations that human beings still perform will increase output, and thus the efficiency of the effort applied. But the real challenge is to figure out ways to optimize the relation between what is possible and what is necessary. Procedures that will associate the output to the many criteria by which humans or the machine determine how meaningful that output is, are more important than raw technological performance. Until now, literacy has not proven to be the suitable instrument for this goal.

People and language change together. Individuals are formed in language; their practical experiences reshape language and lead to the need for new languages. If we cannot uncouple language and the human being, especially in view of the parallel evolution of genetic endowment and linguistic ability, *we will continue to move in the vicious cycle of expression and representation.* The issue is not language *per se,* but the claim that representation is the dominant, one might say exclusive, paradigm of human activity. Neither science nor philosophy has produced an alternative to representation.

There is more to physical reality than what language can lay claim to. And there is much more to the dynamics of our existence in a world whose own dynamics integrates it while extending far beyond it. Skills needed to function in the physical world—skills which children and newborn animals display—are only partially represented in language. The entire realm of instinctive behavior belongs here. This includes coordination and the very rich forms of relating to space, time, and other living beings. Advanced biological and cognitive research (Maturana's work leads in this area) shows that various organisms survive without the benefits of representation. Very personal human experiences—among them, pain, love, hate, and joy—happen without the benefits and constraints of language representation.

There are skills for which we have no representation in language. Various tags are used to name them under the heading of parapsychology, magic, and non-verbal communication. Once these are described through their results only, they cause reactions ranging from doubt to ridicule. The unusual and inexplicable performances of individuals called *idiots savants* belong to this category. An *idiot savant* hears a piano concerto and replays it masterfully, although he or she cannot add two and two. A matchbox falls and the *idiot savant* can state, without looking at the box, the exact number of matches that fell out. These are feats that are on record. Some *idiots savants* are able to go through long sequences of phone numbers, produce complete listings of prime numbers, and execute incredible multiplication and division. Researchers can only observe and record such accomplishments. For other inexplicable phenomena, we simply have no concept available: the amazing last moments before death, the power of illusion, and the visualization aptitudes of some individuals. Researchers have accumulated data on the power of prayer and faith, and on paranormal manifestations. It is not the intention of this book to venture explanations of these phenomena, but to point out the great variety of experiences which could be integrated into human praxis but are not, merely because they still defy explanation in language.

Functioning in a world that we read through the glasses of literacy makes us often blind to what is different, to what literacy does not encompass. A realm of fact and possible abstraction, difficult to compare with the world of existence that language reports about, remains to be explored. When the Nobel Prize winning physicist Richard Feynman reported on a difference in machine and human computation, this report pointed to aspects for which language was not prepared to serve as a useful interface, and to a realm different from representation.

Crises, catastrophes, and breakdowns testify to the borders of a given pragmatic context. They are references as to how far such a context can extend. Beyond the context begins the universe of fundamental change and revolution, constitutive of a new framework. The really interesting level of language, and of any other sign system, is not the referential level but the level of constituting new worlds. These worlds do not necessarily extend the old one. Telecommuting is an extension of the previous pattern of work. Cooperative real-time practical experiences are more than the sum of individual contributions. They are constitutive of non-linear forms of complementarity. The virtual office is but another form of office. Virtual community is a constitutive experience. Nothing of what we have learned in experiences of broadcasting is pertinent to the participatory aspect of human self-constitution in an environment of fluidity and unsettled patterns of interaction. The goal is not to inform, but to enable and empower. The elaborate combinations of chemicals concocted to increase the effectiveness of medicine, of construction materials, or of electronic components continues earlier patterns. Atomic manipulation, intended to synthesize intelligent materials and self-repairing substances and devices, constitutes a new domain of practical experiences.

Each of these examples belongs to a pragmatic framework different in nature from the one that defined literacy and which literacy embodies and forces upon our experience. Centrism—Euro-, ethno-, techno- or any other kind—as well as dualism—good and bad, right and wrong, just and unjust, beautiful and ugly—and hierarchy have exhausted their potential. The attempt to measure the emergent pragmatics against ideals that do not originate from within them can only result in empty slogans firmly entrenched in the avatars of machine-age ideologies. As we experience it at the juncture between literacy and illiteracy, the legacy of language is not only accomplishments but also the diversion from what the world is to descriptions that stand for it in our minds, books, and social concerns. The networks of objects and their properties (qualifiers of objects) exist in the civilization of literacy only through language: things are real insofar as they are in language. To overcome this perception is a challenge well beyond the power of most individuals. What emerges in the new pragmatic framework of distributed practical experience and of cooperative, parallel human interactions is a human being self-constituted in a plurality of interconditioning means of expression, communication, and signification. We might just be on the verge of a new age.

CHAPTER 2: A SENSE OF THE FUTURE

Beyond literacy begins a realm which for many is still science fiction. The name *civilization of illiteracy* is used to define direction and to point out markers. The richness and diversity of this realm is indicative of the nature of our own practical experiences of self-constitution. The landscape mapped out by these experiences is simultaneously its own *Borgesian* map. One marker along the road from present to future leaves no room for doubt: the digital foundation of the pragmatic framework. But this does not mean that the current dynamics of change can be reduced to the victorious march of the digital or of technology, in general.

Having challenged the model of a dominant sign system—language in its literate experience—we suggested that a multitude of various sign processes effectively override the need for and justification of literacy in a context of higher efficiency expectations. We could alternatively define the pragmatic framework of the civilization of illiteracy as semiotic in the sense that human practical experiences become more and more subject to sign processes. The digital engine is, in final analysis, a semiotic machine, churning out a variety of signs. Nevertheless, the semiotization of human practical experiences extends beyond computers and symbolic processing.

As we have seen, in all human endeavors, semiotic awareness is expressed in choices (of means of expression and communication) and patterns of interaction. Successive fashion trends, no less than the new media, global interaction through networks, cooperative work, and distributive configurations are semiotic identifiers. Interfaces are semiotic entities through which difficult aspects of the relation between individuals and society are addressed. More precisely, *to interface* means to advance methods and notions of a new form of cultural engineering, that has the same condition as genetic engineering, although not necessarily based on its mechanism, as the proponents of memetics would like us to believe.

No matter how spectacular new technologies are, and how fast the rate of their adoption, pragmatic characteristics that make the quantum leap of efficiency possible within the new scale of humankind remain the *defining* element of the dynamics of change. To make this point clear no argument is superfluous, and no stone of doubt or suspicion should be left unturned. Our concern is not with the malignant rhetoric against technology of a probably insane *Unabomber,* for example. It is with a false sense of optimism focused on fleeting embodiments of human creativity, not on its integration in meaningful experiences. Whether a spectacular multimedia program, a virtual reality environment, genetically based medicine, broadband human interaction, or cooperative endeavors, what counts are the human cognitive resources, in the form of semiotic processes irreducible to language and literacy, at work under circumstances of globality.

COGNITIVE ENERGY

It is impossible to tire of acknowledging applications from which many will people benefit, but which many resent even before these applications become available. They all become possible once they transcend the pragmatic framework of the civilization of literacy because they are based on structurally different means of expression, communication, and signification. We have all witnessed some of these applications: sensors connected to unharmed nervous terminals allow the quadriplegic to move. A child in a wheelchair who exercises in virtual reality can be helped to function independently in the world that qualifies his condition as a handicap. Important skills can be acquired by interpolating patterns of behavior developed in the physical world in the rough draft of the simulated world. People are helped to recover after accidents and illness, and are supported in acquiring skills in an environment where the individual sets the goals. In Japan, virtual reality helps people prepare for earthquakes and tests their ability to cope with the demand for fast response. Interconnected virtual worlds support human interactions in the space of their scientific, poetic, or artistic interest, or combinations thereof, stimulating the hope, as naive as it may sound, for a new Renaissance.

Not everything need be virtual. *Active badges*™ transmit data pertinent to an individual's identification in his or her world. Not only is it easier to locate a person, but the memory of human interaction, in the form of digital traces, allows people and machines to remember. You step into a room, and your presence is automatically acknowledged. The computer lets you know how many messages are waiting for you, and from whom. It evaluates how far you are from the monitor and displays the information so you can see it from that distance. It reminds you of things you want to do at a certain time. Details relevant to our continuous self-constitution through extremely complex practical experiences play an important role in making such interactions more efficient. A personal diary of actions, dialogues, and thinking out loud can be automatically recorded. Storing data from the active badge and from images captured during a certain activity is less obtrusive than having someone keep track of us. This is a new form of personal diary, protected, to the extent desired, from intrusion or misuse. This diary collects routine happenings that might seem irrelevant—patterns of movement, dialogue, eating, reading, drawing, building models, and analyzing data. The record can be completed by documenting patterns of behavior of emotional or cognitive significance, such as fishing, mountain climbing, wasting time, or dancing—according to one's wish. At the end of the day, or whenever requested, this diary of our living can be e-mailed to the *writer*. One can review the events of a day or search for a certain moment, for those details that make one's time meaningful.

In the world beyond literacy and literacy-based practical experiences, we can search for artistic events. A play by Shakespeare can be projected onto the *screen* of our eyes, where the boundary between reality and fiction starts. The play will feature the actors of one's choosing. The viewer can even intercalate any person in the cast, even himself or herself, and deliver a character's lines. Sports events and games can be viewed in the same way. In another vein, we can initiate dialogues with the persons we care for, or get involved in the community we choose to belong to. Belonging, in this new sense, means going beyond the powerless viewing of political events that seem as alien as almost all the mass-media performances they are fed with. Belonging itself is redefined, becoming a matter of choice, not accident. Belonging goes beyond watching the news and political events on TV, beyond the impotence we feel with respect to the huge political machine. All these can happen as a private, very intense experience, or as interaction with others, physically present or not. *To see the world differently* can lead to taking another person's, or creature's, viewpoint. How does a recent immigrant, or a visitor from abroad, perceive the people of the country he has landed in? What do human beings look like to a whale, a bee, an ant, a shark? We can enter the bodies of the handicapped to find out how a blind person negotiates the merciless world of speeding cars and people in a hurry. The empathy game has been played with words and theatrics in many schools. But once a person assumes the handicapped body in a simulated universe, the insight gained is no longer based on how convincing a description is, but on the limits of self-constitution as handicapped. People can learn more about each other by sharing their conditions and limitations. And, hopefully, they will ascertain a sense of solidarity beyond empty expressions of sympathy.

That all these semiotic means—expression in very complex dynamic sign systems—change the nature of individual practical experiences and of social life cannot be emphasized enough. Everything we conceive of can be viewed, criticized, felt, sensed, experienced, and evaluated before it is actually produced. The active badge

can be attached to a simulated person— an avatar—let loose to walk
through the plans for a new building, or on the paths of an expedition through mountains. The diary of space discovery is at least as
important as the personal diary of a person working in a real factory,
research facility, or at home. Before another tree is cut, before another riverbed is moved, before a new housing development is constructed, before a new trail is opened, people can find out what changes of
immediate and *long-term* impact might result.

It is possible to go even a step beyond the integrated world of digital processing and to entrust extremely complicated processes to
neural networks trained to perform functions of command, control,
and evaluation. Unexpected situations can be turned into learning
experiences. Where individuals sometimes fail—for instance under
emotional stress—neural networks can easily perform as well as
humans do, without the risks associated with the unpredictability of
human behavior. The active badge can be connected, through a local
area network of wall-mounted sensors that collect information, to a
neural network-based procedure designed to process the many *bits
and pieces* of knowledge that are most of the time wasted. People
could learn about their own creativity and about cognitive processes
associated with it. They can derive knowledge from the immense
amount of their aborted thoughts and actions. Ubiquity and unob-
trusiveness qualify such means for the field of medical care, for the
support of child development, and for the growing elderly population. With the advent of optical computers, and even biological data
processing devices, chances will increase for a complete restructuring
of our relation to data, information processing, and interhuman relationships. Individuals will ascertain their characteristics more and
more, thus increasing their role in the socio-political network of
human interaction.

Some people still decide for others on certain matters: How
should children play? How should they study? What are acceptable
rules of behavior in family and society? How should we care for the
elderly? When is medical intervention justified? Where does life end

and biological survival become meaningless? These people exercise power within the set of inherited values that originated in a pragmatic context of hierarchy associated with literacy. This does not need to be so, especially in view of the many complexities hidden in questions like the ones posed above. Our relation to life and death, to universality, permanence, non-hierarchical forms of life and work, to religion and science, and last but not least to all the people who make up our world of experiences, is bound to change. Once individuality is redefined as a *locus of interaction* through rich sign systems, not just as an identity to be explained away in the generality that gnoseologically replaces the individual, politics itself will be redefined.

LITERACY IS NOT ALL IT'S MADE OUT TO BE

Enthusiasm over technology is not an argument; and semiotics, obfuscated by semiologues, is not a panacea. George Steiner pointed out that scientists, who "have been tempted to assert that their own methods and vision are now at the center of civilization, that the ancient primacy of poetic statement and metaphysical image is over." This is not an issue of criteria based on empirical verification, or the recent tradition of collaborative achievement, correctly contrasted to the apparent idiosyncrasy and egotism of literacy. The pragmatic framework reflects the challenge of efficiency in our world of increased population, limited resources, and the domination of nature. This framework is critical to the human effort to assess its own possibilities and articulate its goals. Let us accept Steiner's idea—although the predicament is clearly unacceptable—that sciences "have added little to our knowledge or governance of human possibility." Let us further accept that "there is demonstratably more insight into the matter of man in Homer, Shakespeare, or Dostoyevsky than in the entire neurology of statistics." This, if it were true, would only mean that such an insight is less important to the practical experience of human self-constitution than literacy-based humanities would like us to believe.

Literary taste or preference aside, it is hard to understand the epistemological consequence of a statement like "No discovery of genetics impairs or surpasses what Proust knew of the spell or burden of lineage." All this says is that in Steiner's practical experience of self-constitution, a pragmatics other than genetics proves more consequential. Nobody can argue with this. But from the particular affinity to Proust, one cannot infer that consequences for a broader number of people, the majority of whom will probably never know anything about genetics, are not connected to its discoveries. We may be touched by the elegant argument that "each time Othello reminds us of the rust of dew on the bright blade, we experience more of the sensual, transient reality in which our lives must pass than it is the business or ambition of physics to impart." After all the rhetoric that has reverberated in the castle of literacy, the physics of the first three minutes or seconds of the universe proves to be no less metaphysical, and no less touching, than any example from the arts, literature, or philosophy that Steiner or anyone else can produce. Science only has different motivations and is expressed in a different language. It challenges human cognition and sentiment, and awareness of self and others, of space and time, and even of literature, which seems to have stagnated once the potential of literacy was exhausted. The very possibility of writing as significantly as the writers of the past did diminishes, as the practical experience of literate writing is less and less appropriate to the new experiences of self-constitution in the civilization of illiteracy.

The argument can go on and on, until and unless we settle on a rather simple premise: The degree of significance of anything connected to human identity—art, work, science, politics, sex, family— is established in the act of human self-constitution and cannot be dictated from outside it, not even by our humanistic tradition. The air, clean or polluted, is significant insofar as it contributes to the maintenance of life. Homer, Proust, van Gogh, Beethoven, and the anonymous artist of an African tribe are significant insofar as human self-constitution integrates each or every one of them, in the act of individual identification. Projecting their biological constitution into the world—we all breathe, see, hear, exercise physical power, and perceive the world—humans ascertain their natural reality. The experience of making oneself can be as simple as securing food, water, and shelter, or as complex as composing or enjoying a symphony, painting, writing, or meditating about one's condition. If in this practical experience one has to integrate a stick or a stone, or a noise, or rhythm in order to obtain nourishment, or to project the individual in a sculpture or musical piece, the significance of the stick or stone or the noise is determined in the pragmatic context of the self-constitutive moment.

Many contexts confirm the significance of literacy-based practical experiences. History, even in its computational form or in genetic shape, is an example. Literacy made quite a number of practical experiences possible: education, mass media, political activism, industrial manufacture. This does not imply that these domains are forever wed to literacy. A few contexts, such as crafts, predated literacy. Information processing, visualization, non-algorithmic computation, genetics, and simulation emerged from the pragmatics that ascertained literacy. But they are also relatively independent of it. Steiner was correct in stating that "we must countenance the possibility that the study and transmission of literature may be of only marginal significance, a passionate luxury like the preservation of the antique." His assertion needs to be extended from literature to literacy.

The realization that we must go beyond literacy does not come easy and does not follow the logic of the current *modus operandi* of the scholars and educators who have a stake in literacy and tradition. Their logic is itself so deeply rooted in the experience of written language that it is only natural to extend it to the inference that without literacy the human being loses a fundamental dimension. The sophistry is easy to catch, however. The conclusion implies that the practical experience of language is identical to literacy. As we know, this is not the case. Orality, of more consequence in our day than the majority are aware of, and in more languages that do not have a writing system, supports human existence in a universe of extreme expressive richness and variety.

Many arguments, starting with those against writing enunciated in ancient times and furthered in various criticisms of literacy, point to the many dimensions of language that were lost once it started to be tamed and its regulated use enforced upon people. Again, Steiner convincingly articulates a pluralistic view: "...we should not assume that a verbal matrix is the only one in which articulations and conduct of the mind are conceivable. There are modes of intellectual and sensuous reality founded not on language, but on other communicative energies, such as the icon or the musical note." He correctly describes how mathematics, especially under the influence of Leibniz and Newton, became a dynamic language: "I have watched topologists, knowing no syllable of each other's language, working effectively together at a blackboard in the silent speech common to their craft."

NETWORKS OF COGNITIVE ENERGY

Chemistry, physics, biology, and recently a great number of other practical experiences of human self-constitution, formed their own languages. Indeed, the medium in which experiences take place is not a passive component of the experience. It is imprinted with the degree of necessity that made such a medium a constitutive part of the experience. It has its own *life* in the sense that the experience involves a dynamics of exchange and awareness of its many components. The cuneiform tablets could not hold the *depth* of thinking of the formulas in which the theory of relativity is expressed. They probably had a better *expressive* potential for a more spontaneous testimony to the process of self-identification of the people who projected themselves in the act of shaping damp tablets, inscribing them, and baking them to hardness. Ideographic writing may well explain, better than orality, the role of silence in Taoism and Buddhism, the tension of the act of withdrawal from speech and writing, or the phonetic subtleties at work when more than 2000 ideographs were reduced to the standard 600 signs now in use. The historic articulation of the Torah, its mixture of poetry and pragmatic rules, is different in nature from the writings, in different alphabets and different pragmatic structures, reflected in the language of the New Testament or of the Koran.

Writing under the pragmatics of limited human experiences, and writing after the Enlightenment, not to mention today's automated writing and reading, are fundamentally different. Gombrich recalls that Gutenberg earned a living by making amulet mirrors used by people in crowds to catch the image of sacred objects displayed during certain ceremonies. The animistic thought marks this experience. It is continued in the moving type that Gutenberg invented, yet another mirror to duplicate the life of handwriting, which type imitated. Printed religious texts began their lives as talismans. After powerful printing presses were invented, writing extends a different thought—machines at work—in the sequence of operations that transform raw materials into products.

All the characteristics associated with literacy are characteristics of the underlying structure of practical experiences, values, and aspirations embodied in the printing machines. The linear function, replicated in the use of the lever, was generalized in machines made of many levers. It was also generalized in literacy, *the language machine* that renders language use uniform. Writing originated in a context of the limited sequences of human self-constitutive practical experiences embodied in the functioning of mechanical machines. The continuation of the sequential mode in more elaborate experiences, as in automated production lines, will be with us for quite a while. Nevertheless, sequentiality is increasingly complemented by parallel functioning. Similar or different activities carried through at the same time, at one location or at several, are qualitatively different from sequential activities. Self-constitution in such parallel experiences results in new cognitive characteristics, and thus in new resources supporting higher efficiency. The deterministic component carried over from literacy-based practical experiences reflects awareness of action and reaction. Its dualistic nature is preserved in the right/wrong operational distinctions of the literate use of language, and thus in the logic attached to it.

Pragmatic expectations of efficiency no longer met by conceptual or material experiences based on the model embodied in literacy have led to attempts to transcend determinism, as well as linear functions, sequentiality, and dualism. A new underlying structure prompts a pragmatics of non-linear relations, of a different dynamics, of configurations, and of multi-valued systems. A wide array of methods and technologies facilitates emancipation from the centralism and hierarchy embodied in literacy-based pragmatics. The pragmatic framework of the civilization of illiteracy requires that the centralism of literacy be replaced through massive distribution of tasks, and non-hierarchic forms of human interactions. Augmented by worldwide networking, this pragmatics has become global in scope. Probably just as significant is the role mediation plays in the process. As a specific form of human experience, mediation increases the effectiveness of praxis by affording the benefits of integration to human acts of self-constitution. Mediation replaces the analytic strategy inherited through literacy, opening avenues for reaching a sense of the whole in an experience of building hypotheses and performing effective synthesis. In order to realize what all this means, we can think of everything involved in the conception, design, manufacturing, distribution, and integration of computers in applications ranging from trivial data management to sophisticated simulations. The effort is, for all practical purposes, global.

The brightest minds, from many countries, contribute ideas to new concepts of computation. The design of computers involves a large number of creative professionals from fields as varied as mechanical engineering, chip design, operating systems, telecommunications, ergonomy, interface design, product design, and communication. The scale of the effort is totally different from anything we know of from previous practical experiences. Before such a new computer will become the hardware and software that eventually will land on our desks, it is modeled and simulated, and subjected to a vast array of tests that are all the expression of the hypothesis and goals to be synthesized in the new product.

Some people might have looked at the first personal computers as a scaled-down version of the mainframes of the time. Within the pragmatics associated with literacy, this is a very good representation. In the pragmatics we are concerned with, this linear model does not work, and it does not explain how new experiences come about. Chances are that the mass-produced machines increasingly present in a great number of households reach a performance well above those mainframes with which the PC might have been compared.

Representing the underlying structure of the pragmatics of the civilization of illiteracy, the digital becomes a resource, not unlike electricity, and not unlike other resources tapped in the past for increasing the efficiency of human activity. In the years to come, this aspect will dominate the entire effort of the acculturation of the digital. Today, as in the Industrial Age of cars and other machines, the industry still wants to put a computer on every desk. The priority, however, should be to make computation resources, not machines, available to everyone. Those still unsure about the Internet and the World Wide Web should understand that what makes them so promising is not the potential for surfing, or its impressive publication capabilities, but the access to the *cognitive energy* that is transported through networks.

Expectations stemming from the civilization of literacy differ in their condition from those of the cognitive age. Infinitely more chances open continuously, but the risks associated with them are at least of the same order of magnitude as the changes. Walking along a road is less risky than riding a horse, bicycling, or driving a car. Flying puts the farthest point from us on the globe within our reach, but the risks involved in flight are also greater. Cognitive resources integrated in our endeavors contribute to an efficiency higher than that provided by hydropower, steam engines, and electric energy. With each new step in the direction of their increased participation in our praxis, we take a chance.

There is no reason to compare simulations of the most complex and daring projects to successful or failed attempts to build new cities, modify nature, or create artifacts conceived under cognitive assumptions of lesser complexity than that achieved in our time. A failed connection on today's Internet, or a major scam on the Web, should be expected in these early stages of the pragmatic framework to which they belong. But we should at no moment ignore the fact that cognitive breakdowns are much more than the crash of an operating system or the breakdown of a network application.

We learn more about ourselves in the practical experiences of constituting the post-literate languages of science, art, and the humanities than we have learned during the entire history of humankind. These languages—very complex sign systems indeed—integrate knowledge accumulated in a great variety of experiences, as well as genetically inherited and rationally and emotionally based cognitive procedures. Changes in the very fabric of the human being involved in these practical experiences are reflected in the increased ability to handle abstraction, refocus from the immediate to the mediated, and enter interhuman commitments that result from the practice of unprecedented means of expression, communication, and signification.

During the process, we have reached some of our most critical limitations. Knowledge is deeper, but more segmented. To use Steiner's words once again, there is a "gap of silence" between many groups of people. Our own efficiency made us increasingly vulnerable to drives that recall more of the primitive stages of humankind than all that we believed we accumulated through the humanities. The new means are changing politics and economic activity, but first of all they are changing the nature of human transactions. And they are changing our sense of future.

Let us not forget Big Brother, not to be brushed away just because the year 1984 has come and gone, but to be understood from a viewpoint Orwell could not have had. If the means in question are used to monitor us, too bad. In the emerging structures of human interaction, to exercise control, as done in previous societies, is simply not possible. It is not for the love of the Internet that this constitutes a non-regulated domain of human experiences. Rather it is because by its nature, the Internet cannot be controlled in the same way our driving, drinking, and social behavior are controlled. The opportunity for transparency afforded by systems that replace the domination of literacy is probably too important to be missed or misused. The dynamics of the civilization of illiteracy results from its implicit condition. We can affect some of its parameters, but not its global behavior. For instance, the integration required by parallelism and the massive distribution of tasks cannot take place successfully if the network of interactions is mined by gates, filters, and veils of secrecy, by hierarchic control mechanisms, and by authorization procedures. Imagine if a person's arms, eyes, ears, or nostrils had to obtain permission to participate in the self-constitution of the whole human being. Individuals in the new pragmatic context are the eyes, arms, brains, and nostrils of the complex human entity involved in an experience that integrates everyone's participation. It is an intense effort, not always as rewarding as we expect it to be, a self-testing endeavor whose complexity escapes individual realization. Feedback loops are the visible part of the broader system, but not its essential part.

The authenticity of each and every act of our self-making contributes to the integrity of the overall process—our ascertainment through what we do. Relative insularity and a definite alienation from the overall of the system's goals—meeting higher demands by higher performance—are part of the picture described. Complemented by a sense of empowerment—the ability to self-determine—and a variety of new forms of human interaction, the resulting human pragmatics can be more humane than the pragmatics of the huge factories of industrial society—commuters rushing from home to job to shopping mall, to entertainment. It is not Big Brother who will be watching. Each and every individual is part of the effort, entitled to know everything about it, indeed wanting to know and caring. Without transparency that we can influence, the effort will not succeed. We are our own active badge. The record is of interest in order to justify the use of our time and energy, but foremost to learn about those instances when we are less faithful to ourselves than our newly acquired liberty affords. It is much easier to submit to outside authority, as literacy educates us to do. But once self-control and self-evaluation, as feedback mechanisms under our own control become the means of optimization, the burden is shifted from Big Brother, bureaucracies, and regulations to the individual.

It is probably useful at this point to suggest a framework for action in at least some of the basic activities affected by the change brought about in the civilization of illiteracy. The reason for these suggestions is at hand. We know that literate education is not appropriate, but this observation remains a critical remark. What we need is a guide for action. This has to translate into positive attitudes, and into real attempts to meet the challenge of present and shape the future in full awareness of forces at work.

Literacy-based education, as all other literacy experiences, assumes that people are *the same*. It presumes that each human being can and must be literate. Just as the goal of industry was to turn out standardized products, education assumes the same task through the *mold* of literacy. Diplomas and certificates testify how like the mold the product is. To those who have problems with writing or reading, the labels *legasthenic* and *dyslexic* are applied. *Dyscalculus* is the name given to the inability to cope with numbers. The question of why we should expect uniform cognitive structures covering the literate use of language or numbers, but not the use of sounds, colors, shapes, and volume, is never raised. Tremendous effort is made to help individuals who simply cannot execute the sequentiality of writing or the meaning of successive numbers. Nothing similar is done to address cognitive characteristics of persons inclined to means different from literacy.

In order to respond to the needs of the pragmatics of high efficiency leading to the civilization of many literacies, education needs first of all to *rediscover* the individual, and his or her extensive gamut of cognitive characteristics. I use the word *rediscover* having in mind incipient forms of education and training, which were more on a one-to-one or one-to-few basis. Education also needs to reconsider its expectation of a universal common denominator, based on the industrial model of standardization. Rather than taming and sanitizing the minds of students, education has not only to *acknowledge* differences in aptitudes and interests, but also to *stimulate* them. Every known form of energy is the expression of difference and not the result of leveling.

During this process of re-evaluation, the goals of education will have to be redefined, methods of education rethought, and content reassessed. A new philosophy, embodied in a dynamic notion of education, has to crystallize as we work towards educational alternatives that integrate the visual, the kinetic, the aural, and the synesthetic. In the spirit of the pragmatic context, education ought to become an environment for interaction and discovery. Time taken with reiterations of the past deserves to be committed to inferences for the present, and, to the extent possible, for the future.

Some of the suggestions to be made in the coming lines might sound utopian or have the ring of techno-babble. Their purpose is to present *possibilities*, not to conjure up miraculous solutions. The path from present to future is the path of human practical experiences of self-constitution. To achieve goals corresponding to the requirements and expectations of the civilization of no dominant literacy, education needs to give up the *reductionist* perspective that has marked it since generalized education became the norm. Education has to recognize its students as the individuals they are, not as some abstract or theoretic entity.

Basic education should be centered around the major forms of expression and communication: language, visual, aural, kinetic, and symbolic. Differences among these systems need to be explored as students familiarize themselves with each of them, as well as combinations. Concrete forms of acculturation should be geared towards using these elements, not dispensing instructions and assigning exercises. Each student will discover from within how to apply these systems. Most important, students will share their experiences among themselves. There will be no right or wrong answer that is not proven so by the pragmatic instance.

Fundamental to the educational endeavor is the process of heuristic inquiry, to be expressed through programs for further investigation. These programs require many languages: literate inquiry, mathematics, chemistry, computation, and so on. By virtue of the fact that people from different backgrounds enter the process, they bear the experience of their respective languages. Relevance to the problem at hand will justify one approach or another. Frequently, the wheel will be re-invented. Other times, *new wheels* will emerge as contributions of authentic ingenuity and inventiveness. In their interaction, those involved in the process share in the experience through which they constitute themselves at many levels. One is to provide access to the variety of perspectives reflecting the variety of people.

INTERACTIVE LEARNING

Education has to become a living process. It should involve access to all kinds of information sources, not only to those stored in literate formats. These resources have their specific epistemological condition—a printed encyclopedia is different from a database. To access a book is different from accessing a multimedia knowledge platform. Retrieval is part of the practice of knowledge and defines a horizon for human interaction. All these differences will become clear through use, not through mere assertion or imitation. The goal of education cannot be the dissemination of imitative behavior, but of procedures. In this model of education, *classes* are groups of people pursuing connected goals, not compartments based on age or subject, even less bureaucratic units. A class is an expression of interest, not the product of statistical distribution based on birth and zoning. The physical environment of the class is the world, and not the brick and mortar confined room of stereotyped roles and interactions. This might sound hollow, or too grandiose, but the means to make this happen are progressively becoming available.

Here is one possible scenario: Students approach *centers of interactive education* after the initial phase of acculturation. Perhaps the word *center* recalls one of the characteristics of the civilization of literacy. By their own nature, though, these centers are distributed repositories of knowledge stored in a variety of forms—databases, programs pertinent to various human practical experiences, examples, and evaluation procedures. With such a condition, such *centers* lend themselves to making refreshable knowledge available in all imaginable formats. On request, its own programs (known as *intelligent agents*) search for appropriate sources through the guidance of those in need, independent of them, or parallel to them. Requests are articulated in voice command: "I would like to know ...." Or the requests can be handwritten, typed, or diagrammed. Such interactive education centers are simultaneously libraries of knowledge, heuristic environments, laboratories, testing grounds, and research media. The hybrid human-machine *machine* that constitutes their nucleus alters as the individual involved in the interaction changes.

As we all know, the best way to learn is to teach. Students should be able to teach their neural network partners subjects of interest to their own practical experiences. In many cases, the neural networks, themselves networked with others, will become partners in pursuing practical goals of higher and higher complexity. The fact that students interact not based on their address and school district, not based on homogeneity criteria of age or cultural background, but on *shared interests* and *different perspectives* gives this type of education a broader social significance: There is nothing we do that does not affect the world in its entirety. Repeating these words *ad nauseam* will not affect the understanding of what this means, as one practical endeavor of global consequential nature can.

In the model suggested, interests are identified and pursued, and results are compared. Questions are widely circulated. What students appropriate in the process are ways of thinking, procedures for testing hypotheses, and means and methods for ascertaining progress in the process. Professional educators, aware of cognitive processes and freed from the burden of administrative work, no longer rehash the past but design interactive environments for students to learn in. Teachers involve themselves in this interaction, and continue to evolve as knowledge itself evolves. Instead of inculcating the discipline of one dominant language, they leave open choices for short and long-term commitments, their own included.

Not having to force themselves to think in an imposed language, students are freed from the constraints of assigned tasks. They are challenged by the responsibility to make their own choices and carry them through. In the process, differences among students will become apparent, but so will the ability to understand how being different, in a context of cooperative interactions, is an asset and not a liability. Motivation is seeded in the satisfaction of discovery and the ability to easily integrate in a framework of practical experiences that are no longer mimicked in education, but practiced in discovery.

FOOTING THE BILL

Instead of an education financed by the always controversial redistribution of social resources, interactive learning will be supported by its real beneficiaries. That a biogenetics company, for instance, can do this better than an organization engaged in bureaucratic self-perpetuation is a fair assumption. Freed from the costs associated with buildings and high administrative overhead, education should take place in the environment of interactions characteristic of the pragmatic framework. As extensions of industries and services, of institutions and individual operations, education would cease to be training for a hypothetical employer. Like the practical experience for which it is constituted, education points to the precise reward and fulfillment, not to vague ideals that prove hollow after the student, or society, has paid tens of thousands of dollars to learn them. Vested in the benefits of a company whose potential depends on their future performance, students can be better motivated. Will business cooperate? As things stand now, business is in the paradoxical situation of criticizing the inadequacies of an education that has many of the same characteristics as outmoded ways of doing business.

Once students reach a level of confidence that entitles them to attempt to continue on their own or to associate with the company, the alumni of such educational experiences have better control over their destinies and can follow the cognitive path of their choosing. There will be analytically oriented and synthetically oriented individuals, many embracing the experience of articulating hypotheses and testing them. Some will follow cognitive inclinations to induction, to making observations and drawing generalizations. Others will follow the path of deduction, noticing general patterns and seeing how they apply in concrete cases. Others will follow abductions, i.e., applying knowledge about a representative sample in order to infer for a broader collection of facts or processes.

No cognitive path should be forbidden or excluded, as long as human integrity, in all aspects, is maintained and human interaction supported in the many possible forms it can assume. Motivation reflected in integrity is the element that will bring individual direction into focus. As it is practiced today, education cultivates motivations that exclude integrity and the development of skills appropriate to understanding that you can cheat your teacher but not yourself without affecting the outcome. In the current system of education, integrity appears as something incidental to the experience. Collaboration on a project of common interest introduces elements of reciprocal responsibility in respect to the outcome. Since outcome affects everyone's future, education is no longer a matter of grades, but of successful collaboration in pursuing a goal.

In order to accomplish these goals—obviously in a greater number of manifestations than the ones just described—we need to free education from its many inherited assumptions. Progress can no longer be understood as exclusively linear. Neither can we continue to apply a deterministic sequence of cause and effect in domains of non-deterministic interdependencies, characteristic of distributed cooperative efforts. Neither hierarchy nor dualism can be cultivated in the educational environment because the dynamics of association and interaction is based on patterns of changing roles within a universe focused on optimal parameters, not threatened by the radical disjunction of success vs. failure. Complexity must be acknowledged, not done away with through methods that worked in the Industrial Age but which fail in the new pragmatic context.

Unless and until one discovers through practical experience the need for a different viewpoint, for values outside the immediate object of interest, nothing should be imposed on the individual. Shakespeare and Boole are neither loved, nor understood, nor respected more by those who were forced to learn how to spell their names, learn dates by heart, or learn titles of works, fragments of plays or logical rules. The very presence of art and science, sport and entertainment, politics and religion, ethics and the legal system in educational forms of interactive media, books, artworks, databases, and programs for human interaction opens the possibility for discoveries. As serious as all these matters are, no education will ever succeed without making its students happy, without satisfaction. In each instance of education, good or bad, the human being, as a natural entity, is broken in. Tension will always be part of education, but instead of rewarding those more adept at acculturation, education should integrate complementary moments. No, I do not advocate interactive study from the beach or from a remote mountain ski resort; and I am not for extending human integration in the world of practical experiences around the clock. But as education frees itself from the industrial model—factory-like buildings, classes that correspond to shifts, holidays and vacation time—it should also let students make choices that are closer to their natural rhythms. Instead of physical co-presence, there should be interactive and cooperative creativity that does not exclude the playful, the natural, and the accidental.

If all this sounds too far-fetched to bring about, that is because it is. Even if the computer giants of the world were to open interactive learning centers tomorrow, it would be to little avail. Students will bring with them attitudes rooted in traditional expectations. There is more consensus in our world for what is right with the current system of education than for what can or should be done to change it. But with each nucleus of self-organization, such as on-line classes on subjects pertinent to working on the network, seeds are sown for future development. In our time, when the need for qualified people surges in one field or another—computational genetics, nanotechnology, non-linear electronic publishing—the model I presented is the answer. Waiting for the educational system to process students and to deliver them, at no cost to the corporations that will employ them, is no longer an acceptable strategy. Instead of endowing university chairs dedicated to the study of the no longer meaningful, corporations should invest in training and post-academic life-long learning.

To preach that in order to be a good architect one has to know history and biology and mathematics, and to know who Vitruvius was, equals preaching the rules of literacy in a world that effectively does not need them. To create an environment for the revelation of such a need, if indeed it is acknowledged as humans discover new ways to deal with their questions, is a very different task. How much reading, how much writing, mathematics, drawing, foreign language, or chemistry an architect needs is the wrong question. It assumes that someone knows, well in advance of the changing pragmatic context, what is the right mixture and how future human practical experiences will unfold. The ingredients change, the proportions change, and the context changes first of all.

As opposed to the current hierarchy, which proclaims drawing or singing as extraneous but orthography and reading as necessary, education needs to finally acknowledge complementarity. It has to encourage self-definition in and through skills best suited to practical experiences of self-constitution in a world that has escaped the cycle of repetition, and pursues goals unrelated to previous experiences. Instead of doing away with or rationalizing intuition, or being suspicious of irrationality, education will have to allow the individual to pursue a search path that integrates them. Students should be able to define goals where intuition, and even irrationality and the subconscious, are applicable. They should be freed from the constraints and limitations of the paradigm of problem solving, and engaged in generating alternatives.

All this relies heavily on the maturity of the student and the ability of educators to design environments that stimulate responsibility and self-discipline. The broad-stroke educational project sketched up to here will have to address the precise concerns connected to how and when education actually starts, what the role of the family should be—if the family remains a valid entity—and how variety and multiplicity will be addressed. In today's words and expectations, even in today's prejudices, education is of national interest in one main respect: to equip students with skills so they can contribute to the national coffers in the future. But the arena of economic viability is the global economy, not an economy defined by national boundaries. The trans-national marketplace is the real arena of competition. Re-engineering, far from being finished, made it quite clear that for the sake of efficiency, productive activities are relocated without any consideration for patriotism or national pride, never mind human solidarity and ethics.

In today's world, and to some extent in the model described so far, the unfolding of the individual through cultivation of the mind and spirit is somehow lost in the process of inculcating facts. It is its own reward to enjoy subtleties, or to generate them, to partake in art, or be part of it, to challenge the mind, or indulge in the rich world of emotions. Prepared for work that is usually different from what educators, economists, and politicians anticipate, people face the reality of work that becomes more and more fragmented and mediated. On the assembly line, or in the "analysis of symbols" (to use Robert Reich's term), work is, in the final analysis, a job, not a vocation. Physicians, professors, businessmen, carpenters, and burger flippers perform a job that can be automated to some degree. Depriving work of its highest but often neglected motivation—the unfolding of individual abilities, becoming an identity in the act—negates this motivation. Replaced by external rationale—the substance of commercial democracy—the decline of inner motivation leads to lack of interest, reduced commitment, and declining creativity. Education that processes humans for jobs promises access to abundance, but not to self-fulfillment. The decline of family, and new patterns of sexuality and reproduction, tell us that expectations, sublime on their own merit, of improved family involvement will be the exception, not the rule. Accordingly, the challenge is to understand the nature of change and to suggest alternatives, instead of hoping that, miraculously or by *divine intervention* of the almighty dollar (or yen, franc, mark, pound, or combinations thereof), families will again become what literacy intended they should be. If the challenge is not faced, education will only become a better machine for processing each new generation.

Many scholars of education have set forth various plans for saving education. They do not ignore the new pragmatic requirements. They are unaware of them. Therefore, their recommendations can be classified as *more of the same.* The sense of globality will not result from taking rhymes from *Mother Goose* (with its implicit reference and culturally determined rhythm) and adding to them the *Mother Goose* of other countries. The Victorian and post-Victorian vision transferred upon children, the expectation of "everything will be fine if you just do as you're told," reflects past ideals handed down through the moralizing fiction of the Industrial Age.

The most ubiquitous presence in modern society is the television set. It replaced the book long ago. Notwithstanding, TV is a passive medium, of low informative impact, but of high informative ability. Digital television, which extends the presence of computers, will make a difference, whether it is implemented in high resolution or not. Television in digitally scalable formats is an active medium, and interactivity is its characteristic. Education centers will integrate digital television, and open ways to involve individuals regardless of age, background and interests. We can all learn that there are several ways of seeing things, that the physics of time and music report on different aspects of temporal characteristics of our experience in the world. The movement of a robot, though different from the elegant dance of a ballerina, can benefit from a sense and experience of choreography, considered by many incompatible with engineering. The new media of interaction that are embodied in educational centers should be less obsessed with conveying information, and more with allowing human understanding of instances of change.

But these are only examples. What I have in mind is the creation of an environment for exploration in which knowledge of aesthetic aspects is learned parallel to scientific knowledge. The formats are not those of classes in the theory or history of art, or of similar art oriented subjects. As exploration takes place, aesthetic considerations are pursued as a means of optimizing the effort. It is quite clear that as classes dynamically take shape, they will integrate people of different ages and different backgrounds. Taking place in the public domain of networked resources, this education will benefit from a sense of creative competition. At each moment in time, projects will be accessible, and feedback can be provided. This ensures not only high performance from a scientific or technological viewpoint, but also aesthetic relevance.

The literacy-based educational establishment will probably dismiss the proposals set forth as *pie-in-the-sky*, as futuristic at best. Its representatives will claim that the problem at hand needs solutions, not a futuristic model based on some illusory self-organizing nuclei supported by the economy. They will argue that the suggested model of education is less credible than perfecting a practice that at least has some history and achievements to report. The public, no matter how critical of education, will ask: Is it permissible, indeed responsible, to assume that a new philosophy of education will generate new student attitudes, especially in view of the reality of metal detectors installed in schools to prevent students from carrying weapons? Is it credible to describe experiences in discovery involving high aesthetic quality, while mediocrity makes the school system appear hopelessly damned? Self-motivation is described as though teenage pregnancy and classes where students bring their babies are the concern of underpaid teachers but not of visionaries. More questions in the same vein are in the air. To propose an analogy, selling water in the desert is not as simple as it sounds.

We can, indeed, dream of educational tools hooked up to the terminals at the Kennedy Space Center, or to the supercomputers of the European Center for Research of the Future. We can dream of using digital television for exploring the unknown, and of on-line education in a world where everyone envisions high accomplishments through the use of resources that until now were open to very few. But unless society gives up the expectation of a homogeneous, obligatory education that forces individuals who want—or do not want—to prepare themselves for a life of practical experiences into the same mold, education will not produce the desired results. Good intentions, based on social, ethnic, or racial criteria, on love of children, and humanistic ideals, will not help either. While all over the world real spending per student in public education and private institutions increased well above the levels of inflation, fewer students do homework, and very few study beyond the daily assignment. This is true not only in the USA but also in countries with high admission standards for college, such as France, Germany, and Japan.

Translated into the language of our considerations, all this means that education cannot be changed independent of change in society. Education is not an autonomous system. Its connections to the rest of the pragmatic context are through students, teachers, parents, political institutions, economic realities, racial attitudes, culture, and patterns of behavior in our commercial democracy. In today's education, parochial considerations take precedence over global concerns. Bureaucratic rules of accumulated imbecility literally annihilate the changes for a better future of millions of students. What appears as the cultivation of the mind and spirit is actually no more than the attempt to polish a store window while the store itself lost its usefulness long ago. It makes no sense to require millions of students to drive daily to schools that can no longer be maintained, or to pass tests when standards are continuously lowered in order to somehow justify them.

In view of the fundamental changes in patterns of human activity, not only students need education, but practically everyone, and probably educators first of all. Connection to education centers needs to be different from the expectation of children sitting in a class dominated by a teacher. On the interactive education networks, age no longer serves as a criterion. Learning is self-paced, motivated by individual interests and priorities and by the perspectives that learning opens. A sense of common interest is expressed through interaction, unfolding through a diversity of perspectives and ways of thinking and doing. Nothing can help generations that are more different and more antagonistic than ours to find a common ground than an experience of education emancipated from hierarchies, freed of authoritarian expectations, challenging and engaging at the same time. Education will be part of the continuous self-definition of the human being throughout one's entire life.

Whether we like it or not, the economy is driven by consumer spending. This does not automatically mean that we can or should let the feedback loop follow a course that will eventually lead to losing the stability of the system to which we belong. If consumption were to remain the driving force, however, we would all end up enjoying ourselves to death. But the solution to this state of affairs is not to be found in political or educational sermonizing. To blame consumption, expectations of abundance, or entertainment will not help in finding answers to educational worries. Education will have to integrate the human experience of consumption and facilitate the acquisition of common sense. A sense of quality can be instilled by pursuing cooperative projects involving not only the production of artifacts, but also self-improvement. Generations that grow up with television as their window to reality cannot be blamed for lack of interest in reading, or for viewing reality as a show interrupted by thirty-second messages. Young minds acquire different skills, and education ought to provide a context for their integration in captivating practical experiences, instead of trying to neutralize them. Television is here for good, although changes that will alter the relation between viewers and originators of messages will change television as well.

The cognitive characteristics and motor patterns of *couch potatoes* and moderate viewers in the age of generalized TV and interactive networking are very different from those of people educated as literate. These characteristics will be further reshaped as digital television becomes part of the networked world. Where reading about history, or another country, is marginally relevant to praxis in the new context of life and work, the ability to view, understand images, perceive and effect changes, and the ability to edit them and reuse, to complete them, moreover to generate one's own images, is essential to the outcome of the effort. Without *engaging* the student, education heads into oblivion. As difficult as it is to realize that there are no absolute values, unless this realization is shared by all generations, we will face more inter-generational conflicts than we already face. Television is not the panacea for such conflicts, but a broad ground for reaching reciprocal awareness of what it takes to meet an increasingly critical challenge. Sure, we are focused here on a television that transcended its mass communication industrial society status, and reached the condition of individual interaction.

Understanding differences cannot be limited to education, or reduced to a generalized practice of viewing TV (digital or not). It has to effectively become the substance of political life. While all are equal with respect to the law, while all are free and encouraged to become the best they can be, society has to effectively abandon expectations of homogeneity and uniformity, and to dedicate energies to enhancing the significance of what makes its members different. This translates into an education freed from expectations that are not rooted in the process of self-affirmation as scientists, dancers, thinkers, skilled workers, farmers, sportspeople, and many other pragmatically sanctioned professionals. The direction is clear: to become less obsessed with a job, and more concerned with work that satisfies them, and thus their friends and relatives. The means and methods for moving in this direction will not be disbursed by states or other organizations. We have to discover them, test, and refine, aware of the fact that what replaces the institution of education is the open-ended process through which we emerge as educated individuals.

Does education henceforth become a generic trade school? For those who so choose, yes. For others, it will become what they themselves make of it through their involvement. Remaining an *open* enterprise, education will allow as many adjustments as each individual is willing to take upon oneself for the length of one's life. The education of interactive skills, of visualization technologies, of methods of search and retrieval, of thinking in images, sounds, colors, odors, textures, and haptic perception requires contexts for their discovery, use, and evaluation which no school or university in the world can provide. But if all available educational resources are used to establish learning centers based on the paradigms of interactivity, data processing, multimedia, virtual reality, neural networks, and genetic engineering, using powerful carriers such as digital TV or high-speed and broadband networks, we will stop managing a bankrupt enterprise and open avenues for successful alternatives.

As humanity ages, and societies have to cope with a new age structure, education will have to focus also on how to constitute one's identity past the biological optimum. Among the fastest growing segments on the Internet, the elderly represent a very distinct group, of high motivation, and of abilities that can better benefit society.

Access to knowledge in the form of interactive projects, pursued by classes constituted of individuals as different as the world is, is not trivial, and obviously not cheap. The networked world, the many challenges of new means of communication already in place, the new medium of digital TV—closer to reality than many realize—and computers, are already widely available. A major effort to provide support to many who are not yet connected to this world, at the expense of the current bureaucracy of education, will make the rest avialable. Instead of investing in buildings, bureaucracies, norms, and regulations, instead of rebuilding crumbling schools, and recycling teachers who intellectually died long ago in the absence of any real challenge, we can, and should, design a global education system. Such a system will effect change not only in one country, not only in a group of rich countries, but all over the world. The practice of networking and the competence in integrating work produced independently in functional modules can be attained by tackling real problems, as these are encountered by each person, not invented assignments by teachers or writers of manuals.

Education can succeed or fail only on the terms of efficiency expected in our pragmatic framework. Scores, religiously accounted for in literacy-based political life, are irrelevant. Practical experiences of self-constitution are not multiple-choice examinations. They involve the person in his entirety, and result in instances of personal growth and increased social awareness. A global world requires a live global system of education that embodies the best we can afford, and is driven by the endless energy of variety.

UNEXPECTED OPPORTUNITIES

We have heard the declaration over and over: This is the age of knowledge. The statement describes a context of human practical experiences in which the major resources are cognitive in nature. In the civilization of literacy, knowledge acquisition could take place at a slow pace, over long periods of time. The interlocking factors that defined the pragmatic context were such that no other gnoseological pattern was possible. Knowledge arising from practical experiences of industrial society progressively contributed to making life easier for human beings. Eventually, everything that had been done through the power of human muscle and dexterity—using mainly hands, arms, and legs—was assigned to machines and executed using energy resources found in the environment. Cognition supported the incremental evolution of machines through a vast array of applications.

Human knowledge allowed for the efficient use of energy to move machines which executed tasks that might have taken tens, even hundreds of men to perform.

To make this more clear, let us compare some of the tasks of the Machine Age with those of the Age of Cognition we live in. Within industrial pragmatics, the machine supplanted the muscle and the limited mechanical skills needed for processing raw materials, manufacturing cars, washing clothes, or typing. Discoveries of more sources of coal, gas, and oil kept the machine working and led to its extension from the factory to the home. Literacy, embodying characteristics of industrial pragmatics, kept pace with the demands and possibilities of the Machine Age. In our age, computer programs supplant our thinking and the limited knowledge involved in supervising complex production and assembly lines that process raw materials or synthesize new material. Computer programs are behind the manufacture of automobiles; they integrate household functions—heating, washing clothes, preparing meals, guarding our homes. Publishing on the World Wide Web relies on computers. The scale of all these efforts is global. Many languages, bearing the data needed by each specific sub-task, go into the final product or outcome. Older dependencies on natural resources and on a social model shaped to optimally support industrial praxis are partially overcome as the focus changes from permanence to transitory communities of interest and to the individual—the locus of the Cognitive Age.

Cognitive resources arise from experiences qualitatively different from those of the Machine Age. Digital engines do not burn coal or gas. *Digital engines burn cognition.* The source of cognition lies in the mind of each human being. The resources of the Machine Age are being slowly depleted. Alternative resources will be found in what was typically discarded. Recycling and the discovery of processes that extract more from what is available depend more on human cognition than on brute force processing methods. The sources of cognition are, in principle, unlimited. But if the cognitive component of human practical experiences were to stagnate or break down for some unimaginable reason, the pragmatics based on the underlying digital process of the Age of Cognition would break down also. To understand this, one need only think of being stuck in a car on an untravelled road, all because the gasoline ran out. Compare this situation with what would happen if the most complex machine, more complicated than anything science fiction could describe, came to a halt because there was no human thought to keep it going.

In the current context, the dynamics of cognition, distributed between processing information and acquiring and disseminating knowledge, stands for the dynamics of the entire system of our existence. Embodied in technologies and processing procedures, cognition contributes to the fundamental separation of the individual human from the productive task, and from a wide variety of nonproductive activities. It is not necessary that an individual possess all knowledge that a pragmatic experience requires. This means, simply, that operators in nuclear power plants need not be eminent physicists or mathematicians. Neither do all workers in a space research program need to be rocket scientists. A programmer might be ignorant of how a disk drive works. A brain surgeon does not know how the tools he or she uses are made. Each facet of a pragmatic instance entails specific requirements. The whole pragmatic experience requires knowledge above and beyond what the individuals *directly* involved can or should master. Instead of limited knowledge uniformly dispensed through literate methods, knowledge is distributed and embodied in tools and methods, not in persons. The advantage is that programs and procedures are made uniform, not human beings. For example, data management does not substitute for advanced knowledge, but a data management system as such can be endowed with knowledge in the form of routines, procedures, operation schemes, management, and self-evaluation.

Just as everyone kept the mechanical engine going, everyone, layperson or expert, contributes to the functioning of the digital engine. The only source of cognition that we can count on is within people self-constituted through practical experiences involving the digital. This does not mean that everyone will become a thinker and everyone will produce knowledge. Two sources of knowledge are relevant in the Age of Cognition within which the civilization of illiteracy unfolds. One source is the advanced work of experts and researchers, in areas of higher abstraction, way beyond what literacy can handle. The other, much more critical, source is to be found in common-sense human interaction, in day-to-day human experience.

We know that the knowledge of experts will continue to be integrated in the pragmatics of this age. The specific motivations of human practical experiences resulting in knowledge have to be recognized and stimulated. And we must also be aware of circumstances that could have a negative effect on these experiences.

We know less about the second source of knowledge because in previous pragmatic contexts it was less critical, and widely ignored. In particular, we do not know how to tap into the infinite reservoir of cognitive resources that are manifested through the routine work and everyday life of the overwhelming portion of the world's population. Taken individually, each person can contribute cognitive resources to the broader dynamics of the world. But these individual contributions are random, difficult to identify, and do not necessarily justify the effort of *mining* them. In our lives, many decisions and choices are made on the basis of extremely powerful procedures of which we, as individuals, are almost never aware. There is a grain of genius in some of the most mundane ways of doing things. Here the nodal points of integration in the multi-dimensional array that constitutes the globality of humankind are what counts. Delving into the dynamic collective persona makes such an effort worthwhile.

Years ago, in a dialogue with a prominent researcher in education, who used to maintain interactive simulations for youngsters who logged in at his institute, I discussed the then fashionable Game of Life (developed by John Horton Conway). As an open-ended simulation of the rules of birth and death, and based on the theory of cellular automata, the game required quite a bit of thinking. There is no winner or loser in the Game of Life. Although the rules of the game are relatively simple, highly complex forms of artificial life arise on the matrix: a cell going from empty to full describes birth, from full to empty, death. Satisfaction in playing is derived from reaching complex forms of life.

The idea we discussed was to make the game widely available on the network. The hundreds of thousands of players would leave traces of cognitive decisions that, over time, would add up to an expression of the intelligence of the collective body who shared an interest in the game. The cognitive sum total is of a Gestalt nature—much higher than the sum of its parts. That is, the sum has a different *qualitative* condition, probably comparable to that of the experts and geniuses, or even much higher! Considering all the instances of human application to tasks that range from being frankly useless to highly productive, one can surmise that the second source of knowledge and intelligence is much more interesting than that of the dedicated thinkers. There is more to what we do and how we choose than rationality and thinking, never mind literate rationality.

This collective persona need not comprise the entire population of the world (minus the knowledge professionals). It would help to start with groups formed *ad hoc,* groups which share an interest in a certain activity, such as playing games, or surfing for a particular piece of information, from the trivial "How do I get from here to there?" to whatever people are looking for—football scores, pornography, crossword puzzles, recipes, investment information, support in facing a certain problem, love, inter-generational conflicts, religion—anything. The challenge comes in capturing the cognitive resources at work, making inferences from the small or vast collective bodies of common focus, and coming up with viable procedures that can be utilized to enhance individual performance—all this without shaping future individual performance into grotesque repetitive patterns, no matter how successful they might be.

If there is validity to the notion that we are in the age of knowledge, we cannot limit ourselves to the knowledge of a few, no matter how exceptional these few are. The civilization of illiteracy transcends the literate model of individual performance considered a guarantee of the performance of society at large.

As practical experiences become more complex, breakdowns can be avoided only at the expense of more cognitive resources. We know that it took millennia before primitive notation progressed to writing and then to generalized literacy. In the Age of Cognition, we cannot afford such a long cycle for integrating human cognitive resources. Marvin Minsky once pointed out how much mind activity is lost in the leisure of watching football games on TV. While relaxation is essential to human existence, nobody can claim, in good faith, that what has resulted from the enormously increased efficiency of cognition-based practical experiences is not wasted to a great extent. Short of giving up, one has to entertain alternatives. But alternatives to this situation cannot be legislated. It is clear that within the motivations of the global economy, the need to identify and tap more sources of cognition will result in ways to stimulate human interaction. Watching TV probably generates thoughts that only die on the ever larger screens in our homes. Surfing the Web, where millions of hits are counted on the pornography sites—not on mathematics or literature sites—is also a waste and a source of mediocrity. *Mouse potatoes* are not necessarily better than the couch variety.

If we could derive cognition even from the many experiences of human self-constitution in computer games, we could not only further the success of the industry that changed the way humans play, but gain some insight into motivations, cognitive and emotional aspects of this elementary form of human identity. Above and beyond the speculation on playful man (*Homo Ludens*), there are quantifiable aspects of competition, satisfaction, and pleasure. And as the Internet effectively maps our journey through a maze of data, information, and sources of knowledge, we can ask whether such cognitive maps are not too valuable to be abandoned to marketing experts, instead being utilized for understanding what makes us tick as we search for a word, an image, an experience. Data regarding how and what we buy is not always representative of what we are. For many people, buying a book or a work of art, a fashionable shirt, a home, or a car is only an experience in mediation performed by the agents of these objects. But there are authentic experiences in which no one can replace us human beings. Games belong to this domain, and so do joking and interactions with friends. No agent can replace us. Within such authentic moments of self-constitution, cognitive resources of exceptional value are at work.

Many people from very different locations and of different backgrounds might simultaneously be present on a certain Web site, without ever knowing it. The server's performance could suggest that there is quite a crowd at a Web site, but it cannot say who the others are, what they are looking for, what kind of cognition drives the digital engine of their particular experiences.

While the medium of networking is more transparent than literacy experiences, it still maintains a certain opaqueness, enhanced by the firewalls meant to protect us from ourselves. Many individuals present at the same time on a Web site is not a situation one can duplicate in literacy, in which the ratio was one reader to one book, or one magazine, or even one videotape (although more than one can watch it on the family TV set, in a class, or on an airplane). Thousands of viewers simultaneously landing on a Web site is a chance and a challenge. We should accordingly think of methods for identifying ourselves, to the extent desired, and declare willingness to interact. This next level of self-constitution and identification is where the potential of rich interactions and further generation of cognition becomes possible. Tapping into cognitive resources in such situations is an opportunity we should not postpone.

Burning cognition, digital engines allow us to reach efficiency that is higher by many orders of magnitude in comparison to the efficiency attained by engines burning coal and oil. But the experience introduces the pressure of accelerated accumulation of data, information processing, and knowledge utilization. To understand the intimate relation between the performance of the digital engine and our own performance, one has only to think of a coal-burning steam engine driving a locomotive uphill. The civilization of illiteracy is a rather steep ascent, facing many obstacles—our physical abilities, limited natural resources, ecological concerns, ability to handle social complexity. To pull the brake will only make the effort of the engine more difficult, unless we want to tumble downhill, head first. Feeding the furnace faster is the answer that every sensible engineer knows. This would sound like a curse, were it not for the excitement of discovery, including that of our own cognitive resources.

Analogy aside, what drives the digital engine is not abstract computing cycles of faster chips, but human cognition embodied in experiences that support further diversification of experiences. It has yet to be the case that we had enough computing cycles to burn and we did not know what to do with the extra computing power available. On the contrary, human practical experiences are always ahead of technology, as we challenge ourselves with new tasks for which the chips of yesterday and the memory available are as inappropriate as the methods and means of literacy.

Bio-electric signals associated with the activity of our minds have been measured for quite a number of years. We learned from such measurements that minds are constituted in anticipation of our practical experience of self-identification as human beings. The idea seemed far-fetched, despite the strong scientific evidence on which it was ultimately founded. Cognition is process, and bio-electric signals are indicative of cognitive processes in our minds. Sensors attached to the skin, such as through a simple finger glove, can read such signals. In effect, they read unfolding mind processes based on our cognitive resources. Feeding digital engines hungry to burn cognition, we arrive not only at mind-controlled prosthetic devices for people with disabilities, but also at a mind-driven painter's brush, or desktop film directing, allowing us to get involved with cinematographic projects of scripting and affecting variations of the plot. From pinball games to tennis and skiing, from virtual bowling to virtual football, our thoughts make new experiences possible. For those affected by disabilities, this is a qualitatively new horizon. Einstein, but many others as well, was quite convinced that only 10 percent of our cognitive abilities are effectively engaged in what we do. As the digital engine burns more and more cognition, this number will change, as probably our physical condition, already marked by forms of degeneration, will change too.

If, by using only one-tenth of our cognitive resources, we reach the level of possibilities presently open to us, it is not too hard to imagine what only one more tenth might bring. The civilization of illiteracy, with all the dangers and inequities it has to address, is only at its beginning. That its duration will be shorter than the one preceding it is another subject.

1982-1996: Providence RI; Rochester NY; Bexley OH; New York NY; Little Compton RI; Wuppertal, Germany.

REFERENCES AND INDEX

REFERENCES

INTRODUCTION

Literacy in a Changing World

During the writing of this book, several articles were published and lectures presented on themes pertinent to the subject. None was taken over in this work. Among these are:

J. Deely and M. Lenhard, editors. The Civilization of Illiteracy, in *Semiotics 1981*. New York: Plenum, 1983.

H. Stachowiak, editor. Pragmatics in the Semiotic Framework, in *Pragmatik,* vol. II. Hamburg: Felix Meiner Verlag, 1986.

La civilization de l'analphabetisme, in *Gazette de Beaux-Arts,* vol. iii, no. 1430, March 1988, pp. 225-228.

Writing is Rewriting, in *The American Journal of Semiotics,* vol. 5, no. 1, 1987, pp. 115-133.

Sign and Value. (Lecture)Third Congress of the International Association of Semiotic Studies, Palermo, Italy, June 25-29, 1984.

The Civilization of Illiteracy. (Lecture) Sixth Annual Meeting of the Semiotic Society of America, Vanderbilt University, Nashville, October 1-4, 1981.

Philosophy in the Civilization of Illiteracy. (Lecture) XVII World Congress of Philosophy, Montreal, August, 1983.

Values in the Post-Modern Era: The Civilization of Illiteracy. (Lecture) Institute Forum, Rochester Institute of Technology, November 9, 1984.

A Case for the Hacker. (Lecture) University of Oregon, Oct. 27, 1987.

Communication in a time of integration and awareness. (Lecture) New York University, April, 1989.

De plus ça change... Creativity in the context of scientific and technological change. (Lecture) University of Michigan, January, 1993.

The bearable impertinence of rationality. (Lecture) Multimediale, the1st International Festival of Multimedia, Hamburg: February, 1993.

From a very broad literature on literacy, including the emergence of writing and early written documents, the following proved useful in defining the position stated in this book:

John Hladczuk, William Eller, and Sharon Hladczuk. *Literacy/Illiteracy in the World. A Bibliography.* New York: Greenwood Press, 1989.

David R. Olson, Nancy Torrance, and Angela Hildyard, editors. *Literacy, Language, and Learning: The Nature and Consequences of Reading and Writing.* New York: Cambridge University Press, 1985.

Robert Pattison. *On Literacy: The Politics of the Word from Homer to the Age of Rock.* New York: Oxford University Press, 1982.

Gerd Baumann, editor. *The Written Word: Literacy in Transition.* New York: Oxford University Press, 1986.

National Advisory Council on Adult Education. Literacy Committee. *Illiteracy in America: Extent, Causes and Suggested Solutions,* 1986.

Susan B. Neuman. *Literacy in the Television Age. The Myth of the TV Effect.* Norwood, NJ: Ablex, 1991.

Edward M. Jennings and Alan C. Purves, editors. *Literate Systems and Individual Lives. Perspectives on Literacy and Schooling.* Albany: SUNY Press, 1991.

Harald Haarman. *Universalgeschichte der Schrift.* Frankfurt/Main: Campus Verlag, 1990.

David Diringer. *The Alphabet. A Key to the History of Mankind* (3rd edition). New York: Funk & Wagnalls, 1968.

Colin H. Roberts. *The Birth of the Codex.* London: Oxford University Press, 1987.

Martin Koblo. *Die Entwicklung der Schrift*. Wiesbaden: Brandsetter, 1963.

R. Hooker. *Reading the Past. Ancient Writing from Cuneiform to the Alphabet*. Berkeley: University of California Press, 1990.

Donald Jackson. *The Story of Writing*. New York: Taplinger Publishing Co., 1981.

Hannsferdinand Dobler. *Von der Keilschrift zum Computer. Schrift, Buch, Wissenschaften*. Munich: Bertelsmann, 1974.

Colin Clair. *A History of European Printing*. New York: Academic Press, 1976.

Lucien Paul Victor Febre. *The Coming of the Book. The Impact of Printing 1450-1800*. Trans. David Gerard. London: N.L.B., 1976.

Karlen Mooradian. *The Dawn of Printing*. Lexington, KY: Association for Education in Journalism, 1972.

Warren Chappel. *A Short History of the Printed Word*. New York: Knopf, 1970.

Peter S. Bellwood. *Prehistory in the Indo-Malaysian Archipelago*. Orlando, FL: Academic Press, 1985.

Andrew Sherrat, editor. *The Cambridge Encyclopedia of Archaeology*. New York: Crown Publishers, 1980.

Peirce's pragmatic perspective was extracted from his writings. In the absence of a finished text on the subject, various scholars chose what best suited their own viewpoint. A selection from an unusually rich legacy of manuscripts and published articles was made available in *The Collected Papers of Charles Sanders Peirce* (eight volumes). Volumes 1-6 edited by Charles Hartshorne and Paul Weiss; volumes 7-8 edited by A. Burks. Cambridge: The Belknap Press of Harvard University Press, 1931-1958.
The standard procedure in citing this work is "volume.paragraph" (e.g., 2.227 refers to volume 2, paragraph 227).
Important references to Peirce's semiotics are found in his correspondence with Victoria, Lady Welby. This was published by Charles Hardwick as *Semiotics and Significs. The Correspondence between Charles S. Peirce and Victoria Lady Welby*, Bloomington and London: Indiana University Press, 1977.
Peirce's manuscripts are currently being published in a new edition, *The Writings of Charles S. Peirce. A Chronological Edition* (E. Moore, founding editor; Max A. Fisch, general editor; C. Kloesel, Director), Bloomington: Indiana University Press, 1984-present.
Peirce's pragmaticism was defined in a text dated 1877, during his return journey from Europe aboard a steamer, "...a day or two before reaching Plymouth,

nothing remaining to be done except to translate it into English," (5.526): "Considerer quels sont les effets pratiques que nous pensons pouvoir être produits par l'objet de notre conception. La conception de tous ces effets est la conception complète de l'objet."

In respect to Peirce, his friends William James and John Dewey wrote words of appreciation, placing him "in the forefront of the great seminal minds of recent times," (cf. Morris R. Cohen, *Chance, Love, and Logic,* Glencoe IL: 1954, p. iii). C. J. Keyser stated, "That this man, who immeasurably increased the intellectual wealth of the world, was nevertheless almost permitted to starve in what in his time was the richest and vainest of lands is enough to make the blood of any decent American boil with chagrin, indignation, and vicarious shame," (cf. Portraits of Famous Philosophers Who Were Also Mathematicians, in *Scripta Mathematica,* vol. III, 1935).

C.P. Snow. *The Two Cultures and a Second Look* (An Expanded Version of The Two Cultures and the Scientific Revolution). Cambridge: At the University Press, 1965 (first printed in 1955).

Gottfried Wilhelm Leibniz (1646-1716). From the few works published during his lifetime, reference is made to *Dissertatio de Arte Combinatoria* (Leipzig, 1666). G.H. Parkinson translated some works in *Leibniz Logical Papers* (London, 1966). Another edition considered for this book is by Gaston Grua, *Leibniz. Textes inédits* (Paris, 1948), which offers some of the many manuscripts in which important ideas remained hidden for a long time.

Humberto R. Maturana. The Neurophysiology of Cognition, in *Cognition: A Multiple View* (P. Garvin, Editor). New York: Spartan Books, 1969.

Humberto R. Maturana and Francisco J. Varela. *El árbol del conocimiento,* 1984. The work was translated as *The Tree of Knowledge. The Biological Roots of Human Understanding.* Boston/London: Shambala New Science Library, 1987.

Terry Winograd. *Understanding Natural Language.* New York: Academic Press, 1972.

—. *Language as Cognitive Process.* Reading MA: Addison-Wesley, 1983.

Terry Winograd and Fernando Flores. *Understanding Computers and Cognition. A New Foundation for Design.* Norwood NJ: Ablex Publishing Corporation, 1986.

George Lakoff and Mark Johnson. *Metaphors We Live By.* Chicago: Chicago University Press, 1980.

George Lakoff. *Women, Fire, and Dangerous Things.* (What Categories Reveal about the Mind). Chicago/London: The University of Chicago Press, 1987.

"The point is that the level of categorization is not independent of who is doing the categorizing and on what basis" (p. 50).

With his seminal work on fuzzy sets, Lotfi Zadeh opened a new perspective relevant not only to technological progress, but also to a new philosophic perspective.

Fuzzy Sets, in *Information and Control*, 8 (1965), pp. 338-353.

Fuzzy Logic and Approximate Reasoning (in Memory of Grigore Moisil), in *Synthèse* 30 (1975), pp. 407-428.

Coping with the impression of the real world, in *Communications of the Association for Computing Machinery*, 27 (1984), pp. 304-311.

George Steiner. *Language and Silence.* New York: Atheneum, 1967.

—. *After Babel. Aspects of Language and Translation.* London: Oxford University Press, 1975.

—. *Real Presence: Is There Anything in What We Say?* London/Boston: Faber & Faber, 1989.

—. The End of Bookishness? in *The Times Literary Supplement,* July 8-14, 1988, p. 754.

Marshall McLuhan. *The Gutenberg Galaxy: The Making of Typographic Man.* Toronto: Toronto University Press, 1962.

Ivan Illich. *Deschooling Society.* New York: Harper & Row, 1971.
Illich states bluntly: "Universal education through schooling is not feasible" (Introduction, p. ix).

Ivan Illich and Barry Sanders. *The Alphabetization of the Popular Mind.* San Francisco: North Point Press, 1988.

Y. M. Lotman. *Kul'tura kak Kollektvinji Intellekt i Problemy Iskusstuennovo Razuma* (Culture as collective intellect and problems of artificial intelligence). Predvaritel'naya Publicacija, Moskva: Akademija Nauk SSSR (Nauchinyi Soviet po Kompleksnoi Problemi Kibernetika), 1977.

Jean Baudrillard. *Simulations.* Trans. Paul Foss, Paul Patton, Philip Beitchman. New York: Semiotext(e), 1983.

BOOK I

Chapter 1: The Chasm Between Yesterday and Tomorrow

Hans Magnus Enzensberger. *Mittelmaß und Wahn. Gesammelte Zerstreuungen.* Frankfurt am Main: 1988.

Norbert Wiener. *The Human Use of Human Beings. Cybernetics and Society.* 1st ed. New York: Avon Books, 1967.
Wiener was very concerned with the consequences of human involvement with machines and the consequences of the unreflecting use of technology. "Once before in history the machine had impinged upon human culture with an effect of the greatest moment. This previous impact is known as the Industrial Revolution, and it concerned the machine purely as an alternative to human muscle" (p.185).
"It is fair to say, however, that except for a considerable number of isolated examples, this industrial revolution up to present [ca. 1950] has displaced man and beast as a source of power, without making any great impression on other human functions" (p. 209).
Wiener goes on to describe a new stage, what he calls the Second Industrial Revolution, dominated by computing machines driving all kinds of industrial processes. He notes: "Let us remember that the automatic machine, whatever we think of any feelings it may have or may not have, is the precise economic equivalent of slave labor. Any labor which competes with slave labor must accept the economic conditions of slave labor" (p. 220).
"What can we expect of its economic and social consequences? In the first place, we can expect an abrupt and final cessation of the demand for the type of factory labor performing purely repetitive tasks. In the long run, the deadly uninteresting nature of the repetitive task may make this a good thing and the source of leisure necessary for a man's full cultural development. It may also produce cultural results as trivial and wasteful as the greater part of those so far obtained from the radio and the movies" (p. 219).

Nick Thimmesch, editor. *Aliteracy. People Who Can Read but Won't.* Washington, DC: American Enterprise Institute for Policy Research, 1983. Proceedings of a conference held on September 20, 1982 in Washington, DC.
According to William A. Baroody, Jr., President of the American Enterprise Institute, the aliterate person scans magazines, reads headlines, "never reads novels or poetry for the pleasures they offer." He goes on to state that aliteracy

is more dangerous because it "reflects a change in cultural values and a loss of skills" and "leads to knowing without understanding."

Marsha Levine, a participant in the conference noted that although educators are concerned with universal literacy, many people read less or not at all: "A revolution in technology is having an impact on education...they [technological means] increase the level of literacy, but they might undermine the practice of what they teach."

At the same conference, an anonymous participant posed a sequence of questions: "Exactly what advantage do reading and literacy hold in terms of helping us to process information? What does reading give us that is of some social advantage that cannot be obtained through other media? Is it entirely certain that we cannot have a functioning society with an oral-aural method of communication, where we use television and its still unexploited resources of communication? [...] Is it impossible to conceive of a generation that has received its knowledge of the world and itself through television?" (p. 22).

John Searle. The storm over the university, in *The New York Review of Books*, 37:19, December 6, 1990, pp. 34-42.

Plato. *Phaedrus, and The Seventh and Eighth Letters*. Trans. Walter Hamilton. Harmondsworth: Penguin Press, 1973.
In *Phaedrus*, Socrates, portrayed by Plato, articulates arguments against writing: "It will implant forgetfulness in their souls [of people, M.N.]: they will cease to exercise memory because they rely on that which is written, calling these things to remembrance no longer from within themselves, but by means of external marks; what you have discovered is a recipe [*pharmakon*, a potion; some translate it as *recipe*, M.N.] not for memory, but for reminder" (274-278e. p. 96). (References to Plato include the Stephanus numbers. This makes them independent of the particular edition used by the reader.)

Claude Lévi-Strauss. *Tristes Tropiques*. Paris: Plon, 1967.
The author continues Socrates' thought: "It [writing] seems to have favored the exploitation of human beings rather than their enlightenment" (p. 298).

From a very broad literature on literacy, including the emergence of writing and early written documents, the following proved useful in defining the position stated in this book:

John Hladczuk, William Eller, and Sharon Hladczuk. *Literacy/Illiteracy in the World. A Bibliography*. New York: Greenwood Press, 1989.

David R. Olson, Nancy Torrance, and Angela Hildyard, editors. *Literacy, Language, and Learning: The Nature and Consequences of Reading and Writing*. New York: Cambridge University Press, 1985.

Robert Pattison. *On Literacy: The Politics of the Word from Homer to the Age of Rock.* New York: Oxford University Press, 1982.

Gerd Baumann, editor. *The Written Word: Literacy in Transition.* New York: Oxford University Press, 1986.

National Advisory Council on Adult Education. Literacy Committee. *Illiteracy in America: Extent, Causes and Suggested Solutions,* 1986.

Susan B. Neuman. *Literacy in the Television Age. The Myth of the TV Effect.* Norwood, NJ: Ablex, 1991.

Edward M. Jennings and Alan C. Purves, editors. *Literate Systems and Individual Lives. Perspectives on Literacy and Schooling.* Albany: SUNY Press, 1991.

Dr. Harald Haarman. *Universalgeschichte der Schrift.* Frankfurt/Main: Campus Verlag, 1990.

David Diringer. *The Alphabet. A Key to the History of Mankind.* 3rd edition. New York: Funk & Wagnalls, 1968.

Colin H. Roberts. *The Birth of the Codex.* London: Oxford University Press, 1987.

Martin Koblo. *Die Entwicklung der Schrift.* Wiesbaden: Brandsetter, 1963.

Donald Jackson. *The Story of Writing.* New York: Taplinger Publishing Co., 1981.

Hannsferdinand Dobler. *Von der Keilschrift zum Computer. Schrift, Buch, Wissenschaften.* Munich: Bertelsmann, 1974.

Colin Clair. *A History of European Printing.* New York: Academic Press, 1976.

Lucien Paul Victor Febre. *The Coming of the Book. The Impact of Printing 1450-1800.* Trans. David Gerard. London: N.L.B., 1976.

Karlen Mooradian. *The Dawn of Printing.* Lexington, KY: Association for Education in Journalism, 1972.

Warren Chappel. *A Short History of the Printed Word.* New York: Knopf, 1970.

C.P. Snow. *The Two Cultures and a Second Look.* An expanded version of *The Two Cultures and the Scientific Revolution.* Cambridge: At the University Press, 1959.

John Brockman. *The Third Culture: Beyond the Scientific Revolution.* New York: Simon & Schuster, 1995.

A recent criticism of the book, by Phillip E. Johnson, on the World Wide Web, states that the scientists contributing to the book "tend to replace the literary intellectuals rather than cooperate with them."

Alan Bloom. *The Closing of the American Mind*. New York: Simon and Schuster, 1987.

Antoine de St. Exupéry. *The Little Prince*. Trans. Katherine Woods. New York: Harcourt, Brace & World, 1943.

Helmut Schmidt, ex-Chancellor of West Germany, Marion Gräfin Dönhoff, editor-in-chief of *Die Zeit*, Edzard Reuter, ex-CEO of Daimler-Benz, along with several prominent German intellectuals and politicians, met during the summer of 1992 to discuss issues facing their country after reunification. In their *Manifesto*, they insisted that any concept for a sensible future needs to integrate the notion of renouncing (*Verzicht*) and sharing as opposed to growing expectations and their export through economic aid to Third World countries. See *Ein Manifest: Weil das Land sich ändern muß* (A Manifesto. Because the country needs to change), Reinbeck: Rowohlt Verlag, 1992

Jean-Marie Guéhenno. *La Fin de la Démocratie*. Paris: Flammarion, 1993.

Edmund Carpenter. *They Became What They Beheld*. New York: Outerbridge and Dienstfrey/Ballantine, 1970.

Nathaniel Hawthorne. Earth's Holocaust, in *The Complete Short Stories of Nathaniel Hawthorne*. Garden City NY: Doubleday & Co., 1959.

George Steiner. The end of bookishness? in *Times Literary Supplement*, July 8-14, 1988.
"To read classically means to own the means of that reading. We are dealing no longer with the medieval chained library or with books held as treasures in certain monastic and princely institutions. The book became a domestic object owned by its user, accessible at his will for re-reading. This access in turn comprised private space, of which the personal libraries of Erasmus and of Montaigne are emblematic. Even more crucial, though difficult to define, was the acquisition of periods of private silence" (p. 754).

Thomas Robert Malthus. An Essay On the Principle of Population, 1798, in *The Works of Thomas Robert Malthus*. E.A. Wrigley and David Souden, editors. London: W. Pickering, 1986.

Mark Twain (Samuel Langhorn Clemens). *The Annotated Huckleberry Finn: The Adventures of Huckleberry Finn*. With introduction, notes, and bibliography by Michael P. Hearn. New York: C.N. Potter and Crown Publishers, 1981.

"Twain drives home just how strongly we are chained to our own literacy through Huck's illiterate silence" (p. 101). "Thus Twain brings into focus the trap of literacy. There is a whole world in *Huck Finn* that is closed to those without literacy. They can't, for ironic example, read this marvelous work, *The Adventures of Huckleberry Finn*. And yet we must recognize a world rich with superstition and folklore, with adventure and beauty, that remains closed to those who are too tightly chained to letters" (p. 105).

George Gilder. *Life After Television: The Coming Transformation of Media and American Life.* New York: Norton, 1992.

Neil Postman. *Technopoly: The Surrender of Culture to Technology.* New York: Knopf, 1992.

Chapter 2: The Epitome of the Civilization of Illiteracy

John Adams. *Letters from a Distinguished American: Twelve Essays by John Adams on American Foreign Policy, 1780.* Compiled and edited by James H. Hutson. Washington, DC: Library of Congress, 1978.

——. *The Adams-Jefferson: the Complete Correspondence between Thomas Jefferson and Abigail and John Adams* (Lester J. Cappon, editor). Chapel Hill: University of North Carolina Press, 1959.

Jean-Jacques Servan-Schreiber. *The American Challenge.* Trans. Robert Steel. With a foreword by Arthur Schlesinger, Jr. New York: Atheneum, 1968.

Neil Postman. Rising Tide of Illiteracy in the USA, in *The Washington Post*, 1985.
　　　"Whatever else may be said of the immigrants who settled in New England in the 17th century, it is a paramount fact that they were dedicated and skillful readers.... It is to be understood that the Bible was the central reading matter in all households, for these people were Protestants who shared Luther's belief that printing was 'God's highest and extremest act of Grace, whereby the business of the Gospel is driven forward.' But reading for God's sake was not their sole motivation in bringing books into their homes."

Lauran Paine. *Captain John Smith and the Jamestown Story.* London: R. Hale, 1973.

Henry Steele Commager. *The American Mind.* New Haven: Yale University Press, 1950.

Charles Dickens. *American Notes.* New York: St. Martin's Press, 1985.

The book is a journal of Dickens's travels from Boston to St. Louis, from January through June, 1842.

Alexis de Toqueville. *Democracy in America*, Vol. 1 (Henry Reeve text as revised by Francis Bowen). New York: Vintage Books, 1945.

Several other writers have attempted to characterize the USA, or at least some of its aspects:

Jean Baudrillard. *Amérique*. Paris: Grasset, 1986.

—. *America*. Chris Turner, London/New York: Verso, 1988.

Gerald Messadie. *Requiem pour superman. La crise du mythe américain*. Paris: R. Laffont, 1988.

Rodó, José Enrique. *Ariel. Liberalismo y Jacobinismo*. Buenos Aires: Ediciones Depalma, 1967.

In practically all her novels, Jane Austen extols the improvement of the mind (especially the female mind) through reading; see especially *Pride and Prejudice*, Vol. 1, chapter 8. (New York: The New American Library, 1961, p. 35).

Thomas Jefferson. Autobiography, in *Writings*. New York: The Library of America/Literary Classics of the United States, 1984.
Jefferson's father placed him in the English school when Thomas was five years old, and at age nine in the Latin school, where he learned Latin, Greek, and French until 1757. In 1758, Jefferson continued two years of the same program of study with a Reverend Maury. In 1760, he attended the College of William and Mary (for two years), where he was taught by a Dr. William Small of Scotland (a mathematician). His education consisted of Ethics, Rhetoric, and Belles Lettres. In 1762, he began to study law.

Joel Spring. *The American School 1642-1990*. 2nd ed. New York/London: Longman, 1990.
Benjamin Franklin's model academy embodied his own education. " '...it would be well if [students] could be taught every thing that is useful, and every thing that is ornamental. But Art is long, and their Time is short. It is therefore propos'd that they learn those things that are likely to be most useful and most ornamental.' [...] Franklin's early life was a model for getting ahead in the New World [...] The 'useful' elements in Franklin's education were the skills learned in apprenticeship and through his reading. The 'ornamental´ elements,... were the knowledge and social skills learned through reading, writing, and debating" (p. 23).

Theodore Sizer, editor. *The Age of the Academics,* New York: Teachers College Press, 1964.
"The academy movement in North America was primarily a result of the desire to provide a more utilitarian education as compared with the education provided in classical grammar schools" (p. 22).

Lester Frank Ward. *The Psychic Factors of Civilization.* 2nd ed. New York: Johnson Reprint Corp, 1970.
"The highest duty of society is to see that every member receives a sound education" (p. 308).

Transcendentalism: "A 19th century New England movement of writers and philosophers who were loosely bound together by adherence to an idealistic system of thought based on a belief in the essential unity of all creation, the innate goodness of man, and the supremacy of insight over logic and experience for the revelation of deepest truths." The main figures were Ralph Waldo Emerson, Henry David Thoreau, and Margaret Fuller (cf. *Encyclopedia Britannica, Micropedia.* 1990 ed.).

Paul F. Boller. *American Transcendentalism, 1830-1860. An Intellectual Inquiry.* New York: Putnam, 1974.

Major philosophers of pragmatics:
Charles Sanders Peirce (1839-1914). Although no finished work deals explicitly with his pragmatic conception, this conception permeates his entire activity. His semiotics is the result of the fundamental pragmatic philosophy he developed.
John Dewey (1859-1952). Dewey bases his pragmatic conception on the proven useful. This explains why this conception was labeled *instrumentalism* or *pragmatics of verification.* Among the works where this is expressed are *How We Think* (1910), *Logic, the Theory of Inquiry* (1938), *Knowing and Known* (1940).
William James (1842-1910). James expressed his pragmatic conception from a psychological perspective. His main works dedicated to pragmatism are *Principles of Psychology* (1890), *Pragmatism* (1907), and *The Meaning of Truth* (1909).
Josiah Royce (1855-1916). He is the originator of a conception he called *absolute pragmatics.*

John Sculley, ex-CEO of Apple Computer, Inc took the bully pulpit for literacy (at President-elect Clinton's economic summit in December, 1992), stating that the American economy is built on ideas. He and other business leaders confuse ideas with invention, which is their main interest, and for which literacy is not really necessary.

Sidney Lanier. The Symphony, 1875, in *The Poems of Sidney Lanier.* (Mary Day Lanier, editor). Athens: University of Georgia Press, 1980.

Thorstein Veblen (1857-1929). American economist and social scientist who sought to apply evolutionary dynamic approach to the study of economic constructions. Best known for his work *The Theory of the Leisure Class* (1899), in which he coined the term *conspicuous consumption.*

Theodore Dreiser. *American Diaries,* 1902-1926. (Thomas P. Riggio, editor). Philadelphia: University of Pennsylvania Press, 1982.

—. *Sister Carrie* (the Pennsylvania Edition). Philadelphia: University of Pennsylvania Press, 1981.

—. *Essays.* Selected magazine articles of Theodore Dreiser: Life and art in the American 1890's. (Yoshinobu Hakutani, editor). 2 volumes. Rutherford: Fairleigh Dickinson University Press, 1985-1987.

Henry James. *The American Scene.* London: Chapman and Hall, 1907.

—. *The Bostonians.* London: John Lehmann Ltd. 1952.
"I wished to write a very American tale," James wrote in his *Notebook* (two years prior to the publication of the novel in 1886). He also stated, "I asked myself what was the most salient and peculiar point of our social life. The answer was: the situation of women, the decline of the sentiment of sex...."

Henry Steele Commager. *The American Mind.* New Haven: Yale University Press, 1950.
In the section aptly entitled "The Literature of Revolt," Commager noticed that the tradition of protest and revolt (dominant in American literature since Emerson and Thoreau) turned, at the beginning of the 20th century (that is, with the New Economics), into an almost unanimous repudiation of the economic order. "...most authors portrayed an economic system disorderly and ruthless, wasteful and inhumane, unjust alike to working men, investors, and consumers, politically corrupt and morally corrupting," (p. 247). He goes on to name William Dean Howell (with his novels), Sinclair Lewis, Theodore Dreiser, F. Scott Fitzgerald, John Dos Passos, and others. In the same vein, Denis Brogan (*The American Character*), J.T. Adams (*Our Business Civilization*), Harold Stearns (*America: A Reappraisal*), Mary A. Hamilton (*In America Today*), André Siegfried (*America Comes of Age*) are also mentioned.

Howard Gardner. *Frames of Mind: Theory of Multiple Intelligences.* New York: Basic Books, 1983.

Diane Ravitch. *The Schools We Deserve.* New York: Doubleday, 1985.

Peter Cooper (1791-1883). Self-taught entrepreneur and inventor. As head of North American Telegraph Works, he made a fortune manufacturing glue and establishing iron works. In 1830, his experimental locomotive made its first 13-mile run.

The Corcoran case. The incredible secret of John Corcoran, *20/20*, ABC News, April 1, 1988. (Text by by *Transcripts:* Journal Graphics, Inc. pp. 11-14.)

Noah Webster. *The American Spelling Book: containing an easy standard of pronunciation. Being the first part of a Grammatical Institute of the English Language.* Boston: Isaiah Thomas and Ebenezer T. Andrews, 1793.

William Holmes McGuffey. *McGuffey's Newly Revised Eclectic First Reader: containing progressive lessons in reading and spelling* (revised and improved by Wm. H. McGuffey). Cincinnati: Winthrop B. Smith, 1853.

It is doubtful that all the clever remarks attributed to Yogi Berra came from him. What matters is the dry sense of humor and logical irreverence that make these remarks another form of Americana.

Akiro Morita, et al. *Made in Japan.* New York: Dutton, 1989.

United We Stand, the political interest group founded by H. Ross Perot, is probably another example of how difficult it is, even for those who take an active stand (no matter how controversial), to break the dualistic pattern of political life in the USA. This group became the Reform Party.

Gottfried Benn. *Sämtliche Werke.* (Gerhard Schuster, editor). Vols. 3-5 (Prosa). Stuttgart: Klett Cotta, 1986. Benn maintains that the language crisis is actually the expression of the crisis of the white man.

Andrei Toom. A Russian Teacher in America, in *Focus*, 16:4, August 1996, pp. 9-11 (reprint of the same article appearing in the June 1993 issue of the *Journal of Mathematical Behavior* and then in the Fall 1993 issue of *American Educator*).
Among the many articles dealing with American students' attitudes towards required subject matter, this is one of the most poignant. It involves not literature, philosophy, or history, but mathematics. The author points out not only the expectations of students and educational administrators, but also the methods in which the subject matter is treated in textbooks. Interestingly enough, he recounts his experience with students in a state university, where generalized, democratic access to mediocrity is equated with education.

Chapter 1: From Signs to Language

Louis Leonor Hammerich. *The Eskimo Language,* Oslo: Universitets forlaget, 1970.

Steven Jacobson. *Yupik Eskimo Dictionary,* Fairbanks: Alaska Native Language Center, University of Alaska, 1984.

Handbook of American Indian Languages. Washington, D.C.: Smithsonian Institution. Part 1, 1917; Part 2, 1922.

Edward Sapir. *American Indian Languages.* (Vol. 1 edited by William Bright; Vol. 2 edited by Victor Golla). Berlin/New York: Mouton de Gruyter, 1991-1992.

Franz Boaz. *Race, Language and Culture.* 1940. rpt. Chicago: University of Chicago Press, 1982.

Geoffrey Pullum. *The Great Eskimo Vocabulary Hoax and Other Irreverent Essays on the Study of Language.* Chicago: University of Chicago Pre, 1991.
The author takes issue with the reported number of words for *snow* that B.J. Whorf made public. Linguistic aspects of this matter go beyond the scope of my analysis.

Willet Kempton. *The Folk Classification of Ceramics. A Study of Cognitive Prototypes.* New York: Academic Press, 1981 (p. 36). He also mentions that Texans have more specific names than the English for the same number of boots (pp. 28-29).

George Lakoff. *Women, Fire, and Dangerous Things. What Categories Reveal about the Mind.*
"...the Australian aboriginal language Dyirbal, which has a category, *balan,* that actually includes women, fire and dangerous things. It also includes birds that are *not* dangerous, as well as exceptional animals, such as the platypus, bandicoot, and echidna" p. 35. Lakoff goes on to quote R.M.W. Dixon (1982), who gave an overview of Dyirbal classification:
I. *Bayi:* men, kangaroos, possum, bats, most snakes, most fishes, some birds, most insects, the moon, storms, rainbows, boomerangs, some spears, etc.

II. *Balan:* women, bandicoots, dogs, platypus, echidna, some snakes, some fishes, most birds, fireflies, scorpions, crickets, the hairy mary grub, anything connected with water or fire, sun and stars, shields, some spears, some trees
III. *Balam:* all edible fruit and plants that bear them, tubers, ferns, honey, cigarettes, wine, cake
IV. *Bala:* parts of the body, meat, bees, wind, yamsticks, some spears, most trees, grass, mud, stones, noises and language (p.93).

Jesús Salinas Pedraza. Anthropologists and computers help people preserve their ancient cultures in *New York Times*, December 31, 1991, p. C1, C7: "In a publishing coup, books in 'unwritten' languages." The article describes the activity of the Oaxaca (Mexico) literacy center. Works in Chatino, Amuzgo, Chinantec, Mazatec, Mixtec, Tzotzil, Zapotec were produced using word processing programs adapted to each of these languages.

Jack Goody, ed. and Ian Watt. The Consequences of Literacy, in *Literacy in Traditional Societies*. Cambridge: Cambridge University Press, 1968, pp. 27-84.

Sylvia Scribner and Michael Cole. *Culture and Thought*. New York: John Wiley, 1973.

—. Literacy without schooling: testing for intellectual effects, in *Harvard Educational Review*, 48, 1978, pp. 448-462.

Dr. Harald Haarman. *Universalgeschichte der Schrift*. Frankfurt/Main: Campus Verlag, 1990.

Eric A. Havelock. *Schriftlichkeit. Das griechische Alphabet als Kulturelle Revolution*. Weinheim: Verlag VCH, 1990.

As stated by Lakoff, Rosch "set out to challenge one of Whorf's hypotheses, namely, that language determines one's conceptual system." In the same book (*Op. cit.*, p. 40, p. 310), Lakoff reports that Dani is a New Guinea language that has only two basic color categories: *mili* (dark-cool, including black, green, and blue) and *mola* (light-warm, including white, red, yellow).

Regarding *semeion:* The three acknowledged activities in which semiotics is constituted are medicine (symptoms of a disease), linguistics (how languages are related to the world in which people speaking them live), and philosophy or logic (in reflecting upon the nature of mind processes) In each of the three practical contexts, the sign, which the Greeks called *semeion*, is the focusing entity.

Derek Bickerton, *Language and Species*. Chicago/London: University of Chicago Press, 1990.

"For the foundations of language lie far back in the evolutionary history of animate creatures with goals and purposes derived from their own needs. Most of those foundations we share with other species. Only evolutionary chance triggered, in our ancestors, the emergence of the first stumbling attempts at language" (p. 256).

Port Royal Logic. La Logique ou l'art de penser, contenant outre les Règles communes, plusieurs observations nouvelles, propre à former le jugement (Logic or the art of thinking, containing in addition the common Rules, several new observations able to form judgement), Paris, 1662. The text was written by Antoine Arnauld (1612-1694) and Pierre Nicole (1625-1695). The basis for the Port Royal Logic is Descartes *Regulae ad Directionem Ingenii (Rules for the Conduct of the Intellect*, written some time after 1649 and published posthumously in 1701) and Blaise Pascal's (1623-1662) *Rules* (for definitions, axioms, demonstrations, as expressed in *De l'art de persuader*, 1657, *The Art of Persuasion*). The expectation is of "evident propositions."

Terence McKenna and Dennis McKenna. *Psilocybin: The Magic Mushroom Growers' Guide.* A talking book of McKenna's Amazon adventures, *True Hallucinations,* was produced by the Edge Foundation in March, 1990.

Kim Sterelny. *The Representational Theory of Mind. An Introduction.* Oxford, England/Cambridge MA: Basil Blackwell, 1990.
"Jerry Fodor has argued that human (and nonhuman) mental processes involve a medium of mental representation, a medium that has all the central features of a language" (p. 23).

Stevan Harnad. *The Origin of Words: A Psychological Hypothesis.* Text presented in 1992 at the Zif Conference on Biological and Cultural Aspects of Language Development. The author introduced the criterion of intertranslatability for defining a language. His work is cognitively based.

Charles Morris, in his writing on semiotic themes, gives the appearance of basing his work on the contributions of Charles S. Peirce. He divides semiotics into semantics, syntax, and pragmatics, all of which could be pure, descriptive, or applied. Semiotics generates a vocabulary for speaking about signs and represents a step towards the unification of science (cf. Foundations of the Theory of Signs, in *The International Encyclopedia of Unified Science,* Vol. 1, Chicago: Chicago University Press, 1938 and *Writings on the General Theory of Signs,* The Hague/Paris: Mouton, 1971).

Scale is a concept applied in various fields: mathematics, music, architecture, economics, anthropology, and system theory. A standard reference in the definition of the scale of society is Godfrey and Monica Wilson's *The Analysis of*

Social Change Based on Observations in Central Africa, Cambridge: At the University Press, 1968. "By the scale of society we mean the number of people in relation and the intensity of those relations" (p. 25), as well as by "the sense of unity and continuity" (p. 28). The authors also approach the increase in scale: "...maybe an increase in the number of relations through increase in population, exploration, or historical and archaeological discovery; or by an increase in the intensity of the more tenuous relations" (p. 40).

Attractor: a concept defined in the mathematical theory of dynamic systems, also known as chaos theory. A dynamic system evolves towards a value that seems pre-defined and which is called an *attractor.*

James Gleick. *Chaos: the Making of a New Science.* New York: Viking Penguin, 1987.

Peter Bellwood. The Austronesian Dispersal and the Origin of Languages, in *Scientific American,* July, 1991, pp. 88-93.

Colin Renfrew. *Archaeology and Language: The Puzzle of Indo-European Origins.* Cambridge: Cambridge University Press, 1987.

Chapter 2: From Orality to Writing

Peter S. Bellwood. *Prehistory in the Indo-Malaysian Archipelago.* Orlando, FL: Academic Press, 1985.

Andrew Sherrat, Editor. *The Cambridge Encyclopedia of Archaeology.* New York: Crown Publishers, 1980.

Eric A. Havelock. *Schriftlichkeit. Das griechische Alphabet als Kulturelle Revolution.* Weinheim: Verlag VCH, 1990.

Ishwar Chandra Rahi. *World Alphabets, Their Origin and Development.* Allahabad: Bhargava Printing Press, 1977.
Current alphabets vary in number of letters from 12 letters of the Hawaiian alphabet (transliterated to the Roman alphabet by an American missionary) to 45 letters in modern Indian (Devnagari). Most modern alphabets vary from 24 to 33 letters: modern Greek, 24; Italian, 26; Spanish, 27; modern Cambodian, 32; modern Russian Cyrillic, 33. Modern Ethiopian has 26 letters representing consonants, each letter modified for the six vowels in the language, making a total of 182 letters.

Walter J. Ong. *Orality and Literacy. The Technologizing of the World*. London and New York: Methuen, 1982.
The comparison between orality and writing has had a very long history. It is clear that Plato's remarks are made in a different pragmatic framework than that of the present. Ong noticed that: "...language is so overwhelmingly oral that of all the many thousands of languages—possibly tens of thousands—spoken in the course of human history, only around 106 have even been committed to writing to a degree sufficient to have produced literature, and most have never been written at all" (p.7). Ong also refers to pictographic systems, noticing that "Chinese is the largest, most complex, and richest: the K'anglisi dictionary of Chinese in 1716 AD lists 40,545 characters" (p. 8).

Recently, the assumption that Chinese writing is pictographic came under scrutiny. John DeFrancis (*Visible Speech. The Diverse Oneness of Writing Systems*. Honolulu: University of Hawaii Press, 1989, p. 115) categorizes the Chinese system as morphosyllabic.

Harald Haarman. *Universalgeschichte der Schrift*. Frankfurt: Campus Verlag, 1990.

David Diringer. *The Alphabet: A Key to the History of Mankind*. 2nd ed. New York: Philosophical Library, 1953.

—. *The Story of Aleph Beth*. New York/London: Yoseloff, 1960.

—. *Writing. Ancient Peoples and Places*. London: Thames of Hudson, 1962.

Ignace J. Gelb. *A Study of Writing*. Chicago: Chicago University Press, 1963.
Gelb, as well as Ong, assumes that writing developed only around 3500 BCE among the Sumerians in Mesopotamia. Many scripts are on record: Mesopotamian cuneiform, Egyptian hieroglyphs, Minoan or Mycenean Linear B, Indus Valley script, Chinese, Mayan, Aztec, and others.

Ritual: a set form or system of rites, religious or otherwise.

Ralph Merrifield. *The Archaeology of Ritual and Magic*. London: B. T. Ratsford, 1987.

Catherine Bell. *Ritual Theory, Ritual Practice*. New York: Oxford University Press, 1992.

Rite: a ceremonial or formal, solemn act, observance, or procedure in accordance with prescribed rule or custom, as in religious use (cf. *Webster's Unabridged Dictionary*).

Roger Grainger. *The Language of the Rite*. London: Darton, Longman & Todd, 1974.

Mythe-rite-symbole: 21 essais d'anthropologie littéraire sur des textes de Homère. Angers: Presses de l'Université d'Angers, 1984.

Weltanschauung: one's philosophy or conception of the universe and of life (cf. *Webster's Unabridged Dictionary*). A particular philosophy or view of life; a conception of the world (cf. *The Concise Oxford Dictionary of Current English*).

Francesco d'Errico. Paleolithic human calendars: a case of wishful thinking? in *Current Anthropology,* 30, 1989, pp. 117-118.
He regards petroglyphs were looked at as a possible mathematical conception of the cosmos, a numbering or even a calculation system, a rhythmical support for traditional recitation, a generic system of notation.

B.A. Frolov. Numbers in Paleolithic graphic art and the initial stages in the development of mathematics, in *Soviet Anthropology and Archaeology,* 16 (3-4), 1978, pp. 142-166.

A. Marshack. Upper paleolithic notation and symbol, in *Science,* 178: 817-28, 1972.

E.K.A. Tratman. Late Upper Paleolithic Calculator? Gough's Cave, Cheddar, Somerset, in *Proceedings,* University of Bristol, Speleological Society, 14(2), 1976, pp. 115-122.

Iwar Werlen. *Ritual und Sprache: Zum Verhältnis von Sprechen und Handeln in Ritualen.* Tübingen: Narr Verlag, 1984.

Inner clock, or *biological clock,* defines the relation between a biological entity and the time-based phenomena in the environment. As with the so-called circadian cycles (circadian meaning almost the day and night cycle, *circa diem*), rhythms of existence persist even in the absence of external stimuli. The appearance, at least, is that of an inner *clock.*

The notion of genetic code describes a system by which DNA and RNA molecules carry genetic information. Particular sequences of genes in these molecules represent particular sequences of amino acids (the building blocks of proteins) and thereby embody *instructions* for making of different types of proteins. On the same subject, but obviously at a deeper level than a dictionary definition, is James D. Watson's celebrated book, *The Double Helix: a personal account of the discovery of the structure of DNA.* (A new critical edition, including text, commentary, reviews, original papers, edited by Gunther S. Stent). London: Weidenfeld and Nicolson, 1981.

Homeostasis: the tendency towards a relatively stable equilibrium between inter-dependent elements of the human body. Physiological processes leading to body equilibrium are interlocked in dynamic processes.
References to the oral phase of language in Claude Lévi-Strauss:
La Pensée Sauvage (1962). Translated as *The Savage Mind.* Chicago: University of Chicago Press, 1966.
Le Cru et le Cuit (1964) *The Raw and the Cooked.* Trans. John and Doreen Weight-man. New York: Harper and Row, 1970.

Andrew and Susan Sherrat (quoted by Peter S. Bellwood, *Op.cit*): A distinction accepted is that between unvocalized (Hebrew, Arabic) and vocalized alpha-bets (starting with the Greek, in which the vowels are no longer omitted). Some languages use syllabaries, reuniting a consonant and a following vowel (such as in the Japanese *Katakana*: ka, ke, ki, ko, ku). When two different con-ventions are applied, the writing system is hybrid: the Korean language has a very powerful alphabet, *hangul*, but also uses Chinese characters, but pro-nouned in Korean. The hangul system (15th century) expressed, for Koreans, a desire for self-identity.

Plato. *Phaedrus, and The Seventh and Eighth Letters* (translated from the Greek), with an introduction by Walter Hamilton. Harmondsworth: Penguin Press, 1973.
In *Phaedrus*, Socrates, portrayed by Plato, articulates arguments against writ-ing: "it will implant forgetfulness in their souls [of people, M.N.]; they will cease to exercise memory because they rely on that which is written, calling these things to remembrance no longer from within themselves, but by means of external marks; what you have discovered is a recipe [*pharmakon*, a potion; some translate it as recipe] not for memory, but for reminder" (274-278e).

Chapter 3: Orality and Language Today: What Do People Understand When They Understand Language?

Ludwig Wittgenstein. *Tractatus Logico-Philosophicus.* Translated by D.F. Pears and B.F. Guinness. London: Routledge & Kegan Paul, 1961.

Amos Oz refers to self-constitution in language as follows: "...a language is never a 'means' or a 'framework' or a 'vehicle' for culture. It is culture. If you live in Hebrew, if you think, dream, make love in Hebrew, sing in Hebrew in the shower, tell lies in Hebrew, you are 'inside'. [...] If a writer writes in Hebrew, even if he rewrites Dostoyevksy or writes about a Tartar invasion of

South America, Hebrew things will always happen in his stories. Things which are ours and which can only happen with us: certain rhythms, moods, combinations, associations, longings, connotations, atavistic attitudes towards the whole of creation, and so forth," (*Under This Blazing Light*, Cambridge, England: University Press, 1979, p. 189).

J. Lyons. *Semantics*. Cambridge: Cambridge University Press, 1977.
Semantics requires that one "abstract from the user of the language and analyze only the expressions and their designata" (Vol. 1., p.115).

Noam Chomsky. The distinction between competence and performance in *Aspects of the Theory of Syntax*. Cambridge, MA: MIT Press, 1965.
Many scholars noticed the dualism inherent in the Chomskyan theory. Competence is "the speaker-hearer's knowledge of his language;" performance is "the actual use of language in concrete situations" (p.4).

Noam Chomsky started to formulate the idea of the innate constitution of a speaker's competence in the famous article *A review of B.K. Skinner's Verbal Behavior* in *Language*, 35 (1959), an idea he has developed through all his scholarly work. In the review, he considered the alternatives: language is learned (within Skinner's scheme of stimulus-response), or it is somehow innate. In *Aspects of the Theory of Syntax* (Cambridge MA: MIT Press, 1965), *Reflections on Language* (London: Fontana, 1976), and *Rules and Representations* (Oxford: Blackwell, 1980), the thought is constantly refined, though not necessarily more convincing (as his critics noticed).

Roman Jakobson. *Essais de Linguistique Générale*, Paris: Editions de Minuit, 1963. Jakobson refused to ascertain any "private property" in the praxis of language. Everything in the domain of language "is socialized" (p. 33).

Feedback: "The property of being able to adjust future conduct by past performance" (Norbert Wiener, *The Human Use of Human Beings*, p.47).

In 1981, Martin Gardner and Douglas Hoffstaedter shared a column in *Scientific American*, which Hoffstaedter called *Metamagical Themes*. In his first article, he defined self-reference: "It happens every time anyone says 'I' or 'me' or 'word' or 'speak' or 'mouth.' It happens every time a newspaper prints a story about reporters, every time someone writes a book about writing, designs a book about design, makes a movie about movies, or writes an article about self-reference. Many systems have the capability to represent or refer to themselves, or elements of themselves, within the system of their own symbolism" (*Scientific American*, January, 1981, vol. 244:1, pp. 22-23). Hofstaedter finds that self-reference is ubiquitous.

Para-linguistic elements are discussed in detail in Eduard Ataian's book *Jazyk i vneiazykovaia deistvitelnost: opyt ontologicheskovo sravnenia* (Language and paralinguistic activity, an attempt towards an ontological comparison). Erevan: Izd. Erevanskovo Universiteta, 1987.

Luciano Canepari. *L'internazione linguistica e paralinguistica,* Napoli: Liguori, 1985.
Canepari insists on prosodic elements.

The pragmatic aspect of arithmetic is very complex. Many more examples relating to the use of numbers and their place in language can be found in Crump (the examples given are referenced in *The Anthropology of Numbers,* Cambridge/New York: Cambridge University Press, 1990, pp. 34 and 37).

Face-to-face communication, or iteration, attracted the attention of semioticians because codes other than those of language are at work. Adam Kendon, among others, thought that non-verbal communication captures only a small part of the face-to-face situation. The need to integrate non-verbal semiotic entities in the broader context of a communicative situation finally leads to the discovery of non-verbal codes, but also to the question of how much of the language experience is continued where language is not directly used. Useful reading can be found in *Aspects of Non-Verbal Communication* (Walburga Raffler-Engel, Editor), Lisse: Swets & Zeitlinger, 1980.

Steven Pinker. *The Language Instinct: How the Mind Creates Language.* New York: William Morrow & Co, 1994. (His book appeared eight years after this chapter was written.)

As opposed to pictograms, which are iconic representations (based on likeness) of concrete objects, ideograms are composites (sometimes diagrams) of more abstract representations of the same. Chao Yuen Ren (in *Language and Symbolic Systems,* Cambridge: At the University Press, 1968) shows how Chinese ideograms for the sequence 1,2,3 are built up: *yi,* represented as — ; *ér* as 二 ; *san* as 三 .

François Cheng. *Chinese Poetic Writing,* Bloomington: Indiana University Press, 1982. (Translation by D.A. Riggs and J.P. Seaton of *L'écriture poétique chinoise,* Paris: Editions du Seuil, 1977).
"The ideogram for *one,* consisting of a single horizontal stroke, separates (and simultaneously unites) heaven and earth" (p. 5). He goes on to exemplify how, "By combining the basic strokes...one obtains other ideograms." The example given is that of combining [one] and [man, house] to obtain [large, big] and further on [sky, heaven].

On protolanguage: Thomas V. Gamkredlidze and V.V. Ivanov, The Early history of Indo-European Languages, in *Scientific American*, March 1990, pp.110-116.

Reading by machines, i.e., scanning and full text processing (through the use of optical character recognition programs) led some companies to advertise a new literacy. Caere and Hewlett-Packard, sponsors of *Project Literacy US* and *Reading is Fundamental* came up with the headline "We'd Like to Teach the World to Read" to introduce optical character recognition technology (a scanner and software), which makes machine *reading* (of texts, numbers, and graphics) possible. In another ad, Que Software depicts English grammar, punctuation and style books, and the dictionary opposite a red key. The ad states: "RightWriter improves your writing with the touch of a hot key." The program is supposed to check punctuation and grammar. It can also be customized for specific writing styles (inquiry to your insurance agent, answer to the IRS, complaints to City Hall or a consumer protection agency). As a matter of fact, the phenomena referred to are not a matter of advertisement slogans but of a new means for reading and even writing. A program such as VoiceWorks (also known as VoiceRad) was designed for radiologists who routinely review X-rays and generate written reports on their findings. Based on patterns recognized by the physician, the program accepts dictation (from a subset of natural language) and generates the ca. 150-word report without misspelling difficult technical terms. VoiceEm (for Emergency Room doctors) is activated by voice clues (e.g., "auto accident"), displaying a report from which the physician chooses the appropriate words: "(belted/non-belted,) (driver/passenger) in (low/moderate/high) velocity accident struck from (rear/head-on/broadside) and (claims/denies) rolling vehicle." *Canned* medical and legal phrases summarize situations that correspond to circumstances on record. When the doctor states "normal throat," the machine spells out a text that reproduces stereotype descriptions: "throat clear, tongue, pharynx without injections, exudate tonsilar hypertrophy, teeth normal variant." The 1,000-word lexicon can handle the vast majority of emergencies. Those beyond the lexicon usually surpass the competence of the doctor.

The subject of visual mnemonic devices used in the interpretation of Shakespeare's plays is marvelously treated in Frances A. Yates's book *The Art of Memory* (Harmondsworth: Penguin Press, 1966). She discusses Robert Fludd's memory system of theater, from his *Ars memoriae* (1619), based on the Shakespearean Globe Theater. In ancient Greece, orators constructed complex spatial and temporal schemata as aids in rehearsing and properly presenting their speeches.

Chapter 4: The Functioning of Language

Research on memory and language functions in the brain is being carried out at the University of Minnesota, Institute of Child Development. Work is focused on individuals who are about to undergo partial lobotomies to treat intractable epilepsy. The goal is to provide a functional map of the brain.

"History remains a strict discipline only when it stops short, in its description, of the nonverbal past." (Ivan Illich and Barry Sanders, *The Alphabetization of the Popular Mind*, p. 3).

Derrick de Kerkhove, Charles J. Lumsden, Editors. *The Alphabet and the Brain. The Lateralization of Writing*. Berlin/Heidelberg: Springer Verlag, 1988.
In this book, Edward Jones and Chizato Aoki report on the different cognitive processing of phonetic (*Kana*) and logographic (*Kanji*) characters in Japanese (p. 301).

André Martinet. *Le Langage*. Paris: Encyclopédie de la Pléiade, 1939.

Maurice Merleau-Ponty. *Phénoménologie de la perception*. Paris: Gallimard, Bibliothèque des Idées, 1945.

André Leroi-Gourhan. Moyens d'expression graphique, in *Bulletin du Centre de Formation aux Recherches Ethnologiques*, Paris, No. 4, 1956, pp. 1-3.

—. Le geste et la parole, Vol. I and II. Paris: Albin Michel, 1964-1965.

—. Les racines du monde, in *Entretiens avec Claude-Henri Rocquet*. Paris: Pierre Belfond, 1982.

Gordon V. Childe. *The Bronze Age*. New York: Biblio and Tannen, 1969.

John DeFrances. *The Chinese Language: Fact and Fantasy*. 1983.

Marshall McLuhan. *Understanding Media: the Extensions of Man*. New York: McGraw Hill 1964.

In many of his writings, Roland Barthes suggested characteristics of the oral and visual culture. The distinction between the two preoccupied him.

Klingon is a language crafted by Marc Okrand, a linguist, for use by fictional characters. The popularity of *Star Trek* explains how *Klingon* spread around the world.

By eliminating sources of ambiguity and prescribing stylistic rules, controlled languages aim for improved readability. They are easier to maintain and they support computational processing, such as machine translation (cf. Willem-Olaf Huijsen, *Introduction to Controlled Languages*, a Webtext of 1996).

An example of an artificial language of controlled functions and logic is Logics Workbench (LWB), developed at the University of Berne, in Switzerland. The language is available through the WWW.

Drawing: The trace left by a tool drawn along a surface particularly for the purpose of preparing a representation or pattern. Drawing forms the basis of all the arts.

Edward Laning, *The Act of Drawing*, New York: McGraw Hill, 1971.

Design: Balducinni defined design as "a visible demonstration by means of those things which man has first conceived in his mind and pictured in the imagination and which the practised hand can make appear."

"Before Balducinni, its primary sense was drawing." (cf. *Oxford Companion to Art*). More information is given in the references for the chapter devoted to design.

Alan Pipes, *Drawing for 3-Dimensional Design: Concepts, Illustration, Presentation*, London: Thames and Hudson, 1990.

Thomas Crump. *The Anthropology of Numbers*, Cambridge/New York: Cambridge University Press, 1990.

Referring to Yoshio Yano's article of 1973, in Japanese, entitled Communication Life of the Family, Crump writes: "...age, in the absence of other over-reaching criteria, determines hierarchy: this rule applies, for instance, in Japan, and is based on the antithesis of *semmai-kohai*, whose actual meaning is simply senior-junior. The moral basis of the precedence of the elder over the younger (*cho-yo-no-jo*) originated in China, and is reflected in the first instance in the precedence of siblings of the same sex, which is an important structural principle within the family" (p. 69).

On the issue of context affecting language functions, see George Carpenter Barker, *Social Functions of Language in a Mexican-American Community*. Phoenix: The University of Arizona Press, 1972.

Arthur M. Schlesinger, Jr. *The Disuniting of America. Reflections on a Multicultural Society*. New York: W.W. Norton, 1992.

Sneja Gunew and Jan Mahyuddin, Editors. *Beyond the Echo. Multicultural Women's Writing*. St. Lucia: University of Queensland Press, 1988.

Stephen J. Rimmer. *The Cost of Multiculturalism*. Belconnen, ACT: S.J.Rimmer, 1991.

Chapter 5: Language and Logic

A.E. Van Vogt. *The World of Null-A.* 1945. The novel was inspired by a work of Alfred Korzybski, *Science and Sanity. An Introduction to Non-Aristotelian Systems and General Semantics* (1933).

Walter J. Ong seems convinced that "...formal logic is the invention of Greek culture after it had interiorized the technology of alphabetic writing, and so made a permanent part of its noetic resources the kind of thinking that alphabetic writing made possible" (*Op. cit.,* p. 52). He reports on A.R. Luria's book, *Cognitive Development: Its Cultural and Social Foundations* (1976). After experiments designed to define how illiterate subjects react to formal logical procedures (in particular, deductive reasoning), Luria seems to conclude that no one actually operates in formally stated syllogisms.

Lucien Lévy-Bruhl. *Les fonctions mentales dans les sociétés inférieures.* Paris: Alcan, 1910. (Translated as *How Natives Think* by Lilian A. Clave, London: Allen & Unwin, 1926.)
Lévy-Bruhl reconnects to the notion of participation that originates in Plato's philosophy and applies it to fit the so-called pre-logic mentality.

Anton Dumitru. *History of Logic.* 4 vols. Turnbridge Wells, Kent: Abacus Press, 1977.
In exemplifying the law of participation, Dumitru gives the following example: "In Central Brazil there lives an Indian tribe called Bororó. In the same region we also find a species of parrots called Arara. The explorers were surprised to find that the Indians claimed to be Arara themselves. [...] Put differently, a member of the Bororó tribe claims to be what he actually is and also something else just as real, namely an Arara parrot" (vol. 1, pp. 5-6).

René Descartes (1596-1650), under his Latinized name Renatus Cartesius, sees logic as "teaching us to conduct well our reason in order to discover the truths we ignore" ("qui apprend à bien conduire sa raison pour découvrir les vérités qu'on ignore"). For Descartes, mathematics is the general method of science. *Oeuvres de Descartes.* Publiées par Charles Adam and Paul Tannery, Eds. 11 vols. Nouvelle présentation en co-édition avec le Centre National de la Recherche Scientifique. Paris: Vrin. 1965-1973 (reprint of the 1897-1909 edition). In English, the rendition by Elizabeth S. Haldane and George R.T. Ross was published in London, Cambridge University Press, 1967.

"Logic is the art of directing reason aright, in obtaining the knowledge of things, for the instruction both of ourselves and of others. It consists of the reflections which have been made on the four principal operations of the mind: conceiving, judging, reasoning, and disposing" (*Port Royal Logic*, Introduction).

John Locke (1632-1704) was looking for simple logical elements and rules to compound them. Certainty is not the result of syllogistic inference. "Syllogism is at best nothing but the art of bringing to light, in debate, the little knowledge we have, without adding any other to it." *An Essay Concerning Human Understanding* (London, 1690) sets an empirical, psychologically based perspective of logic.

George Boole (1815-1864) conceived of a logical calculus, in *An Investigation of the Laws of Thought on which are founded the Mathematical Theories of Logic and Probabilities* (London, 1854), which eventually became the basis for digital computation.

Fung-Yu-lan. *Précis d'histoire de la philosophie chinoise.* Paris: Plon, 1952.
"It is very difficult for somebody to understand fully Chinese philosophical works, if he is not able to read the original text. The language is indeed a barrier. Due to the suggestive character of Chinese philosophical writings, this barrier gets more daunting, these writings being almost untranslatable. In translation, they lose their power of suggestion. In fact, a translation is nothing but an interpretation" (p. 35).

Chang-tzu. cf. Anton Dumitru, *Op.cit.*, p. 13.

Kung-Fu-tzu (551-479, BCE), whose Latinized name is Confucius, expressed the logical requirement to "rectify the names." This translates as the need to put things in agreement with one another by correct designations. "The main thing is the rectification of names (*cheng ming*) [...] If the names are not rectified, the words cannot fit; if the words do not fit, the affairs [in the world] will not be successful. If these affairs are not successful, neither rites nor music can flourish. If rites and music do not flourish, punishments cannot be just. If they are not just, people do not know how to act." The conclusion is, "The wise man should never show levity in using words;" (Lun-yu, cf. Wing-Tsit-chan, *A Source Book in Chinese Philosophy*, Princeton: Princeton University Press, 1963).

Aristotle (384-322 BCE). Logic in his view is thinking about thinking. The whole logical theory of the syllogism is presented in the *Analytica Priora*. The *Analytica Posteriora* gives the structure of deductive sciences. The notion of *political animal* is part of the Aristotelian political system (cf. *Politics*).

Takeo Doi. *Amae no kozo.* Tokyo: Kobundo. 1971. (Translated as *The Anatomy of Dependence* by John Bester, Tokyo/New York: Kodansho International and Harper & Row, 1973.)

Vedic texts, the collective name for Veda, defined as the science (the root of the word seems to be similar to the Greek for idea, or the Latin *videre*, to see) of direct intuition, convey the experience of the Rsis, ancient sages who had a direct perception of things. The writings that make up Veda are: *Rig Veda*, invocatory science; *Yajur Veda*, sacrificial; *Sama Veda*, melody; *Atharva Veda*, of incantation. In each Veda, there is a section on the origin of the ritual, on the meaning, and on the esoteric aspect.

Mircea Eliade. *Yoga*. Paris: Gallimard, 1960.
"India has endeavoured...to analyze the various conditioning factors of the human being. ...this was done not in order to reach a precise and coherent explanation of the human being, as did, for instance, Europe of the 19th century,... but in order to know how far the zones of the human being go and see whether there is anything else beyond these conditionings" (p. 10).

The logic of action, as part of logical theory, deals with various aspects of defining what leads to reaching a goal and what are the factors involved in defining the goal and testing the result.

Raymond Bondon, in *Logique du social* (translated by David and Gillian Silverman as *The Logic of Social Action: An Introduction to Sociological Analysis*, London/Boston: Routledge & Kegan Paul, 1981), gives the subject a sociological perspective. Cornel Popa, in *Praxiologie si Logica* (*Praxiology and Logic*, Bucharest: Editura Academiei, 1984) deals with social action. Authors such as D. Lewis, A. Salomaa, B.F. Chelas, R.C. Jeffrey, and Jaako Hintikka, whose contributions were reunited in a volume celebrating Stig Kanger, pay attention to semantic aspects and conditional values in many-valued propositional logics (cf. *Logical Theory and Semantic Analysis*, edited by Soren Stenlund, Dordrecht/Boston: Reidel, 1974).

The term *culture* originates in human practical experiences related to nature: cultivating land, breeding and rearing animals. By extension, culture (i.e., cultivating and breeding the mind) leads to the noun describing a way of life. In the late 18th century, Herder used the plural *cultures* to distinguish what was to become civilization. In 1883, Dilthey made the distinction between cultural sciences (*Geisteswissenschaften*, addressing the mind) and natural sciences. The objects of cultural sciences are man-made and the goal is understanding (*Verstehen*). For more information on the emergence and use of the term culture, see A.L. Kroeber and C. Kluckholm, Culture: a Critical Review of Concepts and Definitions, in *Peabody Museum Papers*, XLVII, Harvard University Press, 1952.

Ramon Lull (Raymundus Lullus, 1235-1315) suggested a mechanical system of combining ideas, an *alphabet* (or repertory) and a *calculus* for generating all possible judgments. Called *Ars Magna* (The Great Art), his work attracted both ironic remarks and enthusiastic followers.

Athanasius Kircher, in *Polygraphia nova et universalis ex combinatoria arte detecta* (*New and universal polygraphy discovered from the arts of combination*, Rome, 1663), tried to introduce an arithmetic of logic.

George Delgarus, in *Ars signorum* (*The art of signs*, London, 1661), suggested a universal language of signs.

John Wilkins dealt with it as a *secret language* (1641, *Mercury, or the Secret and Swift Messenger*, and 1668, *An Essay Towards a Real Character and a Philosophical Language*).

Lotfi Zadeh introduced *fuzzy logic:* a logic of vague though quantified relations among entities and of non-clear-cut definitions (What is young? tall? bold? good?).

Felix Hausdorf/Paul Mongré. *Sant 'Ilario. Gedanken aus der Landschaft Zarathustras.* 1897. p. 7.

W.B. Gallie (Peirce's Pragmatism, in *Peirce and Pragmatism,* Harmondsworth: Penguin Books, 1952) noticed that Peirce, "in the *Pragmaticism Papers,* approaches the subject of vagueness from a number of different sides. He claims, for instance, that all our most deeply grounded and in practice indubitable beliefs are essentially vague" (cf. Peirce, 5.446). According to Peirce, vagueness is a question of representation, not a peculiarity of the object of the representation. He goes on to specify that the source of vagueness is the relation between the sign and the interpretant ("Indefiniteness in depth may be termed vagueness," cf. MSS 283, 141, 138-9). Additional commentary in Nadin, The Logic of Vagueness and the Category of Synechism, in *The Monist,* Special Issue: The Relevance of Charles Peirce, 63:3, July, 1980, pp. 351-363.

Richard Dawkins. *The Selfish Gene.* New York: Oxford University Press, 1976.

—. *The Extended Phenotype.* New York: Oxford University Press, 1982.

Elan Moritz, of the Institute for Memetic Research, provides the historic and methodological background to the subject in *Introduction to Memetic Science.*

E.O. Wilson. *Sociobiology: The New Synthesis.* Cambridge: Belknap/Harvard University Press, 1975.

Mihai Nadin. *Mind—Anticipation and Chaos* (from the series *Milestones in Thought and Discovery*). Stuttgart/Zurich: Belser Presse. 1991.
"Minds exist only in relation to other minds" p. 4. The book was based on a lecture delivered in January 1989 at Ohio State University.

BOOK III

Chapter 1: Language as Mediating Mechanism

Richard Dawkins. *The Selfish Gene*. New York: Oxford University Press, 1976.

—. *The Extended Phenotype*. New York: Oxford University Press, 1982.

Elan Moritz, of the Institute for Memetic Research, provides the historic and methodological background to the subject in *Introduction to Memetic Science.*, a Webtext.

E.O. Wilson. *Sociobiology:* The New Synthesis. Cambridge: Belknap/Harvard University Press, 1975.

Mediation: a powerful philosophic notion reflecting interest in the many ways in which something different from what we want to know, understand, do, or act upon intercedes between the object of our interest, action, or thought.

G.W. Hegel. *Hegels Werke*, vollständige Ausgabe durch einen Verein von Freunden des Verewigten, vols. I-XIX. Berlin. 1832-1845, 1887
The dialectics of mediation includes a non-mediated mode, generated by the suppression of mediation, leading to the *Thing-in-itself:* "Dieses Sein ist daher eine Sache, die an und für sich ist die Objektivität" (vol. V, p. 171) (This being is, henceforth, a thing in itself and for itself, it is objectivity.) Everything else is mediated.
In all post-Hegelian developments—right wing (Hinrichs, Goeschel, Gabler), left-wing (Ruge, Feuerback, Strauss), center (Bauer, Köstlin, Erdmann)— mediation is a major concept.

Emile Durkheim. *De la Division du Travail Sociale*. 9th ed. Paris: Presses Univérsitaires de France, 1973. (Translated as *The Division of Labor in Society* by W.D. Halls. New York: Free Press, 1984).

Michel Freyssenet. *La Division Capitaliste du Travail.* Paris: Savelli, 1977.

Elliot A. Krause. *Division of Labor, A Political Perspective.* Westport CT: Greenwood Press, 1982.

Gunnar Tornqvist, Editor. *Division of Labour, Specialization, and Technical Change: Global, Regional, and Workplace Level.* Malmo, Sweden: Liber, 1986.

Marcella Corsi. *Division of Labour, Technical Change, and Economic Growth.* Aldershot, Hants, U.K.: Avebury/Brookfield VT: Gower Publishing Co., 1991.

Leonard Bloomfield. *Language.* 1933. rpt. New York: Holt, Rinehart & Winston. 1964.
In this work, the author maintains that the division of labor, and with it the whole working of human society, is due to language.

Charles Sanders Peirce. "Anything that determines something else (its interpretant) to refer to an object to which itself refers (its object) in the same way, the interpretant becoming in turn a sign, and so on *ad infinitum*" (2.303). "Something which stands to somebody in some respect or capacity" (2.228). Other sign definitions have been given: "In the language, reciprocal presuppositions are established between the expression (signifier) and the expressed (signified). The sign is the manifestation of these presuppositions," (A. J. Greimas and J. Courtés, *Semiotics and Language. An Analytical Dictionary,* Bloomington: Indiana University Press, 1983, p. 296; translation of *Sémiotique. Dictionnaire Raisonné de la Théorie du Langage,* Paris: Classique Hachette, 1979).
According to L. Hjelmslev, the sign is the result of semiosis taking place at the time of the language act. Benveniste considers that the sign is representative of another thing, which it evokes as a substitute.

Herbert Marcuse. *The One-Dimensional Man. Studies in the Ideology of Advanced Industrial Society.* Boston: Beacon Press, 1964.

Plato. *Phaedrus,* and The Seventh and Eighth Letters (translated from the Greek), with an introduction by Walter Hamilton. Harmondsworth: Penguin Press, 1973.

Regarding cave paintings, see:

Mihai Nadin. Understanding prehistoric images in the post-historic age: a cognitive project, in *Semiotica*, 100:2-4, 1994. Berlin, New York: Mouton de Gruyter. pp. 387-405.

B. Campbell. *Humankind Emerging.* Toronto: Little, Brown & Co., 1985.

W. Davis. The origins of image making, in *Current Anthropology*, 27 (1986). pp. 193-215.

Luigi Bottin. *Contributi della Tradizione Greco-Latina e Arabo-Latina al Testo della Rhetorica di Aristotele*. Padova: Antenore, 1977.

Marc Fumaroli. *L'Age de l'Éloquence: Rhétorique et 'Res Literaria' de la Renaissance au Seuil de l'Époque Classique*. Geneva: Droz and Paris: Champion, 1980.

William M.A. Grimaldi. *Aristotle, Rhetoric: A Commentary*. New York: Fordham University Press, 1980-1988.

Rhetoric is generally seen as the ability to persuade. Using many kinds of signs (language, images, sounds, gestures, etc.), rhetoric is connected to the pragmatic context. In ancient Greece and Rome, as well as in China and India, rhetoric was considered an art and practiced for its own sake. Some consider rhetoric as one of the sources of semiotics (together with logic, hermeneutics, and the philosophy of language (cf. Tzvetan Todorov, *Théorie du Symbole*, Paris: Ed. du Seuil, 1977). Gestures are a part of rhetoric. Quintillian, in *De institutione oratoria*, dealt with the *lex gestus* (law of gesture). In the Renaissance, the code of gesture was studied in detail. In our days of illiterate rhetoric based on stereotypes and increasingly compressed messages, gestures gain a special status indicative of the power of non-literacy-based ceremonies. The rhetoric of advertisement pervades human interaction.

George Boole (1815-1864) conceived of a logical calculus, in *An Investigation of the Laws of Thought on which are founded the Mathematical Theories of Logic and Probabilities* (London, 1854), which eventually became the basis for digital computation.

Howard Rheingold. *Virtual Reality*. New York: Summit Books, 1991.
Rheingold offers a description that can substitute for a definition: "Imagine a wraparound television with programs, including three-dimensional sound, and solid objects that you can pick up and manipulate, even feel with your fingers and hands. Imagine immersing yourself in an artificial world and actively exploring it, rather than peering at it from a fixed perspective through a flat screen in a movie theater, on a television set, or on a computer display. Imagine that you are the creator as well as the consumer of your artificial experience, with the power to use a gesture or a word to remold the world you see and hear and feel" (p. 16).

In an Internet interview with Rheingold, Sherry Turkel points out that computers and networks are objects-to-think-with for a networked era. She predicts, "I believe that against all odds and against most current expectations, we are going to see a rebirth of psychoanalytic thinking" (cf. *Brainstorms*, http://www.well.com, 1996).

Chapter 2: Literacy, Language, and Market

Reference is made to the works of Margaret Wheatley (*Management and the New Science*); Michael Rothschild (*Bionomics*); Bernardo Huberman (*Dynamics of Collective Actions and Learning in Multi-agent Organizations*); Robert Axtel and Joshua Epstein (creators of *Sugarscape*, a model of trade); and Axel Leijonhufvud (*Multi-agent Systems*), all published as Webtexts.

Transactions as extensions of human biology evince the complex nature of human interactions. Maturana and Varela indirectly refer to human transactions: "Coherence and harmony in relations and interactions between the members of a human social system are due to the coherence and harmony of their growth in it, in an ongoing social learning which their own social (linguistic) operation defines and which is possible thanks to the genetic and ontogenetic processes that permit structural plasticity of the members" (*Op. cit.*, p.199). They diagram the shift from minimum autonomy of components (characteristic of organisms) to maximum autonomy of components (characteristic of human societies).

A Walk Through Wall Street, in *US News and World Report*, Nov. 16, 1987, pp. 64-65. One from among many reminiscences by Martin Mayer, author of *Madison Avenue, Wall Street, Men and Money.*
"Wall Street as price setter for the country dealt with much more than pieces of paper. Commodities markets proliferated. The fish market was on the East River at Fulton; the meat market on the Hudson just to the north.... The 'physicals' of all commodities markets were present...there were cotton sacks in the warehouse of the Cotton Exchange, coffee bags stored here for delivery against the contracts at the Sugar and Coffee Exchange on Hanover Square and often a smell of roasting coffee.
"In the 1950's, this was a male world—women were not allowed to work on the floor of the Stock Exchange, let alone become members. The old-timers explained with great sincerity that there was no ladies room."
The report points out that today Wall Street "sees less of the real world outside, depends more on abstract information processed through data machinery and more than ever responds to forces far from its borders."

Zoon semiotikon, the semiotic animal, labeled by Paul Mongré (also known as Felix Hausdorf).

Charles S. Peirce gave the following definitions:
Representamen: a Sign is a Representamen of which some interpretant is a cognition of a mind (2.242).
Object: the Mediate object is the object outside the Sign; ...the sign must indicate it by a hint (*Letter to Lady Welby*, December 23, 1908).
Interpretant: the effect that the sign would produce upon any mind (*Letter to Lady Welby*, March 14, 1909).

In reference to the symbolic nature of market transactions, another Peircean definition is useful: "Symbols grow. They come into being by development out of other signs.... We think only in signs.... If a man makes a new symbol, it is by thoughts involving concepts" (2.307).
The pragmatic thought is, nevertheless, inherent in any sign process. Markets embody sign processes in the pragmatic field.

Winograd and Flores state bluntly "A business (like any other organization) is constituted as a network of recurrent conversations" (*Op. cit.*, p. 168).

Alfred D. Chandler, Jr. (with the assistance of Takashi Hikino) *Scale and Scope. The Dynamics of Industrial Capitalism.* Cambridge MA/London, England: The Belknap Press of Harvard University Press, 1990.
"...the modern industrial Enterprise...has more than a production function." (p. 14). Chandler further notes that "expanded output by a change in capital-labor ratios is brought about by economies of scale which incorporate economies of speed.... Wholesalers and retailers expand to exploit economies of scale" (p. 21).

James Gordley. *The Philosophical Origins of Modern Contract Doctrine.* New York: Oxford University Press, 1991.

Mariadele Manca Masciadri. *I Contratti di Baliatico*, 2 vols. Milan: (s.n.), 1984.

John H. Pryor. *Business Contracts of Medieval Provence. Selected Notulae from the Cartulary of Girard Amalric of Marseilles, 1248.* Toronto: Pontifical Institute of Medieval Studies, 1981.

ECU: In 1979, the process of European unification led to the creation of the European Monetary System (EMS), with its coin being the European Currency Unit (ECU) and the Exchange Rate Mechanism (ERM). As a *basket* of European currencies, the ECU serves as a reserve currency in Europe and probably beyond. It is not the currency of choice for international transactions, and as of the Maastricht negotiations, which affirmed the need for a

Community currency, the ECU was not adopted for this purpose. Although predominant weight in the basket (over 30%) is given to the German mark, the ECU is designed on the assumption that it is quite improbable that a certain currency will move in the same direction against all others. Therefore, exchange rates are statistically stabilized.

Michael Rothschild. *Bionomics: Economy as Ecosystem.* Webtext, 1990.

Robert L. Heilbroner. The Demand for the Supply Side, in *The New York Review of Books,* June 11, 1981, p.40.
He asks rhetorically: "How else should one identify a force that debases language, drains thought, and undoes dignity? If the barrage of advertising, unchanged in its tone and texture, were devoted to some other purpose—say the exaltation of the public sector—it would be recognized in a moment for the corrosive element that it is. But as the voice of the private sector it escapes this startled notice. I mention it only to point out that a deep source of moral decay for capitalism arises from its own doings, not from that of its governing institutions."

Chapter 3: Language and Work

Noam Chomsky started to formulate the idea of the innate constitution of a speaker's competence in the famous "A review of B.F. Skinner's Verbal Behavior" in *Language,* 35 (1959), and continued through his entire scholarly work. In the review, he considered the alternatives: language is learned (within Skinner's scheme of stimulus-response), or it is somehow innate. In *Aspects of the Theory of Syntax* (Cambridge MA: MIT Press, 1965), *Reflections on Language* (London: Fontana, 1976), and *Rules and Representations* (Oxford: Blackwell, 1980), the thought is constantly refined, though not necessarily made more convincing (as his critics point out).
Roman Jakobson refused to ascertain any "private property" in the praxis of language. Everything in the domain of language "is socialized" (*Essais de Linguistique Générale,* Paris: Editions de Minuit, 1963, p. 33.)

According to Charles S. Peirce, semiosis is the "triadic nature of the operations of a sign process" (Peirce, 1931-66:5.484); cf. *Encyclopedic dictionary of semiotics* (Thomas A Sebeok, general editor). Berlin/New York: Mouton de Gruyter, 1986.

Karl Marx. The power of money in bourgeois society, in *Economic and Philosophic Manuscripts of 1844*. Trans. Martin Milligan). Moscow: Progress Publishers, 1974.
"Money is the universal mediator" (p. 119). Some translations read: "Silver is the 'universal coin....'"

Ferruccio Rossi-Landi devoted a great amount of his research to a semiotics based on Marxist principles. See *Language as Work and Trade. A Semiotic Homology for Linguistics and Economics*. South Hadley MA: Bergin & Garvey Publishers, Inc., 1983. (This is a translation by Martha Adams, et al, of *Il linguaggio come lavoro e come mercato*, published by Bompiani in Milan, 1968.)

Henry George (1839-1897). British economist. *Progress and Poverty: Inquiry into the cause of industrial depressions and of increase of want with increase of wealth*. New York: Robert Schalkenbach Foundation, 1979.
"Here is the difference between the animal and the man. Both the jayhawk and the man eat chickens, but the more jayhawks, the fewer chickens, while the more men the more chickens. Both the seal and the man eat salmon, but when a seal takes a salmon there is a salmon less and were seals to increase past a certain point salmon must diminish; while by placing the spawn of the salmon under favorable conditions man can so increase the number of salmon as more than to make up for all he may take, and thus, no matter how much men may increase, their increase need never outrun the supply of salmon" (Book II, chapter 3, p. 131).

Discovery of oil in the USA took place in Titusville, Pennsylvania in 1859 and was followed by building many oil wells (*Collier's Encyclopedia*, Vol. 18, 1989.)

Keith Branigan. *The Tombs of Mesara: a Study of Funerary Architecture and Ritual in Southern Crete, 2800-1700 B.C.* London: Duckworth, 1970.
Tombs contained a range of artifacts: clay cups, pots, vases, beads, and figures, as well as tools and razors of bronze and obsidian, reassured personal artifacts, and jewelry of gold (cf. pp. 56-85). Minoan burial culture, not unlike others, involved the burial of precious objects to accompany the deceased.

Harald Haarman. *Universalgeschichte der Schrift*. Frankfurt/Main: Campus Verlag, 1990.
Haarman mentions that Phoenician traders used notation in their commerce. He discusses many other examples of notation systems involved in trade and the role such notation had in the stabilization of language and stimulation of commerce.

Geoffrey Sampson. *Writing Systems*. London: Hutchinson, 1985.

"Archaic Sumerian was used for administrative purposes, in particular for keeping brief records of such matters as tax payments or distribution of rations" (p. 47).

J.David Bolter. *Turing's Man: Western Culture in the Computer Age*. Chapel Hill: University of North Carolina Press, 1984.
"Very often a device will take on a metaphoric significance and be compared in art and philosophy to some part of the animate or inanimate world. [...] Today, the computer is constantly serving as a metaphor for the human mind or brain.... [...] A defining technology develops links, metaphorical or otherwise, with a culture's science, philosophy, or literature; it is always available to serve as a metaphor, example, model or symbol" (p. 11).

Edsger Dijkstra. On the Cruelty of Really Teaching Computer Science, in *Communications of the ACM* 32 (12), 1989, pp. 1398-1404.
"Computers represent a radical novelty in our history" (p. 1398).
"The first radical novelty is a direct consequence of the raw power of today's computing equipment" (p. 1399).

Chapter 4: Literacy and Education

Will Seymour Monroe. *Comenius and the Beginnings of Educational Reform*. New York: Arno Press, 1971, (originally printed in 1900).

Adolphe Erich Meyer. *Education in Modern Times. Up from Rousseau*. New York: Avon Press, 1930.

Linus Pierpont Brockett. *History and Progress of Education from the Earliest Times to the Present*. New York: A.S. Barnes, 1860, (Originally signed "Philobiblius," with an introduction by Henry Barnard.)

James Bowen. *A History of Western Education*. 3 Vols. London: Methuen, 1972-1981.

Pierre Riché. *Education et culture dans l'occident barbare 6-8 siècles*. Paris: Editions du Seuil, 1962.

Bernard Bischoff. Elementärunterricht und *probationes pennae* in der ersten Hälfte des Mittelalters, in *Mittelalterliche Studien* I, 1966, pp. 74-87.

James Nehring. *The Schools We Have. The Schools We Want. An American Teacher on the Frontline*. San Francisco: Jossey-Bass, 1992.

Irenée Henri Marron. *A History of Education in Antiquity.* New York: Sheed and Ward, 1956.

Jacques Barzun. *The Forgotten Conditions of Teaching and Learning* (Morris Philipson, Editor). Chicago: The University of Chicago Press, 1991.
The review mentioned was written by David Alexander, Begin Here, in *The New York Review of Books,* April 21, 1991, p. 16.

Polis (Greek) signifies settled communities that eventually evolved into cities.

The City-State in Five Cultures. Edited with an introduction by Robert Griffeth and Carol G. Thomas. Santa Barbara CA: ABC-Clio, 1981.

J.N. Coldstream. *The Formation of the Greek Polis: Aristotle and Archaeology.* Opladen: Westdeutscher Verlag, 1984.

Individual and Community: The Rise of the Polis, 800-500 BC. New York: Oxford University Press, 1986.

Will Durant. *The Story of Civilization.* Vol. 4, *The Age of Faith.* New York: Simon and Schuster, 1950.
In 825, the University of Pavia was founded as a school of law. The University of Bologna was founded in 1088 by Irnevius, also for the teaching of law. Students from all over Latin Europe came to study there. Around 1103, the University of Paris was founded; by the middle of the 13th century, four faculties had developed: theology, canon law, medicine and the seven arts. (The seven liberal arts were comprised of the *trivium*—grammar, rhetoric, and logic—and the *quadrivium*—arithmetic, geometry, music, and astronomy.) Some time in the 12th century, a *studium generale* or university was established at Oxford (pp 916-921).
The name *university* derives from the fact that the essences or universals were taught (cf. *Encyclopedia Britannica*, 15th Edition, *Micropedia*, Vol. 12, 1990).

Logos: (noun, from the Greek, from the verb *lego:* "I say"): word, speech, argument, explanation, doctrine, principle, reason; signified word or speech.

Ratio (from the Latin "to think"): reason, rationale; signified measure or proportion.

Some of the work linking the early knowledge of the Latin and Greek heritage of European thought, especially that part shut off to Christendom in Moorish Jerusalem, Alexandria, Cairo, Tunis, Sicily, and Spain, was transmitted by the Jews, who translated works in Arabic to Latin. The Moslems preserved the texts of Euclid and works dealing with alchemy and chemistry. In 1165, Gerald of Cremona studied Arabic in Spain in order to translate works of Aristotle (*Posterior Analysis, On the Heavens and the Earth,* among others), Euclid (*Elements, Data*), Archimedes, Apollonius of Perga, Galen, works of Greek astronomy and Greco-Arabic physics, 11 books of Arabic medicine and 14 works of Arabic astronomy and mathematics from the Arabic to Latin. Beginning 1217, Michael Scot translated a number of Aristotle's works from the Arabic to Latin (cf. Will Durant, *Op. cit.,* pp. 910-913).

Galileo Galilei. *Discorsi e dimostrazioni matematiche* (*Two New Sciences: Including Centers of Gravity and Force of Percussion,* translated, with a new introduction and notes, by Stillman Drake) Toronto: Wall & Thompson, 1989.

—. *Galileo's Early Notebooks. The Physical Questions* (translated from the Latin, with historical and paleographical commentary, by William A. Wallace). Notre Dame IN: University of Notre Dame Press, 1977.

Sir Isaac Newton (1642-1727). In 1687, he published *Philosophiae Principia Mathematica,* in which he offered explanations for the movement of planets. In this work, the abstraction of force (of attraction) is constituted and a postulate is formulated: every particle of matter in the universe attracts every other with a force whose magnitude depends directly upon the product of their masses and inversely upon the square of the distance between the two.

Albert Einstein (1879-1955) published in 1916 his contribution as *Die Grundlagen der allgemeinen Relativitätstheorie,* in which he referred to the attraction of massive objects. The cosmic reality of such objects and of huge distances and high velocities is quite different from the mechanical universe under consideration by Galileo and Newton. Movement of planets cause the curving of space. Einstein's theory shows that the curvature of space time evolves dynamically. Newton's theory turned out to be an approximation of Einstein's more encompassing model.

John Searle. The Storm Over the University, in *The New York Review of Books,* 37:19, December 6, 1990, pp. 34-42.

Mathematization: the use of mathematical methods or concepts in particular sciences or in the humanities. The conception of mathematics as a model for the sciences as well as for the humanities has been repeatedly expressed throughout history. In some cases, mathematization represents the search for abstract structures. Today mathematization is often taken to mean modeling on computer programs.

Académie Française: French library academy established by Cardinal Richelieu in 1634. Its original purpose was to maintain standards of literary taste and to establish the literary language. Membership is limited to 40 (*Encyclopedia Britannica*, 15th Edition, Micropedia, Vol. 1, 1990. p. 50).

Alan Bloom. *The Closing of the American Mind. How Education Has Failed Democracy and Impoverished the Souls of Today's Students.* New York: Simon and Schuster, 1987
"Those despised millionaires who set up a university in the midst of a city that seems devoted only to what they had neglected, whether it was out of a sense of what they themselves had issued, or out of bad conscience about what their lives were exclusively devoted to, or to satisfy the vanity of having their names attached to the enterprise" (p. 244).

Bart Simpson, the main character of the animated cartoon series of the same name, created by Matt Groening. Bart was first sketched in 1987; the television series first aired in the winter of 1990.

Terry Winograd and Fernando Flores. *Understanding Computers and Cognition. A New Foundation for Design.* Norwood NJ: Ablex Publishing Corporation, 1986.
"Organizations exist as networks of directives and commissives. Directives include orders, requests, consultations, and offers; commissives include promises, acceptances, and rejections" (p. 157).
They state also: "In fulfilling an organization's external commitments, its personnel are involved in a network of conversations" (p. 158).

Ludwig Wittgenstein. *Philosophical Investigations* (Translation by G.E.M. Anscombe of *Philosophische Untersuchungen*). Oxford: Basil Blackwell, 1984 (reprint of the 1968 edition.)

If a multiple choice test in World History (given in June, 1992 at Stuyvesant High School in New York City) asks whether the Holocaust is an Italian revolutionary movement, and if *Mein Kampf* was Hitler's bodyguard or his summer retreat, why should anyone be surprised that American students show no better choices than those they are supposed to choose from?

Steve Waite. Interview with Bill Melton, *Journal of Bionomics,* July 1996.

BOOK IV

Chapter 1: Language and the Visual

Fred R. Barnard. One look is worth a thousand words, in *Printer's Ink*, 1921.

Gutenberg (ca. 1400-ca.1468). Member of the Goldsmiths' Guild in Mainz, he invented the printing press in 1438. The famous *Mazarin Bible* was published in 1455. His backers (who today would be called "venture capitalists") printed on the colophon of the first published book: "This work is fashioned and by diligence finished for the service of God, not with ink of quill nor brazen reed, but with a certain invention of printing and reproduction by John Fust, citizen of Mainz, and Peter Schoeffer of Gernsheim, 17 December 1465 A.D." Gutenberg's name simply disappeared.

In China, Pi Shong had invented movable type some 400 years earlier (ca. 1041-1048). The document acknowledging this invention gives the following description: "He took sticky clay and cut it into characters as thin as the edge of a coin" (Robert K.G. Temple, *China. Land of Discovery*, London: Patrick Stephens, 1986).

Photography was invented by Joseph Nicéphore Niépce while he was trying to transfer drawings (a result of his interest in lithography). He used a *camera obscura*, as many tried down through history: from Aristotle to the 10th-century Arabian scholar Alhazen, to artists of the Renaissance, Thomas Wedgewood in 19th-century England, among others. Rays of light passing through a pinhole form images of what is in front of the device. Niépce used a sheet of pewter covered with the so-called bitumen of Judea, a substance that hardens when exposed to light. The exposure time (in the range of eight hours) and the expectation of intense light made his method (which he called heliography, i.e., writing with light) quite impractical. Louis-Jacques Maudé Daguerre, in touch with Niépce, perfected the process by using a highly polished silver surface plated on a copper sheet. This surface was sensitized to light by treating it with vapors of iodine. After being exposed, the light sensitive compound, silver iodide, had to be processed with mercury. The result was the well known daguerreotype, images of extreme detail on highly polished metal. Only three weeks after Daguerre announced his technique (in the last week of January, 1839), William Henri Fox Talbot announced (prematurely) his method, called Calotype (from the Greek *kalos*, beautiful, and *typos*, impression). He actually invented photographs on paper and the procedure known today as contact printing. From here on, the process accelerated, and only 35 years later (1870), gelatin emulsion and role film were born.

Paul Jay. *Niépce, Genèse d'une Invention.* Châlon-sur-Saône: Société des Amis du Musée Nicéphore Niépce, 1988.

Gail Buckland. *Fox Talbot and the Invention of Photography.* Boston: D. R. Godine, 1980.

Photography: Discovery and Invention. (Papers delivered at a symposium celebrating the invention of photography). Malibu CA: J. Paul Getty Museum, 1990.

Samuel Morse, referring to photography, in respect to the daguerreotype of 1840, wrote: "...painted by nature's self with a minuteness of detail, which the pencil of light in her hands alone can trace...they cannot be called copies of nature, but portions of nature herself."

Peter C. Wensberg. *Land's Polaroid. A Company and the Man Who Invented It.* Boston: Houghton Mifflin, 1987.

Ansel Easton Adams. *Polaroid Land Photography.* 1st edition, revised. Boston: New York Graphic Society, 1978.

The word *Kodak* was coined in 1888 by George Eastman; it means nothing: "as meaningless as a child's first 'goo'", but was interpreted as "snaps like a camera shutter in your face," "terse, abrupt to the point of rudeness, literally bitten off by firm unyielding consonants at both ends."

Mihai Nadin. *The Digital Eye/I.* Lecture presented at the symposium Photography: The Second Revolution, Columbus, Ohio, April 21-23, 1988.
An updated version of the text was printed in *Living,* (Cologne, Germany), vol. 8, no. 2, 1996, pp. 35-36.

Motion pictures started with pseudo-motion afforded by stereographic photographs and continued in the sequence of photographs shot by the father of cinematography, Eadweard Muybridge (his motion studies of a horse were published in 1878). The celluloid roll film (1887) and William Dickson's kinetograph (patented in 1893) were steps toward what became the commercially successful cinematography. Contributions in this direction were made by the Lumière brothers, with their projector, by George Méliès, who pioneered stop-action camera techniques (1899) that allowed the expansion from the original peep-show format to fictional narratives on film. In 1923, experimental sound movies were demonstrated by Lee DeForest, and in 1929, color film emerged as an alternative to black and white images.

Leo Sauvage. *L'Affaire Lumière: du Mythe à l'Histoire.* Paris: L'Herminier, 1985.

Frank E. Beaver. *On Film: A History of the Motion Picture.* New York: McGraw Hill, 1983.

David B. Thomas. *The Origins of the Motion Picture.* London: H.M. Stationery Off., 1964.

At the projection of Lumière's film *L'Arrivée d'un Train en Gare* (Paris, 1895), the spectators were so scared that the arriving train might hit somebody that they started running.

Siegfried Kracauer. *Kino. Essays, Studien, Glossen z. Film* (Hrsg. von Karsten Witte, 1 Aufl.). Frankfurt/Main: Suhrkamp, 1974.

The invention of television was a long process during which display technology, image capturing, transmission, and reception were progressively developed. One can expand the history as to integrate James Maxwell's mathematical formulation of the electromagnetic field (1864), the use of high frequency waves (for radio, at the beginning), the discovery of photosensitive materials (selenium among these, in 1873), the line-by-line scanning (discovered in the USA in 1880 by W.E. Sawyer and in France by Maurice Leblanc). In 1884, Paul Nipkow patented the earliest form of image transmission (a mechanically driven rotating disk). Many other discoveries—the vacuum tube (1906), the fluorescent screen cathode ray tube (1906), the photoelectric cell (1913)—led to the patents issued to Vladimir K. Zworykin (1923 and 1925) for a camera and a color encoding scheme, as well as to the first public demonstration of black-and-white television by J. L. Baird in 1926 and two years later for color television. The British Broadcasting Company started a broadcasting service in 1936 (with 405 scanning lines), while in 1941, a similar service was offered in the USA. Other milestones include: videotape recording system-1956; first demonstration (in London) of a home video recorder-1963; use of satellite for relayed television images-1964; first live TV broadcast from the moon-1969; High Definition TV working system-1981; digital television-1989.

The Federal Communication Commission (FCC) appointed an advisory committee on Advanced Television Service (ACATS) to recommend the new digital standard. A computer industry coalition (CICATS), representing the most important companies (Microsoft, Apple, Silicon Graphics, Intel), worked on alternative standards for digital TV. The differences between the two commissions are relevant not only on the technical level, but also from the perspective of the public audience. It is estimated that no less than an additional 100 billion dollars, some from taxation, is at stake, in addition to the important aspect of computer-television integration.

This information, with ample commentary, has been made available by Alvy Ray Smith, a leading researcher of computer graphics. Last updated in September, 1996, this information can be accessed at http://www.research.microsoft.com.

Jan Marie Lambert Peters. *Fotographie, Film, Televisie. Logica, Magie en Esthetik van het mechanische Beeld.* Antwerp: De Nederlandsche Boekhandel, 69.

Stan Prentiss. *Television: from Analog to Digital.* Blue Ridge Summit PA: Tab Professional and Reference Books, 1985.

George E. Whitehouse. *Understanding the New Technologies of the Mass Media.* Englewood Cliffs, NJ: Prentice Hall, 1986.

Arun N. Netravali and Birendra Prasada, Editors. *Visual Communication Systems.* New York: IEEE Press, 1989.

CD-ROM, 2 volumes. Redmond WA: Microsoft Press (distributed to the book trade in the USA by Harper and Row), 1986-1987.
Vol. 1, *The New Papyrus,* edited by Steve Lambert and Suzanne Ropiequet. Vol. 2, *Optical Publishing. A Practical Approach to Developing CD-ROM Applications,* edited by Suzanne Ropiequet, John Einberger, and Bill Zoellick.

A.M. Hendley. *CD-ROM and Optical Publishing Systems.* An Assessment of the Impact of Optical Read-Only Memory Systems on the Information Industry and a Comparison Between Them and Traditional Paper, Microfilm, and On-line Publishing systems. Westport CT: Meckler Publishing Corp., 1987.

Judith Paris Roth, Editor. *Essential Guide to CD-ROM.* Westport CT: Meckler Publishing Corp., 1986.

Howard Rheingold. *Virtual Reality.* New York: Summit Books, 1991.
Rheingold describes the implementation of virtual reality as follows: "The head-mounted displays (HMD's) and three-dimensional computer graphics, input/output devices, computer models that constitute a VR system make it possible today to immerse yourself in an artificial world and to reach in and reshape it" (p. 16).

Jaron Lanier. Interview, in *Computer Graphics World,* 15:4, pp. 61-70.
"...with kids that grow up with television, there's this very bizarre world of existence in which they can take in a great deal of experience without moving, and that leads to the famous childhood zombie-hood that's so scary to see. This can affect different people in different ways, but I think one of the more common afflictions that people grow up with is the desire for instant gratification

and a lack of just the basic common sense appreciation for doing work to achieve things" (p. 64).

Gottfried Wilhelm Leibniz. *Zwei Briefe über das binäre Zahlensystem und die chinesische Philosophie.* Stuttgart: Belser Presse, 1968.
The book contains text edited and translated from the originals by Renate Loosen and Franz Vonessen. The letters concerning Chinese philosophy (*Lettre sur la philosophie chinoise à Nicole de Remond*) contain a whole section on the characters discovered by Fu-chi and his dyadic system. The *I Ching* has the binary system as its underlying principle. It implies a pragmatic thought: "If one or another action is followed, what will be the outcome?" represented by choices in eight trigrams (three lines, each of which can be continuous or broken). The visual thought in this system is related to Yin-Yang.

Ted Nelson. The Hypertext, in *Proceedings of the World Documentation Federation*, 1965.

—. Replacing the Printed Word: A Complete Literary System, in *Information Processing 80*, S.H. Lavington, Ed.itor, IFIP, 1980, North Holland Publishing Corp., pp. 1013-1023.

Vannevar Bush's seminal article, As We May Think, in the *Atlantic Monthly*, CLXXVI, July, December, 1945, pp. 101-108, is indeed a conceptual breakthrough.

Aspects of visual literacy are discussed in Donis A. Dondis's *A Primer of Visual Literacy.* Cambridge MA/London: MIT Press, 1963.

Chapter 2: Unbounded Sexuality

Karl Marx. *Early Texts* (translated and edited by David McLellan). Oxford: Basil Blackwell, 1971. pp. 137-138.

Joseph Folliet. *Adam et Eve. Humanisme et Sexualité.* Lyon: Chronique Sociale de France, 1965.

Sam Kash Kachigan. *The Sexual Matrix. Boy Meets Girl on the Evolutionary Scale.* New York: Radius Press, 1990.

Among many attempts to define sexual types are those identifying Mediterranean (Latin), Nordic, Nubian, Pygmy, Japanese, Pacific Islands, East Indian. One has to be skeptical of the attempt to label sexual behavior using pre-defined characteristics. That a typology is possible does not automatically result in the conclusion that it is also necessarily meaningful.

Molecular biology is a field stimulated by progress in physics, chemistry, and genetics. Due to some of its research, hominids and chimpanzees were studied from a perspective that other disciplines could not define. In regard to the methods and concepts used, useful reading is provided in:

J.M. Walker and E.B. Gingold, Editors. *Molecular Biology and Biotechnology.* 2nd ed. London: Royal Society of Chemistry, 1988.

A. Babloyantz. *Molecules, Dynamics, and Life: An Introduction to Self-Organization of Matter.* New York: Wiley, 1986.

Neil Philip. *Working Girls. An Illustrated History of the Oldest Profession.* Bloomsbury, 1991.

Gilgamesh. Trans. William Ellery Leonard. Introduction by Leonard Cottrell. Illustrated by Irving Amen). Avon CT: For the members of the Limited Editions Club, 1974.

The Song of Solomon (English and Hebrew). Woodmere NY: Pardes Rimonim Press, 1990.

The Kamasutra by Vatsyanyana and The Perfumed Garden by Cheikh Nefzaoui Trans. Sir Richard Burton and F.F. Arbuthnot. London: Bibliophile Books, 1988.

Swami Chinmayanda. *Narada Bhakti Sutra* (Love Divine. The Highest Art of Making Love to the Lord of the Heart). Madras: Chinmaya Publications Trust, 1970.

Publius Ovidius Naso. *The Art of Love.* Trans. B.P. Moore. New York: Printed for the members of the Limited Editions Club, 1971.

Giovanni Boccaccio. *Decamerone.* Natalino Sapegno, Editor. 1st ed. Torino: TEA, 1989.

David O. Frantz. *Festum voluptatis. A Study of Renaissance Erotica.* Columbus OH: Ohio State University Press, 1989.

Peter Wagner, Editor. *Erotica and the Enlightenment.* Frankfurt/Main and New York: P. Lang, 1991.

Henry Fielding. *The History of Tom Jones.* New York: Modern Library, 1985.

Richard Manton, Editor. *The Victorian Imagination. A Sampler.* New York: Grove Press, 1984.

Sigmund Freud. *The Essentials of Psycho-Analysis* (selected by and with introduction and commentaries by Anna Freud; translated from the German by James Strachey). London: Hogarth and the Institute of Psycho-Analysis, 1986.

Carl Gustav Jung (1875-1961). After contributions in using Galton's word association text, Jung worked with Freud. Afterwards, critical of Freud's classification of instincts as either sexually driven or preservation driven, he investigated myths, rituals, and legends. Individuation brought his concerns into focus.

Charles Darwin. *The Works of Charles Darwin*. 16 Vols. Edited by Paul H. Barrett and R.B. Freeman. London: Pickering & Chatto Ltd., 1986.

Thomas Laqueur. *Making Sex: Body and Gender from Greeks to Freud*. Cambridge: Harvard University Press, 1991.
Laqueur quotes Galen of Pergamon (130-200 AD): "Turn outward the woman's; turn inward, so to speak, and fold double, the man's [genitals] and you will find the same in both in every respect."

Lady Capulet tells her daughter, in reference to Juliet's coming 14th birthday: "Well, think of marriage now; younger than you/Here in Verona, ladies of esteem/Are made already mothers. By my count/I was your mother much upon these years/That you are now a maid..." (*Romeo and Juliet*, act 1, scene 3, ll. 69-74; New York: Dover Publications, 1963, edited by Horace H. Furness).

James Patterson and Peter Kim. *The Day America Told the Truth*. New York: Prentice Hall Press, 1991.
The book presents worrisome statistics regarding the condition of Americans. Data pertinent to family life, moral standards (91% of Americans lie regularly), confidence levels (in church, state, politicians) provide a collective portrait of a people adapting to circumstances of existence that define the civilization of illiteracy.

How contraceptives, in particular the pill and the abortion pill, are changing the nature of sexuality can be discovered in a number of books:

Lynn S. Baker. *The Fertility Fallacy: Sexuality in the Post-Pill Age*. Philadelphia: Saunders Press, 1981.

Jane Everett. *The Condom Book. The Essential Guide for Men and Women*. New York: New American Library, 1987.

Amy Ong Tsui and M.A. Herbertson, Editors. *Dynamics of Contraceptive Use*. Cambridge, England: Parkes Foundation, 1989.

Shirley Green. *The Curious History of Contraception*. London: Ebury Press, 1971.

Michael J. K. Harper. *Birth Control Technologies. Prospects by the Year 2000.* Austin: University of Texas Press, 1983.

L. Mastroianni, P. J. Donaldson, and T.T. Kane, Editors. *Developing New Contraceptives. Obstacles and Opportunities.* Washington, DC.: National Academy Press, 1990.

Etienne-Emile Baulieu, with Mort Rosenblum. *The "Abortion Pill" RU-486, A Woman's Choice.* New York: Simon and Schuster, 1991.

Herbert Marcuse. *Eros and Civilization. A Philosophical Inquiry into Freud.* Boston: Beacon Press, 1966.
The Eros-Thanatos conflict is definitive of Herbert Marcuse's theory of sexuality.

Michel Foucault. *Histoire de la sexualité.* Paris: Gallimard, 1976. Translated from the French by Robert Hurley as *The History of Sexuality,* New York: Pantheon Books, 1978.

Dr. Simon LeVay. Is This Child Gay? Born or Bred; The Origins of Homosexuality, in *Newsweek,* February 24, 1992, pp. 46-53.
Dr. LeVay was the first to notice the difference between the brain of homosexuals and that of heterosexual men.

Caroline Collier. *The 20th Century Plague.* Tring: Lion, 1987.

Pearl Ma and Donald Armstrong, Editors. *AIDS and Infection of Homosexual Men.* Boston: Butterworths, 1989.

Helene M. Cole and George D. Lundberg, Editors. *AIDS, From the Beginning.* Chicago: American Medical Association, 1986.

Kim Sterelny. *The Representational Theory of Mind. An Introduction.* Oxford, England/Cambridge MA: Basil Blackwell, 1990.
"Jerry Fodor has argued that human (and nonhuman) mental processes involve a medium of mental representation, a medium that has all the central features of a language" (p. 23).

Projesh Banerji. *Erotica in Indian Dance.* New Delhi: Cosmo Publications, 1983.

Susan McClary. *Feminine Endings. Music, Gender, and Sexuality.* Minneapolis: University of Minnesota Press, 1991.

Judith Lynne Hanna. *Dance, Sex, and Gender. Signs of Identity, Dominance, Defiance, and Desire.* Chicago: University of Chicago Press, 1988.

Consumption and sexuality are related at least in the sense that sex became an object of consumption along with anything else that can be bought. More subtle aspects of their interrelation can be found in defining attitudes towards value, that of the human being included, respect for others, and self-respect, the drive for more, and the attempt to escape social responsibility.

Robert Hans van Gulik. *Erotic Colour Prints of the Ming Period. With an Essay on Chinese Sex Life from the Han to the Ch'ing Dynasty, BC. 206 - AD 1644.* Tokyo: Privately published, 1951.

Luis Millones. *Amor brujo. Images and Culture or Love in the Andes.* Syracuse, NY: Maxwell School of Citizenship and Public Affairs, 1990.

Nicole Morin and Jean-Louis Neveu, Editors. *Les amours dans la tradition.* Pranecq, France: U.P.C.P./Geste paysanne, 1988.

Alec Flegon. *Eroticism in Russian Art.* London: Flegon Press, 1976.

Mary D. Sheriff. *Fragonard. Art and Eroticism.* Chicago: University of Chicago Press, 1990.

Edward Lucie-Smith. *Sexuality in Western Art.* London: Thames and Hudson, 1991.

Theodore Bowle and Cornelia V. Christenson, Editors. *Studies in Erotic Art.* New York: Basic Books, 1970.

René Etiemple. *Yun yu. An Essay on Eroticism and Love in Ancient China.* Trans. James Hogarth. Geneva: Nagel, 1970.

The condition of women in Japanese society and sexuality, as this unfolds in a framework of hierarchies and values still dominated by literate circumstances, are reflected in birth control methods applied. Induced abortion remains the preferred method. A high proportion of Japanese married couples take steps to prevent conception. Nevertheless, the repertory of means used is different from that acknowledged in Western Europe and the USA. It seems that Japanese men and women, together with the Japanese state, are reluctant to accept the contraceptive pill. Contraception is dominated by the use of condoms (36%); the calendar method, also known as *ogino* and sometimes in combination with condom use (24.2%); the IUD (16.6%). The status of women and the function of sexuality in Japanese families and outside family life are changing; so is the perception of the health implications of oral contraceptives. A useful reference on the subject is Samuel Coleman's book, *Family Planning in Japanese Society. Traditional birth control in a modern urban culture* (Princeton: Princeton University Press, 1983). Another useful reference is *Basic Read-*

ings on Population and Family Planning in Japan, (edited by Chojiro Kunil and Tameyoshi Katagiri, Tokyo: Japanese Organization for International Cooperation in Family Planning. 1976).

Chapter 3: Family: Discovering the Primitive Future

Statistics on family in the USA and the world are a matter of public record. The processing and interpretation of data, even in the age of electronic processing, takes time once data has been collected. The *Statistical Handbook on the American Family* (Phoenix AZ: The Orynx Press, 1992), for instance, deals with trends covering 1989-1990. The numbers are intriguing. Well over 85% of the adult population married by the time of their 45th birthday, but only around 60% are currently married. 10% are divorced and almost as many widowed. The general conclusions about the family are: There is a decline in marital stability with over one million children per year affected by the divorce of their parents. Less than 20% of the people see marriage as a lifetime relationship. The POSSLQ (persons of opposite sex sharing living quarters) is well over 5% of the population. The size of the average American household shrank from 3.7 persons over 40 years ago to 2.6 recently. Interracial marriages, while triple in number compared to 1970, include slightly below 2% of the population.

A.F. Robertson. *Beyond the Family. The Social Organization of Human Reproduction.* Cambridge, England: Polity Press, 1991.

Martine Fell. *Ça va, la famille?* Paris: Le Hameau, 1983.

Nicolas Caparros. *Crisis de la Familia. Revolución del Vivir.* Buenos Aires: Ediciones Pargieman, 1973.

Adrian Wilson. *Family.* London: Travistock Publications, 1985.

Charles Franklin Thwing. *The Family. An Historical and Social Study.* Boston: Lee and Shepard, 1887.

Edward L. Kain. *The Myth of Family Decline. Understanding Families in a World of Rapid Social Change.* Lexington MA: Lexington Books, 1990.

Herbert Kretschmer. *Ehe und Familie. Die Entwicklung von Ehe und Familie im Laufe der Geschichte.* Dornach, Switzerland: Verlag am Goetheanum, 1988.

André Burguière, Christiane Klapisch-Zuber, Martine Segalen, Françoise Zonabend, Editors. *Histoire de la famille* (preface by Claude Lévi-Strauss).Paris: Armand Colin, 1986.
Family is established in extension of reproductive drives and natural forms of cooperation. Regardless of the types leading to what was called the family nucleus (husband and wife), families embody reciprocal obligations. The formalization of family life in marriage contracts was stimulated by writing.

J.B.M. Guy. *Glottochronology Without Cognate Recognition.* Canberra: Department of Linguistics Research, School of Pacific Studies, Australian National University, 1980.
Although the processes leading to the formation of nations is relatively recent, nations were frequently characterized as an extended family, although the processes reflect structural characteristics of human practical experiences different from those at work in the constitution of the family.

Martin B. Duberman. *About Time. Exploring the Gay Past.* New York: Gay Presses of New York City, 1986.

Jeffrey Weeks. *Against Nature. Essays on History, Sexuality, and Identity.* London: Rivers Oram, 1991.

Bernice Goodman. *The Lesbian. A Celebration of Difference.* Brooklyn: Out & Out Books, 1977.

Jean Bethke Elshtain. Against Gay Marriage, in *Commonweal,* November 22, 1991, pp. 685-686.

Brent Hartinger. A Case for Gay Marriage, in *Commonweal,* November 22, 1991, pp. 675, 681-686.

Not in The Best Interest (Adoption by Lesbians and Gays), in *Utne Reader,* November/December, 1991, p. 57.

William Plummer. A Mother's Priceless Gift, in *People Weekly,* August 26, 1991, pp. 40-41.

Nelly E. Gupta and Frank. Feldinger. Brave New Baby (ZIFT Surrogacy), in *Ladies Home Journal,* October, 1989, pp. 140-141.

Mary Thom. Dilemmas of the New Birth Technologies, in *Ms.,* May, 1988, pp. 4, 66, 70-72.

Cleo Kocol. The Rent-A-Womb Dilemma, in *The Humanist,* July/August, 1987, p. 37.

Marsha Riben. A Last Resort (excerpt from Shedding Light on the Dark Side of Adoption), in *Utne Reader*, November/December, 1991, pp. 53-54.

Lisa Gubernick. How Much is that Baby in the Window? in *Forbes*, October 14, 1991, pp. 90-91.

Self-sufficiency, reflecting contexts of existence of limited scale, marks the Amish and Mennonite families. The family contract is very powerful. Succeeding generations care for each other to the extent that the home always includes quarters for the elderly. Each new generation is endowed in order to maintain the path of self-sufficiency. The Amish wedding (the subject of Stephen Scott's book of the same title, Intercourse PA: Good Books, 1988), as well as the role the family plays in educating children (*Children in Amish Society: Socialization and Community Education*, by J.A. Hosteter and G. Enders Huntington, New York: Holt Rinehart and Winston, 1971) are indicative of this family life.

Andy Grove. *Only the Paranoid Survive*. New York: Doubleday, 1996.
The CEO of Intel, one of the world's most successful companies, discussed the requirement of genetic update and his own, apparently dated, corporate genes.

Adam Smith. *The Theory of Moral Sentiments* (D.D. Raphael and A.L. Macfie, Editors). Oxford: Clarendon Press, 1976.

David Hume. *A Treatise of Human Nature* (L.A. Selby-Bigge, Editor). 2nd edition. Oxford/New York: Clarendon Press, 1978.

—. *Inquiries concerning human understanding and concerning the principles of morals* (L.A. Selby-Bigge, Editor). Oxford: Clarendon Press, 1975.

Takeo Doi. *Amae no kozo*. Tokyo: Kobundo, 1971. Translated as *The Anatomy of Dependence* by John Bester. Tokyo/New York: Kodansho International and Harper & Row, 1973.

Chapter 4: A God for Each of Us

The following books set forth the basic tenets of their respective religions:

Bhagavad Gita: part of the epic poem *Mahabharata*, this Sanskrit dialog between Krishna and Prince Arjuna poetically describes a path to spiritual wisdom and unity with God. Action, devotion, and knowledge guide on this path.

Torah: the books of Moses (also known as the Pentateuch); for Chistians, the first five books of the Old Testament: Genesis, Exodus, Leviticus, Numbers, Deuteronomy. These describe the origin of the world, the covenant between God and the people of Israel, the Exodus from Egypt and return to the Promised Land, and rules for religious and social behavior. Together with the books labeled *Prophets* and *Writings,* they make up the entire Old Testament. The controversy among Jews, Roman Catholics, Eastern Christians, and Protestants about the acceptance of some books, the order of books, and translations reflect the different perspectives adopted within these religions.

New Testament: the Christian addition to the Bible comprises 27 books. They contain sayings attributed to Jesus, his life story (death and resurrection included), the writings of the apostles, rules for conversion and baptism, and the Apocalypse (the end of this world and the beginning of a new one).

Koran (al Qur'an): the holy book of the Moslems, is composed of 114 chapters (called *suras*). Belief in Allah, descriptions of rules for religious and social life, calls to moral life, and vivid descriptions of hell make up most of the text. According to Moslem tradition, Mohammed ascended the mount an illiterate. He came down with the *Koran*, which Allah had taught him to write.

I-Ching: attributed to Confucius, composed of five books, containing a history of his native district, a system for divining the future (*Book of Changes*), a description of ceremonies and the ideal government (*Book of Rites*), and a collection of poetry. In their unity, all these books affirm principles of cooperation, reciprocal respect, and describe etiquette and ritual rules.

Mircea Eliade, Editor-in-Chief. *The Encyclopedia of Religion.* New York: Macmillan, 1987.

Mircea Eliade (with I. P. Couliano and H.S. Wiesner). *The Eliade Guide to World Religions.* San Francisco: Harper, 1991.

Eliot Alexander. *The Universal Myths: Heroes, Gods, Tricksters, and Others.* New York: New American Library, 1990.

P. K. Meagher, T.C. O'Brien, Sister Consuelo Maria Aherne. *Encyclopedic Dictionary of Religion.* 3 Vols. Corpus City Publications, 1979.

In regard to the multiplicity of religions, the following works provide a good reference:

John Ferguson. *Gods Many and Lords Many: A Study in Primal Religions.* Guildford, Surrey: Lutterworth Educational, 1982.

Suan Imm Tan. *Many Races, Many Religions.* Singapore: Educational Publications Bureau, 1971-72.

H. Byron Earhart. *Religions of Japan: Many Traditions within One Sacred Way.* San Francisco: Harper & Row, 1984.

John M. Reid. *Doomed Religions. A Series of Essays on Great Religions of the World.* New York: Phillips & Hunt, 1884.

Although no precise statistics are available, it is assumed that ca. three billion people acknowledge religion in our days. The numbers are misleading, though. For instance, only 2.4% of the population in England attends religious services; in Germany, the percentage is 9%; in some Moslem countries, service attendance is close to 100%. The "3-day Jews" (two days of Rosh Hashana and 1 day of Yom Kippur, also known as "revolving door" Jews, in for New Year and out after Atonement Day), the Christian Orthodox and Catholics of Christmas and Easter, and the Buddhists of funeral ceremonials belong to the vast majority that refers to religion as a cultural identifier. Many priests and higher order ecumenical workers recite their prayers as epic poetry.

Atheism. The "doctrine that God does not exist, that existence of God is a false belief" (cf. M. Eliade, *Encyclopedia of Religion*, vol. 1, pp 479-480). Literature on atheism continuously increases. A selection showing the many angles of atheism can serve as a guide:

The American Atheist (periodical). Austin TX: American Atheists.

Gordon Stein, Editor. *An Anthology of Atheism and Rationalism.* Buffalo NY: Prometheus Books, 1980.

Michael Martin. *Atheism: A Philosophical Analysis.* Philadelphia: Temple University Press, 1990.

Jacques J. Natanson. *La Mort de Dieu: Essai sur l'Athéisme Moderne.* Paris: Presses Univérstaires de France, 1975.

Robert A. Morey. *The New Atheism and the Erosion of Freedom.* Minneapolis: Bethany House Publishers, 1986.

James Thrower. *A Short History of Western Atheism.* London: Pemberton Books, 1971.

Robert Eno. *The Confucian Creation of Heaven. Philosophy and the Defense of Ritual Mastery.* Albany: State University of New York Press, 1990.

Ronald L. Grimes. *Research in Ritual Studies. A Programmatic Essay and Bibliography.* Chicago: American Theological Library Association; Metuchen NJ: Scarecrow Press, 1985.

Evan M. Zuesse. *Ritual Cosmos. The Sanctification of Life in African Religions.* Athens: Ohio University Press, 1979.

Godfrey and Monica Wilson. *The Analysis of Social Change. Based on observations in Central Africa.* Cambridge: The University Press, 1968.
"A pagan Najakunsa believes himself to be dependent upon his deceased father for health and fertility; he acts as if he were, and expresses his sense of dependence in rituals" (p. 41).

References for the study of myths are as follows:

Eliot Alexander. *The Universal Myths: Heroes, Gods, Tricksters, and Others.* New York: New American Library, 1990.

Jane Ellen Harrison. *Prolegomena to the Study of Greek Religion.* New York: Arno Press, 1975.

Walter Burkert. *Ancient Mystery Cults.* Cambridge MA: Harvard University Press, 1987.

John Ferguson. *Greek and Roman Religion: A Source Book.* Park Ridge NJ: Noyes Press, 1980.

Arcadio Schwade. Shinto-Bibliography in Western Languages. Leiden: Brill, 1986.
Japanese Shintoism began before writing.

Hinduism: With one of the highest number of followers (ca. 650 million), Hinduism is an eclectic religion. Indigenous elements and Aryan religions, codified around 1500 BCE in the *Rig Veda, Sama Veda, Yajor Veda, Atharva Veda, Aranyakas, Upanishads,* result in an amalgam of practices and beliefs dominating religious and social life in India. The caste system classifies members of society in four groups: priests (Brahmins), rulers, farmers, and merchants, laborers (on farms or in industry). Devotion to a guru, adherence to the Vedic scriptures, the practice of yoga are the forms of religious action. The divine Trinity of Hinduism unites Brahma (the creator), Vishna (the preserver), and Shiva (the destroyer).

Taoism: In the *Tao Te Ching (Book of the Way and Its Virtue)*, one reads: "The Tao of origin gives birth to the One. The One gives birth to the Two. The Two gives birth to the Three. The Three produces the Ten Thousand Things." With some background in Tao, the poetry becomes explicit: The One is the

Supreme Void, primordial Breath. This engenders Two, Yin and Yang, the duality from which everything sprung once a ternary relation is established. Tao is poetic ontology.

Confucianism: Stressing the relationship among individuals, families, and society, Confucianism is based on two percepts: *li* (proper behavior) and *jen* (cooperative attitude). Confucius expressed the philosophy on which this religion is based on sayings and dialogues during the 6th-5th century BCE. Challenged by the mysticism of religions (Taoism, Buddhism) in the area of its inception, some followers incorporated their spirit in new-Confucianism (during the period known as the Sung dynasty, 960-1279).

Judaism: Centered on the belief in one God, Judaism is the religion of the Book (the Torah), established at around 2000 BCE by Abraham, Isaac, and Jacob. Judaism promotes the idea of human improvement, as well as the Messianic thought. Strong dedication to community and sense of family are part of the religious practice.

Islam: The contemporary religion with the highest number of adherents (almost 9000 million Muslims on record), and growing fast, Islam celebrates Mohammed, who received the Koran from Allah. Acknowledged at 610, Islam (which means "submission to God") places its prophet in the line started with Abraham, continued with Moses, and redirected by Jesus. The five pillars of Islam are: Allah is the only God, prayer (facing Mecca) five times a day, giving of alms, fast of Ramadan, and pilgrimage to Mecca.

Christianity: in its very many denominations (Roman Catholic, Greek Orthodox, Protestant, which split further into various sects, such as Baptist, Pentecostal, Episcopal, Lutheran, Mormon, Unitarian, Quakers), claims to have its origin in Jesus Christ and completes the Old Testament of the Hebrews with the New Testament of the apostles. It is impossible to capture the many varieties of Christianity in characteristics unanimously accepted. Probably the major celebrations of Christianity (some originating in pre-Christian pagan rituals related to natural cycles), i.e., Christmas and Easter, better reflect elements of unity. Christianity promotes respect for moral values, dedication to the family, and faith in one God composed of three elements (the Trinity: Father, Son, and Holy Spirit).

Bahai of Bahá'i: ascertains the unity of all religious doctrines as these embody ideals of spiritual truth. The name comes from Baha Ullah (Glory of God), adopted by its founder Mirza Husain Ali Nuri, in 1863, in extension of the al-Bab religion. Universal education, equality between male and female, and world order and peace are its goals. The religion is estimated to have 5 million adherents world-wide.

Richard Wilhelm. *I Ging; Das Buch der Wandlungen*. Düsseldorf/Köln: Diedrichs, 1982.
Wilhelm states that, in the context described, Fuh-Hi emerged: "He reunited man and woman, ordered the five elements and set the laws of mankind. He drew eight signs in order to dominate the world." The eight signs are the eight basic trigrams of *I Ging*, the *Book of Changes* (which attracted Leibniz's attention).

King Frederick Barbarossa (Frederick I of the Holy Roman Empire, 1123-1190). Well known for challenging the authority of the Pope and for attempting to establish German supremacy in religious matters.

Joan of Arc (1412-1431). A plowman's daughter who, as the story goes, listened to the voices of saints Michael, Catherine, and Margaret. Thus inspiring the French to victory over British invaders, she made possible the coronation of Charles II at Reims. Captured by the English, she was declared a heretic and burned at the stake. In 1920, Pope Benedict XV declared her a saint.

Jan Hus (1372-1415). Religious reformer whose writings exercised influence over all the Catholic world. In *De Ecclesia*, he set forth that scripture is the sole source of Christian doctrine.

Martin Luther (1483-1546). A priest from Saxony, a scholar of Scripture, and a linguist, who is famous for having attacked clerical abuses. Through his writings (The *95 Theses*), he precipitated the Reformation.

Moslem armies defeated the forces of the Holy Roman Empire, led by Charles Martel, at Poitiers (cf. J.H. Roy, *La Bataille de Poitiers, Octobre 733*, Paris: Gallimard, 1966).

Crusades: a series of military expeditions taking place from 1095 to 1270) intent on reclaiming Jerusalem and the holy Christian shrines from Turkish control.

David Kirsch poses the questions: Is 97% of human activity concept-free, driven by control mechanisms we share not only with our simian forebears, but with insects? (Today the Earwig, Tomorrow the Man? in *Artificial Intelligence*, 47:1-3, Jan. 1991, p. 161).

The *Bible on CD-ROM* is a publication of Nimbus Information Systems (1989). The *CD-Word Interactive Biblical Library* (1990), published by the CD-Word

Library, Inc. offers 16 of the world's most used Bible texts and reference sources (two Greek texts, four English versions).

Secular god-building in the Soviet Union: *Ob ateizme i religii. Sbornik Statei, Pisem i drughich materialov* (About atheism and religion. Collected articles, letters, and other materials) by Anatoli Vasilevich Lunacharskii (1875-1933), Moscow: Mysl, 1972. This is a collection of articles on atheism and religion, part of the scientific-atheistic library. See also Maxim Gorky, *Untimely Thoughts* (translated by Herman Erolaev). New York: P.S. Ericksson, 1966.

Ernest Gellner, Scale and Nation, in *Scale and Social Organization* (F. Barth, editor).
"Max Weber stressed the significance of the way in which Protestantism made every man his own priest" (p. 143).

Glen Tinder. Can we be good without God? in *Atlantic Monthly*, December, 1989.

Michael Lewis. God is in the Packaging, in *The New York Times Magazine*, July 21, 1996, pp. 14 and 16.
Lewis describes pastors using marketing techniques to form congregations. The success of the method has led to branch congregations all over the USA.

Tademan Isobe, author of *The Japanese and Religion,* states: "The general religious awareness of the Japanese does not include an ultimate God with human attributes, as the God of Christianity. Instead, Japanese sense the mystery of life from all events and natural phenomena around them in their daily lives. They have what might be called a sense of pathos" (cf. Web positing of August, 1996, http://www.ariadne.knee.kioto-u.ac.jp).

Karen Armstrong. *A History of God. The 4,000-Year Quest of Judaism, Christianity and Islam.* New York: Ballantine Books, 1993.

Frank S. Mead.*Handbook of Denominations in the United States.* 9th ed. Rev. Samuel S. Hill. Nashville: Abingdon Press, 1992.
The book presents the more than 220 religious denominations known in the USA (historical background, doctrine or main teaching, administrative organization). It is quite interesting to note how fast the geography of the faith changes and how many new denominations emerge from year to year.

Chapter 5: A Mouthful of Microwave

From a strictly qualitative perspective, the amount of food people eat is represented by numbers so large that we end up looking at them in awe, without understanding what they mean. The maintenance of life is an expensive proposition. Nevertheless, once we go beyond the energetic equation, i.e., in the realm of desires, the numbers increase exponentially. It can be argued that this increase (of an order of magnitude of 1,000) is higher than that anticipated by Malthus. On the subject of what, how, and why people eat, see:

Claudio Clini. *L'alimentazione nella storia. Uomo, alimentazione, malattie.* Abano Terme, Padova: Francisci, 1985.

Evan Jones. *American Food. The Gastronomic Story.* Woodstock NY: Overlook Press, 1990.

Nicholas and Giana Kurti, Editors. *But the Crackling is Superb. An Anthology on Food and Drink by Fellows and Foreign Members of the Royal Society.* Bristol, England: A. Hilger, 1988.

Carol A. Bryant, et al. *The Cultural Feast. An Introduction to Food and Society.* St. Paul: West Publishing Co., 1985.

Hilary Wilson. *Egyptian Food and Drink.* Aylesbury, Bucks, England: Shire, 1988.

Reay Tannahill. *Food in History.* New York: Stein and Day, 1973.

Charles Bixler Heiser. *Seed to Civilization. The Story of Food.* Cambridge MA: Harvard University Press, 1990.

Margaret Visser. *Much Depends on Dinner. The Extraordinary History and Mythology, Allure and Obsessions, Perils and Taboos, of an Ordinary Meal.* Toronto, Ont.: McClelland and Stewart, 1986.

Esther B. Aresty. *The Delectable Past. The Joys of the Table, from Rome to the Renaissance, from Queen Elizabeth I to Mrs. Beeton.* Indianapolis: Bobbs-Merrill, 1978.

Maria P. Robbins, Editor. *The Cook's Quotation Book.* A Literary Feast. Wainscott NY: Pushcart Press, 1983.

The Pleasures of the Table (compiled by Theodore FitzGibbon). New York: Oxford University Press, 1981.

Charles Dickens. *American Notes.* New York: St. Martin's Press, 1985. (pp. 154-155).

On the symbolism of food, informative reading can be found in:

Carol A. Bryant. *The Cultural Feast: An Introduction to Food and Society.* St. Paul: West Publishing Co., 1985.

Lindsey Tucker. *Stephen and Bloom at Life's Feast: Alimentary Symbolism and the Creative Process in James Joyce's Ulysses.* Columbus: Ohio State University Press, 1984.

In *L'aile ou la cuisse* (Wing or Drumstick), a 1976 French film directed by Claude Zidi, Luis de Funés became, as the French press put it, "the Napoleon of gastronomy" fighting the barbarian taste of industrial food, seen as a real danger to the authentic taste of France.

At the initiative of the Minister of Culture, a *Conseil National des Arts Culinaires* (CNAC) was founded in 1989. Culinary art and gastronomic heritage were made part of the French national identity. *Awakening of Taste (Le reveil du goût)* is a program launched in the elementary schools. A curriculum originating from the French Institute of Taste is used to explain what makes French food taste good. The CNAC provides a nationwide inventory of local foods. A *University of Taste (Centre de Goût)* would be established in the Loire Valley.

Jean Bottero. *Mythes et Rites de Babylone.* Paris: Librairie Honoré Champion, 1985.

Reallexikon der Assyriologie. Vol. III, *Getränke* (Drinks), pp. 303-306; *Gewürze* (Spices), pp. 340-341; Vol. VI, *Küche* (Cuisine), pp. 277-298. Berlin/New York, Walter de Gruyter, 1982.

La Plus Vieille Cuisine du Monde, in *L'Histoire,* 49, 1982, pp. 72-82.

M. Gabeus Apicius. *De re conquinaria* (rendered into English by Joseph Sommers Vehling, New York: Dover Publications, 1977) first appeared in England in 1705, in a Latin version, based on the manuscripts of this work dating to the 8th and 9th centuries. Apicius was supposed to have lived from 80 BCE to 40 CE. This book has since been questioned as a hoax, although it remains a reference text.

Lucius Junius Moderatus Columella. *De re rustica.* (12 volumes on agriculture. Latin text with German translation by Will Richter). München: Artemis Verlag, 1981.

Roland Barthes. *Empire of Signs.* New York: Hill and Wang. 1982. (Originally published in French as *L'Empire des Signes,* Geneva: Editions d'Art Albert Skira, S.A.
"The dinner tray seems a picture of the most delicate order: its frame containing, against a dark background, various objects (bowls, boxes, saucers, chop-

sticks, tiny piles of food, a little gray ginger, a few shreds of orange vegetable, a background of brown sauce)...it might be said that these trays fulfill the definition of painting which according to Piero della Francesca is merely demonstration of surfaces and bodies becoming even smaller or larger according to their term" (p. 11).

"Entirely visual (conceived, concerted, manipulated for sight, and even for a painter's eye), food thereby says that it is not deep: the edible substance is without a precious heart, without a buried power, without a vital secret: no Japanese dish is endowed with a center (the alimentary center implied in the West by the rite which consists of arranging the meal, of surrounding or covering the article of food); here everything is the ornament of another ornament: first of all because on the table, on the tray, food is never anything but a collection of fragments, none of which appears privileged by an order of ingestion; to eat is not to respect a menu (an itinerary of dishes), but to select, with a light touch of the chopsticks, sometimes one color, sometimes another, depending on the kind of inspiration which appears in its slowness as the detached, indirect accompaniment of the conversation...." (p. 22).

The writings of the various religions (*Koran, Torah, New Testament*) contain strictures and ceremonial rules concerning food. For cooking and eating restrictions in various cultures, see *Nourritures, Sociétés et Religions: Commensalités* (introduction by Solange Thierry). Paris: L'Harmattan, 1990.

On the microwave revolution in cooking, see:

Lori Longbotham. *Better by Microwave*. New York: Dutton, 1990.

Maria Luisa Scott. *Mastering Microwave Cooking*. Mount Vernon NY: Consumers Union, 1988.

Eric Quayle. *Old Cook Books: An Illustrated History*. New York: Dutton. 1978; and Daniel S. Cutler. *The Bible Cookbook*. New York: Morrow, 1985, offer a good retrospective of what people used to eat.

In *World Hunger. A Reference Handbook* (Patricia L. Kutzner, Santa Barbara CA: ABC-Clio, 1991), the author gives a stark description of the problem of hunger in today's world:
"With more than enough food in the world to feed everyone, hundreds of millions of men, women, and children still go hungry" (p. ix).
It is not the first time in history that starvation and famine affect people all over the world. What is new is the scale of the problem, affecting well over one billion human beings. In June, 1974, in the Assessment of the World Food Situation, commissioned by the United Nations Economic and Social Council, the situation was described in terms still unchanged: "The causes of inade-

quate nutrition are many and closely interrelated, including ecological, sanitary, and cultural constraints, but the principal cause is poverty. This in turn results from socioeconomic development patterns that in most of the poorer countries have been characterized by a high degree of concentration of power, wealth, and incomes in the hands of relatively small elites of national and foreign individuals or groups. [...] The percentage of undernourished is highest in Africa, the Far East, and Latin America; the hunger distribution is highest in the Far East (in the range of 60%). Of the hungry, the majority (up to 90%) is in rural areas.

Data is collected and managed by the World Food Council. The Bellagio Declaration, Overcoming hunger in the 1990's, adopted by a group of 23 prominent development and food policy planners, development practitioners, and scientists noticed that 14 million children under the age of five years die annually from hunger related causes.

Among the organizations created to help feed the world are CARE, Food for Peace, OXFAM, Action Hunger, The Hunger Project, Save the Children, World Vision, the Heifer Project. This list does not include the many national and local organizations that feed the hungry in their respective countries and cities.

Chapter 6: The Professional Winner

The word *sport* comes from the Old French *ésporte*, derived from the Latin *sporta*, basket. The verb *to disport*, also comes from the Old French, *disporter*, to divert, amuse, please; as well as from the Latin *dis* + *portare*, to carry, in the sense of carrying away from care, to divert.

R. Brasch. *How Did Sports Begin? A Look at the Origins of Man at Play.* New York: David McKay Comp., 1970.
The author defines sports as "adventurous, personal, and vicarious," adding that "Sports are as old as time."

Paul Weiss. *Sport: A Philosophical Inquiry.* Carbondale: Southern Illinois University Press, 1969.
Focusing on philosophical aspects of sport, Weiss notes that "Excellence excites and awes" (p. 3).

Labib Boutrous. *Phoenician Sport: Its Influence on the Origin of the Olympic Games.* Amsterdam: J. C. Gieben, 1981.

Allen Guttman. *From Ritual to Record. The Nature of Modern Sports.* New York: Columbia University Press, 1978.

Wendy J. Raschke, Editor. *The Archaeology of the Olympics: The Olympics and Other Festivals in Antiquity.* Madison: University of Wisconsin Press, 1988.

David Sansone. *Greek Athletics and the Genesis of Sport.* Berkeley: University of California Press, 1988.

Michael B. Poliakoff. *Combat Sports in the Ancient World.* New Haven: Yale University Press, 1987.

From the many historic accounts of sport, one learns that archery was first documented over 10,000 years ago in early hunting (Indian lore), magic (during the eclipse of the sun, arrows were shot at the disappearing disk, maybe against evil forces or in an attempt to revive the sun's power), in ritual (during times of drought), or with the purpose of restoring sexual power (ancient Hittites attempting to cure impotence and even homosexuality). Stringing the bow became the test of recognition in Homer's *Odysseia* when Odysseus returned to Penelope.

Johan Huizinga (1872-1945). *Homo ludens. A Study of the Play Element in Culture.* Trans. R.F.C. Hull. London: Routledge & Kegan Paul, 1980.

Roger Caillois. Structure et classification des jeux, in *Diogène,* 12, 1955. pp. 72-88.
The author classifies games between *agon*—games based on precise rules—and *alea*—games based on chance. He also used the perspective of the individual participant. In this case, games can be for pleasure (*paidia,* a word derived from the Greek word for child) or with a useful outcome (*ludus*). There are other attempts to deal with the competitive aspects of games.

The gamut of wrestling is documented in the tomb of Pharaoh Beni Hasan of Egypt. A hieroglyphic inscription lauds Pharaoh Amenphosis II for his "strong arm, long stride," and as a "skilled charioteer" (cf. R. Brausch, *Op.cit.,* p. 15).

Tony Mason. *Sport in Britain.* London/Boston: Faber and Faber, 1988.

Kathleen E. McCrone. *Playing the Game: Sport and the Physical Emancipation of English Women.* Lexington KY: University Press of Kentucky, 1988.

The business of advertisement rides high on sports events. Almost 60 spots (of 30 seconds), priced at over $800,000.00 a spot (almost $30,000.00 a second) are the trophies won before the Superbowl. At the Olympic Games held in Barcelona in 1992, sponsorship licensing reached 1.4 billion dollars. A sponsor's village of 24 homes served as a reception site for the companies that invested in the event. Kodak offered free processing of 125,000 rolls of film for the press. Coca Cola became the official soft drink of the entire Olympic organization. When Fuji tried an ambush advertisement by flying its blimp over the Olympic stadium, the organizers convinced the Spanish government to invoke national security as a reason for having it grounded. On the winners' podium, the only sneakers accepted were those of co-sponsor Reebok. This created a conflict since many of the basketball players in the USA's Dream Team endorse Nike. More on the business of sport can be found in:

Victor Head. *Sponsorship: the Newest Marketing Skill.* Cambridge, Cambridgeshire: Woodhead-Faulkn, 1981.

Steve Sleight. *Sponsorship: What It is and How to Use It.* New York: McGraw-Hill, 1989.

Sports Marketing News (periodical). Westport CT: Technical Marketing Corporation. From1986.

B. Seebohm Rowntree. *Betting and Gambling. A National Evil.* New York: The Macmillan Co., 1905.

Michael Heim. *A Breed Apart. The Horses and the Players.* New York: H. Holt, 1991.

Gerald Strine. *Covering the Spread. How to Bet Pro Football.* New York: Random House, 1978.

David Dixon. *From Prohibition to Regulation. Bookmaking, Anti-Gambling, and the Law.* New York: Oxford University Press,1991.

The legal money in the sports gambling industry is only a fraction (some consider a ratio of 1:100) of the underground money at stake. The Superbowl can trigger wagering to over one billion dollars. Through one year of racing, probably 35 billion dollars will be wagered in off-track betting (sometimes run from locations outside the USA).

The Official 1996 Olympic Web Site reported on the efforts of the Atlanta Centennial Olympic Properties (ACOP) to make sure that companies that had not paid for the privilege of advertising at the Olympic Games would be kept at bay. The report states: "Under the terms of its supplier agreement, CMR [Creative Media Reporting] ... will monitor network and local television and radio newscasts and advertising in 125 markets across the U.S. [...] CMR will also alert ACOP to advertising or news reports of companies using parasite tactics in an attempt to appear to have an association with the Olympic Games or the Olympic Movement."

Chapter 7: Science and Philosophy: More Questions than Answers

T.S. Elliot. Burnt Norton, in *V. Four Quartets*. London: Faber & Faber, 1936.

For information on the development of science and philosophy in early civilizations, see:

Shigeru Nakayama and Nathan Sivin, Editors. *Chinese Science: Exploration of an Ancient Tradition*. Cambridge: MIT Press, 1973.

Karl W. Butzer. *Early Hydraulic Civilization in Egypt: a Study in Cultural Ecology*. Chicago: University of Chicago Press, 1976.

Heinrich von Staden. *Herophilus: The Art of Medicine in Early Alexandria*. Cambridge/New York: Cambridge University Press, 1989.

The Cultural Heritage of India, (in 6 volumes). Calcutta: Ramakrishna Mission, Institute of Culture, 1953.

James H. MacLachlan. *Children of Prometheus: A History of Science and Technology*. Toronto: Wall & Thompson, 1989.

Isaac Asimov. *Asimov's Biographical Encyclopedia of Science and Technology. The Lives and Achievements of 1195 Great Scientists from Ancient Times to the Present*. Garden City NY: Doubleday, 1972.

Fritz Kraft. *Geschichte der Naturwissenschaft*. Freiberg: Romback, 1971.

G.E.R. Lloyd. *Methods and Problems in Greek Science* Cambridge University Press, 1991.

Robert K.G. Temple. *China, Land of Discovery*. London: Patrick Stephens, 1986. Temple documents discoveries and techniques such as row cultivation and hoeing ("There are 3 inches of moisture at the end of a hoe,"), the iron plow, the horse harness, cast iron, the crank handle, lacquer ("the first plastic"), the decimal system, the suspension bridge as originating from China. In the *Introduction*, Joseph Needham writes: "Chauvinistic Westerners, of course, always try to minimize the indebtedness of Europe to China in Antiquity and the Middle Ages" (p.7).
What is of interest in the story is the fact that all these discoveries occur in a context of configurational focus, of synthesis, not in the sequential horizon of analytic Western languages. In some cases, the initial non-linear thought is linearized. This is best exemplified by comparing Chinese printing methods, intent on letters seen as images, with those following Gutenberg's movable type. Obviously, a text perceived as a holistic entity, such as the Buddhist charm scroll (printed in 704-751) or the Buddhist Diamond Sutra of 868 (cf. p.

836

Civilization of Illiteracy: References

112) are different from the Bibles printed by Gutenberg and his followers. Contributions to the history of science from India and the Middle East also reveal that many discoveries celebrated as accomplishments of Western analytical science were anticipated in non-analytical cultures.

Satya Prakash. *Founders of Science in Ancient India.* Dehli: Govindram Hasanand, 1986.

G. Kuppuram and K. Kumudamani, Editors. *History of Science and Technology in India.* Dehli: Sundeep Prakashan, 1990.

Seyyed Hossein Nasr. *Islamic Science. Persia.* Tihran: Surush, 1987.

Charles Finch. *The African Background to Medical Science: Essays in African History, Science, and Civilization.* London: Karnak House, 1990.

Magic, myth, and science influence each other in many ways. Writings on the subject refer to specific aspects (magic and science, myth as a form of rational discourse) or to the broader issues of their respective epistemological condition.

Richard Cavendish. *A History of Magic.* London: Weidenfeld & Nicholson, 1977.

Gareth Knight. *Magic and the Western Mind: Ancient Knowledge and the Transformation of Consciousness.* St. Paul: Llewellyn Publications, 1991.

Umberto Eco. *Foucault's Pendulum.* New York: Harcourt, Brace Jovanovich, 1989. In this novel, Umberto Eco deals, in a light vein, with the occult considered as the true science.

Jean Malbec de Tresfel. *Abrège de la Théorie et des véritables principes de l'art appelé chymie, qui est la troisième partie ou colonne de la vraye medecine hermetique.* Paris: Chez l'auteur, 1671.

Adam McLean. *The Alchemical Mandala. A Survey of the Mandala in the Western Esoteric Traditions.* Grand Rapids, MI: Phanes Press, 1989.

Titus Burckhardt. *Alchemie, Sinn und Weltbild.* London: Stuart & Watkins, 1967. Translated as *Alchemy. Science of the Cosmos, Science of the Soul,* by William Stoddart. Longmead/Shaftesbury/Dorest: Element Books, 1986.

Marie Louise von Franz. *Alchemy. An Introduction to the Symbolism and the Psychology.* Toronto: Inner City Books, 1980.

Neil Powell. *Alchemy. The Ancient Science.* Garden City, NY: Doubleday, 1976.

Stanislas Klossowski de Rola. *Alchemy. The Secret Art*. London: Thames and Hudson, 1973.

J.C. Cooper. *Chinese Alchemy. The Taoist Quest for Immortality*. Wellingborough, Northamptonshire: Aquarian Press, 1984.

Robert Zoller. *The Arabic Parts in Astrology. The Lost Key to Prediction*. Rochester, VT: Inner Traditions International (distributed by Harper & Row), 1989.

Dane Rudhyar. *An Astrological Mandala. The Cycle of Transformation and Its 360 Symbolic Phases*. 1st ed. New York: Random House, 1973.

Cyril Fagan. *Astrological Origins*. St. Paul: Llewellyn Publications, 1971.

Percy Seymour. *Astrology. The Evidence of Science*. Luton, Bedfordshire: Lennard, 1988.

Rodney Davies. *Fortune-Telling by Astrology. The History and Practice of Divination by the Stars*. Wellingborough, Northamptonshire: Aquarian Press, 1988.

"Astrological herbalism distinguished seven planetary plants, twelve herbs associated with signs of the zodiac and thirty-six plants assigned to decantates and to horoscopes" cf. Lévi-Strauss, *Le cru et le cuit*, p. 42.

Ruth Drayer. *Numerology. The Language of Life*. El Paso, TX: Skidmore-Roth Publications, 1990.

Albert Einstein (1879-1955) Nobel prize laureate, 1921.
He discusses the conditions of existence for which we are not adjusted in *Über den Frieden, Weltordnung und Weltuntergang* (O. Norden and H. Norden, Editors.), Bern. 1975, p. 494.

In a letter to Jacques Hadamard (1945), Einstein explained: "The words of the language, as they are written or spoken, do not seem to play any role in my mechanisms of thought. The physical entities which seem to serve as elements in thought are certain signs and more or less clear images which can be 'voluntarily' reproduced or combined" cf. A Testimonial from Professor Einstein, in *The Psychology of Invention in the Mathematical Field*, edited by J. Hadamard, Princeton: Princeton University Press, 1945, p. 142.

Raymond Kurzweil, *The Age of Intelligent Machines*, Cambridge: MIT Press, 1990.
"Rather than defining intelligence in terms of its constituent processes, we might define it in terms of its goal: the ability to use symbolic reasoning in the pursuit of a goal" (p. 17).

Alan Bundy, *The Computer Modelling of Mathematical Reasoning*. New York: Academic Press, 1983.

Allan Ramsey. *Formal Methods in Artificial Intelligence*. Cambridge/New York: Cambridge University Press, 1991.

M. Reinfrank, Editor. *Non-Monotonic Reasoning: Second International Workshop*. Berlin/New York: Springer Verlag, 1989.

Titus Lucretius Carus. *De rerum natura* (edited with translation and commentary by John Godwin). Warminster, Wiltshire, England: Aris & Phillips,1986.

—. *The Nature of Things*. Trans. Frank O. Copley. 1st ed. New York: Norton., 1977.

Epicurus, called by Timon "the last of the natural philosophers," was translated by Lucretius into Latin. His *Letter to Herodotus* and *Master Sayings* (*Kyriai doxai*) were integrated in *De rerum natura* (*On Nature*). A good reference book is Clay Diskin's *Lucretius and Epicurus,* Ithaca: Cornell University Press, 1983.

Galileo Galilei. *Discorsi e dimostrazioni matematiche* (*Two New Sciences: Including Centers of Gravity and Force of Percussion*, translated, with a new introduction and notes, by Stillman Drake). Toronto: Wall & Thompson, 1989.

—. *Galileo's Early Notebooks. The Physical Questions* (translated from the Latin, with historical and paleographical commentary, by William A. Wallace). Notre Dame IN: University of Notre Dame Press, 1977.

Starting out as a *dictionnaire raisonné* of the sciences, the arts, and crafts, the *Encyclopédie* became a major form of philosophic expression in the 18th century. Philosophers dedicated themselves to the advancement of the sciences and secular thought, and to the social program of the Enlightenment. The *Encyclopédie* showcased new directions of thought in all branches of intellectual activity. The emergent values corresponding to the pragmatic condition of time, tolerance, innovation, and freedom, were expressed in the Encyclopedic writings and embodied in the political program of the revolutions it inspired. One of the acknowledged sources of this orientation is Ephraim Chamber's *Cyclopedia (or an Universal Dictionary of Arts and Sciences),* London, 1728.

The examination of star naming is in some ways an exercise in the *geology* of pragmatic contexts. The acknowledgment of what is high, over, above, and beyond the observer's actions suggested power. The sequence of day and night, of seasons, of the changing weather is a mixture of repetitive patterns and unexpected occurrences, even meteorites, some related to wind, fire, water. Once the shortest and the longest days are observed, and the length of day equal to that of night (the equinox), the sky becomes integrated in the pragmatics of human self-constitution by virtue of affecting cycles of work. Furthermore, parallel to the mytho-magical explanation of what happens follows the association of mythical characters, mainly to stars. Saturn, or Chronos, was the god of time, a *star* known for its steady movement; Jupiter, known by the Egyptians as Ammon, the most impressive planet, and apparently the biggest. Details of this geology of naming could lead to a book. Here are some of the names used:

Mythomagical: Mercury, Venus, Mars, Jupiter, Uranus, Pluto; Zodiacal: Gemini, Capricorn, Sagittarius, Scorpio, etc.

Space: limitless, 3-dimensional, in which objects exist, events occur, movement takes place. Objects have relative positions and their movement has relative directions. The geometric notion of space expands beyond 3-dimensionality.

Paradigm: Since the time Thomas Kuhn published *The Structure of Scientific Revolutions* (1962), the concept of paradigm was adopted in philosophic jargon. The underlying thesis is that science operates in a research space dominated by successive research models, or paradigms. The domination of such a paradigm does not make it more important than previous scientific explanations (paradigms are not comparable). Rather it effects a certain convergence in the unifying framework it ascertains.

Logos: ancient Greek for *word*, was many times defined, almost always partially, as a means to express thoughts. By generalization, *logos* became similar to thought or reason, and thus a way to control the word through speech (*legein*). In this last sense, *logos* was adapted by Christianity as the Word of Divinity.

For a description of holism, see *Holism-A Philosophy for Today,* by Harry Settanni (New York: P. Lang, 1990).

Techné: from the Greek, means "pertaining to the making of artifacts" (art objects included).

Francis Bacon (1561-1626): Statesman and philosopher, distinguished for establishing the empiric methods for scientific research. Intent on analytical tools, he set out methods of induction which proved to be effective in the distinction between scientific and philosophical research. In *The Advancement of Learning* (1605) and especially *Novum Organum* (1620), Bacon set forth principles that affected the development of modern science.

René Descartes (1596-1650): Probably one of the most influential philosophers and scientists, whose contribution, at a time of change and definition, marked Western civilization in many ways. The *Cartesian* dualism he developed ascertains a physical (*res extensa*) and a thinking (*res cogitans*) substance. The first is extended, can be measured and divided; the second is indivisible. The body is part of *res extensa*, the mind (including thoughts, desires, volition) is *res cogitans*. His rules for the *Direction of the Understanding* (1628), influenced by his mathematical concerns, submitted a model for the acquisition of knowledge. The method of doubt, i.e., rejection of everything not certain, expressed in the famous *Discourse on Method* (1637), together with the foundation of a model of science that combines a mechanic image of the universe described mathematically, are part of his legacy.

Edwin A. Abbot. *Flatland. A Romance of Many Dimensions*. By a Square.
A broad-minded square guides the reader through a 2-dimensional space. High priests (circular figures) forbid discussing a third dimension. Abruptly, the square is transported into spaceland and peers astonished into his 2-dimensional homeland.

Spatial reasoning: a type of reasoning that incorporates the experience of space either in direct forms (geometric reasoning) or indirectly (through terms such as *close, remote*, among others).

Linearity: relation among dependent phenomena that can be described through a linear function.

Non-linearity: relations among dependent phenomena that cannot be described through a linear function, but through exponential and logarithmic functions, among others.

Jackson E. Atlee. *Perspectives of Non-Linear Dynamics*. Cambridge/New York: Cambridge University Press, 1990.

S. Neil Rasband. *Chaotic Dynamics of Non-Linear Systems*. New York: Wiley, 1990.

Coherence: the notion that reflects interest in how parts of a whole are connected. Of special interest is the coherence of knowledge.

Ralph C.S. Walker. *The Coherence Theory of Truth: Realism, Anti-Realism, Idealism*. London/New York: Routledge, 1989.

Alan H. Goldman. *Moral Knowledge*. London/New York: Routledge, 1988.

A major survey, focused on the contributions of Keith Lehrer and Laurence Bon Jour, was carried out in *The Current State of the Coherence Theory. Critical Essays on the Epistemic Theories of Keith Lehrer and Laurence Bon Jour, with Replies* (John W. Bender, Editor, Dordrecht/Boston: Kluwer Academic Publishers, 1989).

David Kirsch. *Foundations of Artificial Intelligence*. A special volume of the journal *Artificial Intelligence*, 47:1-3, January 1991. Amsterdam: Elsevier.

Self-organization is a dominant topic in artificial life research. The Annual Conference on Artificial Life (Santa Fe) resulted in *Proceedings* in which self-organization is amply discussed. Some aspects pertinent to the subject can be found in:

H. Haken. *Advanced Synergetics: Instability Hierarchies of Self-Organizing Systems and Devices*. Berlin/New York: Springer Verlag, 1983.

P.C.W. Davies. *The Cosmic Blueprint*. London: Heinemann, 1987.

G. M. Whitesides. *Self-Assembling Materials*, in Nanothinc, 1996. http://www.nanothinc.com/webmaster @nanothinc.com

More information on self-assembling materials and nanotechnology can be found on the Internet at http://www.nanothinc.com/; webmaster@nanothinc.com and at http://www.foresight.org/; webmaster@foresight.org.

Richard Feynman, in a talk given in 1959, stated that "The principles of physics...do not speak against the possibility of maneuvering things atom by atom. [...] The problems of chemistry and biology can be greatly helped if our ability to...do things on an atomic level is ultimately developed, a development which I think cannot be avoided." (cf. http://www.foresight.org).

Preston Prather. Science Education and the Problem of Scientific Enlightenment, in *Science Education*, 5:1, 1996.

The money invested in science is a slippery subject. While direct funds, such as those made available through the National Science Foundation, are rather scarce, funding through various government agencies (Defense, Agriculture, Energy, NASA) and through private sources amounts to hundreds of billions of dollars. How much of this goes to fundamental research and how much to applied science is not very clear, as even the distinction between fundamental and applied is less and less clear.

Ernst Mach. *The Science of Mechanics* (1883). Trans. T.J. McCormick. LaSalle, IL: Open Court, 1960.

Henri Poincaré. *The Foundations of Science* (1909). Trans. G.B. Halsted. New York: The Science Press, 1929.

N.P. Cambell. *Foundations of Science* (1919). New York: Dover, 1957.

Bas C. van Fraasen. *The Scientific Image*. Oxford: Clarendon Press,1980.

Richard Dawkins. *The Selfish Gene*. New York: Oxford University Press, 1976.

—. *The Extended Phenotype*. New York: Oxford University Press, 1982.

Elan Moritz, of the Institute for Memetic Research, provides the historic and methodological background to the subject in *Introduction to Memetic Science*.

E.O. Wilson. *Sociobiology: The New Synthesis*. Cambridge: Belknap/Harvard University Press, 1975.

Mihai Nadin. *Mind—Anticipation and Chaos* (from the series *Milestones in Thought and Discovery*). Stuttgart/Zurich: Belser Presse, 1991.

—. The Art and Science of Multimedia, in *Real-Time Imaging* (P. Laplante & A. Stoyenko, Editors). Piscataway NJ: IEEE Press, January, 1996.

—. Negotiating the World of Make-Believe: The Aesthetic Compass, in *Real-Time Imaging*. London: Academic Press, 1995.

"Philosophers have only *interpreted* the world in various ways; the point is to *change* it," Karl Marx (cf. *Theses on Feuerbach* (from *Notebooks of 1844-1845*). See also *Writings of the Young Marx on Philosophy and Society*, Garden City NY: Anchor Books, 1967, p. 402.

Paul K. Feyerabend. *Against Method. Outline of an Anarchistic Theory of Knowledge*. London: Verson Edition,1978.

—. *Three Dialogues on Knowledge*. Oxford, England/Cambridge MA: Blackwell,1991.

Imre Lakatos. *Philosophical Papers*, in two volumes (edited by John Worrall and Gregory Currie). Cambridge, England/New York: Cambridge University Press, 1978.

—. *Proofs and Refutations. The Logic of Mathematical Discovery* (John Worrall and Elie Zahar, Editors). Cambridge, England/New York: Cambridge University Press, 1976.

Multivalued logic: expands beyond the truth and falsehood of sentences, handling the many values of the equivocal or the ambiguous.

Charles S. Peirce ascertained that all necessary reasoning is mathematical reasoning, and that all mathematical reasoning is diagrammatic. He explained diagrammatic reasoning as being based on a diagram of the percept expressed and on operations on the diagram. The visual nature of a diagram ("composed of lines, or an array of signs...") affects the nature of the operations performed on it (cf. On the Algebra of Logic: A Contribution to the Philosophy of Notation, in *The American Journal of Mathematics*, 7:180-202, 1885).

Brockman, John. *The Third Culture: Beyond the Scientific Revolution.* (A collection of essays with Introduction written by John Brockman.) New York: Simon & Schuster. 1995
Here are some quotations from the contributors:
Brockman maintains that there is a shift occurring in public discourse, with scientists supplanting philosophers, artists, and people of letters as the ones who render "visible the deeper meanings of our lives, redefining who and what we are."
Danny Hillis states: "We're at the stage where things change on the order of decades, and it seems to be speeding up...."

Auguste Comte, in whose works the thought of Positivism is convincingly embodied, attracted the attention of John Stuart Mill, who wrote *The Positive Philosophy of Auguste Compte* (Boston: Lee and Shepard, 1871). Some of Compte's early writings are reproduced in *The Crisis of Industrial Civilization* (Ronald Fletcher, Editor, London: Heinemann Educational, 1974).

Stefano Poggi. *Introduzione al il Positivisma.* Bari: Laterza, 1987.

Sybil de Acevedo. *Auguste Compte: Qui êtes-vous?* Lyons: La Manufacture, 1988.

Emil Durkheim. *De la division du travail social.* 9e ed. Paris: Presses univérsitaires de France, 1973. (Translated as *The Division of Labor in Society* by W.D. Halls, New York: Free Press, 1984.
Durkheim applied Darwin's natural selection to labor division.

Herbert Spencer (1820-1903): very well known for his essay, *Progress: Its Laws and Cause* (1857), attempted to conceive a theory of society based on naturalist principles. What he defined as the "super-organic," which stands for social, is subjected to evolution. In his view, societies undergo, cycles of birth-climax-death. Productive power varies from one cycle to other (cf. *Principles of Sociology*, 1876-1896).

Chapter 8: Art(ifacts) and Aesthetic Processes

Art Spiegelman. *Maus. A Survivor's Tale. My Father Bleeds History.* New York: Pantheon Books, 1986; and *Maus II: A Survivor's Tale—And Here My Troubles Began. From Mauschwitz to the Catskills and Beyond.* New York Pantheon Books, 1991.

Started as a comic strip (in *Raw*, an experimental *Comix* magazine, co-edited by Spiegelman and Françoise Monly) on the subject of the Holocaust, Maus became a book and, on its completion, the Museum of Modern Art in New York dedicated a show to the artist. Over 1500 interlocking drawings tell the story of Vladek, the artist's father, a survivor of the concentration camp, and his relation to his son. The comic book convention was questioned as to its appropriateness for the tragic theme.

Milli Vanilli, the group that publicly acknowledged that the album *Girl You Know It's True*, for which it was awarded the Grammy for Best New Artist of 1989, was vocally interpreted by someone else. The prize winners, Fab Morvan and Rob Pilatus, credited for the vocals, were hardly the first to take advantage of the new means for creating the illusion of interpretation. As the 'visual entertainment," they became the *wrapper* on a package containing the music of less video-reputed singers. Their producer, Frank Tarian (i.e., Franz Reuther) was on his second "fake." Ten years earlier, he revealed that the pop group Boney M. was his own "mouthpiece." Image-driven pop music sells the fantasy of teen idol to a musically illiterate public. Packaged music extends to simulations of instruments and orchestras as well.

Beauty and the Beast is the story of a handsome prince in 18th century France turned into an eight-foot tall, hideous, hairy beast. Unless he finds someone to love him before his 21st birthday, the curse cast upon him by the old woman he tried to chase away will become permanent. In a nearby village, Maurice, a lovable eccentric inventor, his daughter Belle, who keeps her nose in books and her head in the clouds, and Gaston, the macho of the place, go through the usual "he (Gaston) loves/wants her; she does not care for/shuns him, etc." As its 30th full-length animation, this Walt Disney picture is a musical fairy tale that takes advantage of sophisticated computer animation. Its over one million drawings (the work of 600 animators, artists, and technicians) are animated, some in sophisticated 3-dimensional computer animation. The technological performance, resulting from an elaborate database, provided attractive numbers, such as the *Be Our Guest* sequence (led by the enchanted candelabra, teapot, and clock characters, entire chorus lines of dancing plates, goblets, and eating utensils perform a musical act), or the emotional ballroom sequence. Everything is based on the accepted challenge: "OK, go ahead and fool us," once upon a time uttered by some art director to the computer-generated imagery specialists of the company. The story (by Mme. Leprince de Beaumont) inspired Jean Cocteau, who wrote the screenplay for (and also directed) *La Belle et La Bête* (1946), featuring Jean Marais, Josette Day, and Marcel André.

Anselm Kiefer (b. 1945). Seduced by the relation to history, he produces allegories in reference to myth, art, religion, and culture. His compositions are strongly evocative, not lacking a certain critical dimension, sometimes focused on art itself, which repeatedly failed during times of challenge (those of Nazi Germany included).

Terminator 2 is a movie about two *cyborgs* who come from the future, one to destroy, the other to protect, a boy who will affect the future when he grows up. It was reported to be the most expensive film made as of 1991 (over 130 characters are killed), costing 85 to 100 million dollars; cf. Stanley Kauffmann, *The New Republic*, August 12, 1991, pp. 28-29.

Kitsch: defined in dictionaries as gaudy, trash, pretentious, shallow art expression addressing a low, unrefined taste. Kitsch-like images are used as ironic devices in artworks critical of the bourgeois taste.

The relation between art and language occasioned a major show organized by the Société des Expositions du Palais de Beaux-Arts in Brussels. A catalogue was edited by Jan Debbant and Patricia Holm (Paris: Galerie de Paris; London: Lisson Gallery; New York: Marian Goodman Gallery).

Georg Wilhelm Friedrich Hegel (1770-1831). *Ästhetik* (Hrsg. von Friedrich Bassenge). Berlin: Verlag das Europäische Buch, 1985.

Dadaism: Hans Arp defined Dada as "the nausea caused by the foolish rational explanation of the world" (1916, Zurich). Richard Huelsenbeck stated that "Dada cannot be understood, it must be experienced" (1920). More on this subject can be found in:

Raoul Hausmann. *Am Anfang war Dada*. (Hrsg. von Karl Riha & Gunter Kampf). Steinbach/Giessen: Anabas-Verlag G. Kampf, 1972.

Serge Lemoine. *Dada*. Paris: Hazan, 1986.

Dawn Ades. *Dada and Surrealism Reviewed*. London: Arts Council of Great Britain, 1978.

Hans Bollinger, et al. *Dada in Zurich*. Zurich: Kunsthaus Zurich, 1985.

Walter Benjamin. *Art in the Age of its Mechanical Reproduction* is a translation of *Das Kunstwerk im Zeitalter seiner technischen Reproduzierbarkeit: drei studien zur Kunstsoziologie*. Frankfurt/Main: Suhrkamp Verlag, 1963.

Walter de Maria's *Lightning Field* project was carried out with the support of the Dia Art Foundation, which bought the land and maintains and allows for limited public access to the work. As the prototypical example of *land-art*, this lattice of lightning rods covers an area of one mile by one kilometer. Filled with 400 rods placed equidistantly, the lightning field is the interplay between precision and randomness. During the storm season in New Mexico, the work is brought to life by many bolts of lightning. The artist explained that "Light is as important as lightning." Indeed, during its 24-hour cycle, the field goes through a continuous metamorphosis. Nature and art interact in fascinating ways.

Christo's latest work was entitled *Wrapped Reichstag,* Berlin, July 1995. Regarding Christo's many ambitious projects, some references are:

Erich Himmel, Editor. *Christo. The Pont-Neuf Wrapped,* Paris 1975-1985. New York: Abrams, 1990.

Christo: The Umbrellas. Joint project for Japan and the USA, 25 May - 24 June, 1988. London: Annely Juda Fine Art, 1988.

Christo: Surrounded Islands. Köln: DuMont Buch Verlag, 1984.
Christo: Wrapped Walkways, Loose Park, Kansas City, Missouri, 1977-1978. New York: H.N. Abrams, 1978.

Christo: Valley Curtain, Riffle, Colorado. New York: H.N. Abrams, 1973.

The Bauhaus, a school of arts and crafts, was founded in 1919 in Weimar, by Walter Gropius. Its significance results from the philosophy of education expressed in the Bauhaus program, to which distinguished artists contributed, and from the impressive number of people who, after studying at the Bauhaus, affirmed its methods and vision in worlds of art, architecture, and new educational programs. Among the major themes at Bauhaus were the democratization of artistic creation (one of the last romantic ideas of our time), the social implication of art, and the involvement of technology. Collaborative, interdisciplinary efforts were encouraged; the tendency to overcome cultural and national boundaries was tirelessly pursued; the rationalist attitude became the hallmark of all who constituted the school. In 1925, the Bauhaus had to move to Dessau, where it remained until 1928, before it settled in Berlin. After Gropius, the architects Hans Mayer (1930-1932) and Mies van der Rohe (1932-1933) worked on ascertaining the international style intended to offer visual coherence and integrity. In some ways, the Bauhaus was continued in the USA, since many of its personalities and students had to emigrate from Nazi Germany and found safe haven in the USA.

Leon Battista Alberti (15th century) wrote extensively on painting and sculpture: *De pictura* and *De Statua* were translated by Cecil Grayson (London: Phaidon, 1972). Alberti's writings on the art of building, *De re aedificatoria,* was translated by Joseph Rykwert, Neil Leach, and Robert Tavernor (10 volumes, Cambridge MA: MIT Press, 1988).

Marcel Duchamp (1887-1968). Intently against those who were "intoxicated by turpentine," he pursued a "dry art." From the *Nu descendant un escalier*, considered "an explosion in a fireworks factory" to his celebrated ready-mades, Duchamp pursued the call to "de-artify" art. Selection became the major operation in offering objects taken out of context and appropriating them as aesthetic icons. He argued that "Art is a path to regions where neither time nor space dominate."

Happening: An artistic movement based on the interaction among different forms of expression. Allan Kaprow (at Douglas College in 1958) and the group associated with the Reuben gallery in New York (Kaprow, Jim Dine, Claes Oldenburg, Whitman, Hausen) brought the movement to the borderline where distinctions between the artist and the public are erased. Later, the movement expanded to Europe.

Andy Warhol. *The Philosophy of Andy Warhol: from A to B and Back Again.* New York: Harcourt Brace Jovanovich, 1975.

—. *Strong Opinions.* New York: McGraw Hill, 1973.
Andy Warhol is remembered for saying that in the future, everyone will be a celebrity for 15 minutes.

Vladimir (Vladimirovich) Nabokov. *Lectures on Literature.* Edited by Fredson Bowers, introduction by John Updike. New York: Harcourt Brace Jovanovich, 1980-1981.

"A rose is a rose is a rose...," now quite an illustrious (if not trite) line, originated in Gertrude Stein's poem *Sacred Emily.* But "...A rose by any other name/would smell as sweet." from Shakespeares *Romeo and Juliet* can be seen as a precursor.

Symbolism is a neo-romantic art movement of the end of the 19th century, in reaction to the Industrial Revolution and positivist attitudes permeating art and existence. Writers such as Beaudelaire, Rimbaud, Maeterlinck, Huysmans, composers (Wagner, in the first place), painters such as Gauguin, Ensor, Puvis de Chavannes, Moreau, and Odilon Redon created in the spirit of symbolism. At the beginning of the 20th century, symbolism attempted to submit a unified *alphabet* of images. Jung went so far as to identify its psychological basis.

James Joyce (1882-1941). *Ulysses.* A critical and synoptic (though very controviersial) edition, prepared by Hans Walter Gabler with Wolfgang Steppe and Claus Melchior. New York: Garland Publishers, 1984.

Antoine Furetière. *Essais d'un Dictionnaire Universel.* Geneva: Slatkine Reprints, 1968 (reprint of the original published in 1687 in Amsterdam under the same title).

Antonio Gramsci (1891-1937). *2000 Pagine de Gramsci.* A cura di Giansiro Ferrata e Niccolo Gallo. Milano: Il Saggiatore, 1971.

—. *Gramsci: Selections from Cultural Writings.* (Edited by David Forgacs and Geoffrey Newell-Smith; translated by William Boelhower). Cambridge MA: Harvard University Press, 1985.

—. *Le Ceneri di Gramsci.* Milano: Garzanti, 1976.

Pier Paolo Pasolini (1922-1975). *Turc al Friul.* Traduzione e introduzione di Giancarlo Bocotti. Munich: Instituto Italian di Cultura, 1980.

Ken Kesey. *The Further Inquiry.* Photographs by Ron Bevirt. New York: Viking Penguin, 1990.

Gustave Flaubert (1821-1880). *Madame Bovary.* Paris: Gallimard, 1986.

—. *Madame Bovary.* Patterns of provincial life. (Translated, with a new introduction by Francis Steegmuller). New York: Modern Library, 1982.

Donald Barthelme. *Amateurs.* New York: Farrar, Strauss, Giroux, 1976.

—. *The King.* New York: Harper & Row, 1990.

—. *The Slightly Irregular Fire Engine or The Hithering Thithering Djinn.* New York: Farrar, Strauss, Giroux, 1971.

Kurt Vonnegut. *Breakfast of Champions or, Goodbye Blue Monday!* New York: Delacorte Press, 1973.

—. *Galapagos. A Novel.* New York: Delacorte Press, 1985.

—. *Fates Worse than Death. An Autobiographical Collage of the 1980's.* New York: G.P. Putnam's, 1991.

John Barth. *Chimera.* New York: Random House, 1972.

—. *The Literature of Exhaustion and the Literature of Replenishment.* Northridge CA: Lord John Press, 1982.

—. *Sabbatical. A Romance.* New York: Putnam, 1982.

William H. Gass. *Fiction and the Figures of Life.* New York: Knopf, 1970.

—. *Habitations of the Word: Essays.* New York: Simon and Schuster, 1985.

—. *In the Heart of the Heart of the Country and Other Stories.* New York: Harper & Row, 1968.

Gary Percesepe. What's Eating William Gass?, in *Mississippi Review,* 1995.

Gertrude Stein's writing technique is probably best exemplified by her own writing. *How to Write,* initially published in 1931 in Paris (Plain Editions), states provocatively that "Clarity is of no importance because nobody listens and nobody knows what you mean no matter what you mean nor how clearly you mean what you mean." In an interview with Robert Haas, 1946) in *Afterword,* Gertrude Stein stated that "Any human being putting down words had to make sense out of them," (p. 101). "I write with my eyes not with my ears or mouth," (p. 103). Moreover: "My writing is as clear as mud, but mud settles and clear streams run on and disappear."

Gertrude Stein. *How to Write* (with a new preface by Patricia Meyerowitz). New York: Dover Publications, 1975.
The author shows that "the innovative works of an artist are explorations" (p.vi).

—. *Useful Knowledge.* Barrytown NY: Station Hill Press, 1988.

—. *What are Masterpieces?* New York: Pitman Publishing Corp., 1970 (reprint of 1940 edition).

Edmund Carpenter. *They Became What They Beheld.* New York: Outerbridge and Dienstfrey/Ballentine, 1970.
The author maintains that *the book* became the organizing principle for all existence, a model for achieving bureaucracy.

It seems that the first comic strip in America was *The Yellow Kid,* by Richard F. Outcault, in the *New York World,* 1896. Among the early comic strips: George Harriman's *Krazy Kat* (held as an example of American Dadaism); Windsor McKay's *Little Nemo in Slumberland*; Milton Caniff's *Terry and the Pirated.*

Filippo Tommaso Marinetti (1876-1944). *Il Futurismo* was written in 1908 as the preface to a volume of his poetry and was published in 1909. Its manifesto was set forth in the words "We declare that the splendor of the world has been increased by a new beauty: the beauty of speed." Breaking with the livresque past, the Italian Futurism took it upon itself to "liberate this land from the fetid cancer of professors, archaeologists, guides, and antiquarians." The break with the past was a break with its values as these were rooted in literate culture.

Dziga Vertov (born Denis Arkadievich Kaufman,1986-1954). Became known through his innovative montage juxtaposition, about which he wrote in *Kino-*

Glas (Kino-Eye). The film *We* (1922) is a fantasy of movement. *Kino-Pravda* (1922-1925) were documentaries of extreme expressionism, with very rich visual associations.

Experiments in simultaneity are also experiments in the understanding of the need to rethink art as a representation of dynamic events.

Michail Fyodorovich Larionov (1881-1964). Russian-born French painter and designer, a pioneer in abstract painting, after many experiences in figurative art and with a declared obsession with the aesthetic experience of simultaneity. Founder of the Rayonist movement—together with his wife, Natalia Goncharova (1881-1962), painter, stage designer, and sculptor—Larionov went from a neo-primitive painting style to cubism and futurism in order to finally synthesize them in a style reflecting the understanding of the role of light (in particular, as rays). His *Portrait of Tatline* (1911) is witness to the synthesis that Rayonism represented.

Fernand Léger (1881-1955). *Machine Aesthetics*, 1923.
"La vitesse est la loi de la vie moderne." (Speed is the modern law of life.)

Chapter 9: Libraries, Books, Readers

In his Introduction to *A Carlyle Reader*, (Cambridge University Press, 1984), G.B. Tennyson is unequivocal in his appreciation: "No one who hopes to understand the nineteenth century in England can dispense with Carlyle," (p. xiv). Since nineteenth century England is of such relevance to major developments in the civilization of literacy, one can infer that Tennyson's thought applies to persons trying to understand the emergence and consolidation of literacy. Thomas Carlyle (1795-1881) wrote *Signs of Times*. (He took the title from the *New Testament*, Matthew 16:3, "O ye hypocrites, ye can discern the face of the sky, but can ye not discern the sign of the times?") He condemns his age in the following terms: "Were we required to characterize this age of ours by any single epithet, we should be tempted to call it, not a Heroical, Devotional, Philosophical, or Moral Age. It is the Age of Machinery, in every outward and inward sense of that word; the age which, with its whole undivided might, forwards, teaches and practises the great art of adapting means to ends. Nothing is done directly, or by hand; all is by rule and calculated contrivance. For the simplest operation, some helps and accompaniments, some cunning abbreviating process is in readiness. Our old modes of exertion are all discredited, and thrown aside. On every hand, the living artisan is driven from his workshop to make room for a speedier, inanimate one," (cf. *Reader*, p. 34). Parallels to the reactions to new technology in our age are more than obvious.

New Worlds, Ancient Texts. The Cultural Impact of an Encounter, a major public documentary exhibit at the New York Public Library, September 1992-January 1992, curated by Anthony Grafton, assisted by April G. Shelford.
At the other end of the spectrum defined by Carlyle's faith in books comes a fascinating note from Louis Hennepin (1684): "We told them [the Indians] that we know all things through written documents. These savages asked, 'Before you came to the lands where we live, did you rightly know that we were here?' We were obliged to say no. 'Then you didn't know all things through books, and they didn't tell you everything'"

A. Grafton, A. Shelford, and N. Siraisi, *The Power of Tradition and the Shock of Discovery*, Cambridge: Harvard University Press, 1992.

In comparison to Carlyle's criticism of mechanical mediation of the Industrial Age comes this evaluation of the Information Age or Post-Industrial Age: "In the industrial age, when people need to achieve something, do they have to go through a series of motions, read manuals, or become experts at the task? Not at all; they flip a switch.... It isn't necessary to know a single thing about lighting; all one needs to do is flip a switch to turn the light on. [...] To take care of a number of tasks, you push a button, flip a switch, turn a dial. That is the age of industry working at its best, so that you don't have to become an electrical engineer or physicist to function effectively.
"To get the information you need...do you need to go on-line or open a manual? Unfortunately, most of us right now end up going through a series of activities in order to get the precise information we need. In the age of information...you will be able to turn on a computer, come up with the specific question, and it will do the work for you." (cf. Address by Jeff Davidson, Executive Director of the Breathing Space Institute of Chapel Hill, before the National Institute of Health, Dec. 8, 1995; reprinted in Vital Speeches, Vol. 62, 06-01-1996, pp. 495, and in the Electric Library™.)

George Steiner. The End of Bookishness? (edited transcript of a talk given to the International Publishers' Association Congress in London, on June 14, 1988) in *Times Literary Supplement*, 89-14, 1988, p. 754.

Aldus Manutius, the Elder (born Aldo Manuzio, 1449-1515): Known for his activity in printing, publishing, and typography, especially for design and manufacture of small pocket-sized books printed in inexpensive editions. The family formed a short-lived printing empire (ending in 1597 with Aldus Manutius, the Younger) and is associated with the culture of books and with high quality typography.

Ray Bradbury. *Fahrenheit 451*. An abridged version appeared in *Galaxy Science Fiction* (1950) under the title *The Fireman*.

Adolf Hitler (1889-1945). *Mein Kampf* (translated by Ralph Manheim) Boston: Houghton Mifflin, 1971.

Mao (1893-1976). *Comrade Mao Tze-tung on imperialism and all reactionaries are paper tigers*. Peking: Foreign Language Press, 1958.

Umberto Eco. *The Name of the Rose* (translated by William Weaver). San Diego: Harcourt Brace Jovanovich. 1983. Originally published in Italy as *Il nome della rosa*. Milano: Fabbri-Bompiani, 1980.

Topos uranikos, in Plato's philosophy is the heavenly place from which we originally come and where everything is true. Vilém Flusser wrote that, "The library (transhuman memory) is presented as a space (*topos uranikos*)" cf. On Memory (Electronic or Otherwise), in *Leonardo*, 23-4, 1990, p. 398.

Great libraries take shape, under *Libraries*, in *Compton's Encyclopedia* (Compton's New Media), January 1, 1994

Noah Webster (1758-1843) wrote *The Compendious Dictionary of the English Language*, in 2 volumes, in 1828. He was probably inspired by Samuel Johnson (1709-1784), who wrote his *Dictionary of the English Language* in 1755.

Larousse de la Grammaire. Paris: Librairie Larousse. 1983

Dudens Bedeutungswörterbuch: 24,000 Wörter mit ihren Grundbedeutungen (bearbeitet von Paul Grebe, Rudolf Koster, Wolfgang Müller, et al). Zehn Bänden. Mannheim: Bibliographisches Institut. 1980

Vannevar Bush. As We May Think, in *The Atlantic Monthly*, A Magazine of Literature, Science, Art, and Politics. vol. CLXXVI, July-Dec., 1945.
The blurb introducing the article states: "As Director of the Office of Scientific Research and Development, Dr. VANNEVAR BUSH has coordinated the activities of some six thousand leading American scientists in the application of science to warfare. In this significant article, he holds up an incentive for scientists when the fighting has ceased. He urges that men of science should then turn to the massive task of making more accessible our bewildering store of knowledge," (p. 101). In many ways, this article marks the shift from a literacy-dominated pragmatics to one of many new forms of human practical activity.

Ted Nelson. Replacing the Printed Word: A Complete Literary System, in *Information Processing 80*. (S.H. Lavington, Editor). Amsterdam: North Holland Publishing Company, 1980, pp. 1013-1023.

Rassengna dei siti piu' utilizzati, and Bibliotechi virtuali, in Internet e la Biblioteca, http://www.bs.unicatt.it/bibliotecavirtuale.html, 1996.

The Infonautics Corporation maintains the Electric Library™ on the World Wide Web.

Chapter 10: The Sense of Design

The term *design* (of Latin origin) can be understood as meaning "from the sign," "out of the sign," "on account of the sign," "concerning the sign," "according to the sign," "through the medium of the sign." All these possible understandings point to the semiotic nature of design activity. Balducinni defined design as "a visible demonstration by means of lines of those things which man has first conceived in his mind and pictured in the imagination and which the practised hand can make appear." It is generally agreed that before Balducinni's attempt to define the field, the primary sense of design was *drawing*. More recently, though, design is understood in a broad sense, from actual design (of artifacts, messages, products) to the conception of events (design of exhibitions, programs, and social, political, and family gatherings).

"Nearly every object we use, most of the clothes we wear and many things we eat have been designed," wrote Adrian Forty in *Objects of Desire. Design and Society since 1750* (London: Thames and Hudson, 1986; paperback edition, New York: Thames and Hudson, 1992, p. 6).

International Style: generic name attached to the functionalist, anti-ornamental, and geometric tendency of architecture in the second quarter of the 20th century. In 1923, Henri-Russel Hitchcock and Philip Johnson organized the show entitled *International Style-Architecture Since 1922*, at the Museum of Modern Art in New York. Among the best known architects who embraced the program are Gerrit T. Rietveldt, Adolf Loos, Peter Behrens, Le Corbusier, Walter Gropius, Mies van der Rohe, and Eero Saalinen.

H. R. Hitchcock and P. Johnson. *The International Style*. New York: Norton, 1966.

Jay Galbraith. *Designing Complex Organizations*. Reading MA: Addison-Wesley, 1973.

Devoted to the art of drawing, a collection of lectures given at the Fogg Museum of Harvard University in March, 1985, *Drawing Defined* (Walter Strauss and Tracie Felker, Editors, New York: Abaris Books, 1987) is a good reference for the subject. Richard Kenin's *The Art of Drawing: from the Dawn of History to the Era of the Impressionists* (New York: Paddington Press, 1974) gives a broad overview of drawing.

Vitruvius Pollio. *On Architecture* (Edited from the Harleian Manuscripts and translated into English by Frank Granger). Cambridge: Harvard University Press, 1970.

Marcus Cetius Faventius. *Vitruvius and Later Roman Building Manuals.* London: Cambridge University Press. 1973. This book is a translation of Faventius' compendium of Vitruvius' *De Architectura* and of Vitruvius' *De diversis fabricis architectonicae.* Parallel Latin-English texts with translation into the English by Hugh Plommer.

Le Corbusier (Charles-Edouard Jeanneret, 1887-1965). One of the most admired and influential architects and city planners whose work combines functionalism and bold sculptural expression.

Since the time design became a field of study, various design styles and philosophies crystallized in acknowledged design schools. Worthy of mention are the Bauhaus, Art Deco, the Ulm School (which continued in the spirit of the Bauhaus), and Post-modernism.
A good source for information on the becoming of design is Nikolaus Pevsner's *Pioneers of Modern Design,* Harmondsworth, 1960.

The Scholes and Glidden typewriter of 1873, became, with refinements, the Remington model 1 (Remington was originally a gun and rifle manufacturer in the state of New York.) *Encyclopedia Britannica,* 15th Edition, *Micropedia,* Vol. 12, 1990. pp. 86-87). See also *History of the Typewriter* (reprint of the original history of 1923). Sarasota FL: B. R. Swanger, 1965.

Peter Carl Fabergé (1846-1920). One of the most renown goldsmiths, jewelers, and decorative artists. After studying in Germany, Italy, France, and England, he settled in St. Petersburg in 1870, where he inherited his father's jewelry business. Famous for his inventiveness in creating decorative objects—flowers, animals, bibelots, and especially the Imperial Easter Egg—Fabergé is for many the ideal of the artist-craftsman.

Louis Comfort Tiffany (1848-1933). American painter, craftsman, decorator, designer and philanthropist who became one of the most influential personalities in the Art Nouveau style who made significant contributions to glassmaking. Son of Charles Louis Tiffany (1812-1902), the jeweler, he is well known for his significant contributions to glassmaking.

Edward George Earle Bulwer-Lÿtton (1803-1873): British politician, poet, and novelist, famous for *The Last Days of Pompeii*. (*Encyclopedia Britannica*, 15th Edition, *Micropedia*, Vol. 7, 1990, p. 595).

James Gibson. *The Ecological Approach to Visual Perception*. Boston: Houghton Mifflin, 1979.

In our days, design is focused on major themes: design integrity (promoting exemplary forms of typography and form studies, as with the Basel School and its American counterparts), design function (of concern to industry-oriented schools), computation based on design. Originating from Gibson's studies in the psychology of man-nature relations, the ecological approach in design has its starting point in affordance. Thus many designers reflect concern for an individualized approach to the understanding of affordance possibilities.

Costello, Michie, and Milne. *Beyond the Casino Economy*. London: Verso, 1989.

D. Hayes. *Beyond the Silicon Curtain*. Boston: South End Press, 1989.

Mihai Nadin. Interface design: a semiotic paradigm, in *Semiotica* 69:3/4. Amsterdam: Mouton de Gruyter, 1988, pp. 269-302.

—. Computational Design, in *formdiskurs* 2, I, 1997, pp. 40-62.

—. Computers in design education: a case study, in *Visible Language* (special issue: Graphic Design-Computer Graphics),vol. XIX, no. 2, Spring 1985, pp. 282-287.

—. Design and design education in the age of ubiquitous computing, in *Kunst Design & Co*. Wuppertal: Verlag Müller + Busmann, 1994, pp. 230-233.

Kim Henderson. Architectural Innovation: The reconfiguration of existing product technologies, in *Administrative Science Quarterly*, vol. 35, January, 1990.

M. R. Louis and R. I. Sutton. *Switching Cognitive Gears: From habits of mind to active thinking*. Working Paper, School of Industrial Engineering, Stanford University, 1989.

Patrick Dillon. *Multimedia Technology from A-Z*. New York: Oryx Press, 1995.

Chapter 11: Politics: There Was Never So Much Beginning

Friedrich Hölderlin (1770-1843). So viel Anfang war noch nie, in *Poems*. English and German. Selected verses edited, introduced, and translated by Michael Hamburger. London/Dover NH: Anvil Press Poetry, 1986.

Aldous Huxley (1894-1963). *Brave, New World*. New York: Modern Library, 1946, 1956.

Thomas Alva Edison (1847-1931). Noted for inventing, among other things, the phonograph and the incandescent bulb.

Alexander Graham Bell (1847-1922). Inventor of the graphophone. He is credited with inventing the telephone and took out the patent on it.

Otto Nicklaus Otto (1832-1891). Inventor of the four-stroke engine applied in the automotive industry.

Nikola Tesla (1856-1943). Inventor of the electric alternator (among other things).

Lev Nikolaievich Tolstoy (1828-1910). *War and Peace*. Trans. Louise and Aylmer Maude. New York: Oxford University Press, 1965. This is a translation of *Voina i Mir*, published in Moscow at the Tipografia T. Ros, 1868.

The *Declaration of Independence* was approved by a group delegates from the American colonies in July, 1776, with the expressed aim of declaring the thirteen colonies independent of England.

Signed at the Constitutional Convention in 1787, after much dispute over representation, the *Constitution of the United States of America* entered into effect once all thirteen states ratified it. Its major significance derives from its ascertainment of an effective alternative to monarchy. The system of checks and balances contained in the Constitution is meant to preserve any one branch of government from assuming absolute authority.

The *Declaration of Rights of Man and the Citizen* was approved by the French National Assembly on August 26, 1789 and declares the right of individuals to be represented, equality among citizens, and freedom of religion, speech, and the press. The ideals of the French Revolution inspired many other political movements on the continent.

Khrushchev, Nikita Sergeevich (1894-1971). Controversial leader of the Soviet Communist Party and head of the soviet government from 1958-1964. He denounced the personality cult formed around Stalin but remained a staunch communist. He was eventually ousted as the crises of the soviet system entered its final phase.

Written by Karl Marx and Friedrich Engels in a year of many popular uprisings all over Europe against conservative monarchies, the *Communist Manifesto* of 1848 expresses the political program of a revolutionary movement: workers of the world united, leading the way to a classless society. The Romantic impetus of the *Manifesto* and its new messianic tone was of a different tenor from the attempts to implement the program in Russia and later on Eastern Europe, China, Vietnam, Cuba, and Korea.

Married...with Children: A situation comedy at the borderline between satire and vulgarity, presenting a couple, Al and Peggy Bundy, and their teenage children, Kelly and Bud, in life-like situations at the fringes of the consumer society.

Born in 1918, Alexander Solzhenitsyn became known as a writer in the context of the post-Stalin era. His books, *A Day in the Life of Ivan Denisovitch* (1962), *The Gulag Archipelago* (1973-1975), *The Oak and the Calf* (1980), testify to the many aspects of Stalin's dictatorship. In 1974, after publishing *Gulag Archipelago* (about life in Soviet prison camps), the writer was exiled from his homeland. He returned to Russia in 1990.

Yevgeni Alexandrovich Yevtushenko: A rhetorical poet in the tradition of Mayakovsky's poetry for the masses. During the communist regime, he took it upon himself to celebrate the official party line, as well as to poeticallly unveil less savory events and abusive practices: "I am ashamed for Stalin, though not only for him." His poetry is still the best way to know the poet and the passionate human being. See: *A Precious Autobiography.* Trans. Andrew R. McAndrew, New York: E. P. Dutton, 1963; and *Yevtushenko's Reader.* Trans. Robin Milner-Gulland. New York: E. P. Dutton, 1972.

Dimitri Dimitrevich Shostakovich (1906-1975): For a very long time the *official* composer of the Soviet Union. After his death, it became clear how deeply critical he was of a reality he seemed to endorse. He created his harmonic idiom by modifying the harmonic system of classical Russian music. See also Gunter Wolter. *Dimitri Shostakovitch: eine sowjetische Tragödie.* Frankfurt/Main, New York: P. Lang, 1991.

There is no good definition of *Samizdat*, the illegal publishing movement of the former Soviet Block and China. Nevertheless, the power of the printed word—often primitively presented and always in limited, original editions—remains exemplary testimony to the many forces at work in societies where authoritarian rules are applied to the benefit of the political power in place.

From a large number of books on various aspects of Samizdat, the following titles can be referenced:

Samizdat. Register of Documents (English edition). Munich: Samizdat Archive Association. From 1977.

Ferdinand J. M. Feldbrugge. *Samizdat and Political Dissent in the Soviet Union.* Leyden: A.W. Sijthoff, 1975.

Claude Widor. *The Samizdat Press in China's Provinces, 1979-1981.* Stanford CA: Hoover Institution, Stanford University, 1987.

Nicolae Ceausescu (1918-1989). His life can be summed up in John Sweeney's statement: "In Ceausescu's Romania, madness was enthroned, sanity a disease" cf. *The Life and Evil Times of Nicolae Ceausescu,* London: Hutchinson, 1991, p. 105.

Berlin Wall. Erected in August, 1961, the wall divided East and West Berlin. Over the years, it became the symbol of political oppression. Hundreds of people were killed in their attempt to escape to freedom. The political events in East Europe of Fall, 1989 led to destruction of the wall, a symbolic step in the not so easy process of German reunification. See also:
J. Ruhle, G. Holzweissig. *13 August 1961: die Mauer von Berlin* (Hrsg von I. Spittman). Köln: Edition Deutschland Archiv, 1981.

Red. B. Beier, U. Heckel, G. Richter. *9 November 1989: der Tag der Deutschen.* Hamburg: Carlsen, 1989.

John Borneman. *After the Wall: East Meets West in the New Berlin.* New York: Basic Books, 1991.

Political unrest, due to intense resentment of the Soviet occupation, and economic hardship led to the creation of an independent labor union, the *Solidarnosc* (Solidarity) in 1980. In 1981, nationwide strikes brought Poland to a standstill. Martial law was imposed and Solidarity was banned in 1982 after dramatic confrontations at the Gdansk shipyards. Reinstated in 1989, Solidarity became a major political factor in the formation of the new, non-communist government.

Massimo d'Azeglio (1798-1866): *I miei ricordi.* A cura di Alberto M. Ghisalberti. Torino: Einaudi, 1971.

Germany has a rather tortuous history behind its unification. After the peace of Westphalia (1648) ending the Thirty Years' War, a sharp division between Catholic and Protestant states arose. After Napoleon's defeat at Waterloo (1815), the German Confederation (led by Austria) prepared the path towards future unification. In 1850, the attempt to form a central government was blocked, to be resuscitated after the Franco-Prussian War (1870-1871). On his defeat of Ludwig II of Bavaria, the Prussian Wilhelm I became the first emperor of a unified Germany in 1871, and Bismarck his first chancellor.

Prepared by Garibaldi's conquest of the Kingdom of the Two Sicilies (1860), the creation of the Kingdom of Italy by Victor Emmanuelle (1861) ended with the seizure of Rome (1870) from the control of the Vatican. Italy became a republic in 1946.

The establishments of various Arab states is a testimony to the many forces at work in the Arab world. The victory of the Allies in World War 1 brought about the dissolution of the Ottoman Empire. Modern Turkey was established in 1920, ruled initially by a Sultan, becoming a republic in 1923 under the presidency of Kamal Atatürk. At around the same time, Syria (including Lebanon) fell under the mandatë of the French League of Nations. Lebanon became a separate state in 1926. Iraq was established as a kingdom in 1921, falling under the same status as Syria within the British League of Nations. Saudi Arabia was created in 1932, and Jordan became an independent kingdom in 1946. The history of national definition and sovereignty in the Middle East is far from being closed.

For information on the Ustasha organization in Croatia, see Cubric Milan's book *Ustasa hrvatska revolucionarna organizacija,* Beograd: Idavacka Kuca Kujizevne Novine, 1990.

Chetniks (in Serbia), see *A Dictionary of Yugoslav Political and Economic Terminology* (cf. Andrlic Vlasta, *Rjecnik terminologije jugoslavenskog politicko-ekonomskog sistema,* published in 1985, Zagreb: Informator). The reality of the breakdown of the country that used to be Yugoslavia is but one of the testimonies of change that renders words and the literate use of language meaningless.

Omae Kenichi. *The Borderless World. Power and Strategy in the Interlinked World Economy.* New York: Harper Business, 1990.

Isaiah Berlin. *The Crooked Timber of Humanity. Chapters in the History of Ideas.* London: John Murray, 1990.

Fedor Mikhailovich Dostoyevsky (1821-1881). Author of *Crime and Punishment* (*Prestuplenie i nakazanie*), Trans. David McDuff, Harmondsworth: Viking, 1991.

Toqueville noticed that "...scarcely any question arises in the United States which does not become, sooner or later, a subject of judicial debate.... As most public men are, or have been, legal practitioners, they introduce the customs and the technicalities of their profession into the affairs of the country.... The language of the law becomes, in some measure, a vulgar tongue" cf. Alexis de Toqueville, *Democracy in America.*

Gary Chapman. Time to Cast Aside Political Apathy in Favor of Creating a New Vision for America, in *Los Angeles Times,* Aug. 19, 1996, p. D3.

Edward Brent (writing as Earl Babble). Electronic Communication and Sociology: Looking Backward, Thinking Ahead, in *American Sociologist,* 27, Apr. 1, 1996, pp. 4-24.

Regulations, whether protective (such as regarding air quality, water pollution, workplace safety, falily leave, etc.) or protectionist (regarding international treade, foreign aid, work abroad, etc.) have a compliance price tag that cost USA businesses 218 billion dollars in 1995. In a report by Thomas Hopkins of the Center for the Study of American Business this number is detailed for small businesses (under 20 employees) at $38,ooo per employee. For individuals, compliance with tax laws in the USA annually costs taxpayers $950.00 *per capita,* for a total of 225 billion dollars.

Chapter 12: *"Theirs not to reason why"*

A professional description of the initial strike in the Gulf War gives the following account: "In the blitz that launched Desert Storm, Apache and special forces helicopters first took out two early warning radar stations. This opened a corridor for 22 F-15E aircraft following in single file to hit Scud sites in western Iraq. Also, 12 stealth F-117A fighters, benefiting from Compass Call and EF-111 long-distance jamming, hit targets in Baghdad, including a phone exchange and a center controlling air defenses. Other such underground centers were hit in the south. Tomahawk missiles took out power plants. All this occurred within 20 minutes.
"About 40 minutes into the assault, a second wave of strike 'packages' of other aircraft, including 20 F-117As, attacked. They were guided by AWACs (airborne warning and control systems) crafts, which had been orbiting within a range of Iraqi radar for months. Coalition forces flew 2399 sorties the first day, losing only three planes." cf. John A. Adam, Warfare in the information age, in *IEEE Spectrum,* September, 1991, p. 27.
One more detail: "The architects of the huge raid are the Central Commander, Lieutenant General Charles A. Horner, and Brigadier General C. Glosson, an electrical engineer by training. For months they have overseen complete war games and rehearsed precision bombing in the Arabian expanse," p. 26.

Sun Tzu. *The Art of War*. Trans. Thomas Cleary. Boston & London: Shambala Dragon Editions,1988.
"Military action is important to the nation—it is the ground of death and life, the path of survival and destruction, so it is imperative to examine it" p. 41.

"Speed is the most important in war," Epaminondas of Thebes. Battle of Leuctra, 371 BCE.

Helmuth von Moltke (1800-1891). *Geschichte des deutsch-französischen Krieges von 1870-1871. The Franco-German War of 1870-1871*. Trans. Clara Bell and Henry W. Fischer. New York: H. Fertig, 1988. Reprint of the version published in New York by Harper in 1892.

Carl von Clausewitz (1780-1831).*Vom Kriege*. Michael Howard and Peter Paret, Editors. *On War*. Princeton NJ: Princeton University Press, 1976. This first edition (1832-1833) was published by Marie von Clausewitz.

Theodor Heuss (1884-1963). *Theodor Heuss über Staat und Kirche*. Frankfurt/Main: P. Lang, 1986.

C. W. Groetsch. Tartaglia's Inverse Problem in a Resistive Medium, in *The American Mathematical Monthly*, 103:7, 1996, pp. 546-551.

Roland Barthes. *Leçon*, Paris: Editions du Seuil, 1978.
The book is based on the lecture delivered at the inauguration of the Chair of Literary Semiology at the Collège de France on January 7, 1977.
"But Language—the performance of a language system—is neither reactionary nor progressive; it is quite simply fascist, for fascism does not prevent speech, it compels speech."

Alan Mathison Turing (1913-1954). British mathematician, one of the inventors of the programmable computer. During World War 2, Turing worked at the British Foreign Office, helping crack the German secret military code.

William Aspray and Arthur Burks, Editors. *Papers of John von Neumann on Computing and Computer Theory*. Cambridge MA: MIT Press; Los Angeles: Tomash Publishers, 1987. Charles Babbage Institute Reprint Series for the History of Computing, Vol. 12.

John Condry, TV: Live from the Battlefield, in *IEEE Spectrum*, September, 1991. Regarding the role of imagery and how it effectively replaces the written word, the following example is relevant: An Israeli visiting Arizona talked to his daughter in Tel Aviv while simultaneously watching the news on the Cable News Network (CNN). The reporter stated that a Scud missile had been launched at Tel Aviv, and the father informed the daughter, who sought protection in a shelter. "This is what television has become since its initial adoption 40 years ago...The world is becoming a global village, as educator Marshall McLuhan predicted it would. Imagery is its language" p. 47.

Darrell Bott. Maintaining Language Proficiency, in *Military Intelligence*, 21, 1995, p. 12.

Charles M. Herzfeld. Information Technology: A Retro- and Pro-spective. Lecture presented at the Battelle Information Technology Summit. Columbus OH, 10 August 1995. Published in *Proceedings of the DTIC/Battelle Information Technology SummIT*.

Linda Reinberg, *In the Field: the Language of the Vietnam War*, New York: Facts on File, 1991.

The strategic defense initiative (SDI) was focused upon developing anti-missile and anti-satellite technologies and programs. A multi-layered, multi-technology approach to ballistic missile defense (BMD) meant to intercept offensive nuclear weapons after they had been launched by aggressors. The system consisted of the so-called target acquisition (search and detection of an offensive object); tracking (determination of the trajectory of the offensive object); discrimination (distinguishing of missiles and warheads from decoys or chaff); interception (accurate pointing and firing to ensure destruction of the offensive object). The critical components are computer programs and the lasers designed to focus a beam on the target's surface, heating it to the point of structural failure.

The Pentagon. *Critical Technologies Plan*, March, 1990.

Restructuring the U.S. Military, a report by a joint task force of the Committee for National Security and *The Defense Budget Project*. Obviously, the post-Cold War momentum provided many arguments for new plans for a scaled down, but highly technological, defense. The new circumstances created by the end of the Cold War require strategies for conversion of industries that until recently depended entirely upon the needs and desires of the military.

Chapter 1: The Interactive Future: Individual, Community, and Society in the Age of the Web

Elaine Morgan. *Falling Apart: The Rise and Decline of Urban Civilisation.* London: Souvenir Press, 1976.

David Clark. *Urban Decline.* London/New York: Routledge, 1989.

Katharine L. Bradbury. *Urban Decline and the Future of American Cities.* Washington DC: Brookings Institution, 1982.

Hegel's theory of state derives from his philosophy of history. Civil society affords individuals opportunities for freedom. But since the state is the final guarantor, it accordingly has priority over the individual; cf. *Philosophy of Right,* T.B. Knox, Editor. London, 1973.

E.A. Wrigley and David Souden, Editors. Thomas Robert Malthus. An Essay On the Principle of Population, 1798, in *The Works of Thomas Robert Malthus.* London: W. Pickering, 1986.
"Population, when unchecked, increases in a geometrical ratio. Subsistence increases only in an arithmetical ratio" (p. 9).

Jean-Jacques Rousseau (1712-1778). Philosopher of the French Enlightenment. In *Du Contract Social,* he stated the law of inverse proportion between population and political freedom (cf. Book 3, chapter 1, Paris: Livre de Poche, 1978. Also in *Social Contract. Essays by Locke, Hume, and Rousseau.* Sir Ernest Barker, Editor. New York: Oxford University Press, 1976).

Bernard Rubin & Associates. *Big Business and the Mass Media.* Lexington MA: Lexington Books, 1977.

Craig E. Aronoff, Editor. *Business and the Media.* Santa Monica CA: Goodyear Publishing Corp., 1979.

David Finn. *The Business-Media Relationship: Countering Misconceptions and Distrust.* New York: Amacom, 1981.

Observations made by media scholars give at least a quantitative testimony to many facets of the business of media. Ed Shiller, in *Managing the Media*

(Toronto: Bedford House Publishing Corp., 1989) states "The media are every-where and they are interested in everything" (p. 13).
A. Kent MacDougall (*Ninety Seconds to Tell It All. Big Business and the News Media*, Homewood IL: Dow Jones-Irwin, 1981) observed that "To communicate with the American public, companies must first communicate with the media" (p. 43). Interestingly enough, they reach huge audiences by using the *rent free* pub-lic airwaves. Consequently, as the author shows, the news media shine by any measure of profitability. According to *Forbes* magazine's annual study of prof-its, broadcasting and publishing companies led all industry groups in return on stockholder's equity and capital in recent years. Specialized publications also keep track of the profitability of the media.
Study of Media and Markets, a service of Simmons Market Research Bureau, Inc., makes available standard marketing information. *Communications Industry Forecasts*, brought out by Veronis, Suhler & Asso. of New York, gives a detailed financial status of the entire communication industry (radio, television, maga-zines, entertainment media, recorded music, advertising, promotion).

J.H. Cassing and S.L. Husted, Editors. *Capital, Technology, and Labor in the New Global Economy*. Washington DC: American Enterprise Institute for Public Poli-cy Research, 1988.

Raymond Vernon. *Exploring the Global Economy: Emerging Issues in Trade and Investment*. Cambridge: Center for International Affairs, Harvard University Press, 1985.

Stephen Gill. *The Global Political Economy: Perspectives, Problems, and Policies*. New York: Harvester, 1988.

Gene Grossman. *Innovation and Growth in the Global Economy*. Cambridge: MIT Press, 1991.

Facts for Action (periodical). Boston: Oxfam America, from 1982.

John Clark. *For Richer or Poorer: An Oxfam Report on Western Connections with World Hunger*. Oxford: Oxfam, 1986.

J.G. Donders, Editor. *Bread Broken: An Action Report on the Food Crisis in Africa*. Eldoret, Kenya: Gaba Publications, AMECEA Pastoral Institute, 1984.

In his study *Eighteenth Brumaire*, (1852), Karl Marx described bureaucracy as a "semi-autonomous power standing partly above class-divided society, exploit-ing all its members alike."

Harvey Wheeler. *Democracy in a Revolutionary Era*. Santa Barbara: Center for the Study of Democratic Institutions, 1970.

Wheeler defineds bureaucracy as "a vast organism with an assortment of specialized, departmentalized tentacles for coping with the different kinds of reality it may encounter" (pp. 99-100).

Max Weber. *Essay in Sociology.* Edited and translated by H.H. Gerth and C. Wright Mills. London: Oxford University Press, 1946.
In this classical theory of bureaucracy, the author saw its roots in the cultural traditions of Western rationalism. As such, it is characterized by impersonal relations, hierarchy, and specialization.

R. Chackerian, G. Abcarian. *Bureaucratic Power in Society.* Chicago: Nelson Hall, Inc., 1984.

B.C. Smith. *Bureaucracy and Political Power.* Brighton: Wheatsheaf Books, Ltd., 1988.
The author argues that "Bureaucracy is a political phenomenon" (p. ix), not a mere administrative occurrence.

Eva Etzioni-Halevy. *Bureaucracy and Democracy. A Political Dilemma.* London/Boston: Routledge & Kegan Paul, 1983.

George C. Roche. *America by the Throat: The Stranglehold of Federal Bureaucracy.* Old Greenwich CT: Devin Adair, 1983.

Eugene Lewis. *American Politics in a Bureaucratic Age: Citizens, Constituents, Clients, and Victims.* Cambridge MA: Winthrop Publishers, 1977.

Michael Hauben and Ronda Hauben. *Netizens: On the History and Impact of Usenet and the Internet.* A Netbook. http://www.columbia.edu/~rh120/ch106, June, 1996.

Telecommuting reflects the new possibilities for efficient use of ressources. Unfortunately, tax laws in the USA and other advanced countries restrict the use of the home office, thus creating an obstacle to change.

Michael J. A. Howe, The Strange Feats of Idiots Savants, in *Fragments of Genius,* London/New York: Routledge, 1989.
"'Idiots savants' is the term that has most frequently been used to designate mentally handicapped individuals who are capable of outstanding achievements at particular tasks" (p. 5). He also mentions alternative labels: *talented imbecile, parament, talented ament, retarded savant, schizophrenic savant, autistic savant.* Among the examples he gives: A 14-year old Chinese who could give the exact page for any Chinese character in a 400-page dictionary; a 23-year old woman hardly able to speak (her mental age was assessed at 2 years, 9 months), with no musical instruction, who could play on the piano a piece of music that a per-

son around her might hum or play; a subject who knew all distances between towns in the USA and could list all hotels and number of rooms available; a person who knew Abraham Lincoln's *Gettysburg Address* but could not, after weeks of classes on the subject, say who Lincoln was or what the speech means.

In *The Degradation of the Democratic Dogma* (1920), Henry Adams presented a logarithmic curve of the acceleration of history. In 1909, Adams noted that between 1800 and 1900, the speed of events increased 1,000 times.

Gerard Piel. *The Acceleration of History.* New York: A. A. Knopf, 1972.

Nicolas Rashevsky. *Looking at History through Mathematics.* Cambridge: MIT Press, 1968.

Chapter 2: A Sense of Future

George Steiner. *After Babel. Aspects of Language and Translation.* London: Oxford University Press, 1975.
His hypothesis is that scientists assert their own method and vision.

The Unabomber's Manifesto was printed in *The Washington Post* on September 19, 1995, as a separate pullout section.

George Orwell (1903-1950). *Nineteen Eighty-Four.* (Text, sources, criticism by Irving Howe, Editor). New York: Harcourt Brace Jovanovich, 1982.

Active badge™, a product of Xerox Park.

Howard Rheinhold. *Virtual Reality.* New York: Summit Books, 1991.

Robert B. Reich. *The Work of Nations: Preparing Ourselves for 21st Century Capitalism.* New York: A.A. Knopf' 1991.

Information on resources, misery, growth of cities, and aging are available from national and international organizations, as well as from scholars in sociology, economics, and demographics. Data is available plenty, but not necessarily in easy-to-read formats. One can consult:

Nathan Keyfitz and Wilhelm Flieger. *World Population Growth and Aging: Demographic Trends in the Late Twentieth Century.* Chicago: University of Chicago Press, 1990.

Robert P. McIntosh. *The Background of Ecology: Concept and Theory.* New York: Cambridge University Press, 1985.

Paul A. Colinvaux. *Ecology.* New York: Wiley, 1986.

Interest in genetics, biology, evolution, population, and ecology eventually led to the understanding of biological diversity as part of the fiber of life on Earth. Diversity is reflected in the interwoven system of species. Destruction of the Amazon rain forest alone results in the end of about three species every hour, which adds up to 27,000 species per year. Edward O Wilson's *The Diversity of Life* (Cambridge: Harvard University Press, 1992) gives a dramatic account of the problem.

Around 40% of American households own a computer. In the immediate future, spending on computers will surpass that on automobiles (currently 3.5% of the gross domestic product). Although in th rest of the world the numbers are very different, the general trend is the same.

INDEX

Abbott, E. 517, 841
Abcarian, G. 866
Abraham 424, 827
Acevedo, S. de 844
Adam, J. A.
Adams, A. 780
Adams, A. E. 813
Adams, H. 867
Adams, J. 780
Adams, J. T. 783
Ades, D. 846
Aherne, S. C. M. 824
Alberti, L. B. 847
Alexander, D. 809
Alexander, E. 824, 826
Aoki, C. 795
Apicius, M. G. 454, 831
Apollonius of Perga 810
Archimedes 810
Aresty, E. B. 830
Aristotle 114, 175, 180, 181, 182,
    296, 383, 798, 809, 810, 812
Armstrong, D. 819, 829
Arnauld, A. 787
Arnold, M. 285
Aronoff, C. E. 864
Arp, H. 846
Ashcroft, J. 36
Asimov, I. 836
Aspray, W. 862
Ataian, E. 793
Atatürk, M. K. 860
Atlee, J. E. 841
Austen, J. 60, 781

Axtel, R. 804
Axthelm, L. L. 455
d'Azeglio, M. 642, 859

Bable, E. 661, 861
Babloyantz, A. 817
Bacon, F. 516, 840
Baird, J. L. 814
Baker, L. S. 818
Balch, S. 286
Balducinni 796, 854
Balzac, H. de 570
Banerji, P. 819
Bannister, R. 490
Barbarossa (King Frederick I.) 462,
    828
Barker, G. C. 796
Barnard, F. R. 323, 324, 812
Baroody, W. A. 776
Barthe, J. 567, 849
Barthelme, D. 567, 849
Barthes, R. 167, 676, 795, 831, 862
Barzun, J. 285, 317, 809
Baudrillard, J. 12, 775, 781
Bauer, B. 801
Baulieu, E.-E. 819
Baumann, G. 772, 778
Bayer, H. 245
Beaudelaire, C. 848
Beaumont, Mme. Leprice de 845
Beaver, F. E. 814
Beckett, S. 562
Beethoven, L. van 735
Behrens, P. 854

Beier, R. B. 859
Bell, A. G. 623, 857
Bell, C. 789
Bellwood, P. S. 97, 773, 788, 791
Bender, J. W. 841
Benedict, P. K. 97
Beneviste, E. 383
Benjamin, W. 542, 846
Benn, G. 73, 784
Berlin, I. 649, 860
Berra (Yogi) 68, 784
Bevirt, R. 849
Bickerton, D. 786
Bischoff, B. 808
Bismarck, O. von 860
Bloom, A. 41, 302, 779, 811
Bloomfield, L. 207, 802
Blust, R. 97
Boaz, F. 785
Boccaccio, G. 817
Boller, P. F. 782
Bollinger, H. 846
Bolter, J. D. 268, 808
Bon Jour, L. 841
Bondon, R. 799
Boole, G. 186, 206, 220, 348, 749,
    798, 803
Boorstin, D. J. 709
Borges, L. 358, 567
Borneman, J. 859
Bott, D. 679, 863
Bottero, J. 453, 831
Bottin, L. 803
Boutrous, L. 833
Bowen, F. 781
Bowen, J. 808
Bowle, T. 820
Bradbury, K. L. 864
Bradbury, R. 853
Bradley, W. 490
Branigan, K. 807

Brasch, R. 833
Brent, E. 861
Brockett, L. P. 808
Brockman, J. 778, 844
Brodsky, V. 563
Brogan, D. 783
Brown, J. C. 160
Bryant, C. A. 830, 831
Buber, M. 527
Buckland, G. 813
Bulwer-Lytton, E. G. E. 598, 856
Bundy, A. 839
Burckhardt, T. 837
Burgess, A. 160, 161, 564
Burguière, A. 822
Burkert, W. 826
Burks, A. 862
Burnes, R. 563
Burrough, W. 67
Bush, V. 587, 816, 853
Butzer, K. W. 836

Caesar, Julius 670
Caillois, R. 834
Cambell, N. P. 842
Campbell, B. 802
Canepari, L. 793
Caparros, N. 821
Carlyle, W. J. 405, 574, 851
Carpenter, E. 46, 570, 779, 850
Carroll, L. 528
Cassing, J. H. 865
Cavendish, R. 837
Ceausescu, N. 859
Cervantes Saavedra, M. de 563, 579
Cézanne, P. 554
Chackerian, R. 866
Chamber, E. 839
Chandler, A. D. 805
Chapman, G. 861
Chappel, W. 773, 778

Chelas, B. F. 799
Cheng, F. 793
Childe, G. V. 153, 795
Chinmayanda, S. (Yoka) 817
Chomsky, N. 118, 270, 697, 792, 806
Christenson, C. V. 820
Christo 847, (and Jeanne-Claude)
    543, 545
Chuang-tzu 181, 798
Clair, C. 773, 778
Clark, D. 864
Clark, J. 865
Clausewitz, C. von 667, 669, 862
Clini, C. 830
Cocteau, J. 845
Cohen, M. R. 774, 787
Cole, H. M. 819
Cole, M. 80, 786
Colinvaux, P. A. 868
Collier, C. 819
Columella, L. J. M. 831
Commager, H. S. 404, 780, 783
Comte, A. 530, 844
Condry, J. 862
Confucius 424, 798, 824, 827
Conway, J. H. 762
Cooper, J. C. 838
Cooper, P. 784
Corcoran, J. 784
Corsi, M. 802
Costello, N. 856
Couliano, I. P. 824
Courtés, J. 802
Crump, T. 793, 796
Cubric, Milan 860

Daguerre, L.-J. M. 812
Darius 670
Darwin, C. 359, 529, 588, 818, 844
Davidson, J. 852
Davies, P. C. W. 842

Davies, R. 838
Davis, W. 803
Dawkins, R. 197, 800, 801, 843
Deely, J. 771
DeForest, L. 813
DeFrancis, J. 168, 789, 795
Delgarus, G. 800
Derschowitz, A. 655
Descartes, R. 95, 96, 179, 516, 526,
    787, 797, 840
Dewey, J. 65, 774, 782
Dickens, C. 59, 60, 61, 66, 448, 449,
    577, 780, 830
Dickson, W. 813
Dijkstra, E. 268, 520, 808
Dillon, P. 856
Dilthey, W. 799
Dine, J. 848
Diringer, D. 772, 778, 789
Dixon, D. 835
Dobler, H. 773, 778
Doi, Takeo 183, 798, 823
Donaldson, P. J. 819
Donders, J. G. 865
Dondis, D. A. 816
Dönhoff, Marion Gräfin v. 779
Dos Passos, J. 563, 783
Dostoyevsky, F. M. 630, 654, 734,
    860
Drayer, R. 838
Dreiser, T. 66, 783,
Duberman, M. B. 822
Duchamp, M. 544, 848
Dumitru, A. 797
Durant, W. 809
Durkheim, E. 529, 801, 844

Earhart, H. B. 825
Eastman, G. 813
Eco, U. 837, 853
Edison, T. A. 623, 857

Einberger, J. 815
Einstein, A. 296, 504, 506, 517, 766, 810, 838
El Lissitzky 245
Elgin, S. H. 160
Eliade, M. 183, 412, 799, 824
Eller, W. 772, 777
Elliot, T. S. 836
Elshtain, J. B. 822
Emerson, R. W. 62, 405, 782
Emmanuelle, V. 860
Enders Huntington, G. 823
Engels, F. 579, 638, 858
Eno, R. 825
Ensor, J. 848
Enzensberger, H. M. 12, 17, 19, 776
Epaminondas of Thebes 666, 862
Epicurus 512, 839
Epstein, J. 804
Erdmann, J. E. 801
d'Errico, F. 790
Etiemple, R. 820
Etzioni-Halevy, E. 866
Euclid 810
Everett, J. 818

Fabergé, P. C. 598, 855
Fagan, Cyril 838
Faulkner, W. 62
Faventius, M. C. 855
Febre, L. P. V. 773, 778
Feldbrugge, F. J. M. 859
Feldinger, F. 822
Felker, T. 855
Fell, M. 821
Ferguson, J. 824, 826
Feuerback, L. 801
Feyerabend, P. K. 527, 843
Feynman, R. 727, 842
Fielding, H. 817
Finch, C. 837

Finn, D. 864
Fitzgerald, F. S. 783
FitzGibbon, T. 830
Flaubert, G. 849
Flegon, A. 820
Fletcher, R. 844
Flieger, W. 867
Flores, F. 311, 774, 805, 811
Fludd, R. 794
Flusser, V. 853
Fodor, J. 787, 819
Folliet, J. 816
Forster, E. M. 167
Forty, A. 854
Foucault, M. 819
Fox, G. 426
Fraasen, B. C. von 842
Franklin, B. 781
Frantz, D. O. 817
Franz, M. L. von 837
Freud, S. 366, 367, 818
Freyssenet, M. 802
Frolov, B. A. 790
Fu-chi 816
Fuller, M. 782
Fumaroli, M. 803
Funés, Louis de 450, 831
Fung-Yu-lan 181, 798
Furetière, A. 563, 849
Fust, J. F. 423

Gabler, G. A. 801
Galbraith, J. 855
Galen of Pergamum 810, 818
Galileo Galilei 296, 512, 810, 839
Gallie, W. B. 800
Galton, F. 818
Gamkredlidze, T. V. 794
Gardner, H. 67, 783, 792
Gardner, M. 792
Garibaldi, G. 860

Hennepin, L. 852
Hensen, H. K. 407
Herbertson, M. A. 818
Herder, J. G. 799
Herzfeld, Ch. M. 863
Hesse, H. 563
Heuss, T. 672, 862
Hildegard (Abbess) 161
Hildyard, A. 772, 777
Hillis, D. 844
Himmel, E. 847
Hinrichs, C. 801
Hintikka, Jaako 799
Hirsch, E. D. 286, 519
Hitchcock, H.-R. 854
Hitler, A. 579, 811, 853
Hjelmslev, L. 802
Hladczuk, J. 772, 777
Hladczuk, S. 772, 777
Hoffstaedter, D. 792
Hölderlin, F. 614, 857
Holzweissig, G. 859
Homer 98, 299, 308, 563, 567, 734, 735, 790
Hooker, R. 773
Horner, Ch. A. 861
Hosteter, J. A. 823
Howard, M. 862
Howe, M. J. A. 866
Howell, W. D. 783
Huberman, B. 804
Huelsenbeck, R. 846
Huijsen, W.-O. 795
Huizing, J. 482, 834
Hume, D. 405, 823, 864
Hus, J. 426, 828
Husted, S. L. 865
Hutson, J. H. 780
Huxley, A. 617, 857
Huysmans 848

I-Ching 824
Illich, I. 12, 52, 154, 775, 795
Ionesco, E. 562
Irving, W. 62
Isaac 827
Isobe, T. 829
Ivanov, V. V. 794

Jackson, D. 773, 778
Jacob 827
Jacobson, S. 785
Jakobson, R. 792, 806
James, H. 62, 65, 66, 783
James, W. 405, 774, 782
Jay, P. 813
Jeanneret, Ch.-E. 855
Jefferson, T. 59, 632, 780, 781
Jeffrey, R. C. 799
Jennings, E. M. 772, 778
Jesus 424
Joan of Arc 426, 828
Johnson, M. 774
Johnson, P. 854
Johnson, P. E. 779
Johnson, S. 853
Jones, E. 795
Jones, E. 830
Joyce, J. 563, 564, 831, 848
Jung, C. G. 818, 848

Kachigan, S. K. 816
Kafka, F. 563
Kain, E. L. 821
Kane, T. T. 819
Kanger, Stig 799
Kant, I. 527, 528
Kaprow, A. 848
Kauffmann, S. 846
Kaufman, D. A. 851
Kempton, W. 785
Kenichi, O. 860

Kenin, R. 855
Kerkhove, D. de 150, 795
Kesey, K. 565, 849
Keyfitz, N. 867
Keynes, J. M. 405
Keyser, C. J. 774
Khrushchev, N. S. 857, 637
Kiefer, A. 846
Kim, P. 818
Kircher, A. 800
Kirsch, D. 828, 842
Klapisch-Zuber, C. 822
Kluckholm, C. 799
Knight, G. 837
Knox, T. B. 864
Koblo, M. 773, 778
Kocol, G. 8224
Korzybski, A. 140, 797
Köstlin, R. 801
Kracauer, S. 814
Kraft, F. 836
Krause, E. A. 802
Kretschmer, H. 821
Kroeber, A. L. 799
Kuhn, T. 840
Kumudamani, K. 837
Kung-Fu-tzu cf. Confucius
Kuppuram, G. 837
Kurti, G. 830
Kurti, N. 830
Kurzweil, R. 838
Kutzner, P. L. 832

Lacquer, T. 362, 818
Lakatos, I. 527, 843
Lakoff, G. 12, 77, 80, 774, 785, 786
Lambert, S. 815
Lamy, C. A. 96
Lanier, J. 340, 815
Lanier, S. 65, 783
Laning, E. 796

Larionov, M. F. 851
Le Corbusier 595, 854, 855
LeVay, S. 819
Leblanc, M. 814
Léger, F. 851
Lehrer, K. 841
Leibniz, G. W. 12, 186, 346, 347,
    526, 527, 528, 737, 774, 816, 828
Leijonhufvud, A. 804
Lemoine, S. 846
Lenhard, M. 771
Lenice, M. 490
Lenin, V. I. 637
Leo the Wise (Byzantine emperor)
    667
Leonard, W. E. 817
Leonardo da Vinci 330
Leonidas 670
Leroi-Gourhan, A. 166, 795
Lévi-Strauss, C. 33, 105, 460, 777,
    791, 822, 838
Levine, M. 777
Lévy-Bruhl 175, 797
Lewis, D. 799
Lewis, E. 866
Lewis, S. 783
Lindendorf, E. 674
Lloyd, G. E. R. 836
Llul, R. 160
Locke, J. 179, 197, 798, 864
Longbotham, L. 832
Longfellow, H. W. 62
Loos, A. 854
Lotman, Y. M. 12, 775
Louis, M. R. 856
Lucas, L. 490
Lucie-Smith, E. 820
Lucretius (Titus L. Carus) 512, 839
Ludwig II 860
Lull, R. 800
Lumsden, Ch. J. 795

Lun-yu 798
Lunacharskii, A. V. 829
Lundberg, D. 819
Luria, A. R. 797
Luther, M. 426, 828
Lyons, J. 118, 792

Ma, P. 819
MacDougall, A. K. 865
Mach, E. 842
Machiavelli, N. 66
Madonna 54, 353
Maeterlinck, M. 848
Mahyuddin, J. 796
Malthus, T. R. 48, 275, 276, 376, 702,
    779, 830, 864
Manton, R. 817
Manutius, Aldus 574, 852
Manuzio, Aldo 852
Mao Zedong 579, 853
Marcuse, H. 802, 819
Maria, W. de 543, 846
Marinetti, F. T. 850
Marron, I. H. 809
Marshack, A. 790
Martel, C. 428
Martin, M. 825
Martinet, A. 795
Marx, K. 353, 441, 527, 527, 579,
    637, 638, 807, 816, 843, 858, 865
Mary (Queen of England) 575
Masciadri, M. M. 805
Mason, T. 834
Mastroianni, L. 819
Matthew 440
Maturana, R. 12, 726, 774, 804
Maurice (Byzantine emperor) 667
Maximus of Torino 362
Maxwell, J. 814
Mayer, H. 847
Mayer, M. 804

McClary, S. 819
McGuffey, W. H. 784
McIntosh, R. P. 868
McKay, W. 850
McKenna, D. and T. 83, 787
McLachlan, J. H. 836
McLean, A. 837
McLuhan, M. 12, 167, 244, 703, 775,
    795, 863
McNamara, R. S. 680
Mead, F. S. 829
Mead, M. 382
Meagher, P. K. 824
Melanchthon, Ph. 18
Méliès, G. 813
Melton, B. 811
Merleau-Ponty, M. 158, 795
Merrifield, R. 789
Messadie, G. 781
Meyer, A. E. 808
Meyerkowitz, P. 850
Mies van der Rohe, L. 847, 854
Mill, J. S. 844
Miller, H. A. 36
Millones, L. 820
Minsky, M. 764
Mitterand, F. 703
Mohammed 424, 827
Moisil, G. 775
Moltke, H. von 666, 862
Mongré, P. 800
Monly, F. 845
Monroe, W. S. 808
Mooradian, K. 773, 778
Moreau, G. 848
Morey, R. A. 825
Morgan, E. 864
Morin, N. 820
Morita, A. 784
Moritz, E. 800, 801, 843
Morris, Ch. 787

Civilization of Illiteracy: Introduction

Cover: Mihai Nadin, Stefan Lehmann, Thomas
Overberg
Layout: Mihai Nadin, Baruch Gorkin
Text set in: Janson MT, Janson Expert MT
Printing: Grafia-Druck Radeberg GmbH

Recent titles from
Dresden University Press

ARTES LIBERALES
ed. by Horst-Jürgen Gerigk

Vol. 1
Horst-Jürgen Gerigk (Ed.):
THE BROTHERS KARAMAZOV
DOSTOEVSKY`S LAST NOVEL FROM
A CONTEMPORARY PERSPECTIVE
(Text in English, German, Russian, and French)
1997, 8vo., 275 pp., ISBN 3-931828-46-8
cloth with dust jacket
DM 88,-/US$ 53

Vol. 2:
Olga Meerson:
DOSTOEVSKY`S TABOOS
1997, 8vo., ca. 270 pp., ISBN 3-931828-48-4
cloth with dust jacket
ca. DM 68,-/US$ 39

PHILOLOGICA
ed. by Walter Schmitz

Vol. A1:
Guy Stern:
LITERARISCHES LEBEN IM EXIL
LITERACY IN EXILE. SELECTED ARTICLES.
1988-1997